GAZETTEER OF PUNJAB HARYANA AND HIMACHAL PRADESH

VOLUME I

ATLANTIC PUBLISHERS & DISTRIBUTORS
4215/1, Ansari Road, Darya Ganj,
New Delhi - 110002

Published by
ATLANTIC PUBLISHERS AND DISTRIBUTORS
B-2, Vishal Enclave, New Delhi - 27
Phone: 5413460

Sales office
4215/1, Ansari Road, Darya Ganj
New Delhi - 110002
Phone : 3273880

Printed in India at
Mehra Offset Press
New Delhi

PREFACE

THE articles contained in these volumes were originally drafted by Mr. H. A. Rose, I.C.S. A considerable portion of the Provincial article was contributed by officers of scientific departments or heads of departments, while the draft District and minor articles were scrutinized and corrected by District and Political Officers, among whom may be mentioned Messrs. J. Coldstream, R. E. Younghusband, E. R. Abbott, P. J. Fagan, H. Calvert, and Captain R. M. Lowis. In compiling State articles special assistance was received from M. Raghunāth Dās of Jīnd, Pandit Rām Singh Sarma of Patiāla, Sardār Gurbachan Singh of Sirmūr, and Malik Muhammad Dīn of Bahāwalpur. The final revision was carried out by Mr. J. P. Thompson, I.C.S., who has rendered valuable service in revising the statistics and collecting additional matter.

TABLE OF CONTENTS

PROVINCIAL GAZETTEERS OF INDIA

PUNJAB

VOLUME I

Punjab (*Panjāb*).—In its strict etymological sense the Punjab, or 'land of the five rivers,' is the country enclosed and watered by the JHELUM, CHENĀB, RĀVI, BEĀS, and SUTLEJ; but the Province as now constituted includes also the table-land of Sirhind between the Sutlej and the Jumna to the south of the former river, the Sind-Sāgar Doāb or wedge of country between the Jhelum and the INDUS, and west of the latter river the two tracts which form Dera Ghāzi Khān and part of Miānwāli District. The Province lies between 27° 39′ and 34° 2′ N. and 69° 23′ and 79° 2′ E., and with its Native States has an area of 133,741 square miles, being larger by one-tenth than the British Isles, and comprising a tenth of the area of the Indian Empire. Of the total area, 36,532 square miles belong to Native States under the political control of the Punjab Government, and the rest is British territory. The population in 1901 was 24,754,737 (of whom 4,424,398 were in the Native States), or 8·4 per cent. of the whole population of the Indian Empire. General description.

On the north the Himālayan ranges divide the Punjab from Kashmīr and the North-West Frontier Province. On the west the Indus forms its main boundary with the latter Province, except that the Punjab includes the strip of riverain which forms the Isa Khel *tahsīl* of Miānwāli District, west of that river. Its south-western extremity also lies west of the Indus and forms the large District of Dera Ghāzi Khān, thereby extending its frontier to the Sulaimān range, which divides it from Baluchistān. On the extreme south-west the Province adjoins Sind, and the Rājputāna desert forms its southern border. On the east, the Jumna and its tributary the Tons divide it from the United Provinces of Agra and Oudh, its Boundaries.

frontier north of the sources of the latter river being contiguous with Chinese Tibet.

Physical divisions.

The Province falls into five main physical divisions. Three of these—the Himālayan region, the Himālayan submontane which stretches from the Jumna to the Salt Range, and the arid plateaux of that range—are small in area, but the submontane is the most fertile and wealthiest in the Punjab. The other two are the arid south-western plains, and the western portion of the Indo-Gangetic Plain west which extends as far eastward as Lahore. Both these divisions are of vast extent, but infertile towards the south, where they encroach on the plains of Sind and Rājputāna.

The Doābs.

The Punjab proper comprises five *doābs*, or tracts lying between two rivers. These received their names from the emperor Akbar, who formed them by combining the first letters of the names of the rivers between which they lie. They are: the Bīst Jullundur, also called the Sāharwāl Doāb, lying between the Beās and the Sutlej; the Bāri, between the old bed of the Beās and the Rāvi; the Rechna (Rachin-āb, or Rachin-ao), between the Rāvi and the Chenāb; the Chinhath, between the Chenāb and the Bihat (another name for the Jhelum), also called the Chaj; and the Sind-Sāgar, between the Indus and the Jhelum or Bihat.

Mountain system.

The whole Central Punjab is a vast alluvial plain; but the north-east of the Province is formed of a section of the HIMĀLAYAS, stretching up to and beyond the great central ranges so as to include the Tibetan cantons of Lāhul and Spiti. The SALT RANGE, with the plateaux which lie to the north between it and the Indus, forms its north-western angle, and the SULAIMĀN Range forms the southern half of the western frontier of the Province. These are the only mountain systems of importance; but a few insignificant outliers of the ARĀVALLI system traverse Gurgaon District in the extreme south-east, and terminate in the famous Ridge at Delhi.

River system.

All the seven great rivers of the Punjab rise in the Himālayas, and after long courses, sometimes of several hundred miles, amid snow-clad ranges, they debouch on the plains. The slope of the low country is to the south and south west, and is very gradual, seldom exceeding 2 feet in a mile; and this determines the course of the rivers. In the process of time each stream has cut for itself a wide valley, which lies well below the level of the plain, and whose banks mark the extreme limits of the course on either side. Within this valley the river meanders in a narrow but ill-defined and ever-shifting channel. In the winter the stream is comparatively small; but as the mountain snows melt at the approach of the hot season, the waters rise and overflow the surrounding country, often to a distance of several miles on either side. At the close of the rainy season, the waters recede, leaving wide expanses of fertile loam or less fertile sand.

Of these seven rivers the Indus is the greatest. Already a mighty stream when it emerges from the Hazāra hills, it flows almost due south past Attock. Here it enters a deep gorge, terminating at Kālābāgh, where it pierces the Salt Range. Thus far it forms the western boundary; but south of Kālābāgh it enters the Province, and divides the Isa Khel *tahsīl* of Miānwāli from the rest of that District. Farther south again it forms the western boundary until it re-enters Punjab territory near Bhakkar, and divides Dera Ghāzi Khān from Miānwāli and Muzaffargarh Districts and from the State of Bahāwalpur. The Jhelum enters the Punjab east of the Salt Range, flowing south between this and the Pabbi hills, which terminate at Mong Rasūl. Thence the river flows west and then south until it is joined by the Chenāb near Jhang. The Chenāb rises in the Himālayan canton of Lāhul within the Province, and after traversing the Chamba State and the Jammu province of Kashmīr debouches on the plains east of the Jhelum, into which it falls about 225 miles from the hills. The Rāvi, rising in Chamba, reaches the plain below Dalhousie, and joins the combined waters of the Jhelum and Chenāb 50 miles south of Jhang. The united streams of these three rivers form the Trimāb. The Beās, rising on the south of the Rhotang pass on the opposite side of the Central Himālaya to the Rāvi, traverses the Kulū valley southward, and then bends suddenly westward, through the Mandī State and Kāngra District, until it turns the northern flank of the Siwāliks, and enters the plains within a few miles of the Rāvi. Thence its course is more southerly, and it falls into the Sutlej about 70 miles from its debouchure. The Sutlej, rising near the source of the Indus in Tibet, enters the Province near the Shipki Pass, traverses Bashahr and other States of the Simla Hills, and pierces the Siwāliks near Rūpar. Thence it runs almost due west to its junction with the Beās near Sobraon, where it takes a more southerly course for 270 miles, and falls into the Trimāb 9 miles north of Uch. Below this confluence the waters of the Jhelum, Chenāb and Rāvi, Sutlej and Beās form the Panjnad, or 'five rivers,' which fall into the Indus at Mithankot. Lastly, the Jumna, the only one of the great rivers of the Province which ultimately drains into the Bay of Bengal, rises in Tehrī State in the United Provinces, and from its junction with the Tons at the eastern extremity of Sirmūr territory forms the boundary between the Punjab and the United Provinces for a distance of over 200 miles.

Scenery.

The Province presents great varieties of scenery, from the snow peaks and glaciers of the Upper Himālayas to the deserts of shifting sand in the Sind-Sāgar Doāb and Bahāwalpur. The scenery of the Himālayas has often been described. In the Salt Range it is picturesque and even grand in places, and in the interior of the range the slopes are everywhere green with box and bog-myrtle. The southern face exhibits a very rugged and broken appearance, but on the north the contours of the hills are for the most part smooth and undulating. Between the Salt Range and the Himālayas the aspect of the country varies greatly, from the deep, shaly, and infertile ravines of Jhelum to the rich uplands of Gūjar Khān. The Siwāliks and the Pabbi hills are much tamer than the Salt Range, and the vegetation which clothes them is coarser and scantier, though the Jaswān Dūn in Hoshiārpur is not lacking in richness and beauty. But the characteristic scenery of the Punjab is that of the plains, and the contrast between their appearance before and after the crops have been cut is most striking. As harvest approaches, the traveller, especially in the irrigated tracts, rides through an endless expanse of waving crops of different shades of colour, out of which the villages seem to rise like islets in an ocean of green. After the harvest all is changed; and the dull brown of the fields is relieved only by the trees, solitary or in groves and avenues, and by the hamlets and village ponds. The lowlands through which the great rivers work their way retain some of their verdure throughout the year, and, especially in the east of the Province, are studded with groves and gardens. But in the plateaux between the rivers, and in the great sandy plains of the south, where cultivation is impossible without the aid of artificial irrigation, the scanty vegetation takes a more sober hue, and the only relief the eye can find from the stretches of bare soil is afforded by stunted and infrequent bushes.

Geology[1]. **The plains.**

Geologically the Punjab falls into three natural divisions: the plains, the Salt Range, and the Himālayas. The plains consist almost entirely of the Indo-Gangetic alluvium, but contain beds of sedimentary rocks of Peninsular type. These

[1] Condensed from a note by Mr. H. H. Hayden, Geological Survey of India.

comprise a small area of rocks of a transition age, which form a series of outliers of the Arāvalli rocks at Delhi and to the south and south-east, whence they are known as the Delhi system[1]. They are composed of a lower group of slates and limestones, and an upper and much thicker group of quartzites; the upper beds, known as the Alwar quartzites, are exposed on the Ridge at Delhi. Two small outliers, also referred to the Delhi system, are found near the Chenāb, at Chiniot and Kirāna, within 35 miles of the beds of extra-peninsular type found in the Salt Range. From the strong contrast they afford in petrological and dynamic conditions, they are almost certainly older than the oldest rocks of that range and in all probability pre-Cambrian.

In the north of the Province the SALT RANGE stretches from the Jhelum valley on the east to the Indus on the west, and crops up again beyond that river. Its geological features are particularly interesting, and the age of the salt which gives its name to the hills is still uncertain. The lowest beds to which a definite period can be assigned are shales, yielding trilobites, *obolus*, and *hyolithes*, and regarded as Lower Cambrian. They are underlain, with apparent conformity, by purple sandstone, which may also be Cambrian. From its apparent position below this sandstone the salt marl has been classed as Lower Cambrian or pre-Cambrian, but it also occurs at various horizons of higher levels. It has no appearance of stratification, but is a soft, structureless mass, showing no signs of sedimentary origin. In it are found immense masses of rock-salt, and bands and strings of gypsum, with disintegrated patches of dolomite. Magnesian sandstone appears to lie conformably on the *obolus* shales, but has yielded only fragmentary fossils. It is, however, probable that this, together with the overlying salt pseudomorph sandstone, belongs to the Cambrian system. Salt Range.

A great break then occurs, representing the Silurian and Devonian and part of the Carboniferous epochs; and the next formation, a boulder-bed, lies unconformably on all the older deposits. It consists of faceted and striated boulders embedded in a fine matrix, giving evidence of a glacial origin; a few fossils are found, including *Conularia*, and the series is regarded as Lower Permian, of the same age as the Tālcher boulder-bed. The Upper Permian is represented by olive and speckled sandstones and lavender clay, containing *Conularia* and other fossils, and the *Productus* beds which yield *Xenaspis* and *Cyclolobus*. Over these are found Lower Triassic beds of

1 *Manual of the Geology of India*, p. 69 ('The Delhi System').

limestone, sandstone, and marl, containing ammonites, and termed ceratite beds. The Middle and Upper Trias appear to be wanting, the ceratites being overlain by sandstones, oolites, and shales, in the upper beds of which have been found ammonites and belemnites of Upper Jurassic age. They are followed by pisolitic sandstones, containing at the Chichali pass a rich Lower Cretaceous (neocomian) flora, and overlain unconformably by shales and sandstones with coal seams passing into Nummulitic limestone, the coal and limestone being of Lower Tertiary (eocene) age. Above the limestone is another unconformity, followed by a great mass of sandstone, with beds of red clay similar to the Nāhan beds of the Himālayas; this in turn is overlain by typical Siwālik sandstones.

Himā-layas. Northern zone.

The Himālayas fall into three broad divisions: a northern, a central, and a southern. The northern, known as the Tibetan zone, extends through Kanāwār and Spiti into Lāhul, and affords an almost unbroken sequence of sedimentary deposits ranging from Cambrian to Cretaceous. The oldest beds are slates and quartzites, for the most part unfossiliferous, but containing in the higher beds trilobites and other fossils of Middle and Upper Cambrian age. These are overlain, unconformably, by conglomerate, followed by a great mass of red quartzite, believed to be of Lower Silurian age, and passing up into limestone and marl with Silurian fossils (trilobites, corals, &c.). The limestone gradually gives place to a white quartzite which is one of the most characteristic horizons of the Himālayas. Except in Kanāwār and Upper Spiti the quartzite is usually overlain by beds of Upper Permian age, but near Lis in Kanāwār a great thickness of limestone and shale is found; the limestone contains a rich fauna of Lower Carboniferous age and the shales have yielded Upper Carboniferous brachiopods and bryozoa. Next in order is a conglomerate of variable thickness, overlain by calcareous sandstone and a bed of dark micaceous shale representing the Permian. The uppermost bed, known as the *Productus* shales, is found throughout the Himālayas, and contains Upper Permian brachiopods and ammonites. The latter are especially interesting, as they are closely allied to species (*Xenaspis carbonaria* and *Cyclolobus oldhami*) from the upper *Productus* limestone of the Salt Range. Above these shales is a thin shaly band with ammonites, known as the Otoceras beds, which passes into a vast thickness of limestone, intercalated by shale, and representing the whole of the Trias, and the Lower and probably Middle Jurassic. Fossils are numerous throughout, and representatives of all subdivisions in the Alpine Trias have been recognized. The limestones are succeeded by the well-known Spiti shales, famous for their ammonites. They are of Upper Jurassic age, and are overlain by the Giumal sandstone and Chikkim limestone and shales representing the Cretaceous system.

Central and lower zones.

A broad zone of metamorphic, crystalline, and unfossiliferous rocks forms the axis of the Himālayas. The crystallines are partly intrusive, and partly the result of contact with the metamorphism of the Cambrian slates in the northern zone. South of the metamorphics, however, the unfossiliferous sedimentary rocks extend from Chamba through Kāngra and the Simla Hill States to Garhwāl. They consist chiefly of limestones, slates, quartzites, and conglomerates of unknown age, and have been divided into three systems. The Jaunsār system, regarded as the oldest, consists of grey slates overlain by blue limestones, followed by red slates and quartzites exposed near Chakrāta. In Jaunsār-Bāwar and the east of Sirmūr the quartzites are overlain by a considerable thickness of trap and volcanic ash. Above the Jaunsār system a great development of limestones forms most of the higher parts of the mountains running north from Deoban, and is known as the Deoban system. It is also seen in Sirmūr, and in the Shali peak north of Simla. Above this follows the carbonaceous system, covering the greatest part of the Lower Himālayas. At the base is a great thickness of grey slate, with beds of grit and quartzite, resembling the Cambrian slates of the Tibetan zone. The slates, which are known as the infra-Blaini or Simla slates, are overlain by a characteristic series of conglomerates or boulder-slate and pink dolomitic limestone, which has been recognized in many parts of the Simla Hill States, while similar beds occur near Mussoorie on the east and in Chamba to the north-west. These are overlain by carbonaceous shale, followed by a quartzite bed of variable thickness, the two being included in the infra-Krol group, while the overlying Krol beds consist of limestone with subordinate bands of carbonaceous shale, the limestone attaining a great thickness in the Krol mountain near Solon. The age of the Jaunsār and Deoban systems is quite unknown; the carbonaceous system has been referred in part to the Permian and in part (the Krol limestone) to the Trias, but this classification is not final.

Sub-Himālayan zone.

The sub-Himālayan zone consists entirely of Tertiary beds, as a rule abutting against the pre-Tertiary rocks of the central and lower zone. These are comparatively narrow on the east, but gradually widen, till on the north-west they spread over the plains, forming a continuous mantle covering Jhelum and Rāwalpindi Districts, and extending to the northern parts of the Salt Range. The lowest or Sabāthu group consists of grey and red gypseous shales, with subordinate bands of limestone. It is overlain conformably by the Dagshai group, composed of a great thickness of grey sandstones, with bright red nodular clays. These are followed by bright red or purple clays, overlain by sandstones which constitute the Kasauli group. The Sabāthu group yields fossils of Nummulitic age, while no recognizable fossils have been found in the Dagshai, and only plant remains in the Kasauli group; but it is probable that the two last represent the oligocene and lower miocene of Europe. The Upper Tertiary or Siwālik series is separated from all the older beds by one of the most marked structural features of the Himālayas, the main boundary fault, a great dislocation which can be traced for long distances along the lower parts of the range. Sandstones and red clay form the lowest group, being well seen at Nāhan. They are succeeded, often unconformably, by many thousand feet of very soft grey sandstone, with bands of clay. These are overlain by conglomerates which constitute the uppermost portion of the Siwālik series. In the Siwālik Hills the thickness of the series is at least 15,000 feet. The two upper groups contain great quantities of mammalian remains of pliocene age.

Botany.

The flora falls naturally into four primary divisions: the Himālayas, the submontane belt from the Jumna to the Rāvi, the plain proper, and the Salt Range on both sides of the Indus with connected country in the north-west of the Province.

Himālayas.

The Himālayan tract includes the basin of the Sutlej, from the Tibetan border at Shipki to the hill station of Kasauli in Ambāla District; the basins of the Beās and Rāvi, from their sources to the submontane tracts of Kāngra and Gurdāspur; the basins of the Chandra and Bhāga, which unite to form the Chenāb, from the high watershed that divides their sources from the Indus valley to the eastern borders of Kashmīr and Jammu; and a promontory bounding the Kashmīr valley on the south, and culminating in the station of Murree about 6,500 feet above sea-level.

The Sutlej basin is again divided into two well-marked portions, of which the outer includes Simla District and adjoining Hill States, with Kasauli. The trees and shrubs of this portion, to about 6,000 feet, are mainly subtropical; but above this is a temperate belt which begins, roughly speaking, at Simla, and is rich in familiar European forest trees, such as yew, pines, oak and holly, elm, a horse-chestnut, several sorts of spindle-tree and buckthorn, and, among humbler growths, crowfoots, columbines, anemones, cresses, violets, stitchworts, cranesbills and St. John's worts, brambles, roses, spiraeas and wild strawberries, woodbines, guelder-rose and ivy, bell-flowers, gentians, Solomon's seal, meadow-rush, and herb-paris. The *Flora Simlensis* of the late Sir Henry Collett (edited by Mr. W. B. Hemsley) takes in only a part of the Simla Hills, but it describes 1,236 species of flowering plants, a number somewhat less than that of the native plants of the British Islands. The component elements, however, differ materially from those of any European flora, for, apart from the sub-tropical contingent, the Outer Himālayas preserve many forms allied to the plants of north-eastern Asia (e.g. *Hydrangea*), as well as Indo-Malayan types. The *deodār*, which flourishes near Simla, is related to the cedars of the Lebanon and the Atlas. East of Simla the rivers drain into the Jumna, and not towards the Sutlej, but as a matter of convenience certain petty States south-east of Bashahr and the territories of Sirmūr are grouped with the Simla area. In this tract the Chaur mountain, rising almost from the plains to over 12,000 feet, shows successive zones of vegetation, from the almost tropical valleys at its southern base to birch forest and subalpine pastures near its summit.

The upper portion of the Sutlej basin within Indian limits—that is to say, Kanāwār and the Spiti valley, with Lāhul and Pāngi, both drained by the Chenāb—constitutes a mainly alpine field of huge extent and great elevation. The flora is most closely linked with the vegetation of Western Tibet and Middle Asia, and includes few trees and very little forest. A pine, which is also found in the mountains of Afghānistān, extends to the lower levels of the inner Chenāb basin; but, except in Pāngi, a small pencil-cedar, stunted junipers, a few scattered birches, with pollard willows grown from saplings planted by the watercourses, complete the list of trees for this portion of the Punjab Himālayas.

Crossing outwards again to the basins of the Beās and Rāvi, the Kulū valley and the higher glens of Chamba present a far more varied and luxuriant aspect to the forester or botanist. The trees are mainly those of the Simla country; but certain shrubs and herbs reappear that are rare or absent in the Sutlej valley, owing doubtless to its greater indraught from the heated sands of the Punjab and Northern Rājputāna. On the other hand, some West Asian types—for example, the wild olive and the Oriental clematis—are found in the drier parts of Kulū more abundantly than to the eastward, while a few European forms, e.g. the great spearwort and the purple loosestrife, find their eastern limit in the Beās valley. The hill stations of Dalhousie and Dharmsāla come within this area. Epiphytic orchids, which are missing from the Simla country except very locally, reappear near Dharmsāla, but do not pass west of the spurs that divide the Kāngra ranges from the basin of the Rāvi.

The Murree hills, which are separated from the Rāvi country by a long stretch of the Outer Himālayas lying within Jammu territory, differ considerably owing to the presence of a stronger West Asian element in their flora.

Submontane tract. The submontane belt is practically restricted to the Districts of Ambāla (with its adjoining States), Hoshiārpur, and Kangra. The *sāl* tree, which is not found elsewhere to the west of the Jumna, survives in a single *dūn* (or strath) connected with the Kāngra valley, but actually within the northern border of Hoshiārpur District. The Kiārda Dūn in Sirmūr State and the Kalesar forest in Ambāla shelter a number of species that are characteristic or abundant in the Siwālik tract east of the Jumna, though unknown or rare farther westward.

Plains. The plain has also its subdivisions, which are, on the whole, even better marked than those of the Himālayas, an important influence being exercised by the climate of the Great Indian Desert which borders the whole southern limit of the Province, and sends out two arms which embrace the actual country of the five[1] rivers. That on the east takes in a great part of the Phūlkiān States, its apex being near the town of Ludhiāna, on an ancient bed of the Sutlej. The western arm (locally known as the Thal) extends from the Sind border up the Indus valley to the south-west angle of the Salt Range. The eastern chain of sandhills and alternating barriers has of late, however, lost much of its desert character through canal extensions. From Ludhiāna to the Jumna valley, and along the Jumna to the neighbourhood of Delhi, the country is substantially a portion of the great Gangetic plain, though some interesting peculiarities present themselves: a crowfoot (best known from North-Eastern America) occurs, also a rose which is elsewhere most abundant in the swamps of Eastern Bengal, and a kind of scurvy-grass (*Cochlearia*), a genus usually

[1] The Beās, Rāvi, Chenāb, Jhelum, and Indus. The Sutlej is included in Hindustān, of which at the same time it forms the traditional boundary.

partial to far colder latitudes. The south-east portions of the Province, and the upland tract skirting the western valley of the Jumna, present certain features of the Deccan flora, merging ultimately in the Arāvalli system. Trees in the extreme south-east are few, and mostly of Arabian or North African affinity. Similar forms, though seldom reaching the dimensions of a tree, characterize the southern fringe of the Punjab; but towards the Indus, a West Asian or indeed European element becomes prominent, in the case especially of those field annuals which come up each winter with the crops of the season: such as poppy, fumitory, rockets, catchfly, spurrey, chickweed, vetches and trefoils, thistles, blue pimpernel, bindweed, toadflax and veronicas, broomrape, goosefoots, milkspurges, asphodel and others.

Between the desert and the Indus the *doābs* bounded by the great rivers presented formerly a succession of alkaline wastes, often covered with low bushes of the saltwort tribe, or untilled expanses dotted with a scrub of thorny bushes of the *Acacia* family and of *van* (*Salvadora*, a desert representative of the olive), with an occasional row of tamarisks near a creek or waterhole, relieved in the autumn by a short-lived flush of climbing plants, and in good seasons by an abundant crop of grasses, which afforded coarse but invaluable pasture to the cattle of the nomad population. Canal extension and systematic state colonization are now changing all this rapidly, and the flora is approximating to the general spring and autumn series of agrestal species of Northern India, though a strong West Asian admixture maintains itself. Beyond the Indus, in Dera Ghāzi Khān District, this 'Oriental'[1] element begins to predominate, even as regards shrubs and perennials; and it continues northwards to the Salt Range and the hills near Attock, where several types common to the Orient and the Mediterranean, e.g. pinks and larkspurs, may be gathered at less than 2,000 feet above sea-level.

Salt Range.

Himālayan forms are still prevalent in the Salt Range, especially at the higher levels. On the north face of the culminating summit (Sakesar), at about 4,800 feet above the sea, there are a few oaks, of a common North-West Himālayan species, while herbaceous plants of the same region intermingle with trans-Indus representatives; but the slopes abound with box-trees, olives, and other Western forms. The herbs and grasses, moreover, although Indian forms abound, include

[1] The region from the Mediterranean to the Indus, and between the Red Sea and the Steppes, is thus termed by botanists.

a decided proportion of more Western types; but, owing to the dryness of the climate, these are usually such as characterize the arid zone that extends on the west through Africa to the Atlantic Islands.

Wild animals.

Until the beginning of the nineteenth century both lions and tigers appear to have been common, and the Nardak of the Eastern Punjab was a favourite hunting ground of the Mughal emperors. As late as 1827 Major Archer says that lions were sometimes seen within 20 miles of Karnāl, while tigers were exceedingly numerous in its immediate vicinity; and in the neighbourhood of Sirsa and in other parts of the Punjab tigers were abundant until past the middle of the nineteenth century. Lions are now entirely extinct and tigers practically so, though occasionally a straggler from the Arāvalli Hills is found in the South-East Punjab, or one from the eastern Tarai in Nāhan or Ambāla. Another animal practically extinct in the Punjab is the wild elephant, though it is occasionally met with in Nāhan and Ambāla. The only common representatives of the feline tribe are the leopard, the hunting leopard, and wild cat, with the lynx, along the southern border; the leopard is chiefly found in the hills. Two kinds of bear, the black and the brown, are found in the hills; hyenas and wolves are seen in most Districts, but are not common; jackals and foxes on the other hand abound. Ibex and *bharal* are found in the Higher Himālayas, and lower down musk deer, barking-deer, and wild goats; in the Salt Range the *uriāl* (*Ovis vignei*) is not uncommon. In the plains antelope are plentiful, especially in the east and south of the Province, and *nīlgai*, 'ravine deer' (*chinkāra*), and hog deer (*pārha*) are common in places. The wild hog, badger, porcupine, and hare are found in most parts. The grey ape (*langūr*) lives in the hills, and monkeys abound, both in the hills and in the canal-irrigated Districts. The otter and river porpoise are found in all the rivers.

Birds.

Peafowl are plentiful, and so is the lesser bustard; the great bustard is less common. Flocks of sand-grouse (imperial painted, pallas, and pintail) are frequently seen in the dry tracts. The grey partridge is found everywhere, and the black partridge is occasionally met with; in the hills the *chikor* (*Caccabis chukor*) and *sīsī* (*Ammoperdix bonhami*) partridges are common, and the snow partridge is found at high elevations. All the Indian pheasants are found in the Himālayas, including the argus, *monal*, *koklas*, *chīr*, and white-crested pheasant. Bush-quail and rain-quail are found in the plains, and the common grey quail comes in hosts at the ripening of the wheat. In the winter large numbers of waterfowl visit the rivers and *jhīls*. The most common ducks are the sealing-wax bill, pintail, mallard, pinkhead, shoveller, teal, and goose teal; geese, cranes, flamingoes, pelicans, ibises, herons, bitterns, snipe are all also more or less plentiful. The crow, vulture, and kite are ubiquitous, and the adjutant bird is occasionally met with. Hawks of various species are found, and often fetch high prices for sporting purposes. Green parrots fill the air with their screeching in the irrigated tracts, the golden oriole sometimes flashes through the trees, and the blue jay and woodpecker lend a frequent note of colour to the scene. Immense flocks of rosy pastors visit the plains in the hot season, and the *maina* is common everywhere in the neighbourhood of houses.

The sharp-nosed or fish-eating crocodile (*ghariyāl*) is found in all the great rivers, and the blunt-nosed crocodile or *magar* (*Crocodilus palustris*) is also met with in the lower reaches. The poisonous snakes are the *karait*, cobra, *Echis carinata* (*kappa*), and, in the east of the Province, Russell's viper. Lizards of various kinds are common. The commonest fish are the *rohu* (*Labeo rohita*) and mahseer, the latter of which runs up to 50 lb. Reptiles and fish.

Locusts sometimes arrive in swarms, chiefly from the south-west, and do considerable damage. White ants attack timber and garnered grain, which is also much subject to injury from weevils. Mosquitoes abound, and with sandflies combine to make life a burden in the hot season; and house-flies swarm, especially towards the beginning and ending of winter. Scorpions and centipedes are numerous, but not much seen. The honey-bee, hornet, and wasp are common, and the firefly's flashing light is to be seen wherever there is irrigation. Insects.

Over the greater part of the Punjab the climate is of the most pronounced continental character, extreme summer heat alternating with great winter cold; but its diversified surface, including montane, submontane, and plains zones, modifies very largely the temperature, weather, and climate in different parts of the Province. The Punjab has accordingly been divided into four natural divisions, in each of which the general meteorological conditions are believed to be fairly homogeneous. These are the Himālayan (stations, Simla and Murree), the sub-Himālayan (stations, Ambāla, Ludhiāna, Siālkot, and Rāwalpindi), the Indo-Gangetic Plain West (stations, Delhi and Lahore), and the north-west dry area (stations, Khushāb, Montgomery, Multān, and Sirsa). Meteorology.

As a whole, the Punjab has in normal years two well-defined rainy seasons. The first or period of the north-east monsoon includes the 'Christmas rains,' as they are called, which fall between the end of December and the end of February or the middle of March. The second rainfall period is that of the south-west monsoon, from the end of June to the middle of September. The rainfall is naturally heaviest in the Himālayas. The highest average received is 126 inches at Dharmsāla, and the average of the Himālayas is nowhere less than 36. In the plains the rainfall decreases rapidly away from the hills. The submontane zone, which skirts the foot of the hills, and of which Rāwalpindi and Siālkot may be taken as typical stations, has an annual fall of 30 to 40 inches. The eastern plains from Delhi to Lahore belong to the West Gangetic plain, and have a mean rainfall of about 24 inches, the valley of the Jumna having a higher rainfall than the rest. To the west and south-west lies the dry area, characterized by an extremely light and variable rainfall, and a heat and dryness in the hot season extreme even for the Punjab. The ordinary south-west monsoon winds from the Sind and Kāthiāwār coasts encircle, but do not blow into this area, which therefore gets very little rain from this source, though it occasionally receives heavy cyclonic downpours from storms that have travelled westward from the head of the Bay. Montgomery and Multān are typical stations of this tract.

The plains, owing to their arid nature and remoteness from the sea, are subject to extreme vicissitudes of climate. In the winter the cold exceeds anything met with elsewhere in the plains of India. In January and February the night temperature commonly falls below freezing-point, while by day the thermometer does not as a rule rise above 75°; and for four months of the year nothing can be more perfect than the Punjab climate, with its bright sun and keen invigorating air. In summer, on the other hand, the fierce dry heat is surpassed only in Sind. In June the thermometer commonly reaches 115° to 121°, while the night temperature averages from 79° to 83°.

About the end of December the weather conditions ordinarily become disturbed; rain falls in the plains and snow on the hills. The rainfall of this season is almost exclusively due to cold-weather storms or cyclones, which follow each other at varying intervals, averaging about ten days, from the end of December to about the middle of March. Important features of these storms are the rapid changes of weather which accompany them. Their approach is preceded by the appearance of a bank of cirrus cloud, which gradually overspreads the whole sky. Under this canopy the heat rapidly increases, more particularly at night, and temperatures from 5° to 15° higher than usual are registered. In the rear of the disturbance a rapid change takes place, accompanying the clearing of the skies and the change of wind. The thermometer falls with great rapidity, sharp frost on the ground is experienced, and air temperatures of 18° or 19° are occasionally recorded at the hill stations. This fall of temperature appears to be directly related to the snowfall on the hills, and is proportional to the amount of the snowfall, and to the lowness of the elevation to which it descends. As the rainfall of this period accompanies the march of cyclonic storms from west to east across Northern India, it is ordinarily heaviest at the northern and Indus valley stations, and usually diminishes to a very small amount over the south and south-east.

The mean temperature in most parts increases from February to May at about the rate of 10° a month, and by the end of March or beginning of April the hot season is in most years fairly established. From April till near the end of June there is, as a rule, no rain of importance, though occasional thunder and hail storms afford temporary relief from the great heat. A desiccating, scorching west wind blows during the greater part of this period, and the thermometer ranges from about 95° in the early morning to about 115° in the heat of the day. These westerly winds commence to drop towards the end of June, and for a few days still, calm, sweltering heat succeeds the scorching blasts of the hot winds. About the end of June south and east winds bring up heavy cumulus clouds, and in favourable years the monsoon rains are then ushered in with violent thunderstorms and heavy showers. The rainfall is generally very variable and irregular in its advance, and is ordinarily brought up by the approach to the south-east of the Province of a cyclonic storm from the Bay of Bengal. This carries with it the moist south-east air currents from the Bay, and at the same time induces an inrush of moist air from the north of the Arabian Sea across the Sind and Kāthiāwār coasts and eastern and central Rājputāna into the south and east Punjab. The rainfall of the monsoon season is seldom steady or continuous, nor does it, as a rule, extend over the whole Province, as in the west and south the fall is both scanty and uncertain. For two or three days in succession heavy, fairly general rain may fall; but this is succeeded by intervals of oppressively hot and sultry weather, when the rain ceases or only falls as scattered showers. These conditions continue with greater or less intensity till the second or third week of September, when, with not infrequently a second outburst of violent thunderstorms, the rains cease and fine weather commences.

Storms and cyclones. Severe cyclonic storms are practically unknown in the Punjab. Hailstorms are fairly frequent, especially in March and April, and often cause considerable damage to the crops.

Floods. Although the Province is traversed or bounded by seven large rivers, it is not to any serious extent subject to inundations from them, and it is only in the comparatively narrow riverain belts bordering the channels of the rivers that floods do serious harm. An exception to this generalization is to be found in the extreme south-west, where parts of the Districts of Dera Ghāzi Khān, Muzaffargarh, and Multān, bordering on the Chenāb and Indus, are low enough to be subject to frequent inundations even during the passage of normal floods. Protection is afforded by the erection of dikes, but they are not always sufficiently strong to resist a heavy spate. Nearly all the high floods of which records exist have occurred in July or August, when the summer monsoon is at its height. The earliest of these was in 1849, when the town and civil station of Shāhpur were washed away by the Jhelum. In 1856 and in 1878 the Indus rose very high, and on both occasions the towns of Muzaffargarh and Dera Ghāzi Khān were flooded out and large portions of the Districts submerged. In 1892, 1893, and 1905 the Chenāb and the Jhelum were heavily flooded, and in the second of these years the Kohāla suspension bridge on the Kashmīr road was carried away. The great Indus flood of 1878 is said to have been in part the result of heavy landslips in the hills.

Earthquakes. Throughout the period over which authentic records of Indian earthquakes extend, the Punjab has repeatedly suffered from the effects of seismic disturbances of greater or less intensity. This is due to the presence of important lines of weakness in the earth's crust, caused by the stresses involved in the folding of the Himālayas and resulting in the development of faults. The most important of these is that known as the 'main boundary fault,' which runs through the Lower Himālayas from end to end of the Punjab. Along these lines readjustments of the equilibrium of the crust are constantly taking place, and when these readjustments are irregular or spasmodic the movement results in an earthquake. Such earthquakes as are due to this cause are naturally most severe in the neighbourhood of the fault. A striking exemplification is to be found in the Kāngra earthquake of 1905. About 20,000 human beings perished in this catastrophe, which ranks as one of the most disastrous of modern times. The loss of life occurred principally in the Kāngra valley, Dharmsāla, Mandī, and Kulū, but the shock was perceptible to the unaided sense throughout an area of some 1,625,000 square miles. Although this most recent catastrophe dwarfs all earthquakes previously recorded in the Province, those of 1803, 1827, 1842, and 1865 were of considerable severity.

History. Early period.

The Punjab was undoubtedly the seat of the earliest Aryan settlements in India, and the Rig-Veda was probably composed within its borders. In one of its finest hymns the Vipāsa (Beās) and Sutudrī (Sutlej) are invoked by the sage Visvāmitra to allow the host of the Bharatas to cross them dryshod. And in the later Vedic period the centre of Aryan civilization lay farther to the south-east, between the Sutlej and the Jumna, in the still sacred land of KURUKSHETRA round Thānesar, the battle-field of the Mahābhārata, while Indrapat near Delhi still preserves at least the name of Yudhishthira's capital, Indraprastha. For a brief period after 500 B.C. part of the Punjab may have formed a Persian province, the Indian satrapy conquered by Darius, which stretched from Kālābāgh to the sea, and paid a tribute of fully a million sterling.

Alexander.

In invading the territories east of the Indus Alexander yielded to mere lust of conquest, for they no longer owed allegiance to the Persian empire. In 326 B.C. he crossed the river at Ohind or Und, invading thereby a dependency of Porus (Paurava), whose kingdom lay in the Chaj Doāb. The capital of this dependency was Taxila (Sanskrit, Takshaṣilā), now the ruins of Shāhdheri, but then a great and flourishing city, which lay three marches from the Indus. Its governor, Omphis (Ambhi) or Taxiles, was in revolt against Porus, and received the Macedonians hospitably. Leaving Philippus as satrap at Taxila, Alexander, reinforced by 5,000 Indians under Taxiles, marched to the Jhelum (Hydaspes), where he found Porus prepared to dispute his passage of the river, probably near Jhelum town. Alexander, however, turned his enemy's right flank by crossing higher up, and defeated him with great loss. Porus himself was captured, but soon admitted to alliance with the Macedonians and granted the country between the upper reaches of the Jhelum and Chenāb (Bhimbar and Rājauri). His nephew, also named

Porus, ruler of Gandaris (possibly the modern Gondal Bār, between the Chenāb and the Rāvi), had already tendered his surrender; but the Macedonians crossed the Chenāb and drove him across the Rāvi. Here, in the modern District of Amritsar or Gurdāspur, Pimprama, the capital of the Adraistoi, surrendered to Alexander, and he then invested Sangala, the capital of the Kathaians. Having taken it by assault he advanced to the Beās; but his soldiers being reluctant to cross that river, he erected twelve massive altars on its bank to mark the eastern limits of his invasion, and returned to the Jhelum, making Porus governor of all the conquered country west of the Beās.

At his newly founded city of Bucephala (? Jhelum), Alexander now prepared a flotilla to sail down the Jhelum and the Indus to the sea. Starting late in October, 326 B.C., the Macedonians marched in two divisions, one on either side of the river, Alexander himself with some of the troops sailing in the fleet, which numbered nearly 2,000 vessels, great and small. At the capital of Sophytes (probably Bhera) he was joined by Philippus, and thence hastened to invade the territories of the Malloi and Oxydrakoi, two powerful tribes which held the country south of the confluence of the Jhelum with the Chenāb. The strongholds of the former soon fell, as did a Brāhman city (? Atari or Shorkot); but the capital of the Malloi offered a desperate resistance, and had to be carried by assault, in which Alexander himself was wounded. The Malloi and Oxydrakoi now submitted, and the satrapy of Philippus was extended to the confluence of the Chenāb with the Indus, including the Xathroi and Ossadioi tribes. At the confluence of these rivers Alexander founded a city, possibly the modern Uch Sharīf, and thence sailed on down the Indus to the capital of the Sogdoi, where he fortified another city, constructed dockyards, and repaired his ships. His voyage now lay through the kingdom of Mousicanus, corresponding to the modern Sind.

His successors.

Alexander thus made no attempt to hold the Punjab east of the Jhelum. That country he designed to make a dependent kingdom under Porus, while Philippus governed the Sind-Sāgar Doāb as satrap. This arrangement, however, did not endure. In 324 Philippus was murdered by his mercenaries, and no successor was appointed, Eudamus and Taxiles being ordered to carry on the administration. After Alexander's death Porus ousted Peithon from Sind, and in revenge Eudamus decoyed him into his power, and murdered him six years later. His execution was the signal for a national revolt against the Macedonian power. Eudamus withdrew with his Greek garrison, and Chandragupta (Sandrocottus), the Mauryan, made himself master of the Punjab and the lower Indus valley. Himself a native of the Punjab, Chandragupta organized the predatory tribes of the north-west frontier against the Greeks. His mastery of the Punjab enabled him to conquer Magadha; and when, about sixteen years later, in 305 B.C., Seleucus Nicator, king of Syria, marched into India to recover Alexander's Indian conquests, he was content to cede to Chandragupta even the territory west of the Indus, and to give him a daughter in marriage. Under his son Bindusāra and his grandson Asoka, Buddhism became the state religion of the Punjab, as is shown by the pillar erected at Topra and by the Buddhist remains at SUI VEHĀR, in the Bahāwalpur State, and in the Kāngra valley. Under the Mauryan dynasty Taxila remained the capital of the great viceroyalty, which extended from the Sutlej to the Hindu Kush, and probably included Sind. After Asoka's death Euthydemus, who had usurped the Graeco-Bactrian throne, extended the Greek power in India. In 205 or 206 Antiochus III of Syria acknowledged his independence, and then crossed the Paropamisus into India and made a treaty with Sophagasenas (Subhāgasena), returning to Syria in the following year. Ten years later, in 195 B.C., Demetrius, son of Euthydemus, reduced the Punjab, rebuilt Sagala, which he renamed Euthydemia, and extended his conquests so far that Justin calls him 'King of the Indians.' But while engaged in these conquests he lost Bactria, and his successors appear to have ruled only over the Western Punjab and the Kābul valley; but little is known about them until Menander raised the Graeco-Bactrian power to its zenith in India. According to Plutarch, Menander's territories extended to the Narbadā and Indus delta. But this great kingdom was doomed, as we shall so often find its successors were doomed, to fall before barbarian invasion from the west.

Sakas and Kushans.

By 100 B.C. Maues or Moga, king of the Sakas, a tribe expelled from Sogdiana by the Yueh-chi, founded a kingdom in the North-West Punjab, with its capital at Taxila, which endured for about seventy years. This kingdom was overrun by Kozula Kadphises, the chief of the Kushan tribe of the Yueh-chi. He also destroyed the last Greek principality in India, and his son Wemo Kadphises (Himakapisa) had extended his sway all over north-western India by A.D. 10[1]. About

[1] The date of the Kushans is still in dispute.

A.D. 25, however, we find a Parthian satrapy established in Afghānistān and Northern India, with Gondophares, the Gundoferus of St. Thomas's mission, as its founder. The Parthian power was short-lived, for by A.D. 78 the Kushans had recovered their supremacy in the person of Kanishka, under whom the so-called Scythian power reached its zenith. He was succeeded by Hushka (Huvishka) and Jushka (Vāsudeva). Under the latter the Kushan dominions shrank to the Indus valley and Afghānistān; and the dynasty was then supplanted by Ki-to-lo, chief of the Little Yueh-chi, and he in turn by the Ephthalites or White Huns about the middle of the fifth century. Under Toramāna and his son Mihirakula these Huns held Northern India, Sagala being their capital. The latter is doubtless the great Mihirakula of the *Rājatarangini*, who lost his empire in Central India and gained the kingdom of Kashmīr, retaining probably the Punjab until his final overthrow at Karor in 544, after the Ephthalite power had endured for a century. Space precludes any detailed account of the religious history of the Punjab after Asoka made Buddhism its state religion; but the coins of the Kushan kings bear effigies of Zoroastrian, Greek, and Hindu divinities, while Mihirakula's persecution of the Buddhists was terrible in its severity, a policy which probably contributed to his downfall. At all events, Buddhism was now on the decline.

In the latter half of the sixth century arose the great kingdom of THĀNESAR. This, however, included only the Punjab east of the Jhelum river; for in the middle of the seventh century Hiuen Tsiang, the Chinese pilgrim, found Taxila and Singhapura in the Salt Range dependent on Kashmīr, while the Central Punjab from the Indus to the Beās formed the kingdom of Tseh-kia, whose capital lay near Sākala, and to which Multān was a subject principality. Early in the eighth century Thānesar ceased to exist as a great kingdom, and the Tomar dynasty of Kanauj established itself in the South-East Punjab, where it held Hānsi and founded Delhi. After a century's dominion, the Tomars were supplanted by the Chauhāns of Ajmer in 1151.

The Muhammadan invasions. The Muhammadan conquerors of India invaded the Punjab by two distinct routes. As early as the year 38 of the Hijra the Khalīfa Alī had appointed governors to the frontiers of Hind, and six years later, in A.D. 664, a Muhammadan general penetrated to Multān. This inroad, however, resulted in no permanent conquest; and the first real invasion occurred in 712, when Muhammad bin Kāsim, another of the Khalīfa's generals, conquered Sind and took Multān, which then lay on the north bank of the Rāvi, in the dominions of Dāhir, ruler of Sind. He made Multān the base of farther inroads, and garrisoned Bramhapur on the Jhelum, the modern Shorkot, Ajtahād, and Karor; and afterwards, with 50,000 men, he marched via Dipālpur to the foot of the Himālayas near Jhelum. But his ill-deserved execution prevented a farther advance; and it was not till some years later that the whole province of Multān was reduced, and the part of the Punjab dependent on Kashmīr subdued.

By 871 the power of the Khalīfate was on the decline, and Multān became an independent and prosperous kingdom under an Arab dynasty. The rest of the Punjab was divided among Hindu kings, the Brāhman dynasty of Ohind probably holding the Salt Range, while as early as 804 Jālandhara or Trigarta was an established kingdom.

Mahmūd of Ghazni.

More than a century elapsed before the Muhammadan advance was resumed, and Ghazni now becomes its base. In 979 Jaipāl, king of Lahore, advanced on Ghazni to encounter Sabuktagīn, its Amīr, at Laghmān, but effected a treaty and retired, only to be defeated there nine years later, in 988. Jaipāl was then in alliance with the kings of Delhi, Ajmer, Kālinjar, and Kanauj; and his defeat was decisive, as he had to surrender four strongholds towards Ghazni, and Sabuktagīn occupied the country up to the Indus. Shaikh Hāmid, the Afghān governor of Multān, also did homage to him. Sabuktagīn was succeeded by the renowned Mahmūd of Ghazni, who in 1001 commenced a series of inroads into India. In the first, Jaipāl was defeated near Peshāwar, and, having burnt himself to death, was succeeded by his son Anand Pāl. The latter allied himself with the governor of Multān, Abul Fateh Lodī, but was also defeated at Peshāwar in 1006, whereupon Multān was reduced. In 1009 Anand Pāl, who had formed a great coalition of Hindu rulers, including those of Ujjain and Gwalior, met with his second defeat near Peshāwar, after which Mahmūd sacked Nagarkot or Kāngra. Nevertheless in 1010 Mahmūd had again to subdue Multān, where the Karmatian heretics had revolted, and deport its Lodī governor. In 1014 he reduced Nandana, a fastness in the Salt Range, driving Trilochan Pāl, Anand Pāl's son and successor, to seek an asylum in Kashmīr; and in the same year he plundered Thānesar. The subjugation of the greater part of the Punjab was hardly completed before 1021, when Trilochan Pāl was defeated again and slain. It was left, however, to Masūd, son of Mahmūd, to reduce Hānsi, the old capital of Siwālik, in 1036. But the Ghaznivids were already destined to succumb to a stronger power, and as early as 1041 Masūd was compelled by the Seljūk Turks to retreat into the Punjab. Nevertheless Ghazni remained the centre of their authority; and it was only as the Turkish power in Central Asia increased that they gradually withdrew into the Punjab, until their kingdom was virtually confined to that province.

Muhammad of Ghor.

Finally, in 1181, Khusrū, who significantly bore only the title of Malik, not that of Shāh, surrendered Lahore to the invader, usually called Shahāb-ud-dīn, but more correctly Muizz-ud-dīn, Muhammad of Ghor. Muhammad was governor of Ghazni under his brother, the Sultān of Ghor, when in 1175–6 he took Multān from the Karmatians and laid siege to Uch, which was betrayed by its queen. In 1179 he captured Peshāwar. Meanwhile the Kashmīr ruler had invoked his aid against Khusrū, who was endeavouring to consolidate his power in the Punjab, with the result already related. In 1191 Muhammad of Ghor made his first great expedition into the South-East Punjab. After conquering Sirhind, which he garrisoned, he advanced to meet Prithwī Rāj of Ajmer, who, with his brother, the ruler of Delhi, and all the chiefs of Hind, encountered him at Talāwari, near Thānesar. Muhammad was defeated and wounded. In the following year, however, he returned and, though too late to relieve Sirhind, overwhelmed Prithwī Rāj, whom he captured, and whose brother, Rai Govind of Delhi, fell in the battle, which was fought on the scene of Muhammad's former defeat. By this victory Ajmer with all the Siwālik territory, including Hānsi, fell into his hands, and his slave and lieutenant Kutb-ud-dīn Aibak completed his work, taking Delhi in the following year (1193). The tribes of the Salt Range, however, made the communications between Ghazni and Lahore precarious; and, though he suppressed them with ruthless severity, Muhammad was in 1206 assassinated by them on his way to Ghazni.

Slave kings.

On Muhammad's death Kutb-ud-dīn established himself as an independent ruler at Lahore, another slave, Tāj-ud-dīn, obtaining Ghazni. Tāj-ud-dīn soon ousted Nāsir-ud-dīn Kubācha from Lahore, which he held for Kutb-ud-dīn, but the latter, advancing from Delhi, drove him back to Kirmān in the Kurram valley, and for six weeks occupied Ghazni. On his death in 1210 his slave Shams-ud-dīn Altamsh was raised to the throne at Delhi, while Nāsir-ud-dīn secured most of the

Punjab. But Tāj-ud-dīn, driven from Central Asia by the Khwārizmis, retreated into the Punjab, wrested Lahore from Nāsir-ud-dīn, and attacked Altamsh, only to be defeated and taken prisoner at Talāwari. Altamsh then seized Lahore, and thus became master of the Punjab, though Nāsir-ud-dīn maintained himself at Uch. Meanwhile, the Khwārizmis themselves had had to yield to the invading Mongol hordes, and in 1221 their Sultān Jalāl-ud-dīn fled into the Punjab, pursued to the west bank of the Indus by Chingiz Khān. Escaping from his pursuer with a handful of followers, Jalāl-ud-dīn defeated an army of Altamsh, but fearing to attack Lahore turned south towards Multān and Uch, overthrew Nāsir-ud-dīn, and returned to summer in the Salt Range. These events led to the first Mongol invasion of the Punjab. Alarmed by Jalāl-ud-dīn's successes, Chingiz Khān had dispatched against him a force which captured Nandana and invested Multān. In the following year (1223) another Mongol army compelled Jalāl-ud-dīn to evacuate the Punjab, after burning Uch in his retreat.

Mongol raids.

Five years later Altamsh defeated Nāsir-ud-dīn and annexed Multān and Uch, with Sind. His authority, thus extending over nearly the whole Punjab, was confirmed in 1229 by a diploma of investiture from the Abbassid Khalīfa of Baghdād. He failed, however, to extend his frontier beyond the Salt Range, and an unsuccesful expedition against the Mongols in that quarter was followed by his death in 1236. Under the influence of 'the Forty,' a corps of Turkish Mamlūks which he had formed, his dynasty rapidly decayed. His daughter Razia, the only Muhammadan queen who ever ruled at Delhi (1236–40), had to face religious disaffection within the city, where a Karmatian rising was suppressed after much bloodshed. Her feudatories of Lahore, Hānsi, and Multān also rebelled, though unsuccessfully, but such was the weakness of the kingdom in 1241 that a Mongol army sacked Lahore. Uch, with Sind, became independent, and the Turkish Amīrs deposed Razia's successor, Bahrām Shāh, a degenerate son of Altamsh, in the following year. The reign of the next king, Alā-ud-dīn Masūd, was chiefly noteworthy for the rise of Balban, one of 'the Forty' who in 1246 compelled the Mongols to raise the siege of Uch. For the next twenty years, Balban and his cousin, Sher Khān, feudatory of Lahore, kept the Mongols and Karlugh Turks at bay. Under Balban's stern rule the disaffection, which had brought rapine to the very gates of Delhi, was checked. More than once he had to ravage the Mewāt, while the Mongols made good their footing in the Indus valley, and, aided by a disloyal vassal at Uch, placed an intendant at Multān. In 1266 Balban was placed on the throne of Delhi, and devoted his whole reign to organizing resistance to the Mongol encroachments. The power of 'the Forty' was broken. Sher Khān died, not without suspicion of poison. Balban's son Nusrat-ud-dīn Muhammad, the patron of the poet Amīr Khusrū, bid fair to continue his father's work, but in 1285 fell in battle with the Mongols near Dipālpur, and earned his title of 'the Martyr Prince.'

Khiljīs and Tughlaks.

Two years later Balban died, and was succeeded by the Khiljī line of Sultāns in 1290. Its founder, Fīroz Shāh II, had to contend with religious disaffection, and in 1296 was assassinated by Alā-ud-dīn Muhammad Shāh, his nephew and son-in-law, who usurped the throne. Alā-ud-dīn's ambition led him to attempt conquests in Southern India, while from 1296 to 1305 the Mongols overran the Punjāb. In 1298, with 200,000 men, they penetrated to Delhi, but met with severe defeat under its walls. In 1303 they beleaguered the Sultān within the city, and, though compelled to retreat after a few months' siege, invaded Hindustān in the following year. Alā-ud-dīn now reorganized his forces, and rebuilt the frontier towns of Sāmāna and Dipālpur, but failed to protect Multān and the Siwāliks from the Mongol inroads. In 1304, however, Ghāzi Beg Tughlak, governor of the Punjab, routed their retreating forces and secured a respite from their inroads until Muhammad Shāh's death in 1316. Four years of anarchy followed, but eventually Ghāzi Beg seized Delhi and established the Tughlak dynasty. Like his Khiljī predecessor, the founder was assassinated by his eldest son, Muhammad, who in 1325 caused a pavilion to fall on him, and ascended his throne. Muhammad bin Tughlak is the most striking figure in mediaeval Indian history. His father had built the great fortress of Tughlakābād, now a cyclopean ruin, near Delhi, but he endeavoured to transplant his capital to Deogiri in the Deccan. Though unable to withstand the Mongols, who in 1327 ravaged Multān and had to be paid a vast ransom to spare Delhi, he planned the conquest of China, Khorāsān, and trans-Oxiana. A scholar, a poet, and a patron of letters, he was as a ruler ruthlessly severe. His economic measures included the introduction of a token currency, and led to frightful disorders and distress. In and around Delhi a terrible famine, caused by his exactions, raged for years; but the Sultān took vigorous measures to restore prosperity, and organized a system of loans to the starving peasantry. He obtained a formal recognition from the Abbassid Khalīfa of distant Egypt, though he ruled an independent kingdom as wide as that of Aurangzeb. Nevertheless his power was built on sand. The Afghāns, who now appear for the first time on the north-west frontier, overwhelmed Multan in 1343. Even the country round Sunām and Sāmāna was in open revolt, and the Gakhars seized Lahore. Eventually Muhammad bin Tughlak died of fever in 1351 while on an expedition in Sind, leaving the kingdom to his cousin the noble Fīroz Shāh III. With this king's accession the modern history of the Punjab begins to take shape. He dug canals, notably that from the Jumna, and founded Hissār. Sirhind was colonized and became a separate government. Nagarkot (Kāngra) was taken, and Sirmūr and the hills north of Ambāla were subdued.

Anarchy.

Fīroz Shāh reigned for thirty-seven years and was succeeded, after the usual interlude of anarchy, by Muhammad Shāh III in 1390. Mewāt, however, was in revolt and the Khokhars under Shaikha seized Lahore. Prince Humāyūn was about to march against them, when his father's death recalled him to the throne, and the rebellion had to be put down by Sārang Khān, feudatory of Dipālpur, in a regular campaign in 1394. By 1395 the empire had fallen into chaos. Rival puppet Sultāns waged war on one another from their opposing capitals at Delhi, while Sārang Khān attacked Multān on his own account. On this scene of disunion the Mongols reappeared in force. In 1397 Pīr Muhammad laid siege to Uch, Sāraṅg Khān's fief, defeating a relieving force, and also invested Multān, which surrendered in 1398, and thus paved the way for Tīmūr's great inroad of that year. Crossing the Indus south of the Salt Range, Tīmūr plundered Talamba in September, and advanced via Ajodhan to Bhatner. Thence his march lay through Fatehābād, Tohāna, across the Ghaggar, through Kaithal and Pānīpat to Delhi, which he sacked on December 26. Crossing the Jumna he attacked Hardwār, and recrossing the river in January, 1399, defeated Ratn Sain (probably the Rājā of Sirmūr) in the Kiārda Dūn, advanced through the Siwāliks, took Nagarkot and Jammu, and encamped at Bannu early in March. In this incredible march Tīmūr massacred men, women, and children by tens of thousands, and reduced the country along his route to ruin. It is, however, a consolation to read that he killed some thousands of Jats near Tohāna because they were given to robbing travellers. The only immediate result of his inroad was to reinstate Khizr Khān in possession of Multān, which Sārang Khān had wrested from him. On his departure the struggle for Delhi recommenced, with the added miseries of pestilence and famine. The Punjab fiefs remained virtually independent, and indeed Delhi never regained her ascendancy until Bābar founded the Mughal dynasty.

Saiyids and Lodīs.

Eventually in 1414 Khizr Khān, who had been practically master, not only of Multān, but of the whole Punjab since Tīmūr's departure, took Delhi and founded the Saiyid dynasty, which owned a nominal allegiance to the Mongols. But the four Saiyid rulers were as weak as those whom they had supplanted. The Mongol governor of Kābul exercised a fitful control over the Punjab, which was in constant revolt under its Turk and Khokhar feudatories. Again, the necessity for a strong warden of the marches compelled Muhammad Shāh IV to entrust Dipālpur and Lahore to Bahlol, a Lodī Afghān, in 1441, but Bahlol soon patched up peace with the Khokhars, and in 1451 took Delhi and founded the first Pathān dynasty. Multān had become an independent kingdom in 1443. Under the Lodīs the Punjab enjoyed such peace as a country no longer worth plundering might enjoy. The period is remarkable for a popular religious revival, for it produced Nānak (1469–1538), the founder of Sikhism.

Mughals and Sūris.

In 1526 Bābar, a fugitive king of Samarkand, defeated Ibrāhīm, the Lodī king of Delhi, at Pānīpat, and thus established the Indian empire of the Mughals. As usual, disunion and disaffection had led to the ruin of the Afghān domination. Daulat Khān, himself a Lodī, governor of the Punjab, sought the aid of Bābar, then king of Kābul, against his kinsman, and enabled him to seize Lahore in 1524, when he established Alā-ud-dīn, Daulat Khān's uncle, as 'Sultān' at Dipālpur. Daulat Khān, now alarmed for his own safety, raised a force to oppose Bābar, who had returned to recruit fresh troops in Kābul, but offered little resistance; and Bābar, having seized his stronghold in the Siwāliks, marched down the Jaswān Dūn, crossed the Sutlej, and overthrew Ibrāhīm at Pānīpat in April, 1526. Bābar spent the last years of his life in establishing his rule in India from the capital at Agra, and on his death at the age of forty-eight, Humāyūn succeeded him in 1530. But Kāmrān, Bābar's second son, promptly annexed the Punjab, and, though the Afghān power was still far from crushed, Humāyūn frittered away his power in a futile conquest of Gujarāt. In 1540 Sher Shāh drove him out of India, through the Punjab and into the desert country near Uch, whence he fled to Persia. Sher Shāh held effective control of the Punjab, building Rohtās in Jhelum District to overawe the

Gakhars of the Salt Range, who had long been vassals or allies of the Mughals. Aided by the Shāh of Persia, Humāyūn expelled Kāmrān from Kābul in 1547, and eight years later he overthrew Sikandar Sūri, who had seized the Punjab, defeating him at Sirhind in 1555. Sikandar retreated to the Kāngra hills, and Akbar was pressing in pursuit of him when he received news of Humāyūn's death at Delhi in 1556.

With Akbar's accession a new era began. The Mughal empire was finally and firmly established, and the Punjab, after twenty years of incessant war, enjoyed comparative peace. Sikandar was indeed intrenched at Mānkot, and Hīmu, a shopkeeper of Rewāri, who had risen to be Wazīr of the last of the Afghān emperors, seized Delhi and proclaimed himself ruler of India under the title of Vikramājīt. In 1556, however, Akbar routed him at Pānīpat. Mānkot surrendered after an eight months' siege, and only a difficult campaign was required to secure the north-west frontier in 1586. With the rest of India, the Punjab benefited by Akbar's reforms and owes to him the foundations of its modern revenue system. Akbar.

The accession of Jahāngīr in 1605 was followed almost immediately by the revolt of his son Khusrū, who escaped from Agra and laid siege to Lahore. The rebellion was suppressed by the emperor in person, and the adherents of the defeated prince were punished with fearful severity. In 1611 Jahāngīr married Nūr Jahān, who during the remaining years of his reign dominated his policy and his fortunes. Her influence at first was for good; but later she involved the emperor in conflicts with his son, Khurram (Shāh Jahān), and his famous general, Mahābat Khān, who in 1626 seized the emperor in his camp on the Jhelum. After making a spirited attempt to rescue him, the empress consented to share his brief captivity. Jahāngīr did not long survive his release. He died in 1627 at Bhimbar, and was buried at Shāhdara near Lahore. His widow raised a splendid mausoleum over his remains, and herself lived in retirement at Lahore for eighteen years after his death. Jahāngīr.

Shāh Jahān was proclaimed at Agra early in 1628, but his younger brother, Shahryār, had already set up his standard at Lahore. He was speedily overthrown by the energy of Asaf Khān, the father-in-law of the emperor, and the ill-starred enterprise terminated with the execution of the pretender and his principal adherents. During the last five years of Jahāngīr's reign, Lahore had been the capital of the empire, but Shāh Jahān determined to build for himself a new capital on the banks of Shāh Jahān.

the Jumna at Delhi. His reign was the most prosperous period of Mughal rule, a period of profound internal peace and immunity from foreign invasion; but it was, none the less, marked by military activity beyond the frontiers. Kandahār was seized in 1639, only to be lost again ten years later; and the great expeditions of 1652, commanded by the princes Aurangzeb and Dārā Shikoh, failed to recover it. The successes of the imperial army in Balkh and Badakhshān in 1644 were neutralized by the disastrous retreat conducted by Aurangzeb through the passes of the Hindu Kush, but the expedition against Baltistān in 1651 was crowned by the capture of Skārdo. A dangerous illness which prostrated the emperor in 1657 was the signal for the outbreak of strife among his sons. After his defeat near Agra, Dārā fled to the Punjab, trusting to his popularity with the people of the province to gain him adherents. In this he was not altogether disappointed; but the restless activity of his brother compelled him to fly, and in the following year he was captured and put to death at Delhi.

Aurangzeb.

The reign of Aurangzeb dates from June, 1658, though his father survived in confinement at Agra till 1666. It was one long struggle against the powers of the South. In the Punjab the profound peace which the province had known under Shāh Jahān continued for half a century under his successor, broken only by the march of the imperial armies through the province in 1673–5 to crush the Afghān revolt, and by the insurrection of the Satnāmis of Nārnaul in 1676. The war with the Afghān tribes dragged on for two years, and was only brought to a close by a treacherous massacre at Peshāwar. The insurrection of the Satnāmis infected the Hindu population of Agra and Ajmer. Detachments of the imperial army were defeated, and the insurgents advanced on Delhi. A panic spread throughout the army, and it was with difficulty that the soldiers could be brought to face the enemy. Confidence was restored by the personal exertions of the emperor, and a crushing defeat was inflicted on the insurgents. In the closing years of Aurangzeb's reign signs were already visible that the downfall of the empire was not far distant, and the century after his death in 1707 saw the rise of a new power in the Punjab.

Sikhs.

This power was the Sikhs, originally a mere religious sect, founded by Bāba Nānak, who was born near Lahore in the latter half of the fifteenth century, and who died at Dera Nānak, on the Rāvi, in 1538. A full account of the sect will be found in Prinsep's *History of the Punjab* (2 vols., 1846) and Cunningham's *History of the Sikhs* (second edition, 1853), to which works the reader is referred for a complete or detailed narrative. Bāba Nānak was a disciple of Kabīr, and preached as a new religion a pure form of monotheism, eagerly accepted by the peasantry of his neighbourhood. He maintained that devotion was due to God, but that forms were immaterial, and that Hindu and Muhammadan worships were the same in the sight of the Deity. His tenets were handed down by a succession of Gurūs or spiritual leaders, under whom the new doctrine made steady but peaceful progress. Rām Dās, the fourth Gurū, obtained from Akbar a grant of land on the spot now occupied by the city of AMRITSAR, the metropolis of the Sikh faith. Here he dug a holy tank, and commenced the erection of a temple in its midst. His son and successor, Arjun Mal, completed the temple, and lived in great wealth and magnificence, besides widely increasing the numbers of his sect, and thus exciting the jealousy of the Mughal government. Becoming involved in a quarrel with the imperial governor of Lahore, Arjun was imprisoned in that city, where he died, his followers asserting that he had been cruelly put to death.

'This act of tyranny,' writes Elphinstone, 'changed the Sikhs from inoffensive quietists into fanatical warriors. They took up arms under Har Govind, the son of their martyred pontiff, who inspired them with his own spirit of revenge and of hatred to their oppressors. Being now open enemies of the government, the Sikhs were expelled from the neighbourhood of Lahore, which had hitherto been their seat, and were constrained to take refuge in the northern mountains. Notwithstanding dissensions which broke out among themselves, they continued their animosity to the Musalmāns, and confirmed their martial habits until the accession, in 1675, of Gurū Govind, the grandson of Har Govind, and the tenth spiritual chief from Nānak. This leader first conceived the idea of forming the Sikhs into a religious and military commonwealth, and executed his design with the systematic spirit of a Grecian lawgiver.'

But their numbers were inadequate to accomplish their plans of resistance and revenge. After a long struggle, Gurū Govind saw his strongholds taken, his mother and his children massacred, and his followers slain, mutilated, or dispersed. He was himself murdered in 1708 by a private enemy at Nander in the Deccan. The severities of the Musalmāns only exalted the fanaticism of the Sikhs, and inspired a spirit of vengeance, which soon broke out into fury. Under Gurū Govind's principal disciple, Banda, who had been bred a religious ascetic, and who combined a most sanguinary disposition with bold and daring counsels, they broke from their retreat, and overran the east of the Punjab, committing unheard-of cruelties wherever they directed their steps. The mosques were destroyed and the Mullās killed; but the rage of the Sikhs was not restrained by any considerations of religion, or by any mercy for age or sex. Whole towns were massacred with wanton barbarity, and even the bodies of the dead were dug up and thrown out to the birds and beasts of prey. The principal scene of these atrocities was Sirhind, which the Sikhs occupied, after defeating the governor in a pitched battle; but the same horrors marked their route through the country eastward of the Sutlej and Jumna, into which they penetrated as far as Sahāranpur. They at length received a check from the local authorities, and retired to the country on the upper course of the Sutlej, between Ludhiāna and the mountains. This seems at that time to have been their principal seat; and it was well suited to their condition, as they had a near and easy retreat when forced to leave the open country. Their retirement on the present occasion was of no long continuance; and in their next incursions they ravaged the country as far as the neighbourhood of Lahore on the one side and of Delhi itself on the other.

The emperor himself, Bahādur Shāh, was compelled to return from the Deccan in order to proceed against the Sikhs in person. He shut them up in their hill fort at Daber, which he captured after a desperate siege; the leader Banda and a few of his principal followers succeeded by a desperate sally in effecting their escape to the mountains. The death of Bahādur Shāh in 1712 probably prevented the extermination of the sect. During the dissensions and confusion which followed that event the Sikhs were allowed to recruit their strength, and they again issued from their mountain fastnesses and ravaged the country. In 1716, however, Abdus Samad Khān, governor of Kashmīr, was dispatched against them at the head of a large army by the emperor Farrukh Sīyar. He completely defeated the Sikhs in several actions, took Banda prisoner, and sent him to Delhi, where he was barbarously put to death along with several other of the Sikh chieftains. An active persecution ensued, and for some time afterwards history narrates little of the new sectaries.

Invasions. In 1738 Nādir Shāh's invading host swept over the Punjab like a flooded river, defeated the Mughal army at Karnāl in 1739, and sacked the imperial city of Delhi. Though Nādir retired from India in a few months with his plunder, he had given the death-blow to the weak and divided empire. The

Sikhs once more gathered fresh courage to rebel; and though again defeated and massacred in large numbers, the religion gathered new strength from the blood of the martyrs. The next great disaster of the Sikhs was in 1762, when Ahmad Shāh Durrāni, the Afghān conqueror of the Marāthās at Pānīpat in the preceding year, routed their forces completely, and pursued them across the Sutlej. On his homeward march he destroyed the town of Amritsar, blew up the temple, filled the sacred tank with mud, and defiled the holy place by the slaughter of cows. But, true to their faith, the Sikhs rose once more as their conquerors withdrew, and they now initiated a final struggle which resulted in the secure establishment of their independence.

Ranjīt Singh.

By this time the religion had come to present very different features from those of Bāba Nānak's peaceful theocracy. It had grown into a loose military organization, divided among several *misls* or confederacies, with a common meeting-place at the holy city of Amritsar. The Mughals had nominally ceded the Punjab to Ahmad Shāh; but the Durrāni kings never really extended their rule to the eastern portion, where the Sikhs established their authority not long after 1763. The Afghān revolution in 1809 facilitated the rise of Ranjīt Singh, a Sikh adventurer, who had obtained a grant of Lahore from Zamān Shāh, the Durrāni ruler of Kābul, in 1799. Gradually this able chieftain spread his power over the greater part of the Punjab, and even in 1808 attacked the small Sikh principalities on the east or left bank of the Sutlej. (See CIS-SUTLEJ STATES.) These sought the protection of the British, now masters of the North-Western Provinces with a protectorate over the royal family of Delhi; and an agreement was effected in 1809 by which Ranjīt Singh engaged to preserve friendship with the British Government, and not to encroach on the left bank of the Sutlej, on condition of his sovereignty being recognized over all his conquests north of that river, a treaty which he scrupulously respected till the close of his life. In 1818 Ranjīt Singh stormed Mūltān, and extended his dominions to the extreme south of the Punjab; and in the same year he crossed the Indus, and conquered Peshāwar, to which shortly after he added the Derajāt, as well as Kashmīr. He had thus succeeded during his own lifetime in building up a splendid power, embracing almost the whole of the present Province, together with the Native State of Kashmīr.

First Sikh War.

On his death in 1839, his son Kharak Singh succeeded to

the throne of Lahore, but died, not without suspicion of poison, in the following year. A state of anarchy ensued, during which the Sikhs committed depredations on British territory, resulting in what is known as the first Sikh War. The Sikh leaders having resolved on war, their army, 60,000 strong, with 150 guns, advanced towards the British frontier, and crossed the Sutlej in December, 1845. The details of the campaign are sufficiently known. On December 18 the first action was fought at Mūdki, in which the Sikhs attacked the troops in position, but were defeated with heavy loss. Three days afterwards followed the toughly contested battle of Ferozeshāh; on January 22, 1846, the Sikhs were again defeated at Alīwāl; and finally, on February 10, the campaign was ended by the capture of the Sikh entrenched position at Sobraon. The British army marched unopposed to Lahore, which was occupied on February 22, and terms of peace were dictated. These were, briefly, the cession in full sovereignty to the British Government of the territory lying between the Sutlej and the Beās rivers, and a war indemnity of 1½ millions sterling. As the Lahore Darbār was unable to pay the whole of this sum, or even to give satisfactory security for the payment of one million, the cession was arranged of all the hill country between the Beās and the Indus, including Kashmīr and Hazāra; arrangements were made for the payment of the remaining half-million of war indemnity, for the disbandment of the Lahore army, and its reorganization on a reduced scale. The other terms included the cession of the control of both banks of the Sutlej; the recognition of the independent sovereignty of Mahārājā Gulāb Singh of Jammu; a free passage through Sikh territory for British troops; and the establishment of a British Resident at Lahore. In addition, at the request of the Lahore Government, it was settled that a British force should remain at Lahore for a time to assist in the reconstitution of a satisfactory administration. Simultaneously, a treaty was executed with Mahārājā Gulāb Singh by which the English made over to him in sovereignty the Kashmīr territory ceded by the Lahore government, in consideration of a payment of three-quarters of a million sterling. Shortly afterwards difficulties arose regarding the transfer of Kashmīr, which the Sikh governor, instigated by Lāl Singh, the chief of the Lahore Darbār, resisted by force of arms. Lāl Singh was deposed and exiled to British India; and in December, 1846, a fresh treaty was concluded, by which the affairs of the State were to be carried on by a Council of Regency, under the direction and control of the British Resident, during the minority of the young Mahārājā Dalīp Singh.

For a time the work of reorganizing the shattered government of the country proceeded quietly and with every prospect of success. But besides many minor causes of discontent among the people, such as the withdrawal of the prohibition against the killing of kine, and the restored liberty of the much-hated and formerly persecuted Muhammadans, the villages were filled with the disbanded soldiery of the old Sikh army, who were only waiting for a signal and a leader to rise and strike another blow for the power they had lost. At length, in April, 1848, the rebellion of the ex-Dīwān Mūlrāj at Multān, and the murder of two British officers in that city, roused a general revolt throughout the Punjāb. Multān city was invested by hastily raised frontier levies, assisted afterwards by British troops under General Whish; the siege, however, had to be temporarily raised in September, owing to the rapid spread of disaffection among the Sikh troops. The two rebellious Sardārs, Chattar Singh and Sher Singh, invoked the aid of the Amīr of Kābul, Dost Muhammad, who responded by seizing Peshāwar, and sending an Afghān contingent to assist the Sikhs. In October, 1848, the British army, under Lord Gough, assumed the offensive, and crossed the Sutlej. Proceeding from Ferozepore across the Punjab at an angle to the Sikh line of march, it came up with Sher Singh at Rāmnagar, and there inflicted on him a severe check. The Sikh army, consisting of 30,000 men and 60 guns, made a stand at Chiliānwāla, where an indecisive and sanguinary battle was fought on January 13, 1849. Two or three days after the action, Sher Singh was joined by his father Chattar Singh, bringing with him Sikh reinforcements, and 1,000 Afghān horse. Lord Gough awaited the arrival of the column under General Whish (set free by the fall of Multān on January 28), and then followed up the Sikhs from Chiliānwāla to Gujrāt, where the last and decisive battle was fought on February 22, the Sikhs being totally defeated with the loss of 60 guns. The Afghān garrison of Peshāwar were chased back to their hills, the Amīr Dost Muhammad himself narrowly escaping capture. The remnants of the Sikh army and the rebel Sardārs surrendered at Rāwalpindi on March 14, and henceforth the entire Punjab became a Province of British India. The formal annexation was proclaimed at Lahore on March 29, 1849, on which day terms were offered to, and accepted by, the young Mahārājā Dalīp Singh, who received

Second Sikh War.

an annuity of £50,000 a year and resigned for himself, his heirs, and his successors, all right, title, and claim to the sovereignty of the Punjab, or to any sovereign power whatever. He resided till his death in England, where he purchased estates, married, and settled down as an English nobleman.

The Punjab, after being annexed in 1849, was governed by a Board of Administration. It was subsequently made a Chief Commissionership, the first Chief Commissioner being Sir John Lawrence, who afterwards became the first Lieutenant-Governor.

The Mutiny.

At the outbreak of the Mutiny in 1857 there were in the Punjab the following troops: Hindustānis, 35,000; Punjābi Irregulars, 13,000; Europeans, 10,000; there were also 9,000 military police. The Europeans consisted of twelve regiments, of whom no less than seven were either at Peshāwar or in the hills north of Ambāla, leaving only five regiments to hold the country from the Indus to the Sutlej. The news of the massacre at Delhi reached Lahore on May 12. There had not been wanting premonitory signs that the Hindustāni sepoys were disaffected and likely to rise; and, accordingly, on May 13, 3,000 native troops were successfully disarmed at Miān Mīr. At the same time European troops were thrown into the forts of Govindgarh and Phillaur, the first important as commanding Amritsar, the second as containing a large arsenal which subsequently supplied the munitions of war for the siege of Delhi. On May 14 the arsenal at Ferozepore was secured; the sepoys here mutinied on the following day, and escaped without punishment. On the 21st of the same month the 55th Native Infantry rose at Mardān and fled to independent territory; many were killed in pursuit, and the remainder were destroyed by the hillmen. On June 7 and 8 the native troops at Jullundur broke and escaped to Delhi. In the first week of July the sepoys at Jhelum and Siālkot mutinied; they were destroyed, as were the 26th Native Infantry, who mutinied at Peshāwar on August 28.

Simultaneous with the vigorous suppression of open mutiny, 13,000 sepoys were disarmed without resistance during June and July. While the Hindustāni troops were thus disposed of, the dispatch of reinforcements to Delhi, an object of paramount importance, proceeded without a break. About May 17 it had become apparent that the Punjab did not sympathize with the movement in Hindustān, and that a good spirit prevailed in the Punjābi troops. It was therefore safe to augment them; and eighteen new regiments were raised in the

Province during the later months of the year. As these forces were being enrolled to supply the place of those who marched down to Delhi, the stream of reinforcements was steadily maintained. Four regiments from the European garrison of the Punjab formed the greater portion of the force that first marched upon Delhi. Next followed two wings of European regiments of infantry. Then a considerable force of native troops was dispatched, including the Guides, two regiments of Punjab cavalry, a body of Punjab horse, two regiments of Punjab infantry, and a body of 1,200 pioneers raised from the Mazbi Sikhs; 7,000 men, forming the contingent of the cis-Sutlej chiefs of Patiāla, Jīnd, and Nābha, accompanied the regular troops to the siege. An irregular force of 1,000 men was also detached to clear the western part of the Delhi territory. Wagon trains were organized from Multān and Ferozepore via Ambāla to Delhi. Siege trains, treasure, stores, and transport animals were poured down from the Punjab for the besieging force. Finally, in August, one last effort was to be made to send reinforcements, in spite of the risk run in denuding the Province of Europeans and loyal troops. The need for aiding the force at Delhi was, however, imperative; it was therefore resolved to send Brigadier-General Nicholson with the movable column and every European who could be spared. Two half-regiments of European infantry, the 52nd Foot, and three regiments of Punjab infantry were dispatched. These were followed by a siege train from Ferozepore, a wing of the 1st Baloch Regiment from Sind, and a contingent 2,000 strong from the Mahārājā of Kashmīr. There then remained only 4,500 Europeans (including sick) to hold the Punjab.

The crisis had now come. If Delhi were taken speedily, all was well; if otherwise, there would be a struggle for European dominion and existence in the Punjab itself. The next few weeks after the departure of Nicholson's column were weeks of anxious suspense, in which all eyes were turned to Delhi. The first symptoms of the wavering faith of the people in the British power appeared in local outbreaks at Murree in the north, and in the wild and barren tracts south of Lahore, between the Rāvi and Sutlej. Both were, however, soon suppressed, and the fall of Delhi on September 14 put an end to all further cause for apprehension. The first sign that the mass of the inhabitants had regained confidence was that the Sikhs of the Mānjha, or the tract between the Rāvi and the Sutlej rivers, who had hitherto held aloof, came forward for enlistment in the new levies.

The loyal action of the chiefs had an important bearing on keeping the population steady during the crisis. The Rājā of Jīnd was actually the first man, European or native, who took the field against the mutineers; and his contingent collected supplies in advance for the English troops marching upon Delhi, besides rendering excellent service during the siege. The Rājās of Patiāla and Nābha also sent contingents for field service; and with the exception of the Nawāb of Bahāwalpur, who did not stir, every chief in the Punjab, so far as he could, aided the English in preserving order and in suppressing rebellion. Rewards in the shape of grants of territory were made to the chiefs of Patiāla, Jīnd, and Nābha, and a large *talukdāri* estate in Oudh was conferred upon the Rājā of Kapūrthala.

Later events.

Since the Mutiny, the Punjab has made rapid progress in commercial and industrial wealth. In 1858 the Delhi territory lying on the right bank of the Jumna, together with the confiscated territory which had formerly belonged to the Nawābs of Jhajjar and Bahādurgarh, was transferred from the North-Western Provinces to the Punjab. The territory thus transferred included the present Districts of Delhi, Rohtak, and Gurgaon, almost the whole of Hissār, and portions of Karnāl and Ferozepore. The year after the suppression of the rebellion is remarkable for the commencement of the first line of railway in the Punjab, from Amritsar to Multān (February, 1859), and for the admission of water into the Bāri Doāb Canal. With the exception of punitive military expeditions against marauding hill tribes, the history of the Province has been one of uninterrupted progress. Canals have spread irrigation over its thirsty fields; railways have opened new means of communication for its surplus produce; and British superintendence, together with the security afforded by a firm rule, has developed its resources with astonishing rapidity. In October, 1901, the North-West Frontier Province was formed. It comprises all the territories formerly administered or controlled by the Lieutenant-Governor of the Punjab which lie to the west of the Indus, except the trans-Indus portion of the Isa Khel *tahsīl* of Miānwāli District, the District of Dera Ghāzi Khān, and the territory occupied by the protected tribes on its western border and known as the Baloch Trans-frontier. It also includes the District of Hazāra, east of the Indus.

Archaeology. Early period.

Though the Punjab was the earliest seat of Vedic civilization, archaeology has hitherto failed to discover any monuments or traces of the epic period. Not a single relic of the Macedonian invasion has been brought to light, and, as in the rest of India, the oldest archaeological monuments in the Punjab are the Asoka inscriptions. Of these, two were inscribed on pillars which now stand at Delhi, where they were re-erected by Fīroz Shāh in about 1362, one having been originally erected at Topra at the foot of the Siwālik Hills in the Ambāla District of this Province, and the other near Meerut in the United Provinces. Both the inscriptions are in the ancient Brāhmi script, which is found in all the Asoka inscriptions excepting those at Shāhbāzgarhi and MĀNSEHRA in the North-West Frontier Province. The vast ruins of Takshasilā (Taxila), now known as Shāhdheri, in Rāwalpindi District, remain to show the extent of the capital of the great Mauryan province which comprised the modern Punjab and the North-West Frontier Province. South-east of Takshasilā is the tope of Manikyāla, identified by General Sir Alexander Cunningham as one of the four great *stūpas* mentioned by the Chinese pilgrim Fa Hian. It is the largest *stūpa* in Northern India, and is believed to have been built to commemorate the sacrifice of the Bodhisattva, who gave his body to feed a starving tigress. Near this great *stūpa* is a smaller one, which contained a slab with a Kharoshthi inscription recording its erection during the reign of Kanishka early in the Christian era.

In Kāngra District a few remains testify to the prevalence of Buddhism in the Himālayan valleys of the north-east Punjab. Close to PATHYĀR, 6 miles south-east of Kanhiāra (? Krishna-vihāra), a votive inscription of a primitive type in both Brāhmi and Kharoshthi has been found; and at KANHIĀRA itself an inscription, also in both characters, records the foundation of a monastery, and indicates the existence of Buddhism in that locality during the second century A.D. A much later inscription at CHARI contained the formula of the Buddhist faith. The existence of Buddhism in the south-west of the Punjab is demonstrated by the ruined *stūpa* and inscription at SUI VEHĀR in the modern State of Bahāwalpur, and by a similar ruin at Naushahra, 100 miles south-west of Sui Vehār. **Buddhism.**

The Punjab can show but few Hindu antiquities. To some extent this is due to the destructive action of the great rivers on whose banks the ancient cities lay, but the iconoclasm of the Moslem invaders was even more destructive. Thus the Arabic inscriptions on the Jāma Masjid or Kuwwat-ul-Islām at Delhi record that material for the building was obtained by demolishing twenty-seven idol-houses of the Hindus, and their **Hinduism.**

profusely carved but partially defaced pillars are still to be seen in its colonnades. But the early Muhammadans often preserved the ancient Hindu monuments which were free from the taint of idolatry, for in this very mosque stands the iron pillar erected by Rājā Chandra, possibly Chandra Gupta II, an early king of the Gupta dynasty (A.D. 375–413). The Inner Himālayas, however, mostly escaped the Muhammadan inroads, and some ancient Hindu shrines have survived; but owing to the style of construction prevalent in the hills, in which wood enters largely, the remains are few and not of very great antiquity. Stone temples exist at BAIJNĀTH, where there is an inscription of 1239, and at NŪRPUR. Those in the KĀNGRA fort were destroyed by the earthquake of April, 1905. In Kulū the stone *lingam* temple at Bajaura contains some sculptures of great age, and the temple of Parasurāma at NIRMAND on the Sutlej possesses a copperplate of Rājā Samudra Sena of unknown date. The temple of Hidimbā Devi at Manāli, which bears an inscription cut among profuse wood-carving, recording its erection in the sixteenth century, and that at NAGAR have conical wooden roofs presenting a type peculiar to the hills. All these places lie in Kāngra District. In the Chamba State the Devi temples at BARMAUR and CHITRĀDI date from the eighth century A.D. They are of a different style from the two Kulū temples last mentioned, and their wood-carving is superior to that found at Manāli. The temple at Trīloknāth in the Mandī State contains a Sāradā inscription. The temples at MALOT and Kathwar in the Salt Range are built in the Kashmīr style.

Islām.

The Muhammadan period inaugurated a new architectural era, nowhere in India better exemplified than in the Punjab. The early Pathān period (1193–1320) is represented by the Kuwwat-ul-Islām, the Kutb Minār, the tomb of Altamsh, the gateway of Alā-ud-dīn, and the Jamāat-khāna mosque at Delhi. Another noteworthy monument is the tomb of Altamsh's eldest son at Mālikpur. The Tughlak or middle Pathān period (1320–1414) is represented by the vast ruins of Tughlakābād and of Fīrozābād near Delhi, with the Kalān mosque and other monuments in and around that city. The later Pathān period (1414–1556) produced the Moth-kī-masjid near Mubārakpur with its glazed tile decoration, and the impressive Kila-i-Kohna mosque of Sher Shāh at Indrapat, with other monuments round Delhi. The Mughals revived the splendours of Muhammadan architecture. At Delhi Akbar built the tomb of Humāyūn and the tomb of Azam Khān, which dates from

1566, in which year Adham Khān's tomb at Mihrauli was also erected. Jahāngīr's reign saw the construction of the Nīlā Burj (in 1624) and the mausoleum of the Khān-i-Khānān. He also built the first of the three Moti Masjids or 'pearl mosques' in the Punjab at Lahore in 1617–8. Shāh Jahān founded the modern city of Delhi and called it Shāhjahānābād. In it he erected the Red Fort, in which were built the Dīwān-i-ām and the matchless Dīwān-i-khās. Opposite the Red Fort rose the imposing Jāma Masjid, and in the midst of the city the smaller Fatehpuri and Sirhindi mosques. Wazīr Khān, Shāh Jahān's minister, built the mosque still known by his name in LAHORE, and his engineer Alī Mardān made the Shālimār garden near that city. The zealot Aurangzeb added little to the architectural monuments of his predecessors, but his reign produced the great Bādshāhi mosque at Lahore and the beautiful Moti Masjid in the Red Fort at Delhi. His daughter built the Zīnat-ul-masājid or 'ornament of mosques' at Delhi. After Aurangzeb's death ensued a period of decay, which produced the Moti Masjid at Mihrauli, the Fakhr-ul-masājid, and the tomb of Safdar Jang at Delhi. A feature of this period is the mosque with gilded domes, hence called 'Sunahri,' of which type one was built at Lahore and three at Delhi.

The south-west of the Punjab has developed an architectural style of its own, distinguished by a blue and white tile decoration, quite distinct from the *kāshi* tile-work of Lahore and Delhi. This style is exemplified by the tomb of the saint Rukn-ud-dīn at MULTĀN, and that of the Nāhar ruler, Tāhir Khān, at SĪTPUR. The tomb of the famous saint Bahā-ul-Hakk, the grandfather of Rukn-ud-dīn, dates from the thirteenth century, but it was injured at the siege of Multān in 1848, and has been entirely renewed. Lastly may be mentioned the Jahāzi Mahal with its remarkable frescoes at SHUJĀBĀD, built by Muzaffar Khān in 1808.

Population. Density.

The total population of the Punjab in 1901 was 24,754,737, including the Baloch tribes on the border of Dera Ghāzi Khān District. The density of the population was 185 persons per square mile, as compared with 174 in 1891 and 158 in 1881. In British territory alone it is 209, compared with 121 in the Native States. The density is greatest in the natural division called the Indo-Gangetic plain west, where it rises to 314 persons to the square mile, and in the Districts of Jullundur and Amritsar in this area to 641 and 639 respectively. The sub-Himālayan tracts, with 300 persons to the square mile, are nearly as densely populated, Siālkot rising to 544 and thus ranking as the third most densely populated District in the Province. In marked contrast to these two areas are the north-west dry area with 96, and the Himālayan with 77 persons to the square mile. In the latter, Chamba State, with only 40 persons to the square mile, is the most sparsely inhabited tract in the Province.

Cities, towns, and villages. The Punjab contained, in 1901, three cities—Delhi, Lahore, and Amritsar—with more than 100,000 inhabitants, 53 towns with more than 10,000, and 99 with more than 5,000. The principal towns are: Rāwalpindi (87,688), Multān (87,394), Ambāla (78,638), Jullundur (67,735), Siālkot (57,956), and Patiāla (53,545). All these include large cantonment populations. Villages numbered 43,660, of which 14,127 contained 500 inhabitants or more. In the Punjab plains the village is as a rule a compact group of dwellings; but in the south-west and the hill tracts it comprises a number of scattered settlements or hamlets, grouped together under the charge of a single headman for fiscal and administrative convenience.

Growth of population. During the ten years ending 1891 the total population of the Punjab rose from 21,136,177 to 23,272,623, an increase of 10·1 per cent. In the next decade the rate of increase was not so rapid, partly owing to the famines of that period, and partly to emigration to other Provinces in India and beyond the seas. During the twenty years since 1881 the population has risen by 17 per cent. The enumerations of 1854 and 1868 were not extended to the Native States, and even in British Districts were imperfect. Since 1854, however, the increase of the population in British territory may be safely estimated to exceed 45 per cent.

Migration. Migration plays an important part in the movement of the population. The Punjābi is free from that disinclination to emigrate which is so strongly felt in other parts of India; and Uganda, Hong-Kong, the Straits Settlements, Borneo, and other countries attract large numbers for military and other service. More than 25,000 Punjābis are believed to have been resident in Uganda in 1901; and though no precise estimate of the total number of emigrants out of India can be made, it must have largely exceeded the number of immigrants. According to the Census the emigrants to the rest of India numbered more than 500,000, exceeding the immigrants by over 200,000. Immigration is mainly from the contiguous United Provinces and Rājputāna, but Kashmīr also supplies a large number. Emigration is mainly to the same territories, but service in the army and military police takes more than 20,000 persons to Burma and many to other distant places. Within the Province the foundation of the CHENĀB COLONY has led to an extensive movement of the population from the congested submontane Districts to the virgin soil of the new colony.

Age statistics.

In 1891 the mean age of the population was 22·8 years for males and 22·4 years for females. Ten years later the figures were 25 and 24·9, excluding the North-West Frontier Province. Judged by European standards, this mean is low, but it is higher than that of any other Province in India, and, allowing for the general inaccuracy of the age-return, indicates a longevity above the Indian average. It is held luckier to understate rather than overstate one's age in the Punjab, and the number of children in proportion to adults is high, as the following table, which gives the distribution over five main age-periods of every 20,000 of the population, shows:—

	1891. (Old Province.)	1901. (New Province.)
0–10 . . .	6,131	5,306
10–15 . . .	1,961	2,330
15–25 . . .	3,974	3,402
25–40 . . .	4,561	4,478
40 and over . .	3,373	4,484
Total	20,000	20,000

The discrepancies in this return are due to the fact that in 1891 the current year of age was returned, whereas in 1901 the completed year was recorded, as it was in 1881; and comparisons with the figures of that year show that the mean age of males was the same in 1901 as in 1881, while that of females had only risen by a tenth of a year. The figures, however, are affected by migration and various other factors, so that no conclusions of value can be drawn from them. Famine, causing a diminution in the number of children, had in 1901 appreciably affected the figures in the Districts of Hissār, Rohtak, and Jhelum.

Vital statistics.

In rural areas the village watchman is entrusted, under the supervision of the village headman and the higher revenue officials, with the duty of registering births and deaths. Though almost invariably illiterate, this agency is so closely supervised in British Districts that the registration is, in the mass, exceedingly accurate, and its results are in close agreement with the Census returns. In municipalities and cantonments registration is in the hands of the local authorities and is often defective. The system of compilation is anomalous. The cantonment returns are excluded from those of the Province altogether, as are those of such Native States as register births and deaths. Municipal returns go direct to the Civil Surgeon, but those from rural areas are compiled by the Superintendent of police, and forwarded by him to the Civil Surgeon, who sends both the municipal and rural returns to the Sanitary Commissioner. In each Division the inspector of vaccination is also charged with the duty of inspecting the birth and death registers, and his supervision has greatly improved the accuracy of the returns. The following table shows the principal vital statistics for the Province :—

Year.	Population under registration.	Ratio of registered births per 1,000.	Ratio of registered deaths per 1,000.	Deaths per 1,000 from			
				Cholera.	Small-pox.	Fevers.	Bowel com-plaints.
1881	17,251,627	38·69	28·37	0·30	0·20	19·39	0·95
1891	18,763,581	35·04	29·43	0·33	0·14	21·72	0·62
1901	20,108,690	35·43	36·13	0·01	0·31	25·26	0·73
1904		41·48	49·06	0·04	0·05	18·82	0·60

In the first three quinquennia of the period from 1881 to 1901 the birth-rate averaged a little over 39 per mille, but in the last quinquennium it rose to 43, pointing to better registration. The fewest births occur in May, after which the rate rises gradually till July and is high in August and September, reaching its zenith in October. It then falls gradually until it drops suddenly in March. The mean death-rate for the five years ending 1900 was 33·7 per mille; but it rose in 1901 to 36, in 1902 to 44, and in 1903 to 49 per mille, plague alone accounting for 10·22 per mille, or more than a fifth of the deaths in the last year. The unhealthy season in the Punjab is the autumn, and the deaths in October corresponded to an average annual rate of 51 per mille in the ten years 1891–1900. March and April are by far the healthiest months. The number of deaths from fever fluctuates greatly from year to year, according as the autumnal months are unhealthy or the reverse. The deaths from cholera, small-pox, and bowel complaints are relatively very few. Under the last head only deaths from dysentery and diarrhoea have been registered since 1901.

Infirmities. In so far as specific infirmities are concerned, the figures of the latest Census showed a marked improvement on those of 1881, only 421 persons in every 100,000 of the population being returned as infirm, compared with 743 in the latter year.

Lepers now only number 19 in every 100,000 as compared with 26 in 1891 and 45 in 1881; and the blind 305, compared with 349 in 1891 and 528 in 1881. Insanity shows an apparent increase to 35 per 100,000 in 1901 from 29 in 1891, but this infirmity is often confused with deaf-mutism, which shows a marked decrease to 80 per 100,000 in 1901 from 97 in 1891.

Fever. The disease returned in the Punjab as most fatal to life is fever. In this malady the people vaguely include most disorders accompanied by abnormally high temperature; but making all due allowances for this fact, malarial fever is unquestionably the most fatal disease throughout the Province. The death-rates fluctuate greatly. In 1892 the rate was 34·8 per mille, and 33·4 in 1900, but in 1899 it was only 18·6. In the two former years heavy monsoon rains caused extensive floods and an unhealthy autumn. Malarial fever is most prevalent in the riverain valleys. This is especially marked in the tract west of the Jumna, which is naturally waterlogged, and where the faulty alignment of the old Western Jumna Canal used to obstruct the natural drainage lines. Much has been done by realigning the canal and constructing drainage channels to remedy this evil, but the tract remains the most unhealthy in the Province.

Cholera and small-pox. Cholera is hardly endemic, though a year seldom passes without an outbreak, and occasionally a local epidemic. Epidemic cholera caused 65,000 deaths in 1892 and 25,000 in 1900. Small-pox is endemic, but owing to the wide extension of vaccination it is not very fatal to life, the mortality in the ten years 1894–1903 never having exceeded 3 per mille. Vaccination is compulsory only in twenty-three of the more advanced towns, and small-pox is most fatal in towns where it is not enforced.

Plague. The first outbreak of plague occurred in October, 1897, in a village of Jullundur District, but infection had probably been imported from Hardwār in the previous May. For three years the disease was almost entirely confined to the adjacent parts of Jullundur and Hoshiārpur Districts, but in November, 1900, it broke out in Gurdāspur and soon spread to the neighbouring District of Siālkot. In 1901 outbreaks occurred in several Districts; since then the disease has spread widely, and the Province has never been completely free from it. The number of deaths was comparatively small till 1901, when 20,998 were recorded. In the following year mortality increased more than tenfold, and the epidemic still continues. The deaths from plague in 1905 numbered 390,233, or 15·8 per thousand of population. The usual measures have been adopted for dealing with outbreaks of plague and with the object of preventing its spread, including the isolation of plague patients and the segregation of persons who had been exposed to infection, the evacuation of infected houses and villages, and the disinfection of houses and effects. Medical treatment and anti-plague inoculation have always been freely offered; but the people have usually preferred native medicines, and the attempts which have been made to eradicate or diminish plague by means of inoculation have not proved successful. Until May, 1901, most of the precautions, with the exception of medical treatment and inoculation, were compulsory; but since then compulsion has been gradually abandoned, and is now chiefly restricted to the reporting of plague occurrences, and the inspection or detention of persons travelling either by road or railway to certain hill stations.

Infant mortality.

Judged by English standards infant mortality is extremely high, especially in the case of girls. This will be clear from the following table:—

Year.	Infant population in 1901.		Number of deaths under one year.		Deaths per 1,000 of infant population.		Number of births registered.		Deaths per 1,000 registered births.	
	Male.	Female.	Male.	Female.	Male.	Female.	Male.	Female.	Male.	Female.
1901	401,640	372,471	91,894	88,058	270	379	373,466	339,067	246	260
1902			107,832	101,216	316	321	461,952	418,525	233	242
1903			117,891	110,782	346	351	452,622	410,240	260	270
1904			97,610	90,832	286	288	436,678	397,371	223	229

Sex statistics.

The births registered show a marked excess of male births, 111 boys being born to every 100 girls. This initial deficiency in the number of females is accentuated, especially in the first year of life, by the heavy mortality among girls and women up to the age of 40. Of the 24,754,737 persons enumerated in 1901, 13,552,514 were males and 11,402,223 females, so that 53·9 per cent. of the population were males and 46·1 per cent. females. In other words, for every 1,000 males there were 854 females in 1901, compared with 851 in 1891 and 845 in 1881. These figures show that the number of females in the Punjab is increasing more rapidly than the number of males, though improved enumeration probably accounts to some extent for the improved ratios of 1891 and 1901. The proportion of females in the Punjab as a whole is probably not affected by migration. In different parts of the Province the ratio varies, being lowest in the central Districts and highest in the Himālayan and submontane. These variations are not explicable by differences in the position of women. The Sikhs, whose women are comparatively well educated and enjoy more liberty than those of the Muhammadans or Hindus, return a very low ratio of females, the figures for 1901 being Sikhs 778, Hindus 844, and Muhammadans 877 per 1,000 males.

Statistics of civil condition.

Among Muhammadans marriage is a civil contract. Among Hindus, Sikhs, and Jains it is in theory a sacrament, indissoluble save by death, and not even by death as far as the wife is concerned. But practice does not always follow precept; and among the lower Hindu and Sikh castes remarriage (*karewa*) is allowed, while in the Himālayas women are sold from hand to hand, and a system of temporary marriage prevails. On the other hand, the prejudice against widow marriage is almost as strong among Muhammadans of the superior classes as it is among orthodox Hindus. All castes view marriage as desirable for a boy and indispensable for a girl, an unmarried maiden who has attained puberty being a social stigma on her family, especially among the Rājputs. Betrothal is, as a rule, arranged at a very early age, and the wedding takes place while the bride is still a child, though she does not go to live with her husband till a later period. Infant marriage is, however, by no means universal, and 4·5 per cent. of the girls and 26 per cent. of the boys over fifteen are unmarried. Early marriages are commonest among Hindus and in the east of the Province. The ceremonies connected with marriage are of infinite variety, the wedding especially being made an occasion for much costly hospitality and display. As a rule, Hindus and Sikhs observe the rule of exogamy which forbids marriage within the tribe, and that of endogamy which permits it only within the caste; but a third social rule, which has been called the law of hypergamy, also exists. By this a father must bestow his daughter on a husband of higher social status than his own, though he may seek a bride for his son in a lower grade. This law renders it difficult and costly for the middle classes to find husbands for their daughters, or brides for their sons, as the lower grades have no scruple in exacting money for a girl. Among the Hindu agriculturists of the extreme east of the Province, the seven circuits round the sacred fire, prescribed by Hindu law, form the essential part of the marriage ritual, and the strict Hindus of the towns everywhere observe the same usage. Farther west among the agriculturists the number is reduced to four, while in the south-western Districts the important part of the ceremony is the *sir mel* or joining of the heads of the parties. The Muhammadan form of marriage, simple in itself, has almost everywhere been coloured by the Hindu ritual. The following table gives statistics of civil condition as recorded in 1891 and 1901 :—

Civil condition.	1891.			1901.		
	Persons.	Males.	Females.	Persons.	Males.	Females.
Unmarried .	10,397,033	6,516,598	3,880,435	11,241,255	7,027,895	4,213,360
Married .	10,547,329	5,237,107	5,310,222	11,062,125	5,459,012	5,603,113
Widowed .	2,328,261	818,729	1,509,532	2,427,270	852,148	1,575,122

Polygamy is not at all common, and is largely a question of means. Among Hindus and Sikhs only 6 per 1,000 of the married males have more than one wife, and among Muhammadans only 11. Many of the agricultural and menial castes allow the marriage of widows, preferably to the brother of the deceased husband, and it is among them that polygamy is commonest. It is rare among high-caste Hindus, who do not recognize remarriage. The ceremonies of remarriage are much simpler than those of marriage, and the woman never acquires the status she had in the house of her first husband, though the children of the second marriage are regarded as legitimate. Avowed polyandry is confined to the Himālayan tracts, though the practice is not unknown among some socially inferior castes in the plains. In the hills it usually exists in the Tibetan form, in which the husbands are all brothers. Indications of succession through females among the polyandrous tribes are few and obscure, and the general rule is that sons succeed as the children of the brotherhood which owns their mother. Divorce is not common, even among Muhammadans, though their law recognizes a husband's right to put away his wife without assigning a reason. Among the Hindu agricultural tribes of the plains it is extremely rare, though the custom is not unknown among the inferior castes and among the Jats of the central Districts. It is only in the Eastern Himālayas, within the limits of Kāngra and Simla Districts and the Hill States, where the marriage tie is notoriously loose, that the power of divorce belongs by custom to the wife as well as to the husband. The joint-family system of Hindu law is almost unknown to the peasantry of the Province. It prevails only among the Brāhmans and the clerical and commercial classes, and even among them it hardly exists outside the towns of the Delhi Division. Among the agricultural tribes of the plains, sons by different mothers usually inherit in equal shares; but the *chundawand* rule, by which they inherit *per stirpes*, is not uncommon among both Hindus and Muhammadans, especially in the centre and west of the Province.

With the exception of Tibeto-Burman, spoken in its pure form Language.
only in the Himālayan canton of Spiti and in a debased form in Lāhul and Upper Kanāwār, the vernaculars of the Punjab belong entirely to the Aryan family of languages. Of this family the Indian branch greatly predominates, the Irānian being represented only by 52,837 persons speaking Pashtū, 40,520 speaking Baluchi, and 3,074 speaking Persian. The Pashtū is confined to the Pathān tribes settled in Attock District and in the Īsā Khel *tahsīl* of Miānwāli on the banks of the Indus, and to Pathān immigrants. Baluchi is virtually confined to Dera Ghāzi Khān District and the adjacent State of Bahāwalpur. Persian is spoken only by immigrant families and refugees from Persia and Afghānistān.

Western Punjābi is spoken in the Indus valley and east of it as far as the valley of the Chenāb in Gujrānwāla, whence its boundary is a line through Montgomery District and the State of Bahāwalpur. East of it Eastern Punjābi is spoken as far as the meridian passing through Sirhind. East again of that line Western Hindī is the dominant speech. These languages are divided into numerous dialects. The Western Punjābi (also called Jatki, 'the Jats' speech,' and Multāni) comprises the Hindko, Pothwārī, Chibhālī, Dhūndi, Ghebī, and Awānkārī. Eastern Punjābi has two main dialects: the standard of the Mānjha, or central part of the Bāri Doāb, spoken round Amritsar; and that of the Mālwā, the tract south of the Sutlej. Western Hindī comprises Hariānī (the dialect of Hariāna), Bāngarū (that of the Bāngar), Jātu (the Jāt speech), and Ahīrwātī (the Ahīr speech). To these three languages must be added the maze of Sanskritic dialects spoken in the hills, and hence called generically Pahārī. These resemble Rājasthānī rather than Punjābi, and merge into the Tibeto-Burman in Lāhul and Kanāwār. The Gūjarī, or Gujar speech, also deserves mention as a tongue spoken in the Himālayas, but also closely resembling Rājasthānī.

The following table shows the numbers returned in 1901 as speaking the chief languages:—

Western Punjābi	2,755,463
Punjābi	15,346,175
Rājasthānī	603,747
Western Hindī	4,164,373
Western Pahārī	1,554,072

Caste.

As an institution caste plays a far less important part in the social life of the people than in other parts of India. Its bonds are stronger in the east than in the west, and generally in the towns than in the villages, so that in the rural areas of the Western Punjab society is organized on a tribal basis, and caste hardly exists. Ethnically, if the Buddhists of the Himālayan tracts of Lāhul, Spiti, and Kanāwār be excluded, the mass of the population is Aryan, other elements, such as the Mongolian and the Semitic (Saiyids, Kureshis, and other sacred Muhammadan tribes), having by intermarriage with Indian converts to Islām lost nearly all traces of their foreign origin. Socially the landed classes stand high, and of these the Jats (4,942,000) are the most important. The Jat, or Jāt as he is termed in the south-east of the Province, is essentially a landholder (*zamīndār*), and when asked his caste usually replies 'Jat *zamīndār*.' The Jats are divided into numerous tribes and septs, and many of these hold considerable areas which are divided into village communities. By religion they are essentially Hindus, 1,595,000 being so returned in 1901; and they also comprise the great mass of the Sikhs, 1,390,000 being of that creed. The Sikh Jats are mainly confined to the central Districts of the Punjab. Large numbers of them have from time to time been converted to Islām, and the Muhammadan Jats number 1,957,000. As cultivators the Hindu or Sikh Jats rank higher than any other class in the Province, and they make enterprising colonists and excellent soldiers, the Sikh holding a marked pre-eminence in these respects. The Muhammadan Jat lacks the energy of his Hindu and Sikh kinsman, but he is not far behind him as a cultivator. Next in importance are the Rājputs (1,798,000). The majority of them are Muhammadans (1,347,000). They do not rank high as cultivators, but furnish many recruits to the Indian army under the general designation of Punjābi Muhammadans. The Hindu Rājputs are found mainly in the north-east corner of the Province, and in the Himālayan and submontane tracts, the Rājput tribes of the plains having for the most part accepted Islām. As a body the Rājputs stand higher than the Jats in the social system, and this has prevented their adherence to the levelling doctrines of Sikhism. Below these castes, both socially and numerically, stand the Muhammadan Arains (1,007,000), the Hindu and Sikh Sainis (127,000), and the Kambohs (174,000), who live by *petite culture* and rarely enlist as soldiers. In the south-east of the Province the Ahīrs (205,000) hold a position little if at all inferior to the Jāts. In the Himālayas of the North-East Punjab, the Kanets (390,000) and Ghiraths (170,000) form great cultivating classes under Rājput overlords.

In the north-west the Gakhars (26,000), Khokhars (108,000), and Awāns (421,000), and farther west and south the Pathāns (264,000), take the position held by Rājputs elsewhere. In the south-west, especially in Dera Ghāzi Khān District west of the Indus, the Balochs (468,000) form a dominant race of undoubted Irānian descent. Essentially pastoral tribes are the Gūjars, or cowherds (632,000), found mainly in the Lower Himālayas, and the Gaddis, or shepherds (26,000), in the State of Chamba and Kāngra District.

The trading castes in the villages occupy a lower position than the landowning classes, but in the towns they rank higher. The most important are the Baniās (452,000) in the south-east, the Khattrīs (436,000) in the centre and north-west, and the Aroras (653,000) in the south-west. All these are Hindus or, rarely, Sikhs. The principal Muhammadan trading classes are the Shaikhs (321,000) and Khojas (99,000). Attached to these classes by a system of clientship, which is a curious combination of social dependence and spiritual authority, are the various priestly castes, the Brāhmans (1,112,000) ministering to Hindus, and the Saiyids (238,000) to Muhammadans. Both these classes, however, often follow secular occupations, or combine them with religious functions, and similar functions are exercised by countless other religious tribes and orders.

Physical characteristics.

The ethnical type in the Punjab is distinctly Aryan, there being few traces of aboriginal or foreign blood, if the Tibetan element in the extreme north-east be excluded. The typical Punjābi is tall, spare but muscular, broad-shouldered, with full dark eyes and an ample beard. The hair is invariably black, but the complexion varies from a deep olive-brown to wheat-coloured. As a rule the lower classes are darker than the upper, and the complexion is fairer in the north-west than in the south-east. The Jats of the Mānjha and Mālwā exhibit a splendid physique, and the peasantry of the plains are generally a fine people; but in the riverain valleys there is a marked falling-off, and in the south-east of the Province the type approximates to that of Hindustān. In marked contrast to the plains people are those of the Himālayas. Among these the higher or Rājput class is slight, high-bred, and clean-limbed, but sometimes over-refined, while owing to immorality the lower classes are often weakly and under-sized. Nothing is more striking than the influence of hereditary occupation and town life on physique, and the urban and trading populations are markedly inferior physically, though not intellectually, to the peasantry.

Religions. The Punjab by religion is more Muhammadan than Hindu. Of the total population enumerated in 1901, 12,183,345 persons, or 49 per cent., were Muhammadans. In the west and in the submontane tracts Islām is the dominant religion, its followers forming four-fifths of the population in the north-west dry area, but the Hindus are more numerous in the Indo-Gangetic plain, and in the Himālayas they form 95 per cent. of the population. In the south-west, Multān and Uch were the earliest strongholds of the Moslem faith, and the population is deeply imbued with Muhammadan ideas, Hinduism being confined to the trading, landless castes, who are socially despised by their Muhammadan neighbours. The early Sultāns made Delhi a great centre of Muhammadan influence, but they and their successors appear to have left the Hindus of the Punjab unmolested in religious matters until the Mughal empire was firmly established. Akbar's policy of religious toleration lessened the gulf between the two creeds, but many Muhammadan tribes ascribe their conversion to the zeal of Aurangzeb. Islām in the Punjab is as a rule free from fanaticism, but among the more ignorant classes it has retained many Hindu ideas and superstitions. Though the great mass of its followers profess the orthodox Sunni creed, the reverence paid to Saiyids as descendants of Alī, the Prophet's son-in-law, is unusually great; and popularly Islām consists in the abandonment of many Hindu usages and the substitution of a Muhammadan saint's shrine for a Hindu temple. A very important factor in Muhammadan religious life is the Sūfi influence which, originating in Persia, was brought into the Punjab by the early Sultāns of Ghor. Its first great exponent was the saint Kutb-ud-dīn Bakhtiyār, in whose honour the Kutb Minār at Delhi was erected. His disciple Bāba Farīd-ud-dīn, Shakar-ganj, of Pākpattan in Montgomery District, is perhaps the most widely reverenced saint in the Punjab; and the shrine of his disciple Khwāja Nizām-ud-dīn, Aulia, near Delhi, is also a place of great sanctity. Spiritual descendants of these saints founded shrines at Mahārān in the Bahāwalpur State, at Taunsa Sharīf in Dera Ghāzi Khān District, and elsewhere. Thus the Province is studded with Sūfi shrines.

Hinduism in the Punjab is a singularly comprehensive creed. As the Province can boast no great centres of Hindu thought or learning, the Punjābi Hindu looks to Hardwār on the Ganges as the centre of his faith. But Hardwār is accessible only to the eastern Districts, so elsewhere pilgrimages are made to countless minor temples and shrines, even those of Muhammadan saints. Vishnu is worshipped chiefly by the Baniās of the south-east and by the Rājputs, but Sivdiwālas or temples to Siva are nearly as common as Thākurdwāras or temples of Vishnu (Thākur). Far more popular than these are the widely spread cults of Gūga, the snake-god, and Sakhi Sarwar, the benevolent fertilizing earth-god, whose shrine in Dera Ghāzi Khān is the object of regularly organized pilgrimages. Gūga's legend also makes him a Rājput prince converted to Islām, and Sakhi Sarwar has been metamorphosed into a Muhammadan saint. There are countless minor cults, such as that of Sītlā, the 'cool one,' the small-pox goddess, and those of the *siddhs* or 'pure ones.' Ancestor-worship is very common among the Jats.

In the Himālayas Vishnu and Siva have many devotees, the Rājputs especially worshipping the former; but underlying these orthodox cults are those of the innumerable *deotās* (gods or spirits), *devīs* (goddesses), and *bīrs* (heroes), which are probably more ancient than Hinduism. The principal religious orders are the Sanyāsis and Jogis, who follow in theory the philosophical system of Sankarāchārya and Pātanjali. There are also Muhammadan Jogis, whose mysticism has much in common with the practices of the Hindu ascetics. The Bairāgis, a Vaishnava order founded by Rāmānand in the fourteenth century, are likewise numerous.

Arya Samāj.

The Arya Samāj was founded by Pandit Dayānand Saraswati, a Brāhman of Kāthiāwār, about 1875. During his lifetime the doctrine spread rapidly; but since his death in 1883, the growth of the Samāj has been comparatively slow, and in 1901 only 9,105 males over 15 returned themselves as Aryas. The movement has been well described as being 'primarily the outcome of the solvent action of natural science on modern Hinduism.' The Samāj finds its sole revelation in the Vedas, which, rightly interpreted, prove that those who were inspired to write them were acquainted with the truths which modern science is slowly rediscovering. It attaches no merit to pilgrimages or to most of the rites of popular Hinduism. The liberal social programme of the Aryas is the outcome of their religious views, and includes the spread of education, the remarriage of widows, and the raising of the age for marriage. They are drawn, as a rule, from the best-educated classes of the community, Khattrīs, Aroras, and Brāhmans, and the doctrines they preach have met with acceptance chiefly in the progressive tracts north and east of the capital. At Lahore they maintain a college. Since 1893 the Samāj has been divided into two parties. The cause of the schism was the question of the lawfulness of meat as an article of diet. Those in favour of it are known as the 'cultured' or 'college' party, and those against it as the *mahātma* party.

Religious architecture.

Religious architecture still maintains the tradition of each sect or community, with few deviations from the old plans which were designed mainly with a view to the needs of each religion. Ablution is an essential feature of every sect, so that a tank of water, with other necessary facilities, is found in a prominent position in all buildings. Mosques, now usually built of brick, consist of an open courtyard, with the *mihrāb* on the west, surmounted by a dome flanked with *minārs* or pillars. The Hindus enclose their temples in a walled courtyard, containing the shrine for the deity to which the temple is dedicated. Over this is a pyramidal tower, surmounted by a metal finial shaped to represent the emblem of the divinity enshrined. The temples of the Sikhs are usually designed on an orthodox square plan consisting of nine parts, known as the *naukara*. The general arrangement is a courtyard, in which is situated a tank of water for washing and a central open construction (*bāradari*) for the reading of the 'Granth.' Over this is a dome, which may be distinguished from that of a mosque by being generally fluted or foliated in design. The modern Sikhs being adepts in wood-carving, the doors and other details are not unfrequently freely decorated. Jain temples are built on a somewhat similar plan to those of the Hindus, except that more than one shrine is often found in the enclosure and pillared verandas are a feature. In modern examples, however, this latter characteristic is frequently omitted.

Christian missions.

Excluding the Jesuits at the Mughal court, the first Christian missionary to the Punjab was a Baptist preacher who visited Delhi early in the nineteenth century. Delhi and Simla are the only stations now occupied by this mission. The first great missionary movement in the Punjab proper was the establishment of the American Presbyterian Mission at Ludhiāna in 1834. The Ludhiāna Mission, as it thus came to be called, occupies a number of stations in the Central Punjab south of the Rāvi, and maintains the Forman Christian College at Lahore, with a large press at Ludhiāna. The Church Missionary Society began operations in the Punjab in 1851. Its stations comprise a group round Amritsar and Lahore, and a long line of frontier stations stretching from Simla to Karāchi in Sind. It has a college in Lahore which prepares natives of India for holy orders, and the Church of England Zanāna Mission works in many of its stations. The Society for the Propagation of the Gospel began work in Delhi in 1852. In 1877 it was reinforced by the Cambridge Mission, which maintains the St. Stephen's College at Delhi. Other missions are the Methodist Episcopal, the Church of Scotland, the Moravian, the American United Presbyterian, the Zanāna Bible and Medical Missions, and the Salvation Army, besides the missionary work conducted by various Roman Catholic orders.

The following table gives statistics of religion as recorded in 1891 and 1901:—

	1891.	1901.
Hindus	10,122,473	10,344,469
Sikhs	1,851,070	2,102,896
Jains	45,615	49,983
Buddhists	6,236	6,940
Zoroastrians	370	477
Muhammadans	11,198,270	12,183,345
Christians: European and Eurasian	28,971	28,611
Christians: Native	19,561	37,980
Jews and unspecified	57	36

Of the total population at least 56 per cent. are supported by agriculture. Next in importance is the artisan section of the community, which numbers 4,898,080, or 19·8 per cent. of the population. Of these, cotton-weaving, spinning, &c., supports 1,012,314, and leather-working 742,034, while potters number 269,869, carpenters 263,717, and iron-workers 164,814. The making of tools and implements supports 135,786, and building 121,153; goldsmiths number 120,755, and tailors 108,963, but the figures for these smaller groups are subject to several qualifications. Commerce supports only 2·8, and the professions 2·2 per cent., of the population, while public service maintains 2 per cent. The residue is composed of general labourers (812,584 in number), personal domestic servants (1,771,944), and 827,289 persons whose subsistence was independent of occupation. In spite of the caste system, the division of labour has not been pushed very far in the Punjab. The carpenter is often an ironsmith, the shopkeeper a moneylender, the agriculturist a trader, and so on. Occupations.

The staple food consists of the grain grown in the locality. Food. Well-to-do people eat wheat and rice, while the ordinary peasant's food consists chiefly of wheat, barley, and gram in summer, and maize in winter. The poorer classes use inferior grains, such as *chīnā* (*Panicum miliaceum*), *mandua* (*Eleusine coracana*), *jowār* (great millet), &c. In the hill, submontane, and canal-irrigated tracts, where rice is largely grown, it forms the principal diet of the people in general, but elsewhere it is eaten only on festive occasions. In the west and south-west *bājra* (spiked millet) is mostly consumed in the winter. Pulses and vegetables are eaten with bread by prosperous *zamīndārs* and townspeople, but the poorer classes, who cannot always afford them, merely mix salt in their bread and, if possible, eat it with buttermilk. Peasants are especially fond of curds, buttermilk, and green mustard (*sarson*) as relishes with bread. *Ghī* is used only by those who can afford it. Meat is seldom eaten, except by the better classes, and by them only on occasions of rejoicing or by way of hospitality. The common beverages are buttermilk, water mixed with milk and sugar, country sherbets, and *sardai*, a cooling drink made by bruising certain moistened ingredients in a mortar; but the use of the two latter is almost entirely confined to the townsfolk. Aerated waters are coming rapidly into use. Hemp (*bhang*) is ordinarily drunk by the religious mendicants (*fakīrs*), both Hindu and Muhammadan. In towns cow's milk is used, but in rural tracts buffalo's is preferred, as being richer. In the camel-breeding tract camel's milk is also drunk.

Dress. The dress of the people is of the simplest kind and, in the plains, made entirely of cotton cloth. A turban, a loincloth, a loose wrap, thrown round the body like a plaid, and, in the cold season, a vest or jacket of some kind, are the usual garments. White is thc usual colour, but dyed stuffs are often worn, especially on festive occasions. As a rule Muhammadans avoid red, while Saiyids and others claiming descent from the Prophet favour green. Hindus similarly avoid blue, but it is the characteristic dress of Sikh zealots, like the Akālīs. Minor variations in dress are innumerable, and fashion tends to adopt European clothes, often with most incongruous results, among the men.

Women are far more conservative; but the influence of Islām has brought about the adoption of the trouser instead of the Hindu skirt, which is only general in the south-east. Here again local and tribal customs vary. Thus Rājput women, Hindu as well as Muhammadan, wear the trouser, and Gūjars the petticoat, while many Sikh and Hindu Jat women wear both. In the wilder parts of the central area the skirt was little more than a kilt, but the more elaborate garment is coming into fashion. The tight bodice is essentially a Hindu woman's garment, the looser shirt a Muhammadan characteristic. The wrap or *chādar* is universally worn; and the *parda* system compels most Muhammadan, and many Hindu and Sikh ladies of the better classes, to wear, when compelled to leave the house, an ungainly and uncomfortable veil (*burka*) which covers the whole form.

The ordinary peasant's house is not uncomfortable, though hardly attractive. Built of mud, with a flat roof, and rarely decorated, it is cooler in summer and warmer in winter than a house of brick or stone. In the large villages of the Central and South-East Punjab the dwellings are close and confined, but in the south-west a ruder and more spacious type is found. Houses of stone are mainly found in the hills, and slate roofs only in the Himālayas. Brick (*pakkā*) houses in the villages are rapidly increasing in numbers, but in comfort are hardly an improvement on the old. In the cities such houses have long been the rule, but to secure privacy and additional room they are built or rebuilt to several storeys, rendering sanitation an insoluble problem. The furniture of an ordinary house is cheap and simple, comprising a few string beds, stools, boxes, spinning wheels, and cooking utensils, with a grain-receptacle of mud. Dwellings.

Muhammadans bury their dead, while Hindus and Sikhs, with some exceptions, burn them. The casteless people, such as the Chūhrās and Chamārs, who stand outside the pale of Hinduism, imitate whichever religion happens to be dominant in their neighbourhood. Hindus collect the bones from the ashes of the funeral pyre and send them to be thrown into the Ganges, or, if they cannot afford that, cast them into an adjacent stream. Disposal of the dead.

Games are singularly few, especially among children, and this perhaps explains why cricket, and to a lesser extent football, have become popular in the schools. In the villages a kind of prisoner's base, clubs, quoit-throwing (among the Sikhs), tent-pegging, especially in the Salt Range and western plains, and camel racing on the Bīkaner border, are fairly popular. Otherwise athletics are a growth of British rule. Wrestling is virtually confined to professionals. Sport is often keenly followed, hawking, coursing, and shooting being favourite pastimes of the well-to-do in many rural tracts. In the towns quail-fighting is the form of sport most actively pursued. The drama hardly exists, except in a few rude plays (*swāngs*), acted Amusements.

by the professional castes. Folk-songs are fairly numerous, but the music is singularly rude and barbarous. The monotony of village life is rendered bearable by the numerous and costly ceremonies which a birth, a wedding, or a funeral demand.

Pilgrimages offer great distractions, and are regularly organized to shrines like that of Sakhi Sarwar. Fairs also afford excuse for numberless holidays, which are mostly spent in harmless though aimless amusements.

'estivals. The principal Hindu holidays are :—the Basant Panchmi, or feast of Saraswatī, goddess of learning; the Sivarātri, or feast of Siva; the Holi, or the great spring festival and Saturnalia of Northern India; the Baisākhi, or Hindu New Year; the Salono, or day when amulets against evil are solemnly put on; the Janm Ashtmi, or birthday of Krishna; the Dasehra, which recalls Rāma's conquest of Rāvana; and the Dewāli, the Hindu feast of lanterns. Instead of the Holi, Sikhs observe a kindred festival called Hola Mohalla, held the day after, and also Gurū Nānak's birthday.

The chief Muhammadan holidays are, in the Punjab as elsewhere:—the Id-ul-Fitr or day after Ramzān, the Id-uz-Zuha, the Muharram, Bāra Wafāt, Juma-ul-widā, and Shab-i-barāt. Besides these, every locality has a succession of minor fairs and festivals of its own.

Names. The ordinary name generally consists of two words, which are selected from a variety of causes, astrological, religious, and superstitious. The father's name is rarely, if ever, given to the son, and there is seldom anything like a surname, persons being distinguished only by the variety of names employed. Among Hindus it is essential that the religious name given at birth should never be known or used, and the name by which a man is known is more or less a nickname; while both among Hindus and Muhammadans it is often not easy to say what a man's real name is, as a man who is known among his friends as Gotra or Mujjan will on occasions of state entitle himself Govardhan Dās or Murtazā Khān. The second name among Hindus is often in a sense honorific, and originally had a religious meaning, Rām and Lāl distinguishing Brāhmans, Singh Kshattriyās, and Mal, Rai, and Lāl Vaishyas; but these distinctions do not now hold good. All Sikhs indeed have names ending in Singh, but the title is not confined to them; and as to the others, a man who one year is called Parsū will, if things prosper with him, call himself Parasurāma the next.

Muhammadan names generally consist of two words, the *alam* or name and *lakab* or honorary title, such as Muhammad Dīn, though, as above mentioned, the villager will as often as not be known by an abbreviation such as Mamdū. A combination of one of the 'comely' names of God with *abd* ('servant') is also common, such as Abdullah, or Abdul Ghafūr. About half the proper names of Muhammadans are of religious origin, and the rest differ in no way from those of Hindus. Besides the two regular names, both affixes and prefixes are found. Affixes generally denote the caste or clan, such as Ahlūwālia, Rāmgarhia, Seth, or Varma (a purely Khattrī appellation), or are honorific, such as the Muhammadan 'Khān.' This affix sometimes, but rarely, tends to harden into a surname. Prefixes are honorific and answer to the European Mr. or Monsieur: such are among Hindus, Bābā, Lālā, Sodhī, Rājā, and Pandit; and among Muhammadans, Munshi, Fakīr, Wazīrzāda, and Makhdūm. In addition a man may bear honorific titles, many of which, such as Rai Bahādur and Khān Bahādur, are given by Government, so that a Muhammadan's full style and title may run Makhdūm Abdul Azīz Khān Shams-ul-Ulama Khān Bahādur, or a Hindu's Bābā Raghunāth Singh Rai Bahādur Dīwān Bahādur.

The most common endings for place names in the Punjab are the Arabic *ābād* ('abode') and *shahr* ('city') and the Hindu *pur*, *nagar*, and *wāra*, all meaning 'town' or 'place,' and *kot* and *garh* meaning 'fort.' Many are in the genitive, meaning, like Mukeriān or Fāzilka, the place of a certain tribe or people; while the termination *wāla*, meaning 'belonging to,' is one of the most common.

Agriculture. Soils and conditions of cultivation.

Excluding the Himālayan and other hill tracts and the ravines of Rāwalpindi, Attock, and Jhelum Districts, the vast alluvial plain is broken only by the wide valleys of its rivers. Its soil is a sandy loam, interspersed with patches of clay and tracts of pure sand. The soils of the Himālayan and lower ranges resemble those of the plains, but both sand and clay are rarer, and the stony area is considerable. The quality of the soil is, however, of comparatively little importance, facilities for irrigation, natural or artificial, being the primary factor. The monsoon current extends only to the extreme south-eastern Districts. The rainfall is fairly sufficient for agricultural purposes in the hills and in the submontane tracts, but diminishes rapidly as the distance from the hills increases, being as little as 5 and 7 inches in Muzaffargarh and Multān.

It is only in or near the Himālayas that unirrigated cultivation can be said to be fairly secure.

Harvests. The Punjab has two harvests: the *rabi* (*hāri*) or spring, sown mostly in October–November and mostly reaped in April–May; and the *kharīf* (*sāwani*) or autumn, sown in June–August and reaped from early September to the end of December. Both sugar-cane and cotton, though sown earlier, are autumn crops. The spring sowings follow quickly on the autumn harvesting. To the spring succeeds the extra (*zaid*) harvest, chiefly tobacco, melons, and similar crops, harvested late in June. Speaking generally, the tendency, as irrigation develops, is for intensive cultivation in the *rabi* to replace the extensive cultivation of the *kharīf*.

Ploughing. The advantages of frequent ploughing are thoroughly recognized, especially for wheat and sugar-cane, for which a fine seed-bed is essential. The plough used is an implement of simple construction, made of wood with an iron or iron-pointed share, and drawn by a single yoke of oxen. When the soil has been reduced to a fairly fine tilth, a heavy log of wood roughly squared, called *sohāga*, is used to supply the place of a light roller. It breaks up any remaining clods, and also compacts and levels the surface.

Sowing. There are three methods of sowing: by scattering the seed broadcast on the surface, by dropping it into the furrows by hand, or by drilling through a tube attached to the plough handle. The last method, if skilfully used, deposits the seed in the bottom of the furrow, and is employed when the surface is dry. The second is employed in moderately moist, and the first in thoroughly moist soils.

Manure. Land near a town or village is heavily manured, as also is land near a well, since it can be easily irrigated and valuable crops grown on it. Sugar-cane, maize, tobacco, and vegetables are always manured. Wheat, cotton, barley, and melons are manured only when manure is readily available. Spiked millet, gram, *tāra mīra*, and other inferior crops are never manured. Thorough manuring costs from Rs. 60 to Rs. 80 an acre, and is most common in the vicinity of the larger towns, the municipal boards of which make a considerable income by sales of refuse. In such localities two to four very rich crops a year are grown. Irrigated land is manured much more generally than unirrigated. Besides the sweepings of villages, night-soil, the dung of sheep, goats, and camels, the ashes of cow-dung, and nitrous earth are used for manure. The two last are applied as a top-dressing, especially for vegetables and tobacco. The others are spread over the land after the *rabi* has been harvested, and ploughed in before the monsoon rains set in. A top-dressing of thoroughly decomposed manure is often applied to sugar-cane after the cuttings have germinated, the soil being then hoed by hand and irrigated. Cattle, sheep, goats, and camels are often folded in the fields for the sake of their manure, and in the hills shepherds derive much profit by lending their flocks for this purpose. The practice of using cow-dung for fuel seriously diminishes the natural supply of manure.

Weeding and hoeing are resorted to only for the more valuable crops. The crops are cut entirely by hand, and harvesting employs all the menials of a village. Grain is mostly trodden out by cattle. The implements in use, of a primitive type and simple construction, are well adapted to the cultivator's needs, but are capable of improvement. The iron sugar-press has now almost ousted the old cumbrous wooden type.

Population dependent on agriculture. Agriculture affords the main means of subsistence to 13,917,000 persons, or 56 per cent. of the population, exclusive of 214,000 partially supported by it. The Punjab is essentially a country of peasant proprietors, landholders and tenants numbering, with their families, 13,452,000 persons. Of the total number supported by agriculture, 36 per cent. are actual cultivators, only 184,000 being rent-receivers.

Principal spring crops.

Wheat. The principal crops in spring are wheat, gram, and barley. Wheat is the staple crop grown for sale. The development of canals in the past ten or fifteen years has led to a great expansion of the area under spring crops, especially wheat, which ordinarily covers about 10,000 square miles. In good years, such as 1894, 1895, and 1901, it covered more than 10,900, but in the famine years of 1897 and 1900 only about 7,800 square miles. Though best sown between the middle of October and the middle of November, it can be put in later; and in the Northern Punjab, if the winter rains are late, it may be sown up to the first week in January. There are many indigenous varieties, both red and white, bearded and beardless. Rather more than half the area under wheat is irrigated. The out-turn varies from 4 to 12 cwt. on irrigated, and from 4 to 7 cwt. on unirrigated land.

Gram. Next to wheat comes gram, which usually covers more than 3,100 square miles, but the area fluctuates with the rainfall. Sown as a rule earlier than wheat and mainly in the poorer unirrigated lands, it is generally harvested a fortnight earlier, but is not infrequently sown and harvested with it. The yield is about 4 to 9 cwt. on unirrigated land, but may rise to 11 cwt. under irrigation.

Barley.

Barley is often sown mixed with wheat and gram, as it matures even if the rainfall be not sufficient for the wheat. It is also useful as a catch-crop, since it can be sown later than wheat. It is grown extensively for the breweries and as fodder. Barley ordinarily covers about 1,600 square miles. On irrigated land the out-turn is from 5 to 11 cwt., compared with 3 to 9 cwt. on unirrigated land.

Principal autumn crops. Maize.

The staple cereals in autumn are maize, great millet (*jowār*), spiked millet (*bājra*), and rice. Of these, maize is the principal food-grain of the montane, submontane, and central tracts, and is cultivated extensively in all three. In 1904 it covered about 1,900 square miles. It is sown from the middle of June to the middle of August, and harvested between the middle of September and the middle of November. Maize yields from 4 to 11 cwt. on land dependent on rainfall, and from 7 to 13 cwt. where irrigation is available.

Spiked millet.

In the Rāwalpindi and Delhi Divisions spiked millet is the chief crop, but it is also grown throughout the Province. It ordinarily covers more than 2,500 square miles, but in years of good rainfall more than 3,100 square miles. It requires less moisture than great millet, but its stalks are of inferior value as fodder. The yield varies from 2½ to 10 cwt. per acre.

Great millet.

Great millet, grown throughout the Province, ordinarily covers 3,000 square miles. This also is chiefly sown on unirrigated land. When sown as a food-crop, it still yields from 120 to 180 cwt. of green fodder per acre. Sown only as a fodder-crop, it is called *chari*. The out-turn of grain is from 3 to 5 cwt. per acre, increased by 1 or 2 cwt. if irrigated.

Rice.

Rice is grown chiefly in Kāngra, Hoshiārpur, Karnāl, and Ambāla Districts, and throughout the Lahore and Multān Divisions. It ordinarily covers more than 1,100 square miles. There are many recognized varieties. Sowings extend from March to August, and the crop is harvested in September and October.

Other autumn cereals.

Other important autumn cereals are *rāgi* or *mandwi* (*Eleusine coracana*), *chīnā* (*Panicum miliaceum*), and *kangni* or Italian millet (*Setaria italica*). In 1904 these covered more than 300 square miles.

Cotton.

Cotton is increasing rapidly in importance as an export staple. The area sown now amounts to over 1,600 square miles. The crop is generally irrigated, except in the Delhi

Division. Sown from March to July, it is picked from October to December. Ginning mills are springing up in the chief cotton tracts. A hundred lb. of uncleaned cotton gives about 30 lb. of clean lint. The cotton is of the short-stapled variety known as 'Bengals,' but is in brisk demand.

Oilseeds are ordinarily sown on 1,000 to 1,300 square miles, but the area varies with the rainfall. The principal kind is *sarson* or rape-seed (*Brassica campestris*), sown from August to December on unirrigated land and ripening in March. Another kind, *toria*, is sown on irrigated land in August, and cut in November or December. Sesamum or *til* (*Sesamum orientale*) is an autumn crop, and a little linseed or *alsi* (*Linum usitatissimum*) is grown in the spring. Oilseeds.

Indian hemp or *san* is only grown sparsely for the local manufacture of rope. It covered 77 square miles in 1904. Hemp.

Spices covered more than 40 square miles in 1904, generally on manured and irrigated lands close to the villages. Chillies are the most important crop of this class; ginger is grown chiefly in the hills. Spices.

Sugar-cane is an important and valuable crop in Rohtak, Delhi, Karnāl, Jullundur, Hoshiārpur, Amritsar, Gurdāspur, Siālkot, Gujrānwāla, and Jhang Districts. It ordinarily covers about 520 square miles, of which more than 80 per cent. is irrigated and the rest moist land. Usually propagated from sets laid down from the middle of February to the middle of April, the crop is seldom cut till December or even later, thus occupying the land for nearly a year. Sugar-cane.

The poppy is a spring crop sown in September–January, the juice being extracted in April and May. In 1904 it covered more than 14 square miles. Drugs and narcotics. Poppy.

Tobacco is grown more or less in every District as an 'extra' spring crop, sown in March or April and picked in June. In 1904 it covered a little more than 80 square miles, mostly manured lands near the villages. Tobacco.

Tea is grown only in Kāngra District, the States of Mandī and Sirmūr, and on a small area in Simla. In Kāngra there are 112 tea estates (15·5 square miles), of which 33 (with 3,500 acres) are owned by European planters. The out-turn in the latter varies from 150 to 250 lb. per acre, and the total output exceeds 1,000,000 lb. annually[1]. Tea.

The area under indigo has greatly decreased of recent years, owing to competition with chemical indigo. The area in Indigo.

[1] This was written before the earthquake of 1905, which had disastrous effects on the tea industry.

1903–4 was a little more than 80 square miles, of which about 30 square miles were in Muzaffargarh District and 25 in Multān.

Garden produce.

Highly manured land near villages grows turnips, carrots, and similar produce, which occupy 578 square miles. Potatoes, already a valuable crop in the Kāngra and Simla Hills, are increasing in importance. Mangoes are a paying fruit-crop in Hoshiārpur, Jullundur, Multān, and Muzaffargarh; and in the two latter Districts and in Dera Ghāzi Khān the date-palm flourishes, there being nearly 1,500,000 female trees which produce about 33,000 tons of fruit annually. It is consumed entirely in Northern India. There is some export of pears, apples, and other European fruit from the Kulū valley, but inaccessibility hinders the development of the industry.

Rotations.

The successions shown below are generally recognized, but all depends on climatic conditions, soils, the means of irrigation, and the system of agriculture followed in any given tract: Maize, indigo, or hemp, followed by wheat; great millet, followed by *masūr* and gram; rice, followed by barley, *masūr*, and peas; turnips or cotton, followed by maize; cotton or maize, followed by *senji*; *senji*, followed by melons.

Improvements in agricultural practice.

Since annexation, the potato, tea, and English fruits and vegetables have been introduced. The first-named is so important that the people call it 'the hillman's sugar-cane.' Attempts made to acclimatize American maize have succeeded only in the hills, and even there the stock has deteriorated. It requires nearly five months to mature, and the heat of the plains ripens it too rapidly. In 1901 an experimental farm of 55 acres was started at Lyallpur in the Chenāb Colony. A 500-acre seed farm has also been opened in the Jhelum Colony.

A combined Agricultural College and Research Institute is to be established at Lyallpur, with a staff which will include a Principal, a Professor of Agriculture, an Agricultural Chemist, an Economic Botanist, an Entomologist, and a Mycologist. The college will train men for the Agricultural department, and also as teachers of agriculture in normal schools. The present experimental farm at Lyallpur will be largely increased in size, and it is intended to establish similar farms on a smaller scale in localities selected as characteristic of the main divisions of the Province. As the scheme develops, it is hoped that an Agricultural Assistant will be appointed for each District. The Veterinary department is a part of the Agricultural department, under the control of the Director of Agriculture.

Loans.

The working of the Land Improvement and Agriculturists'

Loans Acts varies from District to District. In some, borrowing from Government is unpopular, the cultivators preferring to take loans from the village banker, because, though the rates of interest charged by Government are low, it generally insists on punctual and regular repayment in fixed instalments, whereas the village bankers do not insist on punctual repayment, and often accept grain or cattle in lieu of cash. Moreover, the official formalities necessary before the cash reaches the cultivator's hands often deter him from applying for a loan from Government.

During the decade 1891–1900 about 2½ lakhs a year was advanced under the Land Improvement Loans Act, 3·4 lakhs being advanced in 1900–1 and 1·5 lakhs in 1903–4. Loans are made at 6¼ per cent. per annum interest, and on the security of the borrower's holding. They are seldom misapplied, and are mostly taken for sinking irrigation wells, the number of which rose from 211,000 in 1890–1 to 276,000 in 1903–4. Allowing for the wells which fell out of use, more than 100,000 wells must have been sunk or renewed in this period, and of these a large proportion were made with the aid of loans from Government. Advances under the Agriculturists' Loans Act are made on the personal security of the cultivator, and practically only in or after drought, to enable him to replace cattle that have died and to purchase seed. Between 1891 and 1900 about 4·5 lakhs was advanced annually, 2 lakhs being advanced in 1900–1 and 1 lakh in 1903–4.

The indebtedness of the cultivators has long engaged the attention of Government, and the extent of the evil was illustrated by a special investigation into the conditions of certain tracts in Siālkot, Gujrānwāla, and Shāhpur Districts. The measures taken to cope with reckless alienation of land are described below, under Land Revenue. The creditors are in the great majority of cases small Hindu shopkeepers. Agriculturist money-lenders are found in parts of the Punjab, such as Amritsar, Gurdāspur, Ferozepore, and Ludhiāna, where the Sikh, 'half agriculturist, half soldier, and wholly Baniā,' predominates; and they are said to be even more exacting than the trading classes. The ordinary rate of interest varies from 21 to 25 per cent., except in the case of loans on jewels, which are given at about 12 per cent. A Registrar of Co-operative Credit Societies has been appointed in the Punjab. The number of registered societies on March 31, 1906, was 151, of which 108 were in the Districts of Gurdāspur and Jullundur.

Cattle. Yak.

The yak is found within the geographical limits of the

Punjab, but only in the Northern Kāngra hills. In summer it finds pasturage up to 17,000 feet, but in winter grazes below 8,000 feet. In the Higher Himālayas it is used for ploughing and pack-carriage. At lower elevations it is crossed with the ordinary cattle of the hills.

Kine. The Punjab kine are of the humped Indian type. In the Himālayas the mountain or Pahāri breed is dark in colour, becoming black or red as the elevation increases. The Dhanni or Salt Range breed is similar in size but lighter, tending to white, in colour. In the plains there are several breeds, the principal being those of Montgomery, the Mālwā, and Hariāna, and that of the Kachi, the country between the Chenāb and the Thal steppe. The best animals are reared in the southern Districts, Hissār, Delhi, Rohtak, Gurgaon, and Karnāl. Bulls and bullocks are used for ploughing throughout the Province.

Buffaloes. Wild buffaloes are no longer found in the Punjab, but the domesticated variety is common and highly prized. A good cow-buffalo yields from 25 to 30 seers of a white insipid milk, rich in fat, from which large quantities of *ghī* (clarified butter) are made. The profit from *ghī* is in some Districts very large. Hides are an important article of commerce, and bones are largely exported.

Cattle diseases. The most prevalent cattle diseases are foot-and-mouth disease, haemorrhagic septicaemia, rinderpest, black-quarter, and anthrax. Sheep and goats also suffer from the first-named. Though very common, the losses from it are slight, as only 2 or 3 per cent. of the animals attacked die. Septicaemia is also prevalent, especially during the rains, and the mortality is usually 90 per cent. Buffaloes are its chief victims, but it also attacks kine. Rinderpest is common, more especially in the hills, where it assumes a virulent form, killing 80 or 90 per cent. of the animals attacked. Cattle, sheep, goats, and even camels are subject to this pest. Inoculation, segregation, and other measures for combating cattle diseases are controlled by the qualified assistants who work under the Superintendent of the Civil Veterinary department and the Deputy-Commissioner.

Prices. The prices of cattle vary considerably. A good milch buffalo fetches Rs. 100 or even Rs. 150. A pair of young Hariāna plough bullocks cost Rs. 120 or Rs. 140, and a cow from Rs. 50 to Rs. 70, but as a rule inferior and cheaper cattle are in demand.

Horses. The Baloch and Dhanni breeds of horses are the best known in the Punjab. Generally the Punjab stock has immensely improved during the last thirty years from the infusion of the English and Arab blood of thoroughbred stallions. Large horse-fairs are held at Sargodha (in Shāhpur), Dera Ghāzi Khān, Rāwalpindi, Gujrāt, Amritsar, Multān, and Jalālābād (in Ferozepore).

Sheep and goats. Sheep are important in the South-West Punjab, where wool is a staple product. The *dūmba* or fat-tailed sheep is found in the Salt Range, but does not flourish east of it. In the Himālayas the variety found resembles that of Dartmoor or Exmoor, the *khādu* being the best breed. Goats are kept chiefly for milk and meat, but the hair is also largely used.

Camels. Camels are extensively used throughout the plains and in the Lower Himālayas, but the south and south-west supply the largest numbers. Mostly used as a pack-animal, the camel is also employed for draught, riding, and even ploughing in those parts. Camel fairs are held at Abohar and Bhiwāni (in Hissār).

Donkeys and mules. Donkeys are miserable creatures in the Punjab, except in Rāwalpindi and the Districts west of the Chenāb. Mule-breeding from imported donkey stallions supplied by the Army Remount department is carried on in ten Districts and in both the canal colonies, and elsewhere by the Civil Veterinary department.

Pasture-grounds. Cattle are largely stall-fed. Every village has its grazing-grounds; but the grass is never abundant and fails entirely in years of scanty rainfall, when the cattle are driven off in large numbers to find pasture along the rivers and below the hills.

Cattle fairs. The principal cattle fairs are those held at Amritsar, Jahāzgarh (in Rohtak), Gulū Shāh (in Siālkot), and Hissār.

Irrigation. The extent to which cultivation is dependent on irrigation may be gauged from the fact that 41 per cent. of the cultivated area is irrigated, mainly from wells and canals, and that 7 per cent. more is subject to inundation from the rivers. Hence only 52 per cent. of the cultivated area is wholly dependent on the rainfall. Of the 41 per cent. irrigated, 22 per cent. is irrigated from canals, 14 from wells, 4 from wells and canals combined, and 1 from streams and tanks.

The necessity and demand for irrigation vary with the climatic and physical conditions. Speaking generally, the necessity for perennial irrigation varies inversely with the amount of the rainfall, being therefore greatest in the south-west and least in the north-east submontane tracts. The two principal means of irrigation are canals and wells, the latter including various indigenous kinds of lift, and the area in which each can be used is determined by the depth of the spring-level. Perennial canals are beneficial where the spring-level is not less than 20 feet below the surface; but where it is higher, wells are used in the cold season and the canal is reserved for irrigating the autumn crop during the summer months, to prevent the soil from becoming waterlogged.

Canals.

Native rulers were not blind to the possibilities of irrigation in the Punjab; but, at annexation, the only canals open in the Province, as it stood before the addition of the Delhī territory after the Mutiny, were the Hasli (since merged in the Bāri Doāb Canal) and a good many inundation canals in the south-western Districts. Thus the present canals are almost entirely the creation of British rule. These canals fall into two classes: the perennial canals, with permanent head-works; and (2) the inundation canals which run only in the flood season, and irrigate the lowlands along the rivers. Of the former class there are now six canals: the WESTERN JUMNA, SIRHIND, BĀRI DOĀB, CHENĀB, JHELUM, and SIDHNAI, though there is seldom enough water in the river for a cold-season supply to the last-named. These great canals serve four-fifths of the total area irrigated from Government works. There are six series of inundation canals: the UPPER and LOWER SUTLEJ, CHENĀB, INDUS (right bank), MUZAFFARGARH (from the left bank of the Indus and right bank of the Chenāb), SHĀHPUR, and GHAGGAR. Besides these, numerous small inundation canals are owned by private individuals or District boards. Of these the GREY CANALS in Ferozepore are the chief. The total length of main channels and branches in 1890–1, 1900–1, and 1903–4 was 3,813, 4,644, and 4,744 miles respectively.

Canal revenues.

Canal revenue is direct or indirect. The former is paid by the cultivator according to occupier's rates fixed for different crops. It is assessed on all the great perennial canals by the canal officers, and the rules provide liberal remissions for failed crops. The indirect charges (owner's or water-advantage rate) aim at taxing the landowner for the rent or profits derived by him from the canal. The gross receipts averaged 50 lakhs between 1881 and 1890, 102 lakhs between 1891 and 1900, and amounted to 162 lakhs in 1900–1 and 200 lakhs in 1903–4. In the same periods the expenditure (excluding capital account) was 26 lakhs, 42 lakhs, 60 lakhs, and 66 lakhs. The net profits in 1903–4 were 134 lakhs, and, deducting interest on capital expenditure, 94 lakhs, or 8·7 per cent. The most profitable canal was the Chenāb Canal, which yielded 19·6 per cent. The return on capital has decreased greatly in the case of 'minor' works. This is due to the expenditure of

10 lakhs of capital during the ten years 1881–1890 on protective works, which produced no direct return. The returns from inundation canals fluctuate enormously. For example, on the Upper Sutlej Canals the dividend was only 1·95 per cent. in 1900–1 and as much as 43·2 per cent. in 1901–2.

System of distribution of water.

The efficient distribution of the water depends largely on the telegraph system by which canal officers are kept in constant touch with the gauge stations. Control of the distribution is secured by a systematic devolution of responsibility. The Chief Engineer receives a weekly report on the state of the crops, and is thus enabled to supervise the general distribution of the water throughout the Province; the Superintending Engineer controls its distribution among the divisions of his canal, and so on. Within the village the policy is to leave the distribution of the water in the hands of the cultivators, who see that it is divided in accordance with the share lists based on the area to be irrigated in each holding. On inundation canals the supply depends on the rise of the rivers, and these rarely do more than supply water for sowing a spring crop, which has to be matured by well-irrigation.

Projected canals.

A vast irrigation scheme was sanctioned in 1905. It will comprise three new canals: the Upper Jhelum, Upper Chenāb, and Lower Bāri Doāb. Of these, the first will take off from the Jhelum in Kashmīr territory, 18 miles from the British border, and, skirting the Pabbi hills, pass close to Gujrāt town and tail in above the head-works of the existing Chenāb Canal. It will have only one branch; but its distributaries, 562 miles in length, will irrigate the southern part of Gujrāt and a part of Shāhpur District, which is not supplied by the Jhelum Canal. The Upper Chenāb Canal will take off from the Chenāb river opposite Siālkot, and will irrigate a large part of Gujrānwāla and Lahore Districts and a little of Siālkot; then, crossing the Rāvi river by a siphon 16 miles below Lahore, it will feed the third canal in the series. This, the Lower Bāri Doāb Canal, will run parallel with the Rāvi river through the whole length of Montgomery District and end in Multān District, the northern portion of which it will also irrigate. These projects are estimated to cost 782 lakhs, and will take nine years to complete, provided that sufficient labour is forthcoming. The total length of the three canals will be 230 miles, with 2,714 miles of distributaries.

Navigable canals.

The only navigable canals are portions of the Western Jumna and Sirhind systems. The former is navigable from its head to Delhi. A portion of the Hānsi branch is also navigable, the total length of navigable channels being 207 miles. The Sirhind Canal is navigable for 180 miles from its head at Rūpar, and from the town of Patiāla to Ferozepore, where it connects with the river Sutlej, whence there is a continuous water-way to Karāchi. The boat traffic is insignificant, the boat tolls on both together amounting to less than Rs. 5,000 per annum; but there is a considerable raft traffic, &c., particularly on the Western Jumna Canal, where the dues average about Rs. 40,000 per annum. The rafts consist principally of timber, sleepers, scantlings, and bamboos, which are floated down the hills to the canal head, and are thence passed into the canals.

Wells.

Almost all the irrigation carried on by indigenous methods is from wells. In 1903–4 the Punjab contained over 276,000 masonry wells and 38,000 unlined and lever wells and water-lifts. In that year the total area of the crops matured under well-irrigation was about 5,400 square miles. Masonry wells are worked by cattle, the Persian wheel or a rope and bucket being used. Unlined wells are chiefly found in riverain lands, but small unlined wells are also used in submontane tracts with a high water-level. They are mostly worked by a lever. Masonry wells cost from Rs. 150 to Rs. 750 or more according to depth. Unlined wells cost only about R. 1 per foot, but seldom last more than three years.

Other forms of irrigation.

In the Salt Range and the hilly tracts of Gurgaon and Dera Ghāzi Khān, torrents are embanked and the water spread over the fields as required. In the hills and submontane tracts a considerable area, chiefly under rice, is irrigated by small channels (*kūhls*) taken out of a river or stream and often carried along the hill-sides.

Fisheries.

Fish are plentiful in most of the rivers and canals of the Province. In certain Districts the fisheries are leased by Government to contractors, and in 1904–5 the total income from this source was Rs. 4,342. In accordance with the provisions of the Indian Fisheries Act (IV of 1897), certain methods of fishing, such as the use of the drag-net, have been prohibited in some of the streams of Rāwalpindi District, and in the Jumna for a mile above and a mile below the Okhla weir at the head of the Agra Canal, while in Sirmūr and the hill-country of Patiāla the fish in the Giri and other streams are strictly preserved in the interests of anglers.

Rents, wages, and prices.

Rents.

The state under native rule took all, or nearly all, the produce of the land which was not required for the subsistence of the cultivators, and it is only since the value of land has risen under the more lenient British assessments that anything in the shape of a margin leviable as rent has been in any general way available for the owners of land.

The assessment on land, which under Sikh rule was usually taken direct from the cultivator in kind, is now always taken from the owner in cash, and the latter recovers from the tenant, in kind or in cash, an amount which ordinarily ranges from twice to three times the value of the assessment. The usual practice is to take rent in kind at a share of the produce, and 57 per cent. of the rented area of the Province is now subject to some form of kind rent; but where crops difficult to divide are grown, and in the neighbourhood of towns, or on lands held by occupancy tenants, or in tracts, such as the south-east of the Punjab, where the custom is of some standing, it is not unusual to find rents paid in cash. The exact rate at which a rent in kind is paid is largely a matter of custom; and such rents, while varying considerably from soil to soil, do not change much from time to time. Cash rents, on the other hand, have necessarily increased with the increase in the prices of agricultural produce; and the average incidence of such rents has risen from Rs. 1–13–2 per acre in 1880–1, to Rs. 2–6–5 in 1890–1, and Rs. 4–6–0 in 1900–1.

As nearly one-half of the land in the Punjab is cultivated by the owners themselves, and a fair portion of the rest by owners who pay rent to co-sharers or other owners, the tenant class is neither so large nor so distinctively marked as in the rest of Northern India, and the law affords much less elaborate protection to the tenant than is usual in the United Provinces or in Bengal. A limited number of the tenant class, amounting to nearly one-fifth of the whole, have been marked off by the legislature on certain historical grounds as entitled to rights of occupancy, and the rents of this class cannot be enhanced to a standard higher than 12½ to 75 per cent. (according to circumstances) in excess of the land revenue. In the case of the remaining tenants, who hold at will, no limit is fixed to the discretion of the landlord in the matter of enhancement; but the procedure to be followed in ejectment, and the grant of compensation for improvements legally executed, is provided for by the law in respect of both classes of tenants.

The figures given in the table on the next page are of interest as showing the direction in which rents are developing.

These statistics are subject to a good many reservations which need not be entered into here; but they are sufficient to disprove the usual impression that the increase of the landowning population entails a withdrawal of land from tenants, and that with the development of the country the practice of kind rents is disappearing.

	1880–1.	1890–1.	1900–1.	1903–4.
	Acres.	Acres.	Acres.	
Average area held per proprietor .	30·8	18·8	17·8	Not available.
Average area of tenant's holding .	6·0	3·7	3·3	2·5
Percentage of total cultivated area held by tenants	34·7	46·0	52·3	54·1
Percentage of tenant area held by occupancy tenants	31·3	19·6	17·0	19·0
Percentage of grain-rented to total rented area	49·8	54·1	56·6	57·5

Wages.

With normal prices, the sum required for the food of a labouring family may be taken to be about Rs. 4½ a month, and to this Rs. 1½ a month must be added for a reasonable amount of furniture, clothing, and other necessaries. The ordinary unskilled labourer, therefore, looks to get about Rs. 6 a month or its value, and this may be taken as the ordinary rate roughly prevailing. The labourer in a town is usually paid entirely in cash; in the country he is paid either wholly or partially in kind. The country labourer needs a little more food than the town labourer; but whereas the latter has house-rent to pay, the former generally obtains his house at little or no expense to himself. The cultivator who rents but does not own land lives at a standard of comfort very little higher than the landless labourer. As his expenditure, like his income, is almost entirely in grain, and a large part of his food and clothing is produced by himself, it is difficult to estimate his receipts in money; but it would probably be fair to say that, when the ordinary day labourer receives Rs. 6 a month, the receipts of the cultivator after paying his rent would be represented by something like Rs. 7 or Rs. 8, while if the cultivator were also an owner of land his average income, after payment of Government dues, might be put at Rs. 10, or more. Skilled labourers, such as blacksmiths or masons, get about Rs, 16 a month or its equivalent, and carpenters still more. The ordinary vernacular clerk in a commercial or Government office will as a rule get something between Rs. 15 and Rs. 20, but on this he has to maintain a better style of dress and living than men who work with their hands. Wages are now twice or thrice as high as they were in Sikh times, and there has been a progressive rise in recent years. So far as the labourer's food is concerned, its money value has in the last twenty years increased by 30 to 35 per cent., while the other items of his expenditure have decreased in price; and it would probably be correct to say that during the same period the labourer's wages have risen from 20 to 25 per cent. With artisans the increase has been larger, or from 25 to 30 per cent.

Although there are large piece-goods and other marts at places like Delhi and Amritsar, no official statistics are maintained regarding the prices of any but agricultural staples. For these, three classes of data are available: the prices obtained by agriculturists at harvest time at a fair number of towns and large villages in each District; the wholesale prices prevailing at the end of each fortnight in six representative cities of the Province; and the retail prices prevailing at the end of each fortnight at the head-quarters of each District. The differences between the figures obtained under the first and second of these heads are due partly to the cost of carriage, and partly also to the want of capital among agriculturists, which necessitates their selling while the market is still low. To illustrate the difference which prevails between the three classes, an example may be taken from one of the central Districts in 1904, when wheat sold at the country markets at harvest time for Rs. 19·5 per ten maunds, whereas at the head-quarters the average wholesale price for the year was Rs. 21 and the average retail price Rs. 22. In making rough calculations for assessment purposes, it is usual to assume that the agriculturist gets 4 annas per maund of 82 lb. less than the recorded average retail prices of the year. The rise of prices in the Province at large is best studied in the retail figures, which are available in greater completeness than the others. A table at the end of this article (p. 155) shows prices for a series of years at Delhi, Amritsar, and Rāwalpindi. In wheat, which is the main staple of the Province, the average rate of increase in the three markets noted is 36·7 per cent. for the period 1880–1900; and if wheat, gram, *jowār*, and *bājra* are dealt with in the proportion in which they are grown, the average joint increase is 35·4 per cent. The mileage of railways within the Province has more than quadrupled in the same period, and the large rise in prices is doubtless due in the main to this improvement in communication, accompanied by the opening of foreign markets. Prices.

Village life is still simple and possesses few luxuries. All the articles that the people require, except matches, lamps, and kerosene oil, and, most important of all, piece-goods, are Material condition of the people.

made locally, and are much the same as they were before British rule. The wealth which is being accumulated by the people is hoarded, commonly in ornaments, and less usually in cash. The circulation of Punjab circle currency notes rose from 134 lakhs in 1891–2 to 263 in 1903–4, and the deposits in the Postal savings banks increased from 63 to 80 lakhs in the same period. The peasantry, especially the landowners, have a much higher standard of living than they had forty years ago, their increased means enabling them to travel more, eat better food, wear better clothing, and own more horses, utensils, and jewels. The Sikh Districts of the Central Punjab and the submontane and Himālayan tracts are perhaps the most prosperous. Among the landless labouring classes the increase in general comfort has been marked, owing to the extension of canal-irrigation and the foundation of the Chenāb Colony, which has attracted large numbers of labourers from nearly every part of the Province. In the towns cheap European luxuries, such as German watches, patent leather shoes, and bicycles, find a considerable sale, as do American drugs and cigarettes. Round most of the larger towns suburbs are springing up containing villas built in European style with gardens, to which the wealthier classes resort as a change from their close ill-ventilated homes within the ancient walls.

Forests. Forests of the plains. The forests may be divided into two main classes, those of the hills and those of the plains. For the most part the forests of the plains are of the class known as dry forests, growing in tracts of scanty rainfall and poor, sandy, and often salt-impregnated soil. The characteristic trees are the tamarisk or *farāsh* (*Tamarix articulata*), the leafless caper or *karīl* (*Capparis aphylla*), the *jand* (*Prosopis spicigera*), the *van* (*Salvadora oleoides*), and a few acacias of the species known as *kīkar* in the Punjab and *babūl* in the rest of Northern India (*Acacia arabica*). Forests of this type, interspersed with large treeless wastes, occupy extensive areas in the Lahore, Montgomery, Multān, Chenāb, Jhelum, and Shāhpur Forest divisions, where they are estimated to cover an area of about 4,000 square miles. In the Central Punjab large tracts covered with the *dhāk* (*Butea frondosa*) are common. As they approach the hills these forests become richer in species, and gradually blend with the deciduous forests of the Lower Himālayas, while to the south and west they give place to the deserts of Rājputāna and Sind. On the banks and islands of rivers, and indeed wherever water is near the surface, the *shīsham* (*Dalbergia Sissoo*) often becomes gregarious, and is of some importance, and many other species, such as acacias and the black mulberry, are found. The avenues of *shīsham* and other trees planted along roads and canals are an important feature in the scenery of the Province.

The *sāl* tree (*Shorea robusta*) is found in the small submontane forest of Kalesar in Ambāla, in the adjoining State of Sirmūr, and in a few scattered areas in Kāngra District. This is, however, the extreme western limit of its growth, and it can never be expected to attain any great dimensions. The rocky hills of the Salt Range and Kālā-Chitta are in parts covered with an open forest, in which the olive (*Olea cuspidata*) and the *phulāhī* (*Acacia modesta*) are the principal trees.

Hill forests.

The hill forests fall into groups classified by their elevation. Below 3,000 feet they are composed of scrub and bamboo (*Dendrocalamus strictus*). The bamboo forests are most important in Kāngra, where they cover an area of 14,000 acres; the scrub forests survive in good condition only in places where they have been protected by closure from grazing. Between 2,500 and 5,000 feet of elevation the *chīl* pine (*Pinus longifolia*) is the principal tree. Forests of this tree are found throughout Kāngra proper, in the Murree and Kahūta *tahsīls* of Rāwalpindi, and in the lower portions of the valleys of Kulū, Bashahr, and Sirmūr. Between 5,000 and 8,000 feet occurs the true zone of the valuable *deodār* (*Cedrus Deodara*), which grows either in pure forests or mixed with the blue pine (*Pinus excelsa*), the silver fir (*Abies Webbiana*), the spruce (*Picea Morinda*), and trees of various deciduous species. The principal *deodār* forests are found in the Pārbati valley, and around the head-waters and side streams running into the Beās in Kulū, on either side of the Rāvi in Chamba and the Chenāb in Pāngi, in the valleys of the Sutlej and the tributaries of the Jumna in Bashahr, and in Jubbal. In this zone extensive forests of blue pine, pure or mixed with *deodār*, also occur, principally in Kulū and Bashahr. Above 8,000 feet, extensive areas, especially in the zone between 9,500 and 12,500 feet, are covered with silver fir, spruce, and trees of various deciduous species. Approaching 12,500 feet, which is about the limit of tree growth, rhododendron, birch, and juniper are found. The grassy slopes which extend from the limit of tree growth to the line of perpetual snow afford pasturage, and shepherds and herdsmen migrate thither annually with their flocks and cattle.

Management.

The administration of all the more important forests is

controlled by the Forest department, under a Conservator. There are twelve Forest divisions, including those of the Bashahr and Chamba States, the forests of which are leased by the Punjab Government. The forests of the Simla Hill States are under the general care of the Simla Forest officer, who advises the chiefs. In 1904 the land under the Forest department amounted to 9,278 square miles, of which 1,916 were completely 'reserved,' 4,909 'protected,' 1,914 'unclassed,' or given over with some restrictions to the usc of the public, and 539 'leased.' There were also 112 square miles of 'reserved' forest, and square miles of 'unclassed,' under the Military department; and other civil departments had charge of 4 miles of 'reserved,' 10 acres of 'protected,' and 7,033 square miles of 'unclassed' forests, the last being chiefly waste land in the charge of Deputy-Commissioners.

All *deodār* forests of commercial importance are worked in accordance with working plans, prepared by the Forest department and sanctioned by the Local Government. Under their prescriptions 7,140 *deodār* trees are allowed to be cut annually, and the annual yield of *deodār* timber from the forests under the control of the department is estimated at 659,000 cubic feet. This timber, together with a certain amount of blue pine and *chīl*, is floated down the various rivers to the plains, where it is sold to railways for sleepers, or to the public. Efforts are now being made to introduce exploitation by private enterprise. The *chīl* forests of Murree and Kahūta are also under a working plan, and for those of Kāngra a plan is in preparation. In the Kāngra forests the *chīl* trees are systematically tapped for resin. The spruce and fir forests are for the present principally of value as grazing-grounds, and for supplying local requirements in forest produce. They hold, however, enormous stocks of timber, which may eventually become of commercial value. The scrub forests below 2,500 feet and much of the plains forests are managed as grazing-grounds. The bamboo forests of Kāngra form a valuable property, yielding an annual surplus revenue of about Rs. 20,000.

Fuel and fodder reserves.

All closed forest areas in the lower hills and in the plains may be regarded as fuel and fodder reserves. In times of drought such areas are opened to grazing, and if necessary to lopping, so as to enable the people to keep their cattle alive until the occurrence of more favourable seasons. The area of forest land in the plains is rapidly decreasing as colonization schemes are extended, and the consequent contraction of fuel and fodder-producing areas may be felt in the future.

Chānga Mānga in Lahore District contains a plantation of 8,872 acres fully stocked with *shīsham* and mulberry, and there are smaller *shīsham* plantations at Shāhdara in the same District, and at Jullundur, Ludhiāna, and Jagādhri. Efforts have been made for many years past to increase the stock of *deodār* in the hill forests by artificial sowings and plantings, which have been to a certain extent successful. Plantations.

The wants of the people are fully provided for by the various forest settlements, which record their rights to timber, fuel, grazing, &c., in the Government forests; and in some places the inhabitants have the first option of taking grazing leases, and buying the grass from the adjoining forests. The relations of the department with the people are satisfactory, and offences against the forest laws are usually trivial and are becoming less numerous. Relations with the people.

Attempts are made to protect all the more valuable forests from fire. Fortunately the valuable *deodār* forests are but little exposed to this danger, but the *chīl* forests become highly inflammable in the hot season. The local population at first resented the restrictions imposed by fire conservancy, and many cases of wilful firing of forests used to occur; but such occurrences are now happily less frequent, and the people often give willing help in extinguishing fires in Government forests. Fire protection.

The financial results of the working of the department are shown below:— Financial results.

	1880-1 to 1889-90 (average).	1890-1 to 1899-1900. (average).	1900-1.	1903-4.
	Rs.	Rs.	Rs.	Rs.
Revenue . . .	7,74,362	10,06,412	12,60,234	16,51,077
Expenditure . .	5,49,045	7,08,100	8,35,299	9,55,918
Surplus . . .	2,25,317	2,98,312	4,24,935	6,95,159

Forest revenue is principally realized from the sale of *deodār* timber, which produces about 6 lakhs annually, sales of other timber amounting to only Rs. 60,000. The other chief items are sale of fuel (Rs. 4,60,000), and grazing and grass (Rs. 1,64,000).

The Punjab is not rich in minerals; and nearly all its mineral wealth is found in the hills, the only products of the alluvium being *kankar* or nodular limestone, saltpetre, carbonate of soda, and sal-ammoniac. Mines and minerals.

Saltpetre is found on the sites of used and disused habitations, generally associated with the chlorides of sodium, Saltpetre.

magnesium, or potassium, and the sulphates of sodium, potassium, or calcium. The initial process of manufacture, which consists in allowing water to percolate slowly through the nitrous earth, results in a solution not merely of nitre but of all the associated salts. The separation of the nitre from the rest is the work of the refiner. Refineries exist all over the Province and pay an annual licence fee of Rs. 50, while for the initial process the fee is Rs. 2. Saltpetre is exported to Europe, and is also largely used in India in the manufacture of fireworks and gunpowder for blasting. In 1903-4 there were 35 refineries in the Punjab. These produced 73,917 cwt. of refined saltpetre, the out-turn being nearly 41 per cent. of the crude substance. Impure salt (*sitta*) to the amount of 58,322 cwt. was also educed, the out-turn being over 32 per cent. of the saltpetre so utilized. Of this amount only 4,091 cwt. were excised at Rs. 1-5-9 per cwt. (R. 1 a maund), 54,496 cwt. being destroyed. Pure salt is not educed. An important saltpetre refinery exists at Okāra in Montgomery District.

Kankar. The only other important mineral product of the plains is *kankar*, or conglomerated nodules of limestone, used for metalling roads, which is found in most parts. Carbonate of soda (barilla) is made from the ashes of various wild plants, chiefly in the west and south-west of the Province. Sal-ammoniac is manufactured in Karnāl, by burning bricks made of the clay found in ponds and heating the greyish substance which exudes from them in closed retorts.

Carbonate of soda.

Sal-ammoniac.

Salt and gypsum. The most valuable mineral is rock-salt, which, with gypsum, forms immense beds in the Salt Range. It is worked in that range at KHEWRA and NŪRPUR in Jhelum District, at KĀLĀBĀGH in Miānwāli, and at WĀRCHA in Shāhpur. Salt is also manufactured at Sultānpur, in Gurgaon District, by evaporation of the saline subsoil water. Salt, dark in colour and containing a large proportion of earth and other impurities, is quarried at Drang and Guma in the State of Mandī The total amount of salt made and sold in the Punjab rose from 79,295 tons in 1880-1 to 84,338 tons in 1890-1, 94,824 tons in 1900-1, and 105,163 tons in 1903-4. The average output of the Salt Range and Mandī mines in the six years 1898-1903 was 93,698 tons, of which 89,023 came from the Salt Range; the output of the Salt Range in 1904 was 99,192 tons. Large deposits of gypsum occur in Spiti and Kanāwār, but too inaccessible to be at present of any economic value.

Coal. Although the existence of coal at numerous points throughout the Salt Range had long been recognized, no attempts were made to work it until recently, except at the large colliery near Dandot in Jhelum District. Within the last few years, however, prospecting licences have been taken out at Kālābāgh on the Indus in Miānwāli District, a few other places in Jhelum, and Sandral in Shāhpur; and great hopes are entertained that the coal will prove to be of a paying quality. The Dandot Mines have been worked since 1884 by the North-Western Railway. There is only one seam of coal, which outcrops at various points along the hill-side at a mean distance of 300 feet below the limestone scarp, which here rises 2,300 feet above sea-level. The seam averages 2 feet 9 inches in thickness, and is worked on the long-wall system, all the coal being taken out in one operation. The mines are entered by level or inclined tunnels from the hill-side, the longest stretching 900 yards under the hill. From the mouth of each tunnel the coal is conveyed on an inclined tramway to the edge of the hill, whence a funicular railway runs down the cliff to the North-Western terminus at Dandot. The coal is classed as a bituminous lignite, and, though low in fixed carbon, has a relatively high calorific value. About 1,500 men are employed on the mines, at a daily wage of 8 annas for a miner and 3½ or 4½ annas for a cooly. The workers are chiefly agriculturists, who leave the mines when their fields claim all their time, to return to them again when the crops need less attention. Very few can really be called miners. Makrānis were at one time imported from Karāchi, but the experiment was not a success. In 1891 the out-turn was 60,703 tons, in 1901 67,730, and in 1904 45,594 tons. In 1901 it was estimated that three million tons remained to be worked.

There are no gold-mines in the Punjab, but gold-washing is carried on at various places in the upper reaches of most of the rivers. The industry is not remunerative, a hard day's work producing gold to the value of only 2 or 4 annas[1]. The total recorded output in 1904 was 370 oz. Gold.

Iron is found in Kāngra District at several points along the Dhaola Dhār, in the form of crystals of magnetic oxide of iron imbedded in decomposed and friable mica schists. The supply is practically inexhaustible, and the quality of the ore is equal to the best Swedish iron. The remoteness of the tract, combined with difficulties of carriage and absence of fuel, have hitherto prevented smelting on a large scale. Besides iron, antimony ore is found. Iron mines are also worked at Kot Khai in Simla, and in the Hill States of Jubbal, Bashahr, Iron.

[1] *Punjab Products*, by Baden Powell, pp. 12, 13.

Mandī, and Suket. Sirmūr State possesses several iron mines, but they are not worked owing to their inaccessibility and the poor quality of the ore.

Other metals.

Copper was formerly smelted in considerable quantities in various parts of the Outer Himālayas in Kulū, where a killas-like rock persists along the whole range, and is known to be copper-bearing. Veins of galena and of copper pyrites occur in the Lower Himālayas, in Kulū, and in the Simla Hill States; and stibnite is found at Shigri in the valley of the Chandra river in Lāhul.

Slate.

There are quarries at Bākhli in the State of Mandī, near Kanhiāra in Kāngra District, and throughout Kulū, which turn out a good quality of slate. A quarry at Kund in the Rewāri *tahsīl* of Gurgaon is worked under European management, but the slate and flake are not of good quality.

Petroleum.

Petroleum springs occur in Attock District, and in the hills to the south-east, but the average recorded output during the six years (1898–1903) was only 1,674 gallons. In 1904 the output was 1,658 gallons.

Alum.

Near Kālābāgh in Miānwāli District, on the Indus, considerable quantities of a pyritous shale are extracted for the production of alum, but the mining is carried on in an irregular and fitful way. The output was estimated in 1898 to amount to 750 tons, and to only 129 tons in 1904.

Arts and manufactures. Cotton.

Cotton-spinning is the great domestic industry of the Province, coarse cotton cloth being woven by hand in nearly every village. In 1901 the number of persons returned as supported by cotton-weaving in British territory was 778,947, of whom 322,944 were actual workers and 456,003 dependents. The coarse country cloth is strongly woven and wears well, and is not likely to be entirely displaced by the machine-made article for some time to come. Finer qualities are also manufactured, but these include only longcloths and damasks, white or coloured, with woven patterns. Muslin (*tanzeb*) is made in small quantities at Delhi and Rohtak. The longcloths, when checked and of thick material, are called *khes*, and when striped are termed *sūsī*, the latter being made of machine-spun yarn with sometimes a few silk threads in the warp. The *lungī* or *pagrī* is a long narrow strip of cloth worn by men round the head as a turban or as a band round the waist. Beautiful *khes* are made in the South-West and Central Punjab. The *gabrūns* of Ludhiāna closely resemble similar goods made in Europe, and its *lungīs*, imitations of those made in Peshāwar, are famous. The *lungīs* of Shāhpur and

Multān are more ornate. A special cloth made of a mixture of cotton and wool called *garbi loi* is woven in Gurdāspur District and exported all over India. The glazed fabrics, especially the diaper called *ghāti* or *bulbulchashm* or 'nightingale's eye,' of Jullundur are also famous. Cotton rugs, *darīs* or *shatranjīs*, are turned out at Lahore and Ambāla. Cotton-pile carpets are made at Multān, but recent productions indicate that a crude scheme of colours has ruined the beauty of this manufacture. Cotton-printing is carried on in many parts of the Punjab, and the productions of Kot Kamālia, Sultānpur, and Lahore are specially famous. The printing is done by hand by means of small wooden blocks. Within recent years fairly large quantities have been exported to Europe and America, but the trade is declining owing to the fashion having changed.

Sheep's wool is largely produced in the plains, and is woven or felted into blankets and rugs. Dera Ghāzi Khān and Bhera produce coloured felts (*namdās*) in considerable quantities. The finest wool is that of Hissār, and the western Districts also produce a fair quality. Some of the wool worked up in the Province is imported from Australia, most of this being utilized by the power-loom mills at Dhāriwāl. Of greater interest, however, are the manufactures of *pashm*, the fine hair of the Tibetan goat. This is imported through Kashmīr, Kulū, and Bashahr, and supplies Ludhiāna, Simla, Kāngra, Amritsar, and Gujrāt, the chief seats of artistic woollen manufacture. The industry dates from early in the nineteenth century, when famine drove numbers of artisans from Kashmīr to seek a home in the Punjab. Real Kashmīr shawls continued to be made until the Franco-German War, when the demand ceased; and the manufacture of *pashmīna*, or piece-goods made from *pashm*, is now confined to *alwāns* or serges, curtains, and ordinary shawls. In many Districts sacking, coarse blankets, and rugs are made of goats' and camels' hair. Wool.

Practically the whole of the silk used in the Punjab is imported from China. It is woven in most parts, the chief centres being Amritsar, Lahore, Patiāla, Batāla, Multān, Bahāwalpur, Delhi, and Jullundur, where both spinning and weaving are fairly important industries. The articles manufactured may be divided into three classes: woven fabrics of pure silk, woven fabrics of silk and cotton, and netted fabrics of silk or silk and cotton, of which the second are being turned out in largely increasing quantities. Turbans and waistbands (*lungīs*) of cotton cloth with silk borders woven on to them Silk.

are also very largely made. Netted silk is made in the form of fringes, tassels, girdles, *paijāma* strings, &c.

Embroidery.

Many kinds of wearing apparel are decorated with embroidery. The wraps called *phūlkāris* ('flower-work') are in most Districts embroidered with silk, and the industry has grown from a purely domestic one into a considerable trade, large numbers being exported to Europe for table-covers and hangings. Very similar are the *orhnās* of Hissār, which are embroidered in wool or cotton. Delhi is the centre of the trade in embroideries, in which gold and silver wire, as well as silk thread, is largely used, on silk, satin, and velvet. The purity of the manufacture is guaranteed by the municipality, which supervises the manufacture, fees being paid by the artisans to cover expenses. This practice, a relic of native rule, is highly popular among the workmen, who thereby get a guarantee for the purity of their wares. The embroidery is applied chiefly to caps, shoes, belts, uniforms, turbans, elephant trappings and the like, besides table centres and similar articles of European use.

Carpets and rugs.

The carpet-weaving of Amritsar is a flourishing and important industry, and its products are exported to all parts of the world. *Pashm* is used for the finest carpets, and the work is all done by hand. Woollen carpets used to be made at Multān, but owing to the competition of Amritsar the industry is now confined to the manufacture of mats. Felt mats called *namdās* are made of unspun wool and embroidered.

Jewellery.

Ornaments are universally worn, and Punjābi women display jewellery as lavishly as those in any other part of the plains of India. It has been estimated that Amritsar city alone contains jewels to the value of two millions sterling, and the workers in precious metals in the Province considerably outnumber those in iron and steel. Gold is mainly confined to the wealthier classes, and is not largely worn by them except on special occasions; whereas silver ornaments are in daily use by all but the poorer classes. The late Mr. Baden Powell[1] gave a list of ninety-nine names for ornaments used in the Punjab, and the list is by no means exhaustive; it includes ornaments for the head, forehead, ears, nose, neck, arms, and waist, with bracelets, anklets, and rings for the toes and fingers in great variety. The general character of the gold and silver-work is rough and unfinished. Superior work is turned out at Amritsar and Delhi, and at the latter place a good deal of jewellery is made for the European market.

[1] *Punjab Manufactures*, pp. 181-4.

Iron is largely smelted in Kāngra and Simla Districts, but the out-turn is insignificant compared with the amount imported into the Punjab. Lahore used to be famous for the manufacture of weapons, but the industry is now extinct. In Gujrānwāla and at Bhera in Shāhpur District cutlery is made, but the production is irregular. The finish of these articles, though not perfect, is better than the quality of the steel, which is tough but deficient in hardness. Damascening or inlaying small articles of iron with gold wire is carried on in Siālkot and Gujrāt Districts. Agricultural implements are made by village blacksmiths, who are also often carpenters. In Lahore ironwork has been considerably improved under the influence of the North-Western Railway workshops. **Ironwork.**

All the brass and copper used is, in the first instance, imported, chiefly from Europe. Formerly copper was obtained from Kābul, but the import has entirely ceased. Various copper and zinc ores, found in the Kulū hills and other parts of the Himālayas, used to be mined, but the imported metals are so cheap that there is no immediate likelihood of the mines being reopened. European spelter, chiefly German, has long since driven the Chinese zinc out of the market. Both yellow and grey brass (or bell metal) are manufactured in the Punjab. Brass-ware is either hammered or cast; copper-ware is either cast or made of sheet copper soldered together. The industry is limited to the manufacture of domestic utensils, which are only roughly ornamented. The chief centres of the manufacture are the towns of Rewāri, Delhi, Jagādhri, Pānīpat, Gujrānwāla, Amritsar, Pind Dādan Khān, and various places in Siālkot District. **Brass and copper manufactures.**

Rough unglazed pottery is made in nearly every village, the potters being generally village menials who supply the villagers' requirements in return for a fixed share of the harvest. Unglazed pottery of a rather better kind is made at Jhajjar, and thin or 'paper' pottery at Pānīpat, Jhajjar, Jullundur, Tānda, and a few other places. Glazed pottery is made at Multān. Originally confined to the manufacture of tiles, there is now a large trade in flower-pots, plaques, vases, &c. The predominant colours are light and dark blue, brown, and green. Porcelain of disintegrated felspathic earth, mixed with gum, is made at Delhi. China clay is found near Delhi and in the Himālayas, but has not hitherto been utilized. The manufacture of glass is mainly confined to the production of glass bangles. Bottles, glasses, mirrors, lamps, lamp-chimneys, and other articles are made at Karnāl, Kāngra, Hoshiārpur, Lahore, and Delhi. **Pottery.**

Wood-carving and furniture.

Wood-carving as an indigenous art is almost entirely architectural, but devoted to doors and doorways, balconies and bow windows. Apart from the hill work, which has a character of its own, the wood-carving of the Punjab may be divided into three styles: the earliest or Hindu, the Muhammadan, and the modern Sikh style. Examples of the Hindu work are to be seen principally in the large towns, particularly at Lahore. The forms used are fantastic, tassel shapes, pendants, and bosses being predominant; but the style, except for a very recent revival, may be said to be extinct. With the Muhammadans came the development of lattice-work or *pinjra*, which is to this day the characteristic feature of Punjab wood decoration. Most of the old doorways and *bukhārchās* to be seen in frequent profusion in the old towns belong, broadly speaking, to this style of work. The Sikh style, the work of the present day, may be said to be a modern adaptation of the Muhammadan, with occasional Hindu influence underlying it. It is characterized by clear-cut carving, broad treatment, and as a rule fairly good joinery. The best wood-carvers are to be found at Amritsar, Bhera, Chiniot, and Batāla. Of late years the European demand has led to this handicraft being largely applied to small articles of decorative furniture.

Inlaid work.

Inlaid work is also of Muhammadan origin, and was probably introduced from Arabia. The chief centres are Hoshiārpur and Chiniot. The wood inlay-work of Hoshiārpur has a high local reputation, and is capable of considerable development. For many years pen-cases, walking-sticks, mirror-cases, and the low *chauki*, or octagonal table, common in the Punjab and probably of Arab introduction, have been made here in *shīsham* wood, inlaid with ivory and brass. Since 1880 tables, cabinets, and other objects have also been made, and a trade has sprung up which seems likely to expand.

Lacquer-work.

Turned wood ornamented with lac in various combinations of colours is produced in almost every village. Pākpattan has more than a local reputation for this work, while a family in Ferozepore produces a superior quality.

European furniture.

Furniture after European patterns is made in every station and cantonment, the best-known centres being Gujrāt and Kartārpur in Jullundur District. Gujrāt is known for its wood chairs, chiefly made of *shīsham*, the supply of which is abundant.

Ivory.

Ivory-carving is practically confined to the cities of Amritsar, Delhi, and Patiāla, but at the latter place it has greatly declined. Combs, essential to the attire of an orthodox Sikh, are made in large quantities at Amritsar, where paper-cutters and card-cases ornamented with geometrical open-work patterns, of some delicacy of execution but no great interest of design, are also made. The ivory-carving of Delhi is of a high order of excellence, and miniature painting on ivory is also carried on. Ivory bangles are turned in several Districts, the chief being Amritsar, Dera Ghāzi Khān, Gujrānwāla, Multān, and Lahore. Billiard-balls are made at Ludhiāna.

Paper and fibres. The manufacture of paper is now confined almost entirely to the jails. Siālkot was famous in Mughal and Sikh times for its paper, but the industry has greatly declined owing to the competition of jail-made and mill-made paper; and this is also the case in Multān. Gunny-bags, matting, ropes, baskets, blinds, and the like are largely made of various fibrous plants all over the Province.

Extension of factory industries. The decade 1891–1900 witnessed a striking extension of industrial enterprise. In the cotton industry there were, in 1904, 114 steam factories for ginning and pressing cotton, compared with 12 in 1891, and 6 in 1881. The produce of these factories is still for the most part exported abroad, or to other Provinces in India. **Cotton-mills.** The Punjab contains eight cotton-spinning and weaving mills, of which six have been started since 1891, and a good deal of the Punjab-grown cotton is utilized in the Province. The following table shows their recent development:—

	Number of			Daily average of hands employed.
	Mills.	Looms.	Spindles.	
1900–1 . .	5	426	80,188	2,040
1903–4 . .	8	475	112,508	3,201

These mills have a nominal capital of 60 lakhs. The out-turn of yarn has steadily increased since 1895–6, but that of woven goods shows a tendency to decrease, as appears from the following figures, which give the out-turn in pounds:—

	1895–6.	1899–1900.	1900–1.	1901–2.	1903–4.
Yarn spun	4,361,000	7,601,863	7,235,843	9,629,422	11,578,346
Goods woven	91,254	705,408	404,258	272,695	64,927

The commonest counts spun are 13's, 11's, 15's, 16's, and 12's, in the order given, and these amounted to 8½ of the 9·6 million pounds spun in 1901–2. The goods woven are almost all grey. The estimated out-turn of cleaned cotton in 1903 was

104,496,400 lb., of which more than one-fourth was exported. While the Punjab is of considerable importance as a cotton-producing Province, the staple is short, varying from ½ to ¾ of an inch, and occupies a low position in the market.

Woollen industry.

The Egerton Woollen Mills, established at Dhāriwāl in 1880, are the only woollen mills in the Province. The company has a nominal capital of Rs. 12,00,000. Its progress is shown by the following figures:—

	1890–1.	1901.	1904.
Number of looms . .	115	128	264
" spindles . .	4,564	4,320	6,708
" hands employed	620	820	908

In 1903–4 the mills turned out broadcloths, blankets, great-coats, serges, flannels, tweeds, *loīs* and shawls, travelling rugs, knitting yarns, braids, Berlin wool, socks, caps, gloves, and other kinds of knitted goods to the amount of 572,061 lb., valued at Rs. 7,30,118. The native shawl-weaving industry and manufacture of *pattū* and blankets have not been much affected by foreign imports.

Breweries. Ice. Indigo. Distilleries.

The Province contains eight breweries, from which nearly 2,000,000 gallons of malt liquors were issued in 1903–4. In 1904 there were 15 ice factories worked by steam, compared with 4 in 1891. The number of indigo factories decreased from 27 to 12. There were, in 1891, two distilleries for the manufacture of spirits according to the European method, but the number has now risen to six. In 1903–4, 273,102 gallons (London proof) of spirits were issued from these. Most of the spirit is made from sugar, but some is whisky distilled from barley malt.

Iron foundries.

There were 5 private iron foundries in 1904: namely, three at Delhi, one at Lahore, and one at Siālkot. Steel trunks and boxes are made in large numbers at Multān, Lahore, and Siālkot. At the place last mentioned surgical instruments are made by an enterprising firm. The most important iron-works, however, are the North-Western Railway workshops at Lahore.

Protection of operatives.

Factory operatives are protected by the Indian Factories Act, revised rules under which were promulgated in 1892. The orders of the Inspectors have been enforced without difficulty, and very few prosecutions under the Act have been necessary. In 1892 there were 34 factories in which steam-power was used. The number has now risen to 175. While the conditions of labour of the mill operatives has been decidedly improved, it does not appear that there has been any tendency for wages either to rise or fall during the last ten years. The highest rates are paid in the Government workshops on the North-Western Railway, where many skilled mechanics are employed. The ordinary rates in private factories are 3 annas to 5 annas a day for male operatives; 2 annas to 4 annas for women and children; and from Rs. 30 to Rs. 60 a month for skilled mechanics.

Artisans in the indigenous industries.

The condition of skilled artisans in the indigenous industries of the Punjab, such as carpet-weavers, leather-workers, brass-workers, is not favourable. The capitalists in some cities formerly safeguarded their interests by a trade practice, according to which, when a workman left one employer for another, the second employer was held to be liable to the first to the extent of all advances received, and the thraldom of the artisan to the second employer was maintained. This trade practice has recently been declared illegal by several decisions of the Chief Court, and the growing competition among capitalists for the service of workmen is beginning to have its natural effect in strengthening the position of the artisan. The present transitional stage from the guild or caste system to the system of free competition between capital and labour is one of much interest to the student of sociology. The change is, however, as yet only in its initial stages, and has scarcely affected the village artisans, who still receive their customary dues in kind, and are almost as much dependent on the nature of the harvests as the agriculturists themselves. In towns also the hereditary nature of many caste industries, and the tradition of preserving the trade secrets within the trade caste, still continue. The freedom to learn where and what one wills has not yet been obtained, but is being gradually brought about by the competition of capital for labour, by the industrial schools, and the introduction of steam-power and factory labour, which, having no caste tradition, is open to all.

Commerce and trade. Trade prior to annexation.

Prior to annexation the Punjab proper had practically no trade with the rest of India. It had no surplus agricultural produce to export, and the anarchy which ensued on the decay of the Mughal empire was an effectual barrier to commercial enterprise. Ranjīt Singh's policy aimed at excluding British traders from his kingdom, while the earliest efforts of the British Government were directed to opening up the water-way of the Indus. Since annexation the security afforded to person and property, the improvement of communications, and above all the extension of canal-irrigation, have vastly developed the agricultural resources of the Province.

General character of trade.

The main source of the wealth of the Punjab lies in its export of wheat, of which the largest amounts exported were 550,911 tons in 1891–2, 457,991 in 1894–5, 493,826 in 1898–9[1], 623,745 in 1901–2, 536,374 in 1902–3, and 877,022 in 1903–4. Next to wheat, raw cotton is the principal export, and besides wheat inferior grains are exported on a large scale, chiefly to Southern Europe. During the ten years 1891–1900 the value of the agricultural produce exported exceeded that of the amount imported by an average of nearly 438 lakhs a year, a sum which considerably exceeds the total land revenue, with cesses and irrigation rates, levied in the Province.

Among imports, cotton piece-goods, European and Indian, stand first. The imports of the former fluctuate greatly. Valued at 218 lakhs in 1890–1, they had fallen to 190 lakhs in 1900–1, but rose to 253 lakhs in 1901–2, falling again to 231 lakhs in 1903–4. Indian-made piece-goods, however, tend to oust the European, the imports of the former having increased threefold in value between 1891 and 1904. In the case of twist and yarn this tendency is even more marked. The other considerable imports are iron and steel, sugar, wool (manufactured), gunny-bags and cloth, dyes and tans, and liquors. Wheat and gram are also imported in times of scarcity. The well-to-do classes in the Punjab consume wheaten bread, even when wheat is at famine prices, and are not content with a cheaper grain. Hence the imports of wheat vary inversely with the out-turn of the local wheat harvest. In the prosperous year 1898–9 the value of the wheat imported was only 6 lakhs: the poor harvest of 1899–1900 raised it to 29 lakhs, and, the scarcity continuing into 1900–1, to over 41 lakhs in the latter year. Good harvests in 1901–2 and 1903–4 reduced it to 8 and 10 lakhs respectively. The import statistics of the coarser and cheaper food-grains, such as gram and pulse, are an index to the purchasing power of the poorer classes. Less than 8½ lakhs in value in 1898–9, the imports of these grains exceeded 87 lakhs in 1899–1900, falling to 39 lakhs in 1900–1 and 5½ in 1903–4. The figures show that in periods of acute distress the poorer classes are compelled to fall back on inferior grains, until better harvests and lower prices permit them to resume their wheaten diet.

Trade centres.

The development of the export trade in wheat has created

[1] All figures for the year prior to 1900–1 on pp. 86–8 include the trade of the North-West Frontier Province, whether internal or external (i.e. within India or with other Asiatic countries, including Kashmīr), and those for the subsequent years its internal trade alone.

new centres of trade, in places favourably situated on the lines of communication, especially on the Southern Punjab Railway and on the line from Wazīrābād through the Chenāb Colony. Along the former large grain markets have been established at Rohtak, Kaithal, Bhatinda, and Abohar. The last-named, ten years ago a petty agricultural village, has now become a considerable trade centre, and has attracted much of the wheat trade from Fāzilka. In the Chenāb Colony important trade marts have been established at Gojra, Lyallpur, Sāngla, Chiniot Road, and Toba Tek Singh. Kasūr in Lahore District has likewise benefited at the expense of Ferozepore. Imports are distributed chiefly through the cities and larger towns, such as Delhi, Lahore, Amritsar, and Multān. A Punjab Chamber of Commerce, with its head-quarters at Delhi, has recently been established.

The trading castes are the Khattrīs in the centre and north, the Baniās in the east, and the Aroras in the west. The village trader is the collecting and distributing agent, but he almost always combines money-lending with shopkeeping. Nearly every cultivator is his client, and to him much of the agricultural produce of the village is handed over at a low price, to liquidate debts which have sometimes accumulated for generations. To this, however, there are notable exceptions, the Sikh and Hindu Jats being often themselves keen traders. Moreover, in the case of wheat, the exporter often deals direct with the cultivator, and in the east of the Province many cultivators in the slack season fill their carts with produce and set out to sell it in the best market they can find. Most towns are centres for the collection of agricultural produce, and, as mentioned above, many large grain markets have been established along the lines of rail. These usually have the advantage of being free from municipal octroi duties which, in spite of the system of refunds and bonded warehouses for goods in transit, more or less hamper commerce. No statistics are available to show the volume of this internal trade. Organization of internal trade.

The trade outside the Province is almost entirely with other Provinces and States in India, the amount that comes over the passes from Central Asia being relatively insignificant. More than 90 per cent. of the recorded exports and a still higher proportion of the imports are carried by rail, the remainder being borne partly by rail and partly by boat on the Indus to and from Sind and Karāchi. The bulk of the trade of the Province is with Karāchi, which in 1903–4 sent 37 per cent. of the imports and received 54 per cent. of the exports. Bombay and Organization of external trade.

Calcutta together accounted for 27 per cent. of the imports and 14 per cent. of the exports, and the United Provinces for 23 per cent. of the imports and 19 per cent. of the exports. Wheat, raw cotton, oilseeds, hides, raw wool, and a certain amount of inferior grains go to Karāchi, in exchange for cotton and woollen piece-goods, sugar, metals, and railway plant and rolling stock. The trade with the other seaport towns is on the same lines. Bombay takes a large amount of raw cotton, and sends silk, tea, and tobacco. Hides and skins, leather, dyes, and tans go largely to Calcutta, whence comes a great deal of the wearing apparel, jute, and woollen piece-goods imported. Cotton and woollen manufactured goods are exported to the United Provinces, which send sugar, coal and coke (from Bengal), *ghī*, gram, and pulse.

Trade with Kashmīr.

The trade with Kashmīr is partly by the Jammu-Kashmīr Railway, and partly by the roads leading into the Districts of Gurdāspur, Siālkot, Gujrāt, Jhelum, and Rāwalpindi in the Punjab and Hazāra in the North-West Frontier Province. In the table attached to this article (p. 157) the figures for 1903–4 exclude the trade through Hazāra, now a District of the North-West Frontier Province. The trade with Ladākh passes either through Kashmīr or over the Bāra Lācha (pass) into the Kulū subdivision of Kāngra. The chief imports from Kashmīr are rice and other grains, *ghī*, timber, oilseeds, manufactured wool, raw silk, hides and skins, and fruits; and the chief exports to Kashmīr are cotton piece-goods, wheat, metals, tea, sugar, salt, and tobacco. *Charas*, borax, and ponies are the principal imports from Ladākh, and metals and piece-goods are the chief exports thither.

Trade with countries beyond India.

The direct trade with countries beyond India is small, being confined to that with Chinese Tibet, and an insignificant trade with Kābul through Dera Ghāzi Khān. Trade from Chinese Tibet either comes down the Hindustān-Tibet road to Simla, or enters Kulū from Ladākh or through Spiti. The chief imports are raw wool and borax, and the chief exports are cotton piece-goods and metals. The chief imports from Kābul are fruit, *ghī*, and raw wool; the chief exports are piece-goods, rice, leather, and sugar. The trade with Kābul, which passes down the main trade routes, as well as that with Tīrāh, Swāt, Dīr, Bājaur, and Buner, is registered in the North-West Frontier Province; much, however, passes through to the Punjab, and beyond it to the Lower Provinces of India.

Communications. Railways.

The Punjab is well provided with railways. Karāchi, its natural port near the mouths of the Indus in Sind, is directly connected with the Punjab by the broad-gauge North-Western State Railway from Lahore. Delhi is in direct communication with Karāchi by another line passing through Rewāri and Merta Road Junctions, and also by the Southern Punjab Railway, which runs along the southern border of the Province to join the Karāchi line at Samasata. Karāchi has recently been brought into closer contact with Ludhiāna by the new branch of the Southern Punjab Railway from Ludhiāna via Ferozepore and McLeodganj Road. The north-west corner of the Province is directly connected with Karāchi by the branches of the North-Western Railway, which leave the main line at Campbellpur, Golra, and Lāla Mūsa and converge at Kundiān, whence the Sind-Sāgar branch follows the east bank of the Indus and joins the Karāchi branch at Sher Shāh. The new Wazīrābād-Khānewāl line taps the fertile Chenāb Colony in the Rechna Doāb and also connects with Karāchi via Multān. The Jech Doāb line commences from Malakwāl, a station on the Sind-Sagār branch of the North-Western Railway, and ends at the Shorkot Road station of the Wazīrābād-Khānewāl branch. Another small line is under construction from Shāhdara, 3 miles north of Lahore, to Sangla Hill on the Wazīrābād-Khānewāl Railway. It will serve as an outlet to the immense grain traffic in the interior of the Chenāb Colony.

In the east of the Province the country is covered with a network of branch lines, of which the Delhi-Umballa-Kālka, Simla-Kālka, Rājpura-Bhatinda, Bhatinda-Ferozepore, and Ludhiāna-Dhūrī-Jākhal are the most important. The Rewāri-Bhatinda-Fāzilka (metre-gauge) State Railway links up the important junction of Bhatinda with the Rājputāna-Mālwā line, which also connects with Delhi. The Delhi-Agra branch of the Great Indian Peninsula Railway has recently been opened. In the centre of the Province a branch of the North-Western Railway, recently opened, connects Amritsar with Patti, a town in Lahore District.

The oldest railway is that from Amritsar to Lahore, opened in 1862. That from Multān to Lahore linked up the capital with the Indus Flotilla in 1865; but it was not till 1878 that its extension north-westwards began, and only in 1883 was through communication from Peshāwar to Calcutta and Bombay established. Meanwhile Amritsar and Rewāri had been linked with Delhi in 1870 and 1873 respectively; and though no farther extensions were made till 1883, progress was rapid after that year. In 1891 the Province contained 2,189 miles of railway, which increased to 3,086 in 1901 and 3,325 miles in 1904. In the latest year the total was distributed under—broad gauge, 2,757 miles; metre gauge, 380; and narrow gauge, 198 miles.

The greater portion of the railways in the Punjab is worked by the North-Western State Railway, which included 2,585 miles on the broad gauge, and 138 on narrow gauges in 1904. In January, 1886, when the contract of the Sind, Punjab, and Delhi Railway Company expired, Government took over that line and amalgamated it with the Indus Valley, the Punjab Northern State Railways, and the Sind-Sāgar branch into one imperial system called the North-Western State Railway. The Amritsar-Pathānkot Railway, which originally belonged to the Local Government, was transferred to the North-Western Railway in 1892. The Rājpura-Bhatinda, Ludhiāna-Dhūrī-Jākhal, and Jammu-Kashmīr Railways were built respectively by the Patiāla, the Māler Kotla and Jīnd, and the Kashmīr States, but are worked by the North-Western Railway, with which has also been amalgamated the Southern Punjab Railway. The management of the Kālkā-Simla Railway was taken over by the North-Western Railway on January 1, 1907.

The railways in the Punjab may be classed under two heads, commercial and military. The commercial section of the North-Western Railway cost on an average Rs. 1,32,000 per mile to construct, inclusive of the worked lines and the Amritsar-Pathānkot Railway. The worked lines cost on an average Rs. 55,000 per mile to construct, and the Amritsar-Pathānkot Railway Rs. 82,000 per mile. In 1904 the Punjab had one mile of rail to every 40 square miles of territory. The only Districts not yet traversed by a railway are Dera Ghāzi Khān, Kāngra, and Hoshiārpur. The strategical value of the railway system lies chiefly in the facilities it offers for the transport of troops to the north-west frontier of India; the commercial value lies mainly in the export of cotton, grain (especially wheat), and oilseeds to Karāchi. Combined with the canals the railways have revolutionized economic conditions, the former inducing the production of wheat on a vast scale, and the latter placing it on the world's market. Further, their combined effect renders the Province, as a whole, secure from serious food-famines. In 1899–1900 the canal-irrigated tracts formed a granary whence grain was distributed by the railways. The railways also tend to equalize prices in all parts of the Province and from year to year, but it may be doubted whether by themselves they have raised prices generally. It is, however, true that they are tending to erase local variations in speech, dress, manners, and customs, and to obliterate the few restrictions which the caste system in the Punjab imposes on the ordinary intercourse of daily life.

Roads.

The chief road is a continuation of the grand trunk road, which, starting at Calcutta, runs through Northern India to Delhi. Thence, in the Punjab, it passes through Karnāl, Ambāla, Ludhiāna, Jullundur, Amritsar, Lahore, Jhelum, Rāwalpindi, and Attock, where it enters the North-West Frontier Province and ends at Peshāwar, with a total length of 587 miles, metalled and bridged throughout. The section from Karnāl to Ludhiāna was made in 1852, but that from Phillaur to the Beās was only completed in 1860–1. From the Beās to Lahore the road was opened in 1853, and thence to Peshāwar in 1863–4. It runs alongside the railway, and still continues to carry a certain amount of slow traffic. The other roads are mainly important as feeders to the railway system. On the north the chief routes are the Hindustān-Tibet road, which runs from the Shipki Pass on the frontier of the Chinese empire to the railway termini at Simla and Kālka; the Kāngra Valley cart-road, which brings down tea and other hill products to Pathānkot: the Dalhousie-Pathānkot road; and the Murree-Rāwalpindi road, which now forms the main route from Kashmīr. All these, except the Dalhousie road, are metalled, and all are practicable for wheeled traffic, except that part of the Tibet road which lies north of Simla. In the centre of the Province a metalled road runs in a loop from Lahore via Kasūr and Ferozepore to Ludhiāna, where it rejoins the grand trunk road. The other metalled roads are merely short feeders of local importance connecting outlying towns, such as Hoshiārpur and Kapūrthala, with the railways. As feeders and for local traffic unmetalled roads suffice for the requirements of the people, and the construction of metalled roads has accordingly been of recent years subordinated to that of railways, at least in the plains. Thus in 1880–1 the Province contained 1,381 miles of metalled roads, and though in 1900–1 the mileage had risen to 1,916, in 1903–4 it was only 2,054, compared with 20,874 of unmetalled roads. All roads, except 147 miles of strategic roads in Dera Ghāzi Khān District, are maintained from Provincial or District funds. Most of the important metalled roads are Provincial, while unmetalled roads are maintained by District boards, their metalled roads being often made over to the Public Works department for maintenance. The total annual expenditure on land communications is about 4 lakhs for original works, and 10 to 12 lakhs for repairs.

Vehicles. The chief means of transport of goods by road is the bullock-cart. This is a heavy substantial vehicle without springs or tires, and made by any village carpenter. It is drawn by a pair of bullocks at the rate of 2 miles an hour, and 10 to 15 miles are reckoned a fair day's journey. It will stand the roughest usage and the worst roads, and only in the hills and in the sandy tracts does its weight render its use impossible. In the sandy deserts bordering on the Bīkaner desert, and in the Sind-Sāgar Doāb, including the Salt Range, the camel is the chief means of transport of merchandise, while in the Himālayas goods are carried on mules or by bearers. For passengers by road the light springless cart known as the *ekka* is the almost universal means of locomotion; it will carry four to six passengers, and go at the average rate of 5 miles an hour. On metalled roads, the 'tumtum,' a vehicle with springs not unlike a dog-cart, is much in use. On the important cart-roads to the hills regular passenger services are maintained by means of a two-wheeled carriage called a 'tonga,' drawn by two ponies; at every 4 miles there are stages at which ponies are changed, and journeys are performed at the rate of about 8 miles an hour. Regular services of bullock-carts are also maintained on these roads.

Rivers. All the great rivers are navigable in the rains; and the Indus and the lower reaches of the Jhelum, Chenāb, and Sutlej are navigable throughout the year. Except on the Indus, timber is the most important article of commerce transported by this means. There is a considerable trade on the Indus with Sind. Navigation on all rivers is entirely by means of rude country craft, the Indus Steam Navigation Flotilla having ceased to exist some twenty years ago. The grand trunk road crosses the Rāvi, Jhelum, and Indus by roadways attached to the railway bridges, and the Chenāb by a footway; and roadways cross the Sutlej between Lahore and Ferozepore, and the Chenāb between Multān and Muzaffargarh. There is a bridge of boats on the Rāvi near Lahore; and the Indus is crossed by bridges of boats at Khushālgarh, Dera Ismail Khān, and Dera Ghāzi Khān, the latter two replaced by steam ferries in the summer. All the rivers are provided with ferries at frequent intervals, which are generally managed by the District boards.

Post Office. The Districts and States of the Punjab (except the States of Chamba, Jīnd, Nābha, and Patiāla, which have their own postal arrangements) form, together with the North-West Frontier Province and Kashmīr, one postal circle under the Postmaster-General of the Punjab and North-West Frontier Province. It is divided into seventeen postal divisions. The following table shows the advance in postal business in the Punjab during the two decades since 1880, giving also the figures for 1903–4. The figures exclude the North-West Frontier Province and also (for the most part) Kashmīr.

	1880–1.	1890–1.	1900–1.	1903–4.
Number of post offices and letter-boxes . .	842	1,269	4,900	6,850
Number of miles of postal communication . .	8,397	9,474	13,512	15,318
Total number of postal articles delivered:—				
Letters . . .	16,990,413	18,589,127	26,935,983	27,544,764
Postcards . .	1,906,717	12,632,567	31,430,787	38,130,426
Packets . . .	226,198	891,453	3,159,862*	3,441,282*
Newspapers . .	1,778,007	2,966,000	3,284,176†	3,181,412†
Parcels . . .	199,764	252,332	423,098	536,224
Value of stamps sold to the public . Rs.	6,33,510‡	8,46,980‡	14,63,578	18,33,466
Value of money orders issued . . Rs.	66,30,053‡	1,20,69,110‡	2,42,07,579	2,27,01,278
Total amount of savings bank deposits . Rs.	...	56,49,794	1,09,11,336‡	79,79,023

* Including unregistered newspapers. † Registered as newspapers in the Post Office. ‡ Including Kashmīr.

These figures include both the imperial and the local or District post. The latter system was a substitute for the posts which landowners were in early days bound to maintain for the conveyance of official correspondence in each District. As the District came under settlement, this personal obligation was replaced by a cess levied on the land revenue, and eventually in 1883 the cess was merged in and became part of the local rate. The expenditure on the District post averaged Rs. 1,50,274 during the five years ending 1902–3, and amounted in 1903–4 to Rs. 1,42,253. In 1906 the cess was abolished, and the system was amalgamated with the imperial post. The value of the money orders paid during the year 1903–4 amounted to 329 lakhs, or nearly 102 lakhs more than the value of those issued.

Famine. Area liable to be visited.

The Punjab contains two main tracts which are not secure against drought: one in the south-east comprising most of the plains Districts of the Delhi Division and that of Ferozepore; the other, the Districts of Gujrāt, Jhelum, and Rāwalpindi in the north-west. The north-west of Gurdāspur and the

Sharakpur and Ajnāla *tahsīls* (in Lahore and Amritsar Districts respectively) are also insecure. But hitherto famines have been frequent and severe only in the south-eastern tract, of which Hissār is the centre. This area lies on the edge of the sphere of influence of the south-eastern monsoon, and any deflexion of its currents leaves it almost rainless; but the Western Jumna and Sirhind Canals, especially the former, have greatly circumscribed the area liable to famine. In the north-west the rainfall, though liable to fail, is much less capricious than in the south-east, and here scarcity has never deepened into serious famine. Well-irrigation in the insecure tracts is largely impossible or unprofitable, owing to the depth of the water below the surface.

Generally speaking, the autumn crops used to provide the agricultural population in the Punjab with their staple food and most of the fodder for the cattle, the spring crops only being grown for profit. To a great extent this still holds good, especially as regards fodder; but of late years the area under spring crops has greatly increased, and now, even in the insecure tracts, it almost equals that under autumn crops. The loss of a single harvest, or even of both the annual harvests, does not in itself necessitate measures of relief. Such measures are required only after a succession of lean years, and thus the point when failure of the monsoon spells famine can, as a rule, be accurately gauged. Besides a rise in prices, not always a very trustworthy sign, indications of the necessity for measures of relief are usually afforded by the contraction of private charity and credit, activity in the grain trade, increase in crime, and aimless wandering in search of employment or food.

History of famines.

The first famine in the Punjab of which any information exists occurred in 1783-4 (Samvat 1840), and is popularly called the *chālīsa kāl*, or 'famine of the year 40.' It affected the whole country from the Sutlej to Allahābād, and was acute in the neighbourhood of Delhi. Hariāna was desolated and the people perished or emigrated. The mortality must have been great, and few villages now existing in this area boast a history anterior to the famine. Famine again occurred in 1833-4, 1837-8, 1860-1, 1868-9, 1877-8, 1896-7, and in 1899-1900. In 1833-4 the conditions were those of severe scarcity rather than of famine; and though there was suffering in Hissār and Rohtak Districts and the Fāzilka *tahsīl*, no relief, beyond large suspensions of revenue, was given. The scarcity was, however, the precursor of serious famine in 1837-8, when the tract between Allahābād and Delhi was most seriously affected, but Hissār, Rohtak, and Fāzilka also suffered. Relief works were opened for the able-bodied, but the relief of the infirm and helpless was left to private charity. The main features of this famine were the prevalence of aimless wandering and the extraordinary amount of violent crime.

The famine of 1860–1 affected only the Districts between the Jumna and the Sutlej, and was the result partly of the Mutiny, and partly of deficient rainfall in the two preceding years, followed by a failure of the monsoon in 1860. The principles adopted in 1833–4 were again followed. Gratuitous relief was given mainly in the form of cooked food. 1860–1.

Practically the same tract was again affected in 1868–9, but the great influx of famine-stricken immigrants from Rājputāna exhausted the resources of private charity. The principle that it was the duty of the people to relieve the infirm and weak had to be abandoned, and Government acknowledged its liability to supplement charitable aid. Large works under professional control and minor works under civil officers were also utilized for affording relief. The excess mortality in the two Provinces was estimated at 1,200,000. About 3 lakhs of revenue was remitted in the Punjab. 1868–9.

The great famine of 1877–8 hardly reached this Province, in which only scarcity existed. Fāzilka and the Districts of the Delhi Division, which were not protected by irrigation, suffered most. 1877–8.

After 1878, in spite of occasional short harvests, the Punjab had a respite from actual scarcity till 1896–7. In 1895 the monsoon ceased early in August, and a poor autumn harvest was followed by a deficient spring crop in 1896. In the latter year failure of the monsoon caused widespread scarcity in the Punjab, as in other parts of India. The whole of the Delhi Division, except Simla, and parts of the Lahore and Rāwalpindi Divisions were affected. A total of 22½ million day-units were relieved, of whom half were in Hissār. Relief cost 22⅓ lakhs, 22 lakhs of land revenue was suspended, and at the close of the famine 11½ lakhs was advanced for the purchase of seed and cattle. After one good year the monsoon failed again in 1898 and 1899, and famine supervened in the same tracts. The scarcity of fodder caused immense mortality among cattle, and the distress among the people was intense. Relief was afforded to 52 million day-units at a cost of 48 lakhs. In addition, 44 lakhs of land revenue was suspended, and 19 lakhs granted for the purchase of seed and cattle as soon as favourable rain fell in the autumn of 1900. The Charitable 1896–1900.

Relief Fund also allotted 12 lakhs to the Punjab. Hissār was again the most deeply affected tract, accounting for two-thirds of the numbers relieved.

Effects of famine on population.

Of recent years the immediate effects of scarcity on the population of the Province have been practically negligible. The famine of 1899–1900, the most severe since annexation, affected the health of the people, so that many were unable to withstand disease which under more favourable circumstances might not have proved fatal. It might have been anticipated that the two famines of the decade 1891–1900 would have appreciably affected the population in Hissār and Rohtak Districts, but the Census of 1901 showed an increase of 5,711 since 1891 in the former, and an increase of nearly 10 per cent. in the latter. Generally speaking, as regards mortality, the after-effects of famine are almost more potent than famine itself. Practically no deaths from actual starvation were recorded in the Punjab in the recent famines. During famine cholera is most to be feared; but when famine ceases, after a plentiful monsoon, malaria, acting on a people whose vitality has been reduced by privation, claims a long tale of victims. At such seasons the mortality is naturally greatest among the very old and the very young. This is shown by the fact that, at the recent Census, Hissār returned only 999 children under five in every 10,000 of its population, as compared with the Provincial ratio of 1,340. This paucity of children, however, is to some extent due to a diminished birth-rate. The famine of 1899–1900 lasted exactly thirteen months from September, 1899. Up to December the birth-rate was fairly normal, but after that month it rapidly declined until the close of the famine. In July, 1900, it was only 22·3 per mille, as compared with 40·5, the annual average for the month in the five years 1891–5. On the other hand, the re-establishment of normal conditions, after famine, is followed by an abnormally high birth-rate. Thus, in Hissār, famine ended in August, 1897. Up to July, 1898, the birth-rate remained low; but it then rose rapidly and remained well above the average until September, 1899, the highest figures occurring in October and November, 1898, when they reached 81·7 and 76·7 per mille, as compared with 57 and 50·8 respectively, the averages for those two months in 1891–5.

Protective measures.

Whether it will ever be possible to render the Punjab free from liability to famine is a difficult question at present to answer. The two great remedies are the extension of railways and irrigation. As to the former, from the point of view of famine protection, the Province is as a whole well off, and further schemes are in hand for facilitating distribution of the immense surplus stocks produced in the large canal colonies. As to the latter, much has been done and much more is in contemplation. The Chenāb and Jhelum Canals, by rendering cultivable vast areas of waste, have been of incalculable help in reducing the pressure on the soil in the most thickly populated Districts, and in increasing the productive power of the Province; but, until the insecure tracts themselves are rendered safe by the extension to them of irrigation, scarcity and famine must be apprehended. The new Upper Jhelum, Upper Chenāb, and Lower Bāri Doāb Canals have been described above (p. 67).

Administration. Government.

On the annexation of the Punjab in March, 1849, a Board of Administration was constituted for its government. The Board was abolished in February, 1853, its powers and functions being vested in a Chief Commissioner, assisted by a Judicial and a Financial Commissioner. After the transfer of the Delhi territory from the North-Western (now the United) Provinces, the Punjab and its dependencies were formed into a Lieutenant-Governorship, Sir John Lawrence, then Chief Commissioner, being appointed Lieutenant-Governor on January 1, 1859. In this office he was succeeded by Sir Robert Montgomery (1859), Sir Donald McLeod (1865), Sir Henry Durand (1870), Sir Henry Davies (1871), Sir Robert Egerton (1877), Sir Charles Aitchison (1882), Sir James Lyall (1887), Sir Dennis Fitzpatrick (1892), Sir Mackworth Young (1897), Sir Charles Rivaz (1902), and Sir Denzil Ibbetson (1907).

In 1866 the Judicial Commissioner was replaced by a Chief Court. A Settlement Commissioner was shortly afterwards appointed to supervise the land revenue settlements, but this office was abolished in 1884, and a Second Financial Commissioner appointed. In 1897, however, the old arrangement was reverted to, a Settlement Commissioner replacing the Second Financial Commissioner.

The direct administrative functions of Government are performed by the Lieutenant-Governor through the medium of a Secretariat, which comprises a chief secretary, a secretary, and two under-secretaries. These are usually members of the Indian Civil Service. The following are the principal heads of departments: the Financial Commissioner, the Inspector-General of Police, the Director of Public Instruction, the Inspector-General of Prisons, the Inspector-General of Civil

Hospitals, the Sanitary Commissioner, the Conservator of Forests, the Accountant-General, and the Postmaster-General. The last two represent Imperial departments under the Government of India. The heads of the two branches (Irrigation, and Roads and Buildings) of the Public Works department are also *ex-officio* secretaries to Government, and the heads of the Police and Educational departments are similarly under-secretaries in their respective departments. The Financial Commissioner, who has a senior, a junior, and an assistant secretary, controls the Settlement Commissioner, the Commissioner of Excise (also Superintendent of Stamps), the Director of Agriculture, the Director of Land Records (also Inspector-General of Registration), and the Conservator of Forests. He is also the Court of Wards for the Province.

The civil administration is carried on by the Punjab Commission, a body of officers now recruited exclusively from the Indian Civil Service, though prior to the constitution of the North-West Frontier Province one-fourth of the cadre was drawn from the Indian Staff Corps. The Commission is supplemented by the Provincial Civil Service, which is recruited in the Province either by nomination, or by examination, or by a combination of the two, and is almost entirely of Punjābi origin. With a few exceptions, the higher appointments in the administration are held exclusively by members of the Punjab Commission, while members of the Provincial service, who are graded as Extra or as Extra Judicial Assistant Commissioners, perform the functions of District judges, magistrates, and revenue officials. The minor posts in the administration are held by the Subordinate services, which are recruited entirely from natives of the Province.

Administrative divisions.

The territories under the control of the Lieutenant-Governor consist of 29 Districts, grouped into 5 Divisions, and 43 Native States. Each District is in charge of a Deputy-Commissioner, who is subordinate to the Commissioner in charge of the Division. A District is divided into sub-collectorates called *tahsīls*, varying in number as a rule from three to seven, each under a *tahsīldār* with a *naib* (deputy)-*tahsīldār*. Of the 29 Districts Kāngra, with an area of 9,978 square miles, is the largest, and Simla, in area less than the county of London, the smallest. The average District corresponds in size with one of the larger English counties. In population Lahore, with 1,162,109, is the largest, and Simla, with 40,351, again the smallest District. The average population of a District is 701,046. Particulars regarding each Division, District, and

State will be found in the table on pp. 152–3. For purposes of criminal, civil, and revenue jurisdiction, the District is the unit of administration. The Deputy-Commissioner (as the officer in charge of a District is designated, the Punjab being a non-Regulation Province) is Collector, with judicial powers in revenue suits, and also District Magistrate, being usually invested as such with power to try all offences not punishable with death. The District staff includes a District Judge, whose work is almost entirely civil, though he is also ordinarily invested with magisterial powers, which he exercises in subordination to the District Magistrate. It also includes from three to seven Assistant or Extra Assistant Commissioners, with criminal, civil, and revenue powers, of whom one is in charge of the treasury. It further includes one or more Munsifs or civil judges. The *tahsīldārs* are invested with revenue, criminal, and civil powers, and their assistants, the *naib-tahsīldārs*, with revenue and criminal powers. In ten Districts there are subdivisions, each consisting of one or two outlying *tahsīls*, in charge of an Assistant or Extra Assistant Commissioner, who resides at the head-quarters of his jurisdiction. Lahore city also forms a subdivision, and subdivisional officers are posted to the hill stations of Murree and Dalhousie during the hot season. As a rule, however, there is no intermediate link between the District and the *tahsīl.* In two *tahsīls* a sub-*tahsīl* exists in charge of a *naib-tahsīldār.* The *tahsīldār* has under him from two to five field *kānungos,* each of whom supervises twenty to thirty *patwāris* or revenue accountants, in charge of the revenue records of a group of villages. Each village has one or more headmen, who collect the revenue, and *chaukīdārs* or watchmen. In most Districts the villages are grouped into circles or *zails,* each under a non-official (*zaildār*) of local influence, whose duty it is to render general assistance to all Government officials. Commissioners of Divisions now exercise judicial powers only in revenue appeals, their civil and criminal jurisdiction having been transferred to the Divisional and Sessions Judges.

The Native States under the control of the Lieutenant-Governor of the Punjab are 43 in number, comprising an area of 36,532 square miles, and a population in 1901 of 4,424,398 persons, as shown in the table on pp. 152–3, with a total revenue of 155 lakhs. Kashmīr, formerly included among the Punjab States, was placed under the direct political control of the Government of India in 1877. Of the 43 States, the three Phūlkiān States (Patiāla, Jīnd, and Nābha) and Bahāwalpur *Native States.*

are in charge of a Political Agent under the direct control of the Lieutenant-Governor of the Punjab; Chamba is under the Commissioner of Lahore; Kapūrthala, Farīdkot, Māler Kotla, Mandī, and Suket are under the Commissioner of Jullundur; Sirmūr, Kalsia, Dujāna, Pataudi, and Lohāru are under the Commissioner of Delhi; and the 28 Simla States are under the control of the Deputy-Commissioner of Simla, as *ex-officio* Superintendent, Simla Hill States.

Relations with Government.

The relations of the British Government with Bahāwalpur are regulated by treaty; those with the other States by *sanads* or charters from the Governor-General. The States of Patiāla, Bahāwalpur, Jīnd, Nābha, Kapūrthala, Sirmūr, Farīdkot, and Māler Kotla maintain Imperial Service troops. The other States and also Kapūrthala pay a money tribute, amounting in 1903-4 to a total of Rs. 2,66,434. The States of Patiāla, Jīnd, and Nābha are ruled by members of the Phūlkiān family; and should there be a failure of direct heirs in any of them, the *sanads* provide for the selection of a collateral as successor by the chiefs of the other two States. A *nazarāna* or relief is payable to the British Government by the collateral who succeeds. The Phūlkiān chiefs, and also the Rājā of Farīdkot, are bound by *sanad* to execute justice and to promote the welfare of their people; to prevent *satī*, slavery, and female infanticide; to co-operate with the British Government against an enemy, and to furnish supplies to troops; and to grant, free of expense, land required for railways and imperial lines of road. On the other hand, the British Government has guaranteed them full and unreserved possession of their territories. They, with Bahāwalpur and Kapūrthala, differ from the remaining feudatories in the fact that they possess power to inflict capital punishment upon their subjects. The treaties with Bahāwalpur define the supreme position of the British Government, and bind the Nawāb to act in accordance with its wishes, while in turn the British Government engages to protect the State. *Sanads* of varying import are also possessed by the minor feudatories.

Religion.

Of the chiefs, those of Bahāwalpur, Māler Kotla, Pataudi, Lohāru, and Dujāna are Muhammadans; those of Patiāla, Jīnd, Nābha, Kapūrthala, Farīdkot, and Kalsia are Sikhs; and the rest are Hindus. Of the Muhammadan chiefs, the Nawāb of Bahāwalpur is head of the Daudputra tribe, being a descendant of Bahāwal Khān, who acquired independence during the collapse of the Sadozai dynasty of Afghānistān early in the nineteenth century. The Nawāb of Māler Kotla is a member of an Afghān family which came from Kābul about the time of the rise of the Mughal empire; his ancestors held offices of importance under the Delhi kings and became independent as the Mughal dynasty sank into decay. The chiefs of Pataudi and Dujāna are descended from Afghān adventurers, and the Nawāb of Lohāru from a Mughal soldier of fortune, upon whom estates were conferred by the British Government as a reward for services rendered to Lord Lake in the beginning of the nineteenth century.

Race.

With one exception (Kapūrthala), the Sikh chiefs belong to the Jat race. Chaudhri Phūl, the ancestor of the Phūlkiān houses (Patiāla, Jīnd, and Nābha), died in 1652. His descendants took advantage of the break-up of the Mughal empire in the eighteenth century, and of the confusion which attended the successive Persian, Afghān, and Marāthā invasions of Delhi, to establish themselves, at the head of marauding bands of Sikh horsemen, in the Mughal province of Sirhind, and eventually rose to be independent chiefs. The Rājā of Kapūrthala claims Rājput origin, and his ancestor, Jassa Singh, took rank among the Sikh Sardārs about 1750. The founder of the Farīdkot family, a Barār Jat by tribe, rose to prominence in the service of the emperor Bābar. Jodh Singh founded the Kalsia State about the same time. The remaining chiefs, whose territories lie among the Outer Himālayan hill ranges, are principally of Rājput descent, claiming a very ancient lineage.

Chiefs who are minors.

The rulers of Patiāla, Farīdkot, Jubbal, Bāghal, Kanethi, Mailog, Kunihār, Bījā, Madhān, Dhādi, Tharoch, and Kuthār were minors in 1906[1]. The chiefs of Māler Kotla and Kumhārsain are of unsound mind, the Rājā of Bashahr is of weak intellect, and the Rājā of Bilāspur was in 1903–4 temporarily deprived of his powers as a ruling chief for misconduct. The State of Patiāla is administered by a council of regency, composed of a president and two members. An English guardian and tutor supervises the education of the Mahārājā. The administration of Farīdkot is conducted by a council, presided over by an Extra Assistant Commissioner deputed by Government, and Māler Kotla is administered by the heir-apparent. In Bījā, Kunihār, Mailog, and Madhān the administration is carried on by councils of State officials, in Dhādi it is in the hands of a relative of the chief, and in Tharoch in those of the *wazīr*. Bilāspur, Jubbal, Bashahr, Kumhārsain, and

[1] The Nawāb of Bahāwalpur died at sea in February, 1907, while returning from a pilgrimage to Mecca. He leaves a son two years of age.

Kanethi are administered by native officials of the British service deputed by Government. In Bāghal the council consists of a brother of the late chief and an official deputed by Government, while in Kuthār the manager is a member of the ruling family of Suket.

Legislation and justice. Customary law.

By the Punjab Laws Act of 1872 custom governs all questions regarding succession, betrothal, marriage, divorce, the separate property of women, dower, wills, gifts, partitions, family relations such as adoption and guardianship, and religious usages or institutions, provided that the custom be not contrary to justice, equity, or good conscience. On these subjects the Muhammadan or Hindu law is applied only in the absence of custom.

Legislation.

A Legislative Council was created for the Punjab in May, 1897, consisting of the Lieutenant-Governor and not more than nine members nominated by him, of whom five were non-officials in 1904. The members do not as yet possess the rights of interpellation and of discussing the Provincial budget, which have been granted to the Councils of the older Provinces. The following are the chief legislative measures specially affecting the Punjab which have been passed since 1880:—

Acts of the Governor-General in (Legislative) Council.

Punjab University Act, XIX of 1882.

The District Boards Act, XX of 1883.

The Punjab Municipal Act, XIII of 1884 and XX of 1890.

The Punjab Courts Act, XVIII of 1884 (as amended by Acts XIII of 1888, XIX of 1895, and XXV of 1899).

The Punjab Tenancy and Land Revenue Acts, XVI and XVII of 1889.

Government Tenants Punjab Act, III of 1893.

The Punjab Land Alienation Act, XIII of 1900.

Regulations of the Governor-General in (Executive) Council.

The Frontier Crimes Regulations, IV of 1887, IV of 1889, and III of 1901.

The Frontier Murderous Outrages Regulation, IV of 1901.

Acts of the Punjab Legislative Council.

The Punjab General Clauses Act, I of 1898.

The Punjab Riverain Boundaries Act, I of 1899.

The Punjab Land Preservation (*Chos*) Act, II of 1900.

The Punjab Descent of *Jāgīrs* Act, IV of 1900.

The Sind-Sāgar Doāb Colonization Act, I of 1902.

The Punjab Steam Boilers and Prime Movers Act, II of 1902.

The Punjab Military Transport Animals Act, I of 1903.

The Punjab Court of Wards Act, II of 1903.

The Punjab Pre-emption Act, II of 1905.

The Punjab Minor Canals Act, III of 1905.

The supreme civil and criminal court is the Chief Court, which consists of five Judges, of whom one at least must, under section 4 of the Punjab Courts Act, XVIII of 1884, be a barrister of not less than five years' standing. The Court has from time to time been strengthened by the appointment of temporary Additional Judges, who numbered four in 1906. Of the five permanent judges, three are members of the Indian Civil Service, one is an English barrister, and one an Indian pleader. Supreme Court.

Subordinate to the Chief Court are the Divisional and Sessions Judges, each exercising civil and criminal jurisdiction in a Civil and Sessions division comprising one or more Districts. As Divisional Judges, these officers try most of the appeals in civil suits from the courts of first instance. As Sessions Judges, they try sessions cases, with the aid of assessors, and hear criminal appeals. Thus the Divisional and Sessions Judges in the Punjab fulfil the functions of District and Sessions Judges in the Regulation Provinces. Appeals in minor civil suits from the Munsifs' courts are heard by the District Judge, whose court is also the principal court of original jurisdiction in the District. The Divisional and Sessions Courts are established under Act XVIII of 1884, which also provides for the appointment of Subordinate Judges (exercising unlimited civil jurisdiction) and Munsifs. The latter are of three grades, the jurisdiction of a first-grade Munsif being limited to suits not exceeding Rs. 1,000 in value. There are Small Cause Courts at Lahore, Amritsar, Delhi, and Simla, and many Munsifs are invested with the powers of such courts under Act IX of 1887. Subordinate cases.

Relatively to the population, the Punjab is the most litigious Province in India. In 1901 the number of suits instituted was 11·4 per 1,000 of the population, the next highest figure being 9·6 in Bombay. During the last few years, however, the annual number of suits has declined considerably, from 227,284 in 1900 to 156,354 in 1905. In the year 1904–5 alone there was a decline of no less than 26 per cent., due mainly to an amendment in the law which extended the period of limitation in suits for the recovery of money lent from three to six years. The Punjab Alienation of Land Act of 1900 has also had a considerable effect in checking litigation between money-lenders and agriculturists. Suits of this class show a falling-off of nearly 42 per cent. in the five years (1901–5) during which the Act has been in force. The question of codifying the customary law has of late years Civil cases.

attracted some attention. An attempt has been made to codify the custom as to pre-emption in the Pre-emption Act II of 1905, but it is not possible to say at present what the ultimate effect of that Act will be. During its first year it stimulated litigation to some extent.

Criminal courts.

The District Magistrate is ordinarily (and additional District and subdivisional magistrates and other full-powered magistrates are occasionally) invested with power to try all offences not punishable with death, and to inflict sentences up to seven years' imprisonment. Further, in the frontier District of Dera Ghāzi Khān and in Miānwāli an offender may be tried by a council of elders under the Frontier Crimes Regulation, and in accordance with its finding the Deputy-Commissioner may pass any sentence of imprisonment not exceeding fourteen years; but sentences exceeding seven years require the confirmation of the Commissioner, who has also a revisional jurisdiction in all cases.

Criminal cases.

The litigious spirit of the people is illustrated by their readiness to drag their petty disputes into the criminal courts. About one-third of the charges preferred are ultimately found to be false. In a normal year the number of true cases is about 5 per 1,000 of the population, but this figure naturally fluctuates from year to year. A season of agricultural depression will cause an increase in crime against property and a decline in the number of petty assault cases, the prosecution of which is a luxury reserved for times of prosperity. The commonest form of crime is cattle-lifting, which is rife in the South-Western Punjab and in those Districts of the Eastern Punjab which border on the United Provinces and Rājputāna. Crimes of violence, generally arising out of quarrels connected with women or land, are commonest among the Jat Sikhs of the Central Punjab and the Musalmān cultivators of the northern Districts. Offences relating to marriage have increased during the last five years, probably owing to the ravages of plague, which has caused a proportionately higher mortality among females than among males, and has thus enhanced the value of the surviving women. The same cause has led to an increase in civil suits relating to women. In an average year about 250,000 persons are brought to trial, about 27 per cent. being convicted.

Criminal appeals.

All sentences imposed by magistrates of the second and third classes are appealable to the District Magistrate; and in 1904, out of 28,564 persons sentenced by them, 34 per cent. appealed and 36 per cent. of these appeals were successful.

Sentences imposed by District Magistrates and magistrates of the first class are, as a rule, appealable to a Sessions Judge; and in 1904, out of 21,336 persons sentenced by those courts, 32 per cent. appealed, and of these appeals 37 per cent. were successful. Sentences imposed by Courts of Sessions, and those exceeding four years passed by District Magistrates, are appealable to the Chief Court; and in 1904, out of 1,799 persons so sentenced, 61 per cent. appealed, with success in 28 per cent. of the appeals.

Civil appeals. Of the 6,618 civil appeals filed in the courts of District Judges in 1904, 38 per cent., and of the 9,591 filed in the Divisional Courts, 26 per cent. were successful; but of the 2,374 filed in the Chief Court, only 9 per cent. succeeded.

Revenue courts. The revenue courts established under the Punjab Tenancy Act are those of the Financial Commissioner, Collector (Deputy-Commissioner), and Assistant Collectors of the first grade (Assistant or Extra Assistant Commissioners), and Assistant Collectors, second grade (*tahsīldārs* and *naib-tahsīldārs*). These courts decide all suits regarding tenant rights, rents, and divers cognate matters, in which the civil courts have no jurisdiction. Appeals from Assistant Collectors ordinarily lie to the Collector, from him to the Commissioner, and from the Commissioner to the Financial Commissioner, with certain limitations.

Registration. The Registration Act was extended to the Punjab in 1868. All Deputy-Commissioners are *ex-officio* registrars and all *tahsīldārs* are sub-registrars under the Act, but most of the registrations are performed by non-official sub-registrars, remunerated by a percentage of the fees. General control over them is exercised by the Inspector-General of Registration. The figures below are for the old Province up to 1900-1; those for 1904 are for the Province as now constituted.

	1880-1 to 1889-90 (average).	1890-1 to 1899-1900 (average).	1900-1.	1904.
Number of offices	221	277	297	266
Number of documents registered	70,994	129,067	134,906	75,573

Finance. Under Sikh rule revenue was realized from all known sources of taxation, direct and indirect. Land, houses, persons, manufactures, imports and exports, alike contributed to the income of the Khālsa under Ranjīt Singh. The outlying provinces, in which revenue could be levied only by a military force, were farmed out to men of wealth and influence, who exercised powers of life and death without interference from the court of Lahore, so long as their remittances to the royal treasury were regularly made. The revenue from districts nearer Lahore and more completely under control was collected by local tax-gatherers, called *kārdārs*, whose more important proceedings were liable to review by the ministers of the Mahārājā. The salt revenue was realized by a sale of the monopoly.

Under this system the country was, on the whole, wonderfully prosperous. Every Jat village sent recruits to the Sikh army, who remitted their savings to their homes; and many a heavily assessed village thus paid half its land revenue from its military pay. Money circulated freely, manufactures and commodities were in brisk demand, and commerce flourished despite the burden of taxation. From land revenue Ranjīt Singh raised 165 lakhs, partly in cash and partly, or mostly, in kind. From excise he realized 2 lakhs. In the Province generally the dual system of realizing the land revenue remained in force till 1847, and to a much later period in the Native States and great *jāgīrs*. During the regency, however, from 1845 to 1849, summary revenue settlements were made; and on annexation the assessments thereby imposed were maintained as a temporary measure, quinquennial settlements being made in tracts which had not been assessed. The customs and excise systems were also reformed, and in the year after annexation coin of British mintage replaced the old currency, 50 lakhs of which were withdrawn from circulation. The estimated revenue for 1849–50 was as follows: land revenue (including grazing tax, income from forests, gold-washing, iron mines, and rents of lands), 152 lakhs; excise (on salt, liquors, and drugs), including stamps and canal water rate, 26 lakhs; tribute, 5 lakhs; post office, $3\frac{1}{2}$ lakhs; and miscellaneous receipts, $3\frac{1}{2}$ lakhs—a total of 190 lakhs. After the Mutiny of 1857 the Delhi and Hissār Divisions were added to the Punjab, increasing its revenue by 66·2 lakhs.

Provincial settlements.

All items of revenue other than those derived from purely local sources, such as District and municipal funds, fall into one or other of two classes. They may be treated as Provincial, in which case they are at the disposal of the Local Government, or as Imperial, in which case a portion returns into the Province in the form of payments, the balance being absorbed into the Imperial exchequer (see chapter on Finance, Vol. IV, ch. vi). Since 1871 the financial relations of the Local and Supreme Governments have been regulated by periodical settlements. This arrangement consists in the assignment for Provincial uses of the entire income under certain heads of revenue and a fixed proportion of income under others, termed 'shared heads.'

Under the first Provincial settlement the total receipts rose 1877–82. from 284·44 lakhs (Provincial share 51·39) to 335·01 lakhs in 1882 (Provincial share 80·25), owing to the rapid growth of stamps and excise revenue. In the same period expenditure rose from 179·14 to 216·06 lakhs (the Provincial share rising from 116·57 to 133·85 lakhs), owing to the development of the departments transferred to Provincial control. The Provincial income and expenditure during the quinquennium averaged 65·13 and 129·31 lakhs respectively, compared with 49·22 and 120·11 lakhs estimated in the contract. The Provincial 1882–7. balance was 29·63 lakhs in 1882. Under the second settlement Provincial received 40·7193 per cent. of the land revenue, and was made liable for the same proportion of the cost of settlement and survey operations, and refunds of land revenue. Half the receipts and expenditure under forests became Provincial, and the same division was made of stamps, excise, and registration, formerly wholly Provincial, while half the licence tax collections also became Provincial. On the other hand, the pay of Civil Surgeons and other charges devolved on Provincial. Under this settlement the receipts rose from 344·37 to 351·54 lakhs (Provincial from 140·35 to 150·68 lakhs), while expenditure fell from 237·03 to 218·12 lakhs, but the Provincial share of this rose from 146·36 to 155·77 lakhs. The Provincial income and expenditure averaged 146·84 and 152·98 lakhs respectively, as compared with the estimates of 144·90 and 144·94 lakhs, leaving the balance at 17·36 lakhs, or 7·36 more than the minimum reserve prescribed in 1887. The settlement 1887–92. was renewed on the same terms for the third quinquennium, during which the income rose from 361·03 to 414·50 lakhs (Provincial from 151·93 to 168·30 lakhs), and the expenditure from 224·53 to 245·19 lakhs (Provincial from 153·04 to 175·17 lakhs). The Provincial income and expenditure averaged 160·66 and 162·05 lakhs respectively, compared with the estimates of 144·90 and 144·94 lakhs, while the Provincial balance rose to 27·71 lakhs. The cost of certain measures, of which the most important was the reorganization of the Punjab Commission at a cost of 2·27 lakhs a year, was met by assignments from Imperial.

Under the fourth settlement the Provincial shares were fixed 1892–7. as follows: land revenue 25, stamps 75, and excise 25 per cent. Half the income tax, hitherto wholly Imperial, also became Provincial. The income rose from 421·92 to 473·10 lakhs (Provincial from 134·91 to 142·27 lakhs), chiefly under land revenue (9·43 lakhs), stamps (2·88), excise (1·86), income tax (0·80), registration (0·95), and irrigation (2·20), to take the annual averages. Expenditure increased from 248·22 to 284·20 lakhs (Provincial from 180·39 to 185·34 lakhs), owing to larger outlay on public works, maintenance of canals, salaries and expenditure of civil and political departments, and famine relief. Survey and settlement charges, hitherto shared, became Provincial, raising the total of expenditure. The Provincial income and expenditure averaged 139·49 and 179·41 lakhs respectively, as compared with the contract figures of 132·19 and 167·24 lakhs; but the settlement affected the finances of the Province adversely, and the quinquennium closed with a balance of 5·23 lakhs, or hardly more than half the prescribed minimum.

1897-1905. The fifth settlement made in 1897 was afterwards extended to 1904–5. It was modified in details in consequence of the separation of the North-West Frontier Province in 1901, but the general terms remained unaltered. Famine (which commenced in November, 1896) and plague (which broke out early in 1897) led to diminished receipts and larger outlay, resulting in a complete collapse of the Provincial finances, which had to be supported by special grants from Imperial funds. Famine cost 54·70 and plague 6·58 lakhs during the quinquennium 1897–1901. Miānwāli District was created, and the Chenāb and Jhelum Colonies extended. In 1902–3 arrears of land revenue, aggregating 39·30 lakhs, were remitted, and loans to agriculturists, amounting to 9·06 lakhs, were written off in that and the following year. In 1902–3 the Imperial Government contributed 3·80 lakhs for extensive measures against plague, over and above the ordinary plague expenditure from Provincial funds. In that year the income was 519·36 lakhs, and the expenditure 299·65 lakhs (Provincial 219·23 and 208·94 lakhs respectively). Financially, the conditions in the Punjab since 1897 have been so abnormal that analysis of the figures for 1897–1903 would serve no useful purpose.

From April 1, 1905, the new Provincial settlement came into effect. Its noticeable features are:—

(1) Permanency—leaving the Province to enjoy the fruits of its economy, unless grave problems of Imperial interest call for assistance from Local Governments; (2) in the case of 'shared heads' the expenditure is divided between Imperial

and Provincial in the same proportion as in the case of corresponding heads of income, except land revenue, the expenditure (31·04 lakhs) under which is entirely Provincial, while the Provincial share of the income is three-eighths (95·58 lakhs); (3) the Local Government obtains, for the first time, a direct financial interest in 'major' irrigation works, three-eighths of the income (62·89 lakhs) and expenditure (37·74 lakhs), which includes interest on capital outlay 15·62 lakhs, having been assigned subject to a guarantee of a net income of 28 lakhs per annum.

Since the settlement was sanctioned the famine cess (Provincial rates) has been abolished, and a compensatory assignment of 6½ lakhs per annum given to Provincial. Recoveries from District funds on account of District Post charges were waived and the Patwāri cess abolished from April 1, 1906, and the cantonment police provincialized from April 1, 1905, lump assignments aggregating 17·83 lakhs being given as compensation. Famine expenditure did not enter into the Provincial settlement, and the question of its distribution is now under consideration.

Land revenue. Under native rule.

Prior to annexation, the character of the land tenures in the Punjab was very indefinite and varied considerably from place to place. Usually, however, cultivation was carried on by a number of independent groups of men scattered at uncertain intervals throughout the cultivable area of the country. Each group was, or believed itself to be, of a common stock, and the area it cultivated was known as a village or *mauza*, while the cultivators lived together on a common village site. When the crops were cut, a part of the produce was handed over to the village menials in payment for their services, and the rest was divided between the state and the cultivator. In many cases the state share was taken by some magnate or court official to whom it had been assigned; and there would often be some man of local influence who, from his character or traditional claims, was in a position to attend at the division of the grain heap and demand a small share for himself. When an assignee or intermediary claimant was strong enough, he would break up the waste, settle cultivators, and otherwise interfere in the village arrangements; but he seldom, if ever, ousted the cultivator so long as the latter tilled his land and paid his dues. The land itself was very rarely transferred, and when a transfer did take place it was almost always to some relation or member of the village community.

Subse-

On annexation the three duties which fell on the land

quent development. revenue officials were the determination and record of rights in the land, the assessment of the land, and the collection of the revenue; and the same duties continue to constitute the main features of the land revenue administration at the present day.

The cadastral record. A great deal of time and anxiety were expended in the early days of British rule over the determination of the various parties who had rights to the soil, and more particularly over the question of ownership, the persons recorded as owners being as a rule made responsible for the revenue. In many cases, more especially in the south and west of the Province, intermediaries of the kind above noticed were admitted to have superior claims to the proprietary right; but in most instances the cultivators were held to be the owners of the village lands, either jointly or in severalty.

Zamīndārs. In the Punjab, as in the United Provinces, the ordinary landholder is known as *zamīndār*, the term being applied irrespective of the size of the holding. A distinction used to be made in revenue records between *zamīndāri* and *pattīdāri* tenures on the one hand, and *bhaiyāchārā* tenures on the other—the former referring to estates held as a single unit or portions representing fractions of a single original share, and the latter to estates held in separate portions representing no fractional parts of the whole. The former classes of tenure are, however, less common than formerly, and the distinction is now of little practical importance. The *zamīndārs* in an estate are technically bound by a common responsibility towards Government, each being responsible for any balance of revenue due from other *zamīndārs* in the village; but here too the tendency is towards individualism, and with lighter and more elastic assessments the enforcement of collective responsibility has become practically obsolete. In practice, the owner or owners of each holding are assessed separately to revenue and are responsible to Government for the revenue so assessed. The revenue in each village is collected from the owners by one or more headmen or *lambardārs*, who pay the proceeds into the Government treasury and receive a percentage on the collections as their remuneration.

The persons recorded as owners, while undertaking the responsibility for the Government revenue, obtained a very much fuller right of property over their lands than had been usual in Sikh times. The right of transfer remained at first under some control and was little used; but as the revenue became lighter and land more valuable, the owners gradually began to alienate, and within thirty years of annexation land had already begun to pass freely into the hands of money-lenders. This evil grew more and more marked, until in 1901 the Government was compelled to place considerable restrictions on the powers of alienation enjoyed by agricultural tribes, in order to prevent their being completely ousted from their lands.

The initial examination of rights in land which occupied the first twenty years or so after annexation was a part of the process known as the regular settlement of the various Districts, and was accompanied by measurement of the land and the preparation of a complete cadastral map and record of titles. The arrangement originally contemplated was to undertake a revision of the record of each District only when the District came under reassessment, that is to say, at intervals of twenty or thirty years. But since 1885, when the whole record system was reformed, it has been the practice to enter all changes as they occur in a supplementary register and to rewrite the record of titles once every four years; and this record is in law presumed to be true until the contrary is proved. In the same way, instead of making a fresh cadastral measurement of the District at each settlement, it is now becoming more usual to note changes in field boundaries as they occur, and to provide a fresh map at resettlement from the data thus available instead of by complete remeasurement.

The assessment.

The cadastral record, though it also shows all rights to land, was primarily meant to be a fiscal record indicating the persons liable to pay the land revenue. Having determined the persons thus liable, the next point is to decide the manner in which the assessment should be taken. The Sikh government most frequently took its revenue (as above described) in the form of a share of the crop, an arrangement which proportioned the assessment very satisfactorily to the quality of the harvest, but was attended by much friction and dishonesty. To avoid these disadvantages, and to maintain the tradition imported from the North-Western (now United) Provinces, the British revenue was levied in the form of a fixed cash assessment, payable from year to year independently of the character of the harvests. This form of revenue was, in most parts of the country, a considerable relief to the people after the harassment of the Sikh system, and it has ever since remained the predominant form of assessment in the Province. It subsequently, however, became clear that, in dealing with a people who save little from one year to another, an assessment of a fixed character caused a good deal of hardship where the harvests varied greatly in character; and it has therefore become gradually more usual, especially on river-side areas and in rainless tracts of the Western Punjab, to assess the land by a cash acreage rate on the crops of each harvest, so that the revenue may fluctuate with the area actually cropped.

Share of produce taken.

The prevalent form of assessment prior to annexation absorbed the whole, or nearly the whole, of the produce which was not required for the maintenance of the cultivator. The first rough assessments under British rule aimed at obtaining the money value of a share of the gross produce approximating to that obtained by the Sikh revenue proper, after excluding its superfluous cesses; and as more detailed information became available, it became usual to look upon one-sixth of the gross produce as a fair standard of assessment. Later on, however, when land became more valuable and letting to tenants more common, it became, and has now for many years continued to be, the rule to assess on the net rather than on the gross 'assets,' and to assume, as in the United Provinces, that the normal competition rents paid on rented lands are a fair index to the net 'assets' of the proprietors generally. In the rare cases where competition rents are ordinarily paid in cash, there is little further difficulty; but in the more usual case of kind-rents the value of the net 'assets' can be arrived at only after a number of elaborate and somewhat uncertain calculations as to prices, yields, &c. Although therefore the standard of assessment is represented, as in the United Provinces, by one-half the net 'assets,' this standard has not, as in those Provinces, been looked on as determining the average assessment, but as fixing a maximum which should not be exceeded. In four settlements recently sanctioned, for instance, the proportion of the calculated half net 'assets' taken in each District has been 78, 81, 69, and 87 per cent. respectively. These figures do not include the cesses, which are calculated on the land revenue but are separate from it. The rate at which these cesses are levied varies in the different Districts; but the prevailing rate is one of about $13\frac{1}{3}$ per cent., or about $2\frac{1}{6}$ annas per rupee, on the land revenue, of which 5 per cent. goes to the village headman, and $8\frac{1}{3}$ per cent. to Local funds. Efforts are at the same time made to assist local agriculture, not only by the loan of money for the purchase of seed and bullocks and the construction of wells, but also by remitting temporarily the revenue assessable on improvements such as the construction of gardens and wells. The increased

Cesses.

Allowances.

assessment due to the improvement caused by a new well is remitted for a period of twenty years from the date of the construction of the well.

Term of settlement.

The assessment or settlement of the Province has usually been taken up District by District. The settlements effected immediately after annexation were summary in character, and the revenue then assessed remained payable for four or five years only. The more elaborate settlements subsequently made, which were known as regular settlements, were usually for thirty or twenty-six years; and the prevalent term now in force is one of twenty years.

In a tract where the previous assessment has approximated to the standard of half the net 'assets,' the main grounds for enhancement after twenty or thirty years are the increase of cultivation and the rise in prices. The cultivation of the Province between 1880 and 1900 increased about 19 per cent., and the price of the main staple (wheat) rose in the same period by about 36 per cent., while the land revenue demand of the Province, standing in 1880 at 193 lakhs, was 203 lakhs in 1890, 250 lakhs in 1900, and 283 lakhs in 1904, which at present prices represents an assessment of 460,000 tons of wheat. Adding cesses (60 lakhs) and canal rates (168 lakhs), the total assessment comes to 511 lakhs, representing 813,000 tons of wheat. The assessment in the time of Akbar (1594), when cultivation was quite undeveloped, reached a sum of 282 lakhs, which at the prices then current represented in wheat no less than 1,700,000 tons.

The collection of the revenue.

The collection of the grain assessments imposed by the Sikhs taxed, as may be imagined, the energies of a large staff of officials. Since annexation it has been usual to entrust the collection of cash assessments to the village headman, who, in return for this and other services, receives 5 per cent. of the revenue which he collects. In the early days of British rule, when the assessments were based on imperfect data and were often very severe, the headman frequently failed to collect the revenue; and stringent measures had to be undertaken to recover the Government dues, involving in many instances the wholesale transfer of proprietary rights from the agricultural to the moneyed classes. Even at the present day the collection of dues from a body so numerous as the peasant revenue-payers of the Province is a task which cannot always be accomplished without friction; and the law has reserved for Government very complete powers, by way of attachment, arrest, and sale, for the realization of its demands. The enforced sale of a defaulter's property, which in early days was common, is now, however, almost unknown.

Suspensions and remissions.

In collecting the fixed assessments it is now the rule, on the occurrence of any markedly bad seasons, to arrange for total or partial suspensions of the revenue, calculated on the basis of the cropped area of the harvest as recorded by the revenue staff. The suspended revenue is allowed to lie over till next harvest, and is then collected or further suspended according to the conditions then prevailing. Should it be found necessary to postpone the collection for a considerable time, it is ultimately remitted altogether. When crops suffer from causes not of the ordinary seasonal nature for which allowance is made at assessment, e. g. by locusts or hail, the area damaged is calculated, and the revenue thereon is remitted at once. This system of suspending and remitting revenue has since 1880 become much more developed than it was in the earlier days of British rule, and during the famines of 1896 and 1900 it did much to foster the resources of the affected areas. In Hissār, which suffered most at that time, 5·9 lakhs, representing 83 per cent. of the land revenue of the District, was suspended in 1899–1900; and in 1901–2 a sum of 37·3 lakhs then under suspension in various Districts was entirely remitted.

New restrictions on alienation of land.

Mention has been made of the fact that, owing to the serious extent to which land was passing from the hands of the old agricultural tribes to those of the moneyed classes, the Government was in 1901 compelled to place restrictions on the alienation of land in the Punjab, this being the first occasion on which a general measure of this character has been introduced in India. Under the Land Alienation Act (XIII of 1900), the Government has in each District notified certain tribes as 'agricultural tribes,' and has classed as 'agriculturists' for the purposes of the Act all persons holding land, who either in their own names or in the names of their ancestors in the male line were recorded as owners or as hereditary or occupancy tenants at the first regular settlement. A member of an agricultural tribe may not, without permission, sell or otherwise permanently alienate his land to any one who is not a statutory 'agriculturist' of the same village or a member of the same agricultural tribe or group of tribes (for the present all the agricultural tribes of a District are counted as being in one group). Similarly, a member of an agricultural tribe may not mortgage land to any one who is not a member of the same tribe or group of tribes, unless the mortgage is in certain specified forms which fix a limit to the period of usufructuary possession or else ensure the retention of the cultivating possession by the mortgagor. The Act has not yet been long enough in force for its results to be accurately gauged; but as a general rule the object arrived at appears to have been achieved, and the intention of Government to be duly appreciated by the class for whose benefit the new measure was undertaken.

Moderation in assessments.

The assessments in the Punjab have generally been noted for their moderation. In the first regular settlements the assessments imposed at the summary settlements, which had been hastily conducted after annexation, were much reduced, though the enormous fall in prices which followed the pacification of the country made the burden of the earlier assessments heavier than had been intended. The policy of lenient assessments thus initiated has been adhered to.

Classification of land.

For purposes of assessment land is divided into two main classes, irrigated and unirrigated. The latter includes moist (*sailāb*) land, not actually irrigated, in the valleys of the great rivers and on the banks of hill torrents. This is of the most varying quality, and its assessment varies accordingly. *Sailāb* land on hill torrents is occasionally assessed as high as Rs. 4 per acre. Other unirrigated land pays from 3 or 4 annas to Rs. 2 or Rs. 2–8–0 an acre. Canal-irrigated lands are assessed to land revenue in three different ways: (1) by a fixed assessment on the land calculated on its value if unirrigated, plus a fixed or fluctuating canal-advantage land revenue; (2) by a fluctuating canal (*nahri*) rate or rates, no separate 'dry' rate being imposed; and (3) on the Sirhind Canal, by a (fluctuating) combined occupier's and land revenue canal rate. The first system is in force on the Western Jumna and Bāri Doāb, and the second on the Jhelum and Chenāb Canals. Lands irrigated by wells pay 12 annas to Rs. 6 or Rs. 7 per cultivated acre. The lowest rates are taken in the south-west, where the average area for each well is far larger than the area which can be irrigated from it in any one year, and where a considerable part of the crops grown is consumed by the tenant and his cattle without any return to the landlord. The highest rates are paid in the north-western Districts, where only 3 or 4 acres are attached to each well, the land being double cropped and producing valuable staples.

Miscellaneous revenue. Salt.

Under Sikh rule salt was one of forty-eight articles which were liable to customs, town, or transit duties. The cis-Indus and Kālābāgh salt mines were farmed out to persons of eminence; and the farmer, as long as he paid the amount of his contract, was allowed to dispose of the salt in any manner he might think proper. He was under no restrictions as regards time, place, or price, and might sell wholesale or retail, either at the mines or in distant markets. The prices charged by the farmers do not appear to have been high; but mining and transport difficulties helped to restrict the area within which the rock-salt was consumed, and the cis-Sutlej tract seems to have been almost entirely supplied at this time with salt from Rājputāna.

Upon annexation the management of the cis-Indus and Kālābāgh mines was at once taken over by the British Government. An excise duty of Rs. 2 a maund was levied at the mines, in lieu of all charges to which the salt was formerly subject; and on payment of this duty the salt was allowed to pass free throughout the British dominions, subject only to the additional duty of 8 annas a maund levied on all salt crossing the branch customs line established for the protection of the Bengal revenue. The duty imposed was considerably higher than the prices charged by the farmers for salt under the Sikh government, but all articles except salt and liquor were exempted from excise, customs, and transit duties. The Imperial customs line was at the same time extended along the Sutlej and the Panjnad to the Indus at Mithankot, and a preventive line was established on the Indus to exclude Kohāt salt from the cis-Indus portion of the Province. The manufacture of alimentary earth-salt in the cis-Indus Punjab was also prohibited. The adoption of the principle of a fixed duty on the production of salt, levied at the source, foreshadowed the adoption of the policy now in force throughout India. Salt crossing the customs line into the cis-Sutlej Punjab from Rājputāna was liable to the duty in force in the United Provinces of Rs. 2 a maund. The history of salt taxation in the cis-Indus Punjab from this time merges in the history of salt taxation in British India, and it is unnecessary to specify the enhancements and reductions in the rate of the duty which have since been made. In 1870 a price of one anna a maund was charged on rock-salt excavated on behalf of Government in addition to the duty.

From 1849 to 1869 the salt mines and quarries in the cis-Indus Punjab and at Kālābāgh and the preventive line on the Indus were under the management of the Provincial Government; but in 1869 the Government of India assumed the direct control of the inland customs department, and the administration of the salt revenue in the Punjab was at the same time made over to the Imperial department. In 1878 the customs line was abolished, but the preventive line at the Indus was still retained. Upon the abolition of the customs line the Punjab system of levying duty at the mines was extended to the Rājputāna salt sources, but the change of policy had no material effect upon the salt supply of the Punjab. Cis-Indus rock-salt continued to be the main source of supply for the trans-Sutlej Districts, and with the extension of the railway to Khewra in 1882 the demand for this salt rapidly grew.

By the annexation to the Punjab of the Delhi territory after the Mutiny two additional sources—the Nūh and Sultānpur salt-works in Gurgaon and Rohtak Districts—were brought within the Province. The greater part, however, of the salt produced at these works was consumed in the United Provinces of Agra and Oudh; and the competition of superior salt at a uniform rate of duty after the abolition of the customs line and the lease of the Rājputāna salt sources by the British Government soon proved fatal to these works. The quantities of Nūh and Sultānpur salt which annually crossed the customs line into British territory before 1878 were about 158,000 maunds and 680,000 maunds respectively. By 1883–4 the salt from the Nūh works, which were not on the line of railway, had become unsaleable, and the works were closed. The Sultānpur salt-works, most of which are on the Farrukhnagar branch of the Rājputāna-Mālwā Railway, are still struggling for existence, but the annual sales from the works in the three years ending 1903–4 have averaged only 65,763 maunds.

For some years after annexation earth-salt was made on a considerable scale under a contract system of taxation in the Rājanpur *tahsīl* of Dera Ghāzi Khān District; but in 1881 the prohibition of the manufacture of alimentary earth-salt was extended to the territory west of the Indus, and all licit salt-works were closed.

The preventive line on the Indus was withdrawn in 1896, when the duty on Kohāt salt was raised to Rs. 2 a maund of $102\frac{17}{28}$ lb. The transport of this salt to cis-Indus territory, both in the Punjab and in the recently constituted Frontier Province, is, however, still prohibited.

At present Rājputāna salt is consumed in Delhi and the adjoining Districts, and from Ambāla northwards the Province is supplied with rock-salt from the cis-Indus and Kālābāgh mines. The salt excavated from the cis-Indus mines is the cheapest in India, and of excellent quality, the analysis of a sample showing a percentage of 98·86 of chloride of sodium, and the average percentage may be taken at 97. The trade in salt within the Province is in a satisfactory state. In 1903–4 the number of traders dealing direct with the Salt department was 2,035, and salt is supplied to all parts of the Province without the intervention of middlemen. Salt from the Mayo Mines at Khewra is delivered, sewn up into bags (which are provided by the traders) and loaded into railway wagons, at a price of 1 anna 3 pies a maund. Salt from Wārcha and Kālābāgh, where arrangements for its removal are made by the traders, is sold at 9 pies a maund. The illicit manufacture of salt is still carried on in Rājanpur, and cases occasionally occur in Multān, Muzaffargarh, Delhi, and Gurgaon; but salt is good and cheap, especially in the central and western portions of the Province, and offences against the Salt Law are rare.

Details of the quantities of salt sold for consumption within the Province are given below:—

Period.	Salt made and sold.		Salt imported.		Gross revenue, including licences for the manufacture of saline substances, but excluding miscellaneous receipts.	Consumption in the Province.
	On behalf of Government.	On behalf of Mandi State and by private persons.	From within India.	From other countries.		
	Mds.	Mds.	Mds.	Mds.	Mds.	Mds.
1880–1 to 1889–90 (average) .	1,715,205	611,170	394,619	1,537	50,80,241	2,047,473
1890–1 to 1899–1900 (average) .	2,086,198	243,899	314,154	1,559	57,03,369	2,188,088
1900–1 .	2,405,520	175,817	403,337	2,386	63,97,285	2,459,223
1903–4 .	2,662,780	199,967	365,470	2,384	57,08,188	2,542,282

The incidence of consumption per head was $6\frac{3}{4}$ lb. in 1881, $7\frac{4}{5}$ lb. in 1891, $7\frac{1}{7}$ lb. in 1901, and $7\frac{1}{2}$ lb. in 1904.

Excise. Opium.

The Punjab system of excising opium differs essentially from that of the rest of India, in that the cultivator is allowed to sell the produce of his poppy crop to licensed vendors instead of being compelled to sell it to the state as in other Provinces. Hence the state, not being a monopolist of the drug, has to resort to its taxation, and ever since annexation it has levied a twofold tax upon it: firstly, it levies an acreage duty on the poppy crop; and secondly, it taxes its sale by putting up to auction the licences to purchase the produce and resell it when made into opium. Under this system of direct taxation opium is but lightly taxed in the Punjab. The acreage duty is low (only Rs. 2 per acre in the tracts in which opium is made, and Rs. 4 in those in which the poppy is cultivated chiefly for the poppy-heads), in order to safeguard the cultivator against failure of the crop or inability to realize it; and this involves a low rate of import duty, as a high rate would encourage smuggling. On the other hand, the import duty has to be pitched high enough to prevent the home-produce being undersold.

Cultivation.

In the Punjab opium is made only in the following tracts: Shāhpur and Ambāla Districts, the Thānesar *tahsīl* and Pehowa circle (in Karnāl), the Chuniān *tahsīl* of Lahore, the Rājanpur *tahsīl* of Dera Ghāzi Khān, in the plains; and in the hills, the Kot Khai *tahsīl* of Simla, and the Kulū subdivision of Kāngra. The plant is also cultivated chiefly for poppy-heads in four tracts: Jullundur and Amritsar Districts, the Hoshiārpur *tahsīl* of Hoshiārpur, the Lahore and Kasūr *tahsīls* of Lahore, and the Jāmpur *tahsīl* of Dera Ghāzi Khān. Throughout the rest of British territory in the Province the cultivation of the poppy has now been absolutely prohibited, but it is cultivated in several Native States, especially in those of the Himālayan region. The total area cultivated in British territory averaged 10,000 acres between 1891 and 1900, while it was 4,700 acres in 1900–1, and 8,852 acres in 1903–4. The area varies greatly from year to year. In Shāhpur, Simla, and Kulū it is fairly constant; but elsewhere it depends on the price of wheat, a large area being sown only if wheat is cheap. The area cultivated for poppy-heads varies much more than that sown for opium, and their price in consequence also fluctuates greatly.

Imports and exports.

Opium is imported into British territory from the Native States of the Province, especially the Simla Hill States, Sirmūr, Mandī, and the Himālayan area of Patiāla; but import from Bahāwalpur and certain plains tracts of the other Native States is prohibited. It is also imported from Mālwā, Bengal, Kashmīr, and Afghānistān. The Government of India allows a maximum of 1,116½ maunds of Mālwā opium to be imported at a duty of Rs. 280 per chest, compared with the usual duty of Rs. 725. Of this amount about 330 maunds are delivered annually to the Phūlkiān States, and the duty on this is credited to the States in order to interest them in the prevention of smuggling.

The Opium department also supplies the Punjab Government with Bengal opium, not exceeding 176 maunds a year, at Rs. 8–8 a seer; and this is sold by the Government treasuries at Rs. 15 a seer in the Districts of Hissār, Rohtak, and Delhi, and elsewhere at Rs. 17. All other imported opium pays Rs. 2 per seer when it crosses the border. The Punjab exports no opium except to the North-West Frontier Province, but statistics of this export are not available.

Opium-smoking.

Opium-smoking is not common, being practised only by dissipated coteries in the larger towns, and the sale of *madak* and *chandu* (preparations for smoking) is illegal. Licences for their sale used to be granted; but the shops were all closed in 1890, and even their possession for private use is limited to one tola weight.

Liquors.

Prior to annexation the only spirit made in the Punjab was an uncoloured rum from sugar, and this is still the chief alcoholic drink of the people. To control its production, in 1863 no less than 118 state distilleries were established at District and *tahsīl* head-quarters. Each of these was an enclosure in which private distillers were permitted to set up stills, the spirit manufactured being kept in store by the excise officials and issued by them, after payment of the duty, to retail vendors. This system has now been abolished and replaced by six private licensed distilleries—at Sujānpur, Amritsar, Rāwalpindi, Karnāl, and Simla. The latter chiefly distils whisky from barley malt. The other four distil uncoloured rum for the majority of the population. At each distillery a resident exciseman supervises the output and vend. A duty of Rs. 4 per gallon (raised in 1906 to Rs. 6 in the case of coloured spirit, and the so-called brandy, whisky, and gin which are prepared from a cane-spirit basis) is levied both at the still-head and on all Indian spirit imported into the Province, European liquors paying customs duty at the port of arrival. There are seven breweries, all of which except one are situated in the hills, and a tax of one anna a gallon is levied on the beer before it leaves the brewery. Spirit-drinking is most prevalent among the Sikhs. The recorded consumption of the Province is about 300,000 gallons a year; this, however, does not represent nearly the total amount actually consumed, as illicit distillation is extremely prevalent, and, owing to the universal cultivation of sugar-cane, very hard to detect. The consumption of licit country spirit is on the increase.

Foreign spirits.

The figures for imported spirits shown on p. 121 include the amount consumed by the European population; the quantity sold to the Indian public is about 25,000 gallons annually, and is increasing. In the cities cheap European spirits compete with native spirits.

Although the hemp-plant grows abundantly, *charas*, the drug extracted from its leaves and flowers, cannot be made in the Province. It is imported from Yārkaṇd and Kāshgar, via Leh, to bonded warehouses in the Punjab or United Provinces. Before it is sold, a duty of Rs. 6 per seer is levied. *Charas*-smoking is considered disreputable, and is a dangerous practice, often leading to insanity. *Bhang*, the dried leaves of the hemp-plant, supplies a medicinal beverage with cooling properties, which is drunk chiefly by Sikh ascetics. The plant grows wild in such quantities in the hills and submontane Districts that it is impossible to prohibit the gathering of its leaf, but any person found in possession of more than one seer is liable to a penalty. Licensed vendors may collect *bhang* without restriction within their own Districts, but in Districts where hemp does not grow all *bhang* imported is subject to a duty of Rs. 4 per maund. Thus while the duty on *charas* is easily realized by guarding the routes of import, that on *bhang* is very difficult to collect, and where it grows wild cannot be imposed at all. Drugs.

Details of net excise revenue, &c., are shown below. The figures up to and including the year 1900–1 are for the Punjab as constituted before the separation of the North-West Frontier Province; those for 1903–4 are for the Province as now constituted:— Statistics of revenue.

	Net revenue in rupees.		
	1890–1 to 1899-1900 (average).	1900–1.	1903–4.
Imported spirits (by licence fees) .	69,370	91,982	99,006
Indian spirits (including native fermented liquors made in Kāngra District) made in British India, by still-head duty and licence fees	13,63,906	14,76,443	16,34,463
Beer made in British India (by duty per gallon)	32,109	1,01,114	1,23,594
Charas and *bhang* (by licence fees)	17,869	1,94,114	1,72,612
Charas and *bhang* (by quantitative duty and warehouse dues) . .	38,875	1,27,426	1,83,990
Opium, licence fees, and miscellaneous receipts . . .	5,29,188	6,10,007	5,85,577

The incidence of the gross excise revenue, excluding opium, was 1 anna 1 pie per head in 1881, 1 anna 5 pies in 1891, and 1 anna 9 pies in 1904.

Stamped paper of a primitive kind came into use in the Stamps.

Punjab immediately after annexation. In 1872 the present system was inaugurated by the appointment of a Superintendent of Stamps, an office which is now combined with that of Commissioner of Excise. Every Government treasury is a local dépôt for the sale of stamps, judicial and non-judicial, to the public, and of postage stamps to postmasters. Similarly, sub-treasuries are branch dépôts. All treasurers are *ex-officio* vendors of stamped paper to the public. They are entrusted with stocks of stamps, and are required to meet the detailed demands for stamps made by the public, indenting upon the main stock of the local dépôt when their own runs low. The net revenue from the sale of judicial stamps in the Punjab between 1881 and 1890 averaged 23 lakhs and in the following decade 27 lakhs, while non-judicial stamps in the same periods brought in on an average 11 and 14 lakhs respectively. In the year 1900–1 judicial stamps realized 27 lakhs and non-judicial stamps 15 lakhs, and in 1903–4 (after the separation of the North-West Frontier Province) the net revenue was 27 and 13 lakhs respectively.

Income tax.

The net revenue from income tax rose from an average of 10·1 lakhs between 1886 and 1890 to 11·2 lakhs in the following decade, and amounted to 11·6 lakhs in 1903–4, after the separation of the North-West Frontier Province and the exemption of incomes below Rs. 1,000. The corresponding number of assessees was 40,251, 44,785, and 21,709. The incidence of the tax per head (of the assessees) in 1903–4 was Rs. 53–6–8, and there were 1·1 assessees per 1,000 of the population.

Local and municipal. The village community.

Local government in the Punjab, as in the rest of India, is of two kinds, the local government of the village and that of the District and town; the former is an indigenous institution dating from the remotest antiquity, the latter an exotic of Western importation. The Indian village community is described in Vol. IV, chap. ix. All the three types of village community there described are in one form or another represented in the Punjab. The Jat village of the south and central plains is a perfect type of the joint village, while the villages of the Salt Range, owned by landlords of a dominant race, who have gathered round them dependent communities of cultivators, represent the landlord village. The *ryotwāri* type of village may be said to exist in the south-western plains, where the so-called village is merely a group of isolated homesteads, built wherever a well has been sunk in the arid desert. Here the village is really a fiscal unit; and much the same may be said of the villages of the hills, which are in reality only groups of hamlets, loosely held together by certain common interests and joint rights of grazing or pasture in the forests. In these latter cases village self-government has naturally never existed, but the true village community has from time immemorial administered its own affairs with little outside help or interference. The landowners of the village, connected by common descent, real or fictitious, form among themselves a democracy, which rules its dependent priests, artisans, and menials with oligarchic authority. The informal assembly of the village, comprising every adult male of the proprietary body, is presided over by a headman, *chaudhri*, *mukhia* (lit. 'spokesman'), or, to use the modern term, *lambardār*. Often there are several headmen. The headman of a village is appointed by the Deputy-Commissioner, and, if he is recognized by the community as its natural leader, his influence equals his authority. If not, his authority is limited to such legal powers as are conferred on him, and in the South-East Punjab a leader of the opposition is regularly chosen. The headman transacts the business of the community, including the management of its common fund, to which all contribute, and to supplement which, in many villages, a hearth or door tax is imposed on all residents who are not members of the proprietary body. The communal body has no legal powers; but it is in its power to inflict on recalcitrant members of the community the punishment of social excommunication, and on the menials and artisans various inconveniences. Only the village banker is beyond its authority; and he, by virtue of being the creditor of every man in the village, is able to bring considerable pressure on the council to order things according to his pleasure. There is, however, but little prospect of the village council being utilized as a part of the machinery of Government. As being essentially a tribal organization, it can never be entrusted with legal powers in a community that is daily approaching the industrial stage, and the spread of education makes it increasingly difficult for it to exercise its unauthorized powers of control.

Municipal administration.

In some form or other municipal administration has existed in the Punjab ever since annexation. In its earliest stage committees of townsmen were formed to administer the surplus of the funds raised by cesses or duties for watch and ward purposes. This system worked well, but it lacked the essentials of municipal government, the funds being vested in official trustees. A more regular form of municipal administration was introduced in Simla and Bhiwāni under the Act of 1850; and in 1862 the head-quarters of Districts were formed into regular municipalities, with committees, mostly elected, invested with control over local affairs and power to regulate taxation. In 1864 there were 49 committees, of which 28 had elected members. Hitherto the municipalities had been constituted under the executive authority of Government; but in 1866 doubts arose as to their legal status, and more especially as to the validity of the octroi tax from which their funds were mainly derived. Accordingly, the first Municipal Act for the Punjab was passed in 1867, and renewed for a year in 1872. In 1873 a new enactment, which made election permissive, was passed; and under it 190 committees were constituted, 8 of these (Simla, Dharmsāla, Dalhousie, Murree, Delhi, Lahore, Amritsar, and Multān) being of the first class, 17 of the second, and 165 of the third. They were controlled by the Local Government, the Commissioner, or the Deputy-Commissioner, according to their class. The Local Bodies Loans Act of 1879 empowered the Local Government to make loans to approved municipalities for improvements; and in 1884 a new Municipal Act was passed, with the object of restoring the elective principle and widening the sphere of municipal activity. Two classes of committees were recognized, the first having greater latitude to incur expenditure on public works than the second. The Act of 1867 had, however, been too widely applied, and between 1885 and 1887 no less than 41 committees were abolished. In 1891 was passed an amended Act, which reformed the system of taxation, and provided a simple form of municipal administration for towns which it is inexpedient to constitute regular municipalities. The towns to which this form has been applied are termed 'notified areas.'

Constitution of committees and incidence of taxation.

In 1904 the Province contained 8 municipalities of the first class, 131 of the second, and 48 'notified areas.' Three of these (Lahore, Delhi, and Amritsar) contained over 100,000 inhabitants, 47 more than 10,000 but less than 100,000, and 137 less than 10,000 inhabitants. The average incidence of municipal taxation in 1903–4 was Rs. 1–8–0 per head. The population within municipal limits was 2,299,893, including 210,223 in 'notified areas,' according to the Census of 1901. In 1903–4 the members of municipal committees numbered 1,503, of whom 229 were *ex officio*, 495 nominated, and 779 elected. The committees in the 'notified areas' were composed of 186 members, 84 *ex officio* and 102 nominated. Only 126 Europeans sit on all these committees.

The principal source of municipal income is octroi, which in 1903–4 realized as much as 30 lakhs out of the total of Rs. 55,48,000. Direct taxation of houses and lands is virtually confined to the hill municipalities and Delhi. Water rate is levied only in Ambāla, Simla, Kasumpti, Dharmsāla, Lahore, Dalhousie, and Murree, in all of which water-supply schemes have been carried out. The main features of municipal finance are shown in a table at the end of this article (p. 161). **Municipal taxation.**

Local self-government of the District likewise dates from the early days of British rule. Prior to 1871 each District had a District committee, but it was merely an advisory body. The rules under the Local Rates Act of that year made these committees administrative bodies, and they did excellent work. In 1883 Lord Ripon's Act extended the elective principle to District boards, and under it local boards were also established in *tahsīls*. The system of election at first promised well; but it was soon found that membership of a board was not sought for public ends, and men of good position and local influence were reluctant to stand. It is now an accepted fact that the best men prefer nomination by Government to canvassing for election. Local boards were soon found to be superfluous, as the business of the District boards could not with advantage be delegated, and they are rapidly being abolished. In 1903–4 the Province possessed 26 District boards, excluding Simla, where the Deputy-Commissioner exercises the powers of a District board. These boards were composed of 1,077 members: 207 *ex officio* (the Deputy-Commissioner being nearly always *ex-officio* president), 495 nominated and 375 elected. Only 7 Districts had local boards, 28 in number, with 531 members: 28 *ex officio*, 161 nominated, and 342 elected. **District boards.**

The District fund is mainly derived from the local rate—a cess ordinarily of 1 anna 8 pies per rupee, or Rs. 10–6–8 per cent.[1], on the land revenue of the District, supplemented by grants from Provincial funds. The expenditure of a District board is chiefly devoted to the maintenance of schools and dispensaries, vaccination, roads and resthouses, arboriculture, ferries, cattle-pounds, horse-breeding, and horse and cattle fairs. Its expenditure on education, medical relief, and office establishments is largely of the nature of fixed establishment charges. Famine works have been readily undertaken by District boards in time of necessity; and large expenditure under this head, coinciding as it always must with little or

[1] Now reduced to Rs. 8–5–4 per cent. by the abolition of the cess for famine (1906).

no income from the local rate, has frequently necessitated financial aid from Government. District boards have afforded invaluable assistance to Deputy-Commissioners as consultative bodies, but the necessity of conforming to the rules of the educational, medical, and other departments leaves little scope for local initiative. Even in the case of public works, six-sevenths of the sum available is ear-marked for maintenance and establishment. The income and expenditure for a series of years are shown in a table at the end of this article (p. 162).

Public works. Irrigation.

The Public Works department is divided into two branches: Irrigation, and Buildings and Roads. The former has hitherto been an Imperial branch under a Chief Engineer, who is also *ex-officio* secretary to the Provincial Government. According to the Provincial settlement which came into force in 1905, the Provincial Government participates in the profits earned by the branch, and bears a share of the working expenses. Under the Chief Engineer are Superintending Engineers, who control circles formed of one or more canals. These circles are again divided into divisions, each in charge of an Executive Engineer. The size of a division varies according to circumstances; but, excluding head-works divisions, it usually comprises an irrigated area of about 350,000 acres. The Province is divided into 6 circles and 26 divisions. Each division is further divided into 3 or 4 subdivisions in charge of a subdivisional officer, usually an Assistant Engineer. Not only does the department maintain all the canals in its charge, but its officers are responsible for the registration and measurement of the irrigation and the assessment of the revenue levied on it. For canal revenue purposes each subdivision is divided into sections, generally three in number, each in charge of a *ziladār*, and each section is again subdivided into *patwāris'* circles. For maintenance purposes, a subdivision is divided into sections, in charge of overseers or sub-overseers. The revenue establishment of a whole division is further supervised by a Deputy-Collector, who is also a second-class magistrate. When the supply of water is less than required, the Superintending Engineer controls inter-divisional distribution and the divisional officer that between subdivisions. The internal distribution of water and regulation of supply is primarily in the hands of the subdivisional officers. The *ziladār*, who is constantly in touch with all his *patwāris*, indents for water at distributary heads. The subdivisional officer receives reports for all his channels daily and thus controls the distribution. The Executive Engineer supervises the internal distribution by subdivisional officers, and controls the inter-divisional distribution; and a report on the general state of crops is submitted weekly by each divisional officer direct to the Chief Engineer, who thus controls generally the distribution throughout the Province. The efficient distribution on Punjab canals is mainly due to the very extensive canal telegraph system. The Chief Engineer also controls the irrigation works of the North-West Frontier Province, and is *ex-officio* secretary to the Agent to the Governor-General and Chief Commissioner of that Province.

Buildings and roads. The Buildings and Roads branch is under a Chief Engineer, who is likewise *ex-officio* secretary to Government. It is divided into three circles, each under a Superintending Engineer. The number of divisions varies from time to time according to the funds allotted for expenditure, but is ordinarily between twelve and thirteen, each under an Executive Engineer. Each division embraces from one to four civil Districts. A division is again divided into subdivisions, usually controlled either by Assistant Engineers or by upper subordinates. This branch is maintained from Provincial funds, and its primary object is the construction and maintenance of Imperial and Provincial works; but it also assists municipalities and District boards with advice and the loan of its officers when they can be spared, and all important sanitary works are carried out for such bodies by the branch, a percentage being charged for establishment, tools, and plant, though this charge is frequently remitted.

The appointment of Sanitary Engineer to Government was created in October, 1900, for a period of five years in the first instance, with the rank of Superintending Engineer. The cost of his pay and establishment is met from Provincial revenues, which are credited with the fees recovered from the local bodies which utilize his services. The Sanitary Engineer is a member of the Provincial Sanitary Board, and is its executive officer and expert adviser to Government and the Board in all matters relating to sanitary engineering.

The only railway built from Provincial funds was the 65 miles of line from Amritsar to Pathānkot. Its capital cost up to March 31, 1896, was: direct, 55 lakhs; indirect, 5 lakhs. The actual cash paid from Provincial funds was 6 lakhs, the balance having been advanced on loan at 4 per cent. from Imperial funds. As the net earnings barely exceeded 1 per cent. on the capital cost, the undertaking proved a serious financial loss; and the Government of India took over the proprietorship of the line, including its management, in 1897, the Local Government forgoing the 6 lakhs it had spent on it.

The most important buildings constructed during the decade ending 1901 were the Secretariat offices at Simla and the Chief Court and Jubilee Museum at Lahore. District court buildings have been built at Simla, Amritsar, and Lyallpur, a sessions house at Jhelum, and a residence for the Commissioner at Delhi. Six new jails were constructed and one enlarged; a female penitentiary, nine *tahsīl* buildings, and five combined *tahsīl* and police stations were built, and police accommodation extended in six Districts. The principal educational buildings erected were: the Government College, Lahore, with a boarding-house; new buildings for the School of Arts, Lahore; school-rooms for boys and girls; a reception bungalow, band-room, and restoration of buildings at the Lawrence Military Asylum, Sanāwar; a new Technical school at Lahore; a combined boarding-house for the Central Training College, Lahore; the normal and central model schools, Lahore; and normal schools at Jullundur and Rāwalpindi. The chief medical buildings at Lahore were the following: the new Medical School; a separate ward for Europeans at the Mayo Hospital; the Lady Aitchison Hospital for Women; the Prince Albert Victor wing attached to the Mayo Hospital; new dissecting rooms in connexion with the Mayo Hospital; an ophthalmic ward in connexion with the Mayo Hospital; and a new lunatic asylum for the Punjab. A church was also built at Dalhousie. Additions in the form of realignments, metalling, or bridging have been made on a large number of roads, and feeder-roads to the different railways have been extensively constructed.

Since 1901 a General Post Office, a University Hall, a boarding-house attached to the Medical School, and a female ward in the Lunatic Asylum have been erected at Lahore, the Sāragarhi memorial and the Victoria Jubilee Hospital at Amritsar, and the Walker Hospital and a new wing to the Foreign Office at Simla. Water-works and drainage works have been carried out at Lyallpur, and extensive improvements made in the Upper Mall at Lahore.

The most important bridges constructed were as follows: on the Kāngra valley road, the Lyall viaduct over the Chakki torrent, twenty-eight spans of $39\frac{1}{2}$ feet, and the Dheri bridge, of 214 feet span; a bridge over the Jhelum at Kohāla, two spans of 98 feet and one of 142 feet; the Bāngangā bridge in Kāngra, 85 feet span; and the Leh bridge near Rāwalpindi, three spans of 60 feet.

Owing to the construction of the Chenāb Canal, a large

tract of country embracing portions of Jhang and Gujrānwāla Districts, and known as the Chenāb Colony, has been opened up. For the development and proper administration of the colony, roads and buildings have been and are being constructed. Large sums have been spent on unsuccessful attempts to prevent the encroachment of the Indus in DERA GHĀZI KHĀN.

The following large municipal works have been carried out since 1881: water-supply of Lahore city and suburbs, Simla, Rāwalpindi, Delhi, Amritsar, and Ambāla; drainage and sewage works at Lahore, Delhi, Amritsar, Simla, Ludhiāna, and Jullundur.

For thirty-five years, from 1851 to 1886, a military force known as the Punjab Frontier Force was directly under the orders of the Lieutenant-Governor of the Punjab. In the latter year it was transferred to the control of the Commander-in-Chief. The troops in the Punjab now all belong to the Northern Command, with the exception of those quartered at Delhi, which belong to the Meerut division of the Eastern Command. The Lieutenant-General Commanding has his head-quarters at Rāwalpindi and Murree; and the Punjab is garrisoned by the Rāwalpindi and Lahore divisions and the independent Derajāt brigade of the Northern Command, and by the Meerut division of the Eastern Command. The military stations in 1904 were: *Rāwalpindi division*—Attock, Campbellpur, Jhelum, several stations in the Murree hills, Rāwalpindi, and Siālkot; *Lahore division*—Ambāla, Amritsar, Bakloh, Dagshai, Dalhousie, Dharmsāla, Ferozepore, Jullundur, Jutogh, Kasauli, Lahore (Fort and Cantonment), Multān, Sabāthu, and Solon; *Derajāt brigade*—Dera Ghāzi Khān; and *Meerut division*—Delhi. All these (except Bakloh, Dharmsāla, Jhelum, Campbellpur, and the stations in Dera Ghāzi Khān District) are garrisoned by British infantry, and all but Campbellpur, Murree, Solon, Dagshai, Sabāthu, Lahore (Fort), Dalhousie, Kasauli, and Jutogh by native infantry. British cavalry are stationed at Rāwalpindi, Siālkot, and Ambāla, and native cavalry at those places and at Lahore Cantonment, Ferozepore, Multān, Jullundur, and Jhelum. British artillery are stationed at all the foregoing, except Jhelum, and at Campbellpur, Jutogh, and Attock. Sappers and miners are stationed at Rāwalpindi, and a military railway company at Siālkot. Transport units are permanently located at the following stations: mule corps and cadres at Rāwalpindi, Hassan Abdāl, Siālkot, Jhelum, Lahore Cantonment, Ferozepore, Jullundur,

Army.

and Ambāla; camel corps at Campbellpur, Rāwalpindi, Jhelum, Shāhpur, Multān, Montgomery, Lyallpur, and Lahore Cantonment. There are arsenals at Ferozepore and Rāwalpindi. The total strength of the British and Native regular army stationed within the Province on June 1, 1904, was as follows: British, 17,277; Native, 21,420; total, 38,697. There are four volunteer corps, the total strength of which in 1904 was 2,270. Of these, the Punjab Light Horse, raised in 1893, has its head-quarters at Lahore, with detachments at Delhi, Ambāla, Rāwalpindi, Lyallpur, and Pālampur: its strength in 1904 was 186. The 1st Punjab Volunteer Rifle Corps has its head-quarters at Lahore, with detachments at Amritsar, Dhārīwāl, Gurdāspur, Rāwalpindi, Murree, Siālkot, Delhi, Karnāl, Ferozepore, and Dharmsāla, and at Srīnagar in Kashmīr: its strength is 701. The Simla Volunteer Rifle Corps has its head-quarters at Simla, with a detachment at Kasauli: its strength is 363. The North-Western Railway Volunteer Rifles have their head-quarters at Lahore, with detachments at all important stations. The corps has a strength of 1,267, but many of these are in other Provinces. There are also detachments of the 2nd Bombay, Baroda, and Central India Railway Volunteers and of the East Indian Railway Volunteers, at Sirsa, Ambāla, and Kālka, which have a combined strength of 110.

The Punjab stands first among the Provinces of India in the number of recruits it supplies for the native army, and second to none in the fighting quality of the races recruited. The principal classes recruited in the Province are Sikhs, the recruiting centre for whom is at Jullundur; Punjābi Muhammadans, Jhelum; Dogrās, Jullundur; and Jāts and Hindustāni Muhammadans, Delhi.

The forces maintained by the Native States under the control of the Punjab Government are of two kinds: Imperial Service troops and local troops. Eight of the principal States maintain the former. Thus, the Patiāla contingent consists of a regiment of cavalry and two battalions of infantry; Jīnd, Nābha, and Kapūrthala each maintain a battalion of infantry, and Bahāwalpur a transport corps with a mounted escort of camelmen, while Farīdkot, Māler Kotla, and Sirmūr furnish a company of sappers apiece. No State in India, except Gwalior and Kashmīr, furnishes a larger contingent than Patiāla. The local troops are of all degrees of strength and efficiency. They range in strength from the regiment of cavalry, two battalions of infantry, and one battery of artillery that Patiāla can put into the field, to the half-dozen soldiers of some of the

Hill States. Even in the largest States they are employed more as armed police than as a military force, while in the smaller States their services are utilized in the collection of revenue, as well as in the maintenance of order and the performance of ceremonial functions.

Police and jails. Police. History and development.

On the annexation of the Punjab in 1849 a police force was organized in two branches, a military preventive and a civil detective police, the former consisting of 6 regiments of foot and 27 troops of horse. By the beginning of 1860 its strength had risen from 15,000 to 24,700 men, excluding the Peshāwar and Derajāt Levies, and the *thagi*, cantonment, and canal police, the total cost exceeding 46½ lakhs a year. In 1861 the cis-Indus police were reorganized under the Police Act (V of 1861), which was not completely extended to the six frontier Districts till 1889. Revisions in 1862, 1863, and 1869 reduced the cost of the force to 25 lakhs; and in 1863 the Derajāt, Peshāwar, cantonment, *thagi*, and canal police were brought under the general system of the Punjab. The railway police were organized in 1869. The police of the North-West Frontier Province became a separate force on the constitution of that Province in 1901.

Organization.

The establishment now consists of a single force controlled by an Inspector-General, who is *ex-officio* under-secretary to Government. He is assisted by three Deputy-Inspectors-General, one of whom is in administrative charge of the railway police and the criminal investigation department. Commissioners of Divisions are also Deputy-Inspectors-General *ex officio.* Each District has a Superintendent, and the larger Districts each have one or more Assistant Superintendents who (with the exception of the officers in charge of two subdivisions) work under the Superintendent at head-quarters. The unit of administration is the *thāna* or police station under a sub-inspector, and outposts and road-posts are established where necessary. Nearly half the force is armed with bored out Martini-Henry carbines, swords, and batons. The remainder are armed with swords and batons only. The sole military police now maintained are in Dera Ghāzi Khān District, which has two forces, each under the command of an Assistant Commissioner: the Border Military Police proper, and a militia raised in 1901 to take the place of the regular troops recently withdrawn. The training of constables is carried out in the Districts in which they are enrolled. Before promotion to head constable, constables go through a course of instruction at the Police Training School, established at

Armament.

Military police.

Training.

Phillaur in 1891. Head constables and sub-inspectors have also to go through a course at this school to qualify for promotion to the higher grades, and all men who receive direct appointments are required to qualify at the school before they are confirmed.

Rural police.

The village watchmen or *chaukīdārs*, who are appointed by the District Magistrate on the recommendation of the village headmen, receive on an average Rs. 3 a month as pay from the village community. They are not as a rule armed, though in some places they carry swords or spears. Their duties are similar to those in other Provinces, but they are regarded as acting under the control of the village headmen, who are jointly responsible for reporting crime.

Municipal, canton-ment, ferry, and railway police.

In most municipal towns the regular force is supplemented by a body paid from municipal funds. Cantonments have police paid from Provincial funds, and in some Districts there are ferry police. All these bodies are controlled by the District Superintendent. The railway police, who are responsible for the maintenance of law and order over the whole North-Western Railway system, are organized under a Deputy-Inspector-General.

Detection.

There is no separate detective staff. The system of identification by means of finger-prints is employed, and the training school at Phillaur includes a criminal identification bureau.

Proportion of police to area and popula-tion.

The strength of the regular District police is now one man to 7·8 square miles or to 1,647 persons; the number of village watchmen exceeds 29,600.

Criminal tribes and punitive posts.

Nine tribes have been registered under the Criminal Tribes Act. Of these the most important are the Sānsis, Baurias, and Mahtams; they are usually settled in villages under the charge of a police guard, whose duty it is to see that no registered member of the tribe is absent without leave. The imposition of punitive police posts on villages which have misconducted themselves is not an uncommon feature of the administration.

Jails. Adminis-tration.

The jail administration is under an Inspector-General, who is an officer of the Indian Medical Service, as are generally the Superintendents of Central and District jails. The post of Superintendent of a District jail is generally held by the Civil Surgeon. Jails in the Punjab consist of Central and District jails. There are no subsidiary jails, but their place is taken by large lock-ups. The greater portion of the prisoners are confined in barracks, to which the cubicle system is being gradually applied. A jail on this system is being built at Lyallpur.

Mortality in jails.

The table attached to this article (p. 164) shows how mortality in jails has decreased since 1881. It must, however, be noted that tuberculous diseases have shown a tendency to increase during recent years. It is hoped that this will be checked by improvements now being made in the ventilation of dormitories, and in the arrangements for cleansing and disinfecting clothing and bedding. It is also intended to build special tuberculous wards in the larger jails; indeed, such accommodation is being provided in two of the Central jails. It will be noticed also that the average cost of prisoners has steadily increased since 1881. The increase is mainly due to higher prices of food-grains and of such articles as woollen and cotton yarns used in the manufacture of clothing and bedding, and also in some measure to expenditure incurred in effecting a general amelioration of the conditions of prison life.

Employment of prisoners.

The chief industries carried on in the Central jails are lithographic printing, weaving woollen and cotton fabrics, carpet-making, brick-making, and expressing oil. The greater portion of the out-turn is supplied to Government departments. When opportunity has offered, prisoners have been employed in carrying out large public works: and temporary jails were built at Chenāwan in 1884 and at Mong Rasūl in 1898 in connexion with the excavation of the Chenāb and Jhelum Canals. In District jails the chief industries are paper-making, expressing oil, rope-making, and weaving cotton carpets.

Boy prisoners' reformatories.

Until 1903 the Punjab possessed no reformatory, but in that year one was opened at Delhi and placed under the Educational department. Nothing can be said yet with regard to its working.

Education

Prior to the constitution of the Punjab in 1849, Government schools existed in the Districts of the Delhi territory which then formed part of the old North-Western Provinces, and in the rest of the Province indigenous schools afforded a foundation for the present educational system. Under the Sikhs, teaching as a profession was almost entirely in the hands of the Muhammadans, who, besides teaching the Korān in the mosques, gave instruction in the Persian classics. On these schools were grafted the earliest Government vernacular schools. Purely Hindu schools were rare, being either colleges in which Brāhman boys learnt Sanskrit and received a half-religious, half-professional training, or elementary schools where sons of Hindu shopkeepers were taught to keep accounts and read and write the traders' scripts. The few Gurmukhī schools that existed were of a purely religious character. The best feature of the indigenous schools was that they were not confined to the religious and mercantile classes, but were open to the few agriculturists who cared to attend them. After annexation the Christian missions established several schools, that at Lahore as early as 1849. Government soon followed their example and founded schools in the cities and larger towns, while District officers founded and maintained schools at minor places out of Local funds.

History. In 1854 the Educational department was first organized. It was administered by a Director of Public Instruction, with 2 inspectors, 10 deputy, and 60 sub-deputy-inspectors. The schools directly supported by Government numbered 108 (4 District, 100 *tahsīl*, and 4 normal schools). The department cost about 2 lakhs per annum, and in addition a cess of 1 per cent. on the land revenue provided for the maintenance of numerous village schools. The Persian script, already in use throughout the Western Punjab, and in two-thirds of the indigenous schools of the eastern Districts, was unhesitatingly adopted as the standard; but the choice of a language offered greater difficulties. Punjābi is not a literary language; and Urdū, though unpopular, was so generally in use, especially in the law courts, that it was perforce adopted. Gurmukhī and Hindī schools were, however, to be encouraged wherever the people desired them.

Difficulties in administration soon arose. All the schools were under the direct control of the department, and District officers were dissociated from their working. The lower grades of officials were foreigners, imported from Hindustān and without influence over the people. Accordingly, in 1860, all the vernacular schools were entrusted to the Deputy-Commissioners and *tahsīldārs*, the unpopular inspecting agency being abolished. But this measure failed to provide for the professional supervision of the schools, and it was soon found necessary to appoint an inspector in each District as the Deputy-Commissioner's executive agent and adviser in their management. In the same year provision was made for the levy of school fees. Superior Anglo-vernacular *zila* (District) schools were also established, and the personnel and curriculum in all schools improved. In 1864 Government colleges were established at Lahore and Delhi, and in 1865 a scheme for an Oriental University was formulated. In 1868–70 the status of village schoolmaster was improved, the minimum salary being fixed at Rs. 10 a month; but funds ran short, and, as the immediate result of this measure, a number of schools were closed. The decentralization of finances in 1871, however, enabled the Local Government to devote more adequate funds to education, and the village schools rose rapidly in numbers and efficiency.

As now constituted, the inspecting staff of the department consists of a Director of Public Instruction, 5 Inspectors, 2 Inspectresses, 9 assistant inspectors, 28 District inspectors, 24 assistant District inspectors, and 2 assistants to the Inspectresses. The Director and two of the Inspectors are Europeans and members of the Indian Educational Service, as are the principal and three professors of the Government College, the principal and the vice-principal of the Central Training College, the principal of the Mayo School of Art, and the head master of the Central Model School, Lahore. The rest of the staff is drawn from the Provincial service, which also supplies a professor and five assistant professors to the Government College, the vice-principal of the Mayo School, the assistant superintendent of the Central Training College, the registrar of the office of the Director of Public Instruction, the superintendent, reformatory school, and the reporter on books, Educational department. Four members of this service are Europeans. The assistant inspectors are selected from the Subordinate service, which comprises 197 appointments in all, and supplies teachers to the principal colleges and schools. The majority of the teaching staff, except that of the Government high schools, are, however, employed by local bodies, District boards, and municipal committees, which engage teachers for the schools under their control subject to certain departmental rules, or borrow members from the Subordinate service for the more important posts. Present organization.

The Punjab University at Lahore was established in 1882. Prior to that year colleges and schools had been affiliated to the Calcutta University. In 1868 a proposal to establish a Punjab University had been negatived by the Government of India; but a grant-in-aid of Rs. 21,000, equal to the annual income from private sources, was sanctioned for the improvement of the existing Government College at Lahore, and in 1870 Sir Donald McLeod inaugurated the new Punjab University College. The senate of this institution established an Oriental school and college at Lahore, its objects being to promote the diffusion of European science, as far as possible, through the medium of the vernacular languages, and the improvement and extension of vernacular literature generally; to afford encouragement to the enlightened study of Eastern classical languages and literature; and to associate the learned The Punjab University.

and influential classes with Government in the promotion and supervision of popular education.

In 1877, on the occasion of the Imperial Assemblage at Delhi, the movement in favour of a Punjab University was revived and resulted in its incorporation under Act XVII of 1882. The University was empowered to grant degrees in Medicine in 1886, and degrees in Law and Science in 1891. There are five Faculties—Oriental Learning, Arts, Law, Medicine, Science and Engineering. The Syndicate is the executive committee of the Senate. Under the Indian Universities Act of 1904 the Senate has been reconstituted. It now consists of 75 ordinary fellows, of whom 60 are nominated by the Chancellor and 15 elected by the Chancellor's nominees. There are also 10 *ex-officio* fellows, 2 of whom are also ordinary fellows.

Collegiate education. Prior to 1870 the Calcutta University had dominated the higher secondary education of the Punjab; but soon after that year the Lahore College began to hold its own examinations, which were better adapted to the requirements of the Province. After its incorporation as a university the number of graduates was at first very small, only 16 qualifying in 1883–4, in which year the expenditure was Rs. 21,000. In the next six years, however, progress was rapid. Diplomas, being passports to higher employment under Government, were eagerly sought after, and in 1889–90 as many as 41 students graduated, and the expenditure had risen to Rs. 60,912.

In 1883–4 there were only three Arts colleges: the Government and Oriental Colleges at Lahore, and St. Stephen's College at Delhi. The number of candidates for matriculation was 551, and of passes 224, the average cost of each student's education being Rs. 400, and the total expenditure on colleges Rs. 79,223. By 1889–90 the number of Arts colleges had risen to seven, and that of matriculation candidates to 1,016. Passes had increased to 462, and the expenditure to Rs. 2,06,346, while the cost of each student's education had fallen by Rs. 65, owing to the levy of higher fees and the larger number of students. In 1888 the Dayānand Anglo-Vedic School at Lahore, established by the Arya Samāj, was raised to the status of a college, and became in a few years one of the most largely attended in the Province. Another important unaided institution, the Islāmia College at Lahore, was opened in 1892 by the Muhammadan community; and in 1897 the Sikhs established the Khālsa College at Amritsar. By 1900–1 the number of Arts colleges had risen to 12, with

2,148 matriculation candidates and 1,214 passes. Expenditure had risen to Rs. 2,89,582, but the average cost of a student's education was only Rs. 185, or less than half its cost in 1883-4.

The only college which imparts higher professional teaching is the Lahore Medical College. Established in October, 1860, it was raised to collegiate status in 1870. In the latter year it had 68 students. In 1887-8 a monthly fee of Rs. 2 was imposed. In 1889 the erection of the Lady Lyall Home for female students added to its usefulness.

Law School.

The Law School at Lahore is of collegiate status, and prepares students for the degree of Bachelor of Laws. Founded in 1870 with two departments, an English and a vernacular, and a two years' course, it was remodelled in 1889-90, and the course extended to three years, only graduates in Arts being admitted to the Licentiate in Law examinations. In 1891-2 intermediate and LL.B. classes were formed, and two sets of examinations prescribed, one leading to the Licentiate, the other to the LL.B. degree. In 1897-8 the number of students had reached 434, the highest limit; but the supply for trained lawyers was in excess of the demand, and in the next three years the numbers fell to 248.

The following table shows the chief results of university examinations:—

Passes in	1883-4.	1890-1.	1900-1.	1903-4.
Matriculation	224	384	1,214	1,121
First or Intermediate in Arts or Science	39	87	244	233
Ordinary Bachelors' degrees . .	13	41	127	133
Higher and special degrees . .	3	8	42	42

Secondary education.

Secondary schools are either middle or high. A middle school usually contains a primary as well as a middle department. A high school, in addition to its high department, usually contains these two also. The middle course extends over three classes, and terminates in the case of vernacular schools in the middle school examination. The high-school course extends over two years, and ends with the entrance examination of the Punjab University. English is not taught in the vernacular schools, and is commenced only at the upper primary stage in the Anglo-vernacular schools. The vernacular is thus the medium of instruction for all departments up to the third middle class, English being the medium only in the high department.

The effective organization of secondary education dates from

1860. As education spread, it became easier to obtain men capable of teaching up to the entrance standard, and it was thus found possible to increase the number of high schools at comparatively small cost. The vernacular middle schools progressed even more markedly. In 1877 the Punjab Text-Book Committee was appointed to prepare suitable English and vernacular Readers, and in 1880–1 the establishment of the Central Training College helped to provide better qualified teachers.

In 1883–4 there were 25 high schools with 912 scholars, and 198 middle schools with 5,107 scholars. In the next six years the number of high schools had risen to 41, with a satisfactory increase in the numbers on the rolls; and though the number of middle schools had decreased, the number of scholars had risen. In 1882, in accordance with the recommendations of the Education Commission, all schools except those attached to training institutes were made over to local bodies for management, and rules were framed to encourage their conversion into aided schools, the further extension of secondary education being made dependent on private institutions. Scholarships were made tenable on a uniform system, and Jubilee (now known as Victoria scholarships) and *zamīndāri* scholarships were founded to foster education among Muhammadan and Hindu agriculturists. Fees were raised, and a system of payment by results was introduced into the grant-in-aid rules. Special attention now began to be paid to moral and physical instruction and to school discipline. In furtherance of the new educational policy of the Government of India, one high school in each District has, since 1904, been maintained as a state institution.

Primary education (boys).

The first step in primary education was an attempt to raise the indigenous schools of the Punjab to a higher level of efficiency. But this scheme failed; and it was found necessary to convert the principal indigenous schools into Government schools, or branches of mission schools, or to bring them more or less under the influence of District or municipal committees. The educational cess, however, realized so little that salaries sufficient to attract competent teachers could not be offered, although no attempt was made to provide a school for every group of villages. It was accordingly resolved to reduce a number of schools in order to raise the efficiency of the remainder. The result was that schools were accessible only to a small proportion of the boys of school-going age; and Sir Charles Aitchison recognized the necessity of improving the indigenous schools, without destroying their distinctive character, by the offer of liberal grants-in-aid on easy conditions. The system was accordingly reorganized, the management of the schools being transferred to local bodies, which were, on the other hand, required to devote a fixed proportion of their income to primary education. Revised grant-in-aid rules provided for payment by results and staff grants to certificated teachers employed in aided schools. Specially liberal grants were made to indigenous and low-caste schools. The introduction of inter-school rules and good-conduct registers conduced to the moral, as the gymnastic instruction did to the physical, progress of the boys. The recommendations of the Education Commission of 1883 rendered it possible to give effect in greater detail and with greater precision to the policy inaugurated by Sir Charles Aitchison. Schools and scholars increased in numbers and efficiency, though the imposition in 1886 of higher fees on sons of non-agriculturists reduced the number of boys of that class in the lower primary department. By 1889–90 the number of aided schools had risen to 300, with 10,000 pupils; and they continued to progress until 1896–7, when the growing popularity of the Government schools, combined to some extent with the pressure of bad seasons, checked their advance. On the other hand, the District boards, with many pressing calls on their resources, could not meet the demand for primary education. Numerically, primary schools show but a slow advance, but in efficiency their progress has been marked. The abolition of the lower primary examination in 1898 enabled the course of instruction to be made continuous for fully five years, and permitted controlling officers to devote more time to questions of organization and discipline, methods of instruction, and so on, at their inspections. In the upper primary department more time was allotted to object lessons and elementary science.

Zamīndāri schools.

In 1886 the necessity of a simpler and more practical curriculum for sons of agriculturists led to the establishment of *zamīndāri* schools. In these, half-time attendance only is required, and they are closed during each harvest. Elementary reading and writing, in the character chosen by the people, and arithmetic by native methods, are taught. Qualified teachers in these schools received extra pay, and arrangements were also made to train teachers in those subjects in the normal schools. From 1886 to 1892 the schools prospered; but the people then began to realize that they led to nothing, as they did not fit boys for Government employ, and ever since they have been losing ground. In 1901 the *zamīndāri* schools numbered only 187, with 3,887 pupils. In view of their increasing unpopularity, steps were taken in 1904 to open village schools with a simpler course of studies, planned with special reference to the requirements of agriculturists. The Punjab possesses a few special low-caste schools. These are mainly dependent upon missionary enterprise, and are, like all indigenous schools, eligible for grants-in-aid on easy conditions.

Female education.

Encouraged by results in the United Provinces, several girls' schools were opened in the Punjab as early as 1855, and in 1862 Sir Robert Montgomery held a great *darbār* at Lahore in order to enlist the co-operation of the chiefs and notables of the Province. Under this impulse nearly 1,000 schools with 20,000 girls had been opened by 1866, but the results were unsubstantial and the attendance soon fell off. A sound system of female education was only founded in 1885–6, in which year it was attempted to make the existing schools places of healthy elementary education, adapted to the simple requirements of the people, and rewards for diligent work were substituted for payments for mere attendance. An Inspectress of Schools was appointed in 1889. As yet, however, female education can hardly be said to have taken firm root except in the Central Punjab (Lahore, Amritsar, Gujrānwāla, Siālkot, and Jullundur), where Sikh influences are strong, and among the Hindu element in the western Districts. There is, however, throughout the Province much private teaching, almost exclusively religious, by Hindu, Sikh, and Muhammadan women, and, as far as religious objections allow, by the ladies of the Zanāna and other Christian missions. And the most gratifying feature of recent years has been the steady increase of private enterprise on behalf of female education, several unaided schools, notably the Kanya Mahā Vidyālla at Jullundur, having been opened. The establishment in 1905 of the Normal School for Women at Lahore marks a new era in the development of female education in the Province. Its success, which depends much on the sympathetic co-operation of the educated classes, will to a considerable extent remove one great obstacle in the way of the advancement of the education of girls—the lack of qualified women teachers.

Special education. Training institutions.

The Lahore Central Training College was opened in 1881, the first of its kind in India. Since its foundation most of the secondary schools have been supplied with trained teachers, and a few years ago the Punjab was able to spare a number of trained and experienced men to assist in revising and improving the training school system in the United Provinces. There were at first two classes: the senior English, which prepared teachers for higher work in English secondary schools; and the senior vernacular, which trained men for all kinds of purely vernacular teaching in secondary schools. In 1883-4 a junior English class was opened, to train teachers for the primary classes of Anglo-vernacular schools. With the extension of university education, the preliminary educational qualifications were raised; and since 1896 only B.A.'s, or those who have read up to that standard in a recognized college, are admitted to the senior English class. For admission to the junior English class men must have either passed the intermediate examination or attended the classes of a college for two years. In 1904 this institution was completely reorganized. The staff has been strengthened, the period of study has been raised to two years, a clerical and commercial class has been added, and the number of available stipends much increased. A teacher's degree examination, open to all graduates in Arts who have attended the Central Training College for another year after passing the senior Anglo-vernacular certificate examination, has also been instituted.

Normal schools. Normal schools were originally founded to train teachers for both middle and primary schools, but have been restricted to training for the latter alone since the organization of the Central Training College. The schools are under the control of the Inspectors; and in pursuance of the policy of having one in each circle, normal schools were established at Jullundur in 1887 and at Multān in 1891.

Technical education. Prior to 1886 the Medical and Veterinary Colleges, the Law School, the Engineering Class of the Punjab University, and the Mayo School of Industrial Art were the only real technical institutions in the Province, the few so-called industrial schools being mere workshops in which inferior articles were made at a high cost. In the three following years, however, some progress was made, the chief step being the establishment of the Railway Technical School at Lahore to provide instruction for the children of the railway workshop employés. This school has a primary and a middle department; the course of study is much the same as in the ordinary schools, with a progressive course of carpentry, drawing, and practical geometry. The functions of the Mayo School were also extended, and private industrial schools were encouraged. An entrance examination in science and a clerical and commercial examination were also instituted, the one in 1897, and the other in 1900. The movement thus begun bears fruit, and some industrial schools have sprung up at the larger training centres, such as Amritsar, Ludhiāna, and Delhi; but the number of students is still small. In ordinary schools also the course of study has been remodelled, so as to include practical mensuration and agriculture in primary schools, and to develop the powers of observation by object lessons.

European education.

The schools for Europeans and Eurasians in the Punjab were included in the scope of Archdeacon Baly's inquiry in 1881. No less than 440 children of school-going age were then found to be receiving no education whatsoever. Under the Resolution of the Government of India passed in that year, however, the grants to existing schools were increased, and Rs. 11,945 was given by Government for enlarging school-houses. The absence of an enactment making attendance at school compulsory, the apathy of parents, and the migratory character of the European and Eurasian community have been great obstacles to advancement. The schools, especially in the plains, labour under many disadvantages, the lack of trained teachers being specially felt. Of recent years the progress made has, nevertheless, been considerable. In 1903, 46 Europeans and Eurasians passed the matriculation, 94 the middle, and 102 the primary school examination.

Muhammadan education.

When in 1871 attention was first directed to the backwardness of education among Muhammadans in India, inquiry showed that in the Punjab the Musalmān community had availed itself of the facilities offered as fully in proportion to its numbers as the Hindus. Much had been done to foster the study of Arabic and Persian. Indeed, the latter had been favoured at the expense of vernacular languages and literatures, and it was felt that no special measures for the advancement of Muhammadan education were required. It was, however, found that Muhammadans seldom prosecuted their studies beyond the middle schools, and that few attended colleges. Muhammadan boys spent years in learning the Korān by rote in the mosques, and thus reached manhood before their education could be completed. The poverty of the Muhammadans as a community, and the fact that they were mostly agriculturists, also militated against their higher education. Progress was, however, made, and in 1883–4 the Muhammadan college students were thrice as numerous as in 1870–1. Nevertheless, their number in the secondary schools and colleges remained proportionately far below that of the Hindus, and the necessit of special measures was realized. In 1887 Jubilee scholarships (now called Victoria scholarships), tenable in high schools and colleges, were founded by Government; and local bodies were authorized to establish them for middle schools. In addition, half the free or semi-free studentships in secondary schools and scholarships were reserved for Muhammadan boys. The community itself also began to realize the necessity for self-help, and various societies were started which organized Anglo-vernacular Muhammadan schools in the cities and large towns. The result was a rapid advance in higher Muhammadan education, though the Hindus and Sikhs still retained the lead. In the ensuing decade the community showed a growing preference for the public schools, especially those in which English was taught, and availed itself fully of the scholarships and studentships offered, though the societies continued to maintain many schools with or without Government grants-in-aid. The following table shows the number of Muhammadans under instruction in public institutions:—

	1891.	1901.	1904.
Arts colleges	123	309	338
Secondary schools	13,900	19,512	21,133
Primary schools	36,252	43,772	50,440
Special schools	513	1,224	1,103

In 1883-4 the proportion of the population of school-going age in the Punjab under instruction was 4·2 in 100, and in the course of the next six years it rose to 7·8 per cent., but since then it has showed no advance. This is mainly due to the steady decline of private schools, which do not conform to any of the departmental standards, and are not inspected by the department. People either send their boys to the public schools, or keep them at home to help in domestic or other work. The percentage of males in British Districts able to read and write was 6·8 according to the Census of 1901, and that of females 0·37. The most advanced Districts are Simla, Amritsar, and Multān; the most backward are Hissār, Rohtak, and Gurgaon. **General educational results.**

Fees in Government schools and colleges are fixed, and the proportion of free and half-rate studentships is also specified. Schools and colleges which receive aid from Government are bound to observe the rules laid down for them in this behalf. Unaided schools, however, are quite free in the matter of fees. The majority of them charge very low fees, as compared with **Finance.**

the Government and aided institutions. The following table shows the main features of educational finance in 1903-4:—

EXPENDITURE ON INSTITUTIONS MAINTAINED OR AIDED BY PUBLIC FUNDS

	Provincial revenues.	District and municipal funds.	Fees.	Other sources.	Total.
	Rs.	Rs.	Rs.	Rs.	Rs.
Arts and professional colleges . . .	1,71,718	7,983	68,282	28,198	2,76,181
Training and special schools . . .	1,05,748	10,930	8,760	28,665	1,54,103
Secondary boys' schools	1,00,549	2,77,256	4,42,744	99,424	9,19,973
Primary boys' schools .	8,123	3,58,909	91,897*	...	4,58,929
Girls' schools . .	69,904	63,141	42,303	79,936	2,55,284
Total	4,56,042	7,18,219	6,53,986	2,36,223	20,64,470

* Including receipts from other sources.

Registered publications. In 1901 the number of publications registered under the Printing Press and Books Act was 1,478. Of these, 425 were poetical works and 409 religious treatises. Language and pictures came next, with 113 and 82 respectively. Except perhaps in its popular poetry modern Punjab literature displays little originality, and many of its productions are merely translations of English works into the various languages and scripts of the Province.

Newspapers. The number of newspapers published in 1903 was 209. The only important English newspapers are the *Civil and Military Gazette* and the *Morning Post*, published daily at Lahore and Delhi respectively. The native-owned newspapers include 31 published in English, 1 in English and Urdū, 164 in Urdū, 6 in Hindī, and 7 in Gurmukhī. The leading papers are more or less actively political, their columns being devoted mainly to the criticism of Government measures and policy. Generally speaking, these journals are either sectarian, or the mouthpieces of various classes or cliques of the educated community. Few are of much importance, and many are little more than advertising sheets. The *Tribune* and the *Observer*, published in English at Lahore, are the leading Hindu and Muhammadan organs respectively.

Medical. The Civil Medical department is controlled by an Inspector-General of Civil Hospitals. The department was organized in 1880, prior to which year hospitals were under the Inspector-General of Prisons. Each District is under the medical charge of a Civil Surgeon, who is stationed at the District head-quarters (Simla has two officers of this class); but in the summer months a Civil Surgeon is stationed also at Murree, and the Civil Surgeon of Gurdāspur District is transferred to Dalhousie. As a rule, the chief hospital of each District is at its head-quarters, and is in charge of a Civil Assistant Surgeon, who after a five years' course at the Lahore Medical College has qualified for the diploma of Licentiate of Medicine and Surgery of the Punjab University; the minor hospitals and dispensaries in the outlying towns of the District are in charge of Hospital Assistants who have qualified by a four years' course at the college. Their work is supervised by the Civil Surgeon, who is required to inspect each dispensary four times a year.

The progress made since 1881 may be gathered from the table attached to this article (p. 166). The number of hospitals and dispensaries has risen by 44 per cent., and in-patients in much the same ratio, while out-patients have more than doubled. The contribution from Government has slightly decreased; but the income from Local and municipal funds has more than doubled, and that from fees, endowments, and other sources has also increased very largely.

The only institution maintained by Government is the Mayo Hospital at Lahore, an integral part of the Medical College, to which it affords medical instruction. Before the establishment of this college the Subordinate medical service was recruited from the Calcutta College, whose candidates were mostly Bengalis. Partly to obtain recruits locally, and partly with the object of popularizing Western medicine throughout the Province, a medical school was established in 1860 at Lahore, and in 1870 its status was raised to that of a college. The buildings consist of one large block, containing three class-rooms, a dissecting room, a chemical laboratory, several museums, and a large central hall, to which have been added in recent years a large and well-equipped dissecting room with a lecture theatre capable of accommodating 400 students, and pathological and physiological teaching laboratories, with a post-mortem theatre and mortuary. The teaching staff now consists of 8 professors, 6 lecturers, a demonstrator of anatomy, and 3 class assistants. A hostel for female students was built in 1889 by the Punjab committee of the Countess of Dufferin's Fund, chiefly from a donation of Rs. 50,000 given by the Mahārājā of Kashmīr. Arrangements have been made for a similar hostel for male students at a cost of over Rs. 2,00,000. The growth of the college is apparent from the fact that in

1903 it trained 234 students in the English class and 308 in the Hospital Assistant class, compared with 8 and 44 respectively in 1860.

Lunatics.

In 1900 a central asylum for lunatics was constructed at Lahore at a cost of 2 lakhs. It is controlled by a commissioned medical officer, with a military Assistant Surgeon as deputy-superintendent. It has accommodation for 468 patients; and in 1903 a separate building, capable of accommodating 120 female lunatics, was erected at a cost of Rs. 74,000. The daily average number of inmates in 1904 was 554. The record of the alleged cause of insanity is usually drawn up by the police and has little scientific value. Of the cases treated in 1904 in which any cause is assigned, 16·59 per cent. were attributed to the excessive use of Indian hemp in one form or another, 8·09 to epilepsy, 0·71 to heat, and 7·09 to moral causes, such as grief, worry, and disappointment.

Pasteur Institute and Research Institute.

At Kasauli, a Pasteur Institute was established in 1901 for the treatment of persons bitten by rabid animals, which now treats patients from all parts of India. In 1906 a central Research Institute was founded there, which will provide means for the scientific study of the etiology and nature of disease in India, besides the preparation of curative sera for the diseases of man, and the training of scientific workers. The institution is in charge of a Director, with a staff of assistants.

Vaccination.

The practice of inoculation as a protection from small-pox has prevailed in the Punjab from time immemorial. The method adopted was to keep dry crusts from the pustules mixed with a few grains of rice in a box; when a mild form of the disease was desired, a few of the grains of rice were inserted into a wound near the base of the thumb, while a severe attack was procured by inserting a little of the powdered crusts. The practice was most prevalent among Muhammadans, and was performed by Saiyids and Mullās as a *quasi*-religious ceremony. The Hindus of the South-East Punjab did not protect themselves for fear of offending the goddess of small-pox, but elsewhere Rājputs and Nais (barbers) usually acted as inoculators among Hindus. The practice was largely prevalent in Rāwalpindi, Jhang, and Shāhpur Districts as late as 1887, and to a less extent in Karnāl, Hoshiārpur, Kāngra, Multān, and Dera Ghāzi Khān. With a few exceptions, the attempt to enlist the inoculating classes as vaccinators was not successful. Vaccination is now under the charge of the Sanitary Commissioner, and Civil Surgeons are primarily responsible for vaccinations in their Districts. The staff consists of 5 divisional inspectors, 28 superintendents, and 260 vaccinators. The falling-off of vaccination in 1901 shown in the table attached to this article (p. 166) is chiefly due to plague. Vaccination is compulsory in twenty-three municipal towns.

The success of the system of selling quinine through the post office in Bengal led to its introduction into the Punjab late in 1894. First introduced experimentally in the Delhi Division, it was extended in 1899 to that of Lahore, and it is now proposed to extend it to all the Districts of the Province, although in 1901 the total sales only amounted to 293 parcels, each containing 102 five-grain packets of quinine. The small measure of success which the system has met with is not easily explained, though it may in part be accounted for by the reluctance of the literate classes, from which the post office officials are drawn, to act as drug-vendors. It is, however, apparent that the people are at present indifferent to the advantages of the system, and, as a rule, little aware of the value of quinine as a prophylactic. In Kāngra, however, in 1905 some 2,300 packets, each containing 102 powders of seven grains each, were distributed at a total cost of Rs. 3,669. Sale of quinine.

The chief defects of village sanitation are the impurity and contamination of drinking water, the accumulation of filth, the presence of manure-heaps near the houses, and the existence of ponds of stagnant water in or around the village site. It has been considered inadvisable to legislate for the compulsory sanitation of villages, but District boards are empowered to grant rewards in the form of a reduction of revenue to the villages most active in sanitary improvements. Village sanitation.

Surveys in the Punjab have been carried out by two distinct agencies, the local *patwāris* effecting the cadastral or field surveys, and the Survey of India compiling maps based on triangulation. When the revision of a settlement is undertaken, the maps, measurements, and records-of-rights of ownership and actual possession are thoroughly revised by the Settlement officer and a special staff of *tahsīldārs*, *naib-tahsīldārs*, and field *kānungos*. On the conclusion of the operations these records are transferred to the custody of the Deputy-Commissioner, who is henceforth responsible for their maintenance, and correction when necessary. Briefly, the system in force is this: the *patwāri* makes a field-to-field inspection at each harvest, noting all changes in rights, rents, and possession, and all amendments required in the field map. The changes thus noted are recorded, after attestation by a superior revenue Surveys.

officer, in a revised record-of-rights, which is prepared for each village every fourth year and called the *jamabandi*. The Deputy-Commissioner is assisted in this duty by a revenue assistant (Assistant or Extra Assistant Commissioner), the Director of Land Records acting as his expert adviser in all matters connected with it. The staff consists of a District *kānungo*, with a number of field *kānungos* and *patwāris* or village accountants. In 1904 there were 7,906 *patwāris* and 386 field *kānungos* in the Province. *Patwāris* used to be hereditary village officials, servants of the village community and members of the trading castes; but they are now enlisted without regard to hereditary claims, and more than a third in 1903 were of agricultural castes. Two-thirds have passed the middle-school examination. Candidates go through a practical course in field surveying and land record work in the District *patwāri* school. After passing the examination, they may be appointed on salaries usually rising to Rs. 14 a month. The post is non-pensionable, but a *patwāri* may on retirement receive a gratuity not exceeding Rs. 150. *Patwāris* also receive a share of the fees levied for mutation entries in the record-of-rights. The cadastral survey is made entirely by the *patwāris*, and usually during a resettlement of the land revenue. The system used is a scientific one, known as the square system, and its results are remarkably accurate. It consists in laying out the entire village area into squares, which are also shown on the map. The fields are then plotted in, being co-ordinated to the sides of the squares, and the village maps thus show the boundaries of every field. They are tested by comparison with the survey maps.

In the Chenāb and Jhelum Colonies, in which large areas of Government waste have been brought under cultivation, the square system has been extended to the formation of all fields into squares, equal to $\frac{1}{25}$th of a survey square, i.e. to 1 acre 18 poles. This system of square fields greatly facilitates irrigation and revenue management, and is a safeguard against boundary disputes. It is being gradually extended in some localities to old proprietary lands.

The maps of the Survey of India are based on triangulation carried out between 1850 and 1860. Kashmīr and the North-Western Himālayas were topographically surveyed between 1848 and 1865, and Jhelum and Rāwalpindi Districts (including the recently constituted District of Attock) between 1851 and 1859. These surveys, though excellent, are now out of date in the matter of roads, &c., and do not show village boundaries.

The survey of Kāngra, Kulū, the hills of Hoshiārpur, and the Simla Hill States was completed in 1903. The whole of the Punjab plains, with the exception of Hissār, was surveyed between 1846 and 1886, village by village, on the 4-inch scale, and Hissār was surveyed on the 2-inch scale between 1882 and 1884. In 1883 arrangements were made with the Surveyor-General for the revision of the survey maps on the basis of the village maps; and in 1884 a party of the Survey of India commenced compiling new maps from reductions of these village plans, checking and revising them in the field, and completed maps of Jullundur, Ludhiāna, Ferozepore, Ambāla, and Jhang Districts, and of the plains portions of Hoshiārpur. To enable this work to be extended, traverses were run over Shāhpur, Gujrāt, Gujrānwāla, Siālkot, Gurdāspur, and Amritsar Districts. The party was withdrawn in 1889, but in 1901 the work was recommenced. Lahore was completed by 1906, and the work is progressing in Amritsar, Montgomery, Multān, and Muzaffargarh. In addition to this, riverain surveys are being carried out to enable boundaries to be relaid in the areas subject to floods. Several lines of spirit-levels have also been run through portions of the Province. The Cis-Sutlej States were surveyed during 1846–7 on the 1 inch to the mile scale, and Patiāla, Jīnd, Nābha, &c., in 1861–2 on the same scale. The large State of Bahāwalpur was surveyed during 1869–75, the inhabited area village by village on the 4-inch, and desert tracts on the 2-inch scale. Kapūrthala State was resurveyed when Jullundur was surveyed between 1884 and 1889.

Bibliography.

[K. B. Saiyid Muhammad Latif: *History of the Punjab* (Calcutta, 1891).—J. W. McCrindle: *The Invasion of India by Alexander* (1893).—J. D. Cunningham: *History of the Sikhs* (second edition, 1853).—Sir C. Gough and A. D. Innes: *The Sikhs and the Sikh War* (1897).—Sir H. B. Edwardes: *A Year on the Punjab Frontier*, 2 vols. (1851).—Sir L. H. Griffin: *The Rajas of the Punjab* (second edition, 1873), and *Ranjīt Singh* (Oxford, 1892).—C. J. Rodgers: *Revised List of Objects of Archaeological Interest in the Punjab* (Lahore, 1895).—H. G. Raverty: *Tabakāt-i-Nāsiri.*—W. Francklin: *Memoirs of George Thomas* (Calcutta, 1803).—J. B. Fraser: *Memoirs of James Skinner*, 2 vols. (1851).—H. Pearse: *Memoirs of Alexander Gardner* (1898).—Sir J. W. Kaye: *Life of Lord Metcalfe*, 2 vols. (second edition, 1858).—Sir H. M. Lawrence: *Adventures of an Officer in the Service of Ranjīt Singh*, 2 vols. (1845).—L. J. Trotter: *Life of John Nicholson* (1898).—Sir H. B. Edwardes and H. Merivale: *Life of Sir Henry Lawrence*,

2 vols. (1872).—R. Bosworth Smith: *Life of Lord Lawrence*, 2 vols. (1883).—Bhai Maya Singh and H. M. Clark: *The Panjabi Dictionary* (Lahore, 1895).—Rev. E. P. Newton: *Panjabi Grammar* (Ludhiāna, 1898).—R. C. Temple: *The Legends of the Punjab*, 3 vols. (1881–5); 'Punjab Industrial Monographs' (Lahore): *Cotton* (1885), *Woollen* (1886), *Silk* (1887), *Brass and Copper* (1888), *Wood* (1889), *Gold and Silver* (1890), *Fibres* (1891), *Pottery and Glass* (1892), *Leather* (1893), *Silk* (1899), *Ivory* (1900), *Stone* (1906). *Report on the Famine in the Punjab in* 1896–7 (Lahore, 1898); *The Punjab Famine of* 1899–1900 (Lahore, 1901).—S. S. Thorburn: *Report on Peasant Indebtedness and Land Alienations to Money-lenders in the Rāwalpindi Division* (Lahore, 1896).—*Census Reports*, 1855, 1868, 1881 (by D. C. J. Ibbetson), 1891 (by E. D. Maclagan), 1901 (by H. A. Rose).—*District Gazetteers*.]

TABLE I. TEMPERATURE IN THE PUNJAB

Station.	Height in feet of Observatory above sea-level.	Average temperature (in degrees Fahrenheit) for twenty-five years ending with 1901 in							
		January.		May.		July.		November.	
		Mean.	Diurnal range.	Mean.	Diurnal range.	Mean.	Diurnal range.	Mean.	Diurnal range.
Delhi	718	59·0	22·3	92·6	24·1	87·7	13·6	69·8	26·4
Lahore	702	54·8	27·7	89·3	32·9	90·4	21·1	65·8	36·1
Rāwalpindi	1,676	50·3	24·6	82·9	29·5	87·1	21·1	60·6	33·2
Siālkot *	830	54·4	23·0	88·7	28·2	88·8	18·1	65·8	30·7
Multān	420	56·5	26·6	91·8	28·8	94·0	20·1	68·6	31·6
Montgomery †	558	55·0	26·4	92·9	29·8	94·3	21·2	68·0	33·2
Hill Station—Simla ‡	7,224	39·4	10·1	65·8	14·8	64·8	9·1	50·6	11·0

NOTE.—The diurnal range is the average difference between the maximum and minimum temperatures of each day.
* The figures are for twenty-four to twenty-five years. † The figures are for twelve years only. ‡ The figures are for nine to ten years only.

TABLE II. RAINFALL IN THE PUNJAB

Station.	Average rainfall (in inches) for twenty-five years ending with 1901 in												
	January.	February.	March.	April.	May.	June.	July.	August.	September.	October.	November.	December.	Total of year.
Delhi	1·26	0·70	0·50	0·27	0·69	3·25	7·98	8·03	3·95	0·27	0·11	0·64	27·65
Lahore	1·14	1·20	0·67	0·54	0·83	1·86	5·94	5·00	2·11	0·21	0·12	0·46	20·08
Rāwalpindi	2·92	2·35	1·84	1·90	1·61	1·88	8·00	7·98	3·37	0·55	0·47	1·03	33·90
Siālkot	2·54	1·84	1·12	1·00	1·04	2·77	7·95	9·08	2·86	0·28	0·25	0·73	31·46
Multān	0·41	0·42	0·34	0·15	0·38	0·55	2·12	1·92	0·65	...	0·07	0·26	7·27
Montgomery	0·57	0·80	0·43	0·21	0·52	1·19	2·82	2·20	0·82	0·06	0·08	0·29	9·99
Hill Station—Simla	3·02	3·25	2·22	1·73	3·20	7·41	16·54	17·63	5·57	0·98	0·58	1·50	63·63

TABLE III. DISTRIBUTION OF POPULATION, PUNJAB, 1901

	Area in square miles.	Number of towns.	Number of villages.	Total population. Persons.	Total population. Males.	Total population. Females.	Urban population. Persons.	Urban population. Males.	Urban population. Females.	Persons per square mile in rural areas.
British Territory.										
Hissār	5,217	8	964	781,717	418,167	363,550	97,995	51,602	46,393	131·1
Rohtak	1,797	11	491	630,672	333,217	297,455	92,412	46,625	45,787	299·5
Gurgaon	1,984	8	1,171	746,208	390,443	355,765	76,771	39,410	37,361	337·4
Delhi	1,290	4	714	689,039	371,864	317,175	231,381	126,344	105,037	359·5
Karnāl	3,153	7	1,383	883,225	478,953	404,272	90,308	46,571	43,737	251·5
Ambāla	1,851	7	1,718	815,880	451,581	364,299	125,902	72,210	53,692	372·8
Simla	101	6	45	40,351	26,164	14,187	18,902	13,530	5,372	212·4
Total, Delhi Division	15,393	51	6,486	4,587,092	2,470,389	2,116,703	733,671	396,292	337,379	250·6
Kāngra	9,978	3	715	768,124	399,106	369,018	16,179	9,782	6,397	75·4
Hoshiārpur	2,244	11	2,117	989,782	525,854	463,928	72,324	38,503	33,821	408·8
Jullundur	1,431	10	1,216	917,587	496,690	420,897	134,257	72,785	61,472	547·4
Ludhiāna	1,455	5	864	673,097	369,165	303,932	86,966	46,833	40,133	402·8
Ferozepore	4,302	8	1,503	958,072	524,306	433,766	86,024	50,331	35,693	202·7
Total, Jullundur Division	19,410	37	6,415	4,306,662	2,315,121	1,991,541	395,750	218,234	177,516	201·5
Montgomery	4,771	3	1,371	497,706	268,606	229,100	19,770	11,189	8,581	100·2
Lahore	3,704	7	1,533	1,162,109	640,449	521,660	256,090	147,934	108,156	246·3
Amritsar	1,601	5	1,042	1,023,828	559,855	463,973	186,449	105,988	80,461	526·0
Gurdāspur	1,889	11	2,244	940,334	509,951	430,383	70,565	38,263	32,302	460·4
Siālkot	1,991	7	2,348	1,083,909	573,259	510,650	89,580	47,957	41,623	499·4
Gujrānwāla	3,198	8	1,331	890,577	485,260	405,317	78,221	40,864	37,357	254·0
Total, Lahore Division	17,154	41	9,869	5,598,463	3,037,380	2,561,083	700,675	392,195	308,480	286·1
Gujrāt	2,051	4	1,336	750,548	389,402	361,146	41,893	21,002	20,891	345·5
Shāhpur	4,840	5	789	524,259	273,144	251,115	55,852	28,421	27,431	96·8
Jhelum	2,813	4	888	501,424	253,058	248,366	40,581	21,805	18,776	163·8
Rāwalpindi	2,010	2	1,180	558,699	299,893	258,806	89,532	58,823	30,709	233·4
Attock	4,022	4	614	464,430	242,398	222,032	24,109	13,156	10,953	109·5
Total, Rāwalpindi Division	15,736	19	4,807	2,799,360	1,457,895	1,341,465	251,967	143,207	108,760	161·9

TABLE III. DISTRIBUTION OF POPULATION, PUNJAB, 1901 (*continued*)

	Area in square miles.	Number of towns.	Number of villages.	Total population. Persons.	Total population. Males.	Total population. Females.	Urban population. Persons.	Urban population. Males.	Urban population. Females.	Persons per square mile in rural areas.
Miānwāli	7,816	5	426	424,588	224,008	200,580	29,555	15,055	14,500	50·5
Jhang	6,652	3	1,896	1,002,656	559,295	443,361	49,238	27,198	22,040	143·3
Multān	6,107	6	1,351	710,626	388,570	322,056	108,651	60,430	48,221	98·6
Muzaffargarh	3,635	4	700	405,656	220,207	185,449	12,684	6,998	5,686	108·1
Dera Ghāzi Khān	5,306	5	713	471,149	256,381	214,768	43,276	23,684	19,592	80·6
Total, Multān Division	29,516	23	5,086	3,014,675	1,648,461	1,366,214	243,404	133,365	110,039	93·9
Baloch Trans-Border	...	...	...	24,087	13,459	10,628	...	...	...	...
Total, British Territory	97,209	171	32,663	20,330,339	10,942,705	9,387,634	2,325,467	1,283,293	1,042,174	185·2
Native States.										
Patiāla	5,412	14	3,580	1,596,692	877,197	719,495	175,368	95,719	79,649	262·6
Jind	1,259	7	439	282,003	153,376	128,627	40,487	21,927	18,560	191·8
Nābha	928	4	488	297,949	165,386	132,563	36,614	20,564	16,050	281·6
Bahāwalpur	15,000	10	960	720,877	395,684	325,193	69,864	38,727	31,137	43·4
Sirmūr	1,198	1	973	135,687	75,461	60,226	6,256	3,611	2,645	108·0
Lohāru	222	1	56	15,229	8,160	7,069	2,175	1,117	1,058	58·8
Dujāna	100	1	30	24,174	12,481	11,603	5,545	2,723	2,822	186·3
Pataudi	52	1	40	21,933	11,511	10,422	4,171	2,121	2,050	341·6
Kalsia	168	2	181	67,181	36,980	30,201	10,161	5,382	4,779	339·4
Simla Hill States	5,918	3	1,527	389,349	206,206	183,143	8,376	4,873	3,503	64·4
Kapūrthala	630	6	597	314,351	169,797	144,554	47,520	26,462	21,058	423·5
Mandi	1,200	1	146	174,045	90,896	83,149	8,144	4,928	3,216	138·3
Maler Kotla	167	1	115	77,506	41,915	35,591	21,122	10,815	10,307	337·6
Suket	420	2	28	54,676	28,964	25,712	2,179	1,165	1,014	125·0
Farīdkot	642	2	167	124,912	69,321	55,591	19,924	11,195	8,729	163·5
Chamba	3,216	1	1,670	127,834	66,474	61,360	6,000	3,436	2,564	37·9
Total, Native States	36,532	57	10,997	4,424,398	2,409,809	2,014,589	463,906	254,765	209,141	108·4
GRAND TOTAL, PUNJAB	133,741	228	43,660	24,754,737	13,352,514	11,402,223	2,789,373	1,538,058	1,251,315	164·2

NOTE.—The areas given are supplied by the Surveyor-General of India. Lyallpur District was formed in 1904 out of portions of the Districts of Montgomery and Jhang; it has an approximate area of 3,075 square miles and a population of 654,666, and contains 1 town and 1,141 villages.

TABLE IV

Statistics of Agriculture, Punjab

(In square miles)

	1888-90 (average).	1891-1900 (average).	1900-1.	1903-4.
Total area	89,067	89,711	89,595	89,270
Total uncultivated area	53,644	51,568	48,400	46,958
Cultivable but not cultivated	34,515	32,497	26,635	26,373
Uncultivable (including forests)	19,129	19,071	19,765	20,585
Total cultivated area	35,423	38,143	41,195	42,312
Irrigated from canals	3,160	5,363	8,354	9,336
Irrigated from wells and canals	784	1,117	1,555	1,599
Irrigated from wells	5,674	6,072	5,989	6,124
Irrigated from other sources	86	133	247	311
Total irrigated area	9,704	12,685	16,145	17,370
Unirrigated area (including inundated)	25,719	25,458	25,050	24,942
Total cropped area.				
Rice	1,085	1,055	1,184	1,074
Wheat	9,575	9,847	11,901	12,216
Other food-grains and pulses	16,454	14,899	19,289	16,668
Oilseeds	1,101	1,311	2,705	1,683
Sugar-cane	538	528	514	517
Cotton	1,181	1,231	1,608	1,637
Hemp (*san*)	66	66	73	77
Other fibres	2	4	5	4
Opium	22	14	12	14
Indigo	203	134	142	84
Tea	14	15	16	16
Tobacco	86	80	99	84
Miscellaneous	1,783	2,147	3,366	4,137
Total area cropped	32,110	31,331	40,914	38,211
Area double cropped	3,126	3,507	5,721	5,414

TABLE V

Prices of Staples in the Punjab

(In seers per rupee)

Selected staples.	Selected centres.	Percentage of area under crop in 1900–1.	Average for ten years ending			Average for the year 1904.
			1880.	1890.	1900.	
Wheat	Delhi . .	29·1	20·39	18·16	15·45	15·87
	Amritsar .		23·18	21·41	16·73	18·16
	Rāwalpindi .		22·44	20·46	16·25	17·26
Gram	Delhi . .	12·5	25·77	23·93	21·42	23·35
	Amritsar .		29·61	28·78	21·99	28·42
	Rāwalpindi .		26·37	25·58	20·55	24·6
Jowār	Delhi . .	7·0	27·08	23·28	21·60	27·42
	Amritsar .		31·38	28·37	20·29	29
	Rāwalpindi .		28·37	29·53	24·08	24·96
Bājra	Delhi . .	10·8	23·65	20·64	18·62	21·75
	Amritsar .		26·09	22·06	15·94	24·92
	Rāwalpindi .		28·84	28·63	19·97	22·6
Salt	Delhi . .	...	9·03	11·94	11·24	13·1
	Amritsar .		10·53	14·09	12·05	15·54
	Rāwalpindi .		10·45	14·24	13·40	16·02

Note.—The figures for the famine years 1878, 1879, 1897, and 1900 have been omitted.

TABLE VI. Trade by Rail and River of the Punjab (including North-West Frontier Province) with other Provinces and States (excluding Kashmīr and Ladākh)

(In thousands of rupees)

	1890–1.	1900–1.	1903–4.
Imports.			
Cotton, raw	2,92	4,11	5,01
Cotton twist and yarn	28,56	18,31	32,18
Cotton piece-goods	2,72,83	3,20,03	3,97,20
Grain and pulse	23,20	1,34,15	42,77
Hides and skins	5,99	15,75	14,95
Metals and manufactures of metals	70,33	1,05,73	1,59,07
Oils	13,26	18,97	21,33
Oilseeds	8,50	32,58	25,72
Opium	74	4,06	4,07
Provisions	43,00	31,82	35,31
Salt	6,57	10,65	8,44
Spices	13,54	22,64	26,29
Sugar	1,14,21	1,65,58	2,01,39
Tea	9,57	5,66	10,03
Wood	...	8,16	20,58
Woollen goods	20,70	33,67	37,44
All other articles	2,64,52	3,60,40	4,70,89
Total	8,98,44	12,92,27	15,12,67
Treasure { Government	37,50	1,91,66	1,89,00
Treasure { Commercial	*	*	1,07,81
Total	*	*	2,96,81
Exports.			
Apparel	...	52,31	54,25
Coal and coke	1	19	4
Cotton, raw	35,93	1,06,19	2,55,86
Cotton, manufactured	51,00	75,64	79,24
Wheat	1,97,77	1,65,90	5,43,69
Other grains and pulses	1,02,76	1,06,88	1,04,07
Dyes and tans	10,60	17,47	11,03
Jute and manufactures of jute	4,87	10,55	7,92
Hides and skins	31,32	77,45	63,34
Metals and manufactures of metals	13,44	12,12	17,06
Leather	20,41	13,37	13,73
Oils	2,07	9,68	2,44
Oilseeds	16,08	59,74	43,50
Provisions	29,32	27,43	17,53
Railway plant and rolling stock	10,77	26,73	31,82
Spices	11,30	12,84	12,74
Sugar	21,55	24,62	14,83
Tobacco	86	4,43	2,73
Wool, raw	23,30	23,54	30,04
Wool, manufactured	35,28	57,73	30,07
All other articles	97,22	1,14,82	1,33,26
Total	7,15,86	9,99,63	14,69,19
Treasure { Government	7,19†	36,07	72,01
Treasure { Commercial	*	39,48	40,78
Total	7,19†	75,55	1,12,79

* Not available. † Currency figures only.

TABLE VII

Trade of the Punjab with Kashmīr and Ladākh

(In thousands of rupees)

	1890-1 (including trade through Hazāra).		1900-1 (including trade through Hazāra).		1903-4 (excluding trade through Hazāra).	
	Kashmīr.	Ladākh.	Kashmīr.	Ladākh.	Kashmīr.	Ladākh.
Imports.						
Total imports.	54,32	3,42	1,29,15	4,18	98,01	6,21
Treasure:—						
Government	...	...	...	...	10,11	...
Commercial	1,67	...	5,20	1	9,41	...
Total	1,67	...	5,20	1	19,52	...
Exports.						
Total exports.	56,52	2,76	95,64	2,17	78,66	3,07
Treasure:—						
Government	...	...	6,00	...	...	...
Commercial	10	10	3,24	33	4,10	45
Total	10	10	9,24	33	4,10	45

TABLE VIII

Statistics of Criminal Justice, Punjab

	Average for ten years ending 1890.	Average for ten years ending 1900.	1901.	1904.	Percentage of convictions in 1904.
Number of persons tried:					
(*a*) For offences against person and property	100,186	121,939	116,446	134,070	15
(*b*) For other offences against the Indian Penal Code . .	21,456	23,151	21,713	26,656	20
(*c*) For offences against special and local laws . . .	51,255	70,117	63,010	79,791	53
Total	172,897	215,207	201,169	240,517	28

TABLE IX

Statistics of Civil Justice and Revenue Court Cases. Punjab

	Average for ten years ending 1890.	Average for ten years ending 1900.	1901.	1904.
Suits for money and movable property	212,313	211,844	201,423	180,105
Title and other suits . . .	37,740	34,263	30,811	30,040
Rent suits*	1,778‡	1,201‡	275‡	497
Other Revenue Court cases† .	20,330‡	34,111‡	36,415‡	32,944
Total	272,161	281,419	268,924	243,586

* The figures for rent suits and other Revenue Court cases for 1881–4 are for institutions; those for the remaining years for disposals only.

† Other Revenue Court cases include figures for execution of decrees of Revenue Courts throughout, with the exception of the years 1880–4 and 1888 and 1889, for which the data are not available.

‡ These figures are for the old Province.

TABLE X

PRINCIPAL SOURCES OF PROVINCIAL REVENUE, INCLUDING NORTH-WEST FRONTIER PROVINCE UP TO MARCH 31, 1901, BUT FOR PUNJAB AS NOW CONSTITUTED FOR THE YEAR 1903–4

(In thousands of rupees)

	Average for ten years ending March 31, 1890.		Average for ten years ending March 31, 1900.		Year ending March 31, 1901.		Year ending March 31, 1904.	
	Total raised in Province (Imperial, Provincial, and Local).	Amount credited to Provincial revenues.	Total raised in Province (Imperial, Provincial, and Local).	Amount credited to Provincial revenues.	Total raised in Province (Imperial, Provincial, and Local).	Amount credited to Provincial revenues.	Total raised in Province (Imperial, Provincial, and Local).	Amount credited to Provincial revenues.
Land revenue	2,12,73	72,90	2,40,29	98,98	2,43,75	1,12,24	2,33,32	1,41,06
Stamps	35,04	20,84	42,06	29,56	42,80	32,10	40,48	30,36
Excise	13,55	7,98	21,33	6,23	26,01	6,50	28,00	7,00
Provincial rates	33,45	4,84	41,80	5,92	42,28	5,89	44,77	6,18
Assessed taxes	6,96	3,28	12,95	6,47	14,80	7,40	11,70	5,85
Forests	8,52	3,58	10,68	5,34	13,51	6,75	17,18	8,59
Registration	2,10	1,28	3,29	1,65	3,47	1,74	2,19	1,10
Other sources	49,69	40,53	38,80	30,23	44,91	33,16	48,16	30,46
Total	3,62,04	1,55,23	4,11,20	1,84,38	4,31,53	2,05,78	4,25,80	2,30,60

TABLE XI

PROVINCIAL EXPENDITURE, INCLUDING NORTH-WEST FRONTIER PROVINCE UP TO MARCH 31, 1901, BUT FOR PUNJAB AS NOW CONSTITUTED FOR THE YEAR 1903-4

(In thousands of rupees)

	Average for ten years ending March 31, 1890.	Average for ten years ending March 31, 1900.	Year ending March 31, 1901.	Year ending March 31, 1904.
Opening balance	90	2,47	...	25,25
Charges in respect of revenue collection	23,76	31,30	35,05	35,93
Salaries and expenses of Civil Departments:—				
(*a*) General administration	10,05	10,15	10,05	9,25
(*b*) Law and justice .	34,19	41,84	48,68	43,38
(*c*) Police . . .	30,17	38,35	43,81	37,30
(*d*) Education . .	7,08	7,61	7,63	10,50
(*e*) Medical . . .	4,85	6,40	8,72	11,19
(*f*) Other heads . . .	83	1,06	1,06	2,11
Pensions and miscellaneous civil charges . . .	6,06	9,79	12,84	13,14
Famine relief . . .	...	1,20	...	-2
Irrigation	26	76	1,03	53
Public works . . .	25,94	28,32	25,84	43,85
Other charges and adjustments	10,47	10,07	11,07	16,69
Total	1,53,66	1,86,85	2,05,78	2,23,85
Closing balance .	2,47	...	...	32,00

TABLE XII

Income and Expenditure of Municipalities (excluding Notified Areas), Punjab

	1889-90.	Average for ten years 1890-1 to 1899-1900.	1900-1.	1903-4.
Income from—	Rs.	Rs.	Rs.	Rs.
Octroi . . .	22,99,144	25,27,057	27,07,406	30,29,966
Tax on houses and lands . . .	1,17,721	1,37,208	1,37,925	2,37,919
Other taxes . .	42,966	59,162	83,752	1,36,443
Loans . . .	...	2,32,919	1,61,489	6,58,325
Rents and other sources	8,76,838	11,46,599	12,85,011	14,85,673
Total income	33,36,669	41,02,945	43,75,583	55,48,326
Expenditure on—				
Administration and collection of taxes .	4,88,016	5,79,243	6,39,495	7,00,054
Public safety . .	5,14,076	5,66,100	6,39,104	6,93,969
Water-supply and drainage :				
Capital . .	1,32,494	3,19,398	2,70,744	7,53,443
Maintenance .	98,651	1,26,788	1,68,174	2,10,378
Conservancy . .	3,05,986	4,92,286	5,67,395	5,87,339
Hospitals and dispensaries . . .	2,65,265	3,31,091	4,01,272	5,87,909
Public works . .	3,71,801	4,05,426	3,26,225	4,18,253
Education . . .	4,44,628	5,40,690	5,63,852	6,14,382
Other heads . .	8,14,414	7,09,529	8,10,672	8,50,595
Total expenditure	34,35,331	40,70,551	43,86,933	54,16,322

TABLE XIII

Income and Expenditure of District Boards, Punjab

	Excluding the District of Miānwāli.			Whole Province.
	1889–90.	Average for ten years 1890–1 to 1899–1900.	1900–1.	1903–4.
Income from—	Rs.	Rs.	Rs.	Rs.
Provincial rates	19,18,204	20,62,940	20,66,918	24,03,661
Interest	1,100	1,124	1,417	1,361
Education	46,858	80,317	1,11,386	1,20,831
Medical	9,326	21,449	25,050	40,662
Scientific, &c.	85,814	86,125	87,428	94,085
Miscellaneous	70,415	1,28,948	2,35,941	2,88,411
Public works	48,233	1,07,151	1,38,919	1,83,233
Pounds	43,436	55,050	53,944	58,273
Ferries	1,44,383	1,51,965	1,62,528	1,51,629
Total income	23,67,769	26,95,069	28,83,531	33,42,146
Expenditure on—				
Refunds	1,967	2,617	3,168	2,318
General administration	1,05,491	1,14,161	1,28,672	1,35,864
Education	4,68,451	5,76,302	6,12,567	6,68,125
Medical	2,59,894	3,16,238	5,61,538	3,77,654
Scientific, &c.	1,15,152	1,45,678	1,52,350	1,33,809
Miscellaneous	4,59,708	6,91,402	8,01,814	10,25,264
Public works	9,14,242	9,16,148	7,56,918	9,04,418
Total expenditure	23,24,905	27,62,546	30,17,027	32,47,452

TABLE XIV

Police Statistics, Punjab (as now constituted)

	1881.	1891.	1901.	1904.
Provincial and Ferry Police.				
Superintendents and assistant superintendents	47	53	51	56
Inspectors . . .	44	42	43	49
Sub-inspectors . .	407	463	401	526
Head constables . .	1,603	1,666	1,689	1,814
Constables . . .	10,073	9,720	9,767	10,426
Municipal Police.				
Inspectors . . .	6	6	8	8
Sub-inspectors . .	17	27	34	37
Head constables . .	339	388	432	448
Constables . . .	3,451	3,538	3,639	3,791
Town watchmen . .	...	104	124	138
Cantonment Police.				
Inspectors . . .	...	4	4	4
Sub-inspectors . .	2	5	5	6
Head constables . .	28	58	60	69
Constables . . .	391	518	531	574
Military Police.				
Commandants and sub-commandants . .	...	...	3	4
Native officers . .	Not available.	Not available.	37	14
Non-commissioned officers and men . .	...	...	245	606
Railway Police.				
Deputy and assistant superintendents . .	...	...	1	3
Inspectors . . .	5	5	10	10
Sub-inspectors . .	13	13	23	26
European platform sergeants . . .	...	...	9	18
Head constables . .	80	90	200	221
Constables . . .	620	681	957	1,108
Chaukīdārs . . .	84	84	...	7
Rural Police.				
Daffadārs and *chaukīdārs*	...	...	...	29,645
Total expenditure	Rs. 32,23,323	Rs. 32,75,278	Rs. 33,45,684	Rs. 38,62,429

	Average of five years ending 1901 (old Province).	1904 (new Province).
Statistics of cognizable crime.		
Number of cases reported	58,229	85,365
Number of cases decided in the criminal courts .	37,397	43,313
Number of cases ending in acquittal or discharge .	6,552	12,796
Number of cases ending in conviction . .	28,957	30,517

TABLE XV

JAILS STATISTICS, PUNJAB

	1881.	1891.	1901.	1904.
Number of Central jails	2	3	4	3
Number of District jails	28	25	24	25*
Number of subsidiary jails (lock-ups) .	17	20	19	16
Average daily jail population:—				
(*a*) Male prisoners:				
In Central jails .	3,488	2,996	6,406	4,860
In other jails .	8,645	8,033	7,082	6,885
(*b*) Female prisoners:				
In Central jails .	...	...	1	4
In other jails .	512	328	327	270
Total	12,645	11,357	13,816	12,019
Rate of jail mortality per 1,000 . .	62.87	28.26	26.64	19.79
Expenditure on jail maintenance . .	Rs. 7,41,503	Rs. 7,29,382	Rs. 8,98,117	Rs. 7,59,146
Cost per prisoner .	58-10-0	64-4-0	65-0-0	64-13-0
Profits on jail manufactures . . .	1,19,953	1,97,678	1,24,834	1,09,658
Earnings per prisoner .	10-3-0	18-4-0	10-0-0	10-5-0

* Including female jail at Lahore.

TABLE XVI. Colleges, Schools, and Scholars, Punjab

	1883-4.			1890-1.			1900-1.			1903-4.		
	Number of institutions.	Scholars.		Number of institutions.	Scholars.		Number of institutions.	Scholars.		Number of institutions.	Scholars.	
		Males.	Females.		Males.	Females.		Males.	Females.		Males.	Females.
Public.												
Arts colleges	2	152	...	7	468	...	12	1,245	...	15	1,360	...
Professional colleges	1	57	...	2	199	...	2	233	11	3	486	8
Secondary schools:—												
High	25	912	...	48	12,708	511	106	25,199	853	110	26,555	962
Middle	204	5,107	20	215	29,386	1,095	272	35,576	1,822	269	38,143	1,849
Primary schools	1,882	102,876*	10,358*	1,917	77,617	8,907	2,530	98,369	11,852	2,822	109,343	13,705
Training schools	10	206	191	4	267	...	5	256	...	5	248	...
Other special schools	6	300	19	7	773	9	15	2,013	154	22	2,012	244
Private.												
Advanced	...	...	...	794	9,408	...	292	5,108	...	354	5,351	43
Elementary	...	...	...	6,518	83,780	12,124	3,317	46,540	7,349	4,347	58,756	12,565
Total	2,130	109,610	10,588	9,512	214,606	22,646	6,551	214,539	22,041	7,947	242,254	29,376

* Including scholars reading in the primary department of secondary schools.

TABLE XVII

Statistics of Hospitals, Lunatic Asylums, and Vaccination, Punjab

	1881.	1891.	1901.	1904.
Hospitals, &c.				
Number of civil hospitals and dispensaries	170	206	246	263
Average daily number of—				
(*a*) In-patients	1,236	1,472	1,711	1,924
(*b*) Out-patients	8,682	13,526	19,897	21,538
Income from—				
(*a*) Government payments Rs.	59,724	48,391	66,144	59,019
(*b*) Local and municipal payments Rs.	2,33,582	4,06,063	5,05,042	5,53,765
(*c*) Fees, endowments, and other sources Rs.	21,835	30,964	58,749	88,376
Expenditure on—				
(*a*) Establishment Rs.	1,63,437	2,38,612	3,17,249	3,46,700
(*b*) Medicines, diet, buildings, &c. Rs.	1,44,919	2,40,368	3,18,800	3,30,507
Lunatic Asylums.				
Number of asylums	2	2	1	1
Average daily number of—				
(*a*) Criminal lunatics	40	50	109	111
(*b*) Other lunatics	273	278	382	443
Income from—				
(*a*) Government payments Rs.	31,546	31,721	54,289	60,636
(*b*) Fees and other sources Rs.	6,284	19,660	17,203	12,666
Expenditure on—				
(*a*) Establishment Rs.	16,167	14,987	20,376	28,200
(*b*) Diet, buildings, &c. Rs.	21,063	36,394	51,116	45,102
Vaccination.				
Population among whom vaccination was carried on	...	19,629,722	20,734,248	20,293,834
Number of successful operations	...	653,300	629,825	632,240
Ratio per 1,000 of population	...	33·28	30·38	31·15
Total expenditure on vaccination Rs.	...	62,187	87,459	92,017
Cost per successful case As.	...	1–7	2–3	2–4

MOUNTAINS, RIVERS, CANALS, AND HISTORIC AREAS

Himālayas, The.—A system of stupendous mountain ranges, lying along the northern frontiers of the Indian Empire, and containing some of the highest peaks in the world. Literally, the name is equivalent to 'the abode of snow' (from the Sanskrit *hima*, 'frost,' and *ālaya*, 'dwelling-place'). To the early geographers the mountains were known as Imaus or Himaus and Hemodas; and there is reason to believe that these names were applied to the western and eastern parts respectively, the sources of the Ganges being taken as the dividing line. 'Hemodas' represents the Sanskrit *Himāvata* (Prākrit *Hemota*), meaning 'snowy.' The Greeks who accompanied Alexander styled the mountains the Indian Caucasus. **Name.**

Modern writers have sometimes included in the system the Muztāgh range, and its extension the Karakoram; but it is now generally agreed that the Indus should be considered the north-western limit. From the great peak of Nanga Parbat in Kashmīr, the Himālayas stretch eastward for twenty degrees of longitude, in a curve which has been compared to the blade of a scimitar, the edge facing the plains of India. Barely one-third of this vast range of mountains is known with any degree of accuracy. The Indian Survey department is primarily engaged in supplying administrative needs; and although every effort is made in fulfilling this duty to collect information of purely scientific interest, much still remains to be done. **Extent of range.**

A brief abstract of our knowledge of the Himālayas may be given by shortly describing the political divisions of India which include them. On the extreme north-west, more than half of the State of Kashmīr and Jammu lies in the Himālayas, and this portion has been described in some detail by Drew in *Jammu and Kashmīr Territories*, and by Sir W. Lawrence in *The Valley of Kashmīr*. The next section, appertaining to the Punjab and forming the British District of Kāngra and the group of feudatories known as the Simla Hill States, is better known. East of this lies the Kumaun Division of the United Provinces, attached to which is the Tehrī **Political distribution.**

State. This portion has been surveyed in detail, owing to the requirements of the revenue administration, and is also familiar from the careful accounts of travellers. For 500 miles the State of Nepāl occupies the mountains, and is to the present day almost a *terra incognita*, owing to the acquiescence by the British Government in the policy of exclusion adopted by its rulers. Our knowledge of the topography of this portion of the Himālayas is limited to the information obtained during the operations of 1816, materials collected by British officials resident at Kātmāndu, notably B. H. Hodgson, and the accounts of native explorers. The eastern border of Nepāl is formed by the State of Sikkim and the Bengal District of Darjeeling, which have been graphically described by Sir Joseph Hooker and more recently by Mr. Douglas Freshfield. A small wedge of Tibetan territory, known as the Chumbi Valley, separates Sikkim from Bhutān, which latter has seldom been visited by Europeans. East of Bhutān the Himālayas are inhabited by savage tribes, with whom no intercourse is possible except in the shape of punitive expeditions following raids on the plains. Thus a stretch of nearly 400 miles in the eastern portion of the range is imperfectly known.

Divisions of range. In the western part of the Himālayas, which, as has been shown, has been more completely examined than elsewhere, the system may be divided into three portions. The central or main axis is the highest, which, starting at Nanga Parbat on the north-west, follows the general direction of the range. Though it contains numerous lofty peaks, including Nandā Devī, the highest mountain in British India, it is not a true watershed. North of it lies another range, here forming the boundary between India and Tibet, which shuts off the valley of the Indus, and thus may be described as a real waterparting. From the central axis, and usually from the peaks in it, spurs diverge, with a general south-easterly or south-westerly direction, but actually winding to a considerable extent. These spurs, which may be called the Outer Himālayas, cease with some abruptness at their southern extremities, so that the general elevation is 8,000 or 9,000 feet a few miles from the plains. Separated from the Outer Himālayas by elevated valleys or *dūns* is a lower range known as the Siwāliks, which is well marked between the Beās and the Ganges, reappears to the south of central Kumaun, and is believed to exist in Nepāl. Although the general character of the Himālayas in Nepāl is less accurately known, there is reason to suppose that it approximates to that of the western ranges.

Within the limits of this great mountain chain all varieties of scenery can be obtained, except the placid charm of level country. Luxuriant vegetation clothes the outer slopes, gradually giving place to more sombre forests. As higher elevations are reached, the very desolation of the landscape affects the imagination even more than the beautiful scenery left behind. It is not surprising that these massive peaks are venerated by the Hindus, and are intimately connected with their religion, as giving rise to some of the most sacred rivers, as well as on account of legendary associations. A recent writer has vividly described the impressions of a traveller through the foreground of a journey to the snows in Sikkim[1]:— Scenery.

'He sees at one glance the shadowy valleys from which shining mist-columns rise at noon against a luminous sky, the forest ridges, stretching fold behind fold in softly undulating lines—dotted by the white specks which mark the situation of Buddhist monasteries—to the glacier-draped pinnacles and precipices of the snowy range. He passes from the zone of tree-ferns, bamboos, orange-groves, and *dal* forest, through an endless colonnade of tall-stemmed magnolias, oaks, and chestnut trees, fringed with delicate orchids and festooned by long convolvuluses, to the region of gigantic pines, junipers, firs, and larches. Down each ravine sparkles a brimming torrent, making the ferns and flowers nod as it dashes past them. Superb butterflies, black and blue, or flashes of rainbow colours that turn at pleasure into exact imitations of dead leaves, the fairies of this lavish transformation scene of Nature, sail in and out between the sunlight and the gloom. The mountaineer pushes on by a track half buried between the red twisted stems of tree-rhododendrons, hung with long waving lichens, till he emerges at last on open sky and the upper pastures—the Alps of the Himālaya—fields of flowers: of gentians and edelweiss and poppies, which blossom beneath the shining storehouses of snow that encompass the ice-mailed and fluted shoulders of the giants of the range. If there are mountains in the world which combine as many beauties as the Sikkim Himālayas, no traveller has as yet discovered and described them for us.'

The line of perpetual snow varies from 15,000 to 16,000 feet on the southern exposures. In winter, snow generally falls at elevations above 5,000 feet in the west, while falls at 2,500 feet were twice recorded in Kumaun during the last century. Glaciers extend below the region of perpetual snow, descending to 12,000 or 13,000 feet in Kulū and Lāhul, and even lower in Kumaun, while in Sikkim they are about 2,000 feet Snow-line.

[1] D. W. Freshfield in *The Geographical Journal*, vol. xix, p. 453.

higher. On the vast storehouse thus formed largely depends the prosperity of Northern India, for the great rivers which derive their water from the Himālayas have a perpetual supply which may diminish in years of drought, but cannot fail absolutely to feed the system of canals drawn from them.

Rivers.

While all five rivers from which the Punjab derives its name rise in the Himālayas, the Sutlej alone has its source beyond the northern range, near the head-waters of the Indus and Tsan-po. In the next section are found the sources of the Jumna, Ganges, and Kālī or Sārdā high up in the central snowy range, while the Kauriāla or Karnāli, known lower down in its course as the Gogra, rises in Tibet, beyond the northern watershed. The chief rivers of Nepāl, the Gandak and Kosi, each with seven main affluents, have their birth in the Himālayas, which here supply a number of smaller streams merging in the larger rivers soon after they reach the plains. Little is known of the upper courses of the northern tributaries of the Brahmaputra in Assam; but it seems probable that the Dihāng, which has been taken as the eastern boundary of the Himālayas, is the channel connecting the Tsan-po and the Brahmaputra.

Highest peaks.

Passing from east to west the principal peaks are Nanga Parbat (26,182) in Kashmīr; a peak in Spiti (Kāngra District) exceeding 23,000 feet, besides three over 20,000; Nandā Devī (25,661), Trisūl (23,382), Pānch Chūlhī (22,673), and Nandā Kot (22,538) in the United Provinces; Mount Everest (29,002), Devālagiri (26,826), Gosainthān (26,305) and Kinchinjunga (28,146), with several smaller peaks, in Nepāl; and Dongkya (23,190), with a few rising above 20,000, in Sikkim.

Valleys and lakes.

The most considerable stretch of level ground is the beautiful Kashmīr Valley, through which flows the Jhelum. In length about 84 miles, it has a breadth varying from 20 to 25 miles. Elsewhere steep ridges and comparatively narrow gorges are the rule, the chief exception being the Valley of Nepāl, which is an undulating plain about 20 miles from north to south, and 12 to 14 miles in width. Near the city of Srīnagar is the Dal Lake, described as one of the most picturesque in the world. Though measuring only 4 miles by 2½, its situation among the mountains, and the natural beauty of its banks, combined with the endeavours of the Mughal emperors to embellish it, unite to form a scene of great attraction. Some miles away is the larger expanse of water known as the Wular Lake, which ordinarily covers 12½ square miles, but in years of flood expands to over 100. A number of smaller lakes, some of considerable beauty, are situated in the outer ranges in Naini Tāl District. In 1903 the Gohnā Lake, in Garhwāl District, was formed by the subsidence of a steep hill, rising 4,000 feet above the level of a stream which it blocked.

Geology[1].

The geological features of the Himālayas can be conveniently grouped into three classes, roughly corresponding to the three main orographical zones: (1) the Tibetan highland zone, (2) the zone of snowy peaks and Outer Himālayas, and (3) the Sub-Himālayas.

In the Tibetan highlands there is a fine display of marine fossiliferous rocks, ranging in age from Lower Palaeozoic to Tertiary. In the zone of the snowy peaks granites and crystalline schists are displayed, fringed by a mantle of unfossiliferous rocks of old, but generally unknown, age, forming the lower hills or Outer Himālayas, while in the Sub-Himālayas the rocks are practically all of Tertiary age, and are derived from the waste of the highlands to the north.

Age and origin of the range.

The disposition of these rocks indicates the existence of a range of some sort since Lower Palaeozoic times, and shows that the present southern boundary of the marine strata on the northern side of the crystalline axis is not far from the original shore of the ocean in which these strata were laid down. The older unfossiliferous rocks of the Lower Himālayas on the southern side of the main crystalline axis are more nearly in agreement with the rocks which have been preserved without disturbance in the Indian Peninsula; and even remains of the great Gondwāna river-formations which include our valuable deposits of coal are found in the Darjeeling area, involved in the folding movements which in later geological times raised the Himālayas to be the greatest among the mountain ranges of the world. The Himālayas were thus marked out in very early times, but the main folding took place in the Tertiary era. The great outflow of the Deccan trap was followed by a depression of the area to the north and west, the sea in eocene times spreading itself over Rājputāna and the Indus valley, covering the Punjab to the foot of the Outer Himālayas as far east as the Ganges, at the same time invading on the east the area now occupied by Assam. Then followed a rise of the land and consequent retreat of the sea, the fresh-water deposits which covered the eocene marine strata being involved in the movement as fast as they were formed, until the Sub-Himālayan zone river-deposits, no older than the pliocene,

[1] By T. H. Holland, Geological Survey of India.

became tilted up and even overturned in the great foldings of the strata. This final rise of the Himālayan range in late Tertiary times was accompanied by the movements which gave rise also to the Arakan Yoma and the Nāgā hills on the east, and the hills of Baluchistān and Afghānistān on the west.

The rise of the Himālayan range may be regarded as a great buckle in the earth's crust, which raised the great Central Asian plateau in late Tertiary times, folding over in the Baikal region on the north against the solid mass of Siberia, and curling over as a great wave on the south against the firmly resisting mass of the Indian Peninsula.

As an index to the magnitude of this movement within the Tertiary era, we find the marine fossil foraminifer, *Nummulites*, which lived in eocene times in the ocean, now at elevations of 20,000 feet above sea-level in Zāskār. With the rise of the Himālayan belt, there occurred a depression at its southern foot, into which the alluvial material brought down from the hills has been dropped by the rivers. In miocene times, when presumably the Himālayas did not possess their present elevation, the rivers deposited fine sands and clays in this area; and as the elevatory process went on, these deposits became tilted up, while the rivers, attaining greater velocity with their increased gradient, brought down coarser material and formed conglomerates in pliocene times. These also became elevated and cut into by their own rivers, which are still working along their old courses, bringing down boulders to be deposited at the foot of the hills and carrying out the finer material farther over the Indo-Gangetic plain.

The Siwālik series.

The series of rocks which have thus been formed by the rivers, and afterwards raised to form the Sub-Himālayas, are known as the Siwālik series. They are divisible into three stages. In the lowest and oldest, distinguished as the Nāhan stage, the rocks are fine sandstones and red clays without any pebbles. In the middle stage, strings of pebbles are found with the sandstones, and these become more abundant towards the top, until we reach the conglomerates of the upper stage. Along the whole length of the Himālayas these Siwālik rocks are cut off from the older rock systems of the higher hills by a great reversed fault, which started in early Siwālik times and developed as the folding movements raised the mountains and involved in its rise the deposits formed along the foot of the range. The Siwālik strata never extended north of this great boundary fault, but the continued rise of the mountains affected these deposits, and raised them up to form the outermost zone of hills.

The upper stage of the Siwālik series is famous on account of the rich collection of fossil vertebrates which it contains. Among these there are forms related to the miocene mammals of Europe, some of which, like the hippopotamus, are now unknown in India but have relatives in Africa. Many of the mammals now characteristic of India were represented by individuals of much greater size and variety of species in Siwālik times.

Unfossiliferous rocks of Outer Himālayas.

The unfossiliferous rocks which form the Outer Himālayas are of unknown age, and may possibly belong in part to the unfossiliferous rocks of the Peninsula, like the Vindhyans and the Cuddapahs. Conspicuous among these rocks are the dolomitic limestones of Jaunsār and Kumaun, the probable equivalents of the similar rocks far away to the east at Buxa in the Duārs. With these a series of purple quartzites and basic lava-flow is often associated. In the Simla area the unfossiliferous rocks have been traced out with considerable detail; and it has been shown that quartzites, like those of Jaunsār and Kumaun, are overlaid by a system of rocks which has been referred to the carbonaceous system on account of the black carbonaceous slates which it includes. The only example known of pre-Tertiary fossiliferous rocks south of the snowy range in the Himālayas occurs in south-west Garhwāl, where there are a few fragmentary remains of mesozoic fossils of marine origin.

The crystalline axis.

The granite rocks, which form the core of the snowy range and in places occur also in the Lower Himālayas, are igneous rocks which may have been intruded at different periods in the history of the range. They are fringed with crystalline schists, in which a progressive metamorphism is shown from the edge of granitic rock outwards, and in the inner zone the granitic material and the pre-existing sedimentary rock have become so intimately mixed that a typical banded gneiss is produced. The resemblance of these gneisses to the well-known gneisses of Archaean age in the Peninsula and in other parts of the world led earlier observers to suppose that the gneissose rocks of the Central Himālayas formed an Archaean core, against which the sediments were subsequently laid down. But as we now know for certain that both granites, such as we have in the Himālayas, and banded gneisses may be much younger, even Tertiary in age, the mere composition and structure give no clue to the age of the crystalline axis. The position of the granite rock is probably dependent on the development of low-pressure areas during the process of folding, and there is thus a prima facie reason for supposing that much of the igneous material became injected during the Tertiary period. With the younger intrusions, however, there are probably remains of injections which occurred during the more ancient movements, and there may even be traces of the very ancient Archaean gneisses; for we know that pebbles of gneisses occur in the Cambrian conglomerates of the Tibetan zone, and these imply the existence of gneissose rocks exposed to the atmosphere in neighbouring highlands. The gneissose granite of the Central Himālayas must have consolidated under great pressure, with a thick superincumbent envelope of sedimentary strata; and their exposure to the atmosphere thus implies a long period of effectual erosion by weathering agents, which have cut down the softer sediments more easily and left the more resisting masses of crystalline rocks to form the highest peaks in the range. Excellent illustrations of the relationship of the gneissose granites to the rocks into which they have been intruded are displayed in the Dhaola Dhār in Kulū, in the Chor Peak in Garhwāl, and in the Darjeeling region east of Nepāl.

Fossiliferous rocks of the Tibetan zone.

Beyond the snowy range in the Tibetan zone we have a remarkable display of fossiliferous rocks, which alone would have been enough to make the Himālayas famous in the geological world. The boundary between Tibetan territory and Spiti and Kumaun has been the area most exhaustively studied by the Geological Survey. The rocks exposed in this zone include deposits which range in age from Cambrian to Tertiary. The oldest fossiliferous system, distinguished as the Haimanta ('snow-covered') system, includes some 3,000 feet of the usual sedimentary types, with fragmentary fossils which indicate Cambrian and Silurian affinities. Above this system there are representatives of the Devonian and Carboniferous of Europe, followed by a conglomerate which marks a great stratigraphical break at the beginning of Permian times in Northern India. Above the conglomerate comes one of the most remarkably complete succession of sediments known, ranging from Permian, without a sign of disturbance in the process of sedimentation, throughout the whole Mesozoic epoch to the beginning of Tertiary times. The highly fossiliferous character of some of the formations in this great pile of strata, like the *Productus* shales and the Spiti shales, has made this area classic ground to the palaeontologist.

The great Eurasian sea distinguished by the name 'Thetys,'

which spread over this area throughout the Palaeozoic and Mesozoic times, became driven back by the physical revolution which began early in Tertiary times, when the folding movements gave rise to the modern Himālayas. As relics of this ocean have been discovered in Burma and China it will not be surprising to find, when the ground is more thoroughly explored, that highly fossiliferous rocks are preserved also in the Tibetan zone beyond the snowy ranges of Nepal and Sikkim.

Economic minerals. Of the minerals of value, graphite has been recorded in the Kumaun Division; coal occurs frequently amongst the Nummulitic (eocene) rocks of the foot-hills and the Gondwāna strata of Darjeeling District; bitumen has been found in small quantities in Kumaun; stibnite, a sulphide of antimony, occurs associated with ores of zinc and lead in well-defined lodes in Lāhul; gold is obtained in most of the rivers, and affords a small and precarious living for a few washers; copper occurs very widely disseminated and sometimes forms distinct lodes of value in the slaty series south of the snowy range, as in the Kulū, Kumaun, and Darjeeling areas; ferruginous schists sometimes rich in iron occur under similar geological conditions, as in Kāngra and Kumaun; sapphires of considerable value have been obtained in Zāskār and turquoises from the central highlands; salt is being mined in quantity from near the boundary of the Tertiary and older rocks in the State of Mandi; borax and salt are obtained from lakes beyond the Tibetan border; slate-quarrying is a flourishing industry along the southern slopes of the Dhaola Dhār in Kāngra District; mica of poor quality is extracted from the pegmatites of Kulū; and a few other minerals of little value, besides building-stones, are obtained in various places. A small trade is developed, too, by selling the fossils from the Spiti shales as sacred objects.

Botany. The general features of the great variety in vegetation have been illustrated in the quotation from Mr. Freshfield's description of Sikkim. These variations are naturally due to an increase in elevation, and to the decrease in rainfall and humidity passing from south to north, and from east to west. The tropical zone of dense forest extends up to about 6,500 feet in the east, and 5,000 feet in the west. In the Eastern Himālayas orchids are numerically the predominant order of flowering plants; while in Kumaun about 62 species, both epiphytic and terrestrial, have been found. A temperate zone succeeds, ranging to about 12,000 feet, in which oaks, pines, and tree-rhododendrons are conspicuous, with chestnut, maple, magnolia, and laurel in the east. Where rain and mist are not excessive, as for example in Kulū and Kumaun, European fruit trees (apples, pears, apricots, and peaches) have been naturalized very successfully, and an important crop of potatoes is obtained in the west. Above about 12,000 feet the forests become thinner. Birch and willow mixed with dwarf rhododendrons continue for a time, till the open pasture land is reached, which is richly adorned in the summer months with brilliant Alpine species of flowers. Contrasting the western with the eastern section we find that the former is far less rich, though it has been better explored, while there is a preponderance of European species. A fuller account of the botanical features of the Himālayas will be found in Vol. I, chap. iv.

Fauna. To obtain a general idea of the fauna of the Himālayas it is sufficient to consider the whole system as divided into two tracts: namely, the area in the lower hills where forests can flourish, and the area above the forests. The main characteristics of these tracts have been summarized by the late Dr. W. T. Blanford[1]. In the forest area the fauna differs markedly from that of the Indian Peninsula stretching away from the base of the hills. It does not contain the so-called Aryan element of mammals, birds, and reptiles which are related to Ethiopian and Holarctic genera, and to the pliocene Siwālik fauna, nor does it include the Dravidian element of reptiles and batrachians. On the other hand, it includes the following animals which do not occur in the Peninsula—Mammals: the families Simiidae, Procyonidae, Talpidae, and Spalacidae, and the sub-family Gymnurinae, besides numerous genera, such as *Prionodon*, *Helictis*, *Arctonyx*, *Atherura*, *Nemorhaedus*, and *Cemas*. Birds: the families Eurylaemidae, Indicatoridae, and Heliornithidae, and the sub-family Paradoxornithinae. Reptiles: Platysternidae and Anguidae. Batrachians: Dyscophidae, Hylidae, Pelobatidae, and Salamandridae. Compared with the Peninsula, the fauna of the forest area is poor in reptiles and batrachians.

'It also contains but few peculiar genera of mammals and birds, and almost all the peculiar types that do occur have Holarctic affinities. The Oriental element in the fauna is very richly represented in the Eastern Himālayas and gradually diminishes to the westward, until in Kashmīr and farther west it ceases to be the principal constituent. These facts are consistent with the theory that the Oriental constituent of the

[1] 'The Distribution of Vertebrate Animals in India, Ceylon, and Burma,' *Proceedings*, *Royal Society*, vol. lxvii, p. 484.

Himālayan fauna, or the greater portion of it, has migrated into the mountains from the eastward at a comparatively recent period. It is an important fact that this migration appears to have been from Assam and not from the Peninsula of India.'

Dr. Blanford suggested that the explanation was to be found in the conditions of the glacial epoch. When the spread of snow and ice took place, the tropical fauna, which may at that time have resembled more closely that of the Peninsula, was forced to retreat to the base of the mountains or perished. At such a time the refuge afforded by the Assam Valley and the hill ranges south of it, with their damp, sheltered, forest-clad valleys, would be more secure than the open plains of Northern India and the drier hills of the country south of these. As the cold epoch passed away, the Oriental fauna re-entered the Himālayas from the east.

Above the forests the Himālayas belong to the Tibetan sub-region of the Holarctic region, and the fauna differs from that of the Indo-Malay region, 44 per cent. of the genera recorded from the Tibetan tract not being found in the Indo-Malay region. During the glacial epoch the Holarctic forms apparently survived in great numbers.

Owing to the rugged nature of the country, which makes travelling difficult and does not invite immigrants, the inhabitants of the Himālayas present a variety of ethnical types which can hardly be summarized briefly. Two common features extending over a large area may be referred to. From Ladākh in Kashmīr to Bhutān are found races of Indo-Chinese type, speaking dialects akin to Tibetan and professing Buddhism. In the west these features are confined to the higher ranges; but in Sikkim, Darjeeling, and Bhutān they are found much nearer the plains of India. Excluding Burma, this tract of the Himālayas is the only portion of India in which Buddhism is a living religion. As in Tibet, it is largely tinged by the older animistic beliefs of the people. Although the Muhammadans made various determined efforts to conquer the hills, they were generally unsuccessful, yielding rather to the difficulties of transport and climate than to the forces brought against them by the scanty though brave population of the hills. In the twelfth century a Tartar horde invaded Kashmīr, but succumbed to the rigours of the snowy passes. Subsequently a Tibetan soldier of fortune seized the supreme power and embraced Islām. Late in the fourteenth century the Muhammadan ruler of the country, Sultān Sikandar, People.

pressed his religion by force on the people, and in the province of Kashmīr proper 94 per cent. of the total are now Muhammadans. Baltistān is also inhabited chiefly by Muhammadans, but the proportion is much less in Jammu, and beyond the Kashmīr State Islām has few followers. Hinduism becomes an important religion in Jammu, and is predominant in the southern portions of the Himālayas within the Punjab and the United Provinces. It is the religion of the ruling dynasty in Nepāl, where, however, Buddhism is of almost equal strength. East of Nepāl Hindus are few. Where Hinduism prevails, the language in common use, known as Pahāri, presents a strong likeness to the languages of Rājputāna, thus confirming the traditions of the higher classes that their ancestors migrated from the plains of India. In Nepāl the languages spoken are more varied, and Newāri, the ancient state language, is akin to Tibetan. The Mongolian element in the population is strongly marked in the east, but towards the west has been pushed back into the higher portion of the ranges. In Kumaun are found a few shy people living in the recesses of the jungles, and having little intercourse with their more civilized neighbours. Tribes which appear to be akin to these are found in Nepāl, but little is known about them. North of Assam the people are of Tibeto-Burman origin, and are styled, passing from west to east, the Akās, Daflās, Mīris, and Abors, the last name signifying 'unknown savages.' Colonel Dalton has described these people in his *Ethnology of Bengal*.

Agriculture. From the commercial point of view the agricultural products of the Himālayas, with few exceptions, are of little importance. The chief food-grains cultivated are, in the outer ranges, rice, wheat, barley, *maruā*, and amaranth. In the hot, moist valleys, chillies, turmeric, and ginger are grown. At higher levels potatoes have become an important crop in Kumaun; and, as already mentioned, in Kulū and Kumaun European fruits have been successfully naturalized, including apples, pears, cherries, and strawberries. Two crops are obtained in the lower hills; but cultivation is attended by enormous difficulties, owing to the necessity of terracing and clearing land of stones, while irrigation is only practicable by long channels winding along the hill-sides from the nearest suitable stream or spring. As the snowy ranges are approached wheat and buckwheat, grown during the summer months, are the principal crops, and only one harvest in the year can be obtained. Tea gardens were successfully established in Kumaun during the first half of the nineteenth century, but the most important gardens are now situated in Kāngra and Darjeeling. In the latter District cinchona is grown for the manufacture of quinine and cinchona febrifuge.

The most valuable forests are found in the Outer Himālayas, yielding a number of timber trees, among which may be mentioned *sāl, shīsham* (*Dalbergia Sissoo*), and *tūn* (*Cedrela Toona*). Higher up are found the *deodār* and various kinds of pine, which are also extracted wherever means of transport can be devised. In the Eastern Himālayas wild rubber is collected by the hill tribes already mentioned, and brought for sale to the Districts of the Assam Valley. Forests.

Communications within the hills are naturally difficult. Railways have hitherto been constructed only to three places in the outer hills: Jammu in the Kashmīr State, Simla in the Punjab, and Darjeeling in Bengal. Owing to the steepness of the hill-sides and the instability of the strata composing them, these lines have been costly to build and maintain. A more ambitious project is now being carried out to connect the Kashmīr Valley with the plains, motive power being supplied by electricity to be generated by the Jhelum river. The principal road practicable for wheeled traffic is also in Kashmīr, leading from Rāwalpindi in the plains through Murree and Bāramūla to Srīnagar. Other cart-roads have been made connecting with the plains the hill stations of Dharmsāla, Simla, Chakrāta, Mussoorie, Dalhousie, Nainī Tāl, and Rānīkhet. In the interior the roads are merely bridle paths. The great rivers flowing in deep gorges are crossed by suspension bridges made of the rudest materials. The sides consist of canes and twisted fibres, and the footway may be a single bamboo laid on horizontal canes supported by ropes attached to the sides. These frail constructions, oscillating from side to side under the tread of the traveller, are crossed with perfect confidence by the natives, even when bearing heavy loads. On the more frequented paths, such as the pilgrim road from Hardwār up the valley of the Ganges to the holy shrines of Badrināth and Kedārnāth, more substantial bridges have been constructed by Government, and the roads are regularly repaired. Sheep and, in the higher tracts, yaks and crosses between the yak and ordinary cattle are used as beasts of burden. The trade with Tibet is carried over lofty passes, the difficulties of which have not yet been ameliorated by engineers. Among these the following may be mentioned: the Kangwa La (15,500 feet) on the Hindustān-Tibet road through Simla; the Mānā Means of communication.

(18,000 feet), Nitī (16,570 feet), and Balcha Dhurā in Garhwāl; the Anta Dhurā (17,270 feet), Lampiya Dhurā (18,000 feet), and Lipū Lekh (16,750) in Almorā; and the Jelep La (14,390) in Sikkim.

Bibliography. [More detailed information about the various portions of the Himalāyas will be found in the articles on the political divisions referred to above. An admirable summary of the orography of the Himālayas is contained in Lieut.-Col. H. H. Godwin Austen's presidential address to the Geographical Section of the British Association in 1883 (*Proceedings, Royal Geographical Society*, 1883, p. 610; and 1884, pp. 83 and 112, with a map). Fuller accounts of the botany, geology, and fauna are given in E. F. Atkinson's *Gazetteer of the Himālayan Districts in the North-Western* [United] *Provinces*, 3 vols. (1882–6). See also General Strachey's 'Narrative of a Journey to Mānasarowar,' *Geographical Journal*, vol. xv, p. 150. More recent works are the *Kāngra District Gazetteer* (Lahore, 1899); C. A. Sherring, *Western Tibet and the British Borderland* (1906); and D. W. Freshfield, *Round Kangchenjunga* (1903), which contains a full bibliography for the Eastern Himālayas. An account of the Himālayas by officers of the Survey of India and the Geological department is under preparation.]

Siwālik Hills ('belonging to Siva').—A range of hills in Northern India, running parallel to the Himālayas for about 200 miles from the Beās to the Ganges; a similar formation east of the Ganges separates the Pātlī, Patkot, and Kotah Dūns (valleys) from the outer range of the Himālayas as far as Kālādhūngī, where it merges into them, and is believed to reappear still farther east in Nepāl. In the United Provinces the Siwāliks lie between the Jumna and Ganges, separating Sahāranpur District from Dehra Dūn, while in the Punjab they cross the Sirmūr (Nāhan) State and Ambāla and Hoshiārpur Districts. This part of the range is irregular and pierced by several rivers, of which the Ghaggar on the west is the largest. West of the Ghaggar the hills run like a wall, separating Ambāla from the long narrow valley of the Sirsa river in Nālāgarh State, until they are cut through by the Sutlej at Rūpar. Thence the range runs with a more northerly trend through Hoshiārpur, where it terminates near the Beās valley in a mass of undulating hills. Beyond the Sutlej there is merely a broad table-land, at first enclosed by sandy hillocks, but finally spreading into minor spurs. The southern face, in the United Provinces, rises abruptly from the plains and is scored by the bare stony beds of the watercourses which rush down in the rains. On the northern side is a more gentle descent into the elevated valley of Dehra Dūn, which separates this range from the Himālayas. The greatest height does not exceed 3,500 feet, and the range is about ten miles broad. A road from Sahāranpur to Dehra crosses these hills by the Mohan Pass, but has lost its importance since railway communication was opened through the eastern termination near the Ganges. Geologically, the Siwāliks are separated from the Outer Himālayas by a continuous reversed fault. They contain Tertiary strata consisting of fresh-water deposits, celebrated for the fossil remains found in them and described by Falconer and Cautley. The lower hills are thickly clothed with *sāl* (*Shorea robusta*) and *sain* (*Terminalia tomentosa*), while on the higher peaks a cooler climate allows pines to flourish. Wild elephants are found, and also tigers, sloth bears, leopards, hyenas, various kinds of deer, and hog. The term 'Siwālik' has been applied by Muhammadan writers to the area lying south of the hills as far as Hānsi, and also to the Himālayas.

[Falconer and Cautley, *Fauna Antiqua Sivalensis* (1846–9–66).]

Salt Range.—Hill system in the Jhelum, Shāhpur, and Miānwāli Districts of the Punjab, deriving its name from its extensive deposits of rock-salt, and extending from 32° 41′ to 32° 56′ N. and 71° 42′ to 73° E. It was known to the ancient historians as the Makhiālah hills and the Koh-i-Jūd. The main chain commences in the lofty hill of Chail, 3,701 feet above sea-level, which is formed by the convergence of three spurs cropping up from the Jhelum river, and divided from the Himālayan outliers only by the intervening river valley. The most northern of these spurs rises abruptly from the river bank at Sultānpur, and runs nearly parallel with the Jhelum at a distance of 25 miles, till it joins the main chain after a course of 40 miles. It bears the local name of the Nīli hills. The second spur, known as the Rohtās range, runs half-way between the Nīli hills and the river, parallel with both. It contains the fort of Rohtās, and the hill of Tilla in Jhelum District, 3,242 feet above sea-level. The third or Pabbi spur rises south of the Jhelum, dips for a while on approaching the river valley, and rises once more on the northern bank till it finally unites with the two other chains in the central peak of Chail. Thence the united range runs westward in two parallel ridges, till it culminates in the Sakesar hill, on which are the summer head-quarters of Shāhpur, Attock, and Miānwāli Districts, 5,010 feet above sea-level. Between these lines of hills, and topped by their highest summits, lies an elevated and fertile table-land, picturesquely intersected by ravines and peaks. In the midst nestles the beautiful lake of Kallar Kahār. The streams which take their rise in the table-land, however, become brackish before reaching the lowlands. From Jhelum District the Salt Range stretches into Shāhpur and Miānwāli. The long spur which projects into Shāhpur terminates in the hill of Sakesar, and comprises a number of separate rock-bound alluvial basins, the largest of which, the Sūn and Khabbakki valleys, occupy the northern half, while the south consists of a broken country, cut up into tiny glens and ravines by a network of limestone ridges and connecting spurs. In the northern portion of the range, the drainage gathers into small lakes, and trees stud the face of the country; but southward, the streams flow through barren and stony gorges, interspersed with detached masses of rock, and covered with the stunted alkaline plants which grow on soil impregnated with salt. The Miānwāli portion of the range runs north-westward towards the Indus, which it meets at Māri, opposite Kālābāgh, and rising again on the western side is continued in the Khattak-Maidāni hills. The scenery throughout the range is rugged and often sublime, but wanting in softness and beauty. In many parts it becomes simply barren and uninviting.

The beds of salt, from which the range derives its name, occur in the shape of solid rock on the slopes of this table-land, and form the largest known deposits in the world. The mineral is quarried at the MAYO MINES, in the neighbourhood of the village of Khewra, a few miles north-east of Pind Dādan Khān in Jhelum District, at NŪRPUR in Jhelum, at WĀRCHA in Shāhpur, and at KĀLĀBĀGH in Miānwāli District. Coal also occurs in the Salt Range both in oolite and Tertiary strata: the former at Kālābāgh, and the latter between Jalālpur and Pind Dādan Khān. It is of inferior quality, however, consisting of a brown lignite, difficult to burn and yielding a large proportion of ash. Besides salt and coal, other valuable minerals occur in these hills.

Few areas in India are of greater geological interest than the Salt Range, the sedimentary rocks in which have yielded fossils ranging from Cambrian to Tertiary, while the deposits of rock-salt constitute one of the most difficult problems with which the Indian geologist has to deal. A striking feature of the sedimentary beds is their marked variation in different parts of the range, and no single section affords a representative sequence. The following list of formations is compiled from a large number of sections seen in different localities:—

Conglomerates and sandstones (Siwālik) Sandstone and red clay (Nāhan or lower Siwālik)	Upper Tertiary.
Unconformity.	
Nummulitic limestone, underlain by shale, sandstone, and coal	Lower Tertiary.
Unconformity.	
Whitish sandstone	Lower Cretaceous.
Dark shales and limestone, with ammonites and belemnites	Jurassic.
Unconformity.	
Limestone with ceratites (upper ceratite limestone) Sandstone do. (ceratite sandstone) Marl do. (ceratite marl) Limestone do. (lower ceratite limestone)	Lower Trias.
Limestone with ammonites and brachiopods (Chidru group, or upper Productus limestone) Limestone with Xenaspis and brachiopods (Virgal group, or middle Productus limestone) Sandstone with brachiopods (Amb group, or lower Productus beds)	Upper Permian.
Lavender clay Speckled sandstone Olive sandstone Boulder-bed	Lower Permian, perhaps, in part, Upper Carboniferous.
Unconformity.	
Sandstone with pseudomorphs after salt (Salt pseudomorph zone) Magnesian sandstone Shales with *obolus* and trilobites	Cambrian.
Purple sandstone Red salt marl, with rock-salt and gypsum	Age unknown.

[The following publications of the Geological Survey of India may be consulted: *Records*, vols. xix, pt. 2; xxiv, pts. 1 and 4; xxv, pt. 1; *Memoirs*, vols. xiv, xvii, pt. 2; *Palaeontologia Indica*, Series xiii, vols. i, pts. 1–7; iv, pts. 1–2; and New Series i, pt. 1. Also *Neues Jahrbuch für Mineralogie, &c.*, 1896, Bd. ii, p. 61; and 1901, Bd. xiv, p. 369.]

Jumna (*Yamuna*; the *Diamouna* of Ptolemy, *Jomanes* of Pliny, and *Jobares* of Arrian).—A great river of Northern India. Rising in the Tehrī State (31° 1′ N., 78° 27′ E.), eight miles west of the lofty mountain Bandarpūnch (20,731 feet), it flows past the sacred shrine of Jamnotrī, and winds through the Outer Himālayas for eighty miles, receiving a few small streams. At the point where it passes into the Dūn, the valley between the Himālayas and the Siwāliks, it receives the Tons, which is there the larger stream. Its course now runs south-west for 22 miles, dividing the Kiarda Dūn (Punjab) from Dehra Dūn

(United Provinces); two large affluents, the Giri from Sirmūr on the west and the Asan from Dehra on the east, join it here. The Jumna pierces the Siwāliks 95 miles from its source, at Khārā, and divides Ambāla and Karnāl Districts in the Punjab from Sahāranpur and Muzaffarnagar in the United Provinces. It is a large river at Faizābād, where it gives off the WESTERN and EASTERN JUMNA CANALS. Near Bidhaulī in Muzaffarnagar it turns due south, and runs in that direction for 80 miles, dividing Meerut District from the Punjab, till it reaches Delhi. Ten miles below Delhi it gives off the AGRA CANAL from its western bank at Okhla. It then turns south-east for 27 miles to Dankaur, when it again resumes a southerly course. In this portion it receives on the east the Kotha Nadī and the HINDAN, and on the west the Sabī Nadī. Below Delhi the river forms the boundary between Gurgaon District in the Punjab and Bulandshahr and Alīgarh Districts in the United Provinces. It then enters Muttra and, crossing it, turns east till the borders of Agra are reached. Throughout its course in this District, where it receives the BĀNGANGĀ, and also in Etāwah, it winds in a remarkable manner, its bed lying deep between high banks which are furrowed by steep ravines. Just before Jālaun District is reached the great river CHAMBAL from Rājputāna joins it, and the Jumna then divides the three Districts of Cawnpore, Fatehpur, and Allahābād from Jālaun, Hamīrpur, and Bāndā. In Cawnpore District the Sengar, and in Fatehpur the Non and Rind, flow into it; close to Hamīrpur it receives the BETWĀ, and in Bāndā District the KEN. It finally falls into the GANGES below Allahābād, 860 miles from its source.

The Jumna, after issuing from the hills, has a longer course in the United Provinces than the Ganges; but it is not so large or important a stream, and does not carry as much water as is required by the canals taken from it. The supply is therefore increased from the Ganges by means of the cut into the HINDAN; and the Irrigation Commission (1901) recently proposed to make more water from the Ganges available by increasing the supply of the Lower Ganges Canal through a cut from the SĀRDĀ. The Jumna supplies drinking-water to the cities of Agra and Allahābād, which possesses, when fresh, special virtue in destroying the enteric microbe. It is crossed by railway bridges near Sarsāwā in Sahāranpur, at Delhi, Muttra, Agra, Kālpī (2,626 feet in width), and Allahābād (3,230 feet). The breadth of water-surface in the dry season varies from 2,600 feet at Okhla and 1,500 feet at Kālpī to 2,200 feet at

Allahābād. The discharge in flood at Okhla is about 41,000 cubic feet per second, but this dwindles away to less than 200 in the dry season. The Jumna drains a total area of about 118,000 square miles.

The traffic on the Jumna was formerly of some importance, and large sums were spent in clearing away reefs of *kankar* (nodular limestone) and conglomerate in Etāwah District. Before the opening of the East Indian Railway, much cotton grown in Bundelkhand was sent down the river from Kālpī. At present timber is carried down the upper portion, and stone and grain in the lower courses. The principal towns on or near its bank are: Delhi in the Punjab; and Bāghpat, Māt, Brindāban, Muttra, Mahāban, Agra, Fīrozābād, Batesar, Etāwah, Kālpī, Hamīrpur, and Allahābād in the United Provinces.

Chautang.—River in the Ambāla and Karnāl Districts of the Punjab, rising in the plains a few miles south of the SARASWATĪ, to which it runs parallel for a distance. Near Bālchhapar the two rivers apparently unite in the sands, but reappear in two distinct channels farther down, the Chautang running parallel to the Jumna, and then turning westward towards Hānsi and Hissār. The bed in this part of its course affords a channel for the Hissār branch of the Western Jumna Canal. Traces of the deserted waterway are visible as far as the GHAGGAR, which it formerly joined some miles below Bhatnair, after a course of about 260 miles; but the stream is now entirely diverted into the canal. In former days it lost itself in the sand, like others of the smaller cis-Sutlej rivers. Some authorities consider that the Chautang was originally an artificial channel. Cultivation extends along its banks in a few isolated patches, but for the most part a fringe of dense jungle lines its course.

Saraswatī.—River of the Punjab, rising in Sirmūr State close to the borders of Ambāla District. It debouches on the plains at Adh Badri, a place held sacred by all Hindus. A few miles farther on it disappears in the sand, but comes up again about three miles to the south at the village of Bhawānipur. At Bālchhapar it again vanishes for a short distance, but emerges once more and flows on in a south-westerly direction across Karnāl, until it joins the Ghaggar in Patiāla territory after a course of about 110 miles. A District canal takes off from it near Pehowa in Karnāl District. The word Saraswatī, the feminine of Saraswat, is the Sanskrit form of the Zend Haragaiti (Arachosia) and means 'rich in lakes.' The name was probably given to the river by the Aryan invaders in memory of the Haragaiti of Arachosia, the modern Helmand in Seistān.

Ghaggar.—A river of Northern India. It rises on the lower slopes of the Himālayas in the Native State of Sirmūr, in 30° 4′ N. and 77° 14′ E. Passing within three miles of Ambāla town and touching British territory, it traverses the Native State of Patiāla, where it receives the SARASWATĪ, enters Hissār District, and finally loses itself in Bīkaner territory near Hanumāngarh, formerly called Bhatnair. The river was once an affluent of the Indus, the dry bed of the old channel being still traceable. It is not a perennial stream, but depends on the monsoon rainfall for its supply. At present every village through which the stream passes in its upper course diverts a portion of its waters for irrigation, and no less than 10,000 acres in Ambāla District alone are supplied from this source. The dams thus erected check the course of the stream, while the consequent deposit of silt, greatly facilitated by the dams, has permanently diminished the power of the water to force its way across the dead level of the Karnāl or Patiāla plains. Near Jakhāl station on the Southern Punjab Railway a District canal, the Rangoi, takes off from the main stream, and irrigates an average of 12,000 acres annually. The Bīkaner Darbār constantly complained that the dams constructed in Hissār District prevented the water of the river from entering their territory; and in 1896 it was decided to construct a weir at the lower end of the Dhanūr lake at Otu, which supplies two canals, one on the north and the other on the south bank. The work was completed at a cost of 6 lakhs, of which the Bīkaner State contributed nearly half. The two canals are nearly 95 miles in length (51¼ miles in Bīkaner and about 43½ in British territory), and have more than 23 miles of distributaries. They form the most important irrigation works in the Bīkaner State, and have supplied about 10,000 acres annually since 1897–8.

The Ghaggar water, in or near the hills, when used for drinking, produces disastrous results, causing fever, enlarged spleen, and goitre; families are indeed said to die out in the fourth generation, and the villages along its banks are greatly under-populated. Only the prospect of obtaining exceptional returns for their labours can induce cultivators to settle in such an unhealthy region. During the lower portion of its course in Hissār District the bed of the river is dry from November to June, and yields excellent crops of wheat and rice. Even in the rains the water-supply is very capricious, and from time to time it fails entirely except in the immediate neighbourhood of the hills.

Sutlej (*Satlaj*; the *Zaradros* of Ptolemy and Arrian; the *Sutudri* or *Satadru* of the Vedas; 'flowing in a thousand channels').—One of the 'five rivers' of the Punjab from which the Province derives its name. Rising near the more westerly of the Mānasarowar Lakes in Tibet in 30° 20′ N. and 81° 25′ E., at a height of 15,200 feet, the Sutlej flows in a north-westerly direction along the southern slopes of the Kạilās mountains to the Chinese frontier outpost at Shipki. Here its elevation is 10,000 feet above the sea. Thence turning south-west by south it enters the Kanāwār valley in Bashahr State, receiving the waters of the Li or river of Spiti near Dāhlang. Its course in Kanāwār is 80 miles. After leaving that valley it flows west-south-west through deep gorges in the hills, separating the Sarāj *tahṣīl* of Kulū and Mandī State on the north from the Simla Hill States on the south. In this reach lie Rāmpur, the capital of Bashahr, and Bilāspur town. Then winding through Bilāspur State the Sutlej enters the Jaswān Dūn in Hoshiārpur, and turning suddenly south-east, past the town of Anandpur-Mākhowāl in that District, pierces the Siwāliks at Rūpar, after a course of 160 miles from the western extremity of Kanāwār. In the hills, the Sutlej is crossed by bridges at Wangtu, Rāmpur, Lohri, and Seoni. At Rūpar it takes a sudden bend to the west, and debouching upon the plains divides the Jullundur Doāb from the Sirhind plateau. At the south-west corner of Kapūrthala State (31° 11′ N. and 75° 4′ E.) the sluggish waters of the Bein and the broad stream of the Beās flow into the Sutlej. From this point the united stream preserves an almost uniform south-westerly course, dividing the Bāri Doāb to the north from the sandy plains of Ferozepore and Bahāwalpur to the south, until after receiving the Chenāb at Madwāla it joins the Indus at Mithankot in Muzaffargarh District. The total length of the river is 900 miles. In the plains it is fringed by a fertile lowland valley, confined on either side by high banks leading to the naturally barren table-lands that form the watersheds of the Rāvi to the north and the Jumna to the south. The lower valley of the Sutlej is less fertile, and closely resembles the deserts of Rājputāna. As soon as it enters the plains the river is robbed of half its waters by the SIRHIND CANAL, which takes off at Rūpar from the southern bank of the river, and irrigates large tracts in Ludhiāna and Ferozepore Districts and the adjacent Native States. Soon after the Beās joins the Sutlej, the UPPER

Sutlej system of inundation canals takes off from its northern bank to irrigate parts of Lahore and Montgomery Districts. Finally, the Lower Sutlej Canals draw off most of the remaining water to irrigate the rainless tracts of south-west Multān. The river is open to small craft all the year round, but there is little traffic above Ferozepore. It is bridged by the North-Western Railway at Phillaur, Kasūr, and Adamwāhan in Bahāwalpur.

After it leaves the hills the river is never called Sutlej by the people, and it has changed its course more than once in historical times. The history of those changes can be traced with considerable probability and detail. In the time of Arrian, the Sutlej found an independent outlet into the Rann of Cutch. In the year A.D. 1000 it was a tributary of the Hakra, and flowed in the Eastern Nāra. Thence the former bed can be traced back through Bahāwalpur and Bīkaner into the Sirsa *tahsīl* of Hissār, until it is lost near Tohāna. From Tohāna to Rūpar this old bed cannot be traced; but it is known that the Sutlej took a southerly course at Rūpar, instead of turning west, as now, to join the Beās. Thus the Sutlej or the Hakra —for both streams flowed in the same bed—is probably the lost river of the Indian desert, whose waters made the sands of Bīkaner and Sind a smiling garden. By 1245 the Sutlej had taken a more northerly course, the Hakra had dried up, and a great migration took place of the people of the desert—as it thus became—to the Indus valley. The course then taken by the Sutlej was apparently a continuation of the present course of the Ghaggar. About 1593 the Sutlej left the Ghaggar and went north once more. The Beās came south to meet it, and the two flowed in the same channel under various names—Machhu Wah, Hariāni, Dand, Nūrni, Nīli, and Gharah. Then the Sutlej once more returned to its old course and rejoined the Ghaggar. It was only in 1796 that the Sutlej again left the Ghaggar and finally joined the Beās.

Beās (*Hyphasis* of the Greeks; *Arjikūja* of the Vedas; Sanskrit *Vipāsa*).—One of the 'five rivers' of the Punjab from which the Province derives its name. Rising on the southern face of the Rohtang pass in Kulū, 13,326 feet above the sea, the Beās traverses the State of Mandī and enters Kāngra District at Sanghol, 1,920 feet above sea-level. During the early part of its course the fall averages 125 feet per mile. A fine suspension bridge spans the river at Mandī town, and a bridge of boats is kept up during the cold season at Dera Gopipur in Kāngra District. During its lower hill course the Beās is crossed by numerous ferries, at many of which the means of communication consists of inflated skins (*darais*). Lower down it meanders in a westerly course through hilly country, with a fall of 7 feet to the mile, and forms the main channel for the drainage of Kāngra. Near Reh in that District it divides into three channels, which reunite after passing Mirthal, 1,000 feet above sea-level. On meeting the Siwālik Hills in Hoshiārpur, the river sweeps sharply northward, forming the boundary between that District and Kāngra. Then bending round the base of the Siwāliks, it takes a southerly direction, separating the Districts of Hoshiārpur and Gurdāspur. In this portion of its course through the uplands of the Punjab plains, a strip of low alluvial soil fringes its banks, subject in floodtime to inundation from the central stream. The main channel is broad and ill-defined, full of islands and expanding from time to time into wide pools. The depth does not exceed 5 feet in the dry season, increasing to 15 feet during the rains. Broad flat-bottomed country boats navigate this portion of the stream throughout the year. No bridges span the Beās in the Districts of Hoshiārpur or Gurdāspur. After touching Jullundur District for a few miles, the river forms the boundary between Amritsar and the Kapūrthala State. At Beās station it is crossed by a railway bridge on the North-Western Railway; and a bridge of boats on the grand trunk road is also maintained there during the cold season. The channel shifts from year to year through the alluvial valley according to the action of the floods. Finally, the Beās joins the Sutlej at the south-western boundary of the Kapūrthala State, after a total course of 290 miles. It ranks sixth in size among the rivers of the Punjab.

The chief tributaries are the Chakki and the Bein. The Chakki collects the drainage of the Chamba hills and its main stream joins the Beās near Mirthal, while the other branch, formerly a tributary of the Rāvi, has been turned aside by the Bāri Doāb Canal and forced to return to the Beās lower down. The Bein—called the 'Black' (*siyāh*) Bein to distinguish it from the 'White' (*safed*) Bein—rises in the Siwāliks, and joins the Beās 10 miles above its junction with the Sutlej.

The old course of the Beās can be traced from its present point of junction with the Sutlej through Lahore and Montgomery Districts to the place where it used to join the Chenāb, near Shujābād, before the Chenāb turned westwards. The united waters of the Jhelum, Chenāb, and Rāvi joined the Beās in those days 28 miles south of Multān. Since the end of the eighteenth century the course of the Beās has changed but little.

Rāvi (the *Hydraotes* of Arrian, the *Parushni* of the Vedas, and the *Irāvati* of classical Sanskrit authors. The present name means 'sun').—One of the 'five rivers' of the Punjab from which the Province derives its name. Rising in the Kulū subdivision of Kāngra District, it immediately passes into the Chamba State, after which it re-enters British territory on the borders of Gurdāspur District, opposite Basoli in the Jammu district of Kashmīr, forming the boundary of that State for 25 miles, with a general south-westerly course. It leaves the hills at Shāhpur, but still flows between high cliffs, while on the Jammu side the mountains rise from its very brink. At Mādhopur, the head-works of the Bāri Doāb Canal draw off a large portion of its waters. Thenceforward the banks sink in height, and the river assumes the usual character of the Punjab streams, flowing in the centre of an alluvial valley, with high outer banks at some distance from its present bed. In 1870 it carried away the Tāli Sāhib shrine near Dera Nānak, a place of great sanctity with the Sikhs, and still threatens that town. The Rāvi next passes between Siālkot and Amritsar Districts, preserving its general south-westerly direction. The depth here is not more than a foot in March and April, swelling in June and September to 18 or 20 feet. Entering the District of Lahore, it runs within a mile of Lahore city, and throws out several branches which soon, however, rejoin the parent stream. A railway and foot-bridge spans the river a few miles north of Lahore, and the grand trunk road crosses it by a bridge of boats. After entering Montgomery District it receives its chief tributary, the Degh, on its north-western bank. The Degh rises in Jammu and flows through Siālkot and Lahore Districts, bringing with it large deposits of silt and affording great facilities for irrigation by wells. The Rāvi then passes into Multān District, where it is again bridged by the North-Western Railway near Sidhnai, and finally falls into the Chenāb in 30° 31′ N. and 71° 51′ E., after a total course of about 450 miles.

Throughout its course in the plains, the Rāvi flows everywhere in a comparatively narrow valley, often only a couple of miles in width, with generally a very tortuous channel. In one part, however, the river runs a perfectly straight course for 12 miles from Kuchlumba to Sarai Sidhu in Multān District, between high wooded banks, forming a beautiful reach called the Sidhnai, where the SIDHNAI CANAL takes off. Few islands are formed, but the bed shifts occasionally from place to place. The floods of the Rāvi fertilize only a fringe of one or two miles on either side, and it is little employed for direct irrigation, although it supplies water to the Bāri Doāb and Sidhnai Canals. Navigation is difficult, but grain is shipped from Lahore in considerable quantities. *Deodār* timber, floated down in rafts from the Chamba forests during the rains, only finds its way to Lahore in seasons of heavy flood. In 1397 the Rāvi still flowed east and south of Multān and united with the Beās, as it did in the time of Chach (A.D. 800). The change of course northwards has been comparatively slight, and its date is uncertain. Even now, at times of high flood, the water finds its way to Multān by the old channel.

Chenāb (the *Acesines* of the Greeks and *Asikni* of the Vedas).—River in Kashmīr and the Punjab, and one of the 'five rivers' from which the Punjab derives its name. It rises in the Himālayan canton of Lāhul in two streams: the Chandra, which issues from a large snow-bed on the south-east side of the Bāra Lācha at a height of 16,221 feet; and the Bhāga, which rises on the north-west slopes of the pass. The Chandra, after flowing south-east for 55 miles, sweeps round the base of the mid-Himālayas and joins the Bhāga at Tandi, after a total course of 115 miles. The course of the Bhāga to Tandi is only 65 miles, its average fall being 125 feet per mile. The united stream, now known as the Chandra-Bhāga or Chenāb, flows through the Pāngi valley in Chamba State and then enters the Padar district of Kashmīr at an elevation of 6,000 feet. Thence for 180 miles it flows between steep cliffs of the high mountains, and then for 25 miles through the lower hills to Akhnūr, where it becomes navigable. There are three remarkable bends in the Chenāb. Where it reaches Kishtwār from a north-west course it suddenly twists due south; at Jangalwār it tacks from south to west; and at Arnas it leaves its westerly course and flows due south past Riāsi to Akhnūr. At each of these turns the Chenāb is joined by a stream of considerable size, and at every change of course the river seems to cut through the mountain range along which it had been flowing.

The chief tributaries in its passage through Kishtwār, Bhadrawār, and Jammu are the Uniar and Shudi, and the Bhutna and Māru Wardwan rivers. Between Kishtwār and Akhnūr it receives the waters of the Golan Lar and Lidar Kol, and the Bichlari and Ans, and between Riāsi and the western boundary of Jammu it is joined by the Tāwi. There are several bridges, two of which, on the routes from Jammu to Kashmīr and from Kashmīr to Kishtwār respectively, are of a superior description. The rest are of the primitive *jhūla* type—three ropes stretched across the stream in the form of a triangle.

The Chenāb re-enters the Punjab at Khairi Rīhāl in Siālkot District. The Tāwi joins it almost at once, and the first place of importance in British territory is Wazīrābād, where the Alexandra Bridge carries the North-Western Railway across the river. Throughout its course in the plains the river flows in a wide and shifting bed of sand. A few miles south-west of Wazīrābād the main branch of the LOWER CHENĀB CANAL takes off at Khānki; and thence the river flows on greatly diminished in bulk, dividing the Chaj Doāb on the west from the Rechna Doāb on the east, until the Jhelum joins it in Jhang District at Trimmu. Thence the two rivers flow under the name of the Chenāb, till joined by the Rāvi near Sidhu and the Sutlej at Madwāla. The North-Western Railway crosses it again at Sher Shāh. Thence it flows on under the name of the PANJNAD, to join the Indus at Mithankot. Small boats can navigate the river in the plains all the year round, but there is little traffic above Chiniot.

There is evidence to show that the Chenāb flowed to the east of Multān as late as A.D. 1245. The Beās then occupied its old bed, passing Dipālpur; and the Jhelum, Chenāb, and the Rāvi met north-east of Multān, and flowing to the east of that city joined the Beās 28 miles south of it and east of Uch. Thus Multān and Uch were both in the Sind-Sāgar Doāb. By 1397 the Chenāb had altered its course westward and was flowing to the west of Multān, as it still does. The part of the river which divides the modern District of Gujrāt from Gujrānwāla was known to the Muhammadan historians as the Sūdharā (SODHRA), from the town of that name on its left bank.

Bhimbar.—Torrent in Gujrāt District, Punjab. Rising in the second Himālayan range, it drains a considerable valley within the mountain region, passes round the Pabbi hills, runs due south for 25 miles, and fertilizes a low fringe of land upon its banks. Four miles north-west of Gujrāt town it loses itself in the surface of the country, moistening and enriching the surrounding plain; it collects again near the village of Hariālwāla, and runs north-west until it reaches the Jalālia nullah, a branch of the Chenāb. The Bhimbar is an unmanageable stream during the rains, but completely dry in the winter months, leaving its bed a broad waste of sand. It is fordable at all points, except for some hours after heavy rains in the hills.

Jhelum (*Jehlam*).—River of Kashmīr and the Punjab, being the most westerly of the 'five rivers' from which the Punjab derives its name. It was known to the Muhammadan historians as the Bihat, Wihat, or Bihatah, corruptions of its Sanskrit name *Vitastā* (which Alexander's historians graecized into *Hydaspes*, but Ptolemy more correctly as *Bidaspes*), while its modern Kashmīrī name is *Veth*. It may be said to have its source in a noble spring of deep-blue water which issues from the bottom of a high scarp of a mountain spur. The spring is known as Vernāg; and at Khānabal, 15 miles north, its waters join the streams of Adpat, Bring, and Sandran, and form the starting-point of navigation. The river is navigable without a single lock from Khānabal to Bāramūla, 102 miles. In its course to the Wular Lake, which may be regarded as a delta of the river, the fall is 165 feet in the first 30 miles and 55 feet in the next 24 miles. From the Wular Lake to Bāramūla the fall is very slight.

The Jhelum river has many tributaries. On its right bank it receives the Liddar or Lambodri, which comes down from the everlasting snows overhanging the head of the Liddar valley, and from the mountain lake of Tarsar. Below Srīnagar at Shādīpur—the 'place of the marriage' of the two rivers—the Sind river joins the Jhelum, and beyond the Wular Lake the Pohru stream, which drains the Lolāb valley, merges in the great river. On the left bank the chief tributaries are the Vishav, Rembiara, Ramshi, Dudgangā, Suknāg, and Ferozepura. The Dudgangā joins the Jhelum at the lower end of Srīnagar city.

Below Bāramūla (5,000 feet) the placid Jhelum leaves the fertile banks of the valley, and rushes headlong down a deep gorge between lofty mountains of the Kazināg range on the north and an extension of the Pīr Panjāl on the south to Kohāla, 2,000 feet. At Muzaffarābād the Kishangangā river joins the Jhelum on its right bank, while a few miles lower down, and on the same side, the Kunhār river, which drains the Hazāra country, adds no inconsiderable volume of water. Between Khānabal and Bāramūla there are many bridges, but between Bāramūla and Domel, where the Kishangangā joins the Jhelum, the bridges are scarce and primitive. Much of the internal commerce of Kashmīr depends on the Jhelum. An account of the various descriptions of boats used will be found in the article on SRĪNAGAR.

Below its junction with the Kishangangā the Jhelum forms the boundary between Kashmīr State and the British Districts of Hazāra and Rāwalpindi, flowing in a narrow rocky bed, shut in by mountains on either side. Numerous rapids here render navigation impossible, though large quantities of timber are floated down from Kashmīr. A handsome suspension bridge at Kohāla, in Rāwalpindi District, connects Kashmīr with British territory. Below Dangalli, 40 miles east of Rāwalpindi, the Jhelum becomes navigable. Passing into Jhelum District, it skirts the outlying spurs of the Salt Range, receiving the waters of the Kahan, and finally debouches upon the plains a little above the town of Jhelum, about 250 miles from its source. Below Jhelum inundation of the lowlands begins to be possible, and low sandy islands stud the wide bed of the stream. The Bunhā, in the rains a roaring torrent which sometimes spreads over a mile of country, joins the Jhelum at Dārāpur. After a south-westerly course of more than 100 miles, during which the river divides the District of Jhelum from Gujrāt and Shāhpur, it enters the latter District entirely, and trends thenceforth more directly southward. The width in this portion of its course averages 800 yards in flood, dwindling during the winter months to less than half that width. Sudden freshes occur after heavy rains, and cause frequent inundations over the lowlands, greatly increasing the productive power of the soil. The Jhelum next enters the District of Jhang, where it preserves the same general characteristics, but with a wider valley, bounded by the high uplands known as the Bār. It finally joins the Chenāb at Trimmu, in 31° 11′ N. and 72° 12′ E., 10 miles to the south of Maghiāna, after a total course of not less than 450 miles, of which about 200 lie within British territory. The current in the plains has an average rate of 4 miles per hour. The wedge of land between the Jhelum and the Chenāb is known as the Chaj Doāb; while the tract stretching westward to the Indus bears the name of the Sind-Sāgar Doāb.

The principal towns upon the Jhelum are Kashmīr or Srīnagar, Jhelum, Pind Dādan Khān, Miāni, Bhera, and Khushāb. According to General Cunningham, the point where Alexander crossed the Hydaspes may be identified with Jalālpur in Jhelum District; while nearly opposite, on the Gujrāt bank, stands the modern battle-field of Chiliānwāla. Other writers hold that the passage was effected near Jhelum town. A bridge of boats crosses the river at Khushāb. The permanent railway bridge of the North-Western Railway also crosses it at the town of Jhelum, and the Sind-Sāgar line at Haranpur. The LOWER JHELUM CANAL takes off at Mong Rasūl in Gujrāt District.

Panjnad.—River in the Punjab, formed by the united waters of the SUTLEJ, BEĀS, RĀVI, CHENĀB, and JHELUM. Its length is 44 miles to the junction with the Indus.

Indus (Sanskrit, *Sindhu*; Greek, *Sinthos*; Latin, *Sindus*).—The great river of North-Western India. The Indus rises in Tibet, and then flows through Kashmīr, the Frontier Province, and the Punjab, and after a final course through Sind falls into the Arabian Sea in 23° 58′ N. and 67° 30′ E. The drainage basin of the Indus is estimated at 372,700 square miles, and its total length at a little over 1,800 miles. The towns of importance on or near its banks in British territory are, beginning from the south: Karāchi, Kotri, Hyderābād, Sehwān, Sukkur, Rohri, Mithankot, Dera Ghāzi Khān, Dera Ismail Khān, Miānwāli, Kālābāgh, Khushālgarh, and Attock.

Course in Tibet and Kashmīr.

The first section of the course of the Indus lies outside British territory, and must be briefly dealt with here. The river rises, as above stated, in Tibet (32° N. and 81° E.) behind the great mountain wall of the Himālayas, which forms the northern boundary of India, and is said to spring from the north side of the sacred Kailās mountain (22,000 feet), the Elysium of ancient Sanskrit literature. Issuing from the ring of lofty mountains about Lake Mānasarowar, whence also the Sutlej, the Brahmaputra, and the Kauriālā spring, it flows north-west for about 160 miles under the name of Singh-ka-bāb, until it receives the Ghar river on its south-western bank. A short distance below the junction of the Ghar, the Indus, which is supposed to have an elevation of 17,000 feet at its source, enters the south-eastern corner of Kashmīr at an elevation of 13,800 feet, flowing slowly over a long flat of alluvium. Following a steady north-by-west course it skirts Leh at a height of 10,500 feet and drops to 8,000 feet in Baltistān, just before it receives the waters of the Shyok river. At Leh it is joined by the Zāskār river, and is crossed by the great trade route into Central Asia via the Karakoram Pass. Early travellers like Dr. Thomson and Mr. Blane have described this portion of the Indus. The former found numerous hot springs, some of them with a temperature of 174° and exhaling a sulphurous gas. Still flowing north, but more westerly, through Kashmīr territory, it passes near Skārdu in Baltistān, and reaches the Haramosh mountain (24,300 feet) in about 34° 50′ N. and 74° 30′ E. Here it takes a turn southwards

Kashmīr.

at an acute angle, and passing beneath the Hattu Pīr, at an elevation of 4,000 feet, enters Kohistān in the Dīr, Swāt, and Chitrāl Agency near Gur. The steepness of its fall varies, now becoming greater, now less. This inequality of slope has been connected with the changes that occurred in the glacial period from the damming of the river by huge glaciers and the formation of great thicknesses of lacustrine deposit. The Indus has been the cause of serious and disastrous floods; the rapid stream dashes down gorges and wild mountain valleys; and in its lower and more level course it is swept by terrific blasts. Even in summer, when it is said to dwindle down to a fordable depth during the night, it may during the course of the day swell into an impassable torrent from the melting of the snows on the adjoining heights. Opposite Skārdu in Baltistān it is, even in the depth of winter, a grand stream, often more than 500 feet wide and 9 or 10 feet in depth. After leaving Gur, it flows for about 120 miles south-west through the wilds of Kohistān, until it enters the North-West Frontier Province (35° 25′ N. and 73° 51′ E.), near Darband, at the western base of the Mahāban mountain. The only point to which special allusion can be made in the long section of its course beyond British territory is the wonderful gorge by which the river bursts through the western ranges of the Himālayas. This gorge is near Skārdu, and is said to be 14,000 feet in sheer descent.

In the Punjab and the Frontier Province.

The Indus, on entering the Hazāra District of the North-West Frontier Province, 812 miles from its source, is about 100 yards wide in August, navigable by rafts, but of no great depth, and studded with sandbanks and islands. It is fordable in many places during the cold season; but floods or freshes are sudden, and Ranjīt Singh is said to have lost a force, variously stated at from 1,200 to 7,000 horsemen, in crossing the river. Even the large and solid ferry-boats which ply upon it are sometimes swept away. Almost opposite Attock it receives the Kābul river, which brings down the waters of Afghānistān. The two rivers have about an equal volume; both are very swift, and broken up with rocks. Their junction during floods is the scene of a wild confusion of waters. The Kābul river is navigable for about 40 miles above the confluence, but a rapid just above it renders the Indus impracticable. Attock, the limit of the upward navigation of the Indus, forms the first important point on the river within British territory. By this time it has flowed upwards of 860 miles, or nearly one-half of its total length, its further course to the sea being about

940 miles. It has fallen from an elevation of 17,000 feet at its source in Tibet to about 2,000 feet, the height of Attock being 2,079 feet. In the hot season, opposite the fort, its velocity is 13 miles an hour; and in the cold season, 5 to 7 miles. The rise of ordinary floods is from 5 to 7 feet in twenty-four hours, and the maximum is 50 feet above cold-season level. Its width varies greatly with the season—at one time being more than 250 yards, at another less than 100. The Indus is crossed at Attock by the railway bridge opened in 1883, a bridge of boats, and a ferry. The main trunk road to Peshāwar also crosses the river by a subway on the railway bridge.

After leaving Attock, the Indus flows almost due south, forming the western boundary of the Punjab, parallel to the Sulaimān Hills. The great north road from Bannu to Sind runs for several hundred miles parallel with its western bank; and from Attock to Mahmūd Kot the Māri-Attock, Māri, and Sind-Sāgar branches of the North-Western Railway run along its eastern bank. Twelve miles below Attock the Indus receives the waters of the Haroh, a rapid stream which, rising in the Murree hills as the Dhānd, meets the Karrāl coming down from the Mochpuri peak, and rushes through steep banks for a total course of 90 miles. At Makhad, the Sohān brings in all the drainage of Rāwalpindi and Jhelum Districts that is not taken by the Jhelum river. The Indus forms the eastern border of the two frontier Districts of Dera Ismail Khān in the North-West Frontier Province and Dera Ghāzi Khān in the Punjab with the Sind-Sāgar Doāb on its eastern bank, and only a narrow strip of British territory between it and the hill tribes of the Sulaimān ranges on the west. Just above Mithankot, in the south of Dera Ghāzi Khān District, it receives the accumulated waters of the Punjab. Between the Indus and the Jumna flow the five great streams from which the Punjab (Panj-āb, literally 'The five waters') takes its name. These are the JHELUM, the CHENĀB, the RĀVI, the BEĀS, and the SUTLEJ. After various junctions these unite to form the river PANJNAD, literally 'The five streams,' which marks for a short space the boundary between British territory and the Bahāwalpur State, and unites with the Indus near Mithankot, about 490 miles from the sea. In the cold season the breadth of the Indus above the confluence is about 600 yards, its velocity 5 miles an hour, its depth from 12 to 15 feet, and its estimated discharge 10,000 to 25,000 cubic feet per second. During flood-times the breadth sometimes increases to 5 miles, and the discharge to 1,000,000 cubic feet per second. The dimensions of the Panjnad above the point of junction are somewhat less than those of the Indus during the cold season, but during the monsoon floods they are almost as large. The whole course of the Indus through the Punjab is broken by islands and sandbanks; but beautiful scenery is afforded along its banks, which abound with the date, acacia, pomegranate, and other trees.

In Sind. Mithankot has an elevation of only 258 feet above the level of the sea. From Mithankot the Indus forms the boundary between the Punjab and Bahāwalpur State, until, near Kashmor, it enters Sind in 28° 26′ N. and 69° 47′ E. From Bukkur (in Sind) to the sea the river is known familiarly among the Sindīs as the Daryā ('the river'). Pliny writes of *Indus incolis Sindus appellatus*. It first touches Sind close to Kashmor town in the Upper Sind Frontier District, separating it from the Bahāwalpur State and Sukkur District. Formerly in years of high inundation its floods reached Jacobābād, finding their way thence into the Manchhar Lake. To prevent this, the Kashmor embankment, which is the largest in Sind, was erected. Leaving Kashmor the river crosses Sukkur, divides Lārkāna and Karāchi from the Khairpur State and Hyderābād District, finally emptying itself by many mouths into the Arabian Sea near Karāchi after a south-western course of 450 miles through Sind. It ranges in width from 480 to 1,600 yards, the average during the low season being 680 yards. During the floods it is in places more than a mile wide. Its depth varies from 4 to 24 feet. The water, derived from the snows of the Himālayas, is of a dirty brown colour, and slightly charged with saline ingredients, carbonate of soda, and nitrate of potash. Its velocity in the freshes averages 8 miles per hour; at ordinary times 4 miles. The discharge per second varies between a minimum of 19,000 and a maximum of 820,000 cubic feet. On an average the temperature of the water is 10° lower than that of the air. Near the station of Sukkur and again at Kotri the river is spanned by a fine railway bridge. The Sukkur bridge was opened in 1889, and resembles the Forth Bridge in having a central girder with a span of 200 feet, supported at the ends of two cantilever arms, each 310 feet long. The Indus begins to rise in March, attains its maximum depth and width in August, and subsides in September. The maximum rise registered at Kotri, near Hyderābād, was 22 feet 7 inches in 1894. There are many other gauges on the river.

The delta of the Indus covers an area of about 3,000 square miles, and extends along the coast-line for 125 miles. It is almost a perfect level, and nearly destitute of timber, the tamarisk and mangrove alone supplying fuel. In these respects the delta is similar to that of the Nile, but dissimilar to that of the Ganges. The marshy portions contain good pasturage, and rice grows luxuriantly wherever cultivation is possible; but the soil generally is not fertile, being a mixture of sand and clay. In the Shāhbandar *tāluka* are immense deposits of salt. The climate of the delta is cool and bracing in the winter months, hot in the summer, and during the floods most unhealthy. **The Indus delta.**

The Indus formerly flowed down the middle of the THAL. Basira, a village in the centre of the Muzaffargarh Thal, was called Bet Basira; and at Shāhgarh, near the southern end of the Thal, a long lake is still extant which once formed the Indus bed. In 1800 the river at the apex of the delta divided into two main streams, known as the Baghiār and Sītā; but in 1837 it had entirely deserted the former channel. The Khedewāri passage also, which before 1819 was the highway of water traffic to Shāhbandar, was in that year closed by an earthquake. In 1837 the Kakaiwāri, which had then increased from a shallow creek to a river with an average width at low water of 770 yards, was recognized as the highway; but before 1867 this also was completely blocked. In 1897 the river suddenly cut 3 miles inland, north of Rohri, destroying the cultivated fields and the Mando-Dahiro road. Tando Nijābat on the right bank and Mithani on the left have been swept away four times and rebuilt farther off. For the present the Hajāmro, which before 1845 was navigable only by the smallest boats, is the main estuary of the Indus. The shape of the Hajāmro is that of a funnel, with the mouth to the sea; on the east side of the entrance is a beacon 95 feet high, visible for 2 miles; and two well-manned pilot boats lie inside the bar to point out the difficulties of navigation. **Changes in the river course.**

The following facts illustrate further the shifting nature of the Indus. In 1845 Ghorābāri, then the chief commercial town of the delta, was on the river bank; but in 1848 the river deserted its bed. The town of Keti was built on the new bank. The new bank overflowed a few years later, and a second Keti had to be built farther off. At present one of the chief obstructions to navigation is a series of rocks between Tatta and Bhimān-jo-pura, which, in 1846, were 8 miles inland. In 1863 a thousand acres of the Dhāreja forest were swept away. The rapidity and extent of the destructive action in constant progress in the delta may be estimated from the fact that travellers have counted by the reports as many as thirteen bank slips in a minute. In some places the elephant grass (*Typha elephantina*) does good service by driving its roots very deeply (often 9 feet) into the ground, and thereby holding it together.

Inundations and irrigation. The entire course of the Indus in British territory, from Attock to the sea, lies within the zone of deficient rainfall, the annual average being nowhere higher than 10 inches. Cultivation, therefore, is absolutely dependent upon artificial irrigation, almost to as great an extent as in the typical example of Egypt. But the Indus is a less manageable river than the Nile. Its main channel is constantly shifting; at only three places—Sukkur, Jerruck, and Kotri—are the river banks permanent; and during the season of flood the melted snows of the Himālayas come down in an impetuous torrent which no embankment can restrain. From time immemorial this annual inundation, which is to Sind what the monsoons are to other parts of India, has been utilized as far as possible by an industrious peasantry, who lead the water over their fields by countless artificial channels. Many such channels, constructed in the days of native rule, extend 30 and even 40 miles from the river bank. Recently the systematic schemes of British engineers have added numerous perennial canals, such as the Jāmrao, constructed on scientific principles. The first recorded inundation of the Indus took place in 1833; another occurred in 1841 on a much larger scale. This flood was said to have been caused by the bursting of a glacier which formed over an accumulation of water in the Nubra Tso, into which there was a regular and steady flow from the surrounding hills. Eventually, the glacier was burst asunder by the pressure, and the released floods poured down the Shyok valley, carrying everything before them. There was another great flood in August, 1858, when the river rose 90 feet in a few hours, and the greater part of the private property in Naushahra cantonment was destroyed. Lower down in its course considerable damage has been caused in DERA GHĀZI KHĀN DISTRICT, where protective works were undertaken. Of recent years the Indus has been embanked from above Kashmor to the mouth of the Begāri canal, a distance of more than 50 miles. The embankment has proved a great protection to the North-Western Railway, which here runs at right angles to the river.

Principal canals. A full account of irrigation in SIND will be found in the article on that Province. It must suffice in this place to give a list of the principal works, following the Indus downwards from the Punjab. The country has recently been surveyed with a view to a canal being led from Kālābāgh down the Sind-Sāgar Doāb, but the difficulties in the way are at present considerable. The waters of the river are first utilized on a large scale in the INDUS INUNDATION CANALS, which water a narrow strip between the Indus and the Sulaimān mountains. The canals in this tract have an aggregate length of 690 miles, of which 108 have been constructed under British rule. In Muzaffargarh District the MUZAFFARGARH CANALS take off from the Indus and Chenāb, and in the Native State of Bahāwalpur the Chenāb and Sutlej, as well as the Indus, contribute to render cultivation possible. In Sind the following are the chief canal systems:—on the right or west bank, the Desert, Unar Wah, Begāri, Sukkur, Ghar, and Western Nāra; on the left or east, the Nāra Supply Channel, Mahi Wah, JĀMRAO, a branch of the Eastern Nāra, and the EASTERN NĀRA with many distributaries, the principal being the Mithrao and Pinjāri. Other important canals are the Fuleli with two mouths, the Nasrat, and the Dād. The total area irrigated by canals from the Indus in 1903–4 was:—in the Punjab, 714 square miles; in Sind, 4,925 square miles.

Navigation.

As a channel of navigation, the Indus has disappointed the expectations that were at one time formed. Before British arms had conquered Sind and the Punjab, it was hoped that the fabled wealth of Central Asia might be brought by this course down to the sea. But, even so far as local traffic is concerned, experience has proved in this case, as with most other Indian rivers, that the cheapness of water communication cannot compete with the superior speed and certainty of railways. Since the opening of the Indus Valley State Railway (now included in the North-Western system) in the autumn of 1878, navigation on the Indus, whether by steamer or by native boat, has greatly fallen off. The general character of the Indus trade may be inferred from the statistics of imports and exports into the PUNJAB by 'rail and river,' which refer only to traffic borne in part or wholly on the Indus. The original 'Indus Flotilla,' which was broken up in 1862, placed its first steamer on the river in 1835. In 1859 a company established another Indus flotilla in connexion with the Sind Railway, with which it was formally amalgamated in 1870, the joint head-quarters being removed to Lahore. The railway flotilla was abolished in 1882–3. These were not the only flotilla experiments on the Indus. In 1856 the Oriental Inland Steam Company obtained a yearly subsidy of Rs. 50,000 from Government; but, as the current proved too powerful for its steamers, the company stopped the traffic, and eventually collapsed.

For the conservancy of the lower part of the river, Act I of 1863 (Bombay) provides for the registration of vessels, and the levy of pilotage fees by an officer called the Conservator and Registrar of the Indus, the sum realized being expended on the improvement of navigation[1]. A special export board, known as the Indus Commission, was constituted in 1901.

The boats of the Indus are the *dundo* and *zaurak*, both cargo-boats, the *kauntal*, or ferry-boats, and the *dundi*, or fishing-boats. The cargo-boats are sometimes of 60 tons burden, and when laden draw 4 feet of water. The state barges or *jhamptis* of the Sind Mīrs were built of teak, four-masted, and sometimes required crews of thirty men.

Fish.

Fish abound. At the mouths, the salt-water varieties include the *Clupea neowhii*, a species of herring largely consumed along the coast and in the delta. The chief of the fresh-water varieties are the *palla*, placed by Dr. Day under the *Clupeidae*, and nearly allied to, if not identical with, the *hilsa* of the Ganges; and the *dambhro*. The local consumption and also the export of dried *palla* are very large. Otters, turtles, porpoises, water-snakes, and crocodiles of both species are numerous.

[*Notes on the Indus River* (Karāchi, 1901).]

Jumna Canal, Western.—An important perennial irrigation work in the Punjab, taking off from the west bank of the river Jumna, and irrigating Ambāla, Karnāl, Hissār, Rohtak, and Delhi Districts, and parts of the Native States of Patiāla and Jīnd. It is by far the oldest of the great canals in the Province, and originated in 1356, when Fīroz Shāh III utilized the torrent-bed now known as the Chautang to conduct water to the royal gardens at Hissār and Hānsi. This was little more than a monsoon supply-channel, and after about a hundred years water ceased to flow farther than the lands of Kaithal. In 1568 the emperor Akbar re-excavated the work of Fīroz Shāh and brought a supply from the Jumna and the Somb into the Chautang, and so on to Hānsi and Hissār. This was undoubtedly a perennial canal, as is testified by the ancient bridges at Karnāl and Safīdon, and the complete set of water-courses with which the canal was provided, besides the original *sanad* or working-plan of the canal which is still in existence

[1] The Indus Conservancy department and fees levied for its up-keep were abolished in March, 1906.

and promises a supply of water all the year round. A yet more ambitious scheme was undertaken in 1626 by Alī Mardān Khān, the engineer of the emperor Shāh Jahān. The river supply in the western branch of the Jumna was dammed up annually about 14 miles below the present head-works of the canal, and the water led along the drainage line at the foot of the highland through Pānīpat and Sonepat to Delhi. Drainages and escapes were fairly well provided for; and the Pulchaddar aqueduct, which took the canal across the Najafgarh *jhīl* drain near Delhi, was, for the time, a great engineering feat, and was retained, with slight modifications, when the branch was reopened in 1819. The net revenue from the canal was reckoned equal to the maintenance of 12,000 horse. With the decay of the Delhi empire the up-keep of the canal was no longer attended to: water ceased to reach Hānsi and Hissār in 1707, the flow on Fīroz Shāh's line at Safīdon ceased in 1720, and the Delhi branch ceased to flow in 1753–60. The Delhi branch was reopened in 1819, and the Hānsi branch in 1825. The alignment of the canal was, however, by no means satisfactory; and as early as 1846 it was noticed that the concentrated irrigation, the defective drainage, and the high banks which cut off the flow of the natural drainage of the country, all contributed to rapid deterioration of the soil and decline in health of the people. Saline efflorescence was rapidly spreading, and the inhabitants of the waterlogged area were affected with chronic disorders of the liver and spleen. Between 1870 and 1882 various remodelling schemes were sanctioned, with the object of securing increased control over the supply and its distribution, greater facilities for navigation, and improved drainage; and these have resulted in the complete disappearance of the swamps and accumulations of water, and a most marked improvement in the health of the people. The Sirsa branch was sanctioned in 1888, and this and subsequent minor extensions have largely increased the irrigating capacity of the canal. No less than 200,000 acres were rendered secure in 1896–7 by the Sirsa branch alone.

The head of the canal is at Tajewāla in Ambāla District in 30° 17′ N. and 77° 37′ E., about 1½ miles from the point where the river emerges from the lower hills. The river is here crossed by a weir 1,700 feet in length, flanked at each end by a scouring sluice and head regulator for the Eastern Jumna Canal on the left bank and for the Western Jumna Canal on the right, the full capacities authorized being respectively 1,300 and 6,380 cubic feet per second. The Western Jumna Canal has thus a maximum discharge more than three times that of the average flow of the Thames at Teddington. For the first 14 miles of its course the canal runs almost entirely in the old west branch of the Jumna river. It then effects a junction with the Somb river, a masonry dam across which holds up the combined streams and forces them into the canal head at Dādūpur, which is provided with a regulator and a rapid a short distance below. After a farther course of about 38 miles, chiefly in natural channels, there is at Indri a regulator with a lock and escape head, where the canal divides into the Sirsa branch and the new main line. The Sirsa branch has a capacity of 2,000 cubic feet per second, and runs for 115 miles, watering the arid tract of country between Indri and Sirsa. Some 31 miles farther on, the main line bifurcates into the Hānsi and new Delhi branches. The Hānsi branch has a length of 47 miles and a discharge of nearly 2,000 cubic feet a second, and gives off the Būtāna branch with a capacity of 700 cubic feet a second. The new Delhi branch has a capacity of 1,750 cubic feet a second and a length of 74 miles to the point where it meets the Okhla navigation canal at Delhi. The total length of main canal and branches is 343 miles, of distributaries (major and minor) 1,797 miles, of drainage cuts 657 miles, of escapes 76 miles, and of mill channels 9 miles. The total area commanded by the canal is 4,000 square miles, of which 3,300 square miles are cultivable. The average area of crops irrigated during the twenty years ending 1894–5 was 529 square miles, which rose in the four years ending 1903–4 to an average of 944 square miles; and the work is estimated to irrigate altogether 1,259 square miles. The capital outlay to the end of March, 1904 (excluding a contribution of 11½ lakhs from the Patiāla State), was 172·7 lakhs. The gross revenue for the three years ending March, 1904, averaged 23 lakhs, and the net revenue, after paying all interest charges and working expenses, 7·6 lakhs, or 4·4 per cent. on the capital outlay. The main line and the new Delhi branch are navigable from the head-works to Delhi. The Hānsi branch is navigable to where it meets the Southern Punjab Railway at Hānsi. The expenditure on the provision for navigation is estimated at 16 lakhs; and, although near Delhi there is a certain amount of boat traffic, and timber is largely rafted down the canal, this large expenditure has proved hitherto a financial loss, and the combination of navigation with irrigation a failure. There are flour-mills at several of the falls; but the flour and the other mills at Delhi, which at one time were worked advantageously, are now closed, the water being too valuable to be used for this purpose.

Sirhind Canal.—A perennial canal in the Punjab, taking off from the Sutlej, and irrigating the high land between the Sutlej on the north-west and the Patiāla and Ghaggar streams on the south-east, and extending as far south as the borders of Rājputāna, Bahāwalpur, and the Bīkaner State. The canal was constructed by Government, in association with the Native States of Patiāla, Nābha, and Jīnd. The preliminary survey work was begun in 1867, and the canal was formally opened in 1882, though irrigation did not commence until 1883. The area commanded by the canal is 8,320 square miles, of which 4,027 are in British territory, and the remainder in the States of Patiāla, Nābha, Jīnd, Farīdkot, and Kalsia. The head-works are at the town of Rūpar, where the Sutlej issues from the Siwālik Hills into the plains. Here a weir 2,370 feet long crosses the river from bank to bank, having 12 arched undersluices each of 20 feet span. Extending up-stream on the east bank is the canal head regulator, with 13 arched openings of 21 feet span. About 500 feet farther up the river is the lock channel head, to admit of navigation between the river and canal. The crest of the weir is 7¼ feet higher than the canal bed, and along it extends a line of 586 falling shutters 6 feet high. When these are raised and the undersluices closed, the whole of the river supply is turned into the canal, and this is usually the case from early in October to the end of April. The main canal has for 39 miles a bed-width of 200 feet, with a depth of 11½ feet, and can carry 8,000 cubic feet per second, or more than four times the ordinary flow of the Thames at Teddington. At the 39th mile it divides into two large branches, the combined branch on the west and the Patiāla feeder on the east. The former, which has a bed-width of 136 feet and a capacity of 5,200 cubic feet per second, soon divides again into two branches. The northern of these, the Abohar branch, runs parallel to the Sutlej through Ludhiāna and Ferozepore Districts, terminating after a course of 126 miles at the town of Govindgarh. The southern or Bhatinda branch runs through Ludhiāna District and Patiāla territory, with a length of 100 miles. The irrigation from these two branches is mainly in British territory, and the administration is entirely under the British Government, which retains all the revenue derived from them. They receive between them 64 per cent. of the supply of the main line. The Patiāla feeder, the eastern of the two large branches into which the main line bifurcates, runs to the town of Patiāla, having a bed-width of 75 feet, and a capacity of 3,000 cubic feet per second. On its way it gives off to the south the three Native State branches, the Kotla (94 miles long), the Ghaggar (54 miles), and the Choa (25 miles). These three branches irrigate almost exclusively native territory, and the distributaries and irrigation arrangements are under the Native States, who receive the whole of the canal revenue; but the Patiāla feeder and the branches are maintained by an officer of the Canal department as agent for the States, who distributes the water according to a fixed allotment, Patiāla taking 83 per cent., Nābha 9 per cent., and Jīnd 8 per cent.

The distributaries were constructed so as to penetrate the border of every irrigated village, and thus to save the people the expense of making long watercourses and the difficulty of taking them through the land of other villages. This system, though expensive to construct and maintain, has been repaid by the rapidity with which irrigation has spread over the country. As during the cold season the whole of the river supply is turned into the canal, it was necessary to provide a substitute on the canal for the river navigation thus closed. Accordingly the main line, the combined branch, and 48 miles of the Abohar branch were provided with locks at the falls; and from the 48th mile of the Abohar branch a special navigation canal to the Sutlej near Ferozepore, 47 miles long, was constructed with a branch 4 miles long to Ferozepore. The Patiāla feeder was also made navigable as far as Patiāla. There is, however, little navigation along the branches, though the main line from Rūpar to the North-Western Railway is much used, and brings down a considerable amount of timber from the hills. There are 25 flour-mills at different falls along the branches. The greater part of the main line and branches is bordered by rows of trees, and the strip of land reserved for spoil or borrow pits is generally covered with plantations. A telegraph line extends from the canal head down the main line, the two British branches, the Patiāla feeder, and part of the two longer Native State branches. Since 1896–7 the area irrigated has in only one year fallen below 1,560 square miles: the greatest area irrigated was 2,142 square miles in 1899–1900, of which 1,452 were in British territory. The total cost of construction to the end of 1903–4 has been 388·7 lakhs, of which 247·7 lakhs was paid by the Government, and 141 lakhs by the three Phūlkiān States. Of the cost of the head-works and main line, the Government paid 64 per cent. and the Phūlkiān States contributed 36 per cent. The Government defrayed the whole cost of the British branches, and the Native States that of their branches. The charges for annual maintenance are divided in the same way.

The gross revenue on the British branches averages about 28 lakhs, and the net revenue 20 lakhs. On the Native States branches the gross revenue averages about 12·5 lakhs, and the net revenue about 7 lakhs. The return on the British capital outlay was as high as 10·8 per cent. in 1897–8, and averaged 8 per cent. during the six years ending 1902–3. On the Native States capital outlay the return for these six years averaged 5·3 per cent. This canal is now not only a successful commercial scheme paying a handsome profit, but its advantages in years of drought are incalculable. It saves from famine a large tract of country and also provides food for exportation. Since 1896–7 it has been steadily paying off the accumulated interest charges. The tract of country irrigated is now traversed in all directions by several different lines of railway, some of which would not have been required if no canal was in existence.

Bāri Doāb Canāl.—A perennial irrigation canal in the Punjab, taking off from the left bank of the Rāvi, and watering the Districts of Gurdāspur, Amritsar, and Lahore in the Bāri Doab or tract of country between the Beās and Rāvi. The present undertaking originated in a project for the improvement of an older work, the Hasli canal, constructed about the year 1633 by Alī Mardān Khān, the famous engineer of the emperor Shah Jahān. After the occupation of Lahore in 1846, Major Napier (afterwards Lord Napier of Magdāla) turned his attention at once to this project, and set on foot the necessary surveys. The progress of the work was interrupted by the outbreak of war. After annexation the work was pressed on, because the immediate construction of the canal was regarded as almost a matter of political necessity to provide employment for the disbanded Sikh soldiers, who, having their homes in the centre of the tract, would otherwise have had little encouragement to turn to agriculture. The alignment of the Hasli canal proved on examination to be so defective that the officers in charge decided upon the adoption of an entirely independent line, parts only of the original channel being utilized as distributaries. Irrigation began in 1860–1, but the present permanent weir and other regulating head-works were not completed till after 1875. The head-works are at the village of Mādhopur in Gurdāspur District, where the river is crossed by a weir 2,700 feet long. The canal is capable of carrying 6,500 cubic feet per second: the highest average supply in the hot season is 4,850, while in the cold season it varies from 1,270 to 2,170 cubic feet per second. The main line terminates at its 31st mile, there separating into the Kasūr and main branches. The Kasūr branch 7 miles lower down gives off the Sobraon branch, and the main branch after 25 miles gives off the Lahore branch, the four branches following the crests of the ridges into which the tract is divided by its natural drainage. The total length of the main and branch canals is 369 miles, and there are 1,591 miles of distributaries, from which water is brought upon the fields by means of water-courses constructed and maintained by the cultivators. The canal is not navigable. The rainfall is greatest in the upper part of the system, which has necessitated a special system of irrigation in Gurdāspur District and in the portion of Amritsar District north of the North-Western Railway on the Kasūr and Sobraon branches. In that tract the distributaries are closed during the cold season after a watering has been given for sowing the spring crops, the winter rains with some help from wells being sufficient to mature those crops. The water thus set free has been utilized in extending irrigation in the driest part of Lahore District, where it borders on Montgomery—a tract for which it would otherwise have been impossible to provide a perennial supply. The gross area commanded by the canal is 2,710 square miles in Gurdāspur, Amritsar, and Lahore Districts. The lower portion of the Doāb in Montgomery and Multān is not irrigated, as there is not sufficient water available in the Rāvi during the winter. The area irrigated was 297 square miles in 1860, 677 square miles in 1880–1, 1,346 square miles in 1900–1, and 1,464 square miles in 1903–4. The total capital expenditure (exclusive of interest) up to the end of 1903–4 was 197 lakhs. The gross income for that year was about 33 lakhs, or, inclusive of the increase of land revenue due to irrigation (which is credited to the canal in the accounts), 36 lakhs. The working expenses amounted to 11 lakhs, leaving a net profit of 25 lakhs, or 12·68 per cent. on the capital outlay.

Chenāb Canal, Lower.—A perennial canal in the Punjab, taking off from the left bank of the Chenāb river and watering the tract between it and the Rāvi. The greater part of this area was before the introduction of irrigation a desolate region, unpeopled except for a race of pastoral nomads known as

Janglīs. The land was for the most part Government waste, and was thus adapted for colonization on a scale hitherto untried in the history of India, if not of the world. The original work was designed as a small inundation canal and opened as such in 1887, but in 1889 it was decided to convert it into a perennial canal of the first magnitude. The head-works of the canal are at Khānki, a village in Gujrānwāla District, 8 miles below Wazīrābād. Here there is a weir across the river, by which the supply to the canal is regulated and controlled. The main line of the canal has a bed-width of 250 feet, and has been run with a depth of about 11 feet and a discharge of 11,000 cubic feet per second, or about six times the ordinary flow of the Thames at Teddington. This weir was commenced in 1890 and completed in 1892. The largest branch of the canal, the Gugera, carrying about one-half of the total supply, takes off from the left bank of the main line at the 28th mile. It has a length of 55 miles and then bifurcates into two subsidiary branches, the Gugera Lower and the Buralla, with lengths of 77 and 46 miles respectively. On the right bank, not far from the same off-take, is the Kot Nikka branch with a length of 18 miles. The extreme length of the main line is 40 miles, and it then divides into the Jhang, Rakh, and Miān Alī branches. The Jhang is the second largest branch of the system, and carries about 3,000 cubic feet per second. Its length is about 62 miles, before it bifurcates into the Jhang Lower (38 miles) and the Bhowāna (7½ miles long). The lengths of the Rakh and Miān Alī are 55 and 27 miles respectively. The total length of the main channels is 426 miles. For the distribution of the water-supply from the branches to the watercourses which directly irrigate the land there were, at the end of 1903–4, 2,323 miles of distributaries; and for the villages colonized by Government there had been constructed about 11,000 miles of watercourses. The total area commanded by the canal at the end of 1903–4 was 5,255 square miles in Gujrānwāla, Lahore, Jhang, and Montgomery Districts, of which 3,098 square miles were irrigated, an area which is capable of substantial increase. The total area of Government waste in the Doāb is about 3,817 square miles, of which 2,827 square miles of land commanded by the canal had been allotted by the end of 1903–4. The grantees are divided into three classes—capitalists, yeomen, and peasants; the greater part of the land has been distributed to peasants, who are by far the most satisfactory tenants. For the purpose of allotment the whole of the Government waste has been divided into squares, the side of each square being 1,100 feet and the area about 28 acres. A peasant's grant consists of from one-half to three squares, a yeoman's of four or five, and a capitalist's of any number from five to twenty or more; and each settler is practically guaranteed water for the annual irrigation of a certain percentage of his holding. The Government retains the proprietary rights in the land, and the colonists are its tenants, the peasants for a term of years, the yeomen with right of continued occupancy so long as they pay their assessment, while the capitalists have also the right to purchase proprietary rights in their tenancy after the lapse of a certain period. There are also tenures which carry the liability to provide a certain number of camels for military service. For the purpose of distributing the land and of settling the colonists in villages, a special Colonization officer has been appointed with head-quarters at Lyallpur. There were 1,423 villages in 1903-4, the average size being about 50 squares or 1,400 acres. The population of the colony at the Census of 1901 was 782,690, and may ultimately reach two and a half millions. A railway for the transport of produce has been constructed, running the whole length of the Doāb from Wazīrābād to Khānewāl, and several feeder-lines are under consideration. The capital cost of the canal up to the end of 1903-4 was about 280 lakhs. The canal earned a large revenue even while under construction, while the profits in 1903-4 amounted to 24 per cent. on the capital invested. The gross and net revenue derived therefrom in that year amounted to about 84 and 66 lakhs respectively. By 1913 the net revenue is likely to be very considerably increased, and the interest on the capital invested may amount to 30 per cent., while the value of the crops raised in a year is estimated to rise to 650 lakhs. The canal has thus not only enormously relieved the pressure of population in the congested Districts of the Punjab, but has proved a most remunerative investment, besides adding largely to the general wealth of the country. An extensive telegraph system runs from the head of the canal down its main line and branches, and along some of its larger distributaries, thus facilitating rapid regulation of supply.

Jhelum Canal, Lower.—A perennial irrigation work in the Punjab now approaching completion. It takes off from the left bank of the Jhelum, and will eventually supply perennial irrigation to the whole of the country lying between the Jhelum and Chenāb rivers, west of a line joining the town of Miāni on the Jhelum with Pindi Bhattiān on the Chenāb. The head of the canal is near the village of Mong Rasūl in Gujrāt District. The river is dammed by a weir 4,100 feet long, and a regulator across the head of the canal takes the form of a bridge of 8 spans of 24½ feet each. The main line has a bed-width of 140 feet and will have when running full a depth of 7·5 feet, and a discharge of 3,800 cubic feet per second, or twice the flow of the Thames at Teddington. The Shāhpur branch will take off at about the 28th mile of the main line. This branch has been designed to take up the irrigation now performed in Shāhpur District by the existing Imperial, Provincial, and privately owned inundation canals. After a course of 39 miles, in which it gradually approaches the centre of the highlands of the Doāb, the canal bifurcates into two main branches, watering the northern and southern portions of the Doāb respectively. The total length of the main line and main branches is about 167 miles, and about 960 miles of distributing channels will be constructed. The canal will protect an area of 2,400 square miles, and is expected to irrigate annually about 1,200 square miles. Of 2,400 square miles protected, about 850 are Government waste, which it is intended to turn into an immense horse-breeding colony for the supply of remounts to the Indian army. For this purpose the greater portion has been leased out to colonists on the condition of their keeping an approved brood mare, and other areas have been reserved for public and private breeding establishments and horse runs. The work of colonization is under an officer of the Indian Civil Service, who has his head-quarters at Sargodha in Shāhpur District. The land has been divided into squares of nearly 28 acres each, and one brood mare has to be maintained for every 2½ squares. A railway has been constructed from Malakwāl on the Sind-Sāgar line to Shorkot on the Lyallpur-Khānewal line, affording facilities for the immigration of colonists and the export of produce.

Elaborate precautions have been taken to prevent water-logging of the soil by over-irrigation. The depth at which spring-water is found below the surface of the ground has been carefully observed over the whole of the commanded area, and the country has been divided into three zones according to these depths. Where the spring-level is 40 feet or more below the surface, 50 per cent. of the gross area commanded may be irrigated; where the depth lies between 25 and 40 feet, 40 per cent. of the area will be irrigated; and where the water is nearer to the surface than 25 feet, only 25 per cent. will be allowed perennial irrigation, and powers have been reserved to reduce these supplies if they should be found to be in excess of requirements. On the Shāhpur branch 50 per cent. of the area will be irrigated.

The canal was opened on October 30, 1901; and irrigation is now well advanced, except on the Shāhpur branch, the construction of which has only just been commenced. It is estimated that this canal will cost when finished 187·5 lakhs, and will give a return of 15·8 per cent. on the capital spent upon it, and that ten years after completion the net revenue will exceed the interest charges by 192 lakhs.

Shāhpur Inundation Canals.—A system of inundation canals in the Punjab, fed from the Jhelum river and mainly situated in Shāhpur District. About sixteen of them are owned by private persons and six by Government. Of the latter three are classed as Imperial and two as Provincial, while one, the Pind Dādan Khān Canal in Jhelum District, has recently been made over to the municipal committee of Pind Dādan Khān for management. The three Imperial canals lie wholly in the Shāhpur *tahsīl*, and are developments of a canal dug in 1864 by Colonel Sir William Davies, to supply water to the civil station of Shāhpur. In 1870 Government acquired this canal and added two new canals. The Imperial canals command an area of 105 square miles and irrigate 50 square miles a year on an average, yielding a net revenue of Rs. 50,000, or 24 per cent. on the capital outlay. Of the two Provincial canals the largest is the Rānīwāh, an old native canal which had fallen into disuse and was reopened in 1870–1. It commands 72 square miles in the Bhera *tahsīl* and irrigates 30 square miles annually, yielding a net revenue of Rs. 11,000. It has extinguished its capital cost and yielded a net profit of 4·1 lakhs to Government. The Corbynwāh, constructed in 1879, irrigates about 4,500 acres, mostly grass lands, in the Khushāb *tahsīl* on the right bank of the Jhelum.

The Pind Dādan Khān Canal does not pay expenses, but it supplies the town with sweet water. It performs a small amount of irrigation as well, the area irrigated in 1904–5 having been 395 acres. The private canals have a total length of about 227 miles and irrigate 87 square miles. Many of them are old canals which had silted up and were re-excavated, under Sir Donald McNabb and other Deputy-Commissioners of the District, by owners or lessees to irrigate their own lands. They also irrigate the lands of other persons on payment of a water rate. As noted in the article on the LOWER JHELUM

Canal, most of these inundation canals will cease to exist as such when the Shāhpur branch of the Lower Jhelum Canal is constructed.

Sutlej Canals, Upper.—An Imperial system of four inundation canals in the Punjab, known as the Katora, Khānwah, Upper Sohāg, and Lower Sohāg (or Lower Sohāg and Pāra) Canals. They take off from the right bank of the river Sutlej, and irrigate the low-lying land bounded on the north by the old dry bed of the Beās, which separates it from the tracts commanded by the Bāri Doāb Canal. The tract commanded by the Katora Canal lies in Lahore District, and the remainder in Montgomery.

The canals existing at the end of 1903–4 aggregated 325 miles in length with 394 miles of distributaries, and carried an aggregate supply of 4,935 cubic feet per second. During the five years ending 1903–4 they irrigated an average annual area of 409 square miles and yielded an average gross revenue of 3·5 lakhs or, inclusive of the land revenue due to irrigation (which is credited to the canals in the accounts), 5·4 lakhs per annum. The average annual working expenses during the same period were 3·6 lakhs. There was, therefore, an annual profit of 1·8 lakhs. No capital expenditure was recorded against the canals till 1854–5; up to the end of 1903–4 it has amounted to 17 lakhs.

The Katora Canal has a bed-width of 55 feet, and an authorized discharge of 685 cubic feet per second. It was made in 1870–1, and follows the bed of a nullah for 21 miles, when it separates into three channels called the Pakhoki, Atāri, and Chuniān distributaries. The Khānwah has a bed-width of 65 feet, and an authorized full supply of 1,290 cubic feet per second. The date of first opening is not known: it is, however, recorded that the canal was improved by Mirza Khān, a minister of the emperor Akbar; but it was neglected by his successors, and silted up. In the time of Ranjīt Singh, Dīwān Rādha Rām repaired the head and cleared the channel, and the canal flowed from 1807 to 1823. It was again neglected till 1841, when Fakīr Chirāgh-ud-dīn, under the orders of Mahārājā Sher Singh, had the canal repaired, and it was in flow when taken over by the Irrigation department on the annexation of the Punjab. The Upper Sohāg Canal has a bed-width of 60 feet, and an authorized discharge of 1,540 cubic feet per second. It appears to have been made in 1827, and worked till 1840, when it was neglected; and nothing further was done to it till 1855, when, the canal having been taken over by the Irrigation department, the channel was again put into working order. The Lower Sohāg Canal has a bed-width of 90 feet, and an authorized discharge of 1,420 cubic feet per second. It may be said to date from 1816, when the first attempt to irrigate was made by means of a dam across the Sohāg nullah, which caused it to overflow its banks. In 1831 another dam was made, and the water was led on to the lands of Jawand Singh at Dipālpur, who is said to have obtained a large return from the water. After some fighting the dam was demolished in 1835; and from that date the canal existed only in name, irrigation being effected on only 3,000 acres by lifts by means of a narrow cut 20 feet wide. In 1885–6 the present regular canal was opened. The canal follows generally the Sohāg nullah for 33 miles, till it gives off the Pāra nullah. The canal continues in the form of two branches, one along the Pāra nullah and the other along the Sohāg nullah. The channel, however, was not formed in the bed, but consists of an artificial cut, which is crossed and re-crossed by the tortuous dry nullahs. The canal was constructed mainly for the purpose of bringing under cultivation 142 square miles of Government waste. This area was colonized by allotting parcels of land to chosen peasants from adjacent over-populated Districts. For the purpose of allotment the land was divided into squares, 27·7 acres in area, and each allotment consisted of 4 squares or 111 acres. The canals being dry in the cold season the colonists were required to construct wells, at least one well per holding being necessary.

Grey Canals.—A system of inundation canals in the Punjab, taking off from the south bank of the Sutlej and irrigating the low-lying tracts of Ferozepore District. They take their name from Colonel L. J. H. Grey, under whose orders, as Deputy-Commissioner of the District, they were constructed. The work was begun in 1875–6, when 11 canals were made; the number was increased to 13 in 1883; and in 1885, after the incorporation of the Fāzilka *tahsīl* in Ferozepore District, two of the canals were remodelled and extended so as to irrigate this *tahsīl*. In addition to these, a new canal, named Kingwāh, has just been completed at a cost of 1·7 lakhs. The 14 canals as they now exist vary in length from 28 to 107 miles, in bed-width from 30 to 80 feet, and in discharge from 283 to 640 cubic feet per second. Their total length is 1,034 miles, and their aggregate discharge 6,340 cubic feet per second. Being inundation canals, they run only when the Sutlej is at a sufficient height. Up to and including 1905–6 the total cost on original works has been 11·6 lakhs (exclusive of the 1·7 lakhs spent on the new Kingwāh Canal), and on repairs and establishment 23·4 lakhs. The average area irrigated during the five years ending 1905–6 was 277 square miles. The canals are remarkable as being constructed and maintained on the co-operative system without any direct aid from Government, except a small grant towards the cost of establishment in Fāzilka which has been stopped since the last settlement (1902). The excavation work was performed by the agriculturists whose lands the canal was to benefit, supervised by the ordinary revenue staff of the District. Since 1881 the special establishment required for their up-keep has been met by a charge of 3 to 4 annas per *ghumao* (five-sixths of an acre); and the annual silt clearance and other works have been carried out at the expense of the irrigators at the average rate of 8 to 10 annas per irrigated *ghumao*. In addition to these charges for maintenance, a royalty of 12 annas per *ghumao* of superior, and 6 annas per *ghumao* of inferior, crops is taken by Government.

Ghaggar Canals.—An Imperial system of minor canals in the Punjab, taking off from the Ghaggar. Owing to the waste of water in the lakes and swamps of that river, and the insanitary condition to which the low-lying lands in the valley below Sirsa were reduced, it was agreed between the British Government and the State of Bīkaner that the Dhanūr lake, about 8 miles from Sirsa, should be converted into a reservoir by the construction of a masonry weir at Otu, and that irrigation should be effected by two canals, the northern and southern, taking off from each end of the weir, with a combined capacity of 1,000 cubic feet per second. The Bīkaner State was to share the canal supplies and meet a proportionate part of the cost. The canals were constructed with famine labour in 1896–7, and began to irrigate in the monsoon of 1897. The areas commanded in British and Bīkaner territory are 130 and 117 square miles, and the irrigable areas are 53 and 35 square miles, respectively. There are 95 miles of main canals and 24 of distributaries; and the total capital outlay to the end of March, 1904, was 6·3 lakhs, of which 2·8 lakhs was debited to Bīkaner. These canals are never likely to show any return on their capital cost, as only part of the irrigated area is assessed to canal occupiers' rates, the remainder being assessed to land revenue only.

Sutlej Inundation Canals, Lower.—An Imperial system of inundation canals in the Punjab, taking off from the right bank of the Sutlej and irrigating part of Multān District. They were for the most part constructed in the middle of the eighteenth century by the Daudputras, a powerful tribe who were in possession of this part of the country from the downfall of the Mughals to the rise of Ranjīt Singh; but one of the largest, the Dīwānwāh, was excavated in 1831 by Dīwān Sāwan Mal, who also enlarged and improved several others. Excluding the Hājiwāh canal, whose history is separate from that of the rest, there were in 1850 nineteen of these canals; these, however, have been gradually amalgamated, and in 1903 there were only three, the Mailsi, Muhammadwāh-Sardārwāh, and Bahāwalwāh-Lodhrān canals, of which the last two will probably be amalgamated. The gross cultivable area commanded by these canals is 1,414 square miles, of which 424 are at present irrigable. The canals generally flow from April to October; but since the SIRHIND CANAL came into full operation the supply of water at the commencement and end of the flood season has been considerably reduced, and the actual area irrigated in the five years ending 1903-4 was only 263 square miles. The normal autumn crop is sown and matured with canal water alone; but for the spring harvest only the preliminary waterings required for ploughing and sowing are given from the canal, and further irrigation is supplied from wells. The maximum discharge is 5,000 cubic feet per second, and the total length of main canals is 394 miles and of distributaries 328 miles. Properly designed channels are only of recent construction, and have still to be provided on the Mailsi canal. Until recently canal clearance was effected by the labour of the cultivators: this system was, however, finally abolished in 1903 and rates are now paid. No capital account is kept for these canals. The gross revenue during the three years ending 1903-4 averaged 3·8 lakhs and the net revenue Rs. 83,000.

The Hājiwāh canal is included in the Lower Sutlej system. It was a private canal constructed in the time of Ranjīt Singh, and its administration was taken over by Government in 1888 in consequence of the mismanagement of the owners. This action was authorized by the terms of a deed executed in 1886, under which Government had given the owners a grant of 60,000 acres of land served by the canal, and it was upheld by the Privy Council in 1901. The canal has a bed-width of 30 feet, an average supply during the flood season of 500 cubic feet per second, and a length of 39 miles. The average area irrigated is only 53 square miles, as the alignment is defective.

Sidhnai Canal.—An irrigation work in the Punjab, taking

off from the left bank of the Rāvi and watering part of Multān District. It derives its name, meaning 'straight,' from a remarkable reach of the Rāvi, which extends in a perfectly straight cutting for 10 or 12 miles from Tulamba to Sarai Sidhu. It was opened for irrigation in 1886. The head-works consist of a weir 737 feet long, built across this reach. The main line has a bed-width of 90 feet and a maximum discharge of 1,820 cubic feet per second; after 30 miles it divides into two large distributaries, which between them take nearly one-third of the whole supply. The very short length of the canal compared with the area irrigated is one cause of its financial success. There are in all thirteen main distributary channels taking off from the main line, and three subsidiary canals which take off from the river above the dam. The gross area commanded is 595 square miles, of which the greater part was Government waste, and was settled by colonists brought from various parts of the Punjab, the land being given out for the most parts in 90-acre plots. Although the whole of the water in the Sidhnai reach can be turned into the canal, the Rāvi in the winter is often absolutely dry, owing to the supply taken by the Bāri Doāb Canal, so that the spring crop has to be matured by the aid of wells. The average area irrigated during the three years ending 1903-4 was 190 square miles. The capital outlay up to the end of 1903-4 was about 13 lakhs, and the average annual profit more than 11 per cent.

Chenāb Inundation Canals.—A system of inundation canals in the Punjab, taking off from the left bank of the Chenāb below its confluence with the Rāvi, and irrigating part of the Multān and Shujābād *tahsīls* of Multān District. They were for the most part constructed by the Pathān rulers of Multān and Shujābād, and were once thirteen in number; but by amalgamation the heads in the river have been reduced to four, the Mattithal, Walī Muhammad, Sikandarābād, and Sikandarwāh. As the canal-irrigated land is much lower than the river-level in July and August, the outer banks of the canals are made specially high and strong to keep the flood-waters from pouring over the cultivated land, and in certain lengths of the river embankments have been constructed. In this way there is a chain of protection about 80 miles long on the east bank of the river. The maximum discharge of the canals is 5,200 cubic feet per second: there are 252 miles of main canals and 46 miles of Government distributaries. Until recently water was taken from the main canal entirely by private watercourses, but the construction of properly aligned distributaries is now in progress. The system by which the cultivators, in lieu of paying for the water, provided labour for silt clearance has recently been abolished, and occupiers' rates imposed. No capital account is kept for these canals. The gross revenue during the three years ending 1903-4 averaged 3·3 lakhs yearly, and the net revenue Rs. 47,000. The average area irrigated during the six years ending 1903-4 was 214 square miles.

Muzaffargarh Canals.—An Imperial system of inundation canals in the Punjab, taking off from the left bank of the Indus and the right bank of the Chenāb, and irrigating portions of Muzaffargarh District. They were for the most part constructed by the native rulers of the District, and improved by Sāwan Mal, governor under Ranjīt Singh. After annexation the canals remained for many years under the management of the Deputy-Commissioner, and were transferred to the Canal department as a 'minor' work in 1880. The system of canal clearance by the labour of the cultivators was finally abolished in 1903, when occupiers' rates were introduced. The Indus series, which is by far the more important of the two, consists of eight canals with an aggregate length of 1,138 miles of main, branch, and distributary channels, and a total average discharge of 2,570 cubic feet per second. There are five canals in the Chenāb series, with a total length of 232 miles, and a discharge of 740 cubic feet per second. The gross area commanded by the canals is 1,205 square miles, of which 1,055 are cultivable and 547 irrigable, the area irrigated during the five years ending 1903-4 averaging 457 square miles, of which 366 square miles were watered from the Indus. To protect the irrigated country, embankments have been constructed, stretching for 119 miles along the Indus and for 40 miles along the Chenāb. No capital account is kept for the system. The gross revenue in 1903-4 was 6 lakhs and the net revenue 3·3 lakhs.

Indus Inundation Canals.—An Imperial system of inundation canals in the Punjab, taking off from the west bank of the Indus, and irrigating part of Dera Ghāzi Khān District. They are fourteen in number and cover a river frontage of 175 miles, protecting a low-lying narrow strip of country from 6 to 16 miles wide, known as the Sind. These were mostly constructed by the Mirāni chiefs and other native rulers, and were greatly improved by Sāwan Mal, governor under Ranjīt Singh. Five, however, were constructed by Baloch chiefs in 1862-3 for the use of their tribal lands, but proving a financial failure were bought up by Government. The gross area commanded is 1,374 square miles, of which 661 are cultivable.

The greatest area of crops matured is 348 square miles, and the average about 300 square miles. The normal period of flow is from the beginning of May to the end of September; consequently, while the autumn crop is matured entirely by canal water, the supply in the spring harvest is sufficient only for ploughing and sowing, after which wells are used. The average discharge of the whole series is 2,400 cubic feet per second. There are 680 miles of main canals and branches, of which 108 have been constructed under British rule, 75 miles of distributaries, and 7 of drainage cuts and escapes. As the irrigated tract is below the flood-level of the Indus, a system of embankments 75 miles long has been built, and also works for training the river and protecting the irrigation works. The capital sum expended from 1854 to the end of March, 1904, is 8·6 lakhs. Until 1897 there was practically no net revenue; in that year, by the revised settlement of Dera Ghāzi Khān District, the indirect revenue was substantially increased and a low occupier's rate imposed. The gross revenue for 1903–4 was 4·1 lakhs and the net revenue 1 lakh, or 11·88 per cent. on the capital expenditure. A considerable income is derived from Government lands on the Dhundi canal.

Bāri Doāb.—A *doāb* or 'tract between two rivers' (the Beās and Rāvi) in the Punjab, lying between 29° 22′ and 32° 30′ N. and 71° 6′ and 75° 58′ E., and comprising Amritsar District and portions of Gurdāspur, Lahore, Montgomery, and Multān. The name was formed by the Mughal emperor Akbar, by combining the first syllables of the names of the two rivers.

Bhattiāna.—A tract of country in the Punjab, lying between 29° 15′ and 30° 15′ N. and 74° 0′ and 75′ 45′ E., and comprising the valley of the Ghaggar from Fatehābād in Hissār District to Bhatnair in the State of Bīkaner, together with an undefined portion of the dry country stretching north-west of the Ghaggar towards the old bank of the Sutlej. For its physical aspects see HISSĀR DISTRICT. Roughly speaking, the tract is bounded on the east by HARIĀNA, on the south and west by the Bīkaner desert, while on the north its boundary includes Bhatinda in Patiāla, and may be taken as roughly corresponding to the line of the Southern Punjab Railway. Bhattiāna derives its name from the Bhattis, a collection of Muhammadan tribes claiming Rājput origin, who also gave their name to Bhatnair.

Early in the fourteenth century the wild country held by the Bhattis and Mains (Mīnās) was attached to ABOHAR, a dependency of Dipālpur; and the daughter of Rāna Mal, the Bhatti chief, was married to Sipāh Sālār Rajab, and in 1309 became the mother of Fīroz Shāh III. The Bhatti chiefs seem to have maintained a position of semi-independence for a considerable time. Rai Hansu, Bhatti, son of Khul Chain, was employed under Mubārak Shāh II against Pulād in 1430 and 1431. Later, the Bhatti chief Ahmad Khān, who had risen to great power and had 20,000 horse under him, defied prince Bāyazīd in the reign of Bahlol Lodī, and, though at first victorious, was eventually defeated and killed. Mirza Kāmrān was employed against the Bhattis in 1527, and they seem to have been reduced to complete subjection by the Mughals, for nothing is heard of them until the decay of the Delhi empire. For twenty-four years after 1750 Bhattiāna was harassed by the Sikhs and Bhattis in turn, until in 1774 Amar Singh, the Rājā of Patiāla, conquered it. But Patiāla was unable to hold the tract, and lost the whole of it (Rānia in 1780–3, Fatehābād in 1784), the Bhatti reconquest being facilitated by the great famine of 1783 which desolated the country. Sirsa fell to George Thomas in 1795–9; and on his fall in 1801 the Marāthās acquired Bhattiāna, only to lose it in 1803 to the British, who took no steps to establish a strong government. At that time Bhattiāna was divided between the chiefs Bahādur Khān and Zābita Khān, of whom the former held the country in the neighbourhood of Fatehābād, while the latter owned Rānia and Sirsa. In 1810 the raids of Bahādur Khān had become intolerable, and an expedition sent against him annexed Fatehābād, while in 1818 the territories of Zābita Khān were acquired. The country thus obtained formed the subject of a long dispute with the Patiāla chief, who had encroached on it between 1818 and 1837. It was finally awarded to the British Government, and made into a separate District of Bhattiāna, which was transferred to the Punjab under the name of Sirsa District after 1857. (See Hissār.)

Bīst Jullundur Doāb.—A *doāb* or 'tract between two rivers' (the Beās and Sutlej) in the Punjab, lying between 30° 57′ and 32° 7′ N. and 75° 4′ and 76° 38′ E., and comprising Jullundur and Hoshiārpur Districts, and the State of Kapūrthala. The name was formed by the Mughal emperor Akbar, by combining the first syllables of the names of the two rivers. It is also known as the Sāharwāl Doab.

Chaj (Jech) Doāb.—A *doāb* or 'tract between two rivers' (the Chenāb and Jhelum) in the Punjab, lying between 31° 10′ and 33° 0′ N. and 72° 7′ and 74° 3′ E., and comprising

Gujrāt and parts of Shāhpur and Jhang Districts. The name was formed by the Mughal emperor Akbar, by combining the first syllables of the names of the two rivers.

Cis-Sutlej States.—A group of States in the Punjab, lying in the tract of country bounded by the Sutlej on the west and north, the Siwāliks on the north-east, the Jumna on the east, and the old Delhi territory on the south. In 1809 the treaty between the British Government and Mahārājā Ranjīt Singh of Lahore set a limit to the encroachments of the Mahārājā to the east and south of the Sutlej, and the Cis-Sutlej States were formally taken under British protection. These States were mostly held by Sikh chiefs, of whom the most prominent was the Rājā of Patiāla with a revenue of a quarter of a million sterling; and by bands of Sikh horsemen, whose individual shares in some cases did not exceed the twentieth part of a single village. Many of them were of recent origin, and had been founded by Sikh warriors from beyond the Sutlej after the overthrow of the Afghān governor at Sirhind by the united forces of the Sikhs on both sides of the river in 1763. For some time previous to the treaty of 1809 Ranjīt Singh had aimed at establishing his supremacy over the cis-Sutlej territory. Several of the most prominent of the chiefs had been tributaries of the Marāthā power, and it was as the successor of the Marāthās that the British Government claimed the protectorate. The protected States were allowed full sovereignty within their respective territories, but were required to assist the British with all their forces in repelling any invasion of the country. The British Government confined its interference with the States to the settlement of quarrels, and the determination of disputes as to succession, but reserved to itself, as the price of its protection, the right of escheat in case of failure of heirs. Political control over the States was until 1840 exercised through the British representative at Delhi and his assistants, who were also responsible for the administration of the territories which lapsed from time to time in default of heirs. In 1840 a Governor-General's Agent for the North-West Frontier was appointed with his headquarters at Ambāla, and two years later the administration of the lapsed territories was transferred to him.

In the first Sikh War (1845–6) the great majority of the States failed to act up to their obligations. The Lahore army was largely recruited in their territories, and their sympathies, as a rule, were with the enemies of their protectors. As a consequence, at the end of 1846, important modifications were made in the relations between the defaulting States and the paramount power. The most flagrant offenders were punished by confiscation, and the remainder were deprived of their police jurisdiction, and of the right to levy customs and transit duties, while the obligation to furnish troops was commuted for a money payment. Nine chiefs only, those of Patiāla, Nābha, Jīnd, Māler Kotla, Farīdkot, Kalsia, Raikot, Diālgarh, and Mamdot, were exempted from this arrangement, and allowed to retain full powers.

These reforms added largely to the territory under the direct control of the British Government. The head-quarters of the Agent had been transferred to Lahore, and a Commissioner of the Cis-Sutlej States was appointed, subordinate to him. It was speedily found that, without police jurisdiction, the position of the States was an impossible one; and in 1849, after the conquest of the Punjab, the British Government assumed complete control throughout their territories, which were shortly afterwards brought under settlement, and the revenues assessed in cash. The position of the chiefs, and of the representatives of the old communities of horsemen (known as *pattīdārs*), who were thus deprived of their former powers, became that of ordinary *jāgīrdārs*; and the right of succession to the *jāgīrs* is confined to the descendants in the male line of the persons actually in possession in 1809, the date of the declaration of the British protectorate. Of the States which were allowed to retain powers in 1846, Diālgarh lapsed in 1852 and Raikot in 1854, while Mamdot was annexed in 1855 in consequence of the misconduct of the Nawāb. The defunct States are now incorporated in the Districts of Ambāla, Karnāl, Ludhiāna, Ferozepore, and Hissār.

Hariāna.—A tract of country in the Punjab, lying between 28° 30′ and 30° N. and 75° 45′ and 76° 30′ E., chiefly in the eastern half of Hissār District, but also comprising part of Rohtak District and of the States of Jīnd and Patiāla. It is in shape an irregular oval, with its long axis lying north-west and south-east. On the north-west it is bounded by the Ghaggar valley; on the west, south-west, and south by the Bagār and Dhundauti, or sandy tracts which are the continuation of the Bīkaner desert; on the east by the Jumna riverain; and on the north-east by the Nardak country, from which it is divided by a line roughly coinciding with the alignment of the Southern Punjab Railway. The name of Hariāna is most probably derived from *hari* ('green'), and is reminiscent of a time when this was a rich and fertile tract. Archaeological remains show that the country watered by the Saraswatī was once the scene of a flourishing Hindu civilization; and the records of Tīmūr's invasion mention the sugar-cane jungles of Tohāna, a proof that at any rate the valley of the Ghaggar was at that time of high fertility, though the country near Hissār seems already to have been dry and arid. The chief events in the history of the tract will be found in the article on HISSĀR DISTRICT. At the end of the eighteenth century Hariāna was a veritable no-man's-land, acknowledging no master and tempting none. Lying at the point where the three powers, Sikh, Bhatti, and Marāthā, met, it covered an area of nearly 3,000 square miles of depopulated country. Its thousand towns and villages had once produced a revenue of 14 lakhs, but now yielded less than 3 lakhs. The tract thus lay open to attack; and in 1797–8 the adventurer George Thomas, who held the fief of Jhajjar from the Marāthās, took part of Kanhari and overran Hariāna as far as the Ghaggar. At Hānsi, which he found a desert, he established his capital, with a mint and arsenal. He next planned the conquest of the Punjab to the Indus, and actually advanced as far as the Sutlej. His successes appeared to have firmly established his power, and he built Georgegarh or Jahāzgarh; but in 1801 he succumbed after a heroic struggle to the overwhelming power of Perron, De Boigne's successor in Sindhia's service. After the capture of Hānsi by Bourquin, Hariāna passed for a short time into the hands of the Marāthās, and in 1803 came under British rule; a native governor was placed in charge of the Districts of Hariāna and Rohtak, but British authority was not actually established till 1810.

Kurukshetra.—A sacred tract of the Hindus, lying between 29° 15′ and 30° N. and 76° 20′ and 77° E., in the Karnāl District and the Jīnd State of the Punjab. According to the Mahābhārata, which contains the oldest account of the tract, it lies between the Saraswatī and Drishadwatī (now the Rakshi), and was watered by seven or nine streams, including these two. It was also divided into seven or nine *bans* or forests. The circuit of Kurukshetra probably did not exceed 160 miles; and it formed an irregular quadrilateral, its northern side extending from Ber at the junction of the Saraswatī and Ghaggar to Thānesar, and its southern from Sinkh, south of Safīdon, to Rām Rai, south-west of Jīnd. The name, 'the field of Kuru,' is derived from Kuru, the ancestor of the Kauravas and Pāndavas, between whom was fought the great conflict described in the Mahābhārata; but the tract was also called the Dharmakshetra or 'holy land,' and would appear to have been famous long before the time of the Kauravas, for at Thānesar Parasu Rāma is said to have slain the Kshattriyas, and the lake of Sarvanavat on the skirts of Kurukshetra is alluded to in the Rig-Veda in connexion with the legend of the horse-headed Dadhyanch. Nardak is another name for Kurukshetra, probably derived from *nirdukh*, 'without sorrow.' The Chinese pilgrim, Hiuen Tsiang, who visited it in the seventh century, calls it 'the field of happiness.' Kurukshetra contains, it is said, 360 places connected with these legends, or with the cults of Siva and the Sun-god, which have long been places of pilgrimage. Of these the principal are THĀNESAR, PEHOWA, JĪND, SAFĪDON, and KAITHAL, but numerous other sites preserve their ancient names and sanctity.

Mālwā.—Tract in the Punjab, lying between 29° and 31° N. and 74° 30′ and 77° E., and comprising the area south of the Sutlej occupied by the Sikhs. It includes the Districts of Ferozepore and Ludhiāna, and the Native States of Patiāla, Jīnd, Nābha, and Māler Kotla. The tract is a great recruiting ground for Sikh regiments, being in this respect second only to the Mānjha. It is said that the name is a modern one, the title of Mālavā Singh having been conferred on the Sikhs of the tract for their valour by Banda, Bairāgi, who promised that it should become as fruitful as Mālwā.

Mānjha.—A tract of country in the Lahore and Amritsar Districts of the Punjab, lying between 30° 52′ and 21° 35′ N. and 73° 45′ and 75° 21′ E., and forming a portion of the uplands of the Bāri Doāb. In shape it is, roughly speaking, a triangle whose base may be taken as the grand trunk road crossing Lahore and Amritsar Districts from the Rāvi to the Beās, and whose sides are the high banks marking the ancient courses of those rivers. From the point where the Beās now joins the Sutlej, the old Beās bank diverges from the present course of the Sutlej and approaches the old bed of the Rāvi near the borders of Montgomery District. This is the apex of the Mānjha, for, though the upland ridge is continued as far as Multān, from this point it bears the name of the Ganji Bār. Before the construction of the Bāri Doāb Canal the Mānjha was an ill-watered and infertile expanse, described by the Settlement officer of Lahore in 1854 as a jungle in which only the poorer cereals and pulses could be grown. Now, however, the Bāri Doāb Canal runs through the whole length of the tract, which is second in fertility to none in the Province. The Sikhs of the Mānjha are some of the finest specimens of the

Jat race, and the tract is one of the most important recruiting grounds for the Sikh regiments. The expression 'Sikhs of the Mānjha' is, however, sometimes loosely used to denote all Sikhs recruited north of the Sutlej. Punjābi of the Mānjha is the phrase used to express the dialect of Punjābi spoken in and about the Mānjha, as contrasted with Western Punjābi, the Punjābi of the submontane tract, the Punjābi of the Jullundur Doāb, and Mālwā Punjābi, or that spoken south of the Sutlej.

Rechna Doāb.—A *doāb* or 'tract between two rivers' (the Rāvi and Chenāb) in the Punjab, lying between 30° 35′ and 32° 50′ N. and 71° 50′ and 75° 3′ E., comprising the Siālkot, Gujrānwāla, and Lyallpur Districts, and parts of Gurdāspur, Lahore, Montgomery, Jhang, and Multān. The name was formed by the Mughal emperor Akbar, by combining the first syllables of the names of the two rivers.

Sind-Sāgar Doāb.—A *doāb* or 'tract between two rivers' (the Indus and Chenāb, and higher up the Indus and Jhelum) in the Punjab, lying between 29° 58′ and 33° 15′ N. and 70° 33′ and 73° 50′ E. It comprises the Districts of Jhelum, Rāwalpindi, Attock, Miānwāli, and Muzaffargarh, and parts of Shāhpur and Jhang.

Thal.—The great steppe lying between 30° 30′ and 32° 0′ E. and 70° 30′ and 72° N., in the Sind-Sāgar Doāb, Punjab. It stretches southward from the foot of the Salt Range for 150 miles towards the apex of the *doāb* as far as the border of Muzaffargarh District, and comprises most of the cis-Indus territory of Miānwāli and part of the Khushāb *tahsīl* of Shāhpur District, being bounded on the west by the high bank of the Indus and on the east by that of the Jhelum. In places its width exceeds 50 miles. A scanty rainfall, a treeless sandy soil, and a precarious and scattered pasturage mark this out as one of the most desolate tracts now remaining in the Punjab. Much of it is real desert, barren and lifeless, and devoid not only of bird and animal life, but almost of vegetation. At first sight the Thal appears a uniformly monotonous desert, but in reality its character varies. The northern Thal has a substratum of hard level soil, the surface of which is covered by a succession of low sandhills with a general north and south direction; and its appearance is that of a sandy rolling prairie, covered in the rare years of good rainfall with grass and stunted bushes. Cultivation is carried on only in small patches, water is from 40 to 60 feet below the surface, and the sparse population depend chiefly on their flocks and herds. It is traversed from west to east by the Sind-Sāgar branch of the North-Western Railway, which turns abruptly south at Kundiān and runs parallel with the Indus down the western border of the Thal. The eastern part of the steppe is called the Thal Kalān or 'Great Thal'; and here a line of high sandhills, running north-east and south-west, alternates with narrow bottoms of soil, stiff and hard in places, but more often covered with sand. Towards the west the hills become lower and less sandy. Agriculture here replaces pasturage as the occupation of the people, and in the Leiah *tahsīl* a broad strip of nearly level ground runs down from Fatehpur towards Mirhan. This tract is called Daggar in the north and Jandi Thal in the south. The main feature of the Daggar is its central core—a narrow strip of firm, flat, cultivable soil, which runs, like a river, from north to south down its centre. From the line of wells in this portion the Daggar takes its name. The good land ends near Khānpur in a region of smooth sand, to be succeeded near Karor by another fertile strip, which forms a core similar to the Jandi Thal. There is little doubt that the Indus once flowed down the middle of the Thal. Last we come to the Powah, a strip of upland some 3 miles broad forming the high bank of the Indus. In the north this bank rises abruptly 40 feet from the river-level, but towards the south it gradually gets lower, until it disappears at Kot Sultān. Large villages, whose lands lie in the riverain tract below, are built on the Powah, where the floods are less likely to reach them. The Thal is peopled by Jat tribes with scattered septs of Siāl, Khokhar, and other Rājputs, and it was for a time under the Hot Baloch chiefs of MANKERĀ. That its natural characteristics have a depressing effect on the people is hardly a matter of surprise, and they are, to use their own expression, 'camel-hearted.' The tract will probably be irrigated by the projected Indus Canal.

DELHI DIVISION

Delhi Division (*Dehli* or *Dillī*).—The south-eastern Division of the Punjab, stretching along the western bank of the Jumna, between 27° 39′ and 31° 18′ N. and 74° 29′ and 77° 40′ E. The Commissioner's head-quarters are at the city of Delhi, or at Simla during part of the hot season. The total population increased from 4,232,449 in 1881 to 4,434,751 in 1891, and to 4,587,092 in 1901. The area is 15,395 square miles, and the density of population 298 persons per square mile, compared with 209 for the Province as a whole. In 1901 Hindus numbered 3,252,428, or 71 per cent. of the total; Muhammadans, 1,192,331; Sikhs, 100,040; Jains, 30,110; Pārsīs, 65; and Christians, 12,108, of whom 3,909 were natives.

The Division includes seven Districts, as shown below:—

District.	Area in square miles.	Population (1901).	Land revenue with cesses (1903-4), in thousands of rupees.
Hissār . .	5,217	781,717	9,91
Rohtak . .	1,797	630,672	11,45
Gurgaon . .	1,984	746,208	14,39
Delhi . .	1,290	689,039	10,19
Karnāl . .	3,153	883,225	12,29
Ambāla . .	1,851	815,880	13,81
Simla . .	101	40,351	21
Total	15,393	4,587,092	72,25

With the exception of the small District of Simla and the hill station of Kasauli in Ambāla, the Division lies wholly in the plains. It contains 6,486 villages and 51 towns, the largest of which are DELHI (population, 208,575), AMBĀLA (78,638), BHIWĀNI (35,917), REWĀRI (27,295), PĀNĪPAT (26,914), KARNĀL (23,559), and ROHTAK (20,323). The Commissioner has political control over the Native States of Sirmūr, Kalsia, Pataudi, Dujāna, and Lohāru, which have an aggregate area of 1,740 square miles and a population of 264,204. Excepting Delhi, there are few towns of commercial importance, but Rewāri and Ambāla may be mentioned. Pānīpat in Karnāl

District has been the scene of several famous battles. SIMLA, the seat of the Supreme Government for seven months in the year, lies within this Division.

Boundaries, configuration, and hill and river systems.

Hissār District (*Hisār*).—District in the Delhi Division of the Punjab, lying between 28° 36′ and 30° 0′ N. and 74° 29′ and 76° 20′ E., with an area of 5,217 square miles. It is bounded on the north by Ferozeporė District and the State of Patiāla; on the east by the Jīnd *nizāmat* of Jīnd State and the District of Rohtak; on the south by the Dādrī *nizāmat* of Jīnd and the territory of the Nawāb of Lohāru; and on the south-west by the State of Bīkaner. Situated on the borders of the Bīkaner desert, it has in many respects the characteristics of Rājputāna rather than of the Punjab; its general aspect is that of a plain or prairie, unbroken except by some detached peaks of the Arāvalli range in the extreme south-west, the highest of which is Toshām hill with an elevation of 800 feet. The only river, the Ghaggar, enters the District in two branches, known as the Ghaggar and Johiya, meeting below Sirsa.

Geology.

With the exception of some small outliers of gneiss at Toshām, there is nothing of geological interest in the District, which is otherwise entirely of alluvial formation.

Botany.

The north-eastern part resembles as regards its vegetation the Upper Gangetic plain, while the southern border is botanically akin to Rājputāna. The Sirsa subdivision resembles the desert and the Western Punjab. The fodder-grasses of the tracts round Hissār and Hānsi (largely species of *Panicum* and *Pennisetum*) are celebrated. A stunted kind of zizyphus (*Z. nummularia*), common in the drier tracts of Northern India, is conspicuous in this District, and its leaves are valued locally for cattle.

Fauna.

Wild animals are comparatively rare, owing to the absence of water; but antelope and 'ravine deer' (gazelle) are common, and hog are plentiful in parts. Wolves are also fairly numerous. *Nīlgai* are sometimes met with near Hissār.

Climate and temperature.

Owing to the extreme dryness of the climate, the District is healthy. Even the canal-irrigated tracts, where there used to be a great deal of fever and the people presented a striking contrast to the inhabitants of the dry tracts, have been healthy since the cultivation of rice was stopped about ten years ago. Both the heat in summer and the cold in winter are extreme, and epidemics of pneumonia are not uncommon in the winter months.

Rainfall.

As the District lies on the edges of both the Bengal and

Bombay monsoon currents, the most striking feature in the rainfall is its extreme variability, and the partial manner in which it is distributed. The yearly average varies from 14 inches at Sirsa to 16 at Hissār, where 14 inches fall in the summer and 2 in the winter. The greatest annual rainfall recorded during the last twenty years was 37·4 inches at Bhiwāni in 1885–6, and the least 3·1 inches at Sirsa in 1899–1900.

History and archaeology.

A large part of the District is, with parts of Rohtak, better known to history as HARIĀNA. The once fertile tract watered by the Ghaggar had its capital at Hānsi, which was the ancient capital and southernmost point of the Siwālik territory, and which archaeological investigations show to be one of the oldest towns in India. The numerous architectural remains of Hindu origin, found built into the walls of Muhammadan tombs and mosques throughout the District, testify to its having been the abode of an ancient and vigorous Hindu civilization. The most interesting of these are to be found at HISSĀR, HĀNSI, FATAHĀBĀD, and TOSHĀM. An inscription at Toshām seems to commemorate a victory over Ghatotkacha, the second known member of the Gupta line (*circa* A.D. 305), and it appears probable that Hānsi was a stronghold of the Kushan rulers of the Punjab.

The District is said to have been overrun in the eighth century by the Tomar Rājputs, and afterwards to have fallen under the dominion of the Chauhāns. In 1036 Hānsi was captured by Masūd, son of Mahmūd of Ghazni; but in 1043 it was retaken by the Delhi Rājā, probably a Tomar vassal of the Chauhāns. After the defeat of Prithwī Rāj by Muhammad of Ghor in 1192, the Jāts laid siege to Hānsi, but were defeated by Kutb-ud-dīn. Hānsi then became a fief of the Delhi kingdom. The districts of Delhi, Ajmer, Hānsi, and Sirsa fell into the hands of the conqueror; but no settled rule seems to have been at first established in this tract, which in the ensuing anarchy was dominated by the Jātu Rājputs, an offshoot of the Tomars. Muhammadan power was, however, gradually consolidated; and about 1254, in the reign of Mahmūd Shāh I, the District, including Hānsi, Sirsa, Barwāla, and Jīnd, was assigned as a fief to Ulugh Khān-i-Azam, afterwards the emperor Balban.

Until the eighteenth century the tract remained a flourishing division of the Muhammadan empire, and Sirsa or Sarsūti was in the fourteenth century, according to Wassāf, one of the most important towns in Upper India. The towns of Fatahābād and Hissār were founded in 1352 and 1356 respectively by Fīroz Shāh III, and canals were dug from the Ghaggar and Jumna for their use. After the capture of Bhatnair, Tīmūr marched through the District via Sirsa, Fatahābād, Rajabpur, Ahrūni, and Tohāna. It is evident from his account that these towns were wealthy and prosperous, for he took much booty in Sirsa, Fatahābād, and Ahrūni, and drove the Jāts of Tohāna into their sugar-cane fields and jungles.

During the eighteenth century the country appears to have been held by Muhammadan tribes claiming Rājput origin, of whom the chief were the Johiyas round Bhatnair (HANUMĀNGARH) and the Bhattis about Rānia, Sirsa, and Fatahābād, from whom the western part of the District took its name of BHATTIĀNA. The Bīkaner annals tell of the incessant struggles of the Hindu Rājputs of that State with the Johiyas and Bhattis for the possession of Bhatnair and sometimes of Sirsa; and the chronicles of Patiāla are full of raids and counter-raids between the Sikh Jats and their hereditary foes, the Bhattis. On the death of Aurangzeb in 1707 we find Nawāb Shāh Dād Khān, a Pathān of Kasūr, *nāzim* of the *sarkār* of Hissār; and under his rule, from 1707 to 1737, the people and country appear to have prospered exceedingly. He was succeeded by the Nawābs of Farrukhnagar, in Gurgaon, who ruled till 1761. But Nādir Shāh ravaged the land in 1739; and with the disintegration of the Delhi empire Hissār became the scene of a sanguinary struggle between the Sikhs of the north-east, the marauding Bhattis of the north and north-west, and the imperial power of Delhi. In 1731 Ala Singh, the founder of the Patiāla State, had commenced a struggle with the Bhatti chiefs of Bhatnair and Fatahābād which lasted during his lifetime; the Bhattis, though supported by imperial troops, were defeated in 1754 and 1757, and Hissār was sacked in 1757 and Tohāna in 1761. In the latter year Nawāb Amīn Khān, the Bhatti chief of Rānia, was appointed *nāzim* of Hissār; but he had no better fortune, and by 1774 Amar Singh, successor of Ala Singh, had become master of the whole of the Hānsi, Hissār, and Sirsa territories. On Amar Singh's death in 1781, an agreement was made whereby Hissār, Hānsi, Toshām, Rohtak, and Maham were assigned to the empire, Sirsa and Fatahābād to the Bhattis, and the rest of their conquests to the Sikhs; but the great famine of 1783, which entirely devastated the District, compelled the latter to retire to their own country. The territories thus left derelict were in 1798 occupied by the adventurer George Thomas, who for three years maintained an independent kingdom in Hānsi and Hissār. However, in 1801, after an obstinate defence of Hānsi, he surrendered to an army under Bourquin sent against him by Perron, Sindhia's French general, and the country was for a brief space under the Marāthā dominion.

In 1803 Hissār and Sirsa, with the territories ceded by Sindhia, passed nominally to the British; but although a military post was maintained at Hānsi, and *nāzims* or native superintendents were placed in civil charge, little was done towards enforcing order until 1810, when an expedition was rendered necessary by the continued raids of the Bhatti chiefs. In consequence of these the territory of Fatahābād was annexed, and a second expedition in 1818 secured the rest of the territory held by the Bhattis. Thus the whole of the Sirsa *tahsīl* was brought under British rule. Most of the present District was in 1820 included in the Western District of the Delhi territory. During the years that followed, the Sikh Rājās, taking advantage of British neglect and the waste condition of the dry tract beyond the Ghaggar, began a series of irregular colonizations, which continued uninterrupted till 1837. The British Government, after a long boundary contention with Patiāla, asserted its supremacy over the dry tract, which was resumed, and, together with the valley of the Ghaggar, made into a separate District under the name of BHATTIĀNA, in which all the present *tahsīl* of Sirsa was included. Additions were made to the territory by other resumptions from encroaching Native States in 1844, 1847, and 1855.

In the Mutiny of 1857 the troops at Hānsi were the first to rise, followed by those at Hissār and Sirsa; all Europeans who did not fly were murdered, and Hissār and Sirsa were wholly lost for a time to British rule. The Ranghars and Pachhādas of Hissār and the Bhattis of Sirsa, followed by the majority of the Muhammadan villagers, rose in insurrection; but before Delhi had been recovered a force of Punjab levies, aided by contingents from Patiāla and Bīkaner, under General van Cortlandt, utterly routed them. After the Mutiny Hissār and Bhattiāna Districts were transferred from the North-Western Provinces to the Punjab, and the latter became the Sirsa District. In 1884 that District was broken up: the Sirsa *tahsīl* and 126 villages of Dabwāli were transferred to Hissār, while Fāzilka and the remaining 31 villages of Dabwāli were amalgamated with Ferozepore District. The small Budhlāda tract was transferred from Karnāl to Hissār in 1889. In 1904 two villages of the District were transferred, with a cash payment of Rs. 25,000, to the Bīkaner State, in exchange for a few villages held by the Darbār in the Deccan.

The people.

Hissār contains 8 towns and 964 villages. Its population at each of the last three enumerations was: (1881) 672,569, (1891) 776,006 and (1901) 781,717. It increased by less than 1 per cent. during the last decade, the low rate being chiefly due to emigration during the famine years of 1897 and 1900. The District is divided into the five *tahsīls* of HISSĀR, HĀNSI, BHIWĀNI, FATAHĀBĀD, and SIRSA, the head-quarters of each being at the place from which it is named. The chief towns are the municipalities of BHIWĀNI, HĀNSI, HISSĀR, and SIRSA, Hissār being the head-quarters of the District.

The following table shows the distribution of population in 1901:—

Tahsīl.	Area in square miles.	Number of Towns.	Number of Villages.	Population.	Population per square mile.	Percentage of variation in population between 1891 and 1901.	Number of persons able to read and write.
Hissār	810	1	134	128,783	159·0	+ 5·3	3,563
Hānsi	799	1	132	178,933	224·0	+ 8·0	4,283
Bhiwāni	750	1	131	124,429	165·9	− 2·6	5,585
Fatahābād	1,179	1	261	190,921	161·9	+ 5·1	3,218
Sirsa	1,651	4	306	158,651	96·1	− 11·2	4,722
District total	5,217	8	964	781,717	149·8	+ 0·7	21,371

NOTE.—The figures for the areas of *tahsīls* are taken from revenue returns. The total District area is that given in the *Census Report*.

Hindus number 544,799, or more than 70 per cent. of the population; Muhammadans, 202,009; and Sikhs, 28,642. Owing to the large areas of sandy soil, the density of the population is only 150 persons to the square mile, and even on the cultivated area it is only 194, the precarious nature of the cultivation forbidding it to support more. The vernaculars are Hariānī, Bāngru, or Deswālī in the south, Punjābi in the north, and Bāgrī in the south-east. Bāgrī and Hariānī run very much into one another; to a less extent Punjābi blends with Hindī and Bāgrī through Pachhādī, the Punjābi dialect of the Muhammadan Pachhādas.

Castes and occupations.

Most important of the landowning tribes are the Jāts, who number 195,000, and comprise one-fourth of the population. They may roughly be divided into four classes: the Deswāli Jāts of Hariāna, some of whose ancestors appear to have inhabited the District in ancient times; the Bāgrī Jāts, immigrants from the Bāgar country of Bīkāner; the Sikh Jāts of Sirsa, who came from the Mālwā country and from Patiāla; and the Muhammadan Jāts, who form part of the nondescript collection of tribes known as Pachhādas. The Deswālī and Bāgrī Jāts are practically all Hindus and intermarry. The Rājputs number 70,000, or 9 per cent. of the population; 78 per cent. of them are Muhammadans. The oldest clan is the Tonwar or Tomar, who first entered the District during the ascendancy of the Tomar dynasty under Anang Pāl at Delhi. Other important clans are the Jātu, Bhatti, Wattu, Johiya, Chauhān, Ponwār, and Rāthor. As a rule the Rājput, retaining the military traditions of his ancestors, is a lazy and inefficient agriculturist, somewhat prone to cattle-stealing. The Pachhādas (30,000), as they are termed by others, are a congeries of Muhammadan tribes, many of whom claim to be Rājputs, though the claim rests on but slender evidence. Their name and tradition point to their having come from the west (*pachhim*), and their facial type suggests a connexion with the tribes of the Western Punjab. They are indifferent agriculturists, lazy, improvident, and sometimes cattle thieves; in physique inferior to the Deswālī and Sikh Jāts, though perhaps superior to the Bāgrī. The Mālīs, chiefly market-gardeners (13,000), are entirely Hindu; the Arains (5,000) Muhammadan; the Brāhmans (43,000) are Gaur, Sārsut, Khāndelwāl, Dahmīa, Gujrātī, Achārj, and Chamārwa in order of status. The great majority of the Gaur and Sārsut Brāhmans are agriculturists, but all are fed on various occasions and venerated, though disliked. Pushkankar Brāhmans from Ajmer are also found. Of the commercial classes the most important is that of the Baniās (61,000), who are divided into three sub-divisions—Agarwāl, Oswāl, and Mahesrī—who neither smoke, eat, nor intermarry with each other. Of artisan and menial tribes may be noted the Ahīrs (10,000), a vagrant tribe who claim Rājput origin, the Tarkhāns (carpenters, 20,000), Lohārs or blacksmiths (10,000), Chamārs or leather-workers (69,000), Dhānaks (20,000), and Chūhrās or scavengers (25,000). Of the total population of the District 72 per cent. are agricultural, and practically the whole of the rural population is dependent on agriculture.

Christian missions.

Two lady missionary doctors are stationed at Bhiwāni, where the Baptist Mission of Delhi maintains a girls' school. The District is also visited by missionaries of the Society for the Propagation of the Gospel from Delhi. In 1901 it contained 53 native Christians.

General agricultural conditions.

The District is divided into four natural tracts. Of these, the Rohi of the Sirsa *tahsīl* stretches from the northern boundary to the Ghaggar. Its soil is a soft loam with a reddish tinge, interspersed with sand and clay; the water-level in the wells varies from 40 to 180 feet, the crops depend entirely on rainfall, and vegetation is sparse. South of the Rohi lies the western extremity of the Nāli tract, stretching from east to west through the Fatahābād and Sirsa *tahsīls*, and traversed by the Ghaggar and Johiya. Its characteristic feature is a hard iron-clay soil, which permits of no cultivation until well saturated by the summer floods. Here the harvest depends on inundation from the Ghaggar and Johiya, helped in some parts by well-irrigation. The Bāgar tract stretches from the south and south-west of Sirsa along the western border of the District, through Sirsa, Fatahābād, Hissār, and Bhiwāni, gradually widening towards the south. Here the prevailing features are a light sandy soil and shifting sandhills, interspersed in parts with firmer and even loamy bottoms; the spring-level is more than 100 feet below the surface, and the water frequently bitter. Practically the *kharīf* is the only harvest sown, and that depends entirely on a sufficient rainfall. The Hariāna tract stretches from the tract watered by the Ghaggar to the south-east corner of the District; it comprises the whole of Hānsi and the eastern portions of Fatahābād, Hissār, and Bhiwāni, and is traversed by the WESTERN JUMNA CANAL. The leading feature of the tract is its firm clay soil; sandhills are found, and in low-lying parts hard clayey soil. The spring-level is generally below 100 feet, except in canal villages where it rises to 30 or 40 feet. Apart from the canal tract, agriculture is practically confined to the autumn harvest. The small jungle tract of Budhlāda, consisting of 15 outlying villages in the north of the Fatahābād *tahsīl*, is sometimes classed as a fifth tract, but resembles the Rohi. Taking the District as a whole, only 9 per cent. of the cultivation is irrigated, and the rainfall is therefore of the utmost importance; on the rainfall of June and July depends the sowing of the autumn crops, and on that of August and September the ripening of the autumn and the sowing of the spring crops. Until recently the autumn harvest was the mainstay of the District; but of late years, owing to the good prices obtained for wheat, the spring harvest has taken the leading place, and the best season is one in which there is heavy rain at the end of August and all through September.

The area for which details are available from the revenue

records of 1903–4 is 5,180 square miles, as shown in the following table:— Chief agricultural statistics and principal crops.

Tahsīl.	Total.	Cultivated.	Irrigated.	Cultivable waste.
Hissār . . .	810	623	53	98
Hānsi . . .	799	690	180	60
Bhiwāni . .	750	603	6	110
Fatahābād . .	1,179	1,300	69	165
Sirsa . . .	1,642	945	75	300
Total	5,180	4,161	383	733

The principal staples of the spring harvest are gram and barley, the areas under which in 1903–4 were 478 and 168 square miles respectively. Wheat covered only 109 square miles. The chief food-grain of the autumn harvest is spiked millet, which occupied 929 square miles. Great millet comes next in importance with 38 square miles, and then pulses with 175. Practically all the sugar-cane and cotton grown is irrigated, with four-fifths of the maize, three-fifths of the rice, and two-fifths of the wheat. No other crop is irrigated to any appreciable extent.

Improvements in agricultural practice.

The cultivation of rice has of late years been prohibited in canal lands, and its place largely taken by cotton. Experiments are being carried on chiefly with the object of introducing cotton of a longer staple. There is great room for improvement in the methods adopted by the people for utilizing the canal water at their disposal.

Large advances are given both under the Land Improvement Loans Act for digging and clearing wells, and under the Agriculturists' Loans Act for the purchase of bullocks and seed. During the five years ending September, 1904, a total of Rs. 73,000 was advanced under the former and 18 lakhs under the latter Act, of which Rs. 43,627 and 10·5 lakhs respectively was advanced during the famine year 1899–1900.

Cattle, horses, and sheep.

Hariāna has been always famous for its cattle, which were the chief support of its former pastoral inhabitants. The breed is still good, though cattle-breeding is somewhat on the wane owing to the spread of cultivation. The Hissār Government cattle farm was started in 1813, and now covers 66 square miles. The pure breeds of cattle maintained are the Gujarātī, Ungoli, Nagaur, and Mysore, which are also crossed with Hariāna cows. Of late years mule-breeding has been commenced. Large cattle fairs are held at Hissār and Sirsa, at which it is estimated that animals of the total value of 6½ lakhs are sold annually. The camel is used in all parts for riding and carrying loads, and where the soil is light does a large part of the ploughing. The local breed of horses is in no way above the average. The District board maintains five horse and four donkey stallions.

Irrigation.

Of the total area cultivated in 1903-4, 383 square miles, or nearly 9 per cent., were classed as irrigated. Of this area, 6 square miles were irrigated from wells and 377 from canals. In addition, 83 square miles, or 2 per cent., are subject to inundation from the Ghaggar and other streams. The Hānsi branch of the WESTERN JUMNA CANAL irrigates the Hānsi, Hissār, and Bhiwāni *tahsils*, while the Sirsa branch irrigates parts of Fatahābād, Hissār, and Sirsa. The GHAGGAR CANALS supply part of the Sirsa *tahsīl*, and the Budhlāda tract and a portion of Sirsa are watered by the SIRHIND CANAL. The area under canal-irrigation increased from 120 square miles in 1891 to 377 in 1904. The area supplied by wells is insignificant, owing to the great depth to water, and the chief use of well-irrigation is to enable sowings to be made for the spring harvest. The total number of wells in use for irrigation was only 854 in 1903-4, all being worked by cattle on the rope and bucket system.

Forests.

The greater part of the cattle farm, known as the Hissār Bīr, is a 'reserved' forest, measuring 65 square miles, under the Civil Veterinary department, the income from which in 1903-4 was Rs. 4,379. The Bīr at Hānsi is an unclassed forest under the same department. Three pieces of grazing-ground are managed by the Deputy-Commissioner at Hissār, Sirsa, and Hānsi for the town cattle. The total area of forest land is: 'reserved,' 65 square miles; and unclassed, 5 square miles. Trees have been extensively planted with the aid of canal water by the District board in and around the civil station of Hissār and the town of Hānsi, and the Bīr at Hānsi is also being planted with trees to make a fuel reserve.

Minerals.

Kankar is found in many localities. Saltpetre is manufactured from saline earth in the villages, and refined in licensed refineries at Bhiwāni, Hānsi, and Sirsa.

Arts and manufactures.

The District has no manufactures of importance. Coarse country cloth is made almost everywhere; and there are 10 cotton-ginning factories, 3 cotton-presses, and 3 factories where ginning and pressing are combined. Hānsi is the industrial centre; but four of the factories are at Bhiwāni, and one at Narnaund, while the cotton-mills of Messrs. Chandu Lāl & Co. at Hissār are the largest in the District. These industries employed 2,061 hands in 1904. Bhiwāni is known for its plain brass and bell-metal work, and for its carved doors. The District produces cotton *phūlkāris* embroidered with silk, which are of exceptional excellence, and embroidered woollen *phūlkāris* are also made. The carpenters' work is above the average.

Commerce and trade

The chief centres of trade are Bhiwāni, Hānsi, Hissār, Budhlāda, and Sirsa on the railway; but a good deal of local trade does not pass through these places, being brought direct to the consumers by individual speculators, generally Bishnoī or Bāgrī Jāts. Hissār and Hānsi are chiefly distributing centres for local requirements; but Bhiwāni and Sirsa are important as centres of through trade to Rājputāna, wheat, flour, sugar, and cotton goods being largely exported.

Railways and roads.

The Rewāri-Bhatinda branch of the Rājputāna-Mālwā Railway runs through the District for 122 miles, while the Southern Punjab Railway passes through Budhlāda, Jākhal, and Tohāna, and the Jodhpur-Bīkaner Railway runs through part of the Sirsa *tahsīl*. The District has 26 miles of metalled and 949 of unmetalled roads, of which 17 miles of metalled and 90 of unmetalled roads are under the Public Works department and the rest under the District board. The unmetalled roads are fit for cart traffic, except in the sandy tracts where camels are used. The Hānsi branch of the Western Jumna Canal is navigable as far as Hānsi.

Famine.

Hissār has always been most liable to famine of all the Districts of the Punjab, owing to the fact that, while pre-eminently dependent on the autumn harvest and very little protected by irrigation, it suffers from a most capricious monsoon, while it receives the first rush of starving wanderers from Bīkaner. The *chālīsa* famine of 1782–3, as has been related, laid waste the District; and in all the famines that have since visited the Punjab, Hissār has always suffered in a pre-eminent degree. Both in 1896–7 and in 1899–1900 the whole of the unirrigated area, or 3,763 square miles, was affected. In 1896–7 the greatest number relieved on any one day was 82,505 persons, and the highest death-rate in any one week was 81 per 1,000. In 1899–1900 the corresponding figures were 161,561 and 32 respectively. The amount expended by Government was 12·3 lakhs in 1896–7, and 25·7 lakhs in 1899–1900. The severity of the famine of 1899–1900 was emphasized by the fact that the people had not recovered from the preceding famine.

District

The District is in charge of a Deputy-Commissioner, assisted subdivisions and staff.

by three Assistant or Extra Assistant Commissioners, of whom one is in charge of the Sirsa *tahsīl* and subdivision. Each of the five *tahsīls* is in charge of a *tahsīldār* assisted by a *naib-tahsīldār*. Dabwāli in Sirsa and Tohāna in Fatahābād are sub-*tahsīls* under *naib-tahsīldārs*.

Civil justice and crime.

The Deputy-Commissioner as District Magistrate is responsible for the criminal justice of the District. Civil judicial work is under a District Judge. Both officers are supervised by the Divisional Judge of Ferozepore. The District Judge has a Munsif under him at head-quarters, and there are four honorary magistrates. Cattle-theft is the principal crime of the District, for which its position, surrounded by Native States, affords peculiar facilities. It is practised chiefly by the Muhammadan Rājputs and Pachhādas.

Land revenue administration.

The revenue history of Hissār proper is quite distinct from that of the Sirsa *tahsīl*, which was only added to the District on the disruption of the old Sirsa District in 1884. The greater part of Hissār was occupied by the British in 1810, and underwent three summary settlements for ten, five, and ten years successively, between 1815 and 1840. The main feature of these assessments was a demand so high that full collections were the exception, and the frequent remissions demoralized both the revenue officials and the people. A rush of immigrants had taken place on the establishment of settled government, and when disturbances occurred in the neighbouring Native States, Hissār formed a convenient refuge. The land revenue, however, was fixed and collected with such a complete disregard of the chances of bad seasons, that when the cultivators were pressed for payment they moved off into the Native States whence they had come. The demand of the first settlement (1815–25) was so high that it exceeded by 20 per cent. the revenue fixed in 1890 for the same villages. High though this assessment was, it was increased in the two settlements that followed, until between 1835 and 1839 the demand was 4·9 lakhs for a tract which in 1890 was assessed at only about two-thirds of that sum.

The amount fixed at the regular settlement of 1840 was 37 per cent. below the old demand. The canal villages were assessed at irrigated rates for the first time in 1839. The reduction came as a new lease of life to the impoverished landholders, and the progress made since has been steady, interrupted only by famine. A revised settlement was made in 1863, which resulted in a further reduction of half a lakh. The second revised settlement was carried out between 1887 and 1892. Cultivation had more than doubled, while prices had risen 60 per cent., and the result was an increase of 58 per cent. to 6 lakhs. The rates varied from 3 to 8 annas per acre, exclusive of canal rates. About 90 per cent. of the tenants pay rent in cash.

The Sirsa *tahsīl*, with the rest of the old Sirsa District, was summarily settled in 1829 and regularly in 1851. In 1881–2, the last year of the regular settlement, the demand stood at 1·4 lakhs, which was raised by the new assessment to 1·9 lakhs. The assessment was revised for the second time between 1901 and 1903, and a fixed assessment of 2 lakhs was announced. The area subject to the very precarious Ghaggar floods was placed under fluctuating assessment, fixed rates for the various crops grown being applied to the area actually cropped every harvest. It is estimated that the yield from this fluctuating assessment will be Rs. 39,000 per annum.

The collections of land revenue alone and of total revenue are shown below, in thousands of rupees :—

	1880-1.	1890-1.	1900-1.	1903-4
Land revenue . .	4,26	7,60	6,48	8,09
Total revenue .	5,08	9,65	9,99	11,90

Local and municipal.

The District contains four municipalities, HISSĀR, HĀNSI, BHIWĀNI, and SIRSA; and three 'notified areas,' FATAHĀBĀD, TOHĀNA, and Budhlādā. Outside these, local affairs are managed by the District board, whose income amounted in 1903–4 to $1\frac{1}{4}$ lakhs. The expenditure in the same year was 1·3 lakhs, education and public works forming the principal items.

Police and jails.

The regular police force consists of 681 of all ranks, including 180 municipal police, under a Superintendent who is usually assisted by four inspectors. The village watchmen or *chaukīdārs* number 1,474, and 42 *chaukīdārs* are directly under the Superintendent. There are 19 police stations, 4 outposts, and 6 road-posts. The District jail at head-quarters has accommodation for 252 prisoners.

Education.

The District stands twenty-fifth among the twenty-eight Districts of the Province in respect of the literacy of its population. In 1901 the proportion of literate persons was 2·7 per cent. (5 males and 0·1 females). The number of pupils under instruction was 1,753[1] in 1880–1, 3,568 in

[1] For the District as then constituted.

1890–1, 3,803 in 1900–1, and 4,258 in 1903–4. In the last year there were 6 secondary and 73 primary (public) schools, and 3 advanced and 46 elementary (private) schools, with 167 girls in the public and 91 in the private schools. The Anglo-vernacular schools at Hissār, Bhiwāni, and Sirsa are the most important. Two girls' schools at Bhiwāni are maintained by the Baptist Zanāna Mission. The total expenditure on education in 1903–4 was Rs. 40,000, to which Provincial funds contributed Rs. 2,000, municipalities Rs. 11,000, fees Rs. 10,000, and District funds Rs. 16,000, while the rest (Rs. 1,000) was met from subscriptions and endowments.

Hospitals and dispensaries.

Besides the dispensary at Hissār, the District possesses eight outlying dispensaries. In 1904 the number of cases treated was 73,530, of whom 2,216 were in-patients, and 6,027 operations were performed. The expenditure was Rs. 20,000, the greater part of which was met from municipal funds.

Vaccination.

The number of successful vaccinations in 1903–4 was 10,038, or 23·7 per 1,000 of the population.

[J. Wilson, *General Code of Tribal Custom in the Sirsa District* (1883); P. J. Fagan, *District Gazetteer* (1892, under revision); A. Anderson and P. J. Fagan, *Settlement Report of Hissār* (1892); C. M. King, *Settlement Report of Sirsa and Fāzilka Tahsīls* (1905).]

Hissār Tahsīl.—*Tahsīl* of Hissār District, Punjab, lying between 28° 54′ and 29° 32′ N. and 75° 22′ and 76° 2′ E., on the borders of the Bīkaner desert, with an area of 810 square miles. The population in 1901 was 128,783, compared with 122,299 in 1891. HISSĀR (population, 17,647) is the head-quarters, and the *tahsīl* also contains 134 villages. The land revenue and cesses amounted in 1903–4 to 1·6 lakhs. The northern part is a bare plain, forming part of the tract known as Hariāna, where the soil is a firm sandy loam. South of the thin belt of fertility afforded by the Western Jumna Canal, the level stretches of poor cultivation gradually merge into the rolling sandhills characteristic of the neighbouring State of Bīkaner.

Hānsi Tahsīl.—*Tahsīl* of Hissār District, Punjab, lying between 28° 51′ and 29° 27′ N. and 75° 48′ and 76° 20′ E., with an area of 799 square miles. The population in 1901 was 178,933, compared with 165,689 in 1891. It contains the town of HĀNSI (population, 16,523), the head-quarters, and 132 villages. The land revenue and cesses amounted in 1903–4 to 2 lakhs. The whole of the *tahsīl* lies within the tract known as Hariāna. The northern part is irrigated by the Western Jumna Canal, and is comparatively well wooded. South of the canal the country is featureless, but fertile enough in a year of good rainfall.

Bhiwāni Tahsīl (*Bhawāni*).—*Tahsīl* of Hissār District, Punjab, lying between 28° 36′ and 28° 59′ N. and 75° 29′ and 76° 18′ E., with an area of 750 square miles. The population in 1901 was 124,429, compared with 127,794 in 1891. The head-quarters are at the town of BHIWĀNI (population, 35,917); and it also contains 131 villages, among which TOSHĀM is a place of some historical importance. The land revenue and cesses amounted in 1903–4 to 1·2 lakhs. The northern part of the *tahsīl* lies in Hariāna. South of Bhiwāni town rolling sandhills and low rocky eminences are the main features of the landscape.

Fatahābād Tahsīl (*Fatehābād*).—*Tahsīl* of Hissār District, Punjab, lying between 29° 13′ and 29° 48′ N. and 75° 13′ and 76° 0′ E., with an area of 1,179 square miles. The population in 1901 was 190,921, compared with 181,638 in 1891. It contains one town, FATAHĀBĀD (population, 2,786), the head-quarters, and 261 villages, among which TOHĀNA and AGROHA are places of historical or archaeological interest. The land revenue and cesses amounted in 1903–4 to 2·3 lakhs. The Ghaggar has cut for itself a deep channel in the north of the *tahsīl.* To the south of this channel lies a broad belt of stiff clay, covered with sparse jungle interspersed with stretches of precarious cultivation, which depend on occasional floods brought by natural and artificial channels from the Ghaggar. The east of the *tahsīl* lies in Hariāna, but the centre and south are bare and sandy. A portion is irrigated by the Western Jumna Canal.

Tohāna Sub-tahsīl.—Sub-*tahsīl* of the Fatahābād *tahsīl* of Hissār District, Punjab, with an area of 450 square miles. It contains 117 villages, and the land revenue and cesses amounted in 1903–4 to Rs. 86,000. TOHĀNA is the head-quarters.

Sirsa Tahsīl.—*Tahsīl* and subdivision of Hissār District, Punjab, lying between 29° 13′ and 30° 0′ N. and 74° 29′ and 75° 18′ E., on the borders of the Bīkaner desert, with an area of 1,642 square miles. The population in 1901 was 158,651, compared with 178,586 in 1891. The town of SIRSA (population, 15,800) is the head-quarters. It also contains 3 other towns and 306 villages. The land revenue and cesses amounted in 1903–4 to 2·9 lakhs. The whole of the *tahsīl* is sandy, except the belt of stiff clay which forms the Ghaggar basin, and depends for its successful cultivation on the river floods, which, below the Otu lake and dam, are distributed over the country by the Ghaggar canals. There is some irrigation in the north from the Sirhind Canal, and in the south from the Western Jumna Canal.

Dabwāli Sub-tahsīl.—Sub-*tahsīl* of the Sirsa *tahsīl* of Hissār District, Punjab, with an area of 349 square miles. It contains 59 villages, and the land revenue and cesses amounted in 1903–4 to Rs. 96,000.

Skinner Estates.—A group of estates held by the descendants of Lieutenant-Colonel James Skinner, C.B., in the Districts of Hissār, Delhi, and Karnāl, Punjab. The area of the estates is 251 square miles in Hissār, 2·6 in Delhi, and 21·4 in Karnāl, and the total revenue of the estates in Hissār is Rs. 62,683. James Skinner, the son of a Scottish officer in the East India Company's service and a Rājput lady, was born in 1778 and received his first commission from De Boigne, the famous Savoyard adventurer, who had organized Sindhia's brigades. After many years' service under the Marāthās, during which he was employed against the adventurer George Thomas, Skinner joined the British forces under Lord Lake in 1803, and received the command of 2,000 of Perron's Hindustāni Horse, who came over to the British after the battle of Delhi. This body served with great distinction under Skinner for thirty years, and is now represented by the 1st Lancers and 3rd Cavalry (Skinner's Horse) of the Indian Army. Rising to be a Lieutenant-Colonel in the British service, Skinner obtained large grants of land in the Delhi territory, and settled at Hānsi in Hissār District, where he died in 1841. He built St. James's Church at Delhi in fulfilment of a vow. Major Robert Skinner, his younger brother, also served under Perron and eventually entered the Company's service.

Agroha.—Ancient town in the Fatahābād *tahsīl* of Hissār District, Punjab, situated in 29° 20′ N. and 75° 38′ E., 13 miles north-west of Hissār. It is said to be the original seat of the Agarwāl Baniās, and was once a place of great importance. The remains of a fort are still visible about half a mile from the existing village, and ruins and débris half buried in the soil on every side attest its former greatness. It was captured by Muhammad of Ghor in 1194, since which time the Agarwāl Baniās have been scattered over the whole peninsula. The clan comprises many of the wealthiest men in India. The present village is quite unimportant and has (1901) a population of only 1,172.

Bhiwāni Town (*Bhawāni*).—Head-quarters of the *tahsīl* of the same name in Hissār District, Punjab, situated in 28° 48′ N. and 76° 8′ E., on the Rewāri-Bhatinda branch of the Rājputānā-Mālwā Railway; distant by rail from Calcutta 1,059 miles, from Bombay 890, and from Karāchi 857. Population (1901), 35,917. The town is practically a creation of British rule, having been an insignificant village when it was selected in 1817 as the site of a free market. It rapidly rose to importance; and though its trade suffered greatly from the opening of the Rājputāna-Mālwā Railway, the construction of the Rewāri-Ferozepore line has restored it to its former position. Bhiwāni is commercially the most important town in Hissār District. It is one of the great centres of trade with Rājputāna the chief articles of commerce being wheat, flour, salt, sugar, cotton goods, and iron. It possesses three cotton-ginning factories and one cotton-press, which give employment to 379 hands. The principal manufactures are brass vessels, tin boxes, and small wooden tables. The municipality was created in 1867. The municipal receipts during the ten years ending 1902–3 averaged Rs. 54,900, and the expenditure Rs. 56,700. The income and expenditure in 1903–4 were Rs. 49,700 and Rs. 47,700 respectively; the chief source of income was octroi (Rs. 42,700), while the main items of outlay were conservancy (Rs. 7,000), education (Rs. 7,700), medical (Rs. 6,900), public safety (Rs. 13,300), and administration (Rs. 4,800). The town has an Anglo-vernacular middle school and a dispensary.

Fatahābād Town (*Fatehābād*).—Head-quarters of the *tahsīl* of the same name in Hissār District, Punjab, situated in 29° 31′ N. and 75° 27′ E., 30 miles north-west of Hissār. Population (1901), 2,786. The town was founded about 1352 by the emperor Fīroz Shāh, who named it after his son Fateh Khān, and had a canal dug to it from the Ghaggar. The fort contains a pillar inscribed with the genealogy of Fīroz Shāh, and a mosque and inscription of Humāyūn. The town is of no commercial importance. It is administered as a 'notified area,' the income of which in 1903–4 was Rs. 1,700.

Hānsi Town.—Head-quarters of the *tahsīl* of the same name in Hissār District, Punjab, situated in 29° 7′ N. and 75° 58′ E., on the Rewāri-Bhatinda branch of the Rājputāna-Mālwā Railway, 15 miles from Hissār. Population (1901), 16,523. This is one of the most ancient towns in Northern India and appears to have been a stronghold of the Kushans, though local tradition attributes its foundation to Anang Pāl, the Tomar king of Delhi. According to the authorities quoted in Tod's *Rajasthan*, Asī or Hānsi was assigned to the son of Bīsaldeo Chauhān about A.D. 1000. Masūd, son of Mahmūd of Ghazni, took it, after one failure, in 1036, but, according to Firishta, it was recovered by the Delhi Rājā in 1043. Prithwī Rāj made considerable additions to the fort at Hānsi, converting it into an important military stronghold. It fell into the hands of Muhammad of Ghor in 1192, and was, until the foundation of Hissār, the administrative head-quarters of the neighbourhood. Hānsi was depopulated by the famine of 1783, and lay deserted until 1798, when the famous adventurer George Thomas, who had seized upon the greater part of Hariāna, fixed his head-quarters here. Thenceforth the town began to revive, and on the establishment of British rule in 1803 it was made a cantonment, where a considerable force, consisting chiefly of local levies, was stationed. In 1857 the troops mutinied, murdered all Europeans upon whom they could lay their hands, and combined with the wild Rājput tribes in plundering the country. On the restoration of order, the cantonment was given up. A high brick wall, with bastions and loopholes, surrounds the town, while the canal, which flows at its feet, contributes to its beauty by a fringe of handsome trees. Since the Mutiny, however, the houses have fallen into decay and the streets lie comparatively deserted, owing to the removal of the troops. The ruins of the fort overlook the town on the north. It contains two mosques and the tomb of Saiyid Niāmat Ullah, killed in resisting Muhammad of Ghor. The mosque and tombs of Kutb Jamāl-ud-dīn and his successors are on the west of the town, with the tomb of Alī Mīr Tijāra. Near by is a mosque called the Shahīd Ganj, situated probably on the scene of Masūd's first unsuccessful attempt to take Hānsi.

The municipality was created in 1867. The income during the ten years ending 1902-3 averaged Rs. 18,500 and the expenditure Rs. 18,800; and the income and expenditure in 1903-4 were Rs. 30,000 and Rs. 20,000 respectively, the chief source of income being octroi. The town has 6 cotton-ginning factories, 2 cotton-presses, and 2 combined ginning and pressing factories, and is a local centre of the cotton trade. The number of factory hands in 1904 was 1,285. It possesses a vernacular middle school and a dispensary.

Hissār Town.—Head-quarters of the District and *tahsīl* of the same name, Punjab, situated in 29° 10′ N. and 75° 44′ E., on the Rewāri-Bhatinda branch of the Rājputāna-Mālwā

Railway; distant by rail from Calcutta 1,097 miles, from Bombay 979, and from Karāchi 819. Population (1901), 17,647. It was founded in 1356 by Fīroz Shāh Tughlak, and supplied with water by means of the canal now known as the Western Jumna Canal, and became the head-quarters of a *sarkār*. In 1408 Hissar fell into the hands of the rebels against Mahmūd Tughlak, but was recovered in 1411 by the emperor in person. It appears to have been occupied by an imperial garrison at the time of Bābar's invasion, and as the head-quarters of a *sarkār* was of considerable importance under the Mughals. The town was plundered by the Sikhs on several occasions between 1754 and 1768, and after the battle of Jīnd was occupied by Amar Singh of Patiāla, who built a fort. Hissār was depopulated by the famine of 1783, and was taken possession of by George Thomas. The inhabitants began to return, and when it passed to the British in 1803 the town was rapidly recovering. In 1857 detachments of the Hariāna Light Infantry and 14th Irregular Cavalry stationed at Hissār mutinied, and the Collector and eleven other Europeans and native Christians were murdered. The chief relic of antiquity is the fort built by Fīroz Shāh, largely with materials taken from Hindu or Jain temples. Another interesting building is the Jahāj, apparently once a Jain temple converted into a mosque, and used as a residence by George Thomas, of whose Christian name its present title is a corruption. Near Hissār is a handsome group of tombs erected to commanders who fell in Humāyūn's campaign in Gujarāt in 1535. The trade of the town is unimportant, being confined to cotton and red pepper; but it contains a large cotton-ginning and pressing factory, which in 1904 employed 397 hands. The municipality was created in 1867. The municipal receipts and expenditure during the ten years ending 1902–3 averaged Rs. 28,700 and 29,300, and in 1903–4 amounted to Rs. 24,600 and Rs. 27,300 respectively, the chief source of income being octroi. The town possesses an Anglo-vernacular high school managed by the Educational department, and a civil hospital.

Sirsa Town.—Head-quarters of the subdivision and *tahsīl* of the same name in Hissār District, Punjab, situated in 29° 32′ N. and 75° 2′ E., on the Rewāri-Bhatinda branch of the Rājputāna-Mālwā Railway, on the north side of a dry bed of the Ghaggar. Population (1901), 15,800. The old town of Sirsa or Sarsūti is of great antiquity, and tradition ascribes its origin to an eponymous Rājā Sāras, who built the town and fort about 1,300 years ago. Under the name of Sarsūti, it is mentioned as the place near which Prithwī Rāj was captured after his defeat by Muhammad of Ghor in 1192; and according to Wassāf it was in the fourteenth century one of the most important towns in Upper India. It was taken by Tīmūr, the inhabitants fleeing before him, and is mentioned in the reign of Mubārak Shāh as the rendezvous of the expedition against the rebel fortress of Sirhind. In the reign of Sher Shāh, Sirsa became for a time the head-quarters of Rao Kalyān Singh of Bīkaner, who had been driven from his country by the Rao of Jodhpur. In the eighteenth century Sirsa was one of the strongholds of the Bhattis, and was taken by Amar Singh of Patiāla in 1774, but restored to the Bhattis by the agreement of 1781. The town was depopulated by the great famine of 1783, and the site was annexed in 1818 after the expedition sent against the Bhatti chief, Nawāb Zābita Khān. In 1838 Sirsa, which had lain deserted since 1783, was refounded by Captain Thoresby, who laid out the present town, which from 1858 to 1884 was the head-quarters of the Sirsa District. The ruins of Old Sirsa lie near the south-west corner of the modern town, and still present considerable remains, though much of the material has been used for building the new houses. It contains an ancient Hindu fort and tank.

The municipality was created in 1867. The income during the ten years ending 1902–3 averaged Rs. 23,300 and the expenditure Rs. 23,900; and income and expenditure in 1903–4 each amounted to Rs. 18,100, the chief source of income being octroi. The town is a centre of the export trade to Rājputāna, and is in a flourishing condition. Most of the trade is in the hands of Baniās from Rājputāna and the country to the south-east. Sirsa contains a dispensary, an Anglo-vernacular middle school maintained by the municipality, and an aided primary school for European boys.

Tohāna Town.—Town in the Fatahābād *tahsīl* of Hissār District, Punjab, situated in 29° 43′ N. and 75° 54′ E., 40 miles north of Hissār town. Population (1901), 5,931. It was once a city of some size and importance, founded, according to tradition, by Anang Pāl, the Tomar Rājā of Delhi. Ruined during the Chauhān supremacy, it recovered its prosperity in the early Musalmān period; but having suffered many vicissitudes of plunder and famine, it has now sunk into an inferior position. It was the scene of a defeat of the Jāts by Tīmūr in 1398. Numerous remains in the neighbourhood testify to its former importance. The town is administered as a 'notified area,' which in 1903–4 had an income of Rs. 900.

Toshām.—Village in the Bhiwāni *tahsīl* of Hissār District, Punjab, situated in 28° 54′ N. and 75° 56′ E., 23 miles south-west of Hissār town. Population (1901), 2,665. A bare rocky elevation, the highest in the District, rises abruptly above the town and desert plain to a height of 800 feet. A tank cut in the rock, half-way up the hill, forms the scene of a yearly fair, and is frequented by pilgrims, some of them from considerable distances. A *bāradari* on a small hill near the town is called Prithwī Rāj's *kacherī*, and an inscription close by was attributed by Sir Alexander Cunningham to an Indo-Scythian king, Toshāra.

Rohtak District.—District in the Delhi Division of the Punjab, lying between 28° 21′ and 29° 17′ N. and 76° 13′ and 76° 58′ E., on the borders of Rājputāna, in the high level plain that separates the waters of the Jumna and Sutlej, with an area of 1,797 square miles. The eastern part falls within the borders of the tract formerly known as HARIĀNA. In its midst lies part of the small State of DUJĀNA. It is bounded on the north by the Jīnd *nizāmat* of Jīnd State, and by Karnāl District; on the east by Delhi, and on the south-east by Gurgaon; on the south by Pataudi State and the Rewāri *tahsīl* of Gurgaon; on the south-west by territory belonging to the Nawāb of Dujāna; and on the west by the Dādrī *nizāmat* of Jīnd and by Hissār District. Although there is no grand scenery in Rohtak, the canals with their belts of trees, the lines of sandhills, and in the south the torrents, the depressions which are flooded after heavy rain, and a few small rocky hills give the District more diversified features than are generally met with in the plains of the Punjab. The eastern border lies low on the level of the Jumna Canal and the Najafgarh swamp. A few miles west the surface rises gradually to a level plateau, which, speaking roughly, stretches as far as the town of Rohtak, and is enclosed by parallel rows of sandhills running north and south. Beyond the western line of sandhills the surface rises again till it ends on the Hissār border in a third high ridge. The eastern line runs, with here and there an interval, down the east side of the District, and rises to some height in the Jhajjar *tahsīl*. South-west of this ridge the country becomes more undulating, and the soil lighter. The south-eastern corner of the District is crossed by two small streams or torrents, the Sāhibi and Indori; these flow circuitously, throwing off a network of branches and collecting here and there after heavy rain in *jhīls* of considerable size, and finally fall into the Najafgarh swamp.

Boundaries, configuration, and hill and river systems.

Geology.

With the exception of a few small outliers of Alwar quartzite belonging to the Delhi system, there is nothing of geological interest in the District, which is almost entirely of alluvial formation.

Botany.

The District forms an arm from the Upper Gangetic plain between the Central Punjab and the desert. Trees, except where naturalized or planted, are rare, but the *nimbar* (*Acacia leucophloea*) is a conspicuous exception. Mango groves are frequent in the north-east; and along canals and roadsides other sub-tropical species have been planted successfully. The *ber* (*Zizyphus Jujuba*) is common, and is often planted.

Fauna.

Game, including wild hog, antelope, 'ravine deer' (Indian gazelle), *nīlgai*, and hare, is plentiful. Peafowl, partridge, and quail are to be met with throughout the year; and during the cold season sand-grouse, wild geese, bustards, and flamingoes. Wolves are still common, and a stray leopard is occasionally killed. The villages by the canal are overrun by monkeys.

Climate and temperature.

The climate is not inaptly described in the *Memoirs* of George Thomas as 'in general salubrious, though when the sandy and desert country lying to the westward becomes heated, it is inimical to a European constitution.' In April, May, and June the hot winds blow steadily all day from the west, bringing up constant sandstorms from the Rājputāna desert; at the close of the year frosts are common, and strong gales prevail in February and March.

Rainfall.

The average rainfall varies from 19 inches at Jhajjar to 21 at Rohtak. Of the rainfall at the latter place, 18 inches fall in the summer months and 3 in the winter. The greatest fall recorded during the years 1885–1902 was 41 inches at Jhajjar in 1885–6, and the least 8 inches at Rohtak in 1901–2.

History.

The District belongs for the most part to the tract of Hariāna, and its early history will be found in the articles on that region and on the towns of Rohtak, Maham, and Jhajjar. It appears to have come at an early date under the control of the Delhi kings, and in 1355 Fīroz Shāh dug a canal from the Sutlej as far as Jhajjar. Under Akbar the present District lay within the *Sūbah* of Delhi and the *sarkārs* of Delhi and Hissār-Fīroza. In 1643 the Rohtak canal is said to have been begun by Nawāb Alī Khān, who attempted to divert water from the old canal of Fīroz Shāh. On the decay of the Delhi empire the District with the rest of Hariāna was granted to the minister Rukn-ud-dīn in 1718, and was in 1732 transferred by him to the Nawābs of Farrukhnagar in Gurgaon. Faujdār Khān, Nawāb of Farrukhnagar, who seems to have succeeded to the territories of Hissār on the death of Shāhdād Khān in 1738, handed down to his son Nawāb Kāmgār Khān a dominion which embraced the present Districts of Hissār and Rohtak, besides part of Gurgaon and a considerable tract subsequently annexed by the chiefs of Jīnd and Patiāla. Hissār and the north were during this time perpetually overrun by the Sikhs, in spite of the combined efforts of the Bhattis and the imperial forces; but Rohtak and Gurgaon appear to have remained with Kāmgār Khān till his death in 1760. His son, Mūsa Khān, was expelled from Farrukhnagar by Sūraj Mal, the Jāt ruler of Bharatpur; and the Jāts held Jhajjar, Badli, and Farrukhnagar till 1771. In that year Mūsa Khān recovered Farrukhnagar, but he never regained a footing in the Rohtak District. In 1772 Najaf Khān came into power at Delhi, and till his death in 1782 some order was maintained. Bahādurgarh, granted in 1754 to Bahādur Khān, Baloch, was held by his son and grandson; Jhajjar was in the hands of Walter Reinhardt, the husband of Begam Sumrū of Sardhana; and Gohāna, Maham, Rohtak, and Kharkhauda were also held by nominees of Najaf Khān. The Marāthās returned in 1785, but could do little to repel the Sikh invasion; and from 1785 to 1803 the north of the District was occupied by the Rājā of Jīnd, while the south and west were precariously held by the Marāthās, who were defied by the strong Jāt villages and constantly attacked by the Sikhs. Meanwhile the military adventurer George Thomas had carved out a principality in Hariāna, which included Maham, Berī, and Jhajjar in the present District; his head-quarters were at Hānsi in the District of Hissār, and at Georgegarh near Jhajjar he had built a small outlying fort. In 1801, however, the Marāthās made common cause with the Sikhs and Rājputs against him, and under the French commander, Louis Bourquin, defeated him at Georgegarh, and succeeded in ousting him from his dominions. In 1803, by the conquests of Lord Lake, the whole country up to the Sutlej and the Siwāliks passed to the British Government.

Under Lord Lake's arrangements, the northern *parganas* of Rohtak were held by the Sikh chiefs of Jīnd and Kaithal, while the south was granted to the Nawāb of Jhajjar, the west to his brother, the Nawāb of Dādrī and Bahādurgarh, and the central tract to the Nawāb of Dujāna. The latter, however, was unable to maintain order in his portion of the territories thus assigned, and the frequent incursions of Sikh and Bhatti marauders compelled the dispatch of a British officer in 1810 to bring the region into better organization. The few *parganas* thus subjected to British rule formed the nucleus of the present District. Other fringes of territory escheated on the deaths of the Kaithal Rājā in 1818, and the chief of Jīnd in 1820. In the last-named year, Hissār and Sirsa were separated from Rohtak; and in 1824 the District was brought into nearly its present shape by the District of Pānīpat (now Karnāl) being made a separate charge.

Up to 1832 Rohtak was administered by a Political Agent under the Resident at Delhi; but it was then brought under the Regulations, and included in the North-Western Provinces. On the outbreak of the Mutiny in 1857, Rohtak was for a time completely lost to the British Government. The Muhammadan tribes, uniting with their brethren in Gurgaon and Hissār, began a general predatory movement under the Nawābs of Farrukhnagar, Jhajjar, and Bahādurgarh, and the Bhatti chieftains of Sirsa and Hissār. They attacked and plundered the civil station at Rohtak, destroying every record of administration. But before the fall of Delhi, a force of Punjab levies was brought across the Sutlej, and order was restored with little difficulty. The rebel Nawābs of Jhajjar and Bahādurgarh were captured and tried. The former was executed at Delhi, while his neighbour and relative escaped with a sentence of exile to Lahore. Their estates were confiscated, part of them being temporarily included in a new District of Jhajjar, while other portions were assigned to the Rājās of Jīnd, Patiāla, and Nābha as rewards for their services during the Mutiny. Rohtak District was transferred to the Punjab Government; and in 1860 Jhajjar was broken up, part of it being added to the territory of the loyal Rājās, and the remainder united with Rohtak.

Archaeology.

There are no antiquities of any note, and the history of the old sites is unknown. Excavations at the Rohtak Khokra Kot would seem to show that three cities have been successively destroyed there; the well-known coins of Rājā Samanta Deva, who is supposed to have reigned over Kābul and the Punjab about A.D. 920, are found at Mohan Bāri. Jhajjar, Maham, and Gohāna possess some old tombs, but none is of any special architectural merit; the finest are at the first place. There is an old *baoli* or stepped well at Rohtak and another at Maham: the latter has been described by the author of *Pen and Pencil Sketches*, and must have been in much better repair in 1828 than it is now. The Gaokaran tank at Rohtak and the Būāwāla tank at Jhajjar are fine works, while the masonry tank built by the last Nawāb of Jhajjar at Chuchakwās is exceedingly handsome. The *asthal* or Jog monastery at Bohar is the only group of buildings of any architectural pretensions in the District; the Jhajjar palaces are merely large houses on the old Indian plan.

Rohtak contains 11 towns and 491 villages. Its population at each of the last four enumerations was: (1868) 531,118, (1881) 553,609, (1891) 590,475, and (1901) 630,672. It increased by nearly 7 per cent. during the last decade, the increase being greatest in the Sāmpla *tahsīl*, and least in Jhajjar. It is divided into four *tahsīls*—ROHTAK, JHAJJAR, SĀMPLA, and GOHĀNA—the head-quarters of each being at the place from which it is named. The chief towns are the municipalities of ROHTAK, the administrative head-quarters of the District, JHAJJAR, BERI, BAHĀDURGARH, and GOHĀNA. The people.

The following table shows the distribution of population in 1901:—

Tahsīl.	Area in square miles.	Number of Towns.	Number of Villages.	Population.	Population per square mile.	Percentage of variation in population between 1891 and 1901.	Number of persons able to read and write.
Rohtak	592	5	102	197,727	334·0	+ 8·2	7,648
Sāmpla	409	2	122	162,423	397·1	+ 8·4	3,810
Jhajjar	466	1	189	123,227	264·4	+ 3·2	3,598
Gohāna	336	3	78	147,295	438·4	+ 6·3	2,011
District total	1,797	11	491	630,672	350·9	+ 6.8	17,067

NOTE.—The figures for the areas of *tahsīls* are taken from revenue returns. The total area is that given in the *Census Report*.

Hindus number 533,723, or 85 per cent. of the total, and Muhammadans 91,687. About 85 per cent. of the population live in villages, and the average population in each village is 1,096, the largest for any District in the Punjab. The language ordinarily spoken is Western Hindī.

The Jāts (217,000) comprise one-third of the population and own seven-tenths of the villages in the District. The great majority are Hindus, and the few Muhammadan Jāts are of a distinctly inferior type. The Hindu Rājputs (7,000) are a well-disposed peaceful folk, much resembling the Jāts in their ways; the Ranghars or Muhammadan Rājputs (27,000), on the other hand, have been aptly described as good soldiers and indifferent cultivators, whose real *forte* lies in cattle-lifting. Many now enlist in Skinner's Horse and other cavalry regiments. The Ahīrs (17,000) are all Hindus and excellent cultivators. There are 9,000 Mālīs and 3,000 Gūjars. The Castes and occupations.

Brāhmans (66,000) were originally settled by the Jāts when they founded their villages, and now they are generally found on Jāt estates. They are an inoffensive class, venerated but not respected. Of the commercial castes the Baniās (45,000) are the most important; and of the menials the Chamārs (leather-workers, 55,000), Chūhrās (scavengers, 23,000), Dhānaks (scavengers, 21,000), Jhīnwars (water-carriers, 12,000), Kumhārs (potters, 13,000), Lohārs (blacksmiths, 9,000), Nais (barbers, 13,000), Tarkhāns (carpenters, 13,000), and Telis (oil-workers, 7,000). There are 17,000 Fakīrs. About 60 per cent. of the population are agriculturists, and 21 per cent. industrial.

Christian missions.

The Society for the Propagation of the Gospel has a branch at Rohtak town, and in 1901 the District contained 41 native Christians.

General agricultural conditions.

The general conditions with regard to agriculture in different parts depend rather on irrigation than on differences of soil. Throughout the District the soil consists as a rule of a good light-coloured alluvial loam, while a lighter and sandier soil is found on elevations and clay soils in depressions of the land. All soils alike give excellent returns with sufficient rainfall, but, unless irrigated, fail entirely in times of drought, though the sandy soil can do with less rain than the clay or loam. The large unirrigated tracts are absolutely dependent on the autumn harvest and the monsoon rains. Roughly speaking, the part north of the railway may be classed as secure, that to the south as insecure, from famine. The whole of the soil contains salts, and saline efflorescence is not uncommon where the drainage lines are obstructed.

Chief agricultural statistics and principal crops.

The District is held almost entirely on the *pattīdāri* and *bhaiyāchārā* tenures, *zamīndāri* lands covering only about 8,000 acres, and lands leased from Government about 5,500 acres. The following table shows the main agricultural statistics in 1903–4, areas being in square miles:—

Tahsil.	Total.	Cultivated.	Irrigated.	Cultivable waste.
Rohtak . .	592	511	186	47
Sāmpla . .	409	346	122	38
Jhajjar . .	466	382	59	59
Gohāna . .	336	281	159	33
Total	1,803	1,520	526	177

Wheat is the chief crop of the spring harvest, occupying 103 square miles in 1903–4; grain occupied 141 and barley

47 square miles. In the autumn harvest the spiked and great millets are the principal staples, occupying 338 and 335 square miles respectively; cotton occupied 65 square miles, sugar-cane 31, and pulses 138. Indigo is grown to a small extent, but only for seed.

Improvements in agricultural practice.

The cultivated area increased from 1,406 square miles in 1879 to 1,520 square miles in 1903-4, in which year it amounted to 84 per cent. of the total area. The increase of cultivation during the twenty years ending 1901 is chiefly due to canal extensions, and it is doubtful whether further extension is possible. Fallows proper are not practised; the pressure of population and the division of property are perhaps too great to allow them. For rains cultivation the agriculturist generally sets aside over two-thirds of his lands in the autumn and rather less than one-third in the spring, and the land gets rest till the season for which it is kept comes round again; if there is heavy rain in the hot season, the whole area may be put under the autumn crop, and in that case no spring crop is taken at all. These arrangements are due to the nature of the seasons, rather than to any care for the soil. On lands irrigated by wells and canals a crop is taken every harvest, as far as possible; the floods of the natural streams usually prevent any autumn crop, except sugar-cane, being grown on the lands affected by them. Rotation of crops is followed, but in a very imperfect way, and for the sake of the crop rather than the soil. Nothing worth mention appears to have been done in the way of improving the quality of the crops grown.

Except in the Jhajjar *tahsīl*, where there is a good deal of well-irrigation, advances under the Land Improvement Loans Act were not popular till recent years; nor are advances under the Agriculturists' Loans Act common, save in times of scarcity, as the people prefer to resort to the Baniās. During the five years ending September, 1904, a total of 5·3 lakhs was advanced, including 4·9 lakhs under the Agriculturists' Loans Act. Of this sum, 3 lakhs was lent in the famine year 1899-1900.

Cattle, horses, and sheep.

The bullocks and cows are of a very good breed, and particularly fine in size and shape. A touch of the Hānsi strain probably pervades them throughout. The bullocks of the villages round Beri and Georgegarh have a special reputation, which is said to be due to the fact that the Nawāb of Jhajjar kept some bulls of the Nagaur breed at Chuchakwās. This breed is small, hardy, active, and hard-working, but is said to have fallen off since the confiscation of the Jhajjar State. The *zamīndārs* make a practice of selling their bullocks after one crop has come up, and buying fresh ones for the next sowings, thereby avoiding the expense of their keep for four or five months. The extensive breaking-up of land which has taken place since 1840 has greatly restricted the grazing-grounds of the villages; the present fodder-supply grown in the fields leaves but a small margin to provide against seasons of drought; and in many canal estates difficulty is already being experienced on this score. Few large stretches of village jungle are now to be found, and the policy of giving proprietary grants has reduced by more than half the area of the Jhajjar and Bahādurgarh reserves. A large cattle fair is held at Georgegarh. The horses of the District are of the ordinary mediocre type. Goats and sheep are owned as a rule by village menials. The District board maintains three horse and three donkey stallions.

Irrigation. Of the total area cultivated in 1903–4, 526 square miles, or nearly 36 per cent., were classed as irrigated. Of this area, 453 square miles were irrigated from canals, and 72 from wells. The District had 2,903 masonry wells in use, all worked by bullocks on the rope-and-bucket system, besides 864 unbricked wells, water-lifts, and lever wells. Canal-irrigation more than trebled and well-irrigation more than doubled during the twenty years ending 1901. The former is derived entirely from the WESTERN JUMNA CANAL, the Būtāna branch of which (with its chief distributary, the Bhiwāni branch) irrigates the Gohāna and Rohtak *tahsīls*, while various distributaries from the new Delhi branch supply Rohtak and Sāmpla. The area estimated as annually irrigable from the Western Jumna Canal is 278 square miles. There used to be a certain amount of irrigation from the Sāhibi and Indori streams, but this has been largely obstructed by dams erected in the territory of the Alwar State. Wells are chiefly found in the south of Jhajjar and in the flood-affected tracts of Sāmpla.

Forests. The District contains no forests, except 8 square miles of Government waste under the control of the Deputy-Commissioner; and, save along canals and watercourses and immediately round the village, trees are painfully wanting. Reserved village jungles are, however, a feature of the District and are found in nearly every village.

Minerals. The Sultānpur salt sources are situated in five villages in Gurgaon and in one in this District in the Jhajjar *tahsīl*. A large amount of *kankar* is found, some of which is particularly pure and adapted for the preparation of lime. The low hills in the south yield a limestone suitable for building purposes.

Arts and manufactures. The chief manufactures are the pottery of Jhajjar; the saddlery and leather-work of Kalānaur; muslin turbans, interwoven with gold and silver thread, and a muslin known as *tanzeb*, produced at Rohtak; and the woollen blankets woven in all parts. Dyeing is a speciality of Jhajjar. The bullock-carts of the District are well and strongly made. Four cotton-ginning factories and one combined ginning and pressing factory have recently been opened at Rohtak, which naturally absorb a good deal of the raw cotton of the District. In 1904 they employed 279 hands. In other industries the native methods of production are adhered to; and, though in the towns foreign sugar and cloth are making way, in the villages native products hold their own. Owing to the opening of the factories and the Rohtak grain market, the demand for labour has considerably increased and wages have risen.

Commerce and trade. In ordinary seasons the District exports grain, the annual export of cereals being estimated by the Famine Commission of 1896–7 at 89,000 tons. The construction of the Southern Punjab Railway has greatly facilitated exports at all times, and imports in time of scarcity, the monthly average imported by this line during the famine year 1899 being no less than 3,400 tons. Commerce is also much helped by the Rohtak grain market, owing to its favourable position, its exemption from octroi, and the facilities given for grain storage.

Railways and roads. The District is traversed by the Southern Punjab Railway; the Rewāri-Bhatinda branch of the Rājputāna-Mālwā Railway crosses the west side of the Jhajjar *tahsīl*; and the terminus of the branch from Garhi Harsāru to Farrukhnagar is about a mile from the border. The District is well provided with roads, the most important of which are the Delhi-Hissār, Rohtak-Bhiwāni, and Rohtak-Jhajjar roads, all of which are metalled. The total length of metalled roads is 79 miles and of unmetalled roads 605 miles. Of these, 20 miles of metalled and 41 miles of unmetalled roads are under the Public Works department, and the rest under the District board.

Famine. The first famine of which there is any trustworthy record was that of 1782–3, the terrible *chālīsa*. From this famine a very large number of villages in the District date their refoundation, in whole or in part. Droughts followed in 1802, 1812, 1817, 1833, and 1837. The famine of 1860–1 was the first in which relief was regularly organized by Government. Nearly 500,000 daily units were relieved by distribution of food and in other ways; about 400,000 were employed on relief works; Rs. 34,378 was spent on these objects, and

Rs. 2,50,000 of land revenue was ultimately remitted. In 1868–9, 719,000 daily units received relief, 125,000 were employed at various times on relief works, nearly Rs. 1,35,000 was spent in alleviating the calamity, and more than Rs. 2,00,000 of revenue in all was remitted. The special feature of the relief in this famine was the amount raised in voluntary subscriptions by the people themselves, which was nearly Rs. 45,000. There is said to have been great loss of life, and nearly 90,000 head of cattle died. The next famine occurred in 1877–8. Highway robberies grew common, grain carts were plundered, and in the village of Badli a grain riot took place. No relief was, however, considered necessary, nor was the revenue demand suspended: 176,000 head of cattle disappeared, and it took the District many years to recover. Both harvests of 1895–6 were a failure, and in 1896–7 there was literally no crop in the rain-land villages. Relief operations commenced in November, 1896, and continued till the middle of July, 1897, at which time a daily average of 11,000 persons were on the relief works. Altogether, Rs. 96,300 was spent in alleviating distress, and suspensions of revenue amounted to 3·4 lakhs. The famine was, however, by no means severe; more than three-fourths of the people on relief works were menials, and large stores of fodder and grain remained in most of the villages. The famine of 1899–1900 was only surpassed in severity by the *chālīsa* famine above mentioned. The spread of irrigation had, however, largely increased the area protected from famine; and, while in 1896–7 the affected area was 1,467 square miles, in 1899–1900 this had shrunk to 1,234, in spite of the greater severity of the drought. The greatest daily average of persons relieved was in the week ending March 10, 1900, when 33,632, or 9 per cent. of the population affected, were in receipt of relief. The total cost of the famine was 7·5 lakhs. The total deaths from December, 1899, to October, 1900, were 25,006, giving a death-rate of 69 as compared with the average rate of 37 per 1,000. Fever was responsible for 18,279 and cholera for 1,935 deaths. The losses of cattle amounted to 182,000.

District subdivisions and staff.

The District is in charge of a Deputy-Commissioner, assisted by three Assistant or Extra Assistant Commissioners, of whom one is in charge of the District treasury. Each of the four *tahsīls* is under a *tahsīldār*, assisted by a *naib-tahsīldār*.

Civil justice and crime.

The Deputy-Commissioner, as District Magistrate, is responsible for criminal justice. Civil judicial work is under a District Judge; and both officers are supervised by the Divisional

Judge of Delhi, who is also Sessions Judge. The District Judge has two Munsifs under him, one at head-quarters, the other at Jhajjar. There are also six honorary magistrates. The predominant form of crime is burglary.

Land revenue administration.

The villages are of unusual size, averaging over 1,000 persons. They afford an excellent example of the *bhaiyāchārā* village of Northern India, a community of clansmen linked together, sometimes by descent from a common ancestor, sometimes by marriage ties, sometimes by a joint foundation of the village, with no community of property, but combining to manage the affairs of the village by means of a council of elders; holding the waste and grazing-grounds, as a rule, in common; and maintaining, by a cess distributed on individuals, a common fund to which public receipts are brought and expenditure charged.

The early revenue history under British rule naturally divides itself into two parts—that of the older tracts which form most of the area included in the three northern *tahsīls*, and that of the confiscated estates which belonged before the Mutiny to the Nawābs of Jhajjar and Bahādurgarh. Thus the regular settlements made in 1838–40 included only half the present District. The earlier settlements made in the older part followed Regulation IX of 1805, and were for short terms. In Rohtak little heed was paid to the Regulation, which laid down that a moderate assessment was conducive equally to the true interests of Government and to the well-being of its subjects. The revenue in 1822 was already so heavy as to be nearly intolerable, while the unequal distribution of the demand was even worse than its burthen. Nevertheless an increase of Rs. 2,000 was levied in 1825 and Rs. 4,000 shortly after. The last summary settlement made in 1835 enhanced the demand by Rs. 20,000. The regular settlement made between 1838 and 1840 increased the assessment by Rs. 14,000. This was never paid, and the revision, which was immediately ordered, reduced it by 1¼ lakhs, or 16 per cent. The progress of the District since this concession was made has been a continuing proof of its wisdom.

Bahādurgarh and Jhajjar were resumed after the Mutiny. The various summary settlements worked well on the whole, and a regular settlement was made between 1860 and 1863.

The settlement of the whole District was revised between 1873 and 1879. Rates on irrigated land varied from Rs. 2 to Rs. 2–12, and on unirrigated land from 5 annas to Rs. 1–9. Canal-irrigated land was, as usual, assessed at a 'dry' rate, plus owners' and occupiers' rates. The result of the new assessment was an increase of 9½ per cent. over the previous demand. The demand for 1903–4, including cesses, amounted to nearly 11 lakhs. The average size of a proprietary holding is 5 acres.

The collections of land revenue alone and of total revenue are shown below, in thousands of rupees :—

	1880–1.	1890–1.	1900–1.	1903–4.
Land revenue . .	9,69	9,50	7,43	8,15
Total revenue . .	11,09	11,38	10,37	11,34

Local and municipal.

The District contains five municipalities, ROHTAK, BERI, JHAJJAR, BAHĀDURGARH, and GOHĀNA; and ten 'notified areas,' of which the most important are MAHAM, KALĀNAUR, MUNDLĀNA, and BUTĀNA. Outside these, local affairs are managed by a District board, whose income amounted in 1903–4 to Rs. 1,24,000. The expenditure in the same year was Rs. 1,22,000, the principal item being public works.

Police and jails.

The regular police force consists of 433 of all ranks, including 63 municipal police, under a Superintendent, who is usually assisted by 2 inspectors. The village watchmen number 702. The District has 10 police stations, 4 outposts, and 17 road-posts. Three trackers and three camel *sowārs* now form part of the ordinary force. The District jail at head-quarters has accommodation for 230 prisoners.

Education.

The standard of education is below the average, though some progress has been made. Rohtak stands twenty-sixth among the twenty-eight Districts of the Province in respect of the literacy of its population. In 1901 only 2·7 per cent. of the population (5 males and 0·1 females) could read and write. The number of pupils under instruction was 2,396 in 1880–1, 3,380 in 1890–1, 5,097 in 1900–1, and 5,824 in 1903–4. In the last year the District possessed 9 secondary and 65 primary (public) schools and 2 advanced and 42 elementary (private) schools, with 211 girls in the public and 8 in the private schools. The Anglo-vernacular school at Rohtak town with 262 pupils is the only high school. The other principal schools are two Anglo-vernacular middle schools supported by the municipalities of Jhajjar and Gohāna, and 6 vernacular middle schools. The total expenditure on education in 1903–4 was Rs. 44,000, chiefly derived from District funds; fees provided nearly a third, and municipal funds and Provincial grants between them a fifth, of the total expenditure.

Besides the Rohtak civil hospital, the District possesses five outlying dispensaries. These in 1904 treated a total of 59,714 out-patients and 1,016 in-patients, while 2,894 operations were performed. The income was Rs. 10,000, almost entirely derived from Local and municipal funds. Hospitals and dispensaries.

The number of successful vaccinations in 1903-4 was 14,406, representing 22·8 per 1,000 of population. The towns of Rohtak and Beri have adopted the Vaccination Act. Vaccination.

[D. C. J. Ibbetson, *District Gazetteer* (1883-4); H. C. Fanshawe, *Settlement Report* (1880).]

Rohtak Tahsīl.—*Tahsīl* of Rohtak District, Punjab, lying between 28° 38′ and 29° 6′ N. and 76° 13′ and 76° 45′ E., with an area of 592 square miles. The population in 1901 was 197,727, compared with 182,649 in 1891. It contains five towns—ROHTAK (population, 20,323), the head-quarters, BERI (9,723), KALĀNAUR (7,640), KAHNAUR (5,024), and MAHAM (7,824)—and 102 villages, including SĀNGHI (5,126). The land revenue and cesses amounted in 1903-4 to 2·9 lakhs. The plain is broken by a chain of sandhills on the east and by scattered sandy eminences elsewhere, and is partially irrigated by the Western Jumna Canal. Trees are scarce, except round the villages and along the older canal-branches.

Sāmpla Tahsīl.—*Tahsīl* of Rohtak District, Punjab, lying between 28° 35′ and 29° 1′ N. and 76° 35′ and 76° 58′ E., with an area of 409 square miles. The population in 1901 was 162,423, compared with 149,818 in 1891. It contains the towns of BAHĀDURGARH (population, 5,974) and Kharkhauda (3,765); and 122 villages, including the 'notified area' of Sāmpla, its head-quarters. The land revenue and cesses amounted in 1903-4 to 3·1 lakhs. The greater part of the *tahsīl* is an arid upland plain, the northern portion of which is now irrigated by the Western Jumna Canal. In the extreme south-east is a small lowland tract, irrigated by countless water-lifts.

Jhajjar Tahsīl.—*Tahsīl* of Rohtak District, Punjab, lying between 28° 21′ and 28° 41′ N. and 76° 20′ and 76° 54′ E., with an area of 466 square miles. The population in 1901 was 123,227, compared with 119,453 in 1891. It contains one town, JHAJJAR (population, 12,227), the head-quarters, and 189 villages, including GEORGEGARH, founded by George Thomas. The land revenue and cesses amounted in 1903-4 to 2·9 lakhs. The *tahsīl* is intersected in all directions by sand ridges which often rise to a considerable height. On the east the low-lying land used to be regularly flooded by the Sāhibi and Indori streams, and large lakes then formed in the depressions; but of recent years the volume of these torrents has diminished, and the country rarely remains flooded for any considerable period. The north of the *tahsīl* is a continuation of the plateau of Rohtak and Sāmpla, while in the south a few low rocky eminences lend variety to the landscape.

Gohāna Tahsīl.—*Tahsīl* of Rohtak District, Punjab, lying between 28° 57′ and 29° 17′ N. and 76° 29′ and 76° 52′ E., with an area of 336 square miles. The population in 1901 was 147,295, compared with 138,555 in 1891. It contains the three towns of GOHĀNA (population, 6,567), its head-quarters, BARAUDA (5,836), and BUTĀNA (7,509); and 78 villages, including MUNDLĀNA (5,657). The land revenue and cesses amounted in 1903–4 to 2·6 lakhs. The *tahsīl* is flat and well wooded, and ample means of irrigation are available.

Bahādurgarh.—Town in the Sāmpla *tahsīl* of Rohtak District, Punjab, situated in 28° 41′ N. and 76° 56′ E., 18 miles west of Delhi on the Rohtak road, and on the Southern Punjab Railway. Population (1901), 5,974. The name of the town was originally Sharafābād. It was given in *jāgīr* to Bahādur Khān and Tāj Muhammad, Baloch chiefs of Farrukhnagar, in 1754, and its name changed to Bahādurgarh. The *jāgīr* was resumed in 1793 by Sindhia, and in 1803 the town and the surrounding villages were bestowed by Lord Lake on Ismail Khān, brother of the Nawāb of Jhajjar. The estate was confiscated in 1857 owing to the disloyalty of the chief, Bahādur Jang. The municipality was created in 1873. The income and expenditure during the ten years ending 1902–3 averaged Rs. 6,600. Income and expenditure in 1903–4 each amounted to Rs. 6,400, the income being chiefly from octroi. The town is of no commercial importance. The municipality maintains a vernacular middle school and a dispensary.

Barauda (*Baroda*).—Town in the Gohāna *tahsīl* of Rohtak District, Punjab, situated in 29° 9′ N. and 76° 37′ E., on the Butāna branch of the Western Jumna Canal. Population (1901), 5,836.

Beri.—Town in the District and *tahsīl* of Rohtak, Punjab, situated in 28° 42′ N. and 76° 35′ E., 15 miles south of Rohtak town, on the direct road from Delhi to Bhiwāni. Population (1901), 9,723. It formed part of the estate of

George Thomas, who took it by storm from a garrison of Jāts and Rājputs. It is now the great trade centre of the neighbourhood, and the residence of many wealthy merchants and bankers. Two large fairs are held annually in February and October. The municipality was created in 1867. The income and expenditure during the ten years ending 1902–3 averaged Rs. 9,800 and 10,200 respectively. The income in 1903–4 was Rs. 6,200, chiefly derived from octroi; and the expenditure was Rs. 7,300. It maintains a vernacular middle school.

Butāna.—Town in the Gohāna *tahsīl* of Rohtak District, Punjab, situated in 29° 12′ N. and 76° 42′ E., 19 miles north of Rohtak, on a branch of the Western Jumna Canal, to which it gives its name. Population (1901), 7,509. It is administered as a 'notified area.'

Georgegarh (*Jahāzgarh*).—Village in the Jhajjar *tahsīl* of Rohtak District, Punjab, situated in 28° 37′ N. and 76° 36′ E. Population (1901), 1,285. It was founded by George Thomas, who built a fort to overawe the towns of Beri and Jhajjar, which was besieged and taken by a large Marāthā force under Louis Bourquin, Thomas being obliged to retire to Hānsi. A large cattle fair is held here twice a year.

Gohāna Town.—Head-quarters of the *tahsīl* of the same name in Rohtak District, Punjab, situated in 29° 8′ N. and 76° 42′ E., on the Western Jumna Canal, 20 miles north of Rohtak town. Population (1901), 6,567. The town is said to have been the site of a fort belonging to Prithwī Rāj, afterwards destroyed by Muhammad of Ghor. A yearly fair is held here at the shrine of Shāh Zia-ud-dīn Muhammad, a saint who accompanied Muhammad of Ghor to India. There are also two temples in honour of the Jain Arhat Parasnāth, at which an annual festival takes place. The municipality was created in 1873. The income during the ten years ending 1902–3 averaged Rs. 9,300, and the expenditure Rs. 9,500. The income in 1903–4 amounted to Rs. 8,300, chiefly derived from octroi, and the expenditure to Rs. 8,200. The town is of no commercial importance. The municipality maintains a dispensary and an Anglo-vernacular middle school.

Jhajjar Town.—Head-quarters of the *tahsīl* of the same name in Rohtak District, Punjab, situated in 28° 36′ N. and 76° 40′ E., 21 miles south of Rohtak town and 35 miles west of Delhi. Population (1901), 12,227. The town was destroyed by Muhammad of Ghor and refounded by a Jāt clan. It was taken from the Nawābs of Farrukhnagar by the Jāt chieftain Sūraj Mal, and afterwards fell into the hands of Walter Reinhardt, husband of Begam Sumrū. Jhajjar was assigned to George Thomas in 1794, and on annexation in 1803 was granted to Nawāb Nijābat Khān. The estate was confiscated in 1857 owing to the disloyalty of the ruling chief, Abdur Rahmān Khān, who was hanged for his share in the Mutiny. Jhajjar became for a short time the head-quarters of a District of that name, which was abolished in 1860. The principal buildings are the old palace of the Nawābs and the new palace or Bāgh Jahānāra. The municipality was created in 1867. The income and expenditure during the ten years ending 1902–3 averaged Rs. 13,500 and Rs. 14,000 respectively. The income in 1903–4 amounted to Rs. 18,600, chiefly derived from octroi, and the expenditure to Rs. 13,800. The town is noted for its dyeing industry, and for the thin or 'paper' pottery produced. It has a considerable manufacture of muslins and woollen goods, and embroidery is also largely carried on. The municipality maintains a dispensary and an Anglo-vernacular middle school.

Kahnaur.—Town in the District and *tahsīl* of Rohtak, Punjab, situated in 28° 45′ N. and 76° 32′ E., 11 miles south of Rohtak town and 15 miles north-west of Jhajjar. Population (1901), 5,024.

Kalānaur.—Town in the District and *tahsīl* of Rohtak, Punjab, situated in 28° 50′ N. and 76° 24′ E., 12 miles west of Rohtak town on the road to Bhiwāni. Population (1901), 7,640. It was founded by Kaliān Singh and Bhawān Singh, two Ponwār Rājputs, sons-in-law of Anang Pāl, the king of Delhi, and named after the former. Kalānaur remained in the possession of their descendants, who, though dispossessed for a time by the Balochs of Farrukhnagar, were reinstated by the Delhi court. The town is famous for its leather-work, especially saddlery. It has a vernacular middle school.

Maham (*Mahim*).—Town in the District and *tahsīl* of Rohtak. Punjab, situated in 28° 58′ N. and 76° 18′ E., 20 miles west of Rohtak town on the road to Hānsī. Population (1901), 7,824. Tradition alleges its destruction by Muhammad of Ghor; but though doubtless a place of some antiquity, it is not mentioned by historians before Akbar gave it in *jāgīr* to Shāhbāz Khān, an Afghān. Under his descendants it flourished greatly, until it was sacked by the Rājputs under Durga Dās in the reign of Aurangzeb. Since then, though repeopled, it has never recovered its prosperity. It is a picturesque place with many interesting ruins, including a fine *baoli* or stepped well built by a mace-bearer of Shāh Jahān. It has a vernacular middle school.

Mundlāna (*Mandlāna*).—Village in the Gohāna *tahsīl* of Rohtak District, Punjab, situated in 29° 12′ N. and 76° 50′ E. Population (1901), 5,657. It is administered as a 'notified area.'

Rohtak Town.—Head-quarters of the District and *tahsīl* of the same name, Punjab, situated in 28° 54′ N. and 76° 35′ E., on the Southern Punjab Railway, 44 miles north-west of Delhi; distant by rail from Calcutta 1,000 miles, from Bombay 1,026, and from Karāchi 863. Population (1901), 20,323, including 10,404 Hindus and 9,916 Muhammadans. It is plausibly identified with the Rauhitaka or Rauhita of the *Rāja-tarangini* and of Alberūni; but tradition avers that its ancient name was Rohtāsgarh or 'the fort of Rohtās,' a Ponwār Rājā, and points to the mound called the Khokra Kot as the site of the old town. It is also said that Muhammad of Ghor destroyed the town soon after it had been rebuilt by Prithwī Rāj in 1160, but it is not mentioned by the earlier Muhammadan historians. A colony of Shaikhs from Yemen are said to have built a fort; and the Afghāns of Birahma, an ancient site close by, also settled in the town, which became the capital of a fief of the Delhi kingdom. Kai Khusrū, the grandson and heir of Balban, was enticed from Multān by Kaikubād and put to death here about 1286; and in 1410 Khizr Khān, the Saiyid, besieged Idrīs Khān in Rohtak fort, and took it after a six months' siege. After the decline of the Mughal power Rohtak, situated on the border line between the Sikh and Marāthā powers, passed through many vicissitudes, falling into the hands of one chieftain after another. It became the head-quarters of Rohtak District in 1824, and was plundered in the Mutiny of 1857.

The municipality was created in 1867. The income during the ten years ending 1902–3 averaged Rs. 24,900, and the expenditure Rs. 24,400. The income in 1903–4 was Rs. 25,000, chiefly derived from octroi; and the expenditure was Rs. 23,600. The town is an important trade centre; and four factories for ginning cotton and one for ginning and pressing have recently been established. The number of factory hands in 1904 was 279. Muslin turbans interwoven with gold and silver thread and a form of muslin known as *tanzeb* are produced. The Anglo-vernacular high school is managed by the Educational department.

Sānghi.—Village in the District and *tahsīl* of Rohtak, Punjab, situated in 29° 1′ N. and 76° 41′ E. Population (1901), 5,126. It is administered as a 'notified area.'

Boundaries, configuration, and hill and river systems.

Gurgaon District.—District in the Delhi Division of the Punjab, lying between 27° 39′ and 28° 33′ N. and 76° 18′ and 77° 34′ E., in the extreme south-east of the Province, with an area of 1,984 square miles. It stretches towards the outlying hills of the Rājputāna table-land, and its southern part belongs geographically to that part of Northern Rājputāna known as Mewāt or the country of the Meos. It is bounded on the north by the States of Dujāna and Pataudi, and the Districts of Rohtak and Delhi; on the east the river Jumna separates it from Bulandshahr and Alīgarh in the United Provinces; on the south it marches with the Muttra District of the United Provinces and the State of Bharatpur; on the west it is bounded by territories belonging to the States of Alwar, Jaipur, and Nābha. The surface presents a considerable variety of contour. Two low rocky ranges, continuations of the Arāvalli chain, enter its border from the south, and run northward in a bare and treeless mass towards the plain country. The northern plain falls into two natural divisions, divided by the western range. Eastwards, the valley between the two ridges lies wide and open throughout; and below the escarpment of the eastern ridge an alluvial level extends unbroken to the banks of the Jumna. Immediately at the foot of the uplands lie a series of undulating hollows, which during the rains become extensive swamps. West of the western range lies the Rewāri *tahsīl*, consisting of a sandy plain, dotted with isolated hills. Though naturally dry and sterile, it has become, under the careful hands of its Ahīr inhabitants, a well-cultivated tract. Numerous torrents carry off the drainage from the hills, while large pools or *jhīls* collect the water brought down by these torrents.

Geology.

The greater part of the District is covered by alluvium, but outcrops of rocks occur in numerous small hills and ridges. These are outliers of the slates and quartzites (Alwar quartzite) of the Delhi system. The slate is usually a fissile clay slate, and is quarried near Rewāri. There are brine wells in the Sultānpur *mahāl* and sulphur springs at Sohna[1].

Botany.

The flora is mainly that of North-Eastern Rājputāna, and in the south-west includes several desert forms. Trees are few, except where planted; but on the hills that extend

[1] Hacket, 'Geology of the Arāvalli Region,' *Records, Geological Survey of India*, vol. xiv, part iv.

into the District from the Arāvalli ranges, *gugal* (*Boswellia serrata*), yielding frankincense, occurs, and also an acacia yielding catechu; while the south-east portion is characterized by the *dhaok* or *dhao* (*Anogeissus pendula*). The Jumna valley and the north-eastern corner belong botanically to the Upper Gangetic plain.

Fauna. The days when tigers abounded in Gurgaon on the wooded banks of the Jumna are long since gone by, though now and then a straggler from the Alwar hills is seen. The striped hyena is found only in the neighbourhood of the hills. Leopards are not uncommon. Wolves, foxes, and jackals are common in all parts. The sacred monkey is found in great numbers about Hodal, and there are also a few in Rewāri and Gurgaon. Wild hog frequent the low hills near Bhaundī and Sohna and the lowlands of the Jumna. Both antelope and 'ravine deer' (Indian gazelle) are fairly plentiful, the former in the hilly and sandy parts, the latter in the lowlands. The *nīlgai* is also found in the southern parts of the Rewāri *tahsīl*. Hog deer are occasionally met with in the lowlands of the Jumna.

Climate and temperature. Both heat and cold are less extreme than in the Punjab proper, though near the hill ranges and in the Fīrozpur-Jhirka valley the radiation from the rocks makes the heat intense. Fever is the chief cause of mortality, but the District is the least unhealthy of the Division, Simla excepted. The flooded tracts near Nūh are particularly malarious, and fever has come with the Agra Canal into the high plain.

Rainfall. The average rainfall varies from 22 inches at Rewāri to 26 at Gurgaon. Of the total in the latter place, 23½ inches fall in the summer months and 2½ in the winter. The uncertain nature of the monsoon is the most marked feature of the returns, the precipitation having varied from 48 inches at Nūh in 1885–6 to 0·1 inch at Hattīn in 1899–1900.

History. Gurgaon, with the rest of the territory known as MEWĀT, formed in early times part of an extensive kingdom ruled over by Rājputs of the Jaduvansī or Jādon tribe. The Jādon power was broken by Muhammad of Ghor in 1196; but for two centuries they sturdily resisted the Muhammadan domination, and the history of the District is a record of incursions of the people of Mewāt into Delhi territory and of punitive expeditions undertaken against them. Under Fīroz Shāh III the Jādons were converted to Islām; and Bahādur Khān or Bahādur Nahar took a prominent part in the intestine struggles that followed the invasion of Tīmūr, founding the family of the Khānzādas, members of which ruled Mewāt in partial independence of the Delhi empire. Bābar annexed Mewāt, and from this time the power of the Khānzādas rapidly declined. During the decay of the Mughal empire the District was torn between contending powers. In the north were the Nawābs of Farrukhnagar, a principality founded in 1732; in the centre an independent power had risen at Ghasera; Rewāri was held by an Ahīr family, with forts at Gokulgarh and Guraora; while from the south the great Jāt ruler Sūraj Mal of Bharatpur was extending his dominions. He captured Ghasera and Farrukhnagar; but after his death in 1763 Farrukhnagar returned to its former rulers, and a great part of the tract was recovered for the empire by Najaf Kulī Khān. Under the Marāthās the greater part of the District was held by Generals de Boigne, Perron, and Bourquin. Begam Sumrū owned the *pargana* of Jhārsa; and George Thomas had that of Fīrozpur assigned to him in 1793, and once plundered Gurgaon, but lost this part of his possessions in the following year. In Rewāri, Tej Singh, ancestor of the present leading family of Ahīrs, allied himself with the Marāthās and established himself in power.

After Lord Lake's conquests the District passed to the British with the rest of the country ceded by Sindhia in 1803, but was left in the hands of native assignees, the District of Gurgaon being formed piecemeal as their estates for one cause or another escheated. The first of these acquisitions was in 1808, when Rewāri, Nūh, Bahora, and Sohna came under British rule, and a District was formed with its head-quarters at Bharāwās near Rewāri. After the lapse of Hodal and Palwal the head-quarters were transferred to Gurgaon. More escheats followed; and in 1836 the Nawāb of Fīrozpur-Jhirka lost his estates for complicity in the murder of Mr. William Fraser, Commissioner of Delhi, while Jhārsa lapsed on the death of Begam Sumrū. In 1857 the Nawāb of Farrukhnagar, followed by the Meos, rose in rebellion, while in Rewāri the Ahīr chief preserved an armed neutrality. Order was, however, quickly restored after the fall of Delhi, and the estates of Farrukhnagar were confiscated.

Archaeology. The chief objects of antiquarian interest are at PALWAL, HODAL, FARRUKHNAGAR, FĪROZPUR-JHIRKA, and REWĀRI.

The people. The District contains 8 towns and 1,171 villages. The population at each of the last four enumerations was: (1868) 689,034, (1881) 641,848, (1891) 668,929, and (1901) 746,208. It increased by 11·5 per cent. during the last decade. There are five *tahsīls*—GURGAON, FĪROZPUR, NŪH, PALWAL, and

REWĀRI—each named from its head-quarters. The chief towns are the municipalities of REWĀRI, FARRUKHNAGAR, PALWAL, FĪROZPUR-JHIRKA, SOHNA, and HODAL. GURGAON, the head-quarters of the District, is a small place. The following table shows the chief statistics of population in 1901:—

Tahsīl.	Area in square miles.	Number of		Population.	Population per square mile.	Percentage of variation in population between 1891 and 1901.	Number of persons able to read and write.
		Towns.	Villages.				
Gurgaon . .	413	3	207	125,760	304·5	+ 11·9	3,986
Palwal . .	382	2	187	172,557	451·7	+ 15·2	4,301
Fīrozpur . .	317	1	230	132,287	417·3	+ 16·2	2,362
Nūh . . .	403	1	257	145,931	362·1	+ 10·9	2,397
Rewāri . .	426	1	290	169,673	398·3	+ 5·2	6,397
District total	1,984	8	1,171	746,208	376·1	+ 11·5	19,443

NOTE.—The figures for the areas of *tahsīls* are taken from revenue returns. The total District area is that given in the *Census Report*.

Hindus number 499,373, or 67 per cent., and Muhammadans 242,548. About 85 per cent. of the people returned their language as Hindustāni or Urdū; 14 per cent. speak Mewātī, and 2,600 persons Braj.

Castes and occupations.

The Meos (129,000), who number one-sixth of the population, are probably almost pure aborigines, of the same stock as the Mīnās of the Arāvalli Hills, though perhaps with an admixture of Rājput blood. They hold large tracts of land in the southern portion of the District, and are now without exception Muhammadans, though retaining many Hindu customs. The tribe has laid aside its former lawless turbulence; and the Meos, though still thriftless, extravagant, and lazy, now rank among the most peaceable communities in the Punjab. The Jāts (77,000) live chiefly in Palwal and the northern *parganas*; they are almost entirely Hindus. Some of their villages worthily sustain the general high reputation of the tribe, but others are reported to be ill-cultivated. The Ahīrs (78,000) form the majority of the population in Rewāri, and are justly esteemed for the skill and perseverance with which they have developed the naturally poor resources of that sterile region. They are all Hindus. The Gūjars (25,000) also are practically all Hindus. The Rājputs comprise 18,000 Hindus and 9,000 Muhammadans. The Gaurwas (4,000) are Rājputs who have adopted widow remarriage. The Khānzādas (4,000) claim descent from Jādon Rājputs, converted by Fīroz Shāh, who made them rulers of Mewāt. It is possible that they are akin to the Meos, some of whom profess to have been formerly Khānzādas; if so, they may be the representatives of the upper, as the Meos are of the lower, classes of the aboriginal population. The Mālīs (market-gardeners) number 11,000. The Saiyids (3,000) and Balochs (2,000) bear a bad name as indolent and thriftless cultivators, and swell the returns of crime far beyond their just proportion. The criminal class of Mīnās (800) are notorious for their thieving propensities. The chief of the commercial tribes are the Baniās (37,000). Of the menial tribes, the most important are the Chūhrās (scavengers, 21,000), Jhīnwars (water-carriers, 12,000), Kumhārs (potters, 16,000), Lohārs (blacksmiths, 7,000), Nais (barbers, 14,000), Kassābs (butchers, 17,000), Tarkhāns (carpenters, 13,000), and Telis (oilmen, 7,000). There are 26,000 Fakīrs. About 60 per cent. of the population are dependent on agriculture.

Christian missions.

The Society for the Propagation of the Gospel Mission has branches at Gurgaon and Rewāri, with dispensaries at the latter place and at Palwal. In 1901 the District contained 221 native Christians.

General agricultural conditions.

The Jumna in Gurgaon, as elsewhere, is fringed by a strip of alluvial land, the *khādar*, which leads to the broad level plain, known as the *bāngar*. Here the soil is almost uniformly a good loam. Towards the hills the plain sinks into a shallow depression of clayey soil, the *dabar*, which receives the drainage of the higher ground. West of the hills the ground is broken by rocky knolls and sandhills, while even in the level parts the soil is much lighter than that of the *bāngar*.

Chief agricultural statistics and principal crops.

The District is held almost entirely on the *pattīdāri* and *bhaīyāchārā* tenures, though *zamīndāri* lands cover 9,000 acres. The area for which details are available from the revenue records of 1903-4 is 1,941 square miles, as shown below:—

Tahsīl.	Total.	Cultivated.	Irrigated.	Cultivable waste.
Gurgaon	413	299	43	37
Palwal	382	314	130	40
Fīrozpur	317	259	49	7
Nūh	403	329	72	23
Rewāri	426	365	106	23
Total	1,941	1,566	400	130

The chief crops of the spring harvest are gram and barley, which occupied 71 and 167 square miles respectively in

1903–4. Wheat occupied 68 square miles. In the autumn, spiked millet is by far the most important crop, occupying 347 square miles. Next come pulses (275 square miles), great millet (111 square miles), and cotton (86 square miles). There is little sugar-cane (only 12 square miles), and practically no rice.

Improvements in agricultural practice.

The cultivated area has increased but slightly since the settlement of 1872–83, being 1,566 square miles in 1903–4 as compared with 1,555 square miles at settlement; and as four-fifths of the total area is now under cultivation, no great extension is to be expected, or could be possible without unduly reducing the area utilized for grazing. Little attention is paid to any regular course of cropping. Unmanured land is generally cultivated only for one harvest, and the rest it gets during the other harvest is thought sufficient. Great millet is not sown in the same land two years in succession. Cotton is not sown after spiked millet. In all other cases, in deciding what crop to sow, regard is paid to the kind of soil and amount of rainfall, without any consideration as to what the previous crop was. Advances for constructing wells under the Land Improvement Loans Act are fairly popular, Rs. 67,000 having been advanced during the five years ending 1904. During the same period 2·8 lakhs was advanced under the Agriculturists' Loans Act, for the purchase of bullocks and seed.

Cattle, horses, sheep, and goats.

As might be expected from the small proportion of land uncultivated, grazing is scarce, and Gurgaon is not a great cattle-breeding District. A cattle fair is held at Rewāri. The horses and sheep are of no special importance. The District board has two horse and two donkey stallions. Large numbers of goats are grazed on the hills; they are frequently owned by butchers, who make them over to shepherds on condition of receiving a certain share, generally a half, of the increase.

Irrigation.

Of the total area cultivated in 1903–4, 400 square miles, or 25 per cent., were classed as irrigated. Of this area, 222 square miles were irrigated from wells, 152 from canals, and 25 from streams, tanks, and embankments. The District has 9,208 wells in use, all worked by bullocks on the rope-and-bucket system, besides 3,511 unbricked wells, lever wells, and water-lifts. Canal-irrigation is entirely from the Agra Canal, which traverses the eastern portion of the District. The third main source of irrigation is the collection of the water of the hill torrents by means of embankments. These are maintained by the District board, and the total area irrigated from them doubled in the twenty years ending 1901. On the other hand, owing to the diminution of water in the Sāhibi, Indori, and Landoha streams, the low-lying flooded area has considerably decreased.

Forests.

The only forests are about one square mile of unclassed forest and Government waste under the control of the Deputy-Commissioner. As a whole, the District is not well wooded, and some parts, such as the low-lying tracts in the Nūh *tahsīl*, are extremely bare. In Rewāri the tamarisk is especially common, and the ownership of these trees in waste lands and along village roads is often distinct from that of the soil. Palwal is by far the best wooded *tahsīl*, and most of the Jāt villages in it reserve a certain portion of their area from the plough.

Minerals.

The Sultānpur salt sources lie in six villages, five in this District and one in Rohtak. The salt is made entirely from natural brine, 43 wells of which were worked in this District in 1903-4. The brine is about 26 feet below the surface and 15 feet deep, and the supply seems inexhaustible, as some of the works have existed for over 200 years. The salt, known as Sultānpurī, is, however, of poor quality, and the demand for it is dying out. Saltpetre is extracted from the earth of old sites and refined at Hodal. Iron ore exists in the hills, but its manufacture has long been abandoned owing to the scarcity of fuel. Traces of copper exist and mica is occasionally extracted. Plumbago has been found, but is too impure to be of any commercial value. A little gold is sometimes washed out of the sand of the hill torrents. Excellent slates are quarried in the neighbourhood of Rewāri.

Arts and manufactures.

Coarse cotton and woollen fabrics are made in the villages. Muslin is woven at Rewāri, but there is little trade in it. The chief industry is the brass manufacture of Rewāri; the greater part of the out-turn consists of cooking utensils, but articles decorated with chasing, engraving, and parcel tinning are also produced for export. Glass bangles are made at Sohna, shoes at Jharsa, Sohna, and other places, and iron vessels at Fīrozpur-Jhirka, and at Dārāpur and Tānkrī in the Rewāri *tahsīl*. There are two factories for ginning cotton, one at Palwal and one at Hodal, employing 268 hands in 1904. There is an out-still for the distillation of spirit at Fīrozpur-Jhirka.

Commerce and trade.

Trade centres in the town of Rewāri, which ranks as one of the chief emporiums in the Punjab. Its merchants transact a large part of the commerce between the States of Rājputāna and Northern India. Salt from the Sāmbhar Lake and iron are the principal imports; while sugar, grain, and English piece-goods are the staple exports. Hardware of brass, coated with white metal, is also largely exported. The District produces cereals and pulses considerably beyond its needs for home consumption; and of late years, owing to the extension of railway communication, a steady export trade in grain has sprung up. Nūh, Fīrozpur-Jhirka, Palwal, Hattīn, Nagīna, Punahāna, Hodal, Hasanpur, and Farrukhnagar are the chief marts (after Rewāri) for country produce, the last-named being also the market for the Sultānpurī salt.

Railways and roads.

The Rājputāna-Mālwā Railway from Delhi to Ajmer crosses the District with a branch line to Farrukhnagar, and the Bhatinda line leaves it at Rewāri, which is an important junction. The Agra-Delhi chord of the Great Indian Peninsula Railway, opened in 1904, runs through the east, and the Rewāri-Phulera line through the Rewāri *tahsīl.*

The grand trunk road from Delhi to Agra traverses the Palwal *tahsīl*, and there is a metalled road from Gurgaon to Sohna (15 miles), which is to be carried 6 miles farther on to Nūh. A metalled road also runs from Fīrozpur-Jhirka through Nagauna into the State of Alwar. The roads of greatest mercantile importance are, however, still unmetalled, very heavy, and difficult to traverse in the rains. The total length of metalled roads is 81 miles, and of unmetalled roads 509 miles. Of these, 30 miles of metalled roads are under the Public Works department, and the rest are maintained from Local funds. The Jumna is navigable by country craft throughout its course, and is crossed by eight ferries.

Famine.

As might be expected in a District so largely dependent, until lately, on the rainfall, Gurgaon suffered severely in all the famines that have visited the Punjab. The *chālīsa* famine of 1783–4 was very disastrous; and in the famines of 1833–4 and 1837–8 a number of estates were deserted, partly on account of high assessments and partly from too stringent collection of revenue. The effects of the famines of 1860–1 and 1868–9 were greatly mitigated by the relief afforded by Government. In the latter year, the first for which we have full reports, 344,527 daily units were relieved, and 15,324 persons were employed on works, with a total expenditure of Rs. 11,139. The famine of 1877–8, in conjunction with a new and excessive assessment of land revenue and an unsympathetic revenue administration, badly crippled the District for some time; the maximum number on relief on any one day was 2,155, while 313 deaths from starvation were reported, and 150,000 head of cattle died. There was scarcity in 1884. In 1896–7 the famine was by no means severe, as irrigation from the Agra Canal had been developed and a much larger measure of protection insured. Distress lasted from January to May, 1897, and affected none but the menial classes. The daily average of persons relieved in no week exceeded 3,100, and the total cost was only Rs. 14,070. In the famine of 1899–1900, 1,033 square miles, or 53 per cent. of the total area, was affected; the greatest daily number in receipt of relief was 18,153 persons, or 5 per cent. of the population affected, and the total expenditure was 3·8 lakhs.

District subdivisions and staff. The District is divided for administrative purposes into five *tahsīls*, each under a *tahsīldār* and a *naib-tahsīldār*. It is in charge of a Deputy-Commissioner, who has under him two Assistant or Extra Assistant Commissioners, one being in charge of the District treasury.

Civil justice and crime. The Deputy-Commissioner as District Magistrate is responsible for criminal justice, and the District Judge for civil judicial work. Both are under the supervision of the Divisional and Sessions Judge of Delhi. There is only one Munsif, who sits at head-quarters. The predominant forms of crime are cattle-theft and burglary.

Land revenue administration. A notable feature in the system of land tenures is the redistribution of the land among the communal proprietors. This custom has survived in a few villages, but is dying out. The fiscal history is a melancholy one. As each *pargana* came under British rule, it was either summarily settled, or else the Collector managed the whole as a single estate, and made from it what collections he could, no regular engagement being entered into with the proprietors. Regular settlements began in 1836–7, and by 1842 every *pargana* had been dealt with. The working of this settlement, though very uneven, was satisfactory on the whole. The rapid rise in prices which continued to the end of the decade helped to mitigate the severities of the assessment. Thus, by the time prices fell in the next decade, increased cultivation and irrigation had put the people in a better position to fulfil their engagements.

The revised settlement was carried out between 1872 and 1883. The increase in cultivation was estimated at 40 per cent., while the increase taken in revenue was only 17 per cent. The new settlement, however, was most unfortunate in the opening seasons of its term. The autumn harvest of 1877 was a complete failure, and the local officials recommended the suspension of the entire instalment; but sanction was refused on the ground that proprietors whose revenue had just been raised must be in a position of affluence and therefore able to pay in a bad year as well as in a good. The result was widespread distress, and collection of the revenue in full proved impossible. Moreover, it was not until 1882 that counsels of leniency prevailed, and by that time pestilence and famine had stamped upon the people an impress of poverty which years of prosperity could hardly remove. The assessment was lowered by nearly 8 per cent. for a term of seven years, and permanently by 4 per cent. At the expiry of the term in 1889 the larger reduction was made permanent; and though the years 1890–5 were years of plenty, they were overshadowed by the famine lustrum that followed. The District came under resettlement in 1903. The average assessment on 'dry' land is Rs. 1–0–6 (maximum, Rs. 1–12; minimum, 9 annas), and on 'wet' land Rs. 2–8 (maximum, Rs. 3–8; minimum, Rs. 1–8). The demand, including cesses, in 1903–4 was nearly 14 lakhs. The average size of a proprietary holding is 3·7 acres.

The collections of land revenue alone and of total revenue are shown below, in thousands of rupees:—

	1880–1.	1890–1.	1900–1.	1903–4.
Land revenue .	12,47	11,96	10,12	11,31
Total revenue .	13,68	13,72	12,97	14,32

The District contains six municipalities, REWĀRI, FARRUKHNAGAR, PALWAL, FĪROZPUR-JHIRKA, SOHNA, and HODAL, besides four 'notified areas.' Outside these, local affairs are managed by a District board, whose income amounted in 1903–4 to Rs. 1,24,000. Its expenditure in the same year was Rs. 1,46,000, the principal item being public works. Local and municipal.

The regular police force consists of 520 of all ranks, including 117 municipal police, under a Superintendent, who is usually assisted by two inspectors. The village watchmen number 1,428. The District contains 15 police stations, one outpost, and 13 road-posts. There is no jail in the District, and the convicts are sent to Delhi District jail. The Mīnās and Bauriās are proclaimed under the Criminal Tribes Act, and 908 were on the register in 1901. Police and jails.

Gurgaon stands twenty-seventh among the twenty-eight Districts of the Province in respect of the literacy of its population. In 1901 the proportion of literate persons was 2·6 per Education.

cent. (4·9 males and 0·1 females). The number of pupils under instruction was 3,199 in 1880–1, 4,696 in 1890–1, 5,139 in 1900–1, and 5,563 in 1903–4. In the last year the District possessed 7 secondary and 108 primary (public) schools, and 17 elementary (private) schools, the number of girls being 347 in the public and 105 in the private schools. Of the public schools, 11 were supported by municipalities and 18 received a grant-in-aid, the remainder being maintained by the District board. The only high school is an Anglo-vernacular municipal school at Rewāri, managed by the Educational department. The special schools include two for low-caste boys, and one industrial school for boys and another for girls. To encourage education among the criminal tribe of Mīnās, stipends of from R. 1 to Rs. 3 per month are offered to boys of this class to support them at school. The total expenditure on education in 1903–4 amounted to Rs. 51,000, of which Government contributed Rs. 2,000, municipalities Rs. 15,000, District funds Rs. 25,000, and fees Rs. 8,000.

Hospitals and dispensaries.

Besides the Gurgaon dispensary the District has eight outlying dispensaries. At these institutions 77,889 out-patients and 1,716 in-patients were treated in 1904, and 3,707 operations were performed. The expenditure was Rs. 24,000, of which Rs. 13,000 was derived from Local funds and the greater part of the remainder from municipal funds. The Society for the Propagation of the Gospel has a dispensary in charge of a lady doctor at Rewāri, and another at Palwal.

Vaccination.

The number of successful vaccinations in 1903–4 was 23,697, or 31·76 per 1,000 of the population. Vaccination is compulsory only in Rewāri.

[J. Wilson, *Codes of Tribal Custom of Twenty-one Tribes in the Gurgaon District* (1882); D. C. J. Ibbetson, *District Gazetteer* (1884); F. C. Channing and J. Wilson, *Settlement Report* (1882).]

Gurgaon Tahsīl.—*Tahsīl* of Gurgaon District, Punjab, lying between 28° 12′ and 28° 33′ N. and 76° 42′ and 77° 15′ E., with an area of 413 square miles. The population in 1901 was 125,760, compared with 112,390 in 1891. It contains the three towns of GURGAON (population, 4,765), the head-quarters, SOHNA (6,024), and FARRUKHNAGAR (6,136); and 207 villages. The land revenue and cesses amounted in 1903–4 to 2·5 lakhs. At annexation the area covered by the present *tahsīl* was occupied by the *parganas* of Farrukhnagar held by the Nawāb of Farrukhnagar, Jhārsa held by Begam Sumrū, and the greater part of Bahora and Sohna, held by General

Perron. The two last *parganas* were resumed at annexation, and were brought under British administration in 1808–9. Jhārsa lapsed on Begam Sumrū's death in 1835, and Farrukhnagar was confiscated owing to the Nawāb's complicity in the Mutiny of 1857. Dams are built across the torrent-beds which descend from the low rocky hills in the centre and east, and the water is stored up for irrigation. In the north, the soil is a rich mould; in the south, sand predominates; while in the north-west, in the neighbourhood of Farrukhnagar, the sand ridges are separated by depressions of hard soil where the water collects in seasons of heavy rainfall.

Palwal Tahsīl.—*Tahsīl* of Gurgaon District, Punjab, lying between 27° 51′ and 28° 16′ N. and 77° 11′ and 77° 34′ E., with an area of 382 square miles. It is bounded on the east and south by the United Provinces, the river Jumna forming the eastern boundary. The population in 1901 was 172,557, compared with 149,740 in 1891. It contains the two towns of PALWAL (population, 12,830), the head-quarters, and HODAL (8,142); and 187 villages. The land revenue and cesses amounted in 1903–4 to 3·2 lakhs. The *parganas* of Palwal and Hodal, which make up the present *tahsīl*, were once held by General de Boigne. They were assigned by the British Government, and lapsed on the deaths of the assignees in 1813 and 1817. The *tahsīl* is well wooded, and consists of a fertile plain watered by the Agra Canal.

Fīrozpur Tahsīl.—*Tahsīl* of Gurgaon District, Punjab, lying between 27° 39′ and 28° 1′ N. and 76° 53′ and 77° 20′ E., with an area of 317 square miles. It is bounded on the north-east by the Nūh and Palwal *tahsīls*, on the south-east by the Muttra District of the United Provinces and the State of Bharatpur, and on the west by the State of Alwar. The population in 1901 was 132,287, compared with 113,874 in 1891. It contains the town of FĪROZPUR-JHIRKA (population, 7,278), the head-quarters, and 230 villages. The land revenue and cesses amounted in 1903–4 to 2·7 lakhs. The *parganas* of Fīrozpur and Punāhāna, which make up the present *tahsīl*, were assigned for good service to Ahmad Bakhsh Khān, but were forfeited by his son for complicity in the murder of Mr. William Fraser in 1836. Of the two ranges of bare and rocky hills which extend northwards into the *tahsīl*, one forms the western boundary and the other runs north-east for 25 miles and then sinks into the plain. The soil in the low-lying parts of the *tahsīl*, which are liable to be flooded after heavy rains, is a sandy loam.

Nūh (*Noh*).—*Tahsīl* of Gurgaon District, Punjab, lying between 27° 53′ and 28° 20′ N. and 76° 51′ and 77° 19′ E., with an area of 403 square miles. It is bounded on the west by the State of Alwar. The population in 1901 was 145,931, compared with 131,593 in 1891. It contains the village of Nūh, the head-quarters, and the town of Hattīn (4,301), with 257 villages. The land revenue and cesses amounted in 1903–4 to 2·9 lakhs. Of the *parganas* which make up the greater part of the present *tahsīl*, Nūh was brought under British rule in 1808, Hattīn in 1823, and Taoru (which had been assigned to Bharatpur) after the Bharatpur War in 1826. The high plateau of Taoru is separated from the low-lying tract round Nūh by a low range of hills. To the east the country is undulating and water collects in the hollows.

Rewāri Tahsīl (*Riwāri*).—*Tahsīl* of Gurgaon District, Punjab, lying between 28° 5′ and 28° 26′ N. and 76° 18′ and 76° 52′ E., with an area of 426 square miles. It is almost entirely detached from the rest of the District, and is bounded on three sides by Native States. The isolated *pargana* of Shāhjahānpur, situated to the south in Alwar territory, is also included in this *tahsīl*. The population in 1901 was 169,673, compared with 161,332 in 1891. It contains the town of REWĀRI (population, 27,295), the head-quarters, and 290 villages. The land revenue and cesses amounted in 1903–4 to 3·2 lakhs. Rewāri formed during the eighteenth century a semi-independent principality under a family of Ahīr chiefs. On the cession of the country to the British, the revenue was first farmed by the Rājā of Bharatpur and then by the Ahīr chief of the day. It was taken over by the Government in 1808. Shāhjahānpur belonged to the Chauhān Rājputs until the Haldias, dependents of Jaipur, wrested it from them in the eighteenth century. It lapsed to the Government in 1824. The *tahsīl* consists of a sandy plain, the monotony of which is varied towards the west by irregular rocky hills of low elevation. The Kasauti on the extreme west and the Sāhibī on the east are two torrents which contribute largely to the fertility of the land along their banks. In other parts there is copious well-irrigation.

Farrukhnagar.—Town in the District and *tahsīl* of Gurgaon, Punjab, situated in 28° 27′ N. and 76° 50′ E., on a branch of the Rājputāna-Mālwā Railway, 14 miles from Gurgaon. Population (1901), 6,136. It is the dépôt for the salt extracted from saline springs in the neighbourhood, but the industry has greatly declined of late years and threatens soon to be extinct altogether. Farrukhnagar was founded by a Baloch chief, Faujdār Khān, afterwards Dalel Khān, who was made governor by the emperor Farrukh Siyar. He assumed the title of Nawāb in 1732, and the Nawābs of Farrukhnagar played an important part in the history of the tract for the next seventy years. Farrukhnagar was captured by the Jāts of Bharatpur in 1757, but recovered in 1764. On annexation the Nawābs were confirmed in their principality, but it was confiscated in 1858 for the complicity of the reigning chief in the Mutiny. The chief buildings are the Delhi Gate, the Nawāb's palace, and a fine mosque, all dating from the time of Faujdār Khān; also a large octagonal well belonging to the period of Jāt occupation. The municipality was created in 1867. The income during the ten years ending 1902–3 averaged Rs. 6,400, and the expenditure Rs. 5,900. The income in 1903–4 was Rs. 6,800, chiefly derived from octroi; and the expenditure was Rs. 10,600. It maintains a dispensary.

Fīrozpur-Jhirka.—Head-quarters of the *tahsīl* of the same name in Gurgaon District, Punjab, situated in 27° 47′ N. and 76° 58′ E., 50 miles due south of Gurgaon. Population (1901), 7,278. Formerly a trade centre for cotton, it has been ruined by the absence of railway communications. It has an out-still for the distillation of spirit. It is said to have been founded by Fīroz Shāh III as a military post to control the Mewātīs. From 1803 to 1836 it was the seat of the Nawābs of Fīrozpur, to whom the present *tahsīl* had been granted on annexation. The municipality was created in 1867. The income and expenditure during the ten years ending 1902–3 averaged Rs. 7,400 and 7,100 respectively. The income in 1903–4 amounted to Rs. 6,600, chiefly derived from octroi, and the expenditure to Rs. 7,800. It maintains a vernacular middle school and a dispensary.

Gurgaon Town.—Head-quarters of the District and *tahsīl* of the same name, Punjab, situated in 28° 29′ N. and 77° 2′ E., 3 miles from Gurgaon station on the Rājputāna-Mālwā Railway. Population (1901), 4,765. It is of no commercial or historical importance. Gurgaon is also known as Hidāyatpur, the village where at annexation a cavalry cantonment was located in order to watch Begam Sumrū's troops at Jhārsa. The civil head-quarters of the District were transferred here in 1816. Its name is taken from the neighbouring village of Gurgaon-Masāni, where there is a temple of Sītla, goddess of small-pox, which is visited annually by 50,000 or 60,000 people.

The town is administered as a 'notified area,' and contains a vernacular middle school and a dispensary.

Hodal.—Town in the Palwal *tahsīl* of Gurgaon District, Punjab, situated in 27° 53′ N. and 77° 23′ E., on the grand trunk road between Delhi and Muttra, and on the Delhi-Agra branch of the Great Indian Peninsula Railway. Population (1901), 8,142. A cotton-ginning factory gave employment to 61 persons in 1904, but the town has little trade. Saltpetre is refined to a certain extent. The Jāt chief, Sūraj Mal, was connected by marriage with the Jāts of Hodal, and there are the remains of several fine buildings erected by him. The municipality was created in 1867. The income during the ten years ending 1902–3 averaged Rs. 6,100, and the expenditure Rs. 5,000. The income in 1903–4 amounted to Rs. 6,300, chiefly derived from octroi, and the expenditure to Rs. 7,300. It maintains a Government dispensary.

Palwal Town.—Head-quarters of the *tahsīl* of the same name in Gurgaon District, Punjab, situated in 28° 9′ N. and 77° 20′ E., on the grand trunk road between Delhi and Muttra, and also on the Delhi-Agra branch of the Great Indian Peninsula Railway. Population (1901), 12,830. A good road leads to Sohna (17 miles), whence the road is metalled to Gurgaon. Palwal is a dépôt for the cotton of the surrounding country, and a cotton-ginning factory has recently been set up, which employed 207 hands in 1904. Hindu tradition identifies Palwal with the Apelava of the Mahābhārata, which is said to have been restored by Vikramāditya. The mosque at Palwal is supported by pillars, which bear traces of Hindu idols defaced in the time of Altamsh in 1221. An elegant domed tomb of red sandstone, just outside the town on the Muttra road, is said to have been built by a *fakīr*, who levied an impost for this purpose of one slab on every cart-load of stone which passed from Agra to Delhi for the building of the fort of Salīmgarh. The municipality was created in 1867. The income and expenditure during the ten years ending 1902–3 averaged Rs. 15,000 and 14,700 respectively. The income in 1903–4 was Rs. 16,800, chiefly derived from octroi; and the expenditure was Rs. 22,100. It maintains a vernacular middle school and a dispensary.

Rewāri Town (*Riwāri*).—Head-quarters of the *tahsīl* of the same name in Gurgaon District, Punjab, situated in 28° 12′ N. and 76° 38′ E., on the Delhi and Jaipur road, 32 miles south-west of Gurgaon, and the junction of the Rewāri-Bhatinda branch and the main line of the Rājputāna

Mālwā Railway; distant by rail from Calcutta 1,008 miles, from Bombay 838, and from Karāchi 904. Population (1901), 27,295, including 14,702 Hindus and 11,673 Muhammadans. Rewāri was formerly a halting-place on the trade road from Delhi to Rājputāna, celebrated for the manufacture of brass and pewter. These manufactures are still carried on; but since the opening of the railway the chief importance of the town lies in its trade in grain and sugar, sent westward, while salt and iron from Alwar are forwarded to the United Provinces.

The ruins of Old Rewāri, which local tradition connects with a nephew of Prithwī Rāj, lie some distance to the east of the present town, said to have been built about 1000 by Rājā Reo or Rāwat, who called it after his daughter Rewati. Under the Mughals, Rewāri was the head-quarters of a *sarkār*, but its Rājā seems to have been almost independent. In the reign of Aurangzeb the town and territory of Rewāri were obtained by a family of Ahīrs, who held them until annexation by the British. Rewāri was brought directly under British administration in 1808–9, and the village of Bhārāwās in its vicinity was until 1816 the head-quarters of the District. The municipality was created in 1867. The income during the ten years ending 1902–3 averaged Rs. 56,300, and the expenditure Rs. 58,100. The income in 1903–4 amounted to Rs. 48,800, chiefly derived from octroi, and the expenditure to Rs. 56,400. Rewāri contains the only high school in the District, managed by the Educational department. The town has a Government dispensary, and another belonging to the S. P. G. Mission in charge of a lady doctor.

Sohna (*Sonāh*).—Town in the District and *tahsīl* of Gurgaon, Punjab, situated in 28° 15′ N. and 77° 5′ E., 15 miles south of Gurgaon. Population (1901), 6,024. It is of no commercial importance, but claims considerable antiquity. It has been occupied in succession by the Kambohs, the Khānzādās, and the Rājputs; and traces of all three settlements are found in the extensive ruins which surround it. The town was taken in the eighteenth century by the Jāts of Bharatpur, who built a large fort, now in ruins. It has a mosque dating from 1561, and its hot springs are famed for their medicinal properties. The municipality was created in 1885. The income and expenditure during the ten years ending 1902–3 averaged Rs. 5,800 and Rs. 5,900 respectively. The income in 1903–4 was Rs. 4,800, chiefly derived from octroi; and the expenditure was Rs. 5,800. It possesses a vernacular middle school and a dispensary.

Boundaries, configuration, and hill and river systems.

Delhi District (*Dehlī* or *Dillī*).—District in the Delhi Division of the Punjab, lying between 28° 12′ and 29° 14′ N. and 76° 48′ and 77° 31′ E., with an area of 1,290 square miles. The name should be written Dillī or Dhilī, and is said to be derived from an eponymous Rājā Dilu or Dhilu. The District is bounded on the north by Karnāl; on the east by the river Jumna, which separates it from the Districts of Meerut and Bulandshahr in the United Provinces; on the south by Gurgaon; and on the west by Rohtak. The northern portion, like most of the alluvial plains of Upper India, is divided into the *khādar*, or riverain, a strip of land adjoining the Jumna; and the drier and more sandy uplands, known as the *bāngar*. Though monotonous in appearance, this latter tract is well wooded, and, being traversed by the Western Jumna Canal, is fertile in the extreme. A prolongation of the Arāvalli Hills enters Delhi from Gurgaon on the southern border, and immediately expands into a rocky table-land, about 3 miles in breadth, running in a north-easterly direction nearly across the District. Ten miles south of the city the range divides into two branches, one of which, turning sharply to the south-west, re-enters the borders of Gurgaon; while the other, continuing its northerly course as a low, narrow range of sandstone, passes west of Delhi city, where it forms the historic Ridge, and finally terminates on the right bank of the Jumna. The table-land nowhere attains an elevation of more than 500 feet above the lowlands at its base; but its surface consists of barren rock, too destitute of water for the possibility of cultivation, even in the few rare patches of level soil. The Jumna, before reaching the borders of the District, has been so completely drained of its waters for the two older canals which it feeds, that it forms only a narrow stream, fordable at almost any point, except during the rains.

Geology.

The greater part of the District lies on the alluvium; but the small hills and ridges, which abound to the south of Delhi, consist of outliers of Alwar quartzite belonging to the Delhi system of the transition group of Peninsular India. The Ridge at Delhi is composed of the same rock.

Botany.

The natural vegetation is that of the drier parts of the Upper Gangetic plain, with an element akin to that of North-East Rājputāna, while traces of an ancient Deccan flora are found on and near the low spur which ends in the ridge at Delhi. The mango and other sub-tropical species are cultivated in gardens and along canals and roadsides; but large trees, except where planted, are comparatively scarce, and the kinds that reproduce themselves spontaneously are probably, in most cases, not natives of the District.

Wolves are not uncommon and leopards are occasionally met with. Hog are plentiful all along the banks of the Jumna. Antelope are becoming scarce, while *nīlgai* and hog deer are practically extinct. 'Ravine deer' (Indian gazelle) are found in the low hills. **Fauna.**

The cold season is much like that of the Punjab proper, but ends a fortnight sooner than at Lahore. Hot west winds blow steadily till the end of June, when plentiful rain is expected. October brings cool nights and the beginning of the feverish season, which is always very unhealthy. The average mean temperature of January is 57°, of April 85°, of June 97°, and of September 87°. **Climate and temperature.**

The average rainfall varies from 21½ inches at Ballabgarh to 28 at Delhi. Of the rainfall at the latter place 25 inches fall in the summer months, and 3 in the winter. The greatest rainfall recorded during the twenty years ending 1901 was 48 inches at Delhi in 1884–5, and the least one-fifth of an inch at Mahrauli in 1896–7. **Rainfall.**

The history of the District is the history of DELHI CITY, of which it has from time immemorial formed a dependency. Even the towns of SONEPAT, BALLABGARH, and FARĪDĀBĀD hardly possess local histories of their own, apart from the city, in or around which are all its great antiquities. **History.**

The tract conquered by the East India Company in 1803 included a considerable strip to the west of the Jumna both north and south of the Mughal capital. A few native princes, however, still held independent estates within the Delhi territory, the principal in the present District being the Rājā of Ballabgarh. As early as 1819 a District of Delhi was regularly constituted. It included a part of the present Rohtak District; and in 1832 the administration of the Delhi territory, nominally as well as actually, was placed in the hands of the East India Company. The territory continued to form part of the North-Western (now the United) Provinces till the Mutiny of 1857.

On the outbreak of the Mutiny the whole District passed into the hands of the rebels; and though communications with the Punjab were soon restored, and the northern *parganas* recovered, it was not till after the fall of Delhi city that British authority could reassert itself in the southern portion. When the final suppression of the Mutiny enabled the work of reconstruction to proceed, the District was transferred to the

Punjab. At the same time the territories of the insurgent Rājā of Ballabgarh, who had been executed for rebellion, were confiscated and added as a new *tahsīl* to the District; while the outlying villages of the Doāb, hitherto belonging to Delhi, and known as the eastern *pargana*, were handed over to the North-Western Provinces.

The people.

The District contains 4 towns and 714 villages. The population at the last enumerations was: (1881) 643,515, (1891) 638,689, and (1901) 689,039. It increased by 7·8 per cent. during the last decade, the increase being greatest in the Delhi *tahsīl* (8·9) and least in Ballabgarh (5·9). It is divided into the three *tahsīls* of DELHI, SONEPAT, and BALLABGARH, the head-quarters of each being at the place from which it is named. The chief towns are the municipalities of DELHI, the head-quarters of the District, SONEPAT, BALLABGARH, and FARĪDĀBĀD. The following table shows the chief statistics of population in 1901:—

Tahsīl.	Area in square miles.	Number of Towns.	Number of Villages.	Population.	Population per square mile.	Percentage of variation in population between 1891 and 1901.	Number of persons able to read and write.
Delhi	429	1	243	359,008	836·8	+ 8·9	21,854
Sonepat	455	1	224	203,338	446·9	+ 7·3	6,445
Ballabgarh	385	2	247	126,693	329·1	+ 5·9	3,271
District total	1,290	4	714	689,039	534·1	+ 7·8	31,570

NOTE.—The figures for the areas of *tahsīls* are taken from revenue returns. The total District area is that given in the *Census Report*.

Hindus number 510,532, or more than 74 per cent. of the total; Muhammadans, 167,290; and Jains, 7,726. The people of Delhi city share with Lucknow the reputation of speaking the most elegant form of Hindustāni or Urdū.

Castes and occupations.

The Jāts are the chief landowning tribe, numbering 114,000, and are almost entirely Hindus. Those of the south of the District centre about Ballabgarh, and their traditions are connected with the Jāt Rājās of that place. Those of the north are divided into two factions: the Dahiyas, who trace their descent from a grandson of Prithwī Rāj, Dhanij by name, and a Jāt woman: and the Ahūlānas, who say that their ancestors came from Rājputāna. The Gūjars (28,000) are nearly all Hindus; they have a bad reputation as thieves, and levy a kind of blackmail on the residents of the civil station by ensuring that the rash householder who does not employ a

Gūjar watchman shall infallibly have his house robbed. The Tagās (9,000) say that they were once Brāhmans, and derive their name from the fact of their having abandoned (*tyāga*) the practice of mendicancy. They are of the Gaur family, and their tradition is that they were invited from Bengal for the purpose of exterminating snakes. Sir H. Elliot finds in this story an allusion to wars against 'Takshaka Scythians' of a Buddhist creed. The Ahīrs (14,000) are all Hindus and claim a Rājput origin. They are excellent cultivators. The Rājputs (24,000) are mostly Hindus, but 4,000 are Muhammadans. The District contains 62,000 Brāhmans, 71,000 Shaikhs, and 8,000 Meos. The Baniās (47,000) are the most important of the commercial classes, but there are 5,000 Khattrīs. Of the menials may be mentioned the Chamārs or leather-workers (66,000), the Chūhrās (27,000) and Dhānaks (6,000) who are scavengers, the Jhīnwars or water-carriers (17,000), the Kumhārs or potters (14,000), the Lohārs or blacksmiths (6,000), the Nais or barbers (11,000), the Kassābs or butchers (6,000), and the Tarkhāns or carpenters (9,000). As is natural in a District containing so large a city, only 41 per cent. of the total population are supported by agriculture, while 29 per cent. are industrial, 6 commercial, and 3 professional.

Christian missions. The Society for the Propagation of the Gospel was established at Delhi in 1854, and reinforced in 1877 by the Cambridge Mission—a body of graduates of Cambridge living and working together as a brotherhood—who, with the original body, form one mission under the name of the S. P. G. and Cambridge Mission in Delhi and the South Punjab. Among the institutions managed by this united body are St. Stephen's Mission College, a high school, with six branches and 700 boys, and other schools, a hospital for women, a Christian girls' boarding school and industrial school, and St. Mary's Home for convalescent converts and teachers. The first Baptist missionary in Delhi was John Chamberlain, tutor to the son of Begam Sumrū, who visited the city in 1814; but Delhi was not recognized as a mission station till 1818. In the operations of the Baptist Mission are included a training institution, dispensary, school, Zanāna mission, and a girls' school. Of every 10,000 persons in the District 46 are Christians. In 1901 it returned 2,042 native Christians.

General agricultural conditions. North of the city the District is divided into two portions: the low-lying riverain *khādar* lands near the Jumna, and the higher upland, or *bāngar* lands. now removed from the influence of the river. In the *khādar*, where the soil is light and sandy, irrigation from wells is easy, and this tract mainly depends on the spring harvest. The *bāngar* is traversed by the Western Jumna Canal and, until the recent realignment, suffered severely from swamping; in its unirrigated portions the autumn harvest is naturally the more important, and south of Delhi the riverain strip is very narrow. In the lands lying just under the hills, the soil is light, and irrigation is chiefly carried on by dams which hold up the mountain torrents. Round the Najafgarh *jhīl* and in the extreme south are blocks of land, inundated in the rains, with a light soil and water near the surface. Since the Najafgarh *jhīl* was drained, cultivation on its borders has ceased to be as profitable as formerly.

Chief agricultural statistics and principal crops.

The District is held almost entirely by petty peasant proprietors, large estates covering only 50,000 acres, and about 16,000 acres owned by Government being held on temporary leases. The area for which details are available from the revenue records of 1903-4 is 1,284 square miles, as shown below:—

Tahsil.	Total.	Cultivated.	Irrigated.	Cultivable waste.
Delhi	429	294	101	71
Sonepat	460	323	194	82
Ballabgarh	395	250	27	41
Total	1,284	867	322	194

The chief crops in the spring harvest are gram and wheat, which occupied 36 and 159 square miles respectively in 1903-4; barley occupied 47 square miles. In the autumn harvest spiked millet occupied 133 and great millet 114 square miles, these being the staple food-grains of the District. Next in importance are cotton (37 square miles), sugar-cane (25 square miles), and maize (15 square miles). Sugar-cane is the most important and profitable crop of the autumn in the *bāngar* tracts of Delhi and Sonepat; melons are an important crop of the extra spring harvest on the river-side near the city.

Improvements in agricultural practice.

The cultivated area increased only from 821 square miles in 1881 to 867 in 1904, or by slightly more than 5 per cent., and there is little room for further extension. The character of the cultivation has, however, been enormously improved by the remodelling of the Western Jumna Canal, which has caused the saline efflorescences and waterlogging, once characteristic of the canal-irrigated tracts, to disappear in great measure. The draining of the Najafgarh *jhīl* has also added to the cultivated area, besides vastly improving the physical well-being of the people. A good deal has been done in the way of encouraging the people to take advances for the construction of wells, and 1·2 lakhs was advanced under the Land Improvement Loans Act during the five years ending 1904.

Cattle and horses.

The cattle form an important feature of agricultural economy, and few Jāts do not own a yoke of bullocks and a cow or buffalo, but the breeds are in no way peculiar. A horse fair is held at Delhi city, but the District does not produce anything beyond the ordinary village pony. The District board maintains one donkey and two horse stallions.

Irrigation.

Of the total area cultivated in 1903–4, 322 square miles, or 37 per cent., were classed as irrigated. Of this area, 161 square miles were irrigated from wells alone, 941 acres from wells and canals, and 159 square miles from canals alone. The new Delhi branch of the Western Jumna Canal, which traverses Sonepat and the northern part of the Delhi *tahsīl*, is estimated to irrigate 129 square miles yearly. When the canal was reopened under British rule, it was aligned for a great part of its length in a valley, and the watercourses were equally ill-constructed, often intersecting one another and running side by side for long distances. The result was that almost irretrievable damage was done by waterlogging and saline efflorescences, and the health of the people was seriously impaired. Since 1880, however, the distributing system has been entirely remodelled and about 386 miles of drainage channels constructed. The result has been most encouraging, and waterlogging with its attendant evils has almost entirely disappeared. A small area is irrigated by the Najafgarh canal, an escape which drains the Najafgarh *jhīl* and is now in charge of the District board. The Agra Canal takes off from the Jumna below Delhi, but flows at too low a level to give much irrigation in this District.

The District contains 9,943 wells, besides 1,279 temporary wells, lever wells, and water-lifts. The Persian wheel is the commonest way of raising water in the north, and the rope and bucket in the south and centre. As there is no scope for the extension of canal-irrigation, the chief means of protection against famine is afforded by the construction of new wells.

Forests.

The only forests are 35·9 square miles of unclassed forests and Government waste under the control of the Deputy-Commissioner.

Minerals.

Chalk is obtained in small quantities from two villages, where it is dug out of a rude mine, made by sinking a shaft 30 or 40 feet deep, and driving horizontal tunnels. The output is about 15,000 maunds annually. The work is done by menial castes, who get $2\frac{1}{2}$ annas a day for work below, and $1\frac{1}{2}$ or 2 annas for work on the surface. *Kankar* is quarried in about 125 villages, and a quartz-like building-stone is also found. A crystal mine, formerly worked at Arangpur, has long been abandoned. A certain amount of crude saltpetre is manufactured; and a saltpetre refinery in Delhi city turns out about 2,500 maunds annually.

Manufactures and trade.

The District possesses no arts or manufactures of any importance except those of the city. Similarly the commerce of the District all centres in the city, that of the rest of the District consisting merely in the interchange of agricultural produce for piece-goods, iron, and other necessaries. Of the twenty-four factories in the District, which in 1904 employed 3,494 hands, all are in the city except a cotton-ginning and pressing factory at Sonepat, where the number of hands employed in 1904 was 130.

Railways and roads.

Delhi is in connexion with six railway systems. The East Indian, North-Western, and Oudh and Rohilkhand Railways enter it from Ghāziābād junction, crossing the Jumna by an iron bridge. The Delhi-Ambāla-Kālka Railway runs northwards from the city, and the Rājputāna-Mālwā Railway traverses the District for a short distance in the direction of Gurgaon. A line from Delhi to Agra was opened in 1904. The Jumna is navigable during the rainy season, and the Western Jumna Canal, continued as far as Delhi by the Okhla Navigation Canal, is navigable all the year round. Good metalled roads connect the city with Lahore, Agra, Jaipur, and Hissār; while a network of local trade-lines runs in every direction to the various minor towns. The District has altogether 143 miles of metalled and 499 of unmetalled roads, all of which, except 104 miles of metalled and 83 of unmetalled roads under the Public Works department, are maintained by the District board. The Jumna is crossed by four ferries, and the railway bridge at Delhi has a subway for ordinary wheeled traffic.

Famine.

The history of famine goes back to the year 1345 in the time of Muhammad bin Tughlak, when it is recorded that men ate one another. Subsequent famines occurred in 1631, in the time of Shāh Jahān; in 1661, under Aurangzeb, a severe famine: in 1739, under Muhammad Shāh, famine followed the invasion by Nādir Shāh; and again in 1770, 1783–4, 1803–4, 1813–4, and in 1825–6, when the Sonepat *tahsīl* was severely affected and the entire revenue was remitted. In 1832–4 and 1837–8 bread riots occurred, and unlimited relief was offered to those who would work. The famine of 1860–1 was severe, and 2·7 lakhs was expended on relief works and gratuitous relief, representing a total number of 12,000 persons relieved for a whole year. The famine of 1865 was not severe in Delhi. In the famine of 1868–9 relief works were provided, and altogether Rs. 14,000 expended, including Rs. 9,000 from private subscriptions. The famine of 1877–8 did not materially affect Delhi. In 1896–7 there was considerable distress, wheat and *bājra* sold at 7¾ and 8½ seers per rupee respectively, and more than 3,000 persons were employed on relief works, and about 4,000 received food at kitchens. Scarcity again supervened in 1899–1900, but in spite of unfavourable local conditions the people did not resort to the main relief work provided. The District is small; it contains a large city centrally situated, and there is at all times a demand for labour. The greatest daily average of persons relieved in 1899–1900 was 4,374; Rs. 40,694 were spent in wages on earthwork, and the cost incurred by the municipality was Rs. 5,699.

District subdivisions and staff. The District is in charge of a Deputy-Commissioner, aided by five Assistant or Extra Assistant Commissioners, of whom one is in charge of the District treasury. The treasury here is the Bank of Bengal, and there is a currency dépôt at the courthouse. The District is divided into three *tahsīls*, each under a *tahsīldār* and a *naib-tahsīldār*. Delhi city is also the head-quarters of the Superintending Engineer, Western Jumna Canal circle, and of the Executive Engineer, Delhi Provincial division.

Civil justice and crime. Civil judicial work is under a District Judge, from whom appeals lie to the Divisional Judge of the Delhi Civil Division. He is aided by an Extra Assistant Commissioner, who is solely employed on civil judicial work and may be replaced by a Munsif, a Small Cause Court Judge, and one Munsif, besides whom the other Assistant and Extra Assistant Commissioners and the *tahsīldārs* help in civil judicial work. There is an honorary Extra Assistant Commissioner at head-quarters. The civil work, arising mainly out of the large and growing trade of the city, is very heavy. The Divisional Judge is also Sessions Judge of the Delhi Civil Division. There are sixteen honorary magistrates, of whom twelve constitute a bench for the city, two sit at head-quarters, and one in each *tahsīl*. The predominant forms of crime are burglary and theft.

Land revenue administration.

The only peculiarity as regards tenure of land is that in a few villages superior and inferior proprietors are found; the settlement is (with one exception) made with the latter, the superior proprietors merely receiving a charge of 5 to 10 per cent. on the revenue. The nature of the early revenue assessments appears to have been very summary. They were made, as far as possible, on the basis of existing arrangements, and were for short terms only. The administration, from annexation to 1841, was harsh and unsympathetic. The Sonepat and Delhi *tahsīls* were regularly settled in 1842 and 1844, and Ballabgarh after its confiscation in 1857. The Settlement officer in 1842 reduced the demand in Sonepat, and excused himself for so doing by pointing out that the greatest difficulty had been invariably experienced in realizing the Government demand; that notwithstanding strenuous and well-sustained efforts the District officers and their subordinates had been baffled, and that large balances had frequently remained uncollected. Reductions were made in all *tahsīls* at the regular settlement. The settlement of the whole District was revised between 1872 and 1880. The revenue rates on land irrigated from wells varied from Rs. 4 to 8 annas, on flooded land from Rs. 2–8 to Rs. 2, and on unirrigated land from Rs. 1–10 to 10 annas. Canal lands were assessed at 'dry' rates of about Rs. 1–8, Rs. 3 being paid as occupier's rate for the use of the water, plus an extra Rs. 1–8 as owner's rate. Villages on the Najafgarh *jhīl* were charged a fluctuating assessment on the area cultivated, varying from Rs. 6 to Rs. 1–8 according to the nature of the crop. The new assessment resulted in an increase of Rs. 45,000. A change was made in 1895 in the method of realizing canal revenue, and the system then adopted remains in force. The land revenue demand in 1903–4, including cesses, was 10 lakhs. The average size of a proprietary holding is 3 acres.

The collections of land revenue alone and of total revenue are shown below, in thousands of rupees:—

	1880–1.	1890–1.	1900–1.	1903–4.
Land revenue . . .	8,60	8,12	7,68	8,06
Total revenue . . .	11,57	11,94	15,10	16,21

Local and municipal.

The District contains four municipalities, DELHI, SONEPAT, BALLABGARH, and FARĪDĀBĀD; and two 'notified areas,' Mahrauli and Najafgarh. Outside these, local affairs are managed by the District board, whose income amounted in 1903–4 to a lakh. The expenditure in the same year was also a lakh, of which a fifth was devoted to education.

The regular police force consists of 1,023 of all ranks, including 539 municipal police, under a Superintendent, who usually has one Assistant and one Deputy-Superintendent (in charge of the city) and six inspectors under him. Village watchmen number 924. There are 14 police stations, of which 3 are in the city, 8 outposts, and 10 road-posts. The District jail in the city has accommodation for 536 prisoners. Police and jails.

Delhi stands fifth among the twenty-eight Districts of the Province in respect of the literacy of its population. In 1901 the proportion of literate persons was 4·6 per cent. (8 males and 0·6 females). The number of pupils under instruction was 5,210 in 1880–1, 8,124 in 1890–1, 9,525 in 1900–1, and 10,644 in 1903–4. In the last year the District had 2 Arts colleges, 14 secondary, 110 primary, one training, and 3 special (public) schools, and 12 advanced and 123 elementary (private) schools, with 570 girls in the public and 277 in the private schools. The total expenditure on education in 1903–4 was 2 lakhs, of which Rs. 19,000 was derived from District funds, Rs. 18,000 from municipalities, and Rs. 73,000 from Provincial funds. Education.

The public medical institutions are the municipal Dufferin Hospital and two dispensaries in the city, and 6 outlying dispensaries. In 1904 these treated a total of 131,050 out-patients and 2,299 in-patients, and 5,975 operations were performed. The total expenditure was Rs. 30,000, the greater part of which was met from municipal and District funds. Besides the institutions mentioned above, the city possesses the St. Stephen's Hospital (Cambridge Mission) for women, and the Baptist dispensary. The Victoria Memorial Zanāna Hospital, erected at a cost of one lakh, was opened in December, 1906. Hospitals and dispensaries.

The number of successful vaccinations in 1903–4 was 27,280, representing 39·7 per 1,000 of the population. Vaccination is compulsory only in Delhi city and Sonepat town. Vaccination.

[D. C. J. Ibbetson, *District Gazetteer* (1883–4); R. Maconachie, *Settlement Report* (1882).]

Delhi Tahsīl.—Central *tahsīl* of Delhi District, Punjab, lying between 28° 30′ and 28° 53′ N. and 76° 51′ and 77° 17′ E., to the west of the river Jumna, with an area of 429 square miles. The population in 1901 was 359,008, compared with 329,547 in 1891. The head-quarters are at DELHI CITY (population, 208,575), and it also contains 243 villages. The land revenue and cesses amounted in 1903–4 to 3·4 lakhs. The eastern portion of the *tahsīl* lies in the Jumna lowlands. From the city southwards stretches a line of low quartzite hills, while the south-west corner is occupied by the Najafgarh *jhīl*. The rest of the *tahsīl* consists of a fertile upland plain, poorly wooded and with a light rainfall, but for the most part irrigated by the Western Jumna Canal.

Sonepat Tahsīl (*Sonpat*).—Northern *tahsīl* of Delhi District, Punjab, lying between 28° 49′ and 29° 14′ N. and 76° 48′ and 77° 13′ E., with an area of 460 square miles. It lies to the west of the river Jumna, which separates it from the Meerut and Bulandshahr Districts of the United Provinces. The population in 1901 was 203,338, compared with 189,490 in 1891. It contains the town of SONEPAT (population, 12,990), the head-quarters, and 224 villages. The land revenue and cesses amounted in 1903–4 to 4·1 lakhs. The eastern portion of the *tahsīl* lies in the Jumna lowlands. The upland plateau to the west is irrigated by the Western Jumna Canal.

Ballabgarh Tahsīl.—Southern *tahsīl* of Delhi District, Punjab, lying between 28° 12′ and 28° 36′ N. and 77° 7′ and 77° 31′ E., with an area of 395 square miles. It lies to the west of the river Jumna, which separates it from the Bulandshahr District of the United Provinces. The population in 1901 was 126,693, compared with 119,652 in 1891. It contains the towns of BALLABGARH (population, 4,506) the head-quarters, and FARĪDĀBĀD (5,310); and 247 villages. The land revenue and cesses in 1903–4 amounted to 2·7 lakhs. The country is in general bare and treeless. On the east lie the Jumna lowlands, while the hills that run south from the Delhi Ridge cross the western portion of the *tahsīl*. The rest consists of a plain of sandy loam.

Ballabgarh Town.—Head-quarters of the *tahsīl* of the same name in Delhi District, Punjab, situated in 28° 20′ N. and 77° 20′ E., 24 miles south of Delhi on the Delhi-Muttra road and the Delhi-Agra branch of the Great Indian Peninsula Railway. Population (1901), 4,506. The name Ballabgarh is a corruption of Balrāmgarh, 'the fort of Balrām,' a Jāt chief who held the surrounding country under Sūraj Mal of Bharatpur, and built the fort and palace. In 1775 the estate was transferred by the Delhi emperor to Ajīt Singh, whose son Bahādur Singh was recognized in 1803 as chief, and built the town. His successor was hanged for complicity in the Mutiny of 1857 and the estate confiscated. The municipality was created in 1867. The income during the ten years ending 1902–3 averaged Rs. 7,000, and the expenditure Rs. 6,300. The income in 1903–4 was Rs. 8,700, chiefly derived from octroi; and the expenditure was Rs. 6,900. The town possesses a vernacular middle school and a dispensary.

Delhi City (*Dehlī* or *Dillī*).—Head-quarters of the Delhi Division, District, and *tahsīl*, Punjab, and former capital of the Mughal empire, situated in 28° 39′ N. and 77° 15′ E., on the west bank of the Jumna; distant from Calcutta 956 miles, from Bombay 982 miles, and from Karāchi 907 miles. The population at the last three enumerations was: (1881) 173,393, (1891) 192,579, and (1901) 208,575. The increase during the last decade is greatly due to the development of mill industries. The population in 1901 included 114,417 Hindus, 88,460 Muhammadans, 3,266 Jains, 2,164 Christians, and 229 Sikhs.

The area close to where the northernmost spur of the Arāvalli Hills abuts on the Jumna has from remote times been the site of one great city after another. First of these is the city of Indraprastha, founded, according to the tradition preserved in the Mahābhārata, by the Pāndava chief Yudhishthira. Indraprastha was, however, only one of the five *prasthas* or 'plains,' which included Sonepat, Pānīpat, Pilpat, and Bāghpat. Firishta has preserved a tradition that Delhi or Dillī was founded by a Rājā Dhilū before the Macedonian invasion; but as an historical city Delhi dates only from the middle of the eleventh century A.D., when Anang Pāl, a Rājput chief of the Tomar clan, built the Red Fort, in which the Kutb Minār now stands, and founded a town. He also removed the famous iron pillar on which are inscribed the eulogies of Chandra Gupta Vikramāditya, probably from Muttra, and set it up in 1052 as an adjunct to a group of temples. This remarkable relic consists of a solid shaft of metal 16 inches in diameter and about 23 feet in height, set in masonry, 3 feet of it being below the surface. Tradition indeed asserts that a holy Brāhman assured the Rājā that the pillar had been driven so deeply into the earth that it reached the head of Vāsuki, the serpent king who supports the world, and, consequently, had become immovable, whereby the dominion was ensured for ever to the dynasty of its founder. The incredulous Rājā ordered the monument to be dug up, when its base was found reddened with the blood of the serpent king. Thus convinced, Anang Pāl at once commanded that the shaft should be sunk

History.

again in the earth; but as a punishment for his want of faith, it appeared that no force could restore it to its place as before. Hence the city derived its name Dhilī, from the fact that the column remained loose (*dhīla*) in the ground. Unfortunately for the legend, not only does the inscription prove its falsity, but the name of Dillī is undoubtedly earlier than the rise of the Tomar dynasty.

Anang Pāl, who seems to have come from Kanauj, ruled a petty principality extending to Hānsi on the north, the Ganges on the east, and Agra on the south. His dynasty lasted just a century, until 1151, when it was supplanted by Vīsaldev or Bīsaldeo, a Chauhān chief of Ajmer. Bīsaldeo's grandson, the famous Prithwī Rāj or Rai Pithora, ruled both Delhi and Ajmer, and built the city which bore his name at the former place. The walls of this city may still be traced for a long distance round the Kutb Minār. From Delhi Rai Pithora in 1191 led his Hindu vassals and allies to defeat Muhammad of Ghor at TIRĀWARI, but in the following year he met with a decisive overthrow at that place. With his death the history of Hindu Delhi ends. In 1193 Kutb-ud-dīn, Muhammad's slave general, took Delhi; and on his master's death in 1206 it became the capital of the Slave dynasty to whom Old Delhi owes its grandest ruins. Kutb-ud-dīn's mosque was commenced, according to the inscription on its entrance archway, immediately after the capture of the city in 1193. It was completed in three years, and enlarged during the reign of Altamsh, son-in-law of the founder, and the greatest monarch of the line. This mosque consists of an outer and inner courtyard, the latter surrounded by an exquisite colonnade, whose richly decorated shafts have been torn from the precincts of Hindu temples. Originally a thick coat of plaster concealed from the believer's eyes the profuse idolatrous ornamentations; but the stucco has now fallen away, revealing the delicate workmanship of the Hindu artists in all its pristine beauty. Eleven magnificent arches close its western façade, Muhammadan in outline and design, but carried out in detail by Hindu workmen, as the intricate lace-work which covers every portion of the arcade sufficiently bears witness. Ibn Batūta, the Moorish traveller, who was a magistrate in Delhi and saw the mosque about 150 years after its erection, describes it as unequalled for either beauty or extent. The Kutb Minār, another celebrated monument of the great Slave king, stands in the south-east corner of the outer courtyard of the mosque. It rises to a height of 238 feet, tapering gracefully from a diameter of 47 feet at the base to nearly 9 feet at the summit. The shaft consists of five storeys, enclosing a spiral staircase, and was crowned by a now broken cupola, which fell during an earthquake in 1803. The original purpose of the minaret was doubtless as a *muazzin's* tower, whence the call to morning and evening prayer might be heard throughout the whole city. The site chosen for the mosque was that already occupied by the iron pillar, which forms the central ornament of the inner courtyard. Around in every direction spreads a heap of splendid ruins, the most important of which are the tomb of Altamsh and the unfinished minaret of Alā-ud-dīn, commenced in 1311.

During the reign of the Slave kings, a queen, for the only time in its history, sat on the throne of the Muhammadan empire of Delhi. As the patriot Hungarians, in the annals of modern Europe, drew their swords for *Rex* Maria Theresa, so her subjects gave to queen Raziya the masculine title of *Sultān*.

The Slave dynasty retained the sovereignty till 1290, when Jalāl-ud-dīn, Khiljī, founded a new line. During the reign of his nephew and successor, Alā-ud-dīn, Delhi was twice unsuccessfully attacked by Mongol hordes, who swept into the country from Central Asia.

In 1321 the house of Tughlak succeeded to the empire; and Ghiyās-ud-dīn, its founder, erected a new capital, Tughlakābād, on a rocky eminence some 4 miles farther to the east. Remains of a massive citadel, and deserted streets or lanes, still mark the spot on which this third metropolis arose; but no human inhabitants now frequent the vast and desolate ruins. Ghiyās-ud-dīn died in 1325, and was succeeded by his son Muhammad bin Tughlak, who thrice attempted to remove the seat of government and the whole population from Delhi to Daulatābād in the Deccan, more than 800 miles away. Ibn Batūta gives a graphic picture of the desolate city, with its magnificent architectural works, and its bare, unpeopled houses. Fīroz Shāh Tughlak once more removed the site of Delhi to a new town, Fīrozābād, which appears to have occupied all the ground between the tomb of Humāyūn and the Ridge. Amid the ruins of this prince's palace, just outside the modern south gate, stands one of the famous pillars originally erected by Asoka, in the third century B.C. This monolith, 42 feet in height, is known as Fīroz Shāh's *lāt* or pillar, as it was brought by him from Topra near Khizrābād in the District of Ambāla. It is composed of pale pink sandstone, and bears a Pālī inscription, first deciphered by Mr. Prinsep.

In December, 1398, while rival claimants of the house of Tughlak were fighting for the remnants of the kingdom, the hordes of Tīmūr reached Delhi. Mahmūd Shāh II, the nominal king, fled to Gujarāt, after his army had suffered a defeat beneath the walls; and Tīmūr, entering the city, gave it over for five days to plunder and massacre. Dead bodies choked the streets; and when at last even the Mongol appetite for carnage was satiated, the host retired, dragging with them into slavery large numbers of both men and women. For two months Delhi remained absolutely without government, until Mahmūd Shāh recovered a miserable fragment of his former empire. In 1412 he died; and his successors, the Saiyid vassals of the Mongols, held Delhi, with a petty principality in the neighbourhood, until 1450, when the Lodī dynasty succeeded to the Muhammadan empire. In 1503 Sikandar II made Agra the capital of the empire, but Delhi retained much of its former importance. After his defeat of Ibrāhīm II, the last of the Lodīs, at Pānīpat, Bābar entered Delhi in 1526, but resided mainly at Agra. Humāyūn removed to Delhi, and built or restored the fort of Purāna Kila on the site of Indraprastha. The Afghān Sher Shāh, who drove out Humāyūn in 1540, enclosed and fortified the city with a new wall. One of his approaches, known as the Lāl Darwāza or 'red gate,' still stands isolated on the roadside, facing the modern jail. The fortress of Salīmgarh preserves the name of a son of Sher Shāh. Humāyūn's tomb forms one of the most striking architectural monuments in the neighbourhood. Akbar and Jahāngīr usually resided at Agra, Lahore, or Ajmer. Shāh Jahān rebuilt the city on its present site, surrounding it with the existing fortifications and adding the title of Shāhjahānābād from his own name. He also built the Jāma Masjid, and reopened the Western Jumna Canal. From his time, except for brief periods, Delhi remained the head-quarters of the Mughal emperors. In 1737, during the reign of Muhammad Shāh, Bāji Rao, the Marāthā Peshwā, appeared beneath its walls. Two years later, Nādir Shāh entered the city in triumph and re-enacted the massacre of Tīmūr. For 58 days the victorious Persian plundered rich and poor alike, and left the city with a booty estimated at nine millions sterling. Before the final disruption of the decaying empire in 1760, the unhappy capital was twice devastated by civil war, sacked by Ahmad Shāh Durrāni, and finally spoiled by the rapacious Marāthās. Alamgīr II, the last real emperor, was murdered in 1759. Shāh Alam, who assumed the empty title, could not establish his authority in Delhi, which became the alternate prey of Afghāns and Marāthās until 1771, when the latter party restored the emperor to the city of his ancestors. In 1788 a Marāthā garrison permanently occupied the palace, and Shāh Alam remained a prisoner in the hands of Sindhia until the British conquest. On March 14, 1803, Lord Lake, having defeated the Marāthās, entered Delhi, and took the emperor under his protection. Next year, Holkar attacked the city; but Colonel (afterwards Sir David) Ochterlony, first British Resident, successfully held out against overwhelming numbers for eight days, until relieved by Lord Lake. The conquered territory was administered by the British in the name of the emperor, while the palace remained under his jurisdiction.

The story of the Mutiny at Delhi and of the restoration of British sovereignty belongs to Indian rather than to local history. Delhi was recovered in September, 1857, and remained for a while under military government; and it became necessary, owing to the frequent murders of European soldiers, to expel the population for a while from the city. Shortly after, the Hindu inhabitants were freely readmitted; but the Muhammadans were still rigorously excluded, till the restoration of the city to the civil authorities on January 11, 1858.

Delhi has on two occasions since the Mutiny been the scene of Imperial assemblages: in 1877 when Queen Victoria was proclaimed Empress of India, and in 1903 to celebrate the accession of Edward VII.

Modern Delhi.

The modern city of Delhi extends for over 2 miles along the west bank of the river Jumna, and on the other three sides is enclosed by a lofty stone wall 3¼ miles in length, built by Shāh Jahān, and reconstructed by the British at the beginning of the last century. It was once entered by fourteen gates, eight on the land side and six leading to the river; but many of these have now been removed. Of those that remain, the principal are: on the north the Kashmīr Gate, on the west the Farāsh Khāna and Ajmer Gates, and on the south the Delhi Gate. The imperial palace, now known as the Fort, lies to the east of the city, and abuts directly on the river. It is surrounded on three sides by an imposing wall of red sandstone, with small round towers, and gateways on the west and south.

On the north-east of the Fort is the outwork of Salīmgarh. At this point the East Indian Railway enters the city by a magnificent bridge across the Jumna, passing over Salīmgarh and through a corner of the Fort to the railway station within the city walls. North-west of the Fort, up to the Kashmīr Gate, lies an open space in which are situated the public offices and St. James's Church. South of this and separated from it by the railway line lies another open space devoted to the public gardens; and in the south-east corner of the city, in the quarter known as Daryā Ganj, is the cantonment. The area thus occupied covers nearly one-half of the entire city; it presents a comparatively open appearance, and forms a marked contrast to the south-west quarter of the city, which is densely occupied by the shops and dwellings of the native population.

The architectural glories of Delhi are famous alike in Indian and European literature. It is impossible in a brief notice like the present to attempt any adequate description of them. They are described in Mr. Fergusson's *History of Indian and Eastern Architecture* (1876), in Mr. Fanshawe's *Delhi Past and Present* (1902), and in many other works. The palace of Shāh Jahān, perhaps less picturesque and more sober in tone than that of Agra, has the advantage of being built on a more uniform plan, and by the most magnificent of the royal builders of India. It forms a parallelogram, measuring 1,600 feet east and west by 3,202 feet north and south, exclusive of the gateways. Passing the deeply-recessed portal, a vaulted hall is entered, rising two storeys, 375 feet long, like the nave of a gigantic Gothic cathedral—'the noblest entrance,' says Mr. Fergusson, 'to any existing palace.' Facing this entrance is the Naubat Khāna or 'music hall,' and beyond is the great court of the palace, in the middle of which stands the Dīwān-i-ām or 'hall of public audience.' Behind this again is a court containing the Rang Mahal or 'painted chamber.' North of this central range of buildings stands the Dīwān-i-khās or 'private audience hall,' which forms, 'if not the most beautiful, certainly the most ornamented of all Shāh Jahān's buildings.' It overhangs the river, and nothing can exceed the delicacy of its inlaid work or the poetry of its design. It is on the walls of this hall that the famous inscription runs, 'If there is a heaven on earth, it is this—it is this!' South of the central range of buildings an area, measuring about 1,000 feet each way, was occupied by the harem and private apartments of the palace, covering, consequently, more than twice the area of the Escurial, or, in fact, of any palace in Europe.

The buildings in the native city are chiefly of brick, well-built, and substantial. The smaller streets are narrow and tortuous, and in many cases end in *culs-de-sac*. On the other hand, no city in India has finer streets than the main thoroughfares of Delhi, ten in number, thoroughly drained, metalled, and lighted. The principal thoroughfare, the Chāndni Chauk, or 'silver street,' leads eastwards from the Fort to the Lahore Gate, three-quarters of a mile long by 74 feet broad. Throughout the greater part of its length, a double row of trees runs down its centre on both sides of a raised path, which has taken the place of the masonry aqueduct that in former days conducted water from the canal into the palace. A little to the south of the Chāndni Chauk is the Jāma Masjid, or 'great mosque,' standing out boldly from a small rocky rising ground. Begun by Shāh Jahān in the fourth year of his reign, and completed in the tenth, it still remains one of the finest buildings of its kind in India. The front courtyard, 450 feet square, surrounded by a cloister open on both sides, is paved with granite inlaid with marble, and commands a view of the whole city. The mosque itself, a splendid structure forming an oblong 261 feet in length, is approached by a magnificent flight of stone steps. Three domes of white marble rise from its roof, with two tall and graceful minarets at the corners in front. The interior of the mosque is paved throughout with white marble, and the walls and roof are lined with the same material. Two other mosques deserve a passing notice : the Kālī Masjid or 'black mosque,' so called from the dark colour given to it by time, and supposed to have been built by one of the early Afghan sovereigns; and the mosque of Roshan-ud-daula. Among the more modern buildings may be mentioned the Residency, now occupied by the Government high school; the town hall, a handsome building in the Chāndni Chauk, containing a Darbār hall with a good collection of pictures, a museum, and a public library; and the Church of St. James, built at a cost of £10,000 by Colonel Skinner, an officer well-known in the history of the East India Company. About half-way down the Chāndni Chauk is a high clock-tower. North of the Chāndni Chauk lie the Queen's gardens. Beyond the city walls the civil lines stretch away on the north as far as the historic Ridge, about a mile outside. To the west and south-west considerable suburbs cluster beyond the walls, containing the tombs of the imperial family. That of Humāyūn is a noble building of red sandstone with a dome of marble. It lies about 3½ miles from the Delhi Gate in a large garden of terraces, the whole surrounded by an embattled wall, with towers and four gateways. In the centre stands a platform about 20 feet high by 200 feet square, supported by cloisters, and ascended by four great flights of granite steps. Above rises the mausoleum, also a square, with a great dome of white marble in the centre. About a mile to the westward is another burying-ground, or collection of tombs and small mosques, some of them very beautiful. The most remarkable is perhaps the little chapel in honour of a celebrated Muhammadan saint, Nizām-ud-dīn, near whose shrine the members of the Mughal imperial family, up to the time of the Mutiny, lie buried, each in his own little enclosure, surrounded by very elegant lattice-work of white marble.

The palaces of the nobles, which formerly gave an air of grandeur to the city, have for the most part disappeared. Their sites are occupied by structures of less pretension, but still with some elegance of architectural design. The city is now amply supplied with water; and much attention has of late been paid to cleanliness and sanitary requirements generally.

The municipality was created in 1850. The income and expenditure during the ten years ending 1902–3 averaged 5·6 lakhs. The income in 1903–4 was 6·5 lakhs, chiefly derived from octroi (3·1 lakhs), taxes on houses, lands, animals, and vehicles, and tolls (1 lakh), municipal property and fines, &c. (Rs. 79,000), and sale of water (Rs. 40,000); and the expenditure was 5·8 lakhs, including general administration (Rs. 77,000), public safety (Rs. 96,000), water-supply (Rs. 40,000), conservancy (Rs. 83,000), hospitals and dispensaries (Rs. 41,000), public works (Rs. 69,000), and education (Rs. 33,000).

The ordinary garrison consists of a company of garrison artillery and a detachment of British infantry in the Fort; a native infantry regiment at Daryā Ganj; and a native cavalry regiment, for which lines have recently been built in the old cantonment, beyond the Ridge. The income and expenditure of cantonment funds during the ten years ending 1902–3 averaged Rs. 12,200.

Arts and manufactures. The occupations and industries of Delhi are numerous, comprising jewellery, silversmith's work, brass and copper ware, ivory-carving, pottery, weaving, gold and silver embroidery, miniature painting, &c. For centuries the jewellery of Delhi has had a worldwide reputation, but it is doubtful whether the productions of the present day are equal to those of Mughal times. Ivory-carving is carried on successfully by one or two families, and within recent years some very beautiful caskets and similar articles in this material have been produced. A feature of the work is the employment of geometric open-work patterns, which are carried out with a very high degree of finish. The pottery is a kind of rough porcelain and has certain artistic qualities. It is a comparatively modern art, and is in the hands of only one or two craftsmen. An important industry is gold and silver embroidery, chiefly carried on by the dealers of the Chāndni Chauk. Although the designs are now showing signs of European influence, good Oriental patterns are still obtainable, and the art is in a fairly flourishing condition. The manufacture of gold and silver wire to carry on this industry employs a large number of hands. These *kandla kashān*, or wire-drawers, pay the municipality yearly Rs. 25,000, in return for which it supervises the melting and blending of the metal in a central workshop, and thereby gives it a guarantee of purity whose value is undisputed throughout India. Modern mill and factory industries have made great progress in the city. The Delhi Cloth and General Mills in 1904 employed 624 hands, the Hanumān and Mahādeo Spinning and Weaving Mills 895, the Kishen Cotton-Spinning Mill 575, and the Jumna Cotton-Spinning Mills 388. The principal flour-mills are the Northern India Flour-Mills with 107 employés, the Ganesh Flour-Mills with 178, and John's Flour-Mill with 113. The three sugar-cane pressing factories employed 246 hands, and the three cotton-ginning factories 305. Minor industries include printing, biscuit-making, malting, and iron and brass-work. The total number of factories, mills, &c., in 1904 was 23, and the total number of employés 3,364.

Commerce and trade.

Delhi possesses a very considerable trade, though the continuation of the North-Western Railway on the eastern bank of the river has thrown it somewhat off the modern line of traffic. It derives importance as a trade centre at present owing to the fact that grain and piece-goods are free of octroi, and it still forms the main entrepôt for commerce between Calcutta or Bombay on the one side and Rājputāna on the other. The chief imports include chemicals, cotton, silk, fibres, grain, oilseeds, *ghī*, metals, salt, horns and hides, and European piece-goods. The exports consist of the same articles in transit, together with tobacco, sugar, oil, jewellery, and gold or silver lacework. Beyond the borders of the Province, Delhi merchants correspond with those of Jīnd, Kābul, Alwar, Bīkaner, Jaipur, and the Doāb; while with all the Punjab towns they have extensive dealings. European finance is represented by the Bengal, the National, the Delhi and

London, the Allahābād, and the Upper India Banks; and several cotton merchants have agents in the city. The great trade avenue of the Chāndni Chauk, already described, is lined with the shops and warehouses of merchants, and is one of the chief sights of interest to the visitor at Delhi.

Education. The principal educational institution was, until 1877, the Delhi College, founded in 1792, but abolished in 1877, in order to concentrate higher education in the Punjab University at Lahore. The chief school is now the municipal high school, with six branch schools; other high schools are the Anglo-Arabic, the Anglo-Sanskrit, St. Stephen's mission school, and the Shāhzāda high school, maintained chiefly for poor descendants of the Mughal imperial family. All these receive grants-in-aid. The municipal high school has been managed by the Educational department since 1904. The city also has a normal school, which trains vernacular teachers for primary schools, a municipal industrial school, the aided middle boarding-schools for girls of the Baptist Mission and the Society for the Propagation of the Gospel, and a school on the Yūnāni system of native medicine.

Farīdābād.—Town in the Ballabgarh *tahsīl* of Delhi District, Punjab, situated in 28° 25′ N. and 77° 20′ E., 16 miles from Delhi, near the Delhi-Muttra road and on the Delhi-Agra branch of the Great Indian Peninsula Railway. Population (1901), 5,310. The town was founded in 1607 by Shaikh Farīd, Jahāngīr's treasurer, to protect the high-road from Delhi to Agra. It is of no commercial importance. The municipality was created in 1867. The income during the ten years ending 1902–3 averaged Rs. 5,900, and the expenditure Rs. 5,800. The income in 1903–4 was Rs. 6,800, chiefly derived from octroi; and the expenditure was Rs. 6,400. The chief educational institutions are the Victoria Anglo-vernacūlar middle school (unaided), a vernacular middle school maintained by the municipality, and the English station school (middle). There is a Government dispensary.

Indarpat.—Village in Delhi District, Punjab, occupying the site of the ancient Indraprastha, and situated in 28° 36′ N. and 77° 17′ E., close to the modern city of Delhi. The original town stood upon the banks of the Jumna, between the Kotīla of Fīroz Shāh and the tomb of Humāyūn; and although the river has now shifted its channel a mile eastward, the former bed may still be traced past the early site. Scarcely a stone of the ancient capital remains standing; but the village of Indarpat and the Muhammadan fort of Purāna Kila probably occupy the true site, while the modern name is obviously a corruption of the old Hindu name. Indraprastha is commonly believed to have been founded by the earliest Aryan colonists of India; and the Mahābhārata relates how the five Pāndavas, Yudhishthira and his brethren, leading a body of settlers from Hastināpur on the Ganges, expelled the savage Nāgās, and built their capital upon this spot. For later details see DELHI CITY.

Sonepat Town (*Sonpat*; Sanskrit *Suvarnaprastha*).—Head-quarters of the *tahsīl* of the same name in Delhi District, Punjab, situated in 29° N. and 77° 1′ E., on the Delhi-Ambāla-Kālka Railway, 28 miles north of Delhi. Population (1901), 12,990. One popular tradition avers that this is one of the five towns mentioned in the Mahābhārata which Yudhishthira demanded from Duryodhana as the price of peace. Another ascribes its foundation to Rājā Soni, thirteenth in descent from Arjuna, a brother of Yudhishthira. It is of no commercial importance. The municipality was created in 1867. The income and expenditure during the ten years ending 1902–3 averaged Rs. 14,300. The income in 1903–4 was Rs. 16,000, chiefly derived from octroi; and the expenditure was Rs. 16,400. The town possesses an Anglo-vernacular middle school, a Government dispensary, and a cotton-ginning and pressing factory which in 1904 employed 130 hands.

Boundaries, configuration, and hill and river systems.

Karnāl District.—District in the Delhi Division of the Punjab, lying between 29° 11′ and 30° 15′ N. and 76° 11′ and 77° 17′ E., with an area of 3,153 square miles, including 36 outlying villages, scattered throughout the eastern part of the State of Patiāla. The District is bounded on the north by Patiāla State and Ambāla District; on the east by the river Jumna, which separates it from the Districts of Sahāranpur, Muzaffarnagar, and Meerut in the United Provinces; on the south by the Punjab Districts of Delhi and Rohtak; and on the west by the States of Patiāla and Jīnd. It is divided into two parts by the low ridge which forms the watershed between the Indian Ocean and the Bay of Bengal. To the east of this ridge along the Jumna lies the *khādar*, a strip of low-lying land from 5 to 10 miles wide; though it is not so thickly wooded as the rest of the District, date-palms abound, and in places a thick jungle skirts the river bank. West of the ridge lies the *bāngar*, an upland plain watered throughout by the Western Jumna Canal, and stretching parallel to the *khādar* for the whole length of the District. These two tracts fill up practically the whole of the southern *tahsīl* of Pānipat; but in Karnāl and Kaithal, the central *tahsīls*, the *bāngar* rises with a perceptible step into the Nardak[1], a high and once arid country, now traversed by the Sirsa branch of the Western Jumna Canal. In the north of the District nearly the whole of Thānesar and the northern part of the Kaithal *tahsīl* are intersected by mountain torrents which drain the Lower Himālayas, and include large tracts of wild country covered with forests of *dhāk* (*Butea frondosa*).

The Jumna forms the entire eastern boundary for a distance of 81 miles. Its bed varies from half a mile to a mile in width, of which the stream occupies only a few hundred yards in the cold season. The most important of the torrents which traverse the northern portion are the GHAGGAR, with its tributaries the Umla and SARASWATĪ, the CHAUTANG, and the Mārkanda and Purān, the last an old bed of the Ghaggar. Minor drainage channels are the Nai or 'new' Nadi, the Būrhi or 'old' Nadi, and Rākshi.

Geology and botany.

Karnāl District offers nothing of geological interest, as it is situated entirely on the alluvium. The flora of the upper Gangetic plain is well represented in the eastern portion; in the west there is an approach to the desert vegetation; while the Jumna valley produces a few temperate types, e.g. a rose, a kind of scurvy grass (*Cochlearia*), both of which are found again in Lower Bengal, and a crowfoot (*Ranunculus pennsylvanicus*), which extends to Ludhiāna, but is absent from the Himālayas. Relics of a former Deccan flora, of which a wild cotton is the most interesting, survive, especially in the neighbourhood of Thānesar. Indigenous trees, except the *dhāk*, are uncommon; in the Jumna *khādar* a low palm abounds, which is often taken for a wild form of the date-palm, but is almost certainly a distinct species.

Fauna.

The Nardak was a favourite hunting-ground of the Mughal emperors, and as late as 1827 Archer says that lions were sometimes seen within 20 miles of Karnāl, while tigers were exceedingly common. Now, however, even the leopard is only found rarely, but wolves are still common. Antelope, *nīlgai*, 'ravine deer' (Indian gazelle), and hog deer are fairly plentiful where there is suitable cover. Small game is abundant.

Climate and temperature.

Fever is particularly prevalent in the Naili (Nāli) tract, flooded by the Saraswatī, and in the canal-irrigated portions of

[1] The Nardak is properly another name for KURUKSHETRA, but it is extended to include all the high tract.

the District. Owing to the faulty alignment of the canal and the swamping caused thereby, fever used to be terribly prevalent, and in consequence the cantonments were removed from Karnāl; but recent improvements have greatly diminished the evil. The climate of Kaithal resembles that of the plains of the Punjab proper, but the Jumna *tahsīls* are not subject to the same extremes of heat and cold.

Rainfall.

The annual rainfall averages 30 inches at Karnāl, 23 at Pānīpat, and 18 at Kaithal, rapidly decreasing as one goes west or south. The *khādar* receives the most plentiful and frequent rain, as many local showers follow the bed of the river. Of the rainfall at Karnāl, 27·4 inches fall in the summer months and 2·4 in the winter.

History and archaeology.

The early legendary history of the District will be found in the account of KURUKSHETRA or the holy plain of the Hindus, which occupies its north-western portion. The number of Indo-Scythian coins found at Polar on the Saraswatī would seem to show that about the beginning of the Christian era the District was included in the Indo-Scythian empire. In or about A.D. 400 it was traversed by the Chinese pilgrim Fa Hian and in 639 by Hiuen Tsiang, the latter finding a flourishing kingdom with its capital at Thānesar. Though Thānesar was sacked by Mahmūd of Ghazni in 1014, the country remained under Hindu rule until the defeat of Prithwī Rāj at Tirāwari in 1192. Thereafter it was more or less firmly attached to Delhi till after the invasion of Tīmūr, who marched through it on his way to the capital. It then belonged, first to the ruler of Sāmāna, and then to the Lodī kings of the Punjab, and during the century and a half that separated Akbar from Tīmūr was the scene of numerous battles, of which the most important were two fought at PĀNĪPAT. For two centuries Karnāl enjoyed peace under the Mughals, broken only by the raid of Ibrāhīm Ḥusain Mirza in 1573, the flight of prince Khusrū through the District in 1606, and the incursion of Banda Bairāgi in 1709. During this period a canal was constructed from the Jumna and the imperial road put in repair. In 1738 Nādir Shāh defeated Muhammad Shāh near Karnāl, and in 1761 occurred the third great battle of PĀNĪPAT, in which the Marāthās were routed by the Afghān army. A terrible period of anarchy followed, during which the tract formed a sort of no-man's-land between the Sikh and Marāthā powers, coveted by both but protected by neither, and the prey of every freebooter that chanced to come that way. On annexation, in 1803, the greater part of the country was held by Sikh chiefs or by confederacies of Sikh horsemen; and the District was gradually formed out of their territories as they escheated. The most important were the petty principalities of Kaithal, Thānesar, and Lādwa, of which the first two lapsed between 1832 and 1850, while Lādwa was confiscated owing to the conduct of its chief during the first Sikh War. In 1849 the District of Thānesar was formed, but in 1862 it was broken up into the two Districts of Ambāla and Karnāl. During the Mutiny there was a good deal of disorder, but no serious outbreak occurred. Great assistance was given by the Rājās of Patiāla and Jīnd in preserving order. The Pehowa *thāna* was transferred from Ambāla to the Kaithal *tahsīl* of the District in 1888, and the rest of the Pipli *tahsīl* (now Thānesar) was added to it in 1897.

The chief relics of antiquity are to be found at KARNĀL, PĀNĪPAT, THĀNESAR, and PEHOWA. At the village of Sītā Mai in the Nardak is a very ancient shrine of Sītā, and several of the great *sarais* built along the old imperial road still remain.

The people.

The District contains 7 towns and 1,383 villages. Its population at the last three enumerations was: (1881) 820,041, (1891) 861,160, (1901) 883,225. It increased by 2·6 per cent. during the last decade, the increase being greatest in the Pānīpat *tahsīl* and least in Karnāl. In the Thānesar *tahsīl* the population decreased 0·9 per cent. in the twenty years ending 1901, owing to the unhealthiness of the tract; while Kaithal increased by 20 per cent. in the same period, owing to the development of canal-irrigation. The District is divided into the four *tahsīls* of KARNĀL, PĀNĪPAT, KAITHAL, and THĀNESAR, the head-quarters of each being at the place from which it is named. The chief towns are the municipalities of KARNĀL (the District head-quarters), PĀNĪPAT, KAITHAL, SHĀHĀBĀD, THĀNESAR, and LĀDWA.

The table on the next page gives the chief statistics of population in 1901.

Hindus number 623,597, or over 70 per cent. of the total. Monastic communities of Bairāgīs own a good deal of land and exercise considerable influence in the District. Muhammadans (241,412) form 27 per cent. of the population. The Saiyids of the District belong to the Shiah organization known as the Bārā Sādāt, which was founded by Saiyid Abdul Farsh Wasīti, a follower of Mahmūd of Ghazni. Sikhs number 12,294. Hindī is spoken by 96 per cent. of the population, and Punjābi in the scattered villages surrounded by Patiāla territory.

Tahsīl.	Area in square miles.	Number of Towns.	Number of Villages.	Population.	Population per square mile.	Percentage of variation in population between 1891 and 1901.	Number of persons able to read and write.
Karnāl . .	836	1	380	248,544	297·3	+ 2·9	6,117
Thānesar . .	559	3	418	173,208	309·8	– 2·4	4,361
Pānīpat . .	462	1	172	196,284	424·9	+ 6·2	6,377
Kaithal . .	1,288	2	413	265,189	205·9	+ 3·0	4,340
District total	3,153	7	1,383	883,225	280.1	+ 2·6	21,195

NOTE.—The figures for the areas of *tahsīls* are taken from revenue returns. The total District area is that given in the *Census Report*.

Castes and occupations.

The Jāts are the most numerous tribe, numbering 120,000, or 14 per cent. of the total. They own 15½ per cent. of the land, and are mostly Hindus, only 8,000 being Sikhs and 3,000 Muhammadans. Their principal clans are the Ghatwāl, Deswāl, Sindhu, Pawānia, Mān, Katkhar, and Jaglān. The Rājputs (83,000) own 32 per cent. of the land; 67,000 are Muhammadans, known as Ranghars. Their principal clans are the Chauhān, Mandhār, Ghorewāha, and Tonwar. The Rors (42,000) own 17½ per cent. and are almost all Hindus; they seem originally to have held their lands as dependants of the Rājputs. Gūjars (30,000) are mostly Hindus, though 8,000 are Muhammadans. Their reputation is no better here than in other parts of the Division. The Tagās (4,000) claim to be a Brāhman race, which has abandoned the priestly profession and taken to agriculture; half of them in this District are Muhammadans. Of Brāhmans (71,000), the Biās or Gujrātī and the Dakaut are important and interesting clans. The Saiyids (6,000) trace their descent from settlers left by Mahmūd, Tīmūr, and other Muhammadan invaders. Of the Shaikhs (19,000), besides the few properly so called and the large number of converts who have taken that name, there are in many villages one or two families of a menial tribe from which the village watchmen are drawn, who are said to be the relics of the old policy of the emperors of settling one or two Muhammadans in every village. The Mālis (26,000) have of late years immigrated in considerable numbers into the District, especially the irrigable tracts of the Thānesar *tahsīl*, where they have purchased estates. Kambohs number 14,000. Of the commercial classes, the chief are the Baniās (52,000). Among the menial classes may be mentioned the Chamārs (leather-workers, 79,000), Chūhrās (scavengers, 45,000), Jhīnwars (water-carriers, 44,000), Kumhārs (potters, 19,000), and

Tarkhans (carpenters, 20,000). About 58 per cent. of the population are supported by agriculture, 19 are industrial, 3 commercial, and 2 professional.

There is a curious division of the non-Rājput tribes into the Dehia and Haulānia factions, apparently dating from a time when the Haulānias under the leadership of the Ghatwāl Jāts were called in by one of the emperors to help to coerce the Mandhār Rājputs, and were opposed by the Dehia Jāts, who from jealousy of the Ghatwāl supremacy joined the Mandhārs. The leading families of the District are those of the Nawāb of Kunjpura, the Mandals of Karnāl, and the Bhais of Arnauli and Siddhuwāl.

Christian missions.

The Society for the Propagation of the Gospel carries on mission work at Karnāl, Kaithal, and Pānīpat. Its operations include *zanāna* teaching, girls' schools, and a hospital and dispensary for women and children. There are also Methodist Episcopal missions at Karnāl and Pānīpat, and a Presbyterian mission at Thānesar (founded in 1895) and Kaithal, to which the village of Santokh Mājra has been leased for a Christian colony. In 1901 the District contained 225 native Christians.

General agricultural conditions.

The soil of the *khādar* is light, and water lies close to the surface. The Jumna floods are, however, not fertilizing, and the best lands are those which lie beyond their reach. The eastern *bāngar* is almost entirely watered by the Western Jumna Canal; the soil is a fertile and easily worked loam, and the tract is for the most part a sheet of cultivation. The soil of the Kaithal *bāngar* is a strong intractable loam, chiefly irrigated by the new Sirsa branch of the Western Jumna Canal, which also supplies most of the Kaithal Nardak. The Thānesar *tahsīl* is a rich alluvial tract watered by the Mārkanda and Umla, but in the flooded tracts crops are very precarious, owing to the uncertainty of the floods: on the Saraswatī two-thirds of the crops belong to the spring harvest, chiefly gram: on the Umla coarse rice is often the only crop.

Chief agricultural statistics and principal crops.

The District is held almost entirely by small peasant proprietors, large estates covering only about 160 square miles and lands leased from Government 4,000 acres.

The area for which details are available from the revenue record of 1903–4 is 3,147 square miles, as shown in the table on the next page.

The staple products of the spring harvest are wheat and gram, sown on 338 and 265 square miles respectively in 1903–4. Barley covered only 19 square miles. In the autumn harvest great millet covered 256 square miles, and rice and spiked millet 97 and 94 square miles respectively. Cotton covered 66 square miles, maize 72, and sugar-cane 30.

Tahsīl.	Total.	Cultivated.	Irrigated.	Cultivable waste.
Karnāl . .	838	450	164	263
Thānesar . .	559	335	37	151
Pānīpat . .	461	288	192	74
Kaithal . .	1,289	724	208	416
Total	3,147	1,797	601	904

During the thirteen years ending 1904, the cultivated area rose from 1,637 square miles to more than 1,797, or by 10 per cent., the increase being chiefly due to the extensions of canal-irrigation. This has been accompanied by an extended cultivation of maize, cotton, and sugar-cane, as well as of the more valuable spring crops; and the use of manure is said to be increasing. Loans for the construction of wells are fairly popular. In the five years ending 1903–4, Rs. 57,000 was advanced under the Land Improvement Loans Act, and 2 lakhs for the purchase of bullocks and seed. **Improvements in agricultural practice.**

Cattle-raising used to play an important part in the economy of the Nardak before the construction of the Sirsa canal, and the cattle of the District are still noted for their excellence. The local breed of horses is of no particular importance. A remount dépôt, established at Karnāl in 1889, was abolished in 1902, and its lands are now used as a military grass farm. The District board maintains three horse and five donkey stallions. Large flocks of goats and sheep are kept in parts, the sheep being all of the small black-tailed breed. There is a fine breed of pigs at Karnāl, dating from the time of the old cantonment. **Cattle, horses, and sheep.**

Of the total area cultivated in 1903–4, 601 square miles, or 33 per cent., were classed as irrigated. Of this area, 230 square miles were irrigated from wells, 364 square miles from canals, 32 acres from wells and canals, and 4,581 acres from streams and tanks. The District possessed 10,931 masonry wells, besides 223 unbricked wells, lever wells, and water-lifts. In the *khādar*, although little irrigation is necessary, wells worked by Persian wheels are numerous. The new main line of the WESTERN JUMNA CANAL enters the Thānesar *tahsīl*, and within this District gives off the Sirsa, Hānsi, and New Delhi branches, which irrigate the greater portion of the Nardak and *bāngar*, **Irrigation.**

except in Thānesar, where the percolation from the main canal and the stoppage of the natural drainage keep the land so moist that it suffers from excess of water rather than from drought. The total area irrigated from the Western Jumna Canal is 2,493 acres. The *bāngar* in the Kaithal *tahsīl* is also supplied by the Saraswatī canal (an inundation canal made and worked by the District board), and some of the Nardak villages are also watered by floods from the Chautang. The few wells in these tracts are on the rope-and-bucket system. The northern part of the District is irrigated by floods from the hill torrents, and for the most part suffers from capricious water-supply, being waterlogged one year and parched the next. Except in the more favoured tracts, wells are liable to be destroyed by floods and are little used. The villages scattered through Patiāla territory are irrigated from the Sirhind Canal.

Forests. The District contains 17 tracts of unclassed forest, with a total area of 24 square miles, in charge of the Deputy-Commissioner; but these are not true forests, being covered only with scrub and small trees. About 2·6 square miles of 'reserved' forest are under the Military department.

Minerals. Sal-ammoniac has from ancient times been manufactured by the potters of the Kaithal *tahsīl*. About 84 tons, valued at Rs. 3,400, are produced annually, and sold to merchants, who mostly export it. It is prepared by burning bricks made of the dirty clay found in certain ponds, and subjecting the substance that exudes from them to sublimation in closed vessels. The District has four saltpetre refineries. The only other mineral product is *kankar*.

Arts and manufactures. Karnāl used to have a name for shoe-making, but the industry is said to be declining from want of capital. Pānīpat is famous for glass-blowing, the chief product being silvered globes which, when broken up, are used for mirror-covered walls, or sewn on *phūlkāris*; the glass retorts used in the manufacture of sal-ammoniac are also made. The town is noted for its manufacture of brass vessels, small fancy wares in various metals, and silver beads. The District possesses three cotton-ginning factories, at Pānīpat, Kaithal, and Dhātrat; a cotton-press at Pānīpat; and two combined ginning and pressing factories, at Pānīpat and Kaithal. The total number of employés in 1904 was 702. Silver-work and musical instruments are made at Shāhābād. Some good lacquered woodwork is also produced.

Commerce and trade. The chief exports are wheat, cotton, gram, fine rice, *ghī*, brass vessels, glass, sal-ammoniac, and saltpetre; and the chief imports are salt, oil and oilseeds, iron, and piece-goods. Cotton and wheat go chiefly to Delhi and Ambāla; *ghī* and hides to Delhi; oil and oilseeds come from the Punjab and the Doāb; timber from Ambāla; iron and piece-goods from Delhi; and salt from Bhiwāni, Delhi, and Ambāla. Kārnal and Pānīpat on the Delhi-Umballa-Kālka Railway are the chief marts, and a good deal of trade goes through Kaithal, which is on a branch of the Southern Punjab Railway. The local trade is principally conducted through the village dealers; but a very considerable traffic is carried on by the cultivators themselves, especially by Jāts from Rohtak, who in the hot season earn a good deal by plying their carts for hire.

Railways and roads. The Delhi-Umballa-Kālka Railway runs through the District side by side with the grand trunk road, and Kaithal is the terminus of a branch of the Southern Punjab Railway. The new main line and the Delhi and Hānsi branches of the Western Jumna Canal are navigable, as is also the Jumna during the rains. The District has 145 miles of metalled roads, and 684 miles of unmetalled roads, of which 129 miles of metalled and 67 of unmetalled roads are under the Public Works department, the rest being maintained by the District board. Metalled roads connect Karnāl and Kaithal, Thānesar and Lādwa, and the grand trunk road traverses the District from north to south; but the unmetalled roads are bad, especially in the Nardak, and in the flooded tract bordering on the Saraswatī and Ghaggar the tracks are often impassable for weeks together during the rains.

Famine. Including the *chālīsa* famine of 1783 the District has been visited by famine thirteen times in 120 years, one of the most terrible perhaps being that of 1833. Relief works seem first to have been established in the famine of 1861, when 22,237 persons were relieved in one month. In 1869 the famine was more severe in Karnāl than in any other part of the Punjab, and hundreds of people were reduced to semi-starvation. The expenditure was 1·7 lakhs, and the highest daily average of persons relieved was 13,934. Cattle to the number of 65,000 died. From 1875 to 1877 there was not a single good harvest, and though the scarcity hardly deepened into famine, the cattle suffered terribly. There was another grass famine in 1883–4. In 1896–7 the highest daily average relieved was 12,361, and the expenditure barely 2 lakhs. The areas affected were the Nardak tracts of Karnāl and Kaithal and the Naili tract of Kaithal. In 1899–1900 the Nardak in Karnāl and part of that in Kaithal were protected by the Nardak irrigation channel, constructed as a relief work in 1897; the tracts affected were chiefly the Naili and *bāngar* tracts of Kaithal and parts of Thānesar. The highest daily average relieved was 14,075, and the expenditure was 2·6 lakhs.

District subdivisions and staff.

The District is divided into the four *tahsīls* of KARNĀL, PĀNĪPAT, THĀNESAR, and KAITHAL, each under a *tahsīldār* and a *naib-tahsīldār*. In the last the sub-*tahsīl* of Gula is also in charge of a *naib-tahsīldār*. The *tahsil* of Kaithal forms a subdivision. The Deputy-Commissioner holds executive charge of the District, aided by three Assistant or Extra Assistant Commissioners, of whom one is subdivisional officer in charge of Kaithal and one in charge of the District treasury.

Civil justice and crime.

The Deputy-Commissioner as District Magistrate is responsible for the criminal justice of the District, and civil judicial work is under a District Judge. Both officers are supervised by the Divisional and Sessions Judge of the Delhi Civil Division. There is one Munsif, who sits at head-quarters. There are also six honorary magistrates. Cattle-stealing, the normal crime of the District, is now less prevalent than formerly, owing to the increase of cultivation made possible by the development of the canals. Formerly heads of families of respectable birth would demur to giving a daughter in marriage to a man who had not proved his ability to support a family by cattle-lifting.

Land revenue administration.

The tract which passed to the British in 1803, and formed part of the old Pānīpat District, was summarily assessed in the years 1817–24, with the exception of the estates assigned to the Mandal family in exchange for the lands they held in the United Provinces. In accordance with the spirit of the time, the summary settlement was oppressive, and the methods of assessment and collection were vexatious and extortionate; a revision of assessments was necessitated by the famine of 1824, and by degrees a more reasonable system was evolved. The regular settlement, made in 1842, was both moderate and fairly distributed. In the *khādar* the assessment on the whole worked well; in the *bāngar* the deterioration of soil caused by the canal brought absolute ruin to many villages, and in 1859–60 large reductions of revenue were made and principles laid down for annual relief to be afforded when necessary. Meanwhile, in the Mandal estate, the assignees struggled to realize their revenue in kind from a lawless and independent Rājput peasantry till 1847, when their oppression and mismanagement necessitated the tract being brought under settlement. The assessment was revised in 1852 and again in 1856. The revised settlement of 1872–80 comprised both these tracts; the revenue rate for irrigated land varied from Rs. 1–14 to Rs. 2–14, and for unirrigated land from 8 annas to Rs. 1–12; pasture was rated at 8 pies an acre; and canal lands were assessed at 'dry' rates varying from Rs. 1–5 to Rs. 1–13.

The rest of the District, comprising the *tahsīls* of Kaithal, Thānesar, and the Indri tract of Karnāl, formed part of the territories of the Cis-Sutlej chiefs, who were taken under protection by the proclamation of 1809. These territories as they escheated were summarily assessed. Thānesar and Indri were regularly settled in 1848–56 and Kaithal in 1853–6. The whole of this portion of the District came under the Karnāl-Ambāla revision in 1882-9. The average assessment on 'dry' land is R. 0–14–3 (maximum, Rs. 1–6; minimum, R. 0–6–6), and on 'wet' land Rs. 2–14 (maximum, Rs. 3–12; minimum, Rs. 2). The total demand for 1903–4, including cesses, was 12 lakhs. The average size of a holding cultivated by the owner is 5·3 acres. The whole District came under settlement in 1904, the present assessment expiring in 1908.

The collections of land revenue alone and of total revenue are shown below, in thousands of rupees:—

	1880-1.	1890-1.	1900-1.	1903-4.
Land revenue . .	6,36	6,95	8,20	8,29
Total revenue . .	7,65	8,88	12,68	13,45

The District contains six municipalities: KARNĀL, PĀNĪPAT, KAITHAL, SHĀHĀBĀD, THĀNESAR, and LĀDWA. Outside these, local affairs are managed by the District board, whose income amounted to nearly 1¼ lakhs in 1903–4. The expenditure in the same year was 1·2 lakhs, education forming the largest item. **Local and municipal.**

The regular police force consists of 683 of all ranks, including 147 municipal police, under a Superintendent, assisted by 4 inspectors. Village watchmen number 1,540. The District contains 22 police stations, 1 outpost, and 5 road-posts. The Sānsis, Balochs, and Tagās are proclaimed under the Criminal Tribes Act; and 55 Sānsis, 447 Balochs, and 237 Tagās were registered in 1903 under the Act. The District jail at headquarters has accommodation for 155 prisoners. **Police and jails.**

Karnāl is the most backward District in the Province in the matter of education, and in 1901 the proportion of literate **Education.**

persons was only 2·4 per cent. (4·3 males and 0·1 females), as compared with 3·6 in the whole Province. The number of pupils under instruction was: 1,961 in 1880–1, 2,242 in 1890–1, 5,902 in 1900–1, and 5,365 in 1903–4. In the last year the District contained 9 secondary and 90 primary (public) schools, besides 12 advanced and 62 elementary (private) schools, with 53 girls in the public and 72 in the private schools. The only high school is at Karnāl. The indigenous Arabic school at Pānīpat, supported by the voluntary contributions of wealthy Muhammadans, is attended by about 50 boys, chiefly from the middle-class Muhammadan families of the town. The District has three primary schools for girls, and the ladies of the Karnāl branch of the Zanāna Mission teach women and children in the town. The total expenditure on education in 1903–4 was Rs. 47,000, the greater part of which was met from Local funds, though Government contributed nearly Rs. 1,600, and fees brought in Rs. 10,000.

Hospitals and dispensaries. Besides the Karnāl civil hospital the District has 9 dispensaries, one at Karnāl and 8 at out-stations, at which 117,370 out-patients and 1,626 in-patients were treated in 1904, and 6,849 operations performed. The income and expenditure amounted to Rs. 21,000, Local and municipal funds contributing Rs. 11,000 and Rs. 9,000 respectively. The Society for the Propagation of the Gospel also maintains a female hospital at Karnāl.

Vaccination. The number of successful vaccinations in 1903–4 was 20,090, representing 23 per 1,000 of population.

[A. Kensington, *Customary Law of Ambāla District* (1893) (for the Thānesar *tahsīl*); J. M. Douie, *District Gazetteer* (1890), *Settlement Report of Karnāl-Ambāla* (1891), and *Riwāj-i-ām of Tahsīl Kaithal and Pargana Indri, District Karnāl* (1892); D. C. J. Ibbetson, *Settlement Report of the Pānīpat Tahsīl and Karnāl Pargana* (1883).]

Karnāl Tahsīl.—Central *tahsīl* of Karnāl District, Punjab, lying between 29° 26′ and 30° 0′ N. and 76° 40′ and 77° 13′ E., on the west bank of the Jumna, with an area of 838 square miles. The population in 1901 was 248,544, compared with 241,369 in 1891. It contains the town of KARNĀL (population, 23,559), the head-quarters, and 380 villages. The land revenue and cesses amounted in 1903–4 to 3·2 lakhs. On the east lie the Jumna lowlands, fertile but unhealthy, and varying in width from 5 to 10 miles. The western boundary of this tract is the old high bank of the Jumna, and from the crest of this bank the country slopes imperceptibly away into the Nardak.

The upland portion of the *tahsīl* is irrigated by the Western Jumna Canal; but in the Nardak the people have not entirely abandoned their pastoral traditions, and still retain ample grazing-grounds for their cattle.

Thānesar Tahsīl (*Thāneswar*).—Northern *tahsīl* of Karnāl District, Punjab, lying between 29° 55′ and 30° 15′ N. and 76° 36′ and 77° 17′ E., on the west bank of the Jumna, with an area of 559 square miles. The population in 1901 was 173,208, compared with 177,442 in 1891. It contains the towns of THĀNESAR (population, 5,066), the head-quarters, LĀDWA (3,518), and SHĀHĀBĀD (11,009); and 418 villages. The land revenue and cesses amounted in 1903–4 to 2·8 lakhs. Thānesar practically coincides with the old Pipli *tahsīl* of Ambāla District, from which it was transferred in 1897. On the east it has a narrow frontage along the Jumna. The fertile riverain lowlands average about 6 miles in width. The western boundary of this tract is the old bank of the Jumna, and from the crest of this bank the country slopes away westwards. The uplands are intersected by several torrent-beds, and the soil, especially to the south, is for the most part stiff and infertile. *Dhāk* jungle abounds. The Markanda country on the north-west has the advantages of a lighter soil and fertilizing floods.

Pānīpat Tahsīl.—Southern *tahsīl* of Karnāl District, Punjab, lying between 29° 11′ and 29° 30′ N. and 76° 38′ and 77° 10′ E., on the west bank of the Jumna, with an area of 462 square miles. The population in 1901 was 196,284, compared with 184,856 in 1891. It contains the town of PĀNĪPAT (population, 26,914), the head-quarters, and 172 villages. The land revenue and cesses amounted in 1903–4 to 3·5 lakhs. On the east lie the Jumna lowlands, rich, picturesque, and unhealthy. West of the railway line the country lies at a higher level. The soil is in places saline, and considerable tracts are in consequence uncultivated, but the *tahsīl* enjoys a high degree of prosperity. The uplands are irrigated by the Western Jumna Canal.

Kaithal Tahsīl.—Western *tahsīl* and subdivision of Karnāl District, Punjab, lying between 29° 22′ and 30° 12′ N. and 76° 11′ and 76° 47′ E., with an area of 1,289 square miles. The population in 1901 was 265,189, compared with 257,493 in 1891. It contains the towns of KAITHAL (population, 14,408), the head-quarters, and PŪNDRI (5,834); and 413 villages, including PEHOWA, a place of religious importance. The land revenue and cesses amounted in 1903–4 to 2·7 lakhs. The *tahsīl* consists chiefly of the petty principality of Kaithal, which escheated in 1843. North of the Ghaggar, the country is undulating and the soil contains a considerable proportion of sand The tract between the Ghaggar and the southern limits of the Saraswatī depression consists of vast prairies, flooded during the rains and interspersed with numerous trees and patches of cultivation. This tract, known as the Naili (Nāli), is notoriously unhealthy, but the pasture it affords is invaluable in dry years. The southern half of the *tahsīl* is a level plain, now irrigated by the Western Jumna Canal. On the east is the Nardak. The people have not yet entirely abandoned their pastoral traditions, and large tracts are still used for grazing alone. Farther west, cultivation becomes more general, and in the extreme south-west the soil contains a large proportion of sand.

Gula.—Sub-*tahsīl* of the Kaithal *tahsīl* of Karnāl District, Punjab. It has an area of 455 square miles, and contains 204 villages. The head-quarters are at the village of Gula. The land revenue and cesses amounted in 1903–4 to 1·2 lakhs.

Kunjpura ('the heron's nest').—An estate in the District and *tahsīl* of Karnāl, Punjab, founded by Najābat Khān, a Ghorgasht Pathān and soldier of fortune under the Mughal emperors. Najābat Khān built a stronghold in the marshes of the Jumna early in the eighteenth century, and then revolted against the imperial government. Siding with Nādir Shāh in 1739, Najābat Khān was recognized by him as chief of Kunjpura and held it till he was killed in 1760, when the Marāthās razed his stronghold to the ground. His son, Diler Khān, received large grants of territory from the Durrānis, but he and his successor were driven out of their lands west of the Jumna by the Rājā of Jīnd and other Sikh chiefs. In 1787, however, Sindhia expelled the Jīnd Rājā from Karnāl, and ten years later General Perron recognized Gulsher as Nawāb of Kunjpura. His son, Rahmat Khān, allied himself to Lord Lake in 1801, and in 1811 was recognized as a protected chief by the British Government. In 1846 the Nawāb of Kunjpura lost his sovereign powers, and the history of the family has since been one of incessant litigation. The present Nawāb succeeded in 1886. He holds a *jāgīr* of thirty-eight villages with a revenue of Rs. 31,000, besides which his estate yields an income of nearly Rs. 32,000.

Kaithal Town.—Head-quarters of the subdivision and *tahsīl* of the same name in Karnāl District, Punjab, situated in 29° 48′ N. and 76° 24′ E., 38 miles west of Karnāl town, and the terminus of the Kaithal branch of the Southern Punjab

Railway. Population (1901), 14,408. Kaithal is picturesquely situated on an extensive tank, which partly surrounds it, with numerous bathing-places and flights of steps. It lies in KURUKSHETRA, and is said to have been founded by the hero Yudhishthira. It bore in Sanskrit the name of Kapisthala, or the 'abode of monkeys,' and possesses an *asthān* or temple of Anjni, mother of Hanumān, the monkey god. During the time of the earlier Muhammadan emperors it was a place of some importance, and Tīmūr, who says its inhabitants were fire-worshippers, halted here before he attacked Delhi in 1398. The tombs of several saints, the oldest of which is that of the Shaikh Salāh-ud-dīn of Balkh (A.D. 1246), show that it was a centre of Muhammadan religious life. The town was renovated, and a fort built, under Akbar. In 1767 it fell into the hands of the Sikh chief, Bhai Desu Singh, whose descendants, the Bhais of Kaithal, ranked among the most powerful of the Çis-Sutlej chiefs. Their territories lapsed to the British Government in 1843, when Kaithal became the head-quarters of a District; but in 1849 it was absorbed into Thānesar District, which was in turn included in that of Karnāl in 1862. The now somewhat dilapidated fort or palace of the Bhais stands out prominently on the bank of the tank. The municipality was created in 1867. The income and expenditure during the ten years ending 1902–3 averaged Rs. 19,900 and Rs. 20,400 respectively. The income in 1903–4 was Rs. 15,800, chiefly derived from octroi; and the expenditure was Rs. 17,400. It maintains a dispensary and an Anglo-vernacular middle school. Saltpetre is refined at Kaithal, and it has a considerable manufacture of lacquered wood, besides two cotton factories, one for ginning and the other for ginning and pressing. The number of employés in the factories in 1904 was 103.

Karnāl Town.—Head-quarters of the District and *tahsīl* of Karnāl, Punjab, situated in 29° 41′ N. and 76° 59′ E., on the old bank of the Jumna, about 7 miles from the present course of that river, and on the Delhi-Umballa-Kālka Railway; distant 1,030 miles by rail from Calcutta, 1,056 from Bombay, and 895 from Karāchi. Population (1901), 23,559. Its name is derived from Karna, the rival of Arjuna in the epic of the Mahābhārata, by whom it is said to have been founded. It would seem to have been a place of little importance in early historical times, as no mention of it occurs until towards the end of the Pathān period. Karnāl was plundered in 1573 by Ibrāhīm Husain Mirza in his revolt against Akbar, and its neighbourhood laid waste by Banda Bairāgi in 1709. In 1739 it was the scene of the defeat of Muhammad Shāh by Nādir Shāh. After the fall of Sirhind in 1763 the town was seized by Gajpat Singh, Rājā of Jīnd, but in 1775 it was recovered by Najaf Khān, governor of Delhi. It again fell into the hands of Gajpat Singh, but his son Bhāg Singh lost it to the Marāthās in 1787, and it was subsequently made over by them to George Thomas. It then fell into the hands of Gurdit Singh of Lādwa, from whom the British took it in 1805. A cantonment was formed at Karnāl, which was abandoned in 1841 owing to the unhealthiness of the station. Karnāl is still unhealthy, though drainage and sanitation have done much to improve its condition. There is a fine marble tomb, built by the emperor Ghiyās-ud-dīn to the memory of the saint Bū-Alī Kalandar. The Society for the Propagation of the Gospel has a mission at Karnāl. The municipality was created in 1867. The income and expenditure during the ten years ending 1902–3 averaged Rs. 32,500 and Rs. 32,100 respectively. The income in 1903–4 was Rs. 33,800, mainly derived from octroi; and the expenditure was Rs. 33,500. The chief manufactures are country cloth, for local consumption, and shoes. The principal educational institution is the Anglo-vernacular high school, managed by the Educational department. It possesses a civil hospital, with a branch in the town. The Society for the Propagation of the Gospel also maintains a female hospital and dispensary.

Lādwa.—Town in the Thānesar *tahsīl* of Karnāl District, Punjab, situated in 29° 59′ N. and 77° 3′ E. Population (1901), 3,518. The town and neighbourhood belonged to a Sikh family, and were confiscated in 1846 in consequence of their conduct in the first Sikh War. The place is of no commercial importance. The municipality was created in 1867. The income and expenditure during the ten years ending 1902–3 averaged Rs. 5,300. The income in 1903–4 was Rs. 4,500, chiefly derived from octroi; and the expenditure was Rs. 4,900. The town has a vernacular middle school and a dispensary.

Pānīpat Town.—Head-quarters of the *tahsīl* of the same name in Karnāl District, Punjab, situated in 29° 24′ N. and 76° 59′ E., on the Delhi-Umballa-Kālka Railway; 1,009 miles by rail from Calcutta, 1,035 from Bombay, and 916 from Karāchi. Population (1901), 26,914. The town is of high antiquity, and is mentioned in the Mahābhārata as one of the five places demanded by Yudhishthira from Duryodhana as the price of peace. In Muhammadan times it would appear to have been of considerably greater importance than it is now.

It was from Pānīpat that prince Humāyūn plundered Delhi in 1390, and he was defeated in the neighbourhood by Abū Bakr. Pānīpat was seven years later held for Tātār Khān and taken by Ikbāl Khān, and in the next year deserted on Tīmūr's approach. During the reign of Bahlol Lodī his son Nizām Khān, afterwards Sikandar Lodī, seized Pānīpat and made it his head-quarters. But its chief title to fame lies in that it was the scene of the three most decisive battles of Northern India: the defeat of Ibrāhīm Lodī by Bābar in 1526, the defeat by Akbar of Hīmū, the Hindu general of Adil Shāh in 1556, and Ahmad Shāh's victory over the Marāthās in 1761. An indecisive battle was also fought at Pānīpat between the Sikhs and the Delhi emperor in 1767. The *pargana* of Pānīpat was made over to General Perron by the Marāthās, and passed to the British in 1803. The chief monument of antiquity is the tomb of the Muhammadan saint Kalandar (also said to be buried at Karnāl), erected by the sons of Alā-ud-dīn of Ghor. Pānīpat was the head-quarters of the District until 1854. The municipality was created in 1867. The income during the ten years ending 1902–3 averaged Rs. 26,400, and the expenditure Rs. 26,200. The income in 1903–4 was Rs. 27,400, chiefly derived from octroi; and the expenditure was Rs. 28,000. Local manufactures include brass vessels, cutlery, and silvered glass; and the town has a cotton press and a combined ginning and pressing factory. The number of operatives employed in 1904 was 500. The Muhammadan community maintains an Arabic school, and the municipality an Anglo-vernacular middle school. The town contains a dispensary.

Pehowa.—Ancient town and place of pilgrimage in the Kaithal *tahsīl* of Karnāl District, Punjab, situated in 29° 59′ N. and 76° 35′ E., on the sacred Saraswatī river, 16 miles west of Thānesar. It lies in KURUKSHETRA, and its name is a corruption of the Sanskrit Prithūdaka, the 'pool of Prithu,' the son of Rājā Vena. Two inscriptions dating from the end of the ninth century A.D., found at Pehowa, show that it was then included in the dominions of Bhoja and his son Mahendrapāla, kings of Kanauj. The more important inscription records the erection of a triple temple to Vishnu by a Tomar family, but no traces of ancient buildings remain, the modern shrines having been erected within the last century. After the rise of the Sikhs to power Pehowa came into the possession of the Bhais of Kaithal, whose palace is now used as a resthouse; but with Kaithal it lapsed to the British Government, and has since lost its importance, the population having decreased from

3,408 in 1881 to 2,080 in 1901. It is still, however, a place of pilgrimage; and close to it are the temples of Pirthūdakeshwar or Pirthūveshwar, built by the Marāthās during their supremacy in honour of the goddess Saraswatī (Sarsūti), and of Swāmi Kārtik. The latter is said to have been founded before the war of the Mahābhārata in honour of the war-god Kartaya. The town has a dispensary.

Pūndri.—Town in the Kaithal *tahsīl* of Karnāl District, Punjab, situated in 29° 46′ N. and 76° 34′ E., on the bank of a great tank called the Pundrak tank. Population (1901), 5,834. It was formerly one of the strongholds of the Pūndirs, a Rājput tribe who held Thānesar and the Nardak. It has a vernacular middle school.

Shāhābād.—Town in the Thānesar *tahsīl* of Karnāl District, Punjab, situated in 30° 10′ N. and 76° 52′ E., on the Delhi-Umballa-Kālka Railway, 16 miles south of Ambāla. Population (1901), 11,009. The town was founded by one of the followers of Muhammad of Ghor at the end of the twelfth century. It is of no commercial importance. The municipality was created in 1867–8. The income during the ten years ending 1902–3 averaged Rs. 10,900, and the expenditure Rs. 10,200. The income in 1903–4 was Rs. 12,300, chiefly derived from octroi; and the expenditure was Rs. 11,200. The town has a vernacular middle school and a dispensary.

Tirāwari (or Azamābād-i-Talāwari, the *Tarain* of the earlier Muhammadan historians).—Village in the District and *tahsīl* of Karnāl, Punjab, situated in 29° 48′ N. and 76° 59′ E., 14 miles south of Thānesar and 84 north of Delhi, on the Delhi-Umballa-Kālka Railway. Tirāwari is identified as the scene of Muhammad of Ghor's defeat by Prithwī Rāj (Rai Pithora), the Chauhān king of Ajmer, in 1191, and of the former's victory over that king in 1192. In 1216 Tāj-ud-dīn Yalduz, who had made himself master of the Punjab, advanced against Shams-ud-dīn Altamsh, but was defeated by the latter near Tarain. It derives its modern name of Azamābād from Azam Shāh, son of Aurangzeb, who was born in the town. In 1739 Nādir Shāh occupied the place, then a fortified town, after battering its walls, and marched to encounter Muhammad Shāh. A great *rabāt* or fortified *sarai* still exists at Tirāwari, and the walls round the village are in excellent preservation.

Thānesar Town (*Thāneswar*).—Head-quarters of the *tahsīl* of the same name in Karnāl District, Punjab, situated in 29° 59′ N. and 76° 50′ E., on the banks of the Saraswatī, and on the Delhi-Umballa-Kālka Railway. Population (1901), 5,066. It is famous as the most sacred place in the holy land of KURUKSHETRA, its name meaning 'the place of the god' (*sthāneshwara*). In the time of Hiuen Tsiang, Thānesar was the capital of a Vaisya (Bais) dynasty, which ruled parts of the Southern Punjab, Hindustan, and Eastern Rājputāna. In A.D. 648 a Chinese ambassador was sent to Harshavardhana of Thānesar, but found that the Senāpati Arjuna had usurped his kingdom, and the dynasty then became extinct. Thānesar, however, continued to be a place of great sanctity; but in 1014 it was sacked by Mahmūd of Ghazni, and although recovered by the Hindu Rājā of Delhi in 1043, it remained desolate for centuries. By the time of Sikandar Lodī it had, however, been in some measure restored, for that emperor proposed to make a raid on it to massacre the pilgrims. In 1567 Akbar witnessed its great fair; but Aurangzeb desecrated the shrine and built a castle in its sacred lake, whence his soldiers could fire on pilgrims who attempted to bathe. At the annexation of the cis-Sutlej territory, the town and neighbourhood were in the possession of a Sikh family, but they lapsed to the British Government in 1850. Thānesar was the head-quarters of a British District till 1862, but has since steadily declined in importance. The municipality was created in 1867. The income during the ten years ending 1902–3 averaged Rs. 7,900, and the expenditure Rs. 7,300. The income in 1903–4 was Rs. 8,900, chiefly derived from octroi; and the expenditure was Rs. 8,200. The town has a vernacular middle school and a dispensary. The bathing-fairs held here on the occasion of solar eclipses are sometimes attended by half a million pilgrims.

Ambāla District.—Northernmost of the plains Districts of the Delhi Division, Punjab, lying between 30° 2′ and 30° 13′ N. and 76° 19′ and 77° 36′ E., with an area of 1,851 square miles. It extends from the Sutlej, which separates it from the District of Hoshiārpur on the north, to the Jumna, which divides it from the District of Sahāranpur in the United Provinces on the south-east. On the north-east it is bounded by the States of Nālāgarh, Patiāla, Sirmūr, and Kalsia; on the south by the District of Karnāl; and on the west by Patiāla and the District of Ludhiāna. The District is very irregular in shape, and consists of two almost separate portions. The main portion lies between the Ghaggar and the Jumna, comprising the three *tahsīls* of Ambāla, Naraingarh, and Jagādhri. It is formed of the plain which descends from

Boundaries, configuration, and hill and river systems.

the Siwālik Hills towards the south-west. This plain is fertile, generally speaking a good alluvial loam, but intersected by torrents, which pour down from the hills at intervals of a few miles; and it is interspersed with blocks of stiff clay soil, which in years of scanty rainfall are unproductive, so that the tract, especially the Naraingarh *tahsīl*, is liable to famine. In this part of the District lies the Morni *ilāka*, a hilly tract of about 93 square miles, chiefly made up of two main ridges, and culminating in the Karoh peak (4,919 feet) on the Sirmūr border. It is inhabited by tribes of Hindu Kanets. The second portion of the District is the Rūpar subdivision, which comprises the *tahsīls* of Rūpar and Kharar, a submontane plain lying to the north between the Ghaggar and the Sutlej. This plain is of great fertility, highly cultivated, and well wooded, with numerous mango groves; but its south-eastern extremity, which is heavily irrigated from the Ghaggar, is waterlogged, and though of boundless fertility is so unhealthy as to be almost uninhabitable. The District also includes the detached tracts containing the town of Kālka and the hill cantonment of Kasauli.

Besides the great boundary streams of the Sutlej and Jumna, each of whose beds passes through the various stages of boulders, shingle, and sand, the District is traversed in every part by innumerable minor channels. The Ghaggar rises in Sirmūr State, passes through the Morni tract, crosses the District at its narrowest point, and almost immediately enters Patiāla; but near the town of Ambāla it again touches British territory, and skirts the border for a short distance. It is largely used for irrigation, the water being drawn off by means of artificial cuts. Among other streams may be mentioned the Chautang, Tangri, Baliāli, Sirvan, Boli, Budki, and Sombh. The Western Jumna Canal has its head-works at Tajewāla in this District, and the Sirhind Canal takes off from the Sutlej at Rūpar.

Geology. With the exception of the narrow submontane strip running along its north-eastern border, the whole District lies on the Indo-Gangetic alluvium. The submontane tract consists of sandstones and conglomerates, belonging to the Upper Tertiary (Siwālik) series of the Himālayas.

Botany. The District includes three very different botanical tracts: the southern part, which belongs to the Upper Gangetic plain; the Siwāliks in the north-east; and the Kasauli tract, which rises to over 6,000 feet, and is Outer Himālayan, with a flora much the same as that of Simla below 5,000 feet above sea-level. The Kalesar forest and the Morni hills generally, which fall in the second tract, have a fairly rich Siwālik flora, with which a few Himālayan types, such as *chīr* or *chīl* (*Pinus longifolia*), intermingle.

Fauna.

Tigers are occasionally shot in the Kalesar forest and the Morni hills; there are a few bears about Morni, and leopards, hyenas, and wolves are not uncommon, while wild hog abound. Of deer six kinds are found: *sāmbar*, *chītal*, and *kākar* in the hill tracts; and 'ravine deer' (Indian gazelle), antelope, and hog deer in the plains.

Climate and temperature.

The climate of the plains is fairly good, though, owing to the nearness of the hills, subject to severe changes of temperature. The average mean temperature of January is 39·45° and of June 77·55°. The hill station of Kasauli, owing to its moderate height and nearness to the dust of the plains, is the least esteemed for climate of the Punjab hill stations. The chief cause of mortality is fever. Swamping, caused by percolation from the Western Jumna Canal, used to affect the health of the people injuriously; but the careful realignment of the canal which has been carried out of recent years has, it is hoped, completely remedied the evil.

Rainfall.

The rainfall varies widely in the hill, submontane, and plain tracts, and the average fall ranges from 28 inches at Rūpar to 61 at Kasauli. The District on the whole is well off in the matter of rainfall, and there are comparatively few years in which the rains fail altogether; the variations from year to year are, however, considerable. The heaviest rainfall recorded during the twenty years ending 1900–1 was 87 inches at Jagādhri in 1884–5, and the lightest was 0·33 inches at Dādūpur in 1889–90.

History and archaeology.

The earliest authentic information with reference to this District is derived from the itinerary of Hiuen Tsiang, the Chinese Buddhist pilgrim of the seventh century. He found it the seat of a flourishing and civilized kingdom, having its capital at Srughna, a town identified by General Cunningham with the modern village of SUGH, near Jagādhri. The country around Ambāla from its position felt the full force of every important campaign in Northern India, but receives little mention except as an appurtenance of Sirhind. Such references as occur in the Muhammadan historians are given in the articles on AMBĀLA CITY and RŪPAR TOWN.

The practical interest of the local annals begins with the rise of the Sikh principalities south of the Sutlej during the latter half of the eighteenth century. As the central power of the Mughal empire relaxed under the blows of the Marāthās on the one side and the Afghāns on the other, numerous Sikh marauders from the Punjab proper began to extend their encroachments beyond the Sutlej, and ere long acquired for themselves the heart of the country between that river and the Jumna. When the Marāthā power fell before the British in 1803, the whole tract was parcelled out among chiefs of various grades, from the powerful Rājās of Patiāla, Jīnd, and Nābha down to the petty *sardār* who had succeeded in securing by violence or fraud the possession of a few villages; but after Ranjīt Singh began to consolidate the Sikh territories within the Punjab, he crossed the Sutlej in 1808, and demanded tribute from the Cis-Sutlej chieftains. Thus pressed, and fearing for themselves the fate which had overtaken their brethren, the Sikh chieftains combined to apply for aid to the British Government. The responsibility of protecting the minor States from their powerful neighbour was accepted, and the treaty of 1809, between the British Government and Ranjīt Singh, secured them in future from encroachment on the north. Internal wars were strictly prohibited by a proclamation issued in 1811; but with this exception the powers and privileges of the chiefs remained untouched. Each native ruler, great or small, including even the descendants of private troopers of the original invading forces, had civil, criminal, and fiscal jurisdiction within his own territory, subject only to the controlling authority of the Governor-General's Agent at Ambāla. No tribute was taken, nor was any special contingent demanded, although the chieftains were bound in case of war to give active aid to the Government. The right to escheats was the sole return which was asked. The first Sikh War and the Sutlej campaign of 1845 gave Government an opportunity of testing the gratitude of the chieftains. Few of them, however, displayed their loyalty more conspicuously than by abstaining from open rebellion. Their previous conduct had not been such as to encourage Government in its policy towards them; and a sweeping measure of reform was accordingly introduced, for the reduction of their privileges. The Political Agency of Ambāla was transformed into a Commissionership, and police jurisdiction was handed over to European officers. In June, 1849, after the second Sikh War had brought the Punjab under British rule, the chiefs were finally deprived of all sovereign powers. The revenues were still theirs, but the assessments were to be made by British officials and under British regulation. Even previous to this arrangement portions of the modern District had lapsed to Government by death or forfeiture; and the reforms of 1849 brought Ambāla nearly to its present proportions.

During the Mutiny of 1857, although incendiary fires and other disturbances gave much ground for alarm, especially at the first beginning of disaffection, no actual outbreak occurred, and the District was held throughout with little difficulty. In 1862 the dismemberment of Thānesar District brought three new *parganas* to Ambāla; since that date there have been several alterations of boundary, the most important of which were the transfer of the Thānesar *tahsīl* to Karnāl in 1897 and the accession of Kasauli and Kālka from Simla in 1899.

Information as to the principal remains of archaeological interest will be found in the articles on SUGH and SĀDHAURA.

The people.

The District contains 7 towns and 1,718 villages. Its population at the last three enumerations was: (1881) 864,748, (1891) 863,641, and (1901) 815,880. During the last decade the rural population decreased by 6·6 per cent. The decrease was apparent in every *tahsīl*, being greatest in Naraingarh and least in Jagādhri; but the towns, with the exception of Ambāla, Būriya, and Sādhaura, showed an increase. This general decline is attributable to the mortality caused by cholera, fever, and small-pox, and also to scarcity and emigration in the famine years. The District is divided into five *tahsīls*—AMBĀLA, KHARAR, JAGĀDHRI, NARAINGARH, and RŪPAR—the head-quarters of each being at the place from which it is named. The chief towns are the municipalities of AMBĀLA, the head-quarters of the District, JAGĀDHRI, RŪPAR, SĀDHAURA, and BŪRIYA.

The following table shows the chief statistics of population in 1901:—

Tahsīl.	Area in square miles.	Number of		Population.	Population per square mile.	Percentage of variation in population between 1891 and 1901.	Number of persons able to read and write.
		Towns.	Villages.				
Ambāla	355	1	295	218,006	614·1	− 5·4	13,701
Rūpar	290	1	358	139,327	480·4	− 5·1	5,472
Kharar	370	2	369	166,267	449·4	− 5·7	7,122
Naraingarh	436	1	317	131,042	300·5	− 7·2	4,022
Jagādhri	406	2	379	161,238	397·1	− 4·4	5,148
District total	1,851	7	1,718	815,880	440·7	− 5·6	35,465

NOTE.—The figures for the areas of *tahsīls* are taken from revenue returns. The total District area is that given in the *Census Report*.

About 62 per cent. of the people are Hindus, 30 per cent. Muhammadans, and 7 per cent. Sikhs. In the Rūpar and Kharar *tahsīls* the language is Punjābi, a Hindī *patois* being spoken in the rest of the District.

Castes and occupations. Jāts or Jats (125,000) are the chief landowning tribe. They are divided into two widely different classes, those of the northern *tahsīls* being the fine sturdy type found in the Punjab proper, while to the east and south they are inferior in physique and energy. Of the Rājputs (67,000), more than two-thirds are Muhammadans. The Mālis (24,000) and Sainis (26,000) are market-gardening tribes scattered throughout the District, generally as occupancy tenants, though the Sainis hold many villages in Rūpar. The Mālis are nearly all Hindus, the Sainis chiefly Hindus with some Sikhs. The Arains (29,000) are almost all Muhammadans, the Kambohs (9,000) chiefly Hindus or Sikhs. The Gūjars (46,000) are divided almost equally between Hindus and Muhammadans; they chiefly inhabit the Jumna valley and the wild broken tract lying under the hills, and own large herds of goats. In this District the Gūjars have an undeserved reputation as cattle-thieves. In the Morni hills, Kanets (2,500), Koris (4,000), and Brāhmans (44,000) are the chief cultivators. The Kanets claim a Rājput descent, the Koris are of menial status. The whole Morni population are a simple, orderly folk, mixing as little as possible with the people of the plains. The Baniās (29,000) are the most important commercial tribe, but there are also 7,000 Khattrīs. Of the menial tribes may be mentioned the Chamārs (leather-workers, 113,000), Chūhrās (scavengers, 32,000), Jhīnwars (water-carriers, 31,000), Julāhās (weavers, 20,000), Kumhārs (potters, 9,000), Nais (barbers, 11,000), Tarkhāns (carpenters, 19,000), and Telis (oilmen, 12,000). There are 20,000 Shaikhs, 6,000 Saiyids, 16,000 Fakīrs, and 8,000 Jogis and Rāwals. Of the total population, 51 per cent. are supported by agriculture, 19 per cent. are industrial, 4 per cent. commercial, and 3 per cent. professional.

Christian missions. The Ludhiāna American Presbyterian Mission has stations at Ambāla city and cantonment, both occupied in 1849, with out-stations at Jagādhri, Mubārakpur, Naraingarh, Raipur, and Mulāna. With a staff of eight missionaries, it supports a high school, a middle school, a school for Muhammadan girls, two for Hindu girls, and a hospital for women. The District contained 959 native Christians in 1901.

General agricul- Every *tahsīl* except Rūpar contains a large tract of hard clay land, which is fit for cultivation only when the rains are abundant. Hence the autumn harvest, which is sown by aid of the monsoon rains, is more important than the spring harvest. The insecure parts are those in which this heavy clay soil predominates, chiefly in the Ambāla *tahsīl* and in the southern quarter of Kharar. The rest of the four *tahsīls* which abut on the Himālayas contain, with a certain proportion of hilly country, large tracts of good alluvial loam; the Rūpar *tahsīl* is practically secure; and such insecurity as there is in Naraingarh and Jagādhri is due rather to the character of the Rājput inhabitants than to defects of soil or climate. The District is intersected by numerous watercourses which, though to all appearance dry except after heavy rain, constitute a large reserve of moisture, and even in times of drought enable fairly good crops to be cultivated along them.

tural conditions.

Chief agricultural statistics and principal crops.

The District is held almost entirely on the *pattīdāri* and *bhaiyāchārā* tenures; but *zamīndāri* lands cover about 70 square miles, a larger proportion than in most Districts.

The following table shows the main agricultural statistics in 1903-4, areas being in square miles:—

Tahsīl.	Total.	Cultivated.	Irrigated.	Cultivable waste.
Ambāla . . .	355	274	3	38
Rūpar . . .	290	193	28	23
Kharar . . .	370	242	21	28
Naraingarh . .	436	219	5	27
Jagādhri . . .	406	267	14	39
Total	1,857	1,195	71	155

The chief crops of the spring harvest are wheat and gram, which in 1903-4 occupied 309 and 181 square miles respectively. Barley covered only 13 square miles. Maize, the principal crop in autumn, occupied 151 square miles; then came rice (115), pulses (95), great millet (30), and cotton (43). About 2,000 acres were under poppy. In the Morni hills *mandal* (*Eleusine coracana*), *kulthi* (*Dolichos uniflorus*), the tuber *kachālu* (*Arum colocaria*), and ginger are cultivated.

Improvements in agricultural practice.

The area under cultivation increased from 1,171 square miles in 1890-1 to 1,195 square miles in 1903-4, in which latter year it was 64 per cent. of the total area of the District. Experiments were carried out in 1887 with a view to introducing natural khāki-coloured (Nankin) cotton as a staple. The cotton was a fine strong plant with a good fibre, and made up well as coarse cloth; but Government decided that it could not take the place of dyed cotton for army purposes, and the people preferred the ordinary cotton; both on account of its colour and because the Nankin cotton took longer to come to maturity and yielded a smaller proportion of fibre to seed. More recent experiments have been made with Nāgpur, Egyptian, and American cotton, the latter with good results as regards out-turn. There is a tendency to substitute the cultivation of fine rice for coarse. Loans under the Land Improvement Loans Act are not very popular, the people preferring to borrow money from the village banker. Only Rs. 1,400 was advanced under this Act during the five years ending 1904, all for the construction of masonry wells. Loans for seed and bullocks are readily taken in times of scarcity, when credit with the banker has failed. Rs. 31,000 was thus advanced during the five years ending 1903–4.

Cattle, horses, and sheep.

The breed of cattle is capable of improvement; but in the alluvial lands the weak home-bred stock are quite equal to the work required, and being accustomed to stall-feeding do not, like the stronger cattle imported from the upland tracts, feel the change from grazing in the open. For work in heavy clay soils, or with deep irrigation wells, a finer breed of cattle is imported. Hissār bulls have been introduced. A good deal of horse-breeding is carried on in the District; the District board maintains seven horse and five donkey stallions. Large quantities of sheep, pigs, and poultry are kept, the high prices obtainable in Simla making poultry especially remunerative.

Irrigation.

Of the total area cultivated in 1903–4, 71 square miles, or 6 per cent., were irrigated. Of this area, 43 square miles were irrigated from wells, 3,396 acres from canals, and 23 square miles from streams and tanks. The head-works of both the WESTERN JUMNA and SIRHIND CANALS lie in the District, but it receives no irrigation from the latter. About 2,500 acres are estimated as irrigable annually from the main line of the Western Jumna Canal. The District has in use 3,297 masonry wells worked by bullocks, almost all on the rope-and-bucket system, even in the riverain tracts; also 2,095 unbricked wells, lever wells, and water-lifts. The hill torrents afford a certain amount of irrigation. Of the crops harvested in 1903–4, only 4 per cent. was grown on irrigated land, sugar-cane being the only crop irrigated to any great extent. It is proposed to add to the programme of famine relief works projects for the construction of storage tanks for purposes of rice irrigation in the clay tracts which largely depend on that crop.

The Kalesar 'reserved' forest has an area of about 19 square miles, lying principally between two low ranges of hills on the right bank of the Jumna. The chief growth is of *sāl*, but ebony and other trees are also found. This forest contains no bamboo, but a good deal grows south of it. Near Jagādhri is a 'reserved' plantation of *shīsham* (*Dalbergia Sissoo*), and at Ambāla a military Reserve of nearly 3 square miles forms the grass farm. The Morni hills are covered with a dense forest growth of scrub mixed with *chīl* (*Pinus longifolia*) and many other valuable trees, including the *harrar* (*Terminalia Chebula*), the fruit of which yields a considerable revenue. In 1903-4 the total forest revenue was Rs. 2,000. Forests.

A good deal of limestone is burnt in the Morni hills; but since 1887 the industry has been discouraged, as it was found that much harm was being done to the forest growth by reckless cutting for fuel. The District also possesses some block *kankar* quarries, which were largely used when the Sirhind Canal was under construction; and in the Kharar *tahsīl* millstones are prepared. Gold is washed in minute quantities in the sand of some of the mountain torrents, especially the Sombh. Minerals.

Excellent cotton carpets are made at Ambāla; and the town also possessed four ginning factories with 369 employés in 1904, three cotton presses with 180 employés, and two factories in which cotton-ginning is combined with flour-milling, and which between them give employment to 63 hands. The cantonment has two flour-mills, one of which was working in 1904 and gave employment to 54 hands, and a factory for cabinet-making and coach-building with 195 hands. At Sādhaura there is a combined cotton-ginning and pressing factory and flour-mill with 55 employés, and at Khānpur a combined cotton-ginning factory and flour-mill with 40, while the Kālka-Simla Railway workshops at Kālka give employment to 200 operatives. A museum of industrial exhibits has recently been started in a building erected in memory of the late Queen-Empress. Rūpar is famous for small articles of iron-work, and a potter in the town enjoys some celebrity for his clay modelling. The Rūpar canal foundry was closed in 1901. Kharar produces good lacquer-work, and Jagādhri has a well-deserved reputation for its brass-ware. Cotton prints are made in some villages. Arts and manufactures.

Ambāla city is a considerable grain mart, receiving grain and cotton from the Phūlkiān States and Ludhiāna, and exporting them up and down country. It imports English Commerce and trade.

cloth and iron from the south, and salt, wood, and woollen and silk manufactures from elsewhere; and exports cotton goods, especially carpets. It has a considerable trade in hill products, such as ginger, turmeric, potatoes, opium, and *charas*; and Simla and Kasauli are largely supplied from it with various necessaries. Rūpar is also an important mart for commerce between the hills and the plains, and has a considerable traffic in grain, sugar, and indigo; salt is imported and sent to the hills in exchange for iron, ginger, turmeric, and potatoes, and country cloth is manufactured in the town and exported to the hills. Jagādhri carries on a considerable trade in metals, importing copper and iron and exporting the manufactured products. It is also a centre of the borax trade. During the American Civil War, a cotton mart was established at Kurāli, where 5 lakhs' worth is still reported to change hands yearly.

Railways and roads. The North-Western Railway from Sahāranpur to Lahore and the Delhi-Umballa-Kālka line cross each other at Ambāla city, the latter being continued by the narrow-gauge Kālka-Simla line. The grand trunk road passes through Ambāla, where the Kālka road for Simla leaves it. The only other important metalled roads are from Abdullahpur (via Jagādhri) to Chhachhrauli, the capital of the State of Kalsia, and from Būriya to Jagādhri. The total length of metalled roads is 103 miles, and of unmetalled roads 404 miles. Of these, 87 miles of metalled and 32 miles of unmetalled roads are under the Public Works department, and the rest are maintained by the District board. Both the Sirhind and Western Jumna Canals are navigable, taking to a large extent the place of the rivers which they drain almost dry except in the summer months. The Jumna is crossed by a ferry, which is replaced in the cold season by a bridge of boats, and the Sutlej by three ferries.

Famine. Ambāla District has only once suffered from serious famine since its formation in 1847. This was in 1860–1, when wheat rose to 8 seers a rupee. Regarding the distress in 1868–9 very little is recorded. The total number of persons employed on relief works was 46,000, and 57,000 received gratuitous relief. Only about Rs. 2,500 was spent from subscriptions, to which Government added as much again. The crops failed in 1884–5 and 1890. The famine of 1896–7 was due, not so much to any actual failure of the crops in the District (though the spring harvest of 1897 was the third poor harvest in succession), as to the state of the grain market all over India. For months together the prices of all food-grains stood at about 10 seers per rupee in rural tracts; and in the towns, when prices were highest, wheat rose to 7 seers, maize (the staple food of the people) and gram to 8 seers; and the District only escaped worse calamities than it actually suffered owing in no small degree to the resources of the small capitalists. The greatest daily average number relieved was 5,279. Rs. 36,600 was spent from District funds on gratuitous and all other forms of relief, and Rs. 15,000 was received from the Indian Charitable Famine Relief Fund. In the famine of 1899–1900, though prices did not rise so high, the crop failure was more complete; there were heavier losses of cattle, and credit was harder to obtain. The greatest daily number relieved did not, however, exceed 816; the expenditure from District funds was Rs. 4,176, and from the Charitable Relief Fund Rs. 4,925.

District subdivisions and staff. The District is divided for administrative purposes into 5 *tahsīls*: AMBĀLA, JAGĀDHRI, NARAINGARH, RŪPAR, and KHARAR, the two last forming the Rūpar subdivision. Each *tahsīl* has a *tahsīldār* and a *naib-tahsīldār*. The District is in charge of a Deputy-Commissioner, aided by six Assistant or Extra Assistant Commissioners, of whom one is subdivisional officer in charge of Rūpar, and another is in charge of the District treasury. Ambāla is the head-quarters of the Deputy-Inspector-General of Police, Eastern Range, and of an Executive division of the Public Works department.

Civil justice and crime. The Deputy-Commissioner as District Magistrate is responsible for the criminal justice of the District. The civil judicial work is under a District Judge, and both officers are supervised by the Divisional Judge of the Ambāla Civil Division. There are three Munsifs—at head-quarters, Jagādhri, and Rūpar. There are also Cantonment Magistrates at Ambāla and Kasauli, with an assistant cantonment magistrate at the former place, and seven honorary magistrates. The predominant forms of crime are burglary and cattle-theft.

Land revenue administration. In the revenue history two periods of chaos have to be distinguished; the first between 1763 and 1809, when the Sikhs having crossed the Sutlej proceeded to divide the country among themselves and rule it with degrees of extortion which varied with the position, necessities, and temperament of individual chieftains; the second between 1809 and 1847, the period of British protection, when confiscation followed escheat, and so-called settlement followed either, under conditions so diverse as to baffle any uniformity of treatment, fiscal or historical. The summary settlements were invariably pitched too high, the demand being fixed by simply commuting at cash rates the grain collections made by the Sikhs. The only data were the accounts of the former payments, and the estimates made by leading men—not unbiased financiers, as their revenue assignments rose and fell with the Government demand. A regular settlement for the whole cis-Sutlej tract was carried out between 1847 and 1855, and remained practically unaltered until the revision commenced in 1882. The assessment, though not unduly light, was fair and, helped by the rise of prices that began in 1860, worked without any difficulty. The Jagādhri *tahsīl* was resettled in 1882–9, and the rest of the District between 1883 and 1889. The average assessment on 'dry' land is Rs. 1–3–6 (maximum, Rs. 2–2; minimum, 5 annas), and on 'wet' land Rs. 3–10 (maximum, Rs. 5; minimum, Rs. 2–4). The result of these revisions was an increase of one lakh in the assessment of the whole District. The demand, including cesses, for 1903–4 was 13·8 lakhs. The average size of a proprietary holding is 2·7 acres.

The collections of land revenue alone and of total revenue are shown below, in thousands of rupees:—

	1880–1.	1890–1.	1900–1.	1903–4.
Land revenue . .	7,87	9,50	6,61	7,45
Total revenue . .	11,11	13,87	12,26	14,54

Local and municipal.

The District contains five municipalities—AMBĀLA, RŪPAR, JAGĀDHRI, SĀDHAURA, and BŪRIYA—and two 'notified areas' or embryo municipalities, Kharar and KĀLKA. Outside these, local affairs are managed by a District board, whose income amounted in 1903–4 to 1·2 lakhs, while its expenditure was 1·1 lakhs, education accounting for one-fifth of the total.

Police and jails.

The regular police force consists of 803 of all ranks, including 148 cantonment and 86 municipal police, under a Superintendent, who usually has one Assistant and one Deputy-Superintendent and five inspectors under him. The village watchmen number 1,782, including 31 *daffadārs*. The District has 17 police stations, 2 outposts, and 6 road-posts. The District jail at head-quarters has accommodation for 856 prisoners.

Education.

The District stands ninth among the twenty-eight Districts of the Province in respect of the literacy of its population. In 1901 the proportion of literate persons was 4·3 per cent. (7·5 males and 0·4 females). The number of pupils under instruction was 5,262 in 1880–1, 9,359 in 1900–1, and 8,906 in 1903–4. In the last year the District possessed one secondary and 99 primary (public) schools, and 3 advanced and 69 elementary (private) schools, with 421 girls in the public and 393 in the private schools. The Mission school in Ambāla city was the only high school of the District until Government opened one at Jagādhri. The District possesses six girls' schools. The total expenditure on education in 1903–4 was 2·4 lakhs, of which the greater part was provided by Imperial and Provincial funds and endowments.

The District contains a hospital at Ambāla city, and seven outlying dispensaries. In 1904 a total of 98,679 out-patients and 1,982 in-patients were treated at these institutions, and 8,697 operations performed. The aggregate expenditure was Rs. 21,000, which was met in nearly equal shares by District and municipal funds, assisted by a grant from Government of Rs. 2,000. A description of the Pasteur Institute and Research Laboratory will be found under KASAULI. There is a leper asylum at Ambāla under the American Presbyterian Mission. The Philadelphia Hospital for women at Ambāla is also under American management. **Hospitals and dispensaries.**

The number of successful vaccinations in 1903–4 was 15,708, representing 20 per 1,000 of the population. Vaccination is compulsory in Ambāla city and Rūpar town. **Vaccination.**

[A. Kensington, *Customary Law of Ambāla District* (1893), *District Gazetteer* (1892–3), and *Settlement Report* (1893); J. M. Douie, *Settlement Report of Karnāl-Ambāla* (1891).]

Ambāla Tahsīl.—South-western *tahsīl* of Ambāla District, Punjab, lying between 30° 7′ and 30° 27′ N. and 76° 33′ and 77° 12′ E., with an area of 355 square miles. The population in 1901 was 218,006, compared with 230,567 in 1891. The head-quarters are at the city of AMBĀLA (population, 78,638). It also contains 295 villages. The land revenue and cesses amounted in 1903–4 to 2·8 lakhs. The *tahsīl* lies in the open plain, and the hard clay subsoil is almost everywhere covered with alluvial loam.

Rūpar Subdivision.—Subdivision of Ambāla District, Punjab, comprising the *tahsīls* of RŪPAR and KHARAR. Kharar contains the cantonment and sanitarium of KASAULI and the 'notified area' of KĀLKA.

Rūpar Tahsīl.—Northern *tahsīl* of Ambāla District, Punjab, lying at the foot of the Himālayas, between 30° 45′ and 31° 13′ N. and 76° 19′ and 76° 44′ E., with an area of 290 square miles. It is bounded on the north by the Sutlej river, and forms part of the Rūpar subdivision. On the north-east the *tahsīl* runs up into the Lower Siwāliks, and along the

Sutlej is a narrow strip of low-lying country. The rest consists of a loam plateau rich in wells, and intersected by mountain torrent-beds. The head-works of the SIRHIND CANAL are at Rūpar. The population in 1901 was 139,327, compared with 146,816 in 1891. The head-quarters are at the town of RŪPAR (population, 8,888). It also contains 358 villages. The land revenue and cesses amounted in 1903–4 to 2·8 lakhs.

Kharar.—*Tahsīl* of Ambāla District, Punjab, lying at the foot of the Himālayas, between 30° 34′ and 30° 56′ N. and 76° 22′ and 76° 55′ E., with an area of 370 square miles, and forming part of the Rūpar subdivision. The population in 1901 was 166,267, compared with 176,298 in 1891. It contains 369 villages, of which Kharar is the head-quarters. The land revenue and cesses amounted in 1903–4 to 3·1 lakhs. For administrative purposes the hill station of KASAULI (population, 2,192) and the town of KĀLKA (7,045) are included in this *tahsīl*. The northern part lies in the Siwāliks. Between the hills and the Ghaggar, in the east, is an unhealthy tract of jungle and rice-fields. The soil in the centre and west is a fertile loam, which in the south stiffens into clay. Communications are everywhere rendered difficult by the torrent-beds which intersect the country.

Naraingarh.—*Tahsīl* of Ambāla District, Punjab, lying at the foot of the Himālayas, between 30° 19′ and 30° 45′ N. and 76° 52′ and 77° 19′ E., with an area of 436 square miles. The population in 1901 was 131,042, compared with 141,326 in 1891. It contains the town of SĀDHAURA (population, 9,812) and 317 villages, of which Naraingarh is the head-quarters. The land revenue and cesses amounted in 1903–4 to 2·3 lakhs. The *tahsīl* includes a tract of hilly country on the north, culminating in the Karoh peak, 4,919 feet above the sea. The lower hills are devoid of vegetation; and below them comes a tract of rough stony country much cut up by ravines, the continuous advance of which is a most serious difficulty for the farmer. The southern half is fairly level.

Jagādhri Tahsīl.—Eastern *tahsīl* of Ambāla District, Punjab, lying at the foot of the Himālayas, between 30° 2′ and 30° 28′ N. and 77° 4′ and 77° 36′ E., with an area of 406 square miles. It is bounded on the south-east by the Jumna, which separates it from the United Provinces. The population in 1901 was 161,238, compared with 168,634 in 1891. It contains the towns of JAGĀDHRI (population, 13,462), the head-quarters, and BŪRIYA (5,865); and 379 villages. The land revenue and cesses amounted in 1903–4 to 2·9 lakhs.

The *tahsīl* includes a small tract of hilly country in the Siwāliks. On the east lie the Jumna lowlands. The rest is generally level or gently undulating, and is intersected by torrent-beds.

Manauli.—Estate in the Kharar and Rūpar *tahsīls* of Ambāla District, Punjab, with an area of 11 square miles. It was the principal *jāgīr* held till recently by a member of the Faizullahpuria or Singhpuria family, which was one of the twelve great Sikh *misls* or confederacies. Founded early in the eighteenth century by Kapūr Singh, a Jat of Amritsar District, the family played a great part in the Jullundur Doāb under his great-nephew, Budh Singh. In 1811, however, the Singhpurias were expelled from their territories north of the Sutlej by Ranjīt Singh's generals, and confined to the estates south of that river, which they still hold. From 1809 to 1846 the family ranked as independent protected chiefs, but they lost their status in the latter year. The last owner, Sardār Raghubīr Singh, held 81 villages in *jāgīr*. These yield a net revenue of Rs. 36,000, and the *sardār* had also other estates. After his death in 1904, the *jāgīr* was divided among a number of his relatives.

Ambāla City.—Head-quarters of the District and *tahsīl* of Ambāla, Punjab, situated in 30° 23′ N. and 76° 46′ E., on the North-Western Railway and the grand trunk road, at the point where they are crossed by the Delhi-Umballa-Kālka Railway; distant by rail from Calcutta 1,077 miles, from Bombay 1,105 miles, and from Karāchi 848 miles. The population (1901) is 78,638: namely, Hindus, 39,601; Sikhs, 2,168; Muhammadans, 32,149; and Christians, 3,610—of whom 50,438 reside in cantonments. Ambāla is chiefly important as being one of the largest cantonments in India. The garrison, which is under the General Officer commanding the Lahore division, consists of one battery of horse artillery, with an ammunition column; one regiment of British and two regiments of native cavalry; and three regiments of British and one battalion of native infantry. The cantonment also contains a mounted infantry school, companies of the Army Hospital and Bearer corps, and detachments of the Punjab Light Horse and the North-Western and East Indian Railway Volunteers.

The native quarter, which has a separate station on the North-Western Railway, lies four miles north-west of the cantonment. Its name is possibly derived from its mythical founder Amba, but is more probably a corruption of Ambwāla, the 'mango village.' It was of no importance before the lapse of the Ambāla estate in 1823, when it became the residence of the Political Agent for the Cis-Sutlej States. The cantonment was established in 1843, and in 1849 it became the head-quarters of a District. The civil lines are situated near the city, and contain, besides the usual offices, a jail and a hospital. The city is well situated as a commercial centre, and is an important cotton and grain market. It also forms a dépôt for the supply of Simla, and carries on a considerable trade in hill products, such as ginger and turmeric. The article on AMBĀLA DISTRICT gives details of the modern industries. A branch of the Alliance Bank of Simla has been established in the cantonment.

The municipality was created in 1867. The income during the ten years ending 1902–3 averaged Rs. 56,200, and the expenditure Rs. 54,300. The income in 1903–4 was Rs. 70,700, the chief source being octroi (Rs. 45,200); and the expenditure was Rs. 71,900, the principal items being drainage and water-supply (Rs. 22,400), medical (Rs. 8,100), conservancy (Rs. 5,800), education (Rs. 6,100), public safety (Rs. 7,500), and general administration (Rs. 9,400). The income and expenditure of the cantonment fund during the ten years ending 1902–3 averaged 1·3 lakhs. Ambāla has three high schools and two middle schools, besides a civil hospital.

Būriya.—Town in the Jagādhri *tahsīl* of Ambāla District, Punjab, situated in 30° 10′ N. and 77° 22′ E., 3 miles north of the North-Western Railway. Population (1901), 5,865. Founded in the time of the emperor Humāyūn, it was captured by the Sikhs in 1760, and became the head-quarters of a considerable principality, which, before the treaty of 1809 between the British Government and Ranjīt Singh, had been divided into the two chiefships of Būriya and Diālgarh. Dissensions between the widows of the last male holder of the latter led to its subdivision, a few years after it came under British protection, into the estates of Jagādhri and Diālgarh. Jagādhri lapsed in 1829. The Rānī of Diālgarh was one of the nine chiefs exempted from the reforms of 1846 and 1849; and she retained her position as an independent protected chief until her death in 1852, when Diālgarh also lapsed. Būriya proper was reduced to the status of an ordinary *jāgīr* in 1849. The town is of no commercial importance. The municipality was created in 1867. The income during the ten years ending 1902–3 averaged Rs. 4,300, and the expenditure Rs. 5,100. The income in 1903–4 was Rs. 4,500, chiefly from octroi; and the expenditure was Rs. 4,400. There is a vernacular middle school.

Jagādhri Town.—Head-quarters of the *tahsīl* of the same name in Ambāla District, Punjab, situated in 30° 10′ N. and 77° 18′ E., about 5 miles north of the North-Western Railway, on the metalled road connecting Ambāla and Sahāranpur. Population (1901), 13,462. It owes its importance to the Sikh chief Rai Singh of Būriya, who settled a commercial and manufacturing population here. The town had been entirely destroyed by Nādir Shāh, but was rebuilt by Rai Singh in 1783. It lapsed to the British Government in 1829. The name is said to be a corruption of Gangā Dhair, so called from a store of Ganges water enshrined in the foundations. Jagādhri is noted for its manufacture of iron and brass-ware. Borax, imported from the hills, is also refined, and oxide of lead manufactured. The municipality was created in 1867. The income during the ten years ending 1902–3 averaged Rs. 24,700, and the expenditure Rs. 24,300. The income in 1903–4 was Rs. 25,700, chiefly from octroi; and the expenditure was Rs. 25,500. It maintains an Anglo-vernacular high school and a dispensary.

Kālka.—Town attached for administrative purposes to the Kharar *tahsīl* of Ambāla District, Punjab, situated in 30° 50′ N. and 76° 57′ E., at the foot of the outlying range of the Himālayas at an elevation of 2,400 feet, and entirely surrounded by Patiāla territory. It is the junction of the Delhi-Umballa-Kālka and Kālka-Simla Railways. Population (1901), 7,045. Kālka was acquired from Patiāla in 1843 as a dépôt for Simla; it is also an important market for hill produce, such as ginger and turmeric. There is a considerable manufacture of millstones, and a railway workshop is situated here, which employed 200 hands in 1904. It is administered as a 'notified area.'

Kasauli.—Hill station and cantonment in the Punjab, situated in 30° 53′ N. and 76° 58′ E., entirely surrounded by Native States, but attached for administrative purposes to the Kharar *tahsīl* of Ambāla District. It stands on the summit of the long ridge overlooking Kālka, at an elevation of 6,335 feet above the sea, and nearly 4,000 feet above Kālka, from which it is distant about 9 miles. Population (1901), 2,192. Kasauli was founded in 1842 as a military station, and now serves as a convalescent dépôt. It has during the summer months a considerable civil population, for whose accomodation hotels have been built. Owing, however, to its nearness to the plains, it is the least attractive in climate of the Punjab hill stations. The management of the station is in the hands of a Cantonment Magistrate assisted by a cantonment committee; the Cantonment Magistrate proceeds on tour for ten days in each month of the hot season, and is relieved of the charge of the treasury by the Assistant Commissioner in charge of the Rūpar subdivision. The Deputy-Commissioner of Ambāla also resides at Kasauli during part of the hot season. There is an Anglo-vernacular middle school. The Lawrence Military Asylum at Sanāwar is 3 miles away, in a portion of territory attached to Simla District. The income and expenditure of cantonment funds during the ten years ending 1902–3 averaged Rs. 13,000.

The Pasteur Institute at Kasauli was established in 1901 for the treatment of persons bitten by rabid animals, and now treats patients from all parts of Northern India. In 1906 a central Research Institute was founded, which will provide means for the scientific study of the etiology and nature of disease in India, in addition to the preparation of curative sera for the diseases of man and the training of scientific workers. The institution is in charge of a Director, with a staff of assistants. Kasauli is also the head-quarters of the Punjab Nursing Association, and contains a dispensary. There is a brewery in the neighbourhood.

Rūpar Town.—Head-quarters of the subdivision and *tahsīl* of the same name in Ambāla District, Punjab, situated in 30° 58′ N. and 76° 32′ E., at the point where the Sutlej issues from the hills. Population (1901), 8,888. It is a town of considerable antiquity, originally called Rūpnagar after its founder Rājā Rūp Chand. It was occupied about 1763 by Hari Singh, a Sikh chieftain, who seized upon a wide tract south of the Sutlej, stretching along the foot of the Himālayas. In 1792 he divided his estates between his two sons, Charrat Singh and Dewa Singh, the former of whom obtained Rūpar. The estates were confiscated in 1846, in consequence of the part taken by the family during the Sikh War of the preceding year. The head-works of the Sirhind Canal are situated here, and the town is an important mart of exchange between the hills and the plains. Salt is imported from the Khewra mines and re-exported to the hills, in return for iron, ginger, potatoes, turmeric, opium, and *charas*. Cotton twill (*sūsī*) is largely manufactured, and the smiths of Rūpar have a reputation for locks and other small articles of iron. Rūpar was the scene of the celebrated meeting between Lord William Bentinck and Ranjīt Singh in 1831. There are two important religious fairs, one Hindu, one Muhammadan. The municipality was created in 1867. The income during the ten years ending 1902–3 averaged Rs. 12,100, and the expenditure Rs. 11,400. The income in 1903–4 was Rs. 14,500, chiefly from octroi; and the expenditure was Rs. 16,900. There are three Anglo-vernacular middle schools and a dispensary.

Sādhaura.—Town in the Naraingarh *tahsīl* of Ambāla District, Punjab, situated in 30° 23′ N. and 77° 13′ E., at the foot of the outlying range of the Himālayas. Population (1901), 9,812. It dates from the time of Mahmūd of Ghazni, and contains a mosque built in the reign of Shāh Jahān. A fair held yearly at the shrine of the Muhammadan saint, Shāh Kumais, is attended by 20,000 or 30,000 persons. There is some manufacture of cotton cloth; and the town possesses a steam printing press, and a combined cotton-ginning and pressing factory, which in 1904 employed 55 hands. The municipality was created in 1885. The income during the ten years ending 1902–3 averaged Rs. 6,800, and the expenditure Rs. 6,400. The income in 1903–4 was Rs. 7,300, chiefly from octroi; and the expenditure was Rs. 8,100. There is a vernacular middle school and a dispensary.

Sugh (*Srughna*).—Village in the Jagādhri *tahsīl* of Ambāla District, Punjab, situated in 30° 9′ N. and 77° 23′ E., in a bend of the old bed of the Jumna, now a part of the Western Jumna Canal, close to Jagādhri and Būriya towns. Population (1901), 378. Srughna is mentioned by Hiuen Tsiang, the Chinese pilgrim of the seventh century, as a town 3½ miles in circuit, the capital of a kingdom and seat of considerable learning, both Buddhistic and Brāhmanical. He describes the kingdom of Srughna as extending to the mountains on the north, and to the Ganges on the east, with the Jumna flowing through the midst of it. The capital he represents as having been partly in ruins; but General Cunningham thought that there is evidence in the coins found on the spot to show that it was occupied down to the time of Muhammadan conquest. He thus describes the extent and position of the ruins:—

'The village of Sugh occupies one of the most remarkable positions that I have seen during the whole course of my researches. It is situated on a projecting triangular spur of high land, and is surrounded on three sides by the bed of the old Jumna, which is now the Western Jumna Canal. On the north and west faces it is further protected by two deep ravines, so that the position is a ready-made stronghold, which is covered on all sides, except the west, by natural defences. In shape it is almost triangular, with a large projecting fort or citadel at each of the angles. The site of the north fort is now occupied by the castle and village of Dayālgarh. The village of Amadalpur stands on the site of the south-east fort, and that of the south-west is unoccupied. Each of these forts is 1,500 feet long and 1,000 feet broad, and each face of the triangle which connects them together is upwards of half a mile in length, that to the east being 4,000 and those to the north-west and south-west 3,000 feet each. The whole circuit of the position is therefore 22,000 feet or upwards of 4 miles, which is considerably more than the $3\frac{1}{2}$ miles of Hiuen Tsiang's measurement. But as the north fort is separated from the main position by a deep sandy ravine, called the Rohāra nullah, it is possible that it may have been unoccupied at the time of the pilgrim's visit. This would reduce the circuit of the position to 19,000 feet or upwards of $3\frac{1}{2}$ miles, and bring it into accord with the pilgrim's measurement. The small village of Sugh occupies the west side of the position, and the small town of Būriya lies immediately to the north of Dayālgarh.'

Boundaries, configuration, and hill and river systems.

Simla District (*Shamla*).—District in the Delhi Division of the Punjab, consisting of nine small tracts lying among the SIMLA HILL STATES, between 30° 58′ and 31° 22′ N. and 77° 7′ and 77° 43′ E., with a total area of 101 square miles. The town lies on the spurs which run down from Jakko hill, and occupies an area of only 6 square miles. North-east of it lie the *parganas* of Kot Khai and Kotgarh, the former 32 miles by road from Simla in the valley of the Giri, the latter 22 miles (50 by road) on a northern spur of the Hātu range overlooking the Sutlej valley. The Bharauli tract is a narrow strip of hill country, extending from Sabāthu to Kiārighāt, about 8 miles long and from 2 to 6 wide. Besides these tracts, the cantonments of Jutogh, Sabāthu, Solon, Dagshai, and Sanāwar, the site of the Lawrence Military Asylum, are included in the District.

The hills and the surrounding Native States compose the southern outliers of the great central chain of the Western Himālayas. They descend in a gradual series from the main chain itself in Bashahr State to the general level of the Punjab plain in Ambāla District, thus forming a transverse south-westerly spur between the great basins of the Ganges and the Indus, here represented by their tributaries, the Jumna and the Sutlej. A few miles north-east of Simla the spur divides into two main ridges, one of which curves round the Sutlej valley towards the north-west, while the other, crowned by the sanitarium of Simla, trends south-eastward to a point a few miles north of Sabāthu, where it merges at right angles in the mountains of the Outer or Sub-Himālayan system, which run parallel to the principal range. South and east of Simla, the hills between the Sutlej and the Tons centre in the great peak of CHAUR, 11,982 feet above the sea. Throughout all the hills forests of *deodār* abound, while rhododendrons clothe the slopes up to the limit of perpetual snow. The scenery in the immediate neighbourhood of Simla itself presents a series of magnificent views, embracing on the south the Ambāla plains, with the Sabāthu and Kasauli hills in the foreground, and the massive block of the Chaur a little to the left, while just below the spectator's feet a series of huge ravines lead down into the deep valleys which score the mountain-sides. Northwards, the eye wanders over a network of confused chains, rising range above range, and crowned in the distance by a crescent of snowy peaks, which stand out in bold relief against the clear background of the sky. The principal rivers of the surrounding tracts are the Sutlej, Pabar, Giri Gangā, Gambhar, and Sarsa.

The rocks found in the neighbourhood of Simla belong entirely to the carbonaceous system and fall into four groups—the Krol, the infra-Krol, the Blaini, and the infra-Blaini, or Simla slates. The Simla slates are the lowest beds seen; they are succeeded by the Blaini group, consisting of two bands of boulder-slate, separated by white-weathering slates (bleach slates), and overlain by a thin band of pink dolomitic limestone. The Blaini group is overlain by a band of black carbonaceous slate, which follows the outcrop of the Blaini beds. The overlying beds consist of a great mass of quartzite and schist, known as the Boileauganj beds; they cover the greater part of Simla and extend to Jutogh. Above these is the Krol group, consisting of carbonaceous slates and carbonaceous and crystalline limestones, with beds of hornblende-garnet schist which probably represent old volcanic ash-beds; they are largely developed in Prospect Hill and Jutogh. Intrusive diorite is found among the lower limestones of the Krol group on the southern slopes of Jutogh. No fossils have been found in any of these rocks, and in consequence their geological age is unknown[1]. **Geology.**

In the *Flora Simlensis* (edited by Mr. W. B. Hemsley), the late Sir Henry Collett has enumerated 1,237 species of trees and flowering plants; but this number would be raised considerably if a botanical census of the smaller Native States **Botany.**

[1] McMahon, 'The Blaini Group and Central Gneiss in the Simla Himālayas,' *Records, Geological Survey of India*, vol. x, part iv; Oldham, 'Geology of Simla and Jutogh,' ibid., vol. xx, part ii; *Manual of Geology of India*, second edition, p. 132 (The Carbonaceous System).

were available, and if the Alpine region in Bashahr including Kanāwār, with which the work does not deal, were added. *Deodār*, pines, and firs, several oaks and maples, a tree-rhododendron, the Himālayan horse-chestnut, and different kinds of buckthorn and spindle-tree (*Rhamnus* and *Euonymus*), and of *Ficus* with *Celtis*, are common; climbers such as ivy, vines, and hydrangea are frequent, with a host of shrubs and herbs belonging to familiar European genera. In Bashahr the Alpine flora is varied and plentiful, while that of Kanāwār is almost purely Tibetan.

Fauna.

The leopard and bear are common in the Simla hills. The *aimu* or serow, the *gural*, the *kākar* or barking-deer, and the musk deer are found. Pheasants of various kinds are found in the higher ranges, while *chikor* and jungle-fowl abound on the lower.

Climate and temperature.

The climate is admirably adapted to the European constitution, and the District has therefore been selected as the site of numerous sanitaria and cantonments. There are four seasons in Simla. The winter lasts from December to February, when the mean maximum temperature ranges from 49° to 44°, while sharp frosts and heavy snow bring the mean minimum sometimes down to 34°. The temperature rises rapidly from February to March, and from March to June hot-season conditions prevail, the mean maximum ranging from 56° in March to 74° in June. The maximum recorded during recent years was 94° in May, 1879. The rainy season extends from July to September. About the middle of September the monsoon currents withdraw, and during October and November fine weather prevails with rapidly falling temperature. Cholera visited Simla, Sabāthu, and Dagshai in 1857, 1867, 1872, and 1875, though one or other station escaped in each visitation. In 1857 the death-rate among Europeans from cholera was 3·5 per 1,000, and in 1867 it was 4·2 per 1,000. Goitre, leprosy, and stone are prevailing endemic diseases, and syphilis is said to be very common amongst the hill people.

Rainfall.

The annual rainfall averages 65 inches at Simla, 46 at Kotgarh, and 40 at Kilba. During the three monsoon months the average fall at Simla is 41 inches.

History.

The acquisition of the patches of territory composing Simla District dates from the period of the Gurkha War in 1815–6. At a very early time the Hill States, together with the outer portion of Kāngra District, probably formed part of the Katoch kingdom of Jālandhar (JULLUNDUR); and, after the disruption of that principality, they continued to be governed by petty

Rājās till the beginning of the nineteenth century. After the encroachments of the Gurkhas had led to the invasion of their dominions in 1815, the British troops remained in possession of the whole block of hill country between the Sārdā and the Sutlej. Kumaon and Dehra Dūn became a portion of British territory; a few separate localities were retained as military posts, and a portion of Keonthal State was sold to the Rājā of Patiāla. With these exceptions, however, the tract conquered in 1815 was restored to the hill chiefs, from whom it had been wrested by the Gurkhas. Garhwāl State became attached to the United Provinces; but the remaining principalities rank among the dependencies of the Punjab, and are known collectively as the SIMLA HILL STATES. From one or other of these the plots composing the little District of Simla have been gradually acquired. Part of the hill over which the Simla hill station spreads was retained by Government in 1816, and an additional strip of land was obtained from Keonthal in 1830. The spur known as Jutogh, 3½ miles from the centre of the station, was acquired by exchange from Patiāla in 1843, as the equivalent of two villages in Bharauli. Kot Khai and Kotgarh, again, fell into our hands through the abdication of the Rāna, who refused to accept charge of the petty State. Sabāthu hill was retained from the beginning as a military fort; and the other fragments of the District have been added at various dates. As a result of some administrative changes made in 1899, Kasauli and Kālka, which till then belonged to the District, were transferred to Ambāla.

The District contains 6 towns and 45 villages. The population at each of the three enumerations was: (1881) 36,119, (1891) 35,851, and (1901) 40,351. It increased by 12·6 per cent. in the last decade. These enumerations having been made in the winter do not give an adequate idea of the summer population, which in Simla town alone was in the season of 1904, 45,587 (municipal limits 35,250, outside area 10,337). The District is divided into the two sub-*tahsīls* of SIMLA-*cum*-BHARAULI and KOT KHAI-*cum*-KOTGARH, with head-quarters at Simla and Kot Khai respectively. The only town of importance is SIMLA, the summer head-quarters of the Government of India; the cantonments have already been mentioned. The village population is almost entirely Hindu, the few Muhammadans which it includes being for the most part travellers. The density of population is 399·5 persons to the square mile. The language spoken in the villages is Pahārī. The people.

The Kanets (9,000) are by far the most important element Castes and occupations. in the rural population. Like all hill tribes, they are a simple-minded orderly people, quiet and peaceful in their pursuits and submissive to authority. The Dāgīs and Kolīs (4,000) are the principal menial tribes. About 39 per cent. of the total population are returned as agricultural.

Christian missions. The Simla Baptist Mission was started in 1865. The American Presbyterian Mission has an out-station at Sabāthu, occupied in 1837, and supports a leper asylum and various schools. The Kotgarh branch of the Church Missionary Society, established in 1840, is an itinerant mission to the hill tribes. The Church Missionary Society also has a branch, with a mission church, in Simla, and the Society for the Propagation of the Gospel Zanāna Mission has a station. In 1901 the District contained 368 native Christians.

General agricultural conditions. Cultivation is carried on in all the lower valleys. Wherever the slope of the ground will permit, fields are built up in terraces against the hill-side, the earth often having to be banked up with considerable labour. The only classification of soil recognized by the people is that depending on irrigation and manure; lands irrigated or manured generally yield two crops in the year, while the poor sloping fields lying at some distance from the homestead, and neither irrigated nor manured, yield only catch-crops either of wheat or barley in the spring or of the inferior autumn grains. Every husbandman has, besides his plot of cultivated land, a considerable area of grass land which is closed to grazing when the monsoon rains begin, and reaped in October and November.

Chief agricultural statistics and principal crops. The area dealt with in the revenue returns of 1903–4 was 77 square miles, of which 36 per cent. were not available for cultivation, 44 per cent. were cultivable waste other than fallows, and 9,956 acres, or 20 per cent., were cultivated. The chief crop of the spring harvest is wheat, which occupied 3,586 acres in that year; the area under barley was 1,534 acres; practically no gram is grown. There were 274 acres under poppy. Maize and rice, the principal staples of the autumn harvest, covered 1,560 and 875 acres respectively. Of millets *chīna* and *mandal* (*Eleusine coracana*), and of pulses *māsh* (*Phaseolus radiatus*) and *kulthi* (*Dolichos uniflorus*), are the most common. Potatoes, hemp, turmeric, and ginger are largely cultivated. Tea is grown at Kotgarh, where 51 acres were picked in 1904. No increase worth mention has occurred

Improvements in agricultural practice. in the cultivated area during the last ten or fifteen years; the demand made by the expansion of Simla town on the surrounding hills being rather for grass, wood, and labour than for agricultural produce. Practically no advances are taken by the people from Government. The cattle are of the small mountain breed. Very few ponies are kept, and the sheep and goats are not of importance. Of the total area cultivated in 1903-4, 745 acres, or nearly 7 per cent., were irrigated by small channels, by which the waters of the hill streams are led to and distributed over the terraced fields.

Cattle, ponies, and sheep.

Irrigation.

Forests.

Forests of timber abound, but only a small part of the Simla Forest division lies within British territory, the greater portion being leased from the Rājās of the various States. In 1903-4 the District contained 13 square miles of 'reserved' and 510 acres of unclassed forest under the Forest department, and 33 square miles of unclassed forest and Government waste lands under the control of the Deputy-Commissioner. It also contains 457 acres of 'reserved' and 2,678 of unclassed forest belonging to the Simla municipality and preserved as the catchment area for the Simla water-supply. In 1903-4 the total revenue of the forests under the Forest department was Rs. 10,000.

Minerals.

The only mineral product of importance is iron, which is found in the Kot Khai tract and smelted roughly by the natives.

Arts and manufactures.

Most of the artistic industries of Northern India are represented in Simla town by artisans who come up for the season, but very few really belong to the District. Shawls are made at Sabāthu by a colony of Kashmīrīs; basket-weaving and some rough iron-smelting at Kot Khai are the only indigenous arts.

Commerce and trade.

There is a considerable trade with Chinese Tibet, which is registered at Wangtu, near Kotgarh. Most of the trade, however, is with Rāmpur in Bashahr. Imports are chiefly wool, borax, and salt; and the exports are cotton piece-goods. The principal imports from the plains are the various articles of consumption required by the residents at Simla.

Railways and roads.

The Kālka-Simla Railway (2 feet 6 inches gauge) has its terminus at Simla, which is also connected with Kālka by a cart-road and a road through Kasauli. The Hindustān-Tibet bridle-road leads from Simla to Rāmpur and Chīni in Bashahr, and a road from Sultānpur in Kulū joins this at Nārkanda, forming the easiest line of communication between Simla and Leh. A road to Mussoorie branches off from that to Rāmpur. Another runs westwards to Bilāspur, whence it leads to Mandī and Suket on one side, and to Nadaun and Kāngra on the other. Sabāthu, Dagshai, Solon, Sanāwar, and Kasauli are all connected by cross-roads.

Famine.

The District has never been visited by famine, the rainfall being constant and the crops always sufficient for the wants of its small agricultural population.

District subdivisions and staff.

The two sub-*tahsīls*, SIMLA-*cum*-BHARAULI and KOT KHAI-*cum*-KOTGARH, are each under a *naib-tahsīldār*. The Deputy-Commissioner, who is also Superintendent of Hill States, is aided by two Assistant or Extra Assistant Commissioners, of whom one is in charge of the District treasury. Simla and the Hill States form an executive division of the Public Works department, and also a Forest division.

Civil justice and crime.

The Deputy-Commissioner as District Magistrate is responsible for the criminal justice of the District; civil judicial work is under a District Judge; and both officers are supervised by the Divisional Judge of the Ambāla Civil Division (who is also Sessions Judge). The District Judge is also Judge of the Small Cause Courts of Simla and Jutogh. The Cantonment Magistrate of Kasauli, Jutogh, Dagshai, Solon, and Sabāthu has jurisdiction throughout the District. He also has the powers of a Small Cause Court in all these cantonments except Jutogh. The station staff officers of Dagshai, Solon, Sabāthu, and Jutogh are appointed magistrates of the third class in the District, but only exercise powers within their own cantonments. The District is free from serious crime.

Land revenue administration.

Little is known of the revenue systems which obtained in the Simla hills before annexation. After various summary settlements made between 1834 and 1856, a regular settlement was made between 1856 and 1859, the rates varying between Rs. 5-14-0 per acre on the best irrigated land, and R. 0-3-8 on the worst kind of 'dry' land. In 1882 the assessment was revised by Colonel Wace; an increase of 36 per cent. in Kotgarh and Kot Khai, and 20 per cent. in Bharauli, was taken, while the assessment of Simla was maintained. The people are prosperous and well-to-do, and the revenue is easily paid. The demand in 1903-4, including cesses, amounted to Rs. 21,000. The average size of a proprietary holding is 1·2 acres.

The collections of land revenue alone and of total revenue are shown below, in thousands of rupees:—

	1880-1.	1890-1.	1900-1.	1902-3.
Land revenue .	14	17	42	17
Total revenue .	1,44	1,81	4,07	3,77

Local and municipal.

SIMLA is the only municipality in the District, though the Deputy-Commissioner exercises the functions of a municipal committee in KASUMPTI, and those of a District board throughout the District. The income of the District fund, derived mainly from a local rate of Rs. 9–5–4 per cent. on the revenue, except in the Simla and Kotgūru *parganas*, where the rate is Rs. 8–5–4, amounted in 1903–4 to Rs. 2,767, and the expenditure to Rs. 1,971, more than half being devoted to education.

The regular police force consists of 315 of all ranks, including 11 cantonment and 128 municipal police, under a Superintendent, who is usually assisted by two inspectors. There are three police stations and one outpost. The District jail at head-quarters has accommodation for 44 male and 12 female prisoners. Police and jails.

The District stands first among the twenty-eight Districts of the Province in respect of the literacy of its population. In 1901 the proportion of literate persons was 17·4 per cent. (22·2 males and 8·5 females). The number of pupils under instruction was 827 in 1880–1, 2,077 in 1900–1, and 1,881 in 1903–4. In the last year the District possessed 12 secondary, 16 primary (public) schools, and 10 elementary (private) schools, with 492 girls in the public and 42 in the private schools. Most of these are in Simla town. The Lawrence Asylum at Sanāwar, founded in 1847 by Sir Henry Lawrence for the children of European soldiers, and now containing some 450 boys and girls, is supported by the Government of India. The total expenditure on education in the District in 1903–4 was 3·7 lakhs, 1·6 lakhs being derived from Provincial revenues and 1·1 lakhs from fees. Education.

Besides the Ripon Hospital and the Walker Hospital in Simla town, the District has one out-lying dispensary at Kot Khai. In 1904 these three institutions treated a total of 26,032 out-patients and 1,365 in-patients, and 2,399 operations were performed. The expenditure was Rs. 68,000, derived almost entirely from municipal funds and sale of securities. Hospitals and dispensaries.

The number of successful vaccinations in 1903–4 was 641, representing 18 per 1,000 of the population. Vaccination is compulsory in Simla town. Vaccination.

[D. C. J. Ibbetson, *Gazetteer* (1883–4, under revision); E. G. Wace, *Settlement Report* (1884); H. F. Blanford, *The Silver Ferns of Simla and their Allies* (1886); Sir H. Collett, *Flora Simlensis* (1902); E. J. Buck, *Simla, Past and Present* (1904).]

Simla-*cum*-**Bharauli**.—These two isolated tracts form a sub-*tahsīl* of Simla District, Punjab, lying between 30° 58′ and 31° 8′ N. and 77° 1′ and 77° 15′ E., with an area of

25 square miles. It is bounded on all sides by the Simla Hill States. The population in 1901 was 29,668, compared with 25,405 in 1891. SIMLA (population, 13,960) is the head-quarters, and there are 35 villages. The land revenue and cesses amounted in 1903–4 to Rs. 7,000. The sub-*tahsīl* lies entirely in the hills.

Kot Khai-*cum*-**Kotgarh** (*Kotguru*).—These two tracts form a sub-*tahsīl* of Simla District, Punjab, lying between 31° 4′ and 31° 22′ N. and 77° 29′ and 77° 43′ E., with an area of 52 square miles. It is bounded on all sides by the Simla Hill States. The population in 1901 was 10,683, compared with 11,581 in 1891. Kot Khai is the head-quarters. There are ten villages, and the land revenue and cesses amounted in 1903–4 to Rs. 14,000. The sub-*tahsīl* lies entirely in the hills, which, in Kot Khai especially, are covered with forests. Kotgarh stands on a spur of the Hātu range overlooking the Sutlej.

Dagshai.—Hill cantonment in Simla District, Punjab, situated in 30° 53′ N. and 77° 4′ E., overlooking the cart-road from Kālka to Simla, and 40·4 miles from the latter station. The land was given in 1847 by the Mahārājā of Patiāla. Dagshai is the head-quarters of a British infantry regiment, and a detachment of British infantry from the Ambāla garrison is quartered there during the summer months. Population (March, 1901), 2,159.

Jutogh.—Hill cantonment in Simla District, Punjab, situated in 31° 7′ N. and 77° 7′ E., about a mile from the western extremity of the station of Simla. The land was acquired from Patiāla in 1843. During the summer months one battery of British mountain artillery and two companies of the regiment quartered at Sabāthu are stationed here. Population (March, 1901), 375.

Kasumpti.—Suburb of Simla station, Punjab. It lies within the territory of the Rājā of Keonthal, but being practically part of Simla was leased from the Rājā in 1884, and constituted a separate municipality, whose functions are performed by the Deputy-Commissioner of Simla. The municipal income and expenditure during the ten years ending 1902–3 averaged Rs. 5,600. The income in 1903–4 was Rs. 6,200, chiefly from taxes on houses and lands; and the expenditure was Rs. 6,300. Population (March, 1901), 170.

Sabāthu (*Subāthu*).—Hill cantonment in Simla District, Punjab, situated in 30° 59′ N. and 77° 0′ E., on a table-land at the extremity of the Simla range, overlooking the Ghambar river. It lies above the old road from Kālka to Simla, 9 miles from Kasauli and 23 from Simla station. Sabāthu has been held as a military post since the close of the Gurkha War in 1816, and a detachment of a British infantry regiment is usually stationed here. There is a small fort above the parade-ground, formerly of military importance, now used as a store-room. The American Presbyterian Mission maintains a school, and an asylum for lepers is supported by voluntary contributions. Elevation above sea-level, 4,500 feet. Population (1901), 2,177.

Simla Town.—Head-quarters of Simla District, Punjab, and summer capital of the Government of India, situated on a transverse spur of the Central Himālayan system, in 31° 6′ N. and 77° 10′ E., at a mean elevation above sea-level of 7,084 feet. It is distant by rail from Calcutta 1,176 miles, from Bombay 1,112 miles, and from Karāchi 947 miles; from Kālka, at the foot of the hills, by cart-road, 58 miles. The population of the town (excluding Jutogh and Kasumpti) was: (1881) 12,305, (1891) 13,034, (1901) 13,960, enumerated in February or March when it was at its lowest. At a municipal census taken in July, 1904, the population within municipal limits was returned at 35,250. Of the population enumerated in 1901, Hindus numbered 8,563, Muhammadans 3,545, Sikhs 346, Christians 1,471, and Jains and Pārsīs 35.

A tract of land, including part of the hill now crowned by the station, was retained by the British Government at the close of the Gurkha War in 1816. Lieutenant Ross, Assistant Political Agent for the Hill States, erected the first residence, a thatched wooden cottage, in 1819. Three years afterwards, his successor, Lieutenant Kennedy, built a permanent house. Officers from Ambāla and neighbouring stations followed the example, and in 1826 the new settlement had acquired a name. A year later, Lord Amherst, the Governor-General, after completing his progress through the North-West on the conclusion of the successful Bharatpur campaign, spent the summer at Simla. From that date the sanitarium rose rapidly into favour with the European population of Northern India. Year after year, irregularly at first, but as a matter of course after a few seasons, the seat of Government was transferred for a few weeks in every summer from the heat of Calcutta to the cool climate of the Himālayas. Successive Governors-General resorted with increasing regularity to Simla during the hot season. Situated in the recently annexed Punjab, it formed an advantageous spot for receiving the great chiefs of Northern India, numbers of whom annually come to Simla to pay their respects. It also presented greater conveniences than Calcutta as a starting-point for the Governor-General's cold-season tour. At first only a small staff of officials accompanied the Governor-General to Simla; but since the administration of Lord Lawrence (1864) Simla has, except in 1874, the year of famine in Bengal, been the summer capital of the Government of India, with its secretariats and head-quarters establishments. Simla was the regular head-quarters of the Commander-in-Chief before it was that of the Governor-General, and now several of the Army head-quarters offices remain in Simla all the year round. The Punjab Government first came to Simla in 1871, and except for a three years' sojourn at Murree from 1873 to 1875 has had its summer head-quarters at Simla ever since.

Under these circumstances, the station has grown with extraordinary rapidity. From 30 houses in 1830 it increased to upwards of 100 in 1841 and 290 in 1866. In February, 1881, the number of occupied houses was 1,141, and in March, 1901, it was 1,847 (including Kasumpti). Schemes for extending the station are under consideration. At present, the bungalows extend over the whole length of a considerable ridge, which runs east and west in a crescent shape, with its concave side pointing southward. The extreme ends of the station lie at a distance of 6 miles from one another. Eastward, the ridge culminates in the peak of Jakko, over 8,000 feet in height, and nearly 1,000 feet above the average elevation of the station. Woods of *deodār*, oak, and rhododendron clothe its sides, while a tolerably level road, 5 miles long, runs round its base. Another grassy height, known as Prospect Hill, of inferior elevation to Jakko and devoid of timber, closes the western extremity of the crescent. The houses cluster thickest upon the southern slopes of Jakko, and of two other hills lying near the western end, one of which, known as Observatory Hill, is crowned by Viceregal Lodge. The church stands at the western base of Jakko, below which, on the south side of the hill, the native town cuts off one end of the station from the other. The eastern portion bears the name of Chota Simla, while the most western extremity is known as Boileauganj. A beautiful northern spur, running at right angles to the main ridge, and still clothed with oak and old rhododendron trees, has acquired the complimentary designation of Elysium. Not far from the western end, two batteries of artillery occupy the detached hill of Jutogh. The exquisite scenery of the neighbourhood has been described in the article on SIMLA DISTRICT.

Simla, besides being the summer head-quarters of the Governments of India and of the Punjab, and of the various Departments of Army head-quarters, is the head-quarters of the Deputy-Conservator of Forests, Simla division, and the Executive Engineer, Simla division, as well as of the ordinary District staff, and the summer head-quarters of the Commissioner of the Delhi Division. A battalion of Volunteers, the 2nd Punjab (Simla) Rifles, is stationed here. There are four churches of the Church of England: Christ Church (the Station Church) opened in 1844, a chapel of ease at Boileauganj, a chapel attached to Bishop Cotton School, and a native church in the bazar. There are also a Roman Catholic cathedral and two convents, and an undenominational church following the Presbyterian form of worship. The Church Missionary Society, the Society for the Propagation of the Gospel Zanāna Mission, and the Baptist Mission have branches in the town. There are two masonic lodges. Simla also contains the United Service Institution of India, and a large club. The Government offices are for the most part accommodated in large blocks of buildings; and a town hall contains a theatre, reading-room, and ball-room. Annandale, the Simla cricket ground and racecourse, has recently been greatly enlarged. The municipality was created in 1850. The income during the ten years ending 1902-3 averaged 4·2 lakhs, and the expenditure 4·1 lakhs. The income in 1903-4 was 5·5 lakhs, chiefly derived from octroi (1·7 lakhs), taxes on houses and lands (1·3 lakhs), municipal property and fines, &c. (Rs. 51,000), and loans from Government (Rs. 39,000). The expenditure of 5·4 lakhs included: general administration (Rs. 57,000), water-supply (Rs. 89,000), conservancy (Rs. 33,000), hospitals and dispensaries (Rs. 36,000), public safety (Rs. 37,000), public works (1 lakh), interest on loans (Rs. 53,000), and repayment of loans (Rs. 64,000). Water is supplied to the station by a system of water-works constructed at a cost of about 6 lakhs, and supposed to be capable of supplying a minimum of 300,000 gallons a day. The supply is not, however, sufficient for the rapidly growing needs of the town. A drainage system is now being extended at a cost of nearly 6 lakhs. The consolidated municipal debt amounts to about 12 lakhs.

The commerce of Simla consists chiefly in the supply of necessaries to the summer visitors and their dependants, but the town is also an *entrepôt* for the trade with China and Tibet mentioned in the article on SIMLA DISTRICT. There are a large number of European shops, and four banks. The chief exports of the town are beer and spirits, there being two breweries and one distillery.

The chief educational institutions are the Bishop Cotton School, a public school for European boys founded by Bishop Cotton in 1866 in thanksgiving for the deliverance of the British in India during the Mutiny of 1857; the Auckland high school for girls; the Christ Church day schools for boys and girls; two convent schools and a convent orphanage; the Mayo Orphanage for European and Eurasian orphan girls; and a municipal high school. The two chief medical institutions are the Ripon and Walker Hospitals, the latter founded in 1902 through the munificence of Sir James Walker, C.I.E., as a hospital for Europeans.

Solon.—Hill cantonment in Simla District, Punjab, situated in 30° 55′ N. and 77° 7′ E., on the southern slope of the Krol mountain, on the cart-road between Kālka and Simla, 30 miles from the latter station. Ground was acquired for a rifle range in 1863–4, and barracks were afterwards erected. Solon is the head-quarters of a British infantry regiment during the hot season. Population (March, 1901), 61.

JULLUNDUR DIVISION

Jullundur Division (*Jālandhar*).—A Division of the Punjab, stretching from the borders of Tibet on the north-east across the valleys of the Upper Beās and the Sutlej to the borders of the Bīkaner desert on the south-west. It lies between 29° 55′ and 32° 59′ N. and 73° 52′ and 78° 42′ E. The Commissioner's head-quarters are at the town of Jullundur. The Division comprises all varieties of scene and soil, from the tumbled masses of the Outer Himālayas, in Kulū and Kāngra, to the fertile plains of Jullundur or the arid tracts of Ferozepore. The population increased from 3,787,945 in 1881 to 4,217,670 in 1891, and to 4,306,662 in 1901. The area is 19,410 square miles, and the density of population 222 persons per square mile, as compared with 209 for the Province as a whole. In 1901 Hindus formed 52 per cent. of the population (2,242,490), while other religions included 1,457,193 Muhammadans, 591,437 Sikhs, 5,562 Jains, 4,176 Buddhists, 33 Pārsīs, and 5,766 Christians (of whom 1,919 were natives). The Division contains five Districts, as shown below:—

District.	Area in square miles.	Population (1901).	Land revenue and cesses (1903–4), in thousands of rupees.
Kāngra	9,978	768,124	10,73
Hoshiārpur	2,244	989,782	16,41
Jullundur	1,431	917,587	17,75
Ludhiāna	1,455	673,097	12,42
Ferozepore	4,302	958,072	14,27
Total	19,410	4,306,662	71,58

Of these, Kāngra lies entirely in the hills, sloping away to the submontane District of Hoshiārpur. The rest lie in the plains. The Division contains 6,415 villages and 37 towns, of which the following had in 1901 a population exceeding 20,000: JULLUNDUR (67,735), FEROZEPORE (49,341), and LUDHIĀNA (48,649). Besides the administrative charge of these British Districts the Commissioner has political control over five Native States, which are shown on the next page, with their area and population.

The total population of these Native States increased from 620,203 in 1881 to 709,811 in 1891, and 745,490 in 1901, of whom 52½ per cent. are Hindus (392,148), while other religions include 245,403 Muhammadans, 105,304 Sikhs, 1,993 Jains, 573 Buddhists, 4 Pārsīs, and 65 Christians. The density of the population is 244 persons per square mile. The States contain 1,053 villages and 12 towns, of which Māler Kotla (21,122) alone exceeds 20,000 persons.

State.	Area in square miles.	Population (1901).
Kapūrthala . . .	630	314,351
Mandī	1,200	174,045
Māler Kotla . . .	167	77,506
Suket.	420	54,676
Farīdkot	642	124,912
Total	3,059	745,490

Ludhiāna, Ferozepore, and Jullundur are the only towns of commercial importance, while Kāngra and Jawāla Mukhi are famous for their religious associations. The Division practically corresponds to the ancient Hindu kingdom of Trigartta. Kāngra fort has been many times besieged, while more recent battle-fields are those of Mudki, Ferozeshāh, Aliwāl, and Sobraon in the first Sikh War (1845).

Boundaries, configuration, and hill and river systems.

Kāngra District.—North-easternmost District of the Jullundur Division, Punjab, lying between 31° 21′ and 32° 59′ N., and 75° 37′ and 78° 42′ E., with an estimated area of 9,978 square miles. It is bounded on the north-west by Chamba State; on the north by Kashmīr territory; on the east by Tibet; on the south-east by Bashahr State; on the south by the Kotgarh villages of Simla District, and by the States of Kumhārsain, Sangri, Suket, Mandī, and Bilāspur; on the south-west by the District of Hoshiārpur; and on the west by Gurdāspur. It stretches eastwards from the plains of the Bāri and Jullundur Doābs across the Himālayan ranges to the borders of Tibet, and comprises two distinct tracts which lie on either side of the Outer Himālayas and present very diverse natural features. Of these two tracts the western block, which constitutes Kāngra proper, is described in this article. This portion, which lies south of the Dhaola Dhār range of the Outer Himālayas, consists of an irregular triangle, whose base lies upon the Hoshiārpur border, while the Native States of Chamba and Mandī constrict its upper portion to a narrow neck, known as Bangāhal, at one point less than

10 miles in width. Beyond this, the eastern block expands once more like an hour-glass, and embraces the Kulū subdivision, which comprises the *tahsīls* of Kulū and Sarāj and the mid-Himālayan cantons of Lāhul and Spiti, each of which merits separate description.

Of the total estimated area of 9,978 square miles, 2,939 are in Kāngra proper. This is the more important part of the District as regards population and cultivation, and comprises two wide and fertile valleys. The Kāngra valley lies between the Dhaola Dhār and the long irregular mass of lower hills which run, almost parallel to the Dhaola Dhār, from north-west to south-south-east. The second valley runs between these hills and the Sola Singhi range, and thus lies parallel to the Kāngra valley. On the north-west the District includes the outlying spurs which form the northern continuation of the Sola Singhi, running down to the banks of the Beās and Chakki, and it also embraces the western slopes of that range to the south. The Kāngra valley is famous for its beauty, the charm lying not so much in the rich cultivation and perpetual verdure of the valley itself as in the constant yet ever-changing view of the Dhaola Dhār, whose snowy peaks rise sheer above the valley, sometimes to 13,000 feet, and present a different phase of beauty at each turn in the road. The *taluka* of Bangāhal forms the connecting link between Kāngra proper and Kulū, and is divided by the Dhaola Dhār into two parts: to the north Barā or Greater Bangāhal, and to the south Chhotā or Lesser Bangāhal.

Although the general trend of the three main ranges which enclose the valleys of Kāngra proper is from north-west to south-east-by-south, its one great river, the Beās, flows through this part of the District from east to west. Entering the centre of its eastern border at the southern head of the Kāngra valley, it runs past Sujānpur Tīra in a narrow gorge through the central mass of hills, flowing westwards with a southerly trend as far as Nādaun. Thence it turns sharply to the north-west, flowing through the valley past Dera Gopipur; and gradually winding westward, it passes between the northern slopes of the Sola Singhi range and the hills forming its continuation to the north. The remainder of the District is singularly devoid of great streams. The Kāngra valley is drained by several torrents into the Beās, the principal of these flowing in deep gorges through the central hills.

Geology.

All three facies of the stratified rocks of the Himālayas are to be found. To the north in Spiti, the Tibetan zone is represented by a series of beds extending in age from Cambrian to Cretaceous; this is separated from the central zone by the granite range between Spiti and Kulū. The rocks of the central zone consist of slates, conglomerate, and limestone, representing the infra-Blaini and overlying systems of the Simla area. Still farther to the south the third or sub-Himālayan zone consists of shales and sandstones (Sirmūr series) of Lower Tertiary age, and sandstones and conglomerates belonging to the Upper Tertiary Siwālik series. The slate or quartz-mica-schist of the central zone is fissile, and of considerable value for roofing purposes; it is quarried at and round Kanhiāra. Gypsum occurs in large quantity in Lower Spiti.[1]

Botany. The main valley is the chief Siwālik tract in the Province, but its flora is unfortunately little known. An important feature is the existence of considerable forests of the *chīr* (*Pinus longifolia*), at comparatively low elevations. Kulū (or the upper valley of the Beās) has a rich temperate flora at the higher elevations; in the lower valleys and in Outer Sarāj (on the right bank of the Sutlej) the vegetation is largely sub-tropical, with a considerable western element, including *Clematis orientalis*, a wild olive, &c. The flora of British LĀHUL, the Chandra-Bhāga or Chenāb valley, and SPITI, are entirely Tibetan.

Fauna. The forests of Kāngra District used to abound in game of all descriptions; and of the larger animals, leopards, bears, hyenas, wolves, and various kinds of deer are still fairly common. Tigers visit the District occasionally, but are not indigenous to these hills. The ibex is found in Lāhul, Spiti, Kulū, and Barā Bangāhal; and the musk deer in Kulū and on the slopes of the Dhaola Dhār. The wild hog is common in many forests in the lower ranges. Of smaller quadrupeds, the badger, porcupine, pangolin, and otter are commonly found. Different species of wild cat, the flying squirrel, hare, and marmot abound in the hills. The bird-life of both hill and plain is richly represented; and though game is not very abundant, many species are found. These include several varieties of pheasant, among them the *monāl* and argus, the white-crested pheasant, and the red jungle-fowl which is common in the lower valleys. Of partridges many species are

[1] Medlicott, 'The Sub-Himālayan Ranges between the Ganges and Rāvi,' *Memoirs, Geological Survey of India*, vol. iii, part ii; Stoliczka, 'Sections across the North-West Himālayas,' *Memoirs, Geological Survey of India*, vol. v, part i; Hayden, 'Geology of Spiti,' *Memoirs, Geological Survey of India*, vol. xxxvi, part i.

found, from the common grey partridge of the plains to the snow partridge of the Upper Himālayas. Quail and snipe sometimes visit the District in considerable numbers. Ducks, geese, and other water-birds are seen upon the Beās at the beginning and end of summer. Fishing is not carried on to any great extent. Thirty-six fisheries are leased to contractors, mostly on the Beās, only a few being in the lower parts of the hill torrents.

Climate and temperature. The mean temperature at Kāngra town is returned as 53° in winter, 70° in spring, 80° in summer, and 68° in autumn. The temperature of the southern portion of Kāngra proper is much higher than this, while that of the inhabited parts of the Dhaola Dhār is about 8° lower. Endemic diseases include fever and goitre. The widespread cultivation of rice, by which the whole Kāngra valley is converted into a swamp, has a very prejudicial effect upon health.

Rainfall. The rainfall varies remarkably in different parts. The average annual fall exceeds 70 inches; along the side of the Dhaola Dhār it amounts to over 100; while 10 miles off it falls to about 70, and in the southern parts to about 50. Barā Bangāhal, which is on the north side of the Dhaola Dhār, has a climate of its own. The clouds exhaust themselves on the south side of the great range; and two or three weeks of mist and drizzle represent the monsoon. The rainfall in Kulū is similarly much less than that of Kāngra proper, averaging from 30 to 40 inches, while Lāhul and Spiti are almost rainless.

The earthquake of 1905. A disastrous earthquake occurred on April 4, 1905. About 20,000 human beings perished, the loss of life being heaviest in the Kāngra and Pālampur *tahsīls*. The station of Dharmsāla and the town of Kāngra were destroyed. The fort and temples at Kāngra received irreparable damage, and many other buildings of archaeological interest were more or less injured.

History. The hills of Kāngra proper have formed for many centuries the dominions of numerous petty princes, all of whom traced their descent to the ancient Katoch (Rājput) kings of Jullundur. According to the mythical chronology of the Mahābhārata, their dynasty first established itself in the country between the Sutlej and the Beās 1,500 years before the Christian era. In the seventh century A.D., Hiuen Tsiang, the Chinese Buddhist pilgrim, found the Jullundur monarchy still undivided. At some later period, perhaps that of the Muhammadan invasion, the Katoch princes were driven into the hills, where Kāngra already existed as one of their chief fortresses; and their restricted dominions appear afterwards to have fallen asunder into several minor principalities. Of these, Nūrpur, Sība, Goler, Bangāhal, and Kāngra are included in Kāngra proper. In spite of constant invasions, the little Hindu kingdoms, secure within their Himālayan glens, long held out against the aggressive Muhammadan power. In 1009 the riches of the Nagarkot temple attracted the attention of Mahmūd of Ghazni, who defeated the Hindu princes at Peshāwar, seized the fort of Kāngra, and plundered the shrine of an immense booty in gold, silver, and jewels. But thirty-five years later the mountaineers rose against the Muhammadan garrison, besieged and retook the fort, with the assistance of the Rājā of Delhi, and set up a facsimile of the image which Mahmūd had carried away. From this time Kāngra does not reappear in general history till 1360, when the emperor Fīroz Tughlak again led a force against it. The Rājā gave in his submission, and was permitted to retain his dominions; but the Muhammadans once more plundered the temple, and dispatched the famous image to Mecca, where it was cast upon the high road to be trodden under the feet of the faithful.

Two hundred years later, in 1556, Akbar commanded in person an expedition into the hills, and succeeded in permanently occupying the fort of Kāngra. The fruitful valley became an imperial demesne, and only the barren hills remained in the possession of the native chiefs. In the graphic language of Akbar's famous minister, Todar Mal, 'he cut off the meat and left the bones.' Yet the remoteness of the imperial capital and the natural strength of the mountain fastnesses encouraged the Rājput princes to rebel; and it was not until after the imperial forces had been twice repulsed that the fort of Kāngra was starved into surrender to an army commanded by prince Khurram in person (1620). On the last occasion twenty-two chieftains promised obedience and tribute, and agreed to send hostages to Agra. At one time Jahāngīr intended to build a summer residence in the valley, and the site of the proposed palace is still pointed out in the lands of the village of Gargari. Probably the superior attractions of Kashmīr, which the emperor shortly afterwards visited, led to the abandonment of his design. At the accession of Shāh Jahān the hill Rājās had quietly settled down into the position of tributaries, and the commands of the emperor were received and executed with ready obedience. Letters patent (*sanads*) are still extant, issued between the reigns of Akbar and Aurangzeb, appointing individuals to various judicial and revenue offices, such as that of *kāzī*, *kānungo*, or *chaudhri*. In some instances the present representatives of the family continue to enjoy privileges and powers conferred on their ancestors by the Mughal emperors, the honorary appellation being retained even where the duties have become obsolete.

During the period of Muhammadan ascendancy the hill princes appear on the whole to have been treated liberally. They still enjoyed a considerable share of power, and ruled unmolested over the extensive tracts which yet remained to them. They built forts, waged war upon each other, and wielded the functions of petty sovereigns. On the demise of a chief, his successor paid the fees of investiture, and received a confirmation of his title, with an honorary dress from Agra or Delhi. The loyalty of the hill Rājās appears to have won the favour and confidence of their conquerors, and they were frequently deputed on hazardous expeditions, and appointed to places of high trust in the service of the empire. Thus in the time of Shāh Jahān (1646), Jagat Chand, Rājā of Nūrpur, at the head of 14,000 Rājputs, raised in his own country, conducted a most difficult but successful enterprise against the Uzbeks of Balkh and Badakhshān. Again, in the early part of the reign of Aurangzeb (1661), Rājā Māndhāta, grandson of Jagat Chand, was deputed to the charge of Bāmiān and Ghorband on the western frontier of the Mughal empire, eight days' journey beyond the city of Kābul. Twenty years later he was a second time appointed to this honourable post, and created a *mansabdār* of 2,000 horse. In later days (1758), Rājā Ghamand Chand of Kāngra was appointed governor of the Jullundur Doāb and the hill country between the Sutlej and Rāvi.

In 1752 the Katoch principalities nominally formed part of the territories ceded to Ahmad Shāh Durrāni by the declining Delhi court. But the native chieftains, emboldened by the prevailing anarchy, resumed their practical independence, and left little to the Durrāni monarch or the deputy who still held the isolated fort of Kāngra for the Mughal empire. In 1774 the Sikh chieftain, Jai Singh, obtained the fort by stratagem, but relinquished it in 1785 to Sansār Chand, the legitimate Rājput prince of Kāngra, to whom the State was thus restored about two centuries after its occupation by Akbar. This prince, by his vigorous measures, made himself supreme throughout the whole Katoch country, and levied tribute from his fellow chieftains in all the neighbouring States. Every year, on fixed occasions, these princes were obliged to attend his court, and to accompany him with their contingents wherever he undertook a military expedition. For twenty years he reigned supreme throughout these hills, and raised his name to a height of renown never attained by any ancestor of his race. He found himself unable, however, to cope with the Sikhs, and two descents upon the Sikh possessions in the plains, in 1803 and 1804, were repelled by Ranjīt Singh. In 1805 Sansār Chand attacked the hill State of Bilāspur (Kahlūr), which called in the dangerous aid of the Gurkhas, already masters of the wide tract between the Gogra and the Sutlej. The Gurkhas responded by crossing the latter river and attacking the Katochs at Mahal Mori, in May, 1806. The invaders gained a complete victory, overran a large part of the hill country of Kāngra, and kept up a constant warfare with the Rājput chieftains who still retained the remainder. The people fled as refugees to the plains, while the minor princes aggravated the general disorder by acts of anarchy on their own account. The horrors of the Gurkha invasion still burn in the memories of the people. The country ran with blood, not a blade of cultivation was to be seen, and grass grew and tigers whelped in the streets of the deserted towns. At length, after three years of anarchy, Sansār Chand determined to invoke the assistance of the Sikhs. Ranjīt Singh, always ready to seize upon every opportunity for aggression, entered Kāngra and gave battle to the Gurkhas in August, 1809. After a long and furious contest, the Mahārājā was successful, and the Gurkhas abandoned their conquests beyond the Sutlej. Ranjīt Singh at first guaranteed to Sansār Chand the possession of all his dominions except the fort of Kāngra and 66 villages, allotted for the support of the garrison ; but he gradually made encroachments upon all the hill chieftains. Sansār Chand died in 1824, an obsequious tributary of Lahore. His son, Anrudh Chand, succeeded him, but after a reign of four years abandoned his throne, and retired to Hardwār, rather than submit to a demand from Ranjīt Singh for the hand of his sister in marriage to a son of the Sikh minister Dhiān Singh. Immediately after Anrudh's flight in 1828, Ranjīt Singh attached the whole of his territory, and the last portion of the once powerful Kāngra State came finally into the possession of the Sikhs.

Kāngra passed to the British at the end of the first Sikh War in 1846, but the commandant of the fort held out for some time on his own account. When the Multān insurrection broke out in April, 1848, emissaries from the plains incited the hill chieftains to revolt ; and at the end of August in the same year, Rām Singh, a Pathānia Rājput, collected a band of adventurers and threw himself into the fort of Shāhpur. Shortly afterwards, the Katoch chief rebelled in the eastern extremity of the District, and was soon followed by the Rājās of Jaswān and Datārpur, and the Sikh priest, Bedi Bikramā Singh. The revolt, however, was speedily suppressed; and after the victory of Gujrāt, the insurgent chiefs received sentence of banishment to Almorā, while Kāngra subsided quietly into a British District. After the outbreak of the Mutiny in 1857, some disturbances took place in the Kulū subdivision; but the vigorous measures of precaution adopted by the local authorities, and the summary execution of the six ringleaders and imprisonment of others on the occasion of the first overt act of rebellion, effectually subdued any tendency to lawlessness. The disarming of the native troops in the forts of Kāngra and Nūrpur was effected quietly and without opposition. Nothing has since occurred to disturb the peace of the District.

Archaeology. Few Districts are richer in antiquities than Kāngra. The inscription at PATHYĀR is assigned to the third century B.C., and that at KANHIĀRA to the second century A.D. It is impossible to fix the date of the famous fort at KĀNGRA TOWN. A temple in it was plundered by Mahmūd of Ghazni in 1009, and an imperfectly legible rock-inscription, formerly outside one of the gates of the fort and now in the Lahore Museum, is assigned to a period at least 400 years earlier. The small temple of Indreswara at Kāngra dates from the ninth century. The beautiful shrine of Baijnāth at Kiragrāma was until recently attributed to the same period, but recent investigations point to a date three or four centuries later. The present temple of Bajreswari Devi at Bhawan, a suburb of Kāngra, is a modern structure, but it conceals the remains of an earlier building, supposed to date from 1440. It has acquired a repute, to which it is not entitled, as the successor of the temple that was sacked by Mahmūd. Remains found at Kāngra prove that it was once a considerable Jain centre. The fort at NŪRPUR, built in the sixteenth and seventeenth centuries, contains a curious wooden temple; and in 1886 a temple of much earlier date, with sculptures unlike anything hitherto found in the Punjab, was unearthed. At Masrur, in the Dehra *tahsīl*, are some rock-temples of uncertain date. In the Kūlu valley, the principal objects of antiquarian interest are the temples of Bajaura. One of them, probably the older of the two, has been partially freed from the débris and boulders in which it was buried. The other, which shows traces of Buddhist workmanship, and dates from the eleventh century, is decorated with carvings of great beauty. The fort and temples of Kāngra town received irreparable damage in the earthquake of 1905.

The people.

The population of the District at the last four enumerations was: (1868) 743,882, (1881) 730,845, (1891) 763,030, and (1901) 768,124, dwelling in 3 towns and 715 villages. It is divided into the seven *tahsīls* of KĀNGRA, NŪRPUR, HAMĪRPUR, DERA GOPIPUR, PĀLAMPUR, KULŪ, and SARĀJ; of which the first five are in Kāngra proper, the two last forming the Kulū subdivision. The head-quarters of these are at the places from which each is named, except in the case of Kulū and Sarāj, whose head-quarters are at Sultānpur and Banjār respectively. The towns are the municipalities of DHARMSĀLA, the head-quarters of the District, KĀNGRA, and NŪRPUR.

The following table shows the chief statistics of population in 1901:—

Tahsīl.	Area in square miles.	Number of Towns.	Number of Villages.	Population.	Population per square mile.	Percentage of variation in population between 1891 and 1901.	Number of persons able to read and write.
Kāngra	429	2	134	126,335	294·5	+ 1·0	7,242
Pālampur	443	...	113	132,955	300·1	+ 2·6	7,477
Kulū and Sarāj	1,342	...	68	119,585	89·1	+ 3·8	3,183
Hamīrpur	601	...	64	161,424	268.6	− 0·8	6,077
Dera Gopipur	516	...	145	125,536	243·3	...	6,397
Nūrpur	525	1	191	102,289	194·8	− 2·6	4,241
District total	9,978	3	715*	768,124	76·9	+ 0·6	34,617

NOTE.—The figures for the areas of *tahsīls* are taken from revenue returns. The total District area is that given in the *Census Report*.

* These figures are taken from the *Census Report* of 1901, but the correct number of villages is now 714, the number for the Kulū and Sarāj *tahsīls* being 67.

In Kāngra proper Hindus number 608,252, or 94 per cent. of the total; Muhammadans, 38,685, or 6 per cent.; and Sikhs, 1,199. Owing to the vast tracts of uncultivable hill-side, the density of the population is only 77 persons per square mile, varying from 300 in the Pālampur *tahsīl* to 65·4 in Kulū; but if the cultivated area alone be considered, the density is 834, almost the highest in the Province. The people speak a great variety of dialects of the group of languages classed together as Pahārī, or the language of the hills.

Castes and occupations.

The distinguishing feature in the population is the enormous preponderance of the Hindu over the Muhammadan element, the latter being represented only by isolated colonies of immigrants, while the mass of the people has preserved its ancient faith in a manner wholly unknown in the plains. This circumstance lends a peculiar interest to the study of the Hindu tribes—their castes, divisions, and customs.

The Brāhmans (109,000) number nearly one-seventh of the total population. Almost without exception, they profess themselves to belong to the great Sāraswat family, but recognize an infinity of internal subdivisions. The first distinction to be drawn is that between Brāhmans who follow, and Brāhmans who abstain from, agriculture. Those who have restricted themselves to the legitimate pursuits of the caste are considered to be pure Brāhmans; while others are no longer held in the same reverence by the people at large.

The Rājputs number even more than the Brāhmans, 154,000 people returning this honourable name. The Katoch Rājās boast the bluest blood in India, and their prejudices and caste restrictions are those of a thousand years ago. The Katoch clan is a small one, numbering only 4,000. The Rāthis (51,000) constitute the higher of the two great agricultural classes of the valley, and are found chiefly in the Nūrpur and Hamīrpur *tahsīls*. The other is the Ghirths (120,000), who are Sūdras by status. In all level and irrigated tracts, wherever the soil is fertile and produce exuberant, the Ghirths abound; while in the poorer uplands, where the crops are scanty and the soil demands severe labour to compensate the husbandman, the Rāthis predominate. It is as rare to find a Rāthi in the valleys as to meet a Ghirth in the more secluded hills. Each class holds possession of its peculiar domain, and the different habits and associations created by the different localities have impressed upon each caste a peculiar physiognomy and character. The Rāthis generally are a robust and handsome race: their features are regular and well-defined; their colour usually fair, and their limbs athletic, as if exercised and invigorated by the stubborn soil upon which their lot is thrown. On the other hand, the Ghirth is dark and coarse-featured; his body is stunted and sickly, and goitre is fearfully prevalent among his race. The Rāthis are attentive and careful agriculturists; their women take little or no part in the labours of the field. The Ghirths predominate in the valleys of Pālam, Kāngra, and Rihlu. They are found again in the Hal Dūn or Harīpur valley, and are scattered elsewhere in every part of the District, generally possessing the richest lands and the most open spots in the hills. They are a most indefatigable and hard-working race.

Among the religious orders in the hills, the most remarkable are the Gosains (1,000), who are found principally in the neighbourhood of Nādaun and Jawāla Mukhi, but are also scattered in small numbers throughout the District. Many of them are capitalists and traders in the hills, and they are an enterprising and sagacious tribe. By the rules of their caste retail trade is interdicted, and their dealings are exclusively wholesale. Thus they possess almost a monopoly of the trade in opium, which they buy up in Kulū and carry down to the plains of the Punjab. They speculate also in *charas*, shawl-wool, and cloth. Their transactions extend as far as Hyderābād in the Deccan, and, indeed, over the whole of India.

Among the hill tribes the most prominent are the Gaddis (9,000). Some have wandered down into the valleys which skirt the base of the Dhaola Dhār, but the great majority live on the heights above. They are found from an elevation of 3,500 or 4,000 feet up to 7,000 feet, above which altitude there is little or no cultivation. They preserve a tradition of descent from refugees from the Punjab plains, stating that their ancestors fled from the open country to escape the horrors of the Musalmān invasions, and took refuge in these ranges, which were at that period almost uninhabited. The term Gaddi is a generic name under which are included Brāhmans and Khattrīs, with a few Rājputs, Rāthis, and Thākurs. The majority, however, are Khattrīs. Besides the Gosains, the commercial castes are the Khattrīs (7,000) and Sūds (6,000). Of the menial castes the Chamārs (leather-workers) are the most numerous (57,000). About 77 per cent. of the population are returned as agricultural.

Christian missions.

The Church Missionary Society has a station at Kāngra town, founded in 1854, with a branch establishment at Dharmsāla; and there is also a station of the Moravian Mission at Kyelang in Lāhul, founded in 1857, and one of the American United Presbyterian Mission in Sarāj. The District in 1901 contained 203 native Christians.

General agricultural conditions.

In the Kāngra *tahsīl* the subsoil rests on beds of large boulders which have been washed down from the main ranges, and the upper stratum, consisting of disintegrated granite mixed with detritus from later formations, is exceedingly fertile. In the neighbourhood of the secondary ranges the soil, though of excellent quality, is less rich, being composed of stiff marls mixed with sand, which form a light fertile mould, easily broken up and free from stones. A third variety of soil is found wherever the Tertiary formation appears: it is a cold reddish clay of small fertility, containing a quality of loose water-worn pebbles; there are few trees in this soil, and its products are limited to gram and the poorer kinds of pulse, while in the first two descriptions the hill-sides are well forested and every kind of crop can be grown. The cultivated area is divided into fields generally unenclosed, but in some parts surrounded by hedges or stone walls. In the Kāngra valley, where rice cultivation prevails, the fields descend in successive terraces levelled and embanked, and where the slope of the land is rapid they are often no bigger than a billiard table; in the west of the Dera and Nūrpur *tahsīls*, where the country is less broken, the fields are larger in size, and the broad sloping fields, red soil, and thick green hedges are charmingly suggestive of a Devonshire landscape. In many parts, and notably in the Kāngra valley, wide areas bear a double harvest.

In Kulū proper the elevation is the chief factor in determining the nature of the crops sown, a few villages lying as low as 3,000 feet and some as high as 9,000. In both Kāngra and Kulū proper the sowing time varies with the elevation, the spring crop being sown from September to December and the autumn crop from April to July. The whole of Lāhul and Spiti is covered with snow from December to the end of April, and sowings begin as soon as the land is clear. For the District as a whole the autumn crop is the most important, occupying 53 per cent. of the area cropped in 1903-4.

Chief agricultural statistics and principal crops.

The land is held, not as in the plains by more or less organized village communities, but by individual holders whose rights originated in a grant by a Rājā of a right of tenancy in the royal domains. In Kulū only forest and cultivable and cultivated lands have been measured, amounting to 1,342 square miles.

The area for which details are available from the revenue records of 1903-4 is 3,857 square miles, as shown below:—

Tahsīl.	Total.	Cultivated.	Irrigated.	Cultivable waste.	Forest.*
Kāngra	429	102	53	37	264
Pālampur	443	125	62	52	239
Kulū	1,054	67	14	12	963
Sarāj	289	58	2	12	206
Hamīrpur	602	234	5	101	205
Dera Gopipur	515	167	26	121	136
Nūrpur	525	170	22	72	208
Total	3,857	923	184	407	2,221

* The revenue returns include only a portion of the forest area.

Wheat is the chief crop of the spring harvest, covering 342 square miles; barley covered 97 square miles, and gram only 42. Maize and rice are the mainstay of the autumn harvest, covering 223 and 164 square miles respectively. Pulses covered 100 square miles. Of the millets, *mandal*, Italian millet, and *chīna* are the most important. There were 6,039 acres under cotton. The tea industry is an important one in Kāngra, and 15 square miles were under tea. There are thirty-four gardens owned by Europeans, and the total output is estimated at over a million pounds of tea annually[1]. Potatoes, introduced shortly after annexation, are now largely cultivated in the higher hills; and the fields round the Gaddi peasants' houses, which formerly produced maize, wheat, or barley hardly sufficient to feed the families which owned them, now yield a very lucrative harvest of potatoes. In Kulū proper poppy is an important crop, covering 2,102 acres. The climate of Kulū is eminently suited for the production of all kinds of European fruits and vegetables, and several European planters do a large trade in pears and apples. In Lāhul barley, wheat, peas, and buckwheat are the principal crops, and in Spiti barley.

Improvements in agricultural practice.

The chief improvements in agriculture have been the introduction of tea and the potato. The cultivated area increased by about 5 per cent. during the ten years ending 1900, owing to the efforts of individuals who have broken up waste land near their holdings; but there is no scope for any considerable increase. Loans from Government are not greatly in demand, the total amount advanced under the Agriculturists' Loans Act during the five years ending 1903–4 amounting to only Rs. 208.

Cattle, ponies, and sheep.

The indigenous breed of cattle is small but strong, and attempts to improve it by the importation of bulls from Hissār have not been satisfactory, the latter being quite unsuited to the climate, and unfitted to mate with the small hill cows. A few bulls of the Dhanni breed have recently been imported from Jhelum District, and it is hoped that they will prove more suitable. The Gūjars are the only people who make a trade of selling milk and *ghī*, and who keep herds of buffaloes; of these some have a fixed abode in the District and pasture their cattle in the adjoining waste, while others move with their herds, spending the summer on the high ranges, and the winter in the woody parts of the low hills. Buffalo

[1] This was written before the earthquake of 1905, which had disastrous effects on the tea industry.

herds are not allowed to move into the Kulū subdivision. The cattle of Lāhul are a cross between the Tibetan yak and the Himālayan breed of cattle. Sheep and goats form in Kāngra proper the chief support of the pastoral tribe of the Gaddis, who move with their flocks, wintering in the forests in the low hills, retreating in the spring before the heat up the sides of the snowy range, and crossing and getting behind it to avoid the heavy rains in the summer. Large flocks are also kept in the Kulū and Sarāj *tahsīls*. There are few ponies in the District and not many mules; the ponies of Kāngra and Kulū proper are poor, but those of Lāhul and Spiti are known for their hardiness and sureness of foot. One pony stallion is maintained by the District board.

Irrigation. Of the total area cultivated in 1903-4, 184 square miles, or nearly 20 per cent., were classed as irrigated. Irrigation is effected entirely by means of channels from the hill streams which lead the water along the hill-sides, often by tortuous channels constructed and maintained with considerable difficulty, and distribute it over the fields. One of these cuts, from the Gaj stream, attains almost the dimensions of a canal, and the channels from the Beās are also important. Most of these works were engineered by the people themselves, and supply only the fields of the villages by which they were constructed; but a few, for the most part constructed by the Rājās, water wider areas, and an organized staff for their maintenance is kept up by the people without any assistance from Government. In Lāhul and Spiti cultivation is impossible without irrigation, and glacier streams are the chief source.

Forests. The forests are of great importance, comprising little short of a quarter of the uncultivated area. Under the Forest department are 87 square miles of 'reserved,' 2,809 of protected, and 296 of unclassed forests, divided into the two Forest divisions of Kāngra and Kulū, each under a Deputy-Conservator. About 4 square miles of unclassed forests are under the Deputy-Commissioner. Several varieties of bamboo cover the lower hills, the bamboo forests occupying an area of 14,000 acres. The produce exported from the Government forests in Kāngra proper is mainly *chīl* (*Pinus longifolia*) and bamboo, while *deodār* is the chief product of Kulū. In 1903-4 the forest revenue was 2·8 lakhs.

Minerals. Valuable metal ores are known to exist both in Kāngra proper and in Kulū; but, owing chiefly to the want of means of carriage, of fuel, and of labour, they are practically unworked. Iron was smelted for some years in the Kāngra hills, and in 1882 there were eight mines yielding 90 maunds of iron a year; but working ceased entirely in 1897. Ores of lead, copper, and antimony have been found, and in Kulū silver and crystal, while gold in small quantities is sometimes washed from the sands of the Beās and Pārbati; coal, or rather lignite, is also produced, but in insignificant quantities. A lease of the old Shigri mines in Lāhul has recently been granted for the purpose of working stibnite and galena. With this exception, the only minerals at present worked are slates and sandstone for building; the Kāngra Valley Slate Company sells 700,000 slates annually, and three other quarries produce together about 83,000, the total value exceeding Rs. 50,000. Several hot mineral springs near Jawāla Mukhi are impregnated with iodide of potassium and common salt. Hot springs occur at several places in Kulū, the most important being at Manikarn in the Pārbati valley, and at Bashist near the source of the Beās.

Arts and manufactures.

The District possesses no factories except for the manufacture of tea, and there are but few hand industries. The cotton woven in the villages holds its own against the competition of European stuffs, but the industry is seriously handicapped by the small quantity of cotton grown locally. Nūrpur used to be a seat of the manufacture of *pashmīna* shawls, but the industry has long been declining; silver ornaments and tinsel printed cloths are made at Kāngra. Baskets are made in the villages of Kāngra proper and Kulū, and blankets in Kulū, Lāhul, and Spiti.

Commerce and trade.

The principal exports to the plains consist of rice, tea, potatoes, spices, opium, blankets, *pashmīna*, wool, *ghī*, honey, and beeswax; in return for which are imported wheat, maize, gram and other pulses, cotton, tobacco, kerosene oil, and piece-goods. The chief centres of the Kāngra trade in the plains are Hoshiārpur, Jullundur, Amritsar, and Pathānkot. There is a considerable foreign trade with Ladākh and Yārkand through Sultānpur in Kulū, the exports being cotton piece-goods, indigo, skins, opium, metals, manufactured silk, sugar, and tea, and the imports ponies, borax, *charas*, raw silk, and wool. The principal centres of internal trade are KĀNGRA, Pālampur, SUJĀNPUR TIRA, JAWĀLA MUKHI, and NŪRPUR.

Roads.

No railway traverses the District, though one from Pathānkot to Pālampur was contemplated. The principal roads are the Kāngra valley cart-road, which connects Pālampur and Pathānkot, with a branch to Dharmsāla, and the road from Dharmsāla, via Kāngra, to Hoshiārpur and Jullundur. The former is partly metalled and a mail tonga runs daily. A road runs from Pālampur to Sultānpur in Kulū over the Dulchi pass (7,000 feet), which is open summer and winter, going on to Simla. Another road runs through Kulū, and, crossing the Rohtang pass (13,000 feet) into Lāhul, forms the main route to Leh and Yārkand. Ladākh is reached from Lāhul over the Bārā Lācha (16,250 feet). The usual route to Spiti is through Lāhul and over the Kanzam pass. The total length of metalled roads is 56 miles, and of unmetalled roads 1,073 miles. Of these, all the metalled and 353 miles of the unmetalled roads are under the Public Works department, and the rest under the District board.

Famine. Famine is unknown, the abundance of the rainfall always assuring a sufficient harvest for the wants of the people, and the District was classed by the Irrigation Commission of 1903 as secure. The area of crops matured in the famine year 1899–1900 amounted to 69 per cent. of the normal.

District subdivisions and staff. The District is in charge of a Deputy-Commissioner, aided by three Assistant or Extra Assistant Commissioners, one of whom is in charge of the Kulū subdivision and one in charge of the District treasury. Kāngra proper is divided into the five *tahsīls* of Kāngra, Nūrpur, Hamīrpur, Dera Gopipur, and Pālampur, each under a *tahsīldār* and a *naib-tahsīldār*; the Kulū subdivision, consisting of the Kulū *tahsīl* under a *tahsīldār* and a *naib-tahsīldār*, the Sarāj *tahsīl* under a *naib-tahsīldār*, and the mountainous tracts of Lāhul and Spiti, which are administered by local officials termed respectively the *thākur* and *nono*. The *thākur* of Lāhul has the powers of a second-class magistrate and can decide small civil suits; the *nono* of Spiti deals with all classes of criminal cases, but can only punish with fine. The criminal administration of Spiti is conducted under the Spiti Regulation I of 1873. Two officers of the Forest department are stationed in the District.

Civil justice and crime. The Deputy-Commissioner as District Magistrate is responsible for the criminal justice of the District, under the supervision of the Sessions Judge of the Hoshiarpur Sessions Division. The subdivisional officer of Kulū hears appeals from the *tahsīldār* of Kulū, the *naib-tahsīldār* of Sarāj, the *thākur* of Lāhul, and the *nono* of Spiti. Civil judicial work in Kāngra proper is under a District Judge, under the Divisional Judge of the Hoshiārpur Civil Division. In Kulū the subdivisional officer generally exercises the powers of a District Judge, and the Deputy-Commissioner of Kāngra, if a senior official, is appointed Divisional Judge of Kulū. The only

Munsif sits at Kāngra, while there are seven honorary magistrates, including the Rājās of Lambāgraon, Nādaun, and Kutlehr in Kāngra proper. The District is remarkably free from serious crime. Civil suits are chiefly brought to settle questions of inheritance involving the rights *inter se* of widows, daughters, and distant agnatic relatives.

Land revenue administration. The revenue history and conditions differ radically from those of the Punjab proper. The hill states, now combined into Kāngra District, were merely a number of independent manors. Each Rājā enjoyed full proprietary rights, and was a landlord in the ordinary sense of the word, leasing his land at will to individual tenants on separate *pattas* or leases. This fact explains the two prominent characteristics of the revenue system, its variety and its continuity. Just as, on the one hand, the intimate local knowledge of the Rājā and his agent enabled them to impose a rent fixed or fluctuating, in cash or kind, according to the resources and the needs of each estate, so, on the other hand, the conquerors, Mughal and Sikh, imposed their tribute on the several Rājās, leaving them to devise the source and the method of collection. The Mughals, it is true, reserved certain areas as imperial demesnes, and here they introduced *chaudhris* who were responsible both for the collection of the revenue and for the continued cultivation of the soil. They made no change, however, either in assessments or in methods of collection. The Rājās depended on their land-agents (called variously *kārdār*, *hākim*, *amīn*, or *palsara*), and these in turn had under them the *kotwāls*, who were responsible for eight or ten villages apiece. The village accountant, or *kāyāt*, the keeper of the granary (*kotiāla*), with constables, messengers, and forest watchers, made up the revenue staff. Every form of assessment was to be found, from the division of the actual produce on the threshing-floor to permanent cash assessments.

Ranjīt Singh was the first to interfere with the Rājās' system. He appointed a *nāzim*, or governor of the hill territory, who managed not only the revenue, but the whole expenditure also. Under him were *kārdārs*, who either farmed the revenue of their *parganas*, or accepted a nominal salary and made what they could. The ancient system, however, has survived the misrule of the Sikhs. Every field in the valley is clearly defined; and the proportion of its produce payable to Government is so firmly established that, even under the present cash assessments, it forms the basis on which the land revenue is distributed among individual cultivators.

The first act of the British officers was to apply the village system of the plains to the Kāngra valley. The tenants, with their private cultivating rights, became the proprietary body, with joint revenue-paying responsibilities. The waste, formerly regarded as the property of the Rājās, became attached to the village communities as joint common land. The people thus gained the income arising from the common land, which had previously been claimed by the state.

A summary settlement was made in 1846 by John Lawrence, Commissioner of the Jullundur Doāb, and Lieutenant Lake, Assistant Commissioner, based entirely on the Sikh rent-roll with a reduction of 10 per cent. The first regular settlement, made in 1849, reduced the demand on 'dry' land by 12 per cent., maintaining the former assessment on 'wet' land. A revised settlement, made in 1866–71, had for its object the preparation of correct records-of-rights; but the assessment was not revised until 1889–94, when an increase of 19 per cent. was announced. Rates varied from Rs. 1–5–4 to R. 0–14–7. The total demand in 1903–4, including cesses, was about 10·7 lakhs. The average size of a proprietary holding is 2 acres. There are a number of large *jāgīrs* in the District, the chief of which are Lambāgraon, Nādaun, and Dādo Sība in Kāngra proper, and *wazīri* Rūpi in Kulū.

A system of forced labour known as *begār* was in vogue in the Kāngra hills until recently, and dates back from remote antiquity. All classes who cultivate the soil were bound to give, as a condition of the tenure, a portion of their labour for the exigencies of state. Under former dynasties the people were regularly drafted and sent to work out their period of servitude wherever the ruler chose. So inveterate had the practice become that even artisans, and other classes unconnected with the soil, were obliged to devote a portion of their time to the public service. Under the British Government the custom was maintained for the conveyance of travellers' luggage and the supply of grass and wood for their camps, but was practically abolished in Kāngra proper in 1884, and in Kulū in 1896.

The collections of land revenue alone and of total revenue are shown below, in thousands of rupees :—

	1880–1.	1890–1.	1900–1.	1903–4.
Land revenue . .	6,19	6,57	7,35	7,50
Total revenue . .	8,76	9,92	10,57	10,55

Local and municipal.

The District contains three municipalities, DHARMSĀLA, KĀNGRA, and NŪRPUR. Outside these, local affairs are managed by a District board, and by the local boards of Kāngra, Nūrpur, Dera Gopipur, Hamīrpur, and Pālampur, the areas under which correspond with the *tahsīls* of the same names. The chief source of their income is the local rate, a cess of Rs. 8–5–4 per cent. on the land revenue in Kāngra, of Rs. 10–6–8 in Kulū, and of Rs. 7–8–10 in the *wazīri* of Spiti. The expenditure in 1903–4 was Rs. 1,45,000, public works being the principal item.

Police and jails.

The District is divided into 15 police stations, 13 in Kāngra proper and 2 in Kulū, and the police force numbers 412 men, with 901 village watchmen. The Superintendent usually has three inspectors under him. The jail at head-quarters contains accommodation for 150 prisoners. It has, however, been condemned as unsafe, and a new one is in contemplation.

Education.

Kāngra stands seventh among the twenty-eight Districts of the Province in respect of the literacy of its population. In 1901 the proportion of literate persons was 4·5 per cent. (8·4 males and 0·3 females). The number of pupils under instruction was 2,591 in 1880–1, 3,881 in 1890–1, 3,341 in 1900–1, and 3,852 in 1903–4. In the last year the District contained 6 secondary and 57 primary (public) schools for boys and 9 for girls, and 3 advanced and 20 elementary (private) schools, with 266 girls in the public and 38 in the private schools. The principal educational institution is the high school at Pālampur, founded in 1868, and maintained by the District board. There are 5 middle schools for boys, of which 2 are Anglo-vernacular; 3 of these are maintained by the District board and 2 are aided. The total expenditure on education in 1903–4 was Rs. 35,000, of which Rs. 7,000 was derived from fees, Rs. 4,000 from Government grants, and Rs. 2,000 from subscriptions and endowments. Municipalities contributed Rs. 4,000, and the balance was paid out of District funds.

Hospitals and dispensaries.

Besides the civil hospital at Dharmsāla, the District has eight outlying dispensaries. In 1904, 739 in-patients and 101,159 out-patients were treated, and 1,769 operations were performed. The expenditure was Rs. 19,000, of which Rs. 14,000 as met from District and Rs. 3,000 from municipal funds.

Vaccination.

The number of successful vaccinations in 1903–4 was 40,825, representing the high proportion of 53 per 1,000 of the population. Vaccination is compulsory in Dharmsāla.

[H. A. Rose, *District Gazetteer of Kāngra Proper* (1905); A. Anderson, *Settlement Report of Kāngra Proper* (1897); A. H. Diack, *Gazetteer of Kulū, Lāhul, and Spiti* (1897), *The Kulū Dialect of Hindī* (1896), and *Settlement Report of Kulū Subdivision* (1898).]

Kāngra Tahsīl.—*Tahsīl* of Kāngra District, Punjab, lying between 31° 54′ and 32° 23′ N. and 76° 8′ and 76° 41′ E., with an area of 429 square miles. The *tahsīl* lies entirely in the hills, between the Dhaola Dhār, which separates it from Chamba on the north, and the Kālidhār hills on the south. The Bāngangā and the Gaj flow through it in a south-westerly direction to join the Beās. The main range of the Dhaola Dhār and its spurs are in many places covered with forest. The population in 1901 was 126,335, compared with 125,138 in 1891. It contains the towns of Dharmsāla (population, 6,971) and Kāngra (4,746), the head-quarters; and 134 villages, of which Kanhiāra and Chari are of archaeological interest. The land revenue and cesses amounted in 1903–4 to 2 lakhs.

Pālampur Tahsīl.—*Tahsīl* of Kāngra District, Punjab, lying between 31° 49′ and 32° 29′ N. and 76° 23′ and 77° 2′ E., with an area of 443 square miles. The *tahsīl* lies wholly in the hills, extending from the Dhaola Dhār on the north to the Beās on the south. It is traversed by a number of tributaries of the Beās. The population in 1901 was 132,955, compared with 129,599 in 1891. It contains 113 villages, of which Pālampur is the head-quarters. The land revenue and cesses amounted in 1903–4 to 2 lakhs.

Kulū Subdivision.—Subdivision of Kāngra District, Punjab, lying between 31° 21′ and 32° 59′ N. and 76° 49′ and 78° 42′ E. It consists of the Kulū and Sarāj *tahsīls* and the *wazīris* of Lāhul and Spiti. The head-quarters are at Nagar, a residence of the old Rājās.

Lāhul.—Himālayan *wazīri* or canton of the Kulū subdivision of Kāngra District, Punjab, lying between 32° 8′ and 32° 59′ N. and 76° 49′ and 77° 47′ E., with an area of 2,255 square miles. The population (1901) is only 7,205, or less than 4 persons per square mile. It is separated from Kāngra and Kulū proper on the south, and from Spiti on the east, by two mountain ranges which give off southwards the Beās and Rāvi and eastwards the Spiti river, a tributary of the Sutlej; they culminate at their junction in the Shurgan Tunga or Deo-Tibba peak (21,000 feet). On the north Lāhul is bounded by the Ladākh province of Kashmīr, and on the west by Chamba State. The Chandra and Bhāga streams rise on the Bāra

Lācha, or pass (16,500 feet), in the north, and, flowing at first in almost opposite directions, unite at Tandi, whence the combined waters of the Chandra-Bhāga or Chenāb flow into Chamba. Between the two rivers, an isolated mass of mountains attains still greater dimensions, consisting of one almost unbroken ice-field, with, at rare intervals, impassable barriers of naked rock. South of the highest peak, 21,415 feet above the sea, a glacier stretches downward for 12 miles; while east and west the hills, though slightly inferior in elevation, still reach the limits of the snow-line, and flank the valley on every side, except along the narrow outlet of the Chenāb. In such a waste of rock and ice, villages can be planted only in a few comparatively favoured spots, among the lower valleys of the Chandra and Bhāga, from Old Koksar on the former to Dārcha on the latter river. The remainder of Lāhul is completely uninhabited, except for a few weeks in summer, when the Kāngra shepherds bring up their flocks for pasturage. Picturesque knots of houses, however, nestle here and there in sheltered nooks, amid green irrigated fields made beautiful by the exquisite Himālayan flora. The summer is almost rainless, but there is heavy snowfall in winter, the whole country being covered from December to April. The mean temperature at Kardang in the valley of the Bhāga is 29° in December and 59° in June. The inhabitants of the valleys of the Chandra and Bhāga are Buddhists, and of that of the united Chandra-Bhāga Hindus. The inhabited portions of the Lāhul valley have an estimated elevation of 10,000 feet above sea-level. Kangser, the highest village, stands at a height of 11,345 feet. The principal villages are KYELANG and Kardang on opposite sides of the Bhāga, on the trade route between the Rohtang pass from Kulū and the Bārā Lācha leading into Ladākh.

The Lāhul valley is mentioned as early as the seventh century in the itinerary of Hiuen Tsiang, the Chinese Buddhist pilgrim, who notices it under the name of Lo-hu-lo, as a district lying north-east of Kulū. In the earliest times, it probably formed a dependency of the Tibetan kingdom; and on the disruption of that kingdom in the tenth century, it seems to have been included in the principality of Ladākh. We have no information to show the period at which it became independent, though reasons have been adduced for believing that that event preceded the reorganization of Ladākh about 1580. An epoch of native rule under petty chiefs (Thākurs) ensued, during which the various local families appear to have paid tribute to Chamba. Four or five of these families have survived to the present day, and are still in possession of their original territories, which they hold in *jāgīr*, subject to the payment of tribute or *nazarāna*. About the year 1700, the supremacy passed to Kulū, in the reign of Budh Singh, son of Rājā Jagat Singh, a contemporary of Shāh Jahān and Aurangzeb. Thenceforward, Lāhul followed the fortunes of Kulū, until they passed together under British rule in 1846. Out of a total area of 2,255 square miles, less than 5 square miles are returned as under cultivation. Barley forms the principal crop, but wheat grows in the lower glens. Cultivation depends entirely on small irrigation canals, constructed and kept in repair by the village landowners. The grain produced does not suffice for local consumption, and is supplemented by imports from Kulū. The Lāhulīs hold in their hands the trade between Ladākh and Central Asia on the one hand, and Kulū and the Punjab on the other. Collecting the merchandise from the north at Patseo, a few miles north of Dārcha, where a large encampment of traders from Ladākh, Central Asia, Tibet, and Kulū is formed, they pass annually into Kulū at the end of summer, driving their ponies and donkeys, goats and sheep, laden with *pashm* or shawl-wool, borax, and cloth; while on their return journey they bring metal vessels, sugar, rice, wheat, tobacco, pepper, ginger, and turmeric.

The Lāhulīs keep only a few sheep and goats, as the snow lies too long and too deep in the winter for the flocks to live out of doors as they do in Ladākh. For a very long time, therefore, the upper ends of the main valleys, which are uninhabited, and the grounds high above the villages in the inhabited parts, have been utilized by the shepherds of Kāngra, Chamba, and Kulū. The snow begins to disappear in these places about the beginning of June; the shepherds do not ordinarily enter Lāhul before the end of that month, and they leave it again early in September, by which time the frost is keen, and the rainy season in the Outer Himālayas has come to an end. In the fine dry climate of Lāhul the sheep escape foot-rot and other diseases which constantly attack flocks kept during the rains on the southern slopes of the Outer Himālayas. The sheep arrive wretchedly thin, but by the time they are ready to leave are in splendid condition.

Lāhul is administered by the Assistant Commissioner of Kulū, under whom Thākur Amar Chand, a descendant of the old rulers and a magistrate of the second class and a Munsif, exercises considerable local influence. The land revenue, as reassessed in 1891, amounts to Rs. 4,916.

Spiti (*Piti*).—Himālayan *wazīri* or canton of the Kulū subdivision of Kāngra District, Punjab, lying between 31° 42′ and 32° 59′ N. and 77° 26′ and 78° 42′ E., with an area of 2,155 square miles. The population (1901) is only 3,231, or less than 2 persons per square mile. Spiti is completely hemmed in by lofty mountain ranges of an average elevation of 18,000 feet, which divide it from Lāhul on the west, Bashahr on the south, Great Tibet on the east, and Ladākh on the north. It includes the upper valley of the Spiti river, which, rising in the Western Himālayas, at about 16,000 feet, flows south-east into Tibet, and thence enters Bashahr at an elevation of 11,000 feet, and ultimately finds its way into the Sutlej; the upper valley of the Pāra river, which also enters Tibet and then falls into the Spiti, their united streams equalling the Sutlej in volume at their junction with that river; the valley of the Isamp, whose waters fall into the Indus; and the eastern half of the Upper Chandra valley. Of these four valleys, only that of the Spiti is inhabited. The most important tributary of the Spiti river is the Pīn, which rises in the angle of the mid-Himālayan and Mānirang ranges, and joins the Spiti after a course of 45 miles, a short distance above Dankar, the principal village of the valley. The mountains of Spiti are yet more lofty than in the neighbouring country of Lāhul. In the Outer Himālayas is one peak of 23,064 feet, and many along the whole line are considerably over 20,000. Of the mid-Himālayas, two peaks exceed 21,000 feet, and in the southern range the Mānirang is 21,646 feet in height. From the main ranges transverse lines of mountains project far into the valley on either side, leaving in many cases only a narrow gorge, through which flows the Spiti river. Even these minor ranges contain peaks the height of which in many instances exceeds 17,000 feet. The mean elevation of the Spiti valley is 12,981 feet above sea-level. Several villages are situated at an elevation of upwards of 13,000 feet, and one or two as high as 14,000 feet. Scarcely any vegetation clothes the bare and rocky mountain slopes; yet the scenery is not devoid of a rugged grandeur, while the deep and peculiar colour of the crags often gives most picturesque effects to the otherwise desolate landscape. Red and yellow predominate in the rocks, contrasting finely with the white snowy peaks in the background and the deep blue sky overhead. The villages stand for the most part on little flat plateaux, above the cliffs of the Spiti river; and their white houses, dotted about among the green cultivated plots, afford rare oases in the desert of stony débris which covers the mountain sides. There is practically no rainfall, but the snowfall in winter is very severe. The mean temperature of the Upper Spiti valley is 17° in January and 60° in July.

The history of Spiti commences with the first formation of the kingdom of Ladākh, after which event the valley seems for a while to have been separated from that government, and attached to some other short-lived Tibetan principality. About 1630 it fell into the hands of Sinagi Nāmgyāl, king of Ladākh, who allotted it to his third son, Tenchbog. Soon afterwards, it became a part of the Guge principality, which lay to the east, in what is now Chinese Tibet; and it did not again come under the dominion of Ladākh till about 1720. In that year the king of Ladākh, at the conclusion of a war with Guge and Lhāsa, married the daughter of the Tibetan commander, and received Spiti as her dower. Thenceforward the valley remained a province of Ladākh; but, from its remote and inaccessible position, it was practically left for the most part to govern itself, the official sent from Leh usually disappearing as soon as the harvest had been gathered in and the scanty revenue collected. Spiti was always liable to be harried by forays; but the people, being an unwarlike race, preferred the payment of blackmail to the armed defence of their barren valley.

After the Sikhs annexed the neighbouring principality of Kulū in 1841, they dispatched a force to plunder Spiti. The inhabitants, in accordance with their usual tactics, retreated into the mountains, and left their houses and monasteries to be plundered and burnt. The Sikhs retired as soon as they had taken everything upon which they could lay hands, and did not attempt to annex the valley to Kulū, or to separate it from Ladākh. In 1846, however, on the cession of the trans-Sutlej States to the British after the first Sikh War, the Government, with the object of securing a road to the wool districts of Chāng Thāng, added Spiti to Kulū, giving other territory in exchange to the Mahārājā of Kashmīr. In the same year, Captain (afterwards Sir A.) Cunningham and Mr. Vans Agnew demarcated the boundary between Spiti, Ladākh, and Chinese Tibet. Since that date, the valley has been peacefully governed by the native hereditary ruler or *nono*, supported by the Assistant Commissioner of Kulū. The *nono* is assisted by five elders or *gatpos*, and practically manages all the internal affairs of the canton in accordance with the Spiti Regulation (No. I of 1873). The British codes are not applicable to Spiti, unless specially extended.

The people are Tartars by race and Buddhist by religion, and extensive monasteries often crown the lower ridges overhanging the villages. The principal and richest monastery is at Ki; that of Tangiūt receives members of the *nono's* family; while at Dankhar is a less important monastery. The monks of these three all belong to the celibate Gelukpa sect. At Pīn is a smaller monastery, belonging to the Dukhpa sect, which permits marriage, and the descendants of its inmates still practise singing and dancing as allowed by their founder. Talo contains an extensive *lāmāsarai*, built by the gods in a single night. As this was not constructed by Buddhists, it does not rank as a monastery (*gonpa*). It possesses a remarkable collection of nearly life-size idols, and one of Chamba 16 feet high. Unlike the *gonpas*, which are all built on lofty eminences, it stands on a level spot and contains about 300 monks. The monasteries, which are endowed by tithes of grain (*pun*) levied from every field, are extensive buildings, standing apart from the villages. In the centre of the pile are the public rooms, consisting of chapels, refectories, and storerooms; round them are clustered the separate cells in which the monks live. Each landholder's family has its particular *tāsha* or cell in the monastery to which it is hereditarily attached; and in this all the monks of the family—uncles, nephews, and brothers—may be found living together. The monks ordinarily mess in these separate quarters, and keep their books, clothes, cooking utensils, and other private property in them. Some mess singly, others two or three together. A boy monk, if he has no uncle to look after him, is made a pupil to some old monk, and lives in his cell; there are generally two or three chapels—one for winter, another for summer, and a third perhaps the private chapel of the abbot or head *lāma*.

The monks meet in the chapel to perform the services, which ordinarily consist of readings from the sacred books; a sentence is read out and then repeated by the whole congregation. Narrow carpets are laid lengthways on the floor of the chapel, one for each monk; each has his allotted place, and a special position is assigned to the reader; the abbot sits on a special seat of honour, raised a little above the common level of the floor; the chapels are fine large rooms, open down the centre, which is separated from the sides by rows of wooden pillars. At the far end is the altar, consisting of a row of large coloured figures, the images of the *avaṭār* or incarnation of Buddha of the present age, of the coming *avatār* of the next age, and of the gurūs Rimbochi, Atishā, and other saints. In some chapels a number of small brass images from China are ranged on shelves on one side of the altar, and on the other stands a bookcase full of the sacred books, which are bundles of loose sheets printed from engraved slabs in the fashion which has been in use in Tibet for many centuries. The walls all round the chapel are painted with figures of male or female divinities, saints, and demons, or hung with pictures on cloth with silk borders; similar pictures on cloth are also suspended across the chapel on ropes. The best pictures are brought from Great Tibet as presents to the monastery by monks who return from taking the degree of *gelang* at Lhāsa, or who have been living for some years in one of the monasteries of that country. They are painted in a very quaint and conventional style, but with considerable power of drawing and colouring. Huge cylindrical prayer-wheels, which spin round at a slight touch of the finger, stand round the room, or on each side of the altar. In the storerooms among the public property are kept the dresses, weapons, and fantastic masks used in the *chām* or religious plays; also the drums and cymbals, and the robes and quaint head-dresses worn by the superior monks at high ceremonies.

The refectory or public kitchen is only used on the occasion of certain festivals, which sometimes last several days, during which special services are performed in the chapels. While these festivals last, the monks mess together, eating and drinking their fill of meat, barley, butter, and tea. The main source from which the expense of these feasts is met is the *pun*, which is not divided among the monks for everyday consumption in the separate cells. To supply his private larder, each monk has, in the first place, all he gets from his family in the shape of the produce of the '*lāma's* field' or otherwise; secondly, he has his share, according to his rank in the monastery, of the *bula* or funeral offerings and of the harvest alms; thirdly, anything he can acquire in the way of fees for attendance at marriages or other ceremonies or in the way of wages for work done in the summer. The funeral offerings made to the monasteries on the death of any member of a household consist of money, clothes, pots and pans, grain, butter, &c.; the harvest alms consist of grain collected by parties of five or six monks sent out on begging expeditions all over Spiti by each monastery just after the harvest. They go round from house to house in full dress, and standing in a row, chant certain verses, the burden of which is—'We are men who have given up the world, give us, in charity, the means of life; by so doing you will please God, whose servants we are.' The receipts are considerable, as each house gives something to every party. On the death of a monk, his private property, whether kept in his cell or deposited in the house of the head of the family, goes not to the monastery, but to his family—first to the monks of it, if any, and in their default, to the head or *kāng chimpa*. When a monk starts for Lhāsa, to take his degree, his *kāng ch*[illegible] and to give him what he can towards the expenses [illegible]ney, but only the well-to-do men can afford it. Many who go to Lhāsa get high employment under the Tibetan government, being sent to govern monasteries, &c., and remain there for years; they return in old age to their native monastery in Spiti, bringing a good deal of wealth, of which they always give some at once to their families.

The cultivated area in Spiti is only 2 square miles. The principal crop is barley. The exports include cereals, manufactured cloth, yaks, and yaks' tails. The imports comprise salt, tobacco, madder, and tea from Lhāsa; wool, turquoises, amber, and wooden vessels from Kanāwār; coarse cloth, dyes, and soda from Ladākh; and iron from Mandī and Kanāwār. A handsome breed of ponies is imported from Chamarti. There are no police, schools, or dispensaries. The shortest route to Spiti from Kulū is over the Hamta pass (14,200 feet), up the Chandra valley over the Great Shigri glacier, and then over the Kanzam La or pass (14,900 feet), so that this is beyond question the most inaccessible part of the British dominions in India. DANKHAR is the chief village and the head-quarters of the *nono*.

Kulū Tahsīl.—*Tahsīl* in the Kulū subdivision of Kāngra District, Punjab, lying between 31° 50′ and 32° 26′ N. and 76° 56′ and 77° 33′ E., with an area of 1,054 square miles. The population in 1901 was 68,954, compared with 64,630 in 1891. It contains 42 villages, including NAGAR, the head-quarters of the subdivision, and SULTĀNPUR, the *tahsīl* head-quarters. The land revenue and cesses amounted in 1903–4 to Rs. 82,000.

The *tahsīl* nominally includes the *wazīris* of LĀHUL and SPITI. Kulū proper is divided into four *wazīris* (Parol, Lag Sari, Lag Mahārājā, and Rūpi), all lying in the upper basin of the Beās. The Beās basin is enclosed by very high mountain ranges, those which separate it from the Spiti, Chenāb, and Rāvi valleys having a mean elevation of 18,000 feet. The lower range, which separates it from the Sutlej valley, lies in the Sarāj *tahsīl*. The Beās rises in the north of Kulū proper at the crest of the Rohtang pass, 13,326 feet above the sea, and after a course of 60 miles enters Mandī State at an elevation of 3,000 feet; its chief tributaries are the Pārbati, Sainj, and Tīrthan, whose valleys comprise the greater part of the eastern half of the tract. The Beās is bridged by the Duff Dunbar steel-rope suspension bridge at Shamsi, by another suspension bridge between Larji and Bujaura, and by wooden cantilever bridges (*sānghas*) at five other places. Its course presents a succession of magnificent scenery, including cataracts, gorges, precipitous cliffs, and mountains clad with forests of pine, towering above the tiers of *deodār* on the lower rocky ledges. Of the total area of Kulū proper, the cultivated portion amounts to only 60 square miles, and the rest is forest and desolate mountain waste above the limit of tree growth. The highest villages are not more than 9,000 feet above the sea, and the average elevation of the cultivated and inhabited parts is about 5,000 feet. The annual rainfall varies from 31 to 42 inches; in winter the ground is covered with snow for days or months together according to its situation, though snow does not usually lie long at heights of less than 6,000 feet; 55 feet of snow have been measured on the Sirīkand pass (15,000 feet), but the Dulchi pass, over which lies the main road to Kāngra, is generally open all the year round.

The little principality of Kulū formed one of the eleven original Rājput States between the Rāvi and the Sutlej, and probably belonged to some of the minor Katoch dynasties, offshoots from the great kingdom of JULLUNDUR. Hiuen Tsiang, the Chinese Buddhist pilgrim, visited it in the seventh century; and local legends preserve the names of eighty-seven princes who ruled successively in this remote mountain valley. Authentic history, however, first recognizes Kulū in the fifteenth century, when Rājā Sudh Singh, whom tradition places seventy-fourth in descent from the original founder of the dynasty, ascended the throne. His descendants ruled the valley till the beginning of the nineteenth century, their annals being wholly confined to the usual Indian record of court intrigues, assassinations, and dynastic quarrels. When the Gurkhas broke out from their home in Nepāl, and conquered all the country up to the banks of the Sutlej, they found Bikramā Singh upon the throne of Kulū. Like the other neighbouring chieftains, Bikramā Singh paid tribute to the invaders for his cis-Sutlej territory, as well as to Sansār Chand, the Katoch prince of KĀNGRA, for Kulū itself. In 1809, however, Ranjīt Singh, called in by Sansār Chand, made himself master of the hills, and levied tribute from the young Rājā of Kulū, Ajīt Singh, an illegitimate son of Bikramā Singh. Three years later, the Sikhs demanded an annual payment of Rs. 50,000; and on the Rājā's refusal, marched upon his capital of Sultānpur and sacked his palace. Ajīt Singh at length bribed the Sikhs to withdraw, by paying them all the money he could collect. After the expulsion of the Gurkhas, the Rājā became a feudatory of the British for the cis-Sutlej tract. In 1840 General Ventura led a Sikh force against the neighbouring State of Mandī; after conquering which, one of his lieutenants attacked Kulū, on the pretext of hostile dispositions. The Rājā made no resistance, and allowed himself to be taken prisoner; but the brutal discourtesy shown him by his captors roused the hereditary loyalty of the hillmen. A secret muster took place; and as the invaders marched out of Sarāj by the Basleo pass, the hillmen fell upon them in a narrow ravine, rescued their prince, and massacred the Sikhs almost to a man. Ajīt Singh retired across the Sutlej to his fief of Shāngri, which he had held from the British Government since the expulsion of the Gurkhas, and so placed himself beyond reach of vengeance from Lahore. A Sikh army soon after marched into Sarāj, but found it completely deserted, the inhabitants having fled into the inaccessible forests on the mountain-sides. Accordingly they handed over the country in farm to the Rājā of Mandī, leaving a garrison in Kulū to enforce their supremacy. Ajīt Singh died at Shāngri in 1841; and the Sikhs made over *wazīri* Rūpi to his first cousin, Thākur Singh, while Shāngri remained in the hands of another relative. In 1846, at the close of the first Sikh War, the Jullundur Doāb, with the adjoining Hill States, passed into the power of the British; and Kulū, with Lāhul and Spiti, became a *tahsīl* of the new Kāngra District. Government confirmed Thākur Singh in his title of Rājā, and gave him sovereign powers within *wazīri* Rūpi. On his death in 1852, his son, Gyān Singh, of doubtful legitimacy, obtained the inferior title of Rai, with half the land and no political powers. The resumed half has since been restored, with certain reservations in favour of Government. In 1892 the present Rai, Megh Singh, succeeded to the *jāgīr* of Rūpi, with some modifications. The Rai is an honorary magistrate and Munsif in his *jāgīr*.

Sarāj Tahsīl.—*Tahsīl* in the Kulū subdivision of Kāngra District, Punjab, lying between 31° 21′ and 31° 50′ N. and 77° 17′ and 77° 47′ E., with an area of 289 square miles. It is bounded on the north-east by Spiti, on the east and south by Bashahr and the Simla Hill States, and on the west by Suket and Mandī. The population in 1901 was 50,631, compared with 50,551 in 1891. It contains 25 villages, including Banjār, the head-quarters. The *tahsīl* is divided into the two *wazīris* or cantons of Inner and Outer Sarāj, separated from each other by the Jalori ridge, which has an average elevation of 12,000 feet. Inner Sarāj lies in the Beās basin, and in physical aspects resembles the KULŪ *tahsīl.* Outer Sarāj belongs to the Sutlej valley, and the country slopes down from the Jalori ridge to the river, which is here only 3,000 feet above the sea. The land revenue and cesses amounted in 1903–4 to Rs. 46,000.

Hamīrpur Tahsīl.—*Tahsīl* of Kāngra District, Punjab, lying between 31° 25′ and 31° 58′ N. and 76° 9′ and 76° 44′ E., with an area of 602 square miles. It is bounded on the south by Bilāspur State and on the east by Mandī State, and lies between the Beās on the north and the Sutlej on the south. The north-east corner is rugged and inaccessible, and the Sola Singhi range runs along the south-west border. Broken masses of hills cover almost all the *tahsīl*, but in some parts there are stretches of fairly level ground. The population in 1901 was 161,424, compared with 162,705 in 1891. It contains 64 villages, including Hamīrpur, the head-quarters, and SUJĀNPUR TIRA. The land revenue and cesses amounted in 1903–4 to 1·9 lakhs.

Dera Gopipur.—*Tahsīl* of Kāngra District, Punjab, lying between 31° 40′ and 32° 13′ N. and 75° 55′ and 76° 32′ E., with an area of 515 square miles. It extends from the high ridge on the north-east, which separates it from the Kāngra *tahsīl*, across the valley of the Beās, to the Jaswān range on the south-west, which separates it from Hoshiārpur. The rich plain which lies between the Gaj and the Beās is irrigated by cuts from the Gaj and the Buner. The population in 1901 was 125,536, compared with 125,512 in 1891. It contains 145 villages, including Dera Gopipur, the head-quarters, HARĪPUR, and JAWĀLA MUKHI. The land revenue and cesses amounted in 1903–4 to 2 lakhs.

Nūrpur Tahsīl.—*Tahsīl* of Kāngra District, Punjab, lying between 31° 58′ and 32° 24′ N. and 75° 37′ and 76° 9′ E., with an area of 525 square miles. It consists of a confused mass of hills, mostly forest-clad, and is bounded on the north-east by the Dhaola Dhār range which divides it from Chamba. The population in 1901 was 102,289, compared with 104,895 in 1891. The town of NŪRPUR (population, 4,462) is the head-quarters, and there are 191 villages. The land revenue and cesses amounted in 1903-4 to 1·6 lakhs.

Lambāgraon.—Estate in Kāngra District, Punjab, with an area of 125 square miles. The present holder, Rājā Jai Chand, is a descendant of the ancient Katoch kings of Kāngra. On the annexation of that District, Ludar Chand, a nephew of the famous Rājā Sansār Chand, was confirmed in his *jāgīr*; and in 1851, on the death of Sansār Chand's grandson Parmodh Singh, Partāb Chand, the eldest son of Ludar Chand, was acknowledged as head of the Katoch family and received the title of Rājā. The *jāgīr* has descended by primogeniture to the present Rājā, who is an honorary magistrate and Munsif in his *jāgīr*, and a Major in the 37th Dogras. In 1904 he was nominated a member of the Punjab Legislative Council. His *jāgīr* consists of 20 villages and brings in about Rs. 40,000 a year.

Nādaun Estate.—Estate in the Hamīrpur *tahsīl* of Kāngra District, Punjab, with an area of 87 square miles. Its holder is a grandson of the famous Rājā Sansār Chand, and is thus, like LAMBĀGRAON, a representative of the ancient Katoch dynasty of Kāngra. Jodhbīr Chand, Sansār Chand's illegitimate son, gave his two sisters in marriage to Ranjīt Singh, and was created a Rājā, Nādaun, the northern portion of the Katoch dominions, being conferred upon him. Rājā Jodhbīr Chand remained loyal during the Katoch insurrection of 1848, and as a reward his *jāgīr* (then worth Rs. 26,270 a year) was confirmed to him by the British Government on annexation. His son Pirthi Singh earned the Order of Merit for his services during the Mutiny. In 1868 the Rājā was made a K.C.S.I. and received a salute of 7 guns. The estate in 1890 devolved by primogeniture on Narindar Chand, the present Rājā. His *jāgīr* consists of 14 villages and brings in about Rs. 35,000 a year. He is an honorary magistrate and Munsif.

Goler.—Estate in the Dera *tahsīl* of Kāngra District, Punjab, with an area of 25 square miles. Legend says that Hari Chand, the Katoch Rājā of Kāngra, fell into a dry well when hunting. He was missed by his companions, and believed to have been killed, so his heir was proclaimed king. When rescued from the well Hari Chand could not reclaim his throne, but he founded Harīpur as the capital of a separate principality, called Goler. Under Shāh Jahān, Rājā Rūp Chand was employed in subduing a Katoch rebellion; and under Akbar, Kunwar Mān

Singh and his son Jagat Singh played a great part, the fief of Kābul being bestowed on the former in 1585. Under the Sikhs, Rājā Bhūp Singh was at first an ally of Ranjīt Singh against the Katoch kings, but in 1812 his territory was confiscated. On the British annexation, his son, Shamsher Singh, obtained a *jāgīr* of 20 villages. This grant is now held by his nephew, Rājā Raghunāth Singh, and its revenue amounts to about Rs. 26,000.

Baijnāth (the ancient Kīra-grāma).—Village in Kāngra District, Punjab, situated in 32° 2′ N. and 76° 43′ E., 11 miles east of Pālampur. Population (1901), 6,555. Two Hindu temples here bear inscriptions in the ancient Sārada character, giving the pedigree of the Rājānakas or princes of Kīragrāma, who were kinsmen and feudatories of the kings of Jālandhara or Trigartta. The date of the inscriptions is disputed. Formerly attributed to the early part of the ninth century, they are assigned by a recent investigator to a period three or four centuries later. One of these temples was seriously damaged by the earthquake of April 4, 1905.

[*Epigraphia Indica*, vol. i, pp. 97–119; *Journal, Royal Asiatic Society*, 1903, p. 16, note.]

Bangāhal.—Canton of the Outer Himālayas, in Kāngra District, Punjab, lying between 32° 15′ and 32° 29′ N. and 76° 49′ and 76° 55′ E., and separating Kāngra proper from the outlying subdivision of Kulū. The Dhaola Dhār divides the canton into two main valleys, the northern of which is called Barā or Greater Bangāhal, and the southern Chhotā or Lesser Bangāhal. The former, with an area of 290 square miles, contains but a single village, with a few Kanet families, 8,500 feet above sea-level. The Rāvi river has its source in this valley, and is a considerable stream before it issues into the State of Chamba, the mountains rising steeply from its banks into peaks of 17,000 and even 20,000 feet, covered with glaciers and perpetual snow. The lower ravines contain much pine forest, and the upper slopes afford grazing for large flocks. Chhotā Bangāhal is again divided by a range, 10,000 feet in height, into two glens. In the eastern, which contains eighteen scattered hamlets of Kanets and Dāghis, rises the Ul river; and the western, known as Bīr Bangāhal, resembles the higher valleys of Kāngra proper.

Bārā Lācha.—Mountain pass in the Lāhul canton of the Kulū subdivision of Kāngra District, Punjab, situated in 32° 49′ N. and 77° 28′ E., on the Central Asian trade route over the Western Himālayas, from Dārcha in Lāhul to the

Rupshu country in Ladākh. The pass is 16,500 feet above the sea; but though the ascent on both sides is easy, it can be crossed by laden yaks and ponies only during the summer. The Chandra and Bhāga rivers (Chenāb) rise on either side of the pass.

Chari.—Village in Kāngra District, Punjab, situated in 32° 8′ N. and 76° 27′ E., near Kot Kāngra. Population (1901), 2,597. In 1854 the foundations of a temple with an inscribed pedestal (since lost) were discovered here. The inscription contained the formula of the Buddhist faith; and from the figures of seven boars carved on the front of the pedestal, it appeared that the statue to which it belonged was that of the Ṭāntric goddess Vajra-varāhi.

[*Archaeological Survey Reports*, vol. v, p. 177.]

Dankhar.—Ancient capital of the Spiti canton, in the Kulū subdivision of Kāngra District, Punjab, situated in 32° 5′ N. and 78° 15′ E., and still the head-quarters of the *nono* or hereditary governor of SPITI. Population (1901), 713. It is picturesquely placed on a spur 12,700 feet above sea-level, which juts out into the main valley, and ends in a precipitous cliff overtopped by a rude fort, now the property of Government, and flanked by a monastery of Buddhist monks of the Gelukpa order. The inhabitants are pure Tibetans.

Dhaola Dhār.—Mountain chain in Kāngra District, Punjab, formed by a projecting fork of the Outer Himālayan range, marking the boundary between the Kāngra valley and Chamba. The main system here rises steeply from the low lands at its base, unbroken by any minor hills, to an elevation of 13,000 feet above the valley beneath. The chain is formed by a mass of granite, which has forced its way through the superincumbent sedimentary rocks, and crowns the summit with its intrusive pyramidal crests, too precipitous for the snow to find a lodging. Below, the waste of snowfields is succeeded by a belt of pines, giving way to oaks as the flanks are descended, and finally merging into a cultivated vale watered by perennial streams. The highest peak attains an elevation of 15,956 feet above sea-level, while the valley has a general height of about 2,000 feet. Dharmsāla, the head-quarters of Kāngra District, lies on a southern spur of the Dhaola Dhār. The name means the 'white' or rather 'grey range.'

Dharmsāla.—Hill station, the head-quarters of Kāngra District, Punjab, situated in 32° 13′ N. and 76° 11′ E. Population (1901), 6,971. Dharmsāla lies on a spur of the Dhaola Dhār, 16 miles north-east of Kāngra, in the midst of wild and picturesque scenery. It originally formed a subsidiary cantonment for the troops stationed at Kāngra, and was first occupied as a station in 1849, when a site was required for a cantonment to accommodate a native regiment which was being raised in the District. A site was found on the slopes of the Dhaola Dhār, in a plot of waste land, upon which stood an old Hindu resthouse, or *dharmsāla*, whence the name adopted for the new cantonment. The civil authorities, following the example of the regimental officers, and attracted by the advantages of climate and scenery, built themselves houses in the neighbourhood of the cantonment; and in 1855 the new station was formally recognized as the head-quarters of the District. Before the earthquake of 1905, the upper part of the station, which rises to a height of about 7,112 feet, contained the European houses, the station church, and the officers' mess and lines of the 1st Gurkhas, together with the public gardens, post office, and two bazars, the Forsythganj and McLeodganj. The public offices, a bazar, and a few European houses made up the lower station, as low as 4,500 feet. The 1st battalion of the 1st Gurkhas used to be stationed here, but was moved to the upper station in 1894–5. The upper and lower stations are connected by numerous roads, one of which, at a gentle gradient and passable by carts, is 5 miles in length. The other roads are steep paths down the hill-side. In the upper station are three level roads cut in parallel lines along the side of the hill, the lowest of which, called the Mall, is about 2 miles in length, ending on one side at the public gardens and the Gurkha mess, and on the other at the McLeodganj bazar, so called in honour of the late Sir D. McLeod, formerly Lieutenant-Governor of the Province. It is connected with the upper roads by paths, most of which are steep ascents, up the face of the hill. The public gardens, which were, before the earthquake, laid out with much taste in lawns and terraces, contained a valuable collection of indigenous and imported trees and shrubs, and were overlooked by the Assembly Rooms, a handsome building comprising a public hall, a library and reading-room, and a billiard-room. The church was beautifully situated in a recess of the mountain. The churchyard contains a monument erected to the memory of Lord Elgin, who died here in 1863. Immediately above the station rises a hill known as Dharmkot, the summit of which is a favourite resort. There are also some picturesque waterfalls, within a walk, at Bhāgsu Nāth. The station was destroyed by the earthquake of April 4, 1905, in which 1,625 persons perished at Dharmsāla alone, including 25 Europeans and 112 of the Gurkha garrison. It has been decided to retain Dharmsāla as the head-quarters of the District, and new offices will shortly be erected. In the upper station, many of the barracks and officers' houses have already been rebuilt. The garrison consists of two battalions of Gurkhas.

The scenery of Dharmsāla is peculiarly grand. The station occupies a spur of the Dhaola Dhār itself, and is well wooded with oak and other forest trees. Above it the pine-clad mountain-side towers towards the loftier peaks, which, covered for half the year with snow, stand out jagged and scarred against the sky. Below, in perfect contrast, lies the luxuriant Kāngra valley, green with rice-fields and a picture of rural quiet. Much has been done of late years to render Dharmsāla more accessible. Cart-roads connect it with the plains, via Hoshiārpur on the south and via Pathānkot on the west; there is a tonga service from Pathānkot, and a telegraph line connects Dharmsāla and Pālampur with Amritsar and Lahore. The rainfall is very heavy, and the atmosphere is peculiarly damp during the three months of the rainy season. The average fall is 126 inches, by far the highest figure reached at any point of observation in the Province. In January, February, and March also, storms are very frequent. Trade is confined to the supply of necessaries for the European residents, officials, and their servants. The Dal fair, held at the Dal Lake, close to the cantonment, in September, is largely attended by the Gaddis and other Hindus. The famous temple of Bhāgsu Nāth is 2 miles to the east of the station. The municipality was created in 1867. The income during the ten years ending 1902–3 averaged Rs. 9,700, and the expenditure Rs. 9,500. In 1903–4 the income and expenditure were Rs. 13,100 and Rs. 11,700 respectively. The chief source of income is taxes on houses and lands and the sale of trees and grass. The income and expenditure of cantonment funds during the ten years ending 1902–3 averaged Rs. 2,900.

Harīpur.—Old fort and village in the Dera Gopipur *tahsīl* of Kāngra District, Punjab, situated in 32° N. and 76° 10′ E., on the banks of the Bāngangā stream, 9 miles south-west of Kāngra fort. Population (1901), 2,243. It was founded in the thirteenth century by Hari Chand, the Katoch Rājā of Kāngra, whose brother had succeeded to the throne of Kāngra on the Rājā's supposed death. Hari Chand had really fallen into a dry well while out hunting; and when he was extricated and heard of his brother's accession, he resigned his right and founded the town and fort of Harīpur opposite Goler, making it the head-quarters of a separate principality. It continued to be the capital of the State until 1813, when it was treacherously seized by Ranjīt Singh. A younger branch of the Goler family still lives in the town, but the elder branch resides in the neighbouring village of Nandpur, and Harīpur is now of little importance.

Jawāla Mukhi.—Ancient site in the Dera Gopipur *tahsīl* of Kāngra District, Punjab, situated in 31° 52′ N. and 76° 20′ E., on the road from Kāngra town to Nādaun, at the foot of a precipitous range of hills, which form the northern limit of the Beās valley. Population (1901), 1,021. Once a considerable and opulent town, as its ruins testify, it is now chiefly famous for the temple of the goddess Jawāla Mukhi, 'she of the flaming mouth,' which lies in the Beās valley and is built over some natural jets of combustible gas, believed to be a manifestation of the goddess Devi. Another legend avers that the flames proceed from the mouth of the demon Jālandhara, the Daitya king whom Siva overwhelmed with mountains, and who gives his name to the Jullundur Doāb. The building is modern, with a gilt dome and pinnacles, and possesses a beautiful folding door of silver plates, presented by the Sikh Rājā, Kharak Singh. The interior of the temple consists of a square pit about 3 feet deep, with a pathway all round. In the middle the rock is slightly hollowed out about the principal fissure, and on applying a light the gas bursts into a flame. The gas escapes at several other points from the crevices of the walls of the pit. It collects very slowly, and the attendant Brāhmans, when pilgrims are numerous, keep up the flames with *ghī*. There is no idol of any kind, the flaming fissure being considered as the fiery mouth of the goddess, whose headless body is said to be in the temple of Bhawan. The income of the temple, which is considerable, belongs to the Bhojki priests. At one time the Katoch Rājās appear to have appropriated the whole or the greater part of the receipts; and under Muhammadan rule a poll-tax of one anna was levied upon all pilgrims. The number of these in the course of the year is very great; and at the principal festival in September–October as many as 50,000 are said to congregate, many coming from great distances. Another festival of scarcely less importance takes place in March. Six hot mineral springs, impregnated with common salt and iodide of potassium, are found in the neighbourhood. A *sarai* erected by the Rājā of Patiāla is attached to the temple, and there are also eight *dharmsālas* or resthouses for travellers. The temple was slightly damaged by the earthquake of April 4, 1905. The municipality was abolished in 1885.

Kāngra Town (*Nagar Kot*[1], *Kot Kāngra*).—Town in Kāngra District, Punjab, formerly the head-quarters of the District and still the head-quarters of the Kāngra *tahsīl*, situated in 30° 5′ N. and 76° 16′ E. Population (1901), 4,746. Lying on the northern slope of the low ranges which run through the centre of the District, it faces Dharmsāla and commands a fine view of the Kāngra valley. In its lower suburb (called Bhawan) was the temple of Devi Bajreshri, whose gilded cupola was, until the earthquake of 1905, a conspicuous landmark, and which contained a late Sanskrit inscription of about 1430 dedicated to Jawāla Mukhi and mentioning Sansār Chand I, the Katoch king of Kāngra. On the lofty ridge south of and above the town stood Kot Kāngra or 'the fort,' surrounded on three sides by inaccessible cliffs. In its highest part were the dwellings and temples of the old Katoch kings of Kāngra. The town, with the fort and temples, was destroyed by the earthquake of April 4, 1905, in which 1,339 lives were lost in the town. Seven Europeans were among the killed.

Kāngra has from time immemorial been a stronghold of the Katoch Rājās. Firishta, in his introductory chapter narrating the exploits of a former king of Kanauj, who overran the hills from Kumaun to Kashmīr, subduing 500 petty chiefs, distinctly alludes to the Rājā of Nagarkot. The riches of the temple attracted the attention of Mahmūd of Ghazni, who in 1009 took the fort and plundered the temple, carrying off, it is said, 700,000 golden *dīnārs*, 700 *mans* of gold and silver plate, 200 *mans* of pure gold in ingots, 2,000 *mans* of unwrought silver, and 20 *mans* of jewels, including pearls, corals, diamonds, and rubies. The temple plundered by Mahmūd was probably situated within the fort and was not the temple of Devi in Bhawan, as has been supposed. Thirty-five years later the place is said to have been recaptured after a siege of four months by the Hindu princes under the Rājā of Delhi. Kāngra submitted to Fīroz Shāh in 1360, who again plundered the temple; and in 1388 prince Mahmūd Tughlak, when a fugitive from Delhi, found an asylum here till called to the throne in 1390. Kāngra was permanently garrisoned under the Mughals,

[1] Nagarkot appears to have been the name of the town and Kāngra of the fort.

and should have passed to Ahmad Shāh Durrāni in the cession of 1752, but the governor, Saif Alī Khān, refused to surrender it, and maintained himself in the fort for twenty years. After his death in 1774, Sansār Chand, Rājā of Kāngra, laid siege to the fort and, being unable to reduce it, called in the Sikh leader Jai Ṣingh, Kanhaya, to whom, and not to the Rājā, it surrendered. Jai Singh, however, withdrew in 1785, and Sansār Chand possessed himself of the fort. Kāngra was besieged from 1806 to 1809 by the Gurkhas, who were only repelled by the aid of Ranjīt Singh. In return for his services the Mahārājā appropriated for himself the fort, which was held by the Sikhs when the Jullundur Doāb was ceded to the British in 1846. The governor refusing to surrender, the fort was invested and capitulated after a two months' siege. The head-quarters of the District were first fixed at Kāngra, but were transferred to Dharmsāla in 1855.

The temple of Devi above mentioned was one of the most ancient and famous shrines in Northern India, and was largely resorted to by pilgrims from the plains at the great festival held in March, April, and October. The municipality was created in 1867. The income during the ten years ending 1902–3 averaged Rs. 5,500, and the expenditure Rs. 5,300. In 1903–4 the income was Rs. 5,600, chiefly derived from octroi; and the expenditure was Rs. 6,500. Its position on the Kāngra valley cart-road makes it an important centre of internal trade. The chief educational institution is an Anglo-vernacular middle school maintained by the Church Missionary Society, which has a station here. There is a Government dispensary.

Kanhiāra.—Village in the District and *tahsīl* of Kāngra, Punjab, situated in 32° 12′ N. and 76° 24′ E., 4 miles east of Dharmsāla. Population (1901), 3,446. The name is a corruption of Krishna-yashas-ārāma according to Cunningham, or possibly Krishna-vihāra. An inscription cut on two massive granite blocks in the Brahmi and Kharoshthi scripts found here, would appear to prove the existence of a Buddhist monastery (*ārāma*) at this place in the second century A.D. Slate is quarried at and round the village. Kanhiāra suffered seriously from the earthquake of April 4, 1905.

[*Archaeological Survey Reports*, vol. v, p. 177, and *Epigraphia Indica*, vol. vii, p. 116.]

Kyelang (*Kailang*).—Chief village in the Lāhul canton of the Kulū subdivision of Kāngra District, Punjab, situated in 32° 35′ N. and 77° 4′ E., on the right bank of the river

Bhāga, about 4 miles above its junction with the Chandra, and on the main trade route between the Rohtang and Bārā Lācha passes. Population (1901), 388. A post office is maintained here during the summer months, and the village has for many years been a station of the Moravian Mission, which maintains a school and a dispensary. It also contains the court-house of the Thākur of Lāhul, and an observatory 10,087 feet above sea-level.

Nādaun Town.—Petty town in the Hamīrpur *tahsīl* of Kāngra District, Punjab, situated in 31° 46′ N. and 79° 19′ E., on the left bank of the Beās, 20 miles south-east of Kāngra town, and head-quarters of the *jāgīr* of Rājā Amar Chand, son of the late Rājā Sir Jodhbīr Chand. Population (1901), 1,426. It was once a favourite residence of Rājā Sansār Chand, who built himself a palace at Amtar, on the river bank, one mile from the town, where he held his court during the summer.

Nagar.—Village in the Kulū subdivision and *tahsīl* of Kāngra District, Punjab, situated in 32° 7′ N. and 77° 14′ E., on the left bank of the Beās river, 14 miles north of Sultānpur, the *tahsīl* head-quarters. Population (1901), 591. Nagar was the capital of the Kulū Rājās, whose ancient residence crowns an eminence looking down upon the river from a height of about 1,000 feet, and is now used as the residence of the Assistant Commissioner, Kulū. It was greatly damaged by the earthquake of April 4, 1905. It commands a magnificent view, and itself forms a striking feature of the village. Nagar is also the head-quarters of the Kulū Forest division and of the Assistant Engineer, Kulū, and contains a post and telegraph office.

Nirmand.—Village in the Kulū subdivision of Kāngra District, Punjab, situated in 31° 26′ N. and 77° 38′ E. Population (1901), 1,150. Near it stands an ancient temple dedicated to Parasu Rāma, in which is deposited a copperplate deed of grant in Sanskrit, probably of 612–3 A.D., recording the assignment of the village of Sulisagrāma by a king Samudrasena to the Brāhmans who studied the Atharva Veda at Nirmanda, a temple dedicated to the god Triparantaka or Siva under the name of Mihiresvara or the Sun-god.

[*Corpus Inscriptionum Indicarum*, vol. iii, p. 286.]

Nūrpur Town.—Head-quarters of the *tahsīl* of the same name in Kāngra District, Punjab, situated in 32° 18′ N. and 75° 55′ E., 37 miles west of Dharmsāla on the road to Pathānkot, on the western side of a hill which rises sharply from the plain. Population (1901), 4,462. Nūrpur was anciently called Dhameri (or Temmery in the old travellers), and was renamed Nūrpur in honour of the emperor Nūr-ud-dīn Jahāngīr. The fort, begun by one of the local Rājās, was finished in the time of Aurangzeb. It contains a curious wooden temple, and excavations made in 1886 revealed the existence of a stone temple of much earlier date than the fort. The carvings on the temple are of a kind unknown elsewhere in the Province. The Rājās of Nūrpur are known to Muhammadan historians as the *zamīndārs* of Mau and Paithān, and Nūrpur became their capital after the destruction of Mau by Shāh Jahān. They were loyal feudatories of the Mughal empire, but stoutly defended their territory against the Sikhs. Ranjīt Singh finally reduced Nūrpur in 1815.

The principal inhabitants are Rājputs, Kashmīris, and Khattrīs, the last being descendants of fugitives from Lahore, who fled from the exactions of the later Muhammadan rulers. The Kashmīris settled in Nūrpur in 1783, driven from their country by famine; and were reinforced by others from a like cause in 1833. They carried with them the national manufacture of their native valley, that of shawls of *pashmīna* wool, and made the town famous for the production of these and other woollen cloths. Owing to the collapse in the shawl trade which followed the Franco-Prussian War, the trade has dwindled, and is now confined to the manufacture on a small scale of shawls and woollen fabrics of an inferior description. Nūrpur was for long the chief town of the District, in both size and commercial importance; but owing to the decay of its chief industry, shawl-weaving, it is now much reduced, though still a centre of local trade. The municipality was created in 1867. The income and expenditure during the ten years ending 1902–3 averaged Rs. 10,200. In 1903–4 the income was Rs. 9,700, chiefly derived from octroi; and the expenditure was Rs. 11,300. The town possesses a Government dispensary, and the municipality maintains an Anglo-vernacular middle school.

Pathyār.—Village in Kāngra District, Punjab, 12 miles south-east of Dharmsāla. Population (1901), 1,983. An inscription of a primitive type, cut in both the Brahmi and Kharoshthi scripts, in letters of remarkable size, recording the dedication of a tank, probably in the third century B.C., has been found here. The village suffered serious damage in the earthquake of April 4, 1905.

[*Epigraphia Indica*, vol. vii, p. 116.]

Rohtang.—Pass in the Kulū subdivision of Kāngra District, Punjab, situated in 32° 22′ N. and 77° 17′ E., across the Himālayan range which divides the Kulū valley from Lāhul. The pass leads from Koksar in Lāhul to Rālla in Kothi Manāli of Kulū. The elevation is only 13,326 feet, a remarkably low level considering that the sides rise to 15,000 and 16,000 feet, while within 12 miles are peaks over 20,000 feet in height. The high road to Leh and Yārkand from Kulū and Kāngra goes over this pass, which is practicable for laden mules and ponies. The pass is dangerous, and generally impassable between November and the end of March or even later. Through it the monsoon rains reach the Chandra valley, and the Beās rises on its southern slope.

Sujānpur Tīra.—Village in the Hamīrpur *tahsīl* of Kāngra District, Punjab, situated in 31° 50′ N. and 76° 31′ E., on the Beās. Population (1901), 5,267. The place derives the second part of its name from the Tīra or 'palace' commenced by Abhāya Chand, the Katoch king of Kāngra, in 1758. His grandson Sujān Chand founded the town, and Sansār Chand, the great Katoch ruler, completed it and held his court here. The site is picturesque, with a fine parade-ground and grassy plain surrounded by trees; but the palace, a highly finished building of regal proportions, has fallen into disrepair since the Katoch family took up its residence in LAMBĀGRAON.

Sultānpur Village.—Village in the Kulū subdivision and head-quarters of the Kulū *tahsīl*, Kāngra District, Punjab, situated in 31° 58′ N. and 77° 10′ E., at the junction of the Beās and Sarvari and below the Bhubhu pass, at an elevation of 4,092 feet. Population (1901), 1,609. It was founded in the seventeenth century by the Kulū Rājā, Jagat Singh. The place is an important dépôt for the trade between the Punjab and Leh and Central Asia. It has an out-still for the manufacture of country spirit, a vernacular middle school, and a Government dispensary, under an assistant surgeon. The village was nearly destroyed by the earthquake of April 4, 1905.

Boundaries, configuration, and hill and river systems.

Hoshiārpur District.—Submontane District in the Jullundur Division, Punjab, lying between 30° 59′ and 32° 5′ N. and 75° 30′ and 76° 38′ E., with an area of 2,244 square miles. Its eastern boundary consists of the western slopes of the Sola Singhi hills, a range of the Outer Himālayan system, which separates it from Kāngra District and Bilāspur State, and whose highest elevation (3,896 feet) within the District is at Bharwain, its summer station. Parallel with this range and lying north-west-by-south-east runs the northern section of the Siwālik range, locally known as the Katār Dhār. Between these ranges is the Jaswān or Una Dūn, a broad fertile valley, watered by the Sohān stream, which rises in its northern extremity and flows south-east until it falls into the Sutlej near Anandpur. The latter river, breaking through the Sola Singhi range near Bhabaur, flows south-east through the Dūn until at Rūpar it cuts through the Siwāliks and thence flows west. The south-east corner of the District, the Jandbhari *ilāka*, lies on the left bank of the Sutlej; but that river forms its boundary on the extreme south-east and south, separating it from Ambāla. On the north the Beās also breaks through the Sola Singhi hills, and sweeping round the northern end of the Siwāliks flows thence almost due south, dividing the District from Kāngra on the north and Gurdāspur on the west. Hoshiārpur thus consists of a long, irregular oval, the Siwāliks forming its axis and dividing it into two unequal parts, of which the western is the larger. This part is a rich well-wooded submontane tract, which slopes south-westwards from the Siwāliks towards the borders of the Kapūrthala State and Jullundur District. It is watered by only two perennial streams of any size: namely, the western or Black Bein, which rises in the swamps near Dasūya and flows into Kapūrthala; and the eastern or White Bein, which rises near Garhshankar, and, after a short winding course through the *tahsīl* of that name, turns sharply to the north and meanders along the Jullundur borde . The principal feature of this submontane tract is the *chos*, or seasonal torrents, which, rising in the Siwaliks, spread like a network over the plain. At an earlier period the silt washed down from the Siwāliks must have formed the alluvial plain to their west and caused its fertility, but owing to the deforestation of those hills the *chos* have for a considerable time been destroying it. Dry in the rainless months, they become raging torrents after heavy rain; and, passing through the sandy belt which lies below the western slope of the hills, they enter the plain, at first in fairly well-defined channels, but finally spreading over its surface and burying the cultivation under infertile sand. At a special inquiry held in 1895–6, it was found that no less than 147 square miles were covered by these torrent-beds, an increase of 72 since 1852. The Punjab Land Preservation (*Chos*) Act (Act II of 1900) has been extended to the Siwāliks, in order to enable the Local Government to limit the rights of grazing and wood-cutting as a preliminary step towards their reafforestation, which, it is hoped, will remedy the damage now being caused by the hill torrents.

Geologically the District falls into two subdivisions: a south- Geology.

western, composed of alluvium; and a north-eastern, comprising the Siwālik and sub-Himālayan ranges running northwest from the Sutlej. These ranges are formed of the sandstones and conglomerates of the upper Siwālik series, which is of Upper Tertiary (pliocene) age [1].

Botany.

The southern portion of the District hardly differs botanically from the general character of the Central Punjab, though the mango and other sub-tropical trees thrive particularly well in cultivation. The submontane part has a true Siwālik flora, and in one valley in the extreme north of the District the *sāl* (*Shorea robusta*) finds its northern limit. The *ber* (*Zizyphus Jujuba*) is plentiful.

Fauna.

Wild animals include leopards (in the hills), hyenas, wolves, antelope, deer, &c. Feathered game is fairly plentiful.

Climate and temperature.

Owing to the proximity of the hills, the heat in the plains is never excessive, while Bharwain, the summer station of the District, enjoys a mild hot season. The chief cause of mortality is fever. Plague entered the District from Jullundur in 1897; and, in spite of considerable opposition culminating in a serious riot at Garhshankar, vigorous measures were for three years taken to stamp out the disease, and to some extent successfully.

Rainfall.

The annual rainfall varies from 31 inches at Garhshankar to 34 at Hoshiārpur; of the rainfall at the latter place 28 inches fall in the summer months, and 6 in the winter. The greatest fall recorded of late years was 79 inches at Una in 1881–2, and the least 13 inches at Dasūya in 1901–2.

History.

Tradition associates several places, notably DASŪYA, with the Pāndavas of the Mahābhārata, but archaeological remains are few and unimportant. Prior to the Muhammadan invasions, the modern District undoubtedly formed part of the Katoch kingdom of Trigartta or Jullundur; and when at an unknown date that kingdom broke up into numerous petty principalities, the Jaswān Rājās, a branch of the Katoch dynasty, established themselves in the Jaswān Dūn. The plains probably came permanently under Muhammadan rule on the fall of Jullundur in 1088, but the hills remained under Hindu chieftains. In 1399 Tīmūr ravaged the Jaswān Dūn on his way to capture Kāngra fort. At this period the Khokhars appear to have been the dominant tribe in the District; and in 1421 Jasrath, their chief, revolted against the weak Saiyid dynasty, but in 1428 he was defeated near Kāngra. After that event several

[1] Medlicott, 'On the Sub-Himālayan Ranges between the Ganges and Rāvi,' *Memoirs, Geological Survey of India*, vol. iii, pt. ii.

Pathān military colonies were founded in the plain along the base of the Siwāliks, and BAJWĀRA became the head-quarters. The fort of Malot, founded in the reign of Sultān Bahlol by a Pathān grantee of the surrounding country, was Daulat Khān's stronghold. It played an important part in Bābar's invasion, and after its surrender Bābar crossed the Siwāliks into the Jaswān Dūn and marched on Rūpar. Under Sher Shāh, the governor of Malot ruled all the hills as far as Kāngra and Jammu, and organized some kind of revenue system. By this time the Dadwāls, another Katoch family, had established themselves at Datārpur in the Siwāliks. On Akbar's accession, the District became the centre of Sikandar Sūri's resistance to the Mughal domination, but he was soon reduced, and in 1596 the Jaswāns were disposed of without actual fighting. After this the District settled down under the Mughal rule and was included in Todar Mal's great revenue survey.

The Rājās of Jaswān and Datārpur retained possession of their fiefs until 1759, when the rising Sikh adventurers, who had already established themselves in the lowlands, commenced a series of encroachments upon the hill tracts. The Jaswān Rājā early lost a portion of his dominions; and when Ranjīt Singh concentrated the whole Sikh power under his own government, both the petty Katoch chiefs were compelled to acknowledge the supremacy of Lahore. At last, in 1815, the ruler of Jaswān was forced by Ranjīt Singh to resign his territories in exchange for an estate held on feudal tenure (*jāgīr*); and three years later his neighbour of Datārpur met with similar treatment. Meanwhile, the lowland portion of the District had passed completely into the hands of the Sikh chieftains, who ultimately fell before the absorbing power of Ranjīt Singh; and by the close of 1818 the whole country from the Sutlej to the Beās had come under the government of Lahore. A small portion of the District was administered by deputies of the Sikh governors at Jullundur; but in the hills and the Jaswān Dūn, Ranjīt Singh assigned most of his conquests to feudal rulers (*jāgīrdārs*), among whom were the deposed Rājās of Datārpur and Jaswān, the Sodhīs of Anandpur, and the Sikh prelate Bedi Bikramā Singh, whose head-quarters were fixed at Una. Below the Siwālik Hills, Sher Singh (afterwards Mahārājā) held Hājipur and Mukeriān, with a large tract of country, while other great tributaries received assignments elsewhere in the lowland region. Shaikh Sandhe Khān had charge of Hoshiārpur at the date of the British annexation, as deputy of the Jullundur governor.

After the close of the first Sikh War in 1846, the whole tongue of land between the Sutlej and the Beās, together with the hills now constituting Kāngra District, passed into the hands of the British Government. The deposed Rājās of Datārpur and Jaswān received cash pensions from the new rulers, in addition to the estates granted by Ranjīt Singh; but they expressed bitter disappointment that they were not restored to their former sovereign positions. The whole of Bedi Bikramā Singh's grant was resumed, and a pension was offered for his maintenance, but indignantly refused; while part of the Sodhī estates were also taken back. Accordingly, the outbreak of the Multān War and the revolt of Chattar Singh, in 1848, found the disaffected chieftains ready for rebellion, and gave them an opportunity for rising against the British power. In conjunction with the Kāngra Rājās, they organized a revolt, which, however, was soon put down without serious difficulty. The two Rājās and the other ringleaders were captured, and their estates were confiscated. Rājā Jagat Singh of Datārpur lived for about thirty years at Benares on a pension from the British Government. Umed Singh of Jaswān received a similar allowance; Ran Singh, his grandson, was permitted to reside at Jammu in receipt of his pension; and on the assumption by Queen Victoria of the Imperial title in January, 1877, the *jāgīr* confiscated in 1848 was restored to Tikka Raghunāth Singh, great-grandson of the rebel Rājā, and son-in-law of the Mahārājā of Kashmīr. Bedi Bikramā Singh followed Chattar Singh at Gujrāt, but surrendered at the close of the war and obtained leave to reside at Amritsar. His son, Sujān Singh, receives a Government pension, and has been created an honorary magistrate. Many other local chieftains still retain estates, the most noticeable being the Rānās of Mānaswāl and the Rais of Bhabaur. The sacred family of the Sodhīs, lineal descendants of Rām Dās, the fourth Sikh Gurū, enjoy considerable pensions.

The Mutiny did not affect this District, the only disturbances being caused by the incursion of servants from Simla, who spread exaggerated reports of the panic there, and the rapid march of a party of mutineers from Jullundur, who passed along the hills and escaped across the Sutlej before the news had reached head-quarters.

The people.

The population of the District at the last four enumerations was: (1868) 937,699, (1881) 901,381, (1891) 1,011,659, and (1901) 989,782, dwelling in 11 towns and 2,117 villages. It decreased by 2·1 per cent. during the last decade, the decrease being greatest in the Hoshiārpur *tahsīl* (3·6) and least in Garhshankar. The density of the population is high. The District is divided into the four *tahsīls* of HOSHIĀRPUR, DASŪYA, UNA, and GARHSHANKAR, the head-quarters of each being at the place from which it is named. The chief towns are the municipalities of HOSHIĀRPUR, the head-quarters of the District, TĀNDA-URMAR, HARIĀNA, GARHDIWĀLA, UNA, ANANDPUR, MUKERIĀN, DASŪYA, and MIĀNI.

The following table shows the chief statistics of population in 1901:—

Tahsīl.	Area in square miles.	Number of Towns.	Number of Villages.	Population.	Population per square mile.	Percentage of variation in population between 1891 and 1901.	Number of persons able to read and write.
Hoshiārpur .	508	4	489	264,112	519·9	– 3·6	12,388
Dasūya . .	501	4	633	239,004	477·1	– 2·2	6,952
Una . . .	717	2	523	225,198	314·1	– 1·8	11,680
Garhshankar .	509	1	472	261,468	513·7	– 1·0	8,360
District total	2,244	11	2,117	989,782	441·0	– 2·1	39,380

NOTE.—The figures for the areas of *tahsīls* are taken from the revenue returns. The total District area is that given in the *Census Report*.

Hindus (603,710) comprise more than 60 per cent. of the total; Muhammadans number 312,958, or 32 per cent.; and Sikhs, 71,126, or 7 per cent. Punjābi is the language chiefly spoken.

Castes and occupations.

The Jats or Jāts (153,000) are first in point of numbers, comprising 15 per cent. of the total. They are chiefly Hindus, but include 35,000 Sikhs and 26,000 Muhammadans. The next most numerous are the Rājputs (94,000), who comprise more than 9 per cent. of the population; they are mostly Hindus in the hills and Muhammadans in the plains. The Gūjars (78,000) are a pastoral people, who are found mainly in the Siwāliks. The Pathāns (7,000) are descendants of colonists planted by the Afghān invaders; their villages originated in small brick fortifications, and are disposed part in a long line parallel to the Siwāliks, as a protection against invasion from the hills, part in a cluster guarding the Srī Gobindpur ferry on the Beās. The Mahtons (10,000) are by their own account Rājputs who have descended in the social scale owing to their practice of widow marriage. They are either Hindus or Sikhs. The Kanets (1,700) are said to have the same origin as the Mahtons, and are equally divided between Hindus and Sikhs. The Arains (35,000) and

Sainis (45,000) are industrious and careful cultivators; the former are entirely Muhammadan, the latter Hindu or Sikh. Other landowning tribes are the Awāns (13,000) and Dogars (5,000), who are chiefly Muhammadans, and Ghirths (47,000), locally known as Bahtis and Chāhngs, who are almost entirely Hindus. The Brāhmans (80,000) are extensive landholders in the hills and also engage in trade. Of the commercial classes, the Khattrīs (21,000) are the most important. Of the menial tribes may be mentioned the Chamārs (leather-workers, 121,000), Chūhrās (scavengers, 19,000), Jhīnwars (water-carriers, 24,000), Julāhās (weavers, 24,000), Kumhārs (potters, 11,000), Lohārs (blacksmiths, 16,000), Nais (barbers, 14,000), Tarkhāns (carpenters, 33,000), and Telis (oil-pressers, 12,000). About 60 per cent. of the population are dependent on agriculture.

Christian missions. The Ludhiāna Mission has a station at Hoshiārpur, dating from 1867, and five out-stations in the District; its staff consists of 20 persons, with Scripture-readers and catechists, and includes a qualified lady doctor. The District contained 785 native Christians in 1901.

General agricultural conditions. The Siwālik Hills, which form the backbone of the District, are for the most part soft sandstone, from which by detrition is formed a belt of light sandy loam known as the Kandī tract, lying immediately at their foot. This soil requires frequent, but not too heavy, showers, and the tract is to a large extent overspread with shifting sand blown from the torrent beds. Parallel to this comes a narrow belt, in which the loam is less mixed with sand; and this is followed by the exceptionally fertile Sirwāl belt, in which the water-level is near the surface, and the loam, little mixed with sand except where affected by the hill torrents, is of a texture which enables it to draw up and retain the maximum of moisture. South-east of Garhshankar is a tract of clayey loam, probably an old depression connected with the Bein river, while north of Dasūya, and so beyond the range of the Siwālik denudation, is an area probably formed by the alluvion of the Beās, which is one of the most fertile in the District. The soil of the Una valley is for the most part a good alluvial loam, especially fertile on the banks of the Sutlej.

Chief agricultural statistics and principal crops. The District is held almost entirely on the *bhaiyāchārā* and *pattīdāri* tenures, *zamīndāri* lands covering only about 120 square miles. The area for which details are available in the revenue records of 1903–4 is 2,235 square miles, as shown in the table on next page.

Tahsīl.	Total.	Cultivated.	Irrigated.	Cultivable waste.
Hoshiārpur . .	508	261	15	63
Dasūya . .	501	327	30	66
Una . . .	717	267	6	98
Garhshankar .	509	291	40	48
Total	2,235	1,146	91	275

The chief crops of the spring harvest are wheat and gram, which occupied 452 and 225 square miles respectively in 1903–4. Barley occupied only 27 square miles. There were 154 acres of poppy. In the autumn harvest maize is the most important crop (212 square miles), and forms the staple food of the people; pulses occupied 81 square miles and rice 39. Very little great or spiked millet is grown. Sugar-cane is a very valuable crop, covering 38 square miles. Cotton occupied 27 square miles.

Improvements in agricultural practice.

The cultivated area increased by about 3 per cent. during the twenty years ending 1901, its extension having been much hindered by the destructive action of the mountain torrents. Outside their range of influence, almost every cultivable acre is brought under the plough; cash rents rise to as much as Rs. 50 per acre, and holdings as small as half an acre are found. Maize is the only crop for which any pains are taken to select the best seed. Advances under the Land Improvement Loans Act are little sought after; in many places unbricked wells, dug at a trifling cost, answer every purpose, while in others the water lies too deep for masonry wells to be profitable. Even in the Sirwāl tract, where there is a tendency to increase the number of masonry wells, they are more often dug by a large number of subscribers, who each own a small holding, in combination, than by means of loans from Government.

Cattle, horses, goats, &c.

The cattle are mostly small and weak, especially in the hills, and such good bullocks as are to be found are imported. Although Bajwāra and Tihāra are mentioned in the *Ain-i-Akbarī* as famous for their horses, the breed now found is very poor. The District board maintains 2 pony and 5 donkey stallions. The people possess few sheep. Goats, which used to be grazed in the Siwāliks in large numbers, and caused much damage, have now under the provisions of the *Chos* Act been excluded from the western slopes of that range. Camels are kept in a few villages. A good deal of poultry is bred for the Simla market.

Irrigation. Of the total area cultivated in 1903–4, 91 square miles, or 8 per cent., were classed as irrigated. Of this, 57 square miles, or 63 per cent., were irrigated from wells; 23 square miles, or 25 per cent., from canals; and 11 square miles, or 12 per cent., from streams. There were 6,533 masonry wells and 7,511 unbricked wells, lever wells, and water-lifts. Except lever wells (which are worked by hand), these are worked by bullocks, generally with the Persian wheel, but occasionally with the rope and bucket. They are found chiefly in the Sirwāl tract. Canal-irrigation is mainly from a private canal called the Shāh Nahr, an inundation cut taking off from the Beās in the north-west of the District. It was originally constructed during the decline of the Mughal empire, and was reopened in 1846 by a number of local landholders at their own expense. Government in 1890 acquired by agreement the management of the canal, subject to certain rights reserved to the shareholders. There are also some small cuts taking off from the Beās, which belong to private individuals and villages, and irrigate about 10 square miles. The irrigation from streams is by means of artificial watercourses, and is employed in some of the hilly tracts.

Forests. The District has 27 square miles of 'reserved' and 139 of unclassed forests under the Forest department, consisting of the forests of *chīl* pine which cover the slopes of the Sola Singhi range, and 10 square miles of bamboo forest in the Siwāliks. A small *rakh* of 3 square miles on the Outer Siwāliks is under the control of the Deputy-Commissioner. All the *chīl* trees on these hills are also the property of Government. The inner slopes are sparsely clad with pine; the denudation of the outer slopes by the action of the hill torrents has already been referred to. In 1903–4 the forest revenue was Rs. 19,000.

Minerals. Gold is washed in the bed of the Sohān and other hill streams, but in quite insignificant quantities, the average earnings of the workers not amounting to more than 3 annas a day. The District contains quarries of limestone of some value, and *kankar* of an inferior quality is found. Saltpetre is extracted from saline earth in fourteen villages, the output being about 140 maunds a year. There are some valuable quarries of sandstone.

Arts and manufactures. The principal manufacture is that of cotton fabrics, which in 1901 employed 44,000 persons. The chief articles are coloured turbans and cloth of coloured stripes. The town of HOSHIĀRPUR is a centre for the manufacture of ivory or bone and copper inlay work and of decorative furniture, but the demand for inferior work in Europe and America has led to deterioration. Lacquered wooden ware and silver-work, with some ivory-carving, are also produced. The carpenters have a reputation for good work, and there is a considerable manufacture of glass bangles. Ornamented shoes are also made, and buskins, breeches, and coats of soft *sāmbar* (deer) skin. At DASŪYA cups and glasses of coloured glass are made. The light 'paper' pottery is made at TĀNDA, and brass vessels at Bahādurpur.

Trade is chiefly confined to the export of raw materials, including rice, gram, barley, sugar, hemp, safflower, fibres, tobacco, indigo, cotton, lac, and a small quantity of wheat. Of these, sugar forms by far the most important item. The cane grows in various portions of the plains, and sugar is refined in the larger towns and exported to all parts of the Punjab, especially to Amritsar. The principal imports are cotton piece-goods from Delhi and Amritsar, millets and other coarse grains from the south of the Sutlej, and cattle from Amritsar and the south. Commerce and trade.

The District contains no railways, but a line from Jullundur to Hoshiārpur is contemplated. The road from Jullundur to Kāngra runs across the District, and transversely to this two lines of road, one on either side of the Siwāliks, carry the submontane traffic between the Beās and Sutlej. The total length of metalled roads is 37 miles, and of unmetalled roads 737 miles. Of these, 21 miles of metalled and 28 miles of unmetalled roads are under the Public Works department, and the rest under the District board. The Sutlej is navigable below Rūpar during the summer months, and the Beās during the same period from the point where it enters the District. The Sutlej is crossed by six and the Beās by ten ferries, nine of which are managed by the District board. Roads.

None of the famines which have visited the Punjab since annexation affected Hoshiārpur at all seriously; the rainfall is generally so plentiful and the soil so moist that a great part of the District is practically secure from drought. The area of crops matured in the famine year 1899–1900 amounted to 7·6 per cent. of the normal. Famine.

The District is in charge of a Deputy-Commissioner, aided by five Assistant or Extra Assistant Commissioners, of whom one is in charge of the District treasury. For general administrative purposes the District is divided into four *tahsīls*—HOSHIĀRPUR, GARHSHANKAR, UNA, and DASŪYA—each with a *tahsīldār* and a *naib-tahsīldār*. District subdivisions and staff.

Civil justice and crime.

The Deputy-Commissioner as District Magistrate is responsible for criminal justice, and civil judicial work is under a District Judge. Both officers are supervised by the Divisional Judge of the Hoshiārpur Civil Division. There are six Munsifs, three at head-quarters and one at each outlying *tahsīl*. The predominant form of crime is burglary.

Land revenue administration.

Under Sikh rule the District was unusually fortunate, in that Misr Rūp Lāl was appointed to the administration of the *doāb* in 1802. He was able and honest, allied to local families by marriage, and interested in the welfare of the people. His assessments were light and easily paid. In 1839 he was succeeded by a different type of ruler, Shaikh Ghulām Muhī-ud-dīn, whose oppressive administration lasted until the British conquest. The summary settlement of the whole *doāb* was promptly made on annexation by John Lawrence. The demand was 13½ lakhs. Except in Garhshankar, the summary settlement worked well. In 1846 the regular settlement of Jullundur and Hoshiārpur began. Changes in officers and the pressure of other work prevented anything being done until 1851, when a Settlement officer was appointed to Hoshiārpur. His charge, however, did not correspond with the present District, as other officers settled the Una *tahsīl*, part of Garhshankar, and the Mukeriān tract. The result for the District as now constituted was an increased demand of Rs. 9,000. Many assignments of revenue, however, had in the meantime been resumed, and the assessment was really lighter than the summary demand. Between 1869 and 1873 a revision of the records-of-right in the hilly tracts was carried out. The settlement was revised between 1879 and 1882. The total revenue assessed was 13¼ lakhs, of which Rs. 71,000 are assigned, while a water rate was imposed on the lands irrigated by the Shāh Nahr Canal. Government subsequently took over the canal, and the shareholders became annuitants, receiving 8 annas out of every 18 annas imposed as water rate. The canal is managed by the Deputy-Commissioner, and all profits are ear-marked to the improvement and extension of the watercourses. The average assessment on 'dry' land is Rs. 1–15 (maximum Rs. 4–4–0, and minimum 6 annas), and that on 'wet' land Rs. 4–8–0 (maximum Rs. 6, and minimum Rs. 3). The demand for 1903–4, including cesses, was 16·4 lakhs. The average size of a proprietary holding is 1·5 acres.

The collections of land revenue alone and of total revenue are shown in the table on next page, in thousands of rupees.

	1880-1.	1890-1.	1900-1.	1903-4.
Land revenue . .	12,60	13,65	13,57	13,74
Total revenue . .	15,84	17,89	19,93	20,36

The District possesses nine municipalities, HOSHIĀRPUR, TĀNDA- URMAR, HARIĀNA, GARHDIWĀLA, UNA, ANANDPUR, MUKERIĀN, DASŪYA, and MIĀNI; and one 'notified area,' Khānpur. Outside these, local affairs are managed by the District board, which in 1903-4 had an income of Rs. 1,67,000. The expenditure in the same year was Rs. 1,49,000, education being the largest item. **Local and municipal.**

The regular police force consists of 480 of all ranks, including 93 municipal police. The Superintendent usually has three inspectors under him. The village watchmen number 1,765. There are 15 police stations and 4 road-posts. The District jail at head-quarters has accommodation for 106 prisoners. **Police and jails.**

The District stands twelfth among the twenty-eight Districts of the Province in respect of the literacy of its population. In 1901 the proportion of literate persons was 4 per cent. (7·3 males and 0·2 females). The number of pupils under instruction was 4,813 in 1880-1, 9,749 in 1890-1, 9,639 in 1900-1, and 10,772 in 1903-4. In the last year the District had 13 secondary and 146 primary (public) schools, and 3 advanced and 75 elementary (private) schools, with 278 girls in the public and 315 in the private schools. The Hoshiārpur municipal high school was founded in 1848 to teach Persian and Hindī, and was brought under the Educational department in 1856. The study of English was introduced in 1859, Arabic and Sanskrit in 1870, at about which time it was made a high school. There are also three unaided Anglo-vernacular high schools, one vernacular high school, and eight middle schools. The Ludhiāna Mission supports a girls' orphanage and boarding-school, and two day-schools for Hindu and Muhammadan girls. The total number of pupils in public institutions in 1904 was about 7 per cent. of the number of children of school-going age. The total expenditure on education in 1903-4 was Rs. 74,000, the greater part of which was met from Local funds. **Education**

The civil hospital at Hoshiārpur has accommodation for 33 male and 12 female in-patients. The District also contains fourteen outlying dispensaries. At these institutions in 1904 a total of 145,455 out-patients and 1,170 in-patients were **Hospitals and dispensaries.**

treated, and 9,267 operations were performed. Local funds contribute nearly three-fourths of the expenditure, which in 1904 amounted to Rs. 24,000, and municipal bodies the remaining fourth. The Ludhiāna Mission has recently opened a female hospital in Hoshiārpur under a qualified lady doctor.

Vaccination. The number of successful vaccinations in 1903–4 was 29,000, representing 29 per 1,000 of the population.

[H. A. Rose, *District Gazetteer* (1904); J. A. L. Montgomery, *Settlement Report* (1885).]

Hoshiārpur Tahsīl.—*Tahsīl* of Hoshiārpur District, Punjab, lying between 31° 21′ and 31° 50′ N. and 75° 40′ and 76° 7′ E., with an area of 508 square miles. The population in 1901 was 264,112, compared with 273,864 in 1891. It contains the towns of HOSHIĀRPUR (population, 17,549), the head-quarters, GARHDIWĀLA (3,652), HARIĀNA (6,005), and Khānpur (3,183); and 489 villages, including BAJWĀRA, a place of some historical interest. The land revenue and cesses amounted in 1903–4 to 4·3 lakhs. The *tahsīl* comprises the western slopes of the Siwāliks, the poor land at their base, a central strip of fairly productive but sandy soil, and in the west a broad belt of fertile land irrigated by wells. It is well wooded, and the mango groves are a characteristic feature. Torrent-beds, dry except after heavy rain, are met with every few miles.

Dasūya Tahsīl.—*Tahsīl* of Hoshiārpur District, Punjab, lying between 31° 35′ and 32° 5′ N. and 75° 30′ and 75° 59′ E., with an area of 501 square miles. The population in 1901 was 239,004, compared with 244,346 in 1891. It contains the towns of DASŪYA (population, 6,404), the head-quarters, MUKERIĀN (3,589), MIĀNI (6,118), and TĀNDA-URMAR (10,247); and 633 villages. The land revenue and cesses amounted in 1903–4 to 4·6 lakhs. The *tahsīl* is situated in a wide bend of the Beās, which is the boundary on the north-east and west. It comprises a stretch of fertile land on the south, the lowlands along the river, a tract of higher land below the Siwāliks, and the northern extremity of the Siwāliks themselves.

Una Tahsīl.—*Tahsīl* of Hoshiārpur District, Punjab, lying between 30° 59′ and 31° 52′ N. and 75° 56′ and 76° 38′ E., with an area of 717 square miles. It consists of the broad and stony valley of the Sohān between the inner and outer SIWALIK HILLS, which near the Beās rises into the Jaswān Dūn, a plateau or upland valley about 1,400 feet above sea-level.

The Jandbārī *taluka*, a small piece of territory on the left bank of the Sutlej, is also included in this *tahsīl*. The population in 1901 was 225,198, compared with 229,308 in 1891. It contains the towns of UNA (population, 4,746), the head-quarters, and ANANDPUR (5,028); and 523 villages. The land revenue and cesses amounted in 1903–4 to Rs. 3·2 lakhs.

Garhshankar Tahsīl.—*Tahsīl* of Hoshiārpur District, Punjab, lying between 30° 59′ and 31° 31′ N. and 75° 51′ and 76° 31′ E., with an area of 509 square miles. The population in 1901 was 261,468, compared with 264,141 in 1891. GARHSHANKAR (population, 5,803) is the head-quarters. It also contains 472 villages, of which JAIJON is of some historical interest. The land revenue and cesses amounted in 1903–4 to 4·4 lakhs. The physical features of the *tahsīl* are similar to those of Hoshiārpur, except that the hills are steeper and torrent-beds less frequent. The Sutlej forms the southern boundary.

Anandpur.—Town in the Una *tahsīl* of Hoshiārpur District, Punjab, situated in 31° 14′ N. and 76° 31′ E., on the left bank of the Sutlej. Population (1901), 5,028. Founded by the Sikh Gurū, Tegh Bahādur, it became a stronghold of the tenth Gurū, Govind Singh, who was defeated here by the troops of Aurangzeb. It is still of religious importance as the head-quarters of the branch of the Sodhīs descended from Tegh Bahādur's nephew, and contains many Sikh shrines and monuments of interest. The municipality was created in 1867. The income and expenditure during the ten years ending 1902–3 averaged Rs. 2,900. In 1903–4 the income was Rs. 3,000, chiefly derived from octroi; and the expenditure was Rs. 2,600. It maintains a Government dispensary.

Bajwāra.—Ancient town in the District and *tahsīl* of Hoshiārpur, Punjab, situated in 31° 31′ N. and 75° 57′ E., 2 miles south-east of Hoshiārpur. Population (1901), 2,653. It is said to have been founded by immigrants from Ghazni, and was once the chief town of the District, tradition relating that its walls were 18 miles in circumference. It is mentioned in the *Ain-i-Akbarī* as famous for horses. Todar Mal, Akbar's minister, is said to have broken up the town into small divisions as a punishment for the inhabitants not receiving him with proper respect. In later times it was held by Sirdār Bhūp Singh, Faizullahpuria, who was ousted in 1801 by Rājā Sansār Chand. The latter built a fort here, which was taken by Ranjīt Singh in 1825. Since then the town has declined and its ruins have been largely used for road-metal. The fort was utilized as a military prison in the earlier years of the British administration, but was afterwards dismantled; and at the present time only two ruined bastions are in existence. The town has an Anglo-vernacular high school.

Bharwain.—Hill sanitarium in the Una *tahsīl* of Hoshiārpur District, Punjab, situated in 31° 48′ N. and 76° 10′ E. Population (March, 1901), 17. It lies on the Jullundur-Dharmsāla road, 28 miles from Hoshiārpur town, near the borders of Hoshiārpur and Kāngra Districts, on the summit of the Sola Singhi range, at an elevation of 3,896 feet above the sea.

Dasūya Town.—Head-quarters of the *tahsīl* of the same name in Hoshiārpur District, Punjab, situated in 31° 49′ N. and 75° 40′ E., 25 miles north-west of Hoshiārpur town. Population (1901), 6,404. Dasūya is one of the numerous places popularly identified with the capital of the Rājā Virāta of the Mahābhārata. It contains a ruined fort, mentioned in the *Ain-i-Akbarī*, which was one of the strongholds of the Rāmgarhias, and was annexed in 1817 by Ranjīt Singh. The municipality was created in 1867. The income during the ten years ending 1902–3 averaged Rs. 2,900, and the expenditure Rs. 2,700. In 1903–4 the income was Rs. 3,700, chiefly derived from octroi; and the expenditure was Rs. 2,900. It maintains a vernacular middle school and a Government dispensary.

Garhdiwāla.—Town in the *tahsīl* and District of Hoshiārpur, Punjab, situated in 31° 45′ N. and 75° 46′ E., 17 miles from Hoshiārpur. Population (1901), 3,652. The chief trade is in sugar. The municipality was created in 1867. The income during the ten years ending 1902–3 averaged Rs. 2,300, and the expenditure Rs. 2,200. In 1903–4 the income was Rs. 2,900, chiefly derived from octroi; and the expenditure was Rs. 2,600. It maintains a Government dispensary.

Garhshankar Town.—Head-quarters of the *tahsīl* of the same name in Hoshiārpur District, Punjab, situated in 31° 13′ N. and 76° 9′ E. Population (1901), 5,803. A fort built on the site of the present town is said to have been taken by Mahmūd of Ghazni, and subsequently given by Muhammad of Ghor to the sons of Rājā Mān Singh of Jaipur. Its inhabitants are Rājputs, who expelled the Mahtons about A.D. 1175. It possesses a considerable trade in sugar and tobacco. The municipality, founded in 1882, was abolished in 1891. The town has a vernacular middle school and a Government dispensary.

Hariāna Town.—Town in the District and *tahsīl* of Hoshiārpur, Punjab, situated in 31° 38′ N. and 72° 52′ E., 9 miles from Hoshiārpur. Population (1901), 6,005. From 1846 to 1860 it was the head-quarters of the *tahsīl*. Its chief trade is in sugar. The municipality was created in 1867. The income and expenditure during the ten years ending 1902–3 averaged Rs. 3,000. In 1903–4 the income was Rs. 3,200, chiefly derived from octroi; and the expenditure was Rs. 3,100. It maintains a vernacular middle school, and the town has a dispensary.

Hoshiārpur Town.—Head-quarters of the District and *tahsīl* of Hoshiārpur, Punjab, situated in 31° 32′ N. and 75° 52′ E., at the foot of the Siwāliks, on the Jullundur-Dharmsāla road, 25 miles from Jullundur. The Divisional and Sessions Judge of the Hoshiārpur Civil Division has his head-quarters here. Population (1901), 17,549. The town was seized in 1809 by Ranjīt Singh, and formed the head-quarters of the governors of the Jullundur Doāb. It is famous for the production of articles of wood inlaid with ivory. The municipality was created in 1867. The income during the ten years ending 1902–3 averaged Rs. 47,500, and the expenditure Rs. 47,400. In 1903–4 the income was Rs. 58,600, chiefly derived from octroi; and the expenditure was Rs. 44,900. It maintains a high school, the management of which was taken over by the Educational department in 1904. There are two other unaided high schools in the town, which also possesses a civil hospital; and the Ludhiāna Mission maintains a female hospital.

Jaijon.—Ancient town in the Garhshankar *tahsīl* of Hoshiārpur District, Punjab, situated in 31° 21′ N. and 76° 13′ E., on the outer edge of the Siwāliks, 10 miles north of Garhshankar. Population (1901), 2,705. Though now of small importance, it was in early days the seat of the Jaswāl Rājās. Rājā Rām Singh first took up his residence here; and the fort which commanded the pass in the hills is said to have been constructed in 1701, and to have been taken by Ranjīt Singh in 1815. It was dismantled at annexation by the British Government. The ruins of the palaces of the Jaswāl Rājās are still visible above the town. The place was till lately an emporium of trade, second only to Hoshiārpur; and even now a good deal of cloth, both country and English, passes through towards the hills, while the produce of the hills, such as rice, turmeric, &c., passes down to the plains.

Malot.—Ancient fortress, now in ruins, in the District and *tahsīl* of Hoshiārpur, Punjab, situated in 31° 50′ N. and 76° E. It was founded by a Pathān general in the reign of Bahlol Lodī (1451–89), and became under Sher Shāh the capital of the tracts which now form Hoshiārpur and Kāngra Districts. In 1526 it was surrendered to Bābar by Daulat Khān, ruler of the Punjab, and in later times it fell into the hands of the hill Rājputs.

Miāni.—Town in the Dasūya *tahsīl* of Hoshiārpur District, Punjab, situated in 31° 43′ N. and 75° 34′ E., on the Beās. Population (1901), 6,118. It is of no commercial importance. The municipality was created in 1874. The income during the ten years ending 1902–3 averaged Rs. 1,700, and the expenditure Rs. 1,600. In 1903–4 the income was Rs. 1,800, chiefly derived from octroi; and the expenditure was Rs. 2,300. It maintains a Government dispensary.

Mukeriān.—Town in the Dasūya *tahsīl* of Hoshiārpur District, Punjab, situated in 31° 57′ N. and 75° 38′ E. Population (1901), 3,589. It was a stronghold of Sardār Jai Singh Kanhaya, whose power was paramount in the Punjab about 1774–84; and Ranjīt Singh's reputed son, Sher Singh, who afterwards became Mahārājā, was born here. The town has no trade of any importance. The municipality was created in 1867. The income and expenditure during the ten years ending 1902–3 averaged Rs. 3,100. In 1903–4 the income was Rs. 3,200, chiefly derived from octroi; and the expenditure was Rs. 2,900. It maintains a vernacular middle school and a Government dispensary.

Sola Singhi (or Chintpurni).—Mountain range in Hoshiārpur District, Punjab, forming the eastern boundary of the Jaswān Dūn. It commences at a point close to Talwāra, on the Beās river, and runs in a south-eastward direction between the Districts of Hoshiārpur and Kāngra. The range as it passes southwards increases steadily both in width and elevation, until it reaches its highest point at the small hill station of Bharwain, 28 miles from Hoshiārpur town on the Dharmsāla road and 3,896 feet above the sea. At this point the ridge is 14 miles across. Thence it continues till it crosses the valley of the Sutlej, its northern slope sinking gradually into the Beās basin, while the southern escarpment consists in places of an abrupt cliff about 300 feet in height. The space between its central line and the level portion of the Jaswān Dūn is occupied by a broad table-land, thickly clothed with forest, and intersected by precipitous ravines, which divide the surface into natural blocks. Another range of hills in Hoshiārpur

District, which continues the line of the Sola Singhi and finally crosses the Sutlej into Bilāspur, terminates in the hill of Naina Devi, with its famous temple.

Tānda-Urmar.—The two towns of Tānda and Urmar are situated within a mile of one another in the Dasūya *tahsīl* of Hoshiārpur District, Punjab, in 31° 40′ N. and 75° 38′ E., and form with their suburbs a single municipality. Their joint population was, in 1901, 10,247. The suburbs contain a shrine of the saint, Sakhi Sarwar. They form an *entrepôt* for country produce and cotton goods, and good pottery is made. The municipality was created in 1867. The income and expenditure during the ten years ending 1902–3 averaged Rs. 5,400. In 1903–4 the income was Rs. 5,800, chiefly derived from octroi; and the expenditure was Rs. 5,400. It maintains an Anglo-vernacular middle school and a Government dispensary.

Una Town.—Head-quarters of the *tahsīl* of the same name in Hoshiārpur District, Punjab, situated in 31° 28′ N. and 76° 17′ E., in the Jaswān Dūn. Population (1901), 4,746. It is important as the seat of a branch of the Bedi clan descended from Kala Dhāri, a descendant of Nānak, the first Sikh Gurū, but has no commercial importance. The municipality was created in 1867. The income during the ten years ending 1902–3 averaged Rs. 2,700 and the expenditure Rs. 2,600. In 1902–3 the income was Rs. 3,800, chiefly derived from octroi; and the expenditure was Rs. 2,900. It maintains a vernacular middle school and a Government dispensary.

Boundaries, configuration, and hill and river systems.

Jullundur District (*Jālandhar*).—District in the Jullundur Division, Punjab, lying between 30° 56′ and 31° 37′ N. and 75° 5′ and 76° 16′ E., with an area of 1,431 square miles. It occupies the southern part of the *doāb* (called the Bīst Jullundur Doāb), or country between the Beās and Sutlej. The latter river forms its southern border, separating it from Ludhiāna and Ferozepore, and in shape the District is an irregular triangle with its base on that river. The State of Kapūrthala separates it on the west from the Beās and its confluence with the Sutlej. Along its north-east border lies the District of Hoshiārpur; and in the centre of this portion, between the Jullundur and Nawāshahr *tahsīls*, is a detached tract of Kapūrthala territory which forms the Phagwāra *tahsīl* of that State. The valley of the Sutlej is marked by a high, well-defined bank. North of this lies a plateau whose highest point, at Rāhon near the eastern corner of the District, is

1,012 feet above sea-level. Thence it slopes gradually westwards towards the Beās. No hill or rock breaks the level of this plateau, which lies entirely within the zone of rich cultivable soil that skirts the foot of the Himālayas, and was regarded by the Sikhs as the garden of the Punjab. At places a few acres are covered with sand; but, except in these rare spots, one vast sheet of luxuriant and diverse vegetation spreads over the plain from end to end. South of the high bank of the Sutlej lies the Bet or *khādar*, a strip of alluvial soil annually fertilized by deposits of silt from that river, although the opening of the Sirhind Canal has greatly reduced its flow, and it now runs almost dry for eight months in the year. The only important stream is the East or White Bein, which, rising east of Rāhon and running along the Hoshiārpur border, traverses the Phagwāra *tahsīl*, and thence meanders westwards across the District till it falls into the Sutlej near its junction with the Beās. In its earlier course it receives several torrents from the Siwālik Hills in Hoshiārpur. These bring down deposits of sand, which are doing considerable damage to the cultivated lands on its eastern bank.

Geology and botany.

The District is situated entirely in the alluvium, and contains nothing of geological interest. Cultivation has advanced to such a point that there is little in the way of natural vegetation beyond the weeds that come up with the crops throughout North-west India. Trees are almost always planted; and, owing to the proximity of the Himālayas, several kinds succeed very well, among them the mango and *ber* (*Zizyphus Jujuba*). The river banks are in places fringed with a dense growth of high grasses, as in Ferozepore and adjoining Districts.

Fauna.

Wolves are seen but very rarely, and towards Kapūrthala antelope, *nīlgai*, and hares are found. Field-rats abound, and do no small amount of damage to the crops.

Climate and temperature.

The climate is, for the plains, temperate; in the hot season, with the exception of June and July, the heat is not excessive; in the cold season frosts are light, and confined to January and February. The average mean temperature of January is 56°, and of June 93°. The mortality varies very much with the rainfall, owing to the prevalence of malaria in rainy years. Plague made its first appearance in the Punjab in the village of Khatkar Kalān of this District in 1897.

Rainfall.

Owing to the nearness of the hills, the rainfall is fairly constant. The average varies from 24 inches at Phillaur to 27 at Jullundur, 22 inches falling in the summer months and only 5 in the winter. During the ten years ending 1903 the heaviest fall was 60 inches at Nawāshahr in 1900–1, and the lightest 11 inches, in 1899–1900, at Jullundur. There were disastrous floods in 1875 and 1878, owing to the railway embankment giving insufficient passage to the floods caused by the unusually heavy rains.

History and archaeology.

Early legends attribute the name of the *doāb* to the Daitya king Jālandhara, who was overwhelmed by Siva under a pile of mountains. His mouth, the legend says, was at JAWĀLA MUKHI, his feet at Multān, where in ancient times the Beās and Sutlej met, and his back under the upper part of the Jullundur Doāb, including the present District. The earliest mention of Jullundur occurs in the accounts of the Buddhist council held at Kuvana, near that city, early in the Christian era, under the auspices of Kanishka. When visited in the seventh century by Hiuen Tsiang, it was the capital of the Rājput kingdom of Trigartta, which also included the modern Districts of Hoshiārpur and Kāngra and the States of Chamba, Mandī, and Suket. Towards the end of the ninth century the *Rājatarangini* records the defeat of Prithwī Chandra, Rājā of Trigartta, by Sankara Chandra of Kashmīr. The town was taken by Ibrāhīm Shāh Ghori about 1088; and from that time the country appears to have remained under Muhammadan rule, the Jullundur Doāb being generally attached to the Lahore province. During the Saiyid dynasty (1414–51), however, the authority of Delhi was but weakly maintained; and the *doāb* became the scene of numerous insurrectionary movements, and especially of the long campaign of the Khokhar chief Jasrath against the ruling power. Near Jullundur the Mughal forces concentrated in 1555, when Humāyūn returned to do battle for his kingdom, and the neighbourhood was the scene of Bairām's defeat by the imperial forces in 1560. Adīna Beg, the last and most famous of the governors of Jullundur, played an important part during the downfall of Muhammadan power in the Punjab, holding the balance between the Delhi emperor, the Sikhs, and Ahmad Shāh Durrāni. Both Nūrmahal and Kartārpur were sacked by Ahmad Shāh, and to avenge the desecration of the latter place the Sikhs burnt Jullundur in 1757.

The Sikh revolt against the Mughal power early found strong support in the District, and a number of petty chieftains rapidly established themselves by force of arms as independent rulers throughout the *doāb*. In 1766 the town of Jullundur fell into the hands of the Faizullahpuria *misl*, or confederacy, then led by Khushhāl Singh. His son and successor, Budh Singh, built a masonry fort in the town, while several other leaders fortified themselves in its suburbs. Phillaur was seized by Budh Singh, who made it the capital of a considerable State; and the Muhammadan Rājputs of Nakodar (on whom the town had been conferred in *jāgīr* during the reign of Jahāngīr) were early ousted by Sardār Tāra Singh, Ghaiba, who built a fort, and made himself master of the surrounding territory. But meanwhile Ranjīt Singh was consolidating his power in the south; Phillaur fell into his hands in 1807, and he converted the *sarai* into a fort to command the passage of the Sutlej; and in 1811 Dīwān Mohkam Chand was dispatched to annex the Faizullahpuria dominions in the Jullundur Doāb. Budh Singh fled across the Sutlej; and though his troops offered some resistance to the invader, the Mahārājā successfully established his authority in the autumn of that year. Thenceforth Jullundur was the capital of the Sikh possessions in the *doāb* till British annexation. Nakodar was seized in 1816, the petty Sardārs were gradually ousted from their estates, and the whole country brought under the direct management of the Sikh governors. Here, as elsewhere, their fiscal administration proved very oppressive, especially under Shaikh Ghulām Muhī-ud-dīn, the last official appointed from the court of Lahore, a tyrannical ruler, who exacted irregular taxes. He made over the tract to his son, Imām-ud-dīn, but neither resided regularly in the *doāb*, their charge being entrusted to lieutenants, the best known of whom were Sandhe Khān in Hoshiārpur and Karīm Bakhsh in Jullundur.

At the close of the first Sikh War the British annexed the whole of the Jullundur Doāb, and it became the Commissionership of the trans-Sutlej States. For two years the administration was directly under the Supreme Government; but in 1848 the Commissioner became subordinate to the Resident at Lahore, and in the succeeding year, when events forced on the annexation of the Punjab, the administration of the *doāb* was assimilated to the general system. The Commissioner's headquarters were fixed at Jullundur, and the three Districts of Jullundur, Hoshiārpur, and Kāngra were created. The fort at Phillaur was occupied as an artillery magazine, and cantonments formed there and at Nakodar, which continued to be occupied till 1857 and 1854 respectively.

In 1857 the native troops stationed at Jullundur and Phillaur mutinied and marched off to join the rebel forces at Delhi; the authorities were, however, not altogether unprepared, and though the mutineers succeeded in escaping unmolested, they were prevented from doing serious damage. Rājā Randhīr Singh of Kapūrthala rendered invaluable assistance at this time, both in supplying troops and, by the exercise of his personal influence, in helping to preserve the peace of the *doāb*.

The tombs at NAKODAR and Nur Jahān's *sarai* at NŪRMAHAL are the chief remains of antiquarian interest.

The people. The population of the District at the last four enumerations was: (1868) 794,418, (1881) 789,555, (1891) 907,583, and (1901) 917,587, dwelling in 10 towns and 1,216 villages. It increased by 1·1 per cent. during the last decade, the increase being greatest in the Jullundur *tahsīl* and least in Phillaur. The density of population is the highest in the Province. The District is divided into the four *tahsīls* of JULLUNDUR, NAWĀSHAHR, PHILLAUR, and NAKODAR, the head-quarters of each being at the place from which it is named. The chief towns are JULLUNDUR, the head-quarters of the District, and the municipalities of KARTĀRPUR, ALĀWALPUR, PHILLAUR, NŪRMAHAL, RĀHON, NAWĀSHAHR, BANGA, and NAKODAR.

The following table shows the chief statistics of population in 1901:—

Tahsīl.	Area in square miles.	Number of Towns.	Number of Villages.	Population.	Population per square mile.	Percentage of variation in population between 1891 and 1901.	Number of persons able to read and write.
Jullundur .	391	3	409	305,976	782·4	+ 3·6	14,209
Nawāshahr .	299	3	274	196,339	656·7	− 4·5	7,820
Phillaur. .	298	3	222	192,860	647·2	+ 1·7	6,285
Nakodar .	371	1	311	222,412	599·5	+ 2·5	4,789
District total	1,431	10	1,216	917,587	641·2	+ 1·1	33,103

NOTE.—The figures for the areas of *tahsīls* are taken from the revenue returns. The total District area is that given in the *Census Report*.

Muhammadans number 421,011, or more than 45 per cent. of the total; Hindus, 368,051, or 40 per cent.; and Sikhs, 125,817, or nearly 14 per cent. Punjābi is spoken throughout the District.

Castes and occupations. By far the most numerous caste are the Jats or Jāts, who number 185,000, or 20 per cent. of the total, and own half the villages. About 185 clans are enumerated in the District. Some of these claim a Rājput origin; others have no traditions of being anything but Jats. Taken as a whole, they are an honest, industrious, sturdy, and vigorous folk, addicted to no form of serious crime, except female infanticide. The Muhammadan Jats are inferior to the Hindu and Sikh. The Arains (143,000) come next, comprising one-seventh of the total. They are entirely Muhammadans, and are a peaceable people without the sturdy spirit of the Jats, but quite as efficient cultivators. The Rājputs (50,000) come third. More than four-fifths are Muhammadans, but they nearly all preserve Hindu customs. They formerly held a more important position in the District than they do now, and carefully maintain the traditions of their former greatness; and, despising work as beneath their dignity, they are very inferior as agriculturists to the Jats. The Khokhars are entirely Muhammadan; they are often considered Rājputs, but the claim is not generally accepted, and they do not intermarry with Rājputs. The Awāns (12,000) also are all Muhammadans. They claim to have come from Arabia, but their observance of Hindu usages marks them as converts to Islām. Other agricultural tribes worthy of mention are Sainis (16,000), who are clever market-gardeners; Kambohs (6,000), mainly Sikhs; and Gūjars (20,000), who are found everywhere. The Khattrīs (26,000) are the most important of the commercial tribes, the Baniās numbering only 6,000. Of menial tribes the most important are the Chamārs (leather-workers, 96,000), Chūhrās (scavengers, 41,000), Kumhārs (potters, 15,000), Lohārs (blacksmiths, 15,000), Mochīs (cobblers, 20,000), Tarkhāns (carpenters, 32,000, many of whom are landowners), Jhīnwars (watermen, 29,000), Julāhās (weavers, 16,000), Nais (barbers, 15,000), Chhīmbas and Dhobīs (washermen, 12,000), and Telis (oil-pressers, 14,000). Brāhmans number 32,000. Half the population is agricultural and one-fourth industrial.

Christian missions. The Jullundur Mission is one of the stations belonging to the American Presbyterian Board of Foreign Missions. It was established in 1847. In 1901 the District contained 276 native Christians.

General agricultural conditions. Lying as Jullundur does close to the Outer Himālayas, an absolute failure of the rains is almost unknown; and apart from the protection afforded by the numerous wells, the soil is sufficiently charged with moisture to resist anything but absolute drought. More than 40 per cent. of the cultivated area is a good alluvial loam; patches of clay soil, amounting in all to 13 per cent. of the cultivated area, are found all over the District, while 24 per cent. is sandy soil, of which half is found in the Jullundur *tahsīl*. A small proportion is uncultivable, being covered by sandhills.

The District is held almost entirely by communities of peasant proprietors, large estates covering only about 37 square miles.

Agricultural statistics and principal crops.

The area for which details are available from the revenue records of 1903-4 is 1,357 square miles, as shown below:—

Tahsil.	Total.	Cultivated.	Irrigated.	Cultivable waste.
Jullundur . .	391	337	104	23
Nawāshahr . .	304	217	146	43
Phillaur . .	291	244	111	19
Nakodar . .	371	295	118	25
Total	1,357	1,093	479	110

The chief crop of the spring harvest is wheat, which occupied 430 square miles in 1903-4; gram covered 177 square miles; and barley only 16 square miles. Maize is the staple product of the autumn harvest, occupying 149 square miles, while pulses covered 121. Sugar-cane, which occupied 49 square miles, is commercially of the greatest importance to the cultivator, as he looks to this crop to pay the whole or the greater part of the revenue. But little great millet is grown (14 square miles), and practically no spiked millet; cotton covered 28 square miles, and rice 3,188 acres.

Improvements in agricultural practice.

The cultivated area increased by only 800 acres in the ten years ending 1901, and hardly any further increase can be anticipated. There has, however, been a considerable development of well-sinking, more than 8,000 wells having been constructed since the settlement of 1880-5. Practically no cultivable land is now left untilled; and the pressure on the soil, which in 1901 was, excluding the urban population, 718 persons per cultivated square mile, can only be met by emigration. The District has already sent numbers of its sons to the Chenāb Colony, to the Jamrao Canal in Sind, to Australia and East Africa; and many are in civil or military employment in other parts of India. The remittances of these emigrants add enormously to the natural resources of the District, and the greater portion of the Government revenue collected in it is required by the post offices to enable them to cash money orders issued on them. Loans under the Land Improvement Loans Act for the construction of wells are popular and faithfully applied; in the five years ending 1904 more than Rs. 54,000 was advanced for this purpose. Nothing has been done in the way of improving the quality of the crops grown.

Cattle, horses, &c.

Jullundur is not well adapted for breeding cattle, and it is estimated that for ploughing and working the wells no less than 10,000 bullocks per annum have to be imported. These are generally obtained at the Amritsar, Sirsa, and Hissār fairs, and from Patiāla and Ferozepore. Although some places in the Jullundur Doāb are mentioned in the *Ain-i-Akbarī* as famous for a breed of horses, the ponies are not now specially valuable. One horse and four donkey stallions are kept by the District board. There are very few camels, and sheep and goats are not important. The country is so fully cultivated that little ground for grazing is left, except along the Sutlej and in places near the Bein. Large numbers of cattle are driven from a distance to these favoured spots, and considerable sums are levied in grazing fees by the owners of the land.

Irrigation.

Of the total area cultivated in 1903–4, 479 square miles, or 44 per cent., were classed as irrigated. Of this area, 477 square miles were irrigated from wells, and 1,455 acres from streams and tanks. In addition, 56 square miles, or 5 per cent., were subject to inundation from the Sutlej. Wells are the mainstay of the District; and there are 28,609 masonry wells worked by cattle, chiefly on the rope-and-bucket system, besides 464 unbricked wells, water-lifts, and lever wells. The Persian wheel is found where the soil is sandy and water near the surface.

Forests.

The District contains two small plantations 'reserved' under the Forest Act, consisting chiefly of *shīsham* and *kīkar*, and covering 262 acres, with a military Reserve of 885 acres. It is on the whole well wooded, almost every one of the wells which it contains being surrounded by a small coppice; but, as already noticed, waste land is very scarce. Phillaur is the winter head-quarters of the Bashahr Forest division, and a great wood mart, to which quantities of timber are floated down the Sutlej and stored. Much also is brought for sale here from the Beās and the Sirhind Canal.

Minerals.

Kankar is plentiful, the best beds being within a radius of ten miles from Jullundur town. Saltpetre is manufactured from saline earth.

Arts and manufactures.

A great deal of cotton-weaving is carried on, the principal products being the coarse cotton cloth which supplies most of the dress of the people, and coloured stripes and checks. Large quantities of very coarse cotton fabrics (*khaddar*) are exported to Shikārpur and Sukkur in Sind. Rāhon had once a great reputation for a superior cotton longcloth, but the industry is almost extinct. Silk-weaving is carried on at Jullundur, and in 1899 employed 250 looms, the estimated out-turn being valued at 2 lakhs. The gold and silver manufactures are flourishing, but in no way remarkable, and the out-turn is insufficient for local requirements. Besides ornaments, silver wire and gold and silver lace are made. The District has some reputation for carpenter's work, and chairs are made at Kartārpur for the wholesale trade. Brass vessels are manufactured in many parts, the output being valued at Rs. 27,000, of which half is exported. The thin pottery known as 'paper pottery' is made in the District, and glazed and coloured tile-work of unusual excellence is turned out at Jullundur by one man. There are two flour-mills at Jullundur town, and attached to one of them is a small iron and brass foundry. The number of factory employés in 1904 was 73.

Commerce and trade. The traffic of the District is mainly in agricultural produce. In ordinary years grain is imported from Ludhiāna, Ferozepore, and the Sikh States for export to the hills; other articles of import are piece-goods from Delhi, Bombay, and Calcutta, iron from Ferozepore, Amritsar, and Karāchi, brass and copper vessels from Jagādhri, Amritsar, and Delhi, rice from Kāngra, and salt from the Mayo Mines. Sugar and molasses are largely manufactured to supply the markets of Bīkaner, Lahore, the Punjab, and Sind. Wheat, cotton cloth, and silk goods are the other principal exports.

Railways and roads. The District is traversed by the main line of the North-Western Railway, and branch lines are contemplated from Jullundur town to Kapūrthala and Hoshiārpur. It is exceptionally well provided with roads, the total length of metalled roads being 158 miles and of unmetalled roads 337 miles. The most important of the former are the grand trunk road, which traverses the District parallel with the railway, and the road from Jullundur to Hoshiārpur; these, with some minor roads, 62 miles in length in all, are under the Public Works department, the rest being under the District board. The Sutlej is navigable only in the rains; there are twelve ferries.

Famine. Jullundur, thanks to the excellence of its soil and the nearness of the hills, is but little liable to drought. None of the famines that have visited the Punjab since annexation has affected the District at all seriously, and it was classed by the Irrigation Commission of 1903 as secure from famine. The area of crops matured in the famine year 1899–1900 amounted to 76 per cent. of the normal.

District subdivi- The District is in charge of a Deputy-Commissioner, aided by three or four Assistant or Extra Assistant Commissioners,

sions and staff.

It is divided into four *tahsīls*, each under a *tahsīldār* assisted by a *naib-tahsīldār* : Jullundur comprises its northern portion, and Nawāshahr, Phillaur, and Nakodar, which lie in that order from east to west, the southern.

Civil justice and crime.

The Deputy-Commissioner as District Magistrate is responsible for criminal justice. Civil judicial work is in charge of a District Judge, and both these officers are subordinate to the Divisional and Sessions Judge of the Jullundur Civil Division, which consists of the District of Jullundur alone. There are six Munsifs, three at head-quarters and one at each outlying *tahsīl*. There are also a Cantonment Magistrate at Jullundur and eight honorary magistrates. The common forms of crime are burglary and theft.

Land revenue administration.

In the revenue system of Akbar the present District formed part of the Duāba Bīst Jālandhar, one of the *sarkārs* of the Lahore *Sūbah*. The later Mughal emperors soon dropped the cash assessments of Rājā Todar Mal as unprofitably just, and leased clusters of villages to the highest bidder. Under the Sikh confederacies even this remnant of system disappeared, and the ruler took whatever he could get. Ranjīt Singh followed the same principle with a greater show of method, giving large grants of land in *jāgīr* on service tenure, and either leasing the rest to farmers or entrusting the collection of the revenue to *kārdārs*, who paid him as little as they dared. When in 1846 the *doāb* came into British possession, a summary settlement was made by John Lawrence. The assessment, which amounted to $13\frac{1}{4}$ lakhs, worked well, and the total demand of the regular settlement (1846–51) was only Rs. 20,000 less. The assessment was again mainly guess-work, the demand of the summary settlement being varied only where circumstances suggested an increase or demanded some relief. A revision carried out between 1880 and 1885 resulted in a demand of 15 lakhs. This has been paid very easily ever since, and the District is prosperous and contented. The rates average Rs. 4–10–0 (maximum, Rs. 5–8–0; minimum, Rs. 3–12–0) on 'wet' land, and Rs. 1–8–0 (maximum, Rs. 2–4–0; minimum, 12 annas) on 'dry' land. The demand, including cesses, for 1903–4 was 17·8 lakhs. The average size of a proprietary holding is 1·8 acres.

The collections of land revenue alone and of total revenue are shown in the table on next page, in thousands of rupees.

Local and municipal.

The District contains nine municipalities: JULLUNDUR, KARTĀRPUR, ALĀWALPUR, PHILLAUR, NŪRMAHAL, RĀHON, NAWĀSHAHR, BANGA, and NAKODAR. Outside these, local affairs are managed by the District board, which in 1903–4 had an income of Rs. 1,55,000. The expenditure was Rs. 1,48,600, public works and education being the principal items.

	1880–1.	1890–1.	1900–1.	1903–4.
Land revenue . .	12,24	13,82	14,22	14,05
Total revenue . .	17,03	19,74	20,42	20,25

Police and jails

The regular police force consists of 453 of all ranks, including 56 cantonment and 78 municipal police. The Superintendent usually has three inspectors under him. The village watchmen number 1,305. There are twelve police stations, two road-posts, and two outposts. The fort at Phillaur was made over in 1891 to the Police Training School and central bureau of the Criminal Identification department. The District jail at head-quarters contains accommodation for 318 prisoners. The chief industries carried on in the jail are the manufacture of paper and lithographic printing.

Educati

The District stands nineteenth among the twenty-eight Districts of the Province in respect of the literacy of its population. In 1901 the proportion of literate persons was 3·6 per cent. (6·4 males and 0·3 females). The number of pupils under instruction was 7,624 in 1880–1, 15,102 in 1890–1, 13,191 in 1900–1, and 13,874 in 1903–4. The District possessed in 1903–4 a training school, 6 Anglo-vernacular high schools, 4 Anglo-vernacular and 7 vernacular middle schools, and 3 English and 124 vernacular primary schools for boys, and 23 vernacular primary schools for girls. In addition, there were 7 advanced and 262 elementary (private) schools. The number of girls in the public schools was 699, and in the private schools 941. The most important schools are in Jullundur town. The total expenditure on education in 1903–4 was 1·1 lakhs, the greater part of which was met by Local and Provincial funds.

Hospita and dis- pensarie

Besides the Jullundur civil hospital, the District has ten outlying dispensaries. At these institutions 154,504 out-patients and 4,247 in-patients were treated in 1904, and 12,883 operations were performed. The expenditure was Rs. 20,000, contributed in nearly equal shares by District and municipal funds. There is a leper asylum at Dakhni.

Vaccina tion.

The number of successful vaccinations in 1903–4 was 21,801, representing 24 per 1,000 of the population. Vaccination is compulsory in the town of Jullundur.

[H. A. Rose, *District Gazetteer* (in press); W. E. Purser, *Settlement Report* (1892).]

Jullundur Tahsīl (*Jālandhar*).—Northern *tahsīl* of Jullundur District, Punjab, lying between 31° 12′ and 31° 37′ N. and 75° 26′ and 75° 49′ E., with an area of 391 square miles. The population in 1901 was 305,976, compared with 295,301 in 1891. The head-quarters are at the town of JULLUNDUR (population, 67,735); and it also contains the towns of KARTĀRPUR (10,840) and ALĀWALPUR (4,423), with 409 villages. The land revenue and cesses amounted in 1903–4 to 4·8 lakhs. The greater part of the *tahsīl* consists of an upland plateau, with a light soil and frequent sand-hillocks, but along the north-eastern border is a belt of extremely fertile land averaging about 6 miles in width.

Nawāshahr Tahsīl.—Eastern *tahsīl* of Jullundur District, Punjab, lying on the north bank of the Sutlej, between 30° 58′ and 31° 17′ N. and 75° 47′ and 76° 16′ E., with an area of 304 square miles. The population in 1901 was 196,339, compared with 205,625 in 1891. The head-quarters are at the town of NAWĀSHAHR (population, 5,641); and it also contains the towns of RĀHON (8,651) and BANGA (4,697), with 274 villages. The land revenue and cesses amounted in 1903–4 to 4·4 lakhs. The Sutlej forms the southern boundary of the *tahsīl*, and the low-lying tract along the river has an average breadth of 4 miles. The upland plateau above the old high bank is an almost unbroken plain with a stiff loam soil.

Phillaur Tahsīl.—*Tahsīl* of Jullundur District, Punjab, lying on the north bank of the Sutlej, between 30° 57′ and 31° 13′ N. and 75° 31′ and 75° 58′ E., with an area of 291 square miles. The population in 1901 was 192,860, compared with 189,578 in 1891. The head-quarters are at the town of PHILLAUR (population, 6,986); and it also contains the towns of NŪRMAHAL (8,706) and JANDIĀLA (6,620), with 222 villages. The land revenue and cesses amounted in 1903–4 to 4·2 lakhs. The Sutlej forms the southern boundary of the *tahsīl*, and along the right bank is a narrow strip of low-lying alluvial land about 1½ miles in width. The uplands which form the greater part of the *tahsīl* are an unbroken plain with a loam soil.

Nakodar Tahsīl.—Western *tahsīl* of Jullundur District, Punjab, lying on the north bank of the Sutlej, between 30° 56′ and 31° 15′ N. and 75° 5′ and 75° 37′ E., with an area of 371 square miles. The population in 1901 was 222,412, compared with 217,079 in 1891. The head-quarters are at the town of NAKODAR (population, 9,958), and it also contains 311 villages. The land revenue and cesses amounted in 1903–4 to 4·3 lakhs. The Sutlej forms the southern boundary of the *tahsīl*. The alluvial lowlands along the right bank average 7 miles in breadth. The soil of the uplands above the old bank of the river is a light loam, and low sand ridges are not uncommon. The Eastern Bein passes through the *tahsīl*.

Alāwalpur.—Town in the *tahsīl* and District of Jullundur, Punjab, situated in 31° 26′ N. and 75° 40′ E. The chief trade is in *sūsī* and *gabrūn* cloth, and in agricultural produce. Population (1901), 4,423. The municipality was created in 1867. The income during the ten years ending 1902–3 averaged Rs. 2,300, and the expenditure Rs. 2,400. In 1903–4 the income was Rs. 2,100, chiefly from octroi; and the expenditure was Rs. 2,200. The municipality maintains a vernacular middle school.

Banga.—Town in the Nawāshahr *tahsīl* of Jullundur District, Punjab, situated in 31° 11′ N. and 76° 0′ E. Population (1901), 4,697. The principal trade is in sugar, manufactures of brass-ware, and carpenter's work. The municipality was created in 1867. The income during the ten years ending 1902–3 averaged Rs. 5,900, and the expenditure Rs. 5,700. In 1903–4 the income was Rs. 8,000, chiefly from octroi; and the expenditure was Rs. 7,200. The town possesses a vernacular middle school maintained by the municipality, and a Government dispensary.

Jandiāla.—Town in the Phillau [illegible] lundur District, Punjab, situated in 31° 34′ N. [illegible] E. Population (1901), 6,620. It ceased to be a municipality in 1872.

Jullundur Town (*Jālandhar*).—Head-quarters of the Division and District of Jullundur, Punjab, situated in 31° 20′ N. and 75° 35′ E., on the North-Western Railway and grand trunk road. It is distant by rail from Ca[illegible]tta 1,180 miles, from Bombay 1,247 miles, and from Karāchi 916 miles. Population (1901), including cantonments, 67,735, of whom 24,715 were Hindus, 40,081 Muhammadans, 901 Sikhs, and 1,543 Christians. Jullundur was, when visited by Hiuen Tsiang, a large city, 2 miles in circuit, the capital of a Rājput kingdom. It was taken by Ibrāhīm Shāh of Ghor about 1088. Under the Mughals Jullundur was the capital of a *sarkār*; it was burnt by the Sikhs in 1757, and captured by the Faizullahpuria confederacy in 1766. Ranjīt Singh annexed it in 1811, and in 1846 Jullundur became the head-quarters of the territory acquired by the British after the first Sikh War. The town is surrounded by several suburbs known as *bastis*, the most important of which are Basti Dānishmandān (population, 2,770) and Basti Shaikh Darwesh (7,109), founded by Ansāri Shaikhs from Kāniguram in the seventeenth century.

The town contains two flour-mills, to one of which is attached a small iron and brass foundry. The number of hands employed in 1904 was 73. Silk is also manufactured, and good carpenter's work is turned out. The municipality was created in 1867. The income during the ten years ending 1902-3 averaged Rs. 70,600, and the expenditure Rs. 68,800. In 1903-4 the income amounted to Rs. 84,300, chiefly from octroi; and the expenditure to Rs. 86,900, the main items being public health (Rs. 32,300) and administration (Rs. 28,600). The chief educational institutions are four Anglo-vernacular high schools, maintained by the municipality, the Presbyterian Mission, and the two rival branches of the Arya Samāj. There is also a civil hospital.

The cantonment, established in 1846, lies 4 miles to the south-east of the town. Population (1901), 13,280. The garrison consists of two batteries of field artillery, one battalion of British infantry, one regiment of native cavalry, and a battalion of native infantry, with a regimental dépôt. The income and expenditure from cantonment funds during the ten years ending 1902-3 averaged Rs. 40,000 and Rs. 41,000 respectively. There is an aided Anglo-vernacular high school.

Kartārpur.—Town in the District and *tahsīl* of Jullundur, Punjab, situated in 31° 26′ N. and 75° 30′ E., on the North-Western Railway and grand trunk road, 9 miles from Jullundur town. Population (1901), 10,840. Founded by Arjun, the fifth Sikh Gurū, it is a place of great sanctity, as the seat of the line of Gurūs descended from him, and as possessing his original Adi Granth or scripture. It was burnt by Ahmad Shāh in 1756. Kartārpur is a flourishing grain mart, with a market outside octroi limits. Chairs, boxes, tables, and native flutes are made; also cotton twill (*sūsī*). The cantonment established here after the first Sikh War was abolished in 1854. The municipality was created in 1867. The income during the ten years ending 1902-3 averaged Rs. 7,500, and the expenditure Rs. 6,900. In 1903-4 the income was Rs. 7,300, mainly from octroi; and the expenditure was Rs. 10,600. The town has an Anglo-vernacular middle school, maintained by the municipality, and a Government dispensary.

Nakodar Town.—Head-quarters of the *tahsīl* of the same name, Jullundur District, Punjab, situated in 31° 8′ N. and 75° 29′ E. Population (1901), 9,958. Taking its name from the Nikūdari wing or legion of the Mughals, it became a stronghold of the Sikh chief, Tārā Singh, Ghaiba, and was captured by Ranjīt Singh in 1815. The cantonment established here after the first Sikh War was abolished in 1854. Nakodar contains two fine tombs dated 1612 and 1637. It has a considerable trade in agricultural produce, and *hukka* tubes and iron jars are manufactured. The municipality was created in 1867. The income during the ten years ending 1902-3 averaged Rs. 9,100, and the expenditure Rs. 8,800. In 1903-4 the income was Rs. 9,300, chiefly from octroi; and the expenditure was Rs. 10,100. The town has an Anglo-vernacular middle school, maintained by the municipality, and a Government dispensary.

Nawāshahr Town.—Head-quarters of the *tahsīl* of the same name, Jullundur District, Punjab, situated in 31° 8′ N. and 76° 7′ E. Population (1901), 5,641. A stronghold of the Sikh chief, Tārā Singh, Ghaiba, it was annexed after his death by Ranjīt Singh. It is of no commercial importance. The municipality was created in 1867. The income during the ten years ending 1902-3 averaged Rs. 4,600, and the expenditure Rs. 4,700. In 1903-4 the income was Rs. 4,800, chiefly from octroi; and the expenditure was Rs. 5,300. The municipality maintains an Anglo-vernacular middle school.

Nūrmahal.—Town in the Phillaur *tahsīl* of Jullundur District, Punjab, situated in 31° 6′ N. and 75° 36′ E. Population (1901), 8,706. It lay on the old imperial road from Delhi to Lahore and was refounded by Nūr Jahān, wife of Jahāngīr. A large *sarai* was built by her orders, the west gateway of which is still in good preservation. The town has some manufacture of *gabrūn* cloth. The municipality was created in 1867. The income and expenditure during the ten years ending 1902-3 averaged Rs. 6,300. In 1903-4 the income was Rs. 6,100, chiefly from octroi; and the expenditure was Rs. 5,900. The town possesses a vernacular middle school, maintained by the municipality, and a Government dispensary.

Phillaur Town.—Head-quarters of the *tahsīl* of the same name, Jullundur District, Punjab, situated in 31° 1′ N. and 75° 48′ E., on the north bank of the Sutlej, on the North-Western Railway and grand trunk road. Population (1901), 6,986. The town was founded by Shāh Jahān, who built a royal *sarai* here, converted by Ranjīt Singh into a fort in consequence of the British occupation of Ludhiāna. A cantonment was established here after the first Sikh War, but the native troops mutinied in 1857 and it was not reoccupied. The fort was made over in 1891 to the Police department, and is now occupied by the Police Training School and the central bureau of the Criminal Identification department. The chief commercial importance of the place is as a timber market. Its only manufacture is that of cotton cloth. The Sutlej is crossed here by a railway bridge 5,193 feet long, completed in 1870. There is no foot-bridge, but ferry trains are run at frequent intervals. The municipality was created in 1867. The income and expenditure during the ten years ending 1902–3 averaged Rs. 9,400. In 1903–4 the income was Rs. 11,000, chiefly from octroi; and the expenditure was Rs. 11,000. The town has an Anglo-vernacular middle school, maintained by the municipality, and a Government dispensary.

Rāhon.—Town in the Nawāshahr *tahsīl* of Jullundur District, Punjab, situated in 31° 4′ N. and 76° 8′ E. Population (1901), 8,651. It is said to have been founded before the Christian era by one Rājā Raghab, who gave it the name of Raghūpur, which is still used by Hindu scholars. It was captured by the Ghorewāha Rājputs in the time of Muhammad of Ghor, whose leader renamed it Rāhon after a lady called Rāho. It is still considered unlucky to use the name Rāhon before breakfast; till then it is called Zanāna Shahr or 'woman town.' It was seized by the Sikh chief Tārā Singh, Ghaiba, in 1759, and annexed on his death by Ranjīt Singh. The chief manufactures are imitation gold and silver braid and cotton cloth, and there is a considerable trade in sugar. The municipality was created in 1867. The income and expenditure during the ten years ending 1902–3 averaged Rs. 11,200. In 1903–4 the income was Rs. 10,500, chiefly from octroi; and the expenditure was Rs. 10,700. The town possesses an Anglo-vernacular middle school, maintained by the municipality, and a Government dispensary.

Boundaries, configuration, and hill and river systems.

Ludhiāna District.—District in the Jullundur Division of the Punjab, lying between 30° 34′ and 31° 1′ N. and 75° 22′ and 76° 24′ E., with an area of 1,455 square miles. It is bounded on the north by the Sutlej, which separates it from the District of Jullundur; on the east by Ambāla District and the Patiāla State; on the south by the territories of the chiefs of Patiāla, Nābha, and Māler Kotla; and on the west by the District of Ferozepore. In the south several of its outlying villages are scattered among the States of Patiāla, Jīnd, Nābha, and Māler Kotla; while, on the other hand, in the east two or three groups of Patiāla villages lie within its territory. It is divided into two portions by the high bank which marks the ancient bed of the Sutlej. At its foot lies a half-deserted watercourse, called the Budha nullah, still full in all but the driest seasons, and once the main channel of the Sutlej. The principal stream of that river now runs farther north, leaving a broad alluvial strip, 2 to 6 miles in width, between its ancient and its modern beds. This strip, known as the Bet, forms the wider channel of the river, and is partly inundated after heavy rain. It is intersected in every direction by minor watercourses or nullahs, and, being composed of recent alluvium, is for the most part very fertile, but its eastern extremity has been injuriously affected by percolation from the Sirhind Canal. The uplands to the south of the high bank consist of a level plain, sloping gently to the south-west and broken only by some lines of sandhills which are very common in the Jangal, the south-western portion of the uplands; this tract is traversed throughout by the Sirhind Canal.

Geology and botany. There is nothing of geological interest in the District, which is situated entirely in the alluvium. It includes the extreme north-west corner of the Upper Gangetic plain, but to the south-west it approximates to the desert region. Trees are few, unless where planted; but the *rerū* (*Acacia leucophloea*) is locally frequent, and the *kīkar* (*Acacia arabica*), which is perhaps not aboriginal, is plentiful. The *ber* (*Zizyphus Jujuba*) is common in gardens and near homesteads.

Fauna. Wolves are not uncommon. *Nīlgai*, antelope, and 'ravine deer' (Indian gazelle) are found throughout the southern part of the District, and hog in the rank grass near the Sutlej and Budha nullah.

Climate and temperature. The heat in May and June is intense, but no worse than in most parts of the Punjab plains. During the monsoon the air is damp and the climate relaxing, except in the Jangal with its dry climate and pure water; and this tract is free from the outbreaks of autumnal fever, which sometimes occur after heavy rains in September. The Bet is peculiarly liable to these epidemics, and enlarged spleen and anaemia due to malarial poisoning are there common.

Rainfall. The rainfall is normal for the Punjab plains, ranging from 29 inches per annum at Samrāla to 22 at Jagraon.

History and archaeology. The early history of the District is obscure. SUNET, near Ludhiāna, MACHHĪWĀRA, and Tihāra are all places of some antiquity, dating from the pre-Muhammadan period. The last, which lies in the north-west corner of the District, is identified by tradition with the Vairāta of the Mahābhārata, and was a place of some importance; but the ancient site has long been washed away by the Sutlej. The town of LUDHIĀNA dates only from the Lodī period, and the principality of RAIKOT originated in a grant of the Saiyid kings of Delhi. Under

Akbar the tract formed a part of the *sarkār* of Sirhind, but the later Mughals leased the western part of the present District to the Rais of Raikot. Early in the eighteenth century they became semi-independent; and though the imperial forces successfully withstood Ahmad Shāh near Khanna in 1747, his subsequent invasions so weakened the Mughal power that the Rais were suffered to take possession of Ludhiāna town in 1760. Meanwhile the Sikhs had become a political power, especially on the south and south-west borders of the District; and after their capture of Sirhind the Samrāla *tahsīl* fell into the hands of Sikh leaders, while the Rais retained most of the Ludhiāna and Jagraon *tahsīls*. In 1798 the Rai, a minor, was attacked by the Sikhs under Bedi Sāhib Singh of Una, who invested Ludhiāna, but raised the siege when the Rai called in George Thomas. Finally, in 1806, Ranjīt Singh crossed the Sutlej on his first expedition against the cis-Sutlej chiefs, and stripped the Rais of their possessions, leaving a couple of villages for the maintenance of two widows, who were the only remaining representatives of the ruling family.

In 1809, after Ranjīt Singh's third invasion, a treaty was concluded between him and the British Government, by which his further conquests were stopped, although he was allowed to retain all territories acquired in his first two expeditions. At the same time, all the CIS-SUTLEJ STATES that had not been absorbed were taken under British protection. In the same year (1809) a cantonment for British troops was placed at Ludhiāna, compensation being made to the Rājā of Jīnd, in whose possession it then was. In 1835, on the failure of the direct line of the Jīnd family, a tract of country round Ludhiāna came into British possession by lapse, and this formed the nucleus of the present District.

On the outbreak of the first Sikh War, Ludhiāna was left with a small garrison insufficient to prevent part of the cantonments being burnt by the chief of Lādwa or to oppose the passage of the Sutlej by Ranjodh Singh. Sir Harry Smith threw some 4,000 men into the place, after losing nearly all his baggage at the action of Baddowāl. This reverse was, however, retrieved by the battle fought at ALĪWĀL, close to the Sutlej, in which Ranjodh Singh was driven across the river, and the upper Sutlej cleared of the enemy.

On the conclusion of the first Sikh War in 1846, the District assumed very nearly its present limits, by the addition of territory annexed from the Lahore government and its adherents south of the Sutlej. Since the British occupation, the town of

Ludhiāna has grown in wealth and population, but its history has been marked by few noticeable events. The cantonment was abandoned in 1854. During the Mutiny in 1857 an unsuccessful attempt was made by the Deputy-Commissioner, Mr. Ricketts, with a small force, to stop the rebellious sepoys from Jullundur on their way to Delhi; but, with the assistance rendered by the chiefs of Nābha and Māler Kotla, he was able to prevent an outbreak in the turbulent and disaffected town of Ludhiāna. In the villages the Muhammadan Gūjars were the only people to show signs of disaffection, the Hindu and Sikh Jats remaining steadfastly loyal. In 1872 occurred an outbreak of the fanatical sect of Kūkas, 150 of whom, starting from Bhaini in this District, made a raid upon Malaudh and the Muhammadan State of Māler Kotla. No adherents joined them, and the outbreak was at once suppressed; Rām Singh, the leader of the sect, was deported from India. Since the first Afghān War (1838–42), Ludhiāna town has been the residence of the exiled family of Shāh Shujā.

Besides the ruins of Sunet above mentioned there are no antiquities of importance. Under the Mughal emperors the imperial road from Lahore to Delhi ran through the District, and is marked by *kos minārs* and by a large *sarai*, built in the reign of Aurangzeb, at Khanna.

The population of the District at the last four enumerations was: (1868) 585,547, (1881) 618,835, (1891) 648,722, and (1901) 673,097, dwelling in 5 towns and 864 villages. The District is divided into three *tahsīls*—LUDHIĀNA, JAGRAON, and SAMRĀLA—the head-quarters of each being at the place from which it is named. The towns are the municipalities of LUDHIĀNA, the head-quarters of the District, JAGRAON, KHANNA, RAIKOT, and MĀCHHĪWĀRA. The people.

The following table shows the chief statistics of population in 1901:—

Tahsīl.	Area in square miles.	Number of Towns.	Number of Villages.	Population.	Population per square mile.	Percentage of variation in population between 1891 and 1901.	Number of persons able to read and write.
Ludhiāna	683	1	432	333,337	488.0	+ 2.9	16,443
Samrāla	291	2	263	154,995	532.6	− 2.4	7,848
Jagraon	417	2	169	184,765	443.1	+ 11.1	7,605
District total	1,455	5	864	673,097	462.6	+ 3.8	31,896

NOTE.—The figures for the areas of *tahsīls* are taken from the revenue returns. The total District area is that given in the *Census Report*.

Hindus number 269,076, or 40 per cent. of the population; Muhammadans, 235,937, or 35 per cent.; and Sikhs, 164,919, or 24 per cent. The language of the District is Punjābi.

Castes and occupations.

The tribes and castes are distinguished by no local peculiarities. Jats or Jāts number 235,000, or 35 per cent. of the total, 132,000 being Sikhs and 77,000 Hindus. If the Jats are the best peasantry in India, the Jats of the MĀLWĀ (i.e. those of Ferozepore and Ludhiāna) possess in a greater degree than any other branch of the tribe the qualities which have earned for them this distinction. They have a finer physique, and as farmers are more prudent and thrifty, than their brethren in Lahore and Amritsar. The Rājputs (29,000) are undoubtedly the oldest of the agricultural tribes now found in the District. They are almost all Muhammadans, and present a striking contrast to the Sikh and Hindu Jats, being indolent and thriftless cultivators. The Gūjars (33,000) are mainly Muhammadans, behind the Jats in general ability, and as a tribe turbulent, lawless, and discontented. Lastly come the Arains (32,000), who are invariably Muhammadans, excelling as market-gardeners and making more than any one else out of a small plot of land, but incapable of managing large areas. The religious castes include Brāhmans (25,000), who generally live on the Jats of the uplands, and the Muhammadan Madāris (6,000). About 17,000 persons (including the Madāris) are classed as Fakīrs. The Sūds (200) deserve mention, as Ludhiāna is considered the head-quarters of their tribe. They are intelligent, and take readily to clerical service under Government. Among the artisan and menial castes may be mentioned the Chamārs (leather-workers), 63,000; Chūhrās (scavengers), 22,000; Jhīnwars (water-carriers), 18,000; Kumhārs (potters), 10,000; Lohārs (blacksmiths), 9,000; Julāhās (weavers), 17,000; Mochīs (cobblers), 9,000; Nais (barbers), 12,000; Sonārs (goldsmiths), 7,000; Tarkhāns (carpenters), 21,000; and Telis (oil-pressers), 14,000. About 55 per cent. of the total population are returned as agricultural.

Christian missions.

Ludhiāna is the chief station in India of the American Presbyterian Mission. Founded here in 1834, the Mission has established many branches throughout the Punjab and United Provinces, and maintains a large number of dispensaries and schools, among which the Forman Christian College at LAHORE is the best known. In 1901 the District contained 415 native Christians.

General agricul-

The soil of the Sutlej riverain is a stiff moist loam, constantly fertilized in the immediate neighbourhood of the river by the silt deposited by it. In the uplands south of the high bank every variety of soil is found, from stiff clay to the lightest of sand, the lighter soils prevailing along the high bank and to the south-west of the District, while those of the eastern parts are much stiffer. Where there is no irrigation, the light sandy loam is the safest soil: although with copious rain its yield is much less than that of the stiffer soils, it is far more able to resist drought. tural conditions.

Chief agricultural statistics and principal crops.

The District is held almost entirely by communities of peasant proprietors, estates held by large landowners covering only about 24 square miles.

The area for which details are available from the revenue records of 1903-4 is 1,394 square miles, as shown below:—

Tahsīl.	Total.	Cultivated.	Irrigated.	Cultivable waste.
Ludhiāna . .	685	572	148	57
Samrāla . .	291	245	90	19
Jagraon . .	418	376	71	17
Total	1,394	1,193	309	93

The principal crops of the spring harvest are wheat and gram, the areas under which were 364 and 285 square miles in 1903-4. Barley covered 32 square miles and rapeseed 35 square miles. Maize is the chief crop of the autumn harvest with 115 square miles; pulses covered 145 square miles, great millet 47 square miles, and spiked millet 4,110 acres. Sugar-cane covered only 18 square miles, but it is the most valuable autumn crop.

Improvements in agricultural practice.

During the twenty years ending 1901 the cultivated area increased by more than 30,000 acres, the increase being chiefly due to the construction of the SIRHIND CANAL. As no more canal water can be spared for this District, the cultivated area, which now amounts to more than four-fifths of the total, is not likely to increase much farther. Loans under the Land Improvement Loans Act are not very popular, about Rs. 2,000 having been advanced during the five years ending 1904.

Cattle, horses, sheep, &c.

Ludhiāna is not a great cattle-breeding District, owing to the small area available for grazing, and a large proportion of the cattle are imported from the breeding tracts to the south. The horses of the Jangal tract, in which part of the Jagraon *tahsīl* lies, are a famous breed descended from Arab stallions kept at Bhatinda by the Mughal emperors. The District board maintains 4 horse and 11 donkey stallions. Sheep and goats are kept in almost every village, and camels in the Jangal tract.

A large number of ducks and geese are reared in the old cantonment for the Simla market.

Irrigation.

Of the total area cultivated in 1903–4, 309 square miles, or 26 per cent., were classed as irrigated. Of this area, 219 square miles were irrigated from wells, 513 acres from wells and canals, 89 square miles from canals, and 103 acres from streams and tanks. In addition, 66 square miles, or 6 per cent., were subject to inundation from the Sutlej. The canal-irrigation is from the SIRHIND CANAL. The main line traverses the Samrāla *tahsīl* without irrigating it, and then below Doraha (in Patiāla State) gives off the Abohar and Bhatinda branches; the former passes through the Ludhiāna and Jagraon *tahsīls*, supplying them from six distributaries, while the extreme south of the District is watered by a distributary of the Bhatinda branch. Wells in the uplands are of masonry, worked by bullocks on the rope-and-bucket system; in the riverain tract, owing to the nearness of the water to the surface, lever and unbricked wells are largely used. In 1903–4 the District contained 10,481 masonry wells, and 362 unbricked and lever wells and water-lifts.

Forests and minerals.

The only forests are two plantations of *shīsham* (*Dalbergia Sissoo*) on the banks of the Sutlej, 'reserved' under the Forest Act, with an area of 197 acres. There are also 179 acres of forest land under the District board. *Kankar* is found in many places.

Arts and manufactures.

The chief industry is the weaving of shawls, known as Rāmpur *chādars*, from the wool of the Tibetan goat and other fine wools. The industry is chiefly carried on by a colony of Kashmīris, who in 1833 migrated from Kashmīr on account of a famine, and settled in Ludhiāna town, where shawls used to be made until the trade was killed by the Franco-German War. Cotton stuffs are produced largely, and Ludhiāna is famous for its turbans, which are imported from Hoshiārpur and embroidered in the town. Many regiments of the Indian army are supplied with turbans from Ludhiāna. Check cloths known as *gabrūn* are also made in large quantities from English and American yarns. Ivory billiard-balls are turned at Ludhiāna and Jagraon. The sugar industry is important, and a great deal of oil is expressed and exported. The District possesses two factories for ginning cotton, and two flour-mills. Both the ginning factories and one of the flour-mills are at Khanna, and the other flour-mill is at Ludhiāna town. The number of employés in the ginning factories in 1904 was 145, and in the flour-mills 44.

There is a large export of wheat to Karāchi, and of rapeseed, oil, maize, millets, and pulses to the United Provinces and Bengal; woollen and cotton goods are exported all over India. The chief imports are piece-goods, cotton yarn, sugar from the Jullundur Doāb, and iron, salt, brass and copper vessels, and barley and inferior grains from the Native States to the south. Commerce and trade.

The main line of the North-Western Railway passes through Ludhiāna town, from which place the Ludhiāna-Dhūrī-Jākhal Railway (also broad gauge) runs to Dhūrī on the Rājpura-Bhatinda line and Jākhal on the Southern Punjab Railway. A line connecting Ludhiāna with Ferozepore, Fāzilka, and M'Leodganj on the Southern Punjab Railway has recently been opened. The grand trunk road passes through the District by the side of the main line of railway, and an important metalled road runs from Ludhiāna town via Ferozepore to Lahore. The total length of metalled roads is 165 miles and of unmetalled roads 207 miles; of the former, 75 miles are under the Public Works department and the rest under the District board. The main line and Abohar branches of the SIRHIND CANAL are navigable, as is the Sutlej during the rains. The Sutlej is crossed by twelve ferries. Railways and roads.

The District suffered, like the rest of the country, in the *chālīsa* famine of 1783, and famines occurred in 1813 and 1833. In 1861 and 1869 there was considerable scarcity, and Rs. 6,000 and Rs. 7,000 respectively was spent on famine relief. Ludhiāna was unaffected by the scarcity of 1878. The opening of the Sirhind Canal has made the District secure against drought, and food-grains were exported during the famines of 1897 and 1900. The area of crops matured in the famine year 1899–1900 amounted to 72 per cent. of the normal. Famine.

The District is in charge of a Deputy-Commissioner, aided by four Assistant or Extra Assistant Commissioners, of whom one is in charge of the District treasury. It is divided into the *tahsīls* of LUDHIĀNA, SAMRĀLA, and JAGRAON, each under a *tahsīldār* assisted by a *naib-tahsīldār*. District subdivisions and staff.

The Deputy-Commissioner as District Magistrate is responsible for criminal justice. The civil judicial work is under a District Judge, subordinate to the Divisional Judge of the Ambāla Civil Division, who is also Sessions Judge. There are four Munsifs, two at head-quarters and one at each outlying *tahsīl*. There are nine honorary magistrates. The crime of the District presents no features of special interest. Civil justice and crime.

Under Akbar the District formed part of the Sirhind division Land revenue administration.

or *sarkār*. The revenue system was elaborate, being based on uniform measurements of the land and a careful classification of soils. Produce estimates were made, and the Government share fixed at one-third of the gross out-turn. Under Akbar's successors, and still more under the Sikhs, revenue assessment degenerated into a system of direct or vicarious extortion. The government, when it was strong enough, and its lessees when it was not, were restrained in their exactions only by the fear of losing their cultivators altogether. A summary assessment was made in 1847–9, a reduction varying from 3 to 6 annas in the rupee being allowed on the existing demand The regular settlement further reduced the demand by 11 per cent., the amount fixed in 1850 being 9·3 lakhs. This assessment worked well. Despite two periods of scarcity the revenue was punctually paid, and in no case were coercive measures found necessary. Transfers of land were few and credit remained generally good. The current settlement, carried out in 1879–83, was based on an estimated rise since 1860 of 50 per cent. in prices, and an increase of 8 per cent. in cultivation; but the proportion of the 'assets' taken was one-half instead of two-thirds, and the enhancement amounted to 18 per cent. The revenue rates average Rs. 2–7–0 (maximum, Rs. 4; minimum, Rs. 1–6–0) on irrigated land, and Rs. 1–9–0 (maximum, Rs. 2–10–0; minimum, 8 annas) on unirrigated. The demand for the first year was 10·9 lakhs, including 1·6 lakhs *jāgīr* revenue; and in 1903–4, including cesses, amounted to over 12·4 lakhs. The average size of a holding cultivated by an owner is 3·2 acres, by an occupancy tenant 1·9, and by a tenant-at-will 1·6 acres.

The collections of land revenue alone and of total revenue are shown below, in thousands of rupees:—

	1880–1.	1890–1.	1900–1.	1903–4.
Land revenue . .	7,96	9,24	9,33	9,50
Total revenue . .	10,22	12,43	14,40	14,40

Local and municipal.

The District contains five municipalities: LUDHIĀNA, JAGRAON, KHANNA, RAIKOT, and MĀCHHĪWĀRA. Outside these, local affairs are managed by a District board, whose income in 1903–4 was Rs. 1,35,000, and expenditure Rs. 1,47,000. Education is the principal item of local expenditure.

Police and jails.

The regular police force consists of 508 of all ranks, including 117 municipal police, under a Superintendent, who usually has three inspectors to assist him. The village watchmen number

917. There are 12 police stations, 2 outposts, and 16 road-posts. The District jail at head-quarters has accommodation for 318 prisoners.

The District stands fourth among the twenty-eight Districts of the Province in respect of the literacy of its population. In 1901 the proportion of literate persons was 4·7 per cent. (8·3 males and 0·1 females). The number of pupils under instruction was 3,977 in 1880–1, 8,875 in 1890–1, 10,825 in 1900–1, and 8,763 in 1903–4. In the last year the District possessed 19 secondary, 104 primary, and 2 special (public) schools, and 8 advanced and 73 elementary (private) schools, with 633 girls in the public and 351 in the private schools. The comparatively high standard of education is largely due to the energy of the missionaries. The two mission high schools at Ludhiāna, one of them a boarding-school, are aided by Government. There are fifteen middle schools throughout the District, including one for girls at Gujarwāl. The District board maintains a technical school, teaching up to the middle standard, at Ludhiāna. The North India School of Medicine for Christian Women gives professional teaching. The total expenditure on education in 1903–4 was 1·1 lakhs, of which District funds supplied Rs. 25,000 and municipal funds Rs. 18,000. Government grants came to Rs. 5,000, and fees brought in Rs. 28,000. **Education.**

Besides the civil hospital and branch dispensary at Ludhiāna town, the District has six outlying dispensaries. At these institutions 103,764 out-patients and 1,336 in-patients were treated in 1904, and 5,206 operations were performed. The expenditure was Rs. 20,000, of which about half came from municipal funds. **Hospitals and dispensaries.**

The number of successful vaccinations in 1903–4 was 12,090, representing 18 per 1,000 of the population. **Vaccination.**

[H. A. Rose, *District Gazetteer* (in press); T. G. Walker, *Settlement Report* (1884), and *The Customary Law of the Ludhiāna District* (1885).]

Ludhiāna Tahsīl.—*Tahsīl* of Ludhiāna District, Punjab, lying on the south bank of the Sutlej, between 30° 34′ and 31° 1′ N. and 75° 36′ and 76° 9′ E., with an area of 685 square miles. The population in 1901 was 333,337, compared with 323,700 in 1891. The town of LUDHIĀNA (population, 48,649) is the *tahsīl* head-quarters, and there are 432 villages. The land revenue and cesses amounted in 1903–4 to 5·8 lakhs. The northern portion lies in the Sutlej lowlands, and the southern in the upland plain irrigated by the Abohar and Bhatinda branches of the Sirhind Canal.

Samrāla Tahsīl.—*Tahsīl* of Ludhiāna District, Punjab, lying on the south bank of the Sutlej, between 30° 37′ and 30° 59′ N. and 76° 2′ and 76° 24′ E., with an area of 291 square miles. The population in 1901 was 154,995, compared with 158,770 in 1891. It contains the two towns of KHANNA (population, 3,838) and MĀCHHĪWĀRA (5,588), and 263 villages, among which is Samrāla, the head-quarters. The land revenue and cesses amounted in 1903–4 to 3·5 lakhs.

Jagraon Tahsīl.—*Tahsīl* of Ludhiāna District, Punjab, lying on the south bank of the Sutlej, between 30° 35′ and 30° 59′ N. and 75° 22′ and 75° 47′ E., with an area of 418 square miles. It is bounded on the east and south by Patiāla and Māler Kotla States. The population in 1901 was 184,765, compared with 166,252 in 1891. It contains the two towns of JAGRAON (population, 18,760), the head-quarters, and RAIKOT (10,131); and 169 villages. The land revenue and cesses amounted in 1903–4 to 3·3 lakhs. It is divided into the Bet or Sutlej lowlands, and the Dhaia or upland plain, irrigated by the Abohar branch of the Sirhind Canal. The battle-field of ALĪWĀL is in this *tahsīl*.

Alīwāl.—Village in the Jagraon *tahsīl* of Ludhiāna District, Punjab, situated in 30° 56′ N. and 75° 38′ E., the scene of the battle fought by Sir Harry Smith on January 28, 1846, against the Sikhs. The Sikh force, which amounted to about 15,000 men, was posted in the lowlands close to the Sutlej, with the right resting on the village of Bhundri on the high bank, and the left on Alīwāl close to the river. East of Bhundri the high bank or ridge, which separates the valley of the Sutlej from the uplands, sweeps inwards in a semicircle to the distance of 5 or 6 miles, crowned with villages at intervals, and leaving a wide open plain between it and the river. It was across this plain that the British army on the morning of January 28 moved to the attack, the capture of the village of Alīwāl, the key of the position, being the first object. The Sikh guns were as usual well served; but Alīwāl was in the hands of inferior troops and the resistance was spiritless. By the capture of the village the Sikh left was turned; but round Bhundri their right, composed of trained and enthusiastic Khālsa troops, made a most determined stand, and the whole battle is still called by natives the fight of Bhundri. The most gallant part of the action was the charge by the 16th Lancers of the unbroken Sikh infantry, who received them in square. Three times the Sikhs were ridden over, but they reformed at once on each occasion; and it was not till the whole strength of the British was brought to bear on them that they were at length compelled to turn their backs. The Sikh troops were either driven across the river, in which many of them were drowned, or dispersed themselves over the uplands. The British loss was considerable, amounting to 400 men killed and wounded. A tall monument, erected in the centre of the plain to the memory of those who fell, marks the scene of the action.

Bahlolpur (*Bhilolpur*).—Village in the Samrāla *tahsīl* of Ludhiāna District, Punjab, situated in 30° 55′ N. and 76° 22′ E. Population (1901), 2,194. It was founded in the reign of the emperor Akbar by two Afghāns, Bahlol Khān and Bahādur Khān, whose descendants still live here. It is now of no importance. Three tombs, said to date from the time of Akbar, stand on the west side of the village.

Jagraon Town.—Head-quarters of the *tahsīl* of the same name in Ludhiāna District, Punjab, situated in 30° 47′ N. and 75° 28′ E., 26 miles from Ludhiāna town. Population (1901), 18,760. There is a considerable trade in wheat and sugar, and a local industry in ivory-carving, billiard-balls being turned. The municipality was created in 1867. The income during the ten years ending 1902–3 averaged Rs. 18,200, and the expenditure Rs. 15,600. In 1903–4 the income was Rs. 19,500, chiefly derived from octroi; and the expenditure was Rs. 25,000. The town has a Government dispensary, and the municipality maintains an Anglo-vernacular middle school.

Khanna.—Town in the Samrāla *tahsīl* of Ludhiāna District, Punjab, situated in 30° 42′ N. and 76° 13′ E., on the North-Western Railway, 27 miles from Ludhiāna town. Population (1901), 3,838. The town possesses two cotton-ginning factories, with a flour-mill attached to one of them. The number of employés in the factories in 1904 was 145, and in the mill 30. Khanna is a dépôt for the agricultural produce of the neighbourhood. It contains an Anglo-Sanskrit middle school (unaided) and a Government dispensary. The municipality was created in 1875. The income during the ten years ending 1902–3 averaged Rs. 6,400, and the expenditure Rs. 6,100. In 1903–4 the income was Rs. 6,600, chiefly derived from octroi; and the expenditure was Rs. 5,900.

Ludhiāna Town.—Head-quarters of the District and *tahsīl* of Ludhiāna, Punjab, situated in 30° 56′ N. and 75° 52′ E., on the grand trunk road. It is the junction of the North-Western, Ludhiāna-Dhūrī-Jākhal, and the Ludhiāna-Ferozepore-M'Leodganj Railways; distant by rail from Calcutta 1,148 miles, from Bombay 1,215, and from Karāchi 884. Population (1901), 48,649. The town is connected by metalled roads with Jagraon (24 miles) and Samrāla (21 miles). It was founded in 1481 by two Lodī Pathāns, from whom it took its name of Lodiāna, corrupted into Ludhiāna. It was the seat of government for this part of the empire under the Lodīs, but under the Mughals was only the head-quarters of a *mahāl* in the *sarkār* of Sirhind, though it continued to be a place of importance. It passed into the possession of the Rais of Raikot in 1760, and in 1806 was taken by Ranjīt Singh, who gave it to his uncle, Rājā Bhāg Singh of Jīnd. Land west of the town was allotted to the British in 1809 for a cantonment, which was up to 1838 the only outpost on the Sutlej frontier. The town and surrounding country escheated on the death of Rājā Sangat Singh of Jīnd in 1835. Ludhiāna was in 1842 fixed on as the residence of the family of the ex-Amīr Shujā-ul-mulk. The cantonment was abandoned in 1854. The fort, built on the site of that constructed by the original founders, owes its present shape to Sir D. Ochterlony.

The municipality was created in 1867. The receipts and expenditure during the ten years ending 1902–3 averaged Rs. 92,800 and Rs. 92,600 respectively. In 1903–4 the income was 1·2 lakhs, the chief source being octroi (Rs. 92,000); while the expenditure of 1·1 lakhs included conservancy (Rs. 12,000), education (Rs. 24,000), medical (Rs. 10,000), public safety (Rs. 15,000), and administration (Rs. 18,000). Ludhiāna is famous for its manufacture of *pashmīna* shawls, which was introduced by some Kashmīri immigrants in 1833. Cotton fabrics are also largely woven, checks and *gabrūns* being made in considerable quantities. Embroidery is largely carried on. The Ludhiāna turbans are also famous, and a certain amount of ivory turning is carried on, including the manufacture of billiard-balls. The town stands next to Amritsar in the excellence of its dyeing of wool and silk. It is an important centre for ornamental woodwork and furniture, and also a large grain mart. A flour-mill has recently been established, which in 1904 gave employment to 14 hands. The principal educational institutions are the four Anglo-vernacular high schools: one maintained by the municipality, the management of which was taken over by the Educational department in 1904, two by the mission, and the Islāmiya school. Ludhiāna has been since 1834 the head-quarters of the American Presbyterian Mission, which, in addition to the schools mentioned, maintains the North India School of Medicine for Christian Women and a printing press. There is a civil hospital in the town, with a branch dispensary.

Māchhīwāra.—Town in the Samrāla *tahsīl* of Ludhiāna District, Punjab, situated in 30° 55′ N. and 76° 12′ E., 6 miles from Samrāla and 27 from Ludhiāna town. Population (1901), 5,588. It has a small sugar industry, and was the scene of Humāyūn's defeat of the Afghāns in 1555. The municipality was created in 1867. The income and expenditure during the ten years ending 1902–3 averaged Rs. 4,900. In 1903–4 the income was Rs. 4,200, chiefly derived from octroi; and the expenditure was Rs. 5,100. The town has a Government dispensary, and the municipality maintains a vernacular middle school.

Raikot (*Raekot*).—Town in the Jagraon *tahsīl* of Ludhiāna District, Punjab, situated in 30° 39′ N. and 75° 36′ E., 27 miles from Ludhiāna town. Population (1901), 10,131. In the seventeenth century it was made the capital of the Rais of Raikot, whose palaces are still standing; but it declined rapidly after their overthrow, and is now of no commercial importance. The municipality was created in 1867. The income during the ten years ending 1902–3 averaged Rs. 6,800, and the expenditure Rs. 6,500. In 1903–4 the income was Rs. 7,700, chiefly derived from octroi; and the expenditure was Rs. 7,400. It possesses a vernacular high middle school maintained by the municipality, and a Government dispensary.

Sunet.—Ruins in the District and *tahsīl* of Ludhiāna, Punjab, situated in 30° 53′ N. and 75° 50′ E., 3 miles south-west of Ludhiāna town. A large mound clearly marks the ancient site of an important city. Cunningham concludes from the coins here discovered that the town of Sunet must have been in existence before the Christian era, and that it continued to flourish during the whole period of the Indo-Scythians and of their successors who used Sassanian types, down to the time of Samanta Deva, the Brāhman king of Kābul or Ohind. On the other hand, from the absence of coins of the Tomar Rājās of Delhi and of the Muhammadan dynasties, it is inferred that Sunet was destroyed during the invasions of Mahmūd Ghazni, and never reoccupied.

[*Archaeological Survey Reports*, vol. xiv, p. 65.]

Ferozepore District (*Fīrozpur*).—District in the Jullundur Division of the Punjab, lying between 29° 55′ and 31° 9′ N. and 73° 52′ and 75° 26′ E., with an area of 4,302 square miles. On the north-east and north-west, the Sutlej forms the boundary separating the District from Jullundur and the Kapūrthala

Boundaries, configuration, and river system.

State, and, after its confluence with the Beās, from the Districts of Lahore and Montgomery. On the south-west and south, it is bounded by the States of Bahāwalpur and Bīkaner, and by Hissār District; on the south-east, by the Farīdkot State, and by detached pieces of territory belonging to Patiāla and Nābha; and on the east by the District of Ludhiāna. Farīdkot State lies across the centre of the District, extending from the south-eastern border to within a few miles of the Sutlej on the north-west. A detached area forming a part of the Moga *tahsīl* lies east of the Farīdkot State. The District consists of a flat, alluvial plain, divided into three broad plateaux by two broken and shelving banks which mark ancient courses of the Sutlej. The upper bank, which crosses the District about 35 miles east of the present stream, is from 15 to 20 feet high; and the river seems to have run beneath it until 350 or 400 years ago, when its junction with the Beās lay near Multān. In the second half of the eighteenth century the river ran under part of the lower bank and, in its changes from this to its present bed, has cut out two or three channels, now entirely dry, the most important of which, the Sukhar Nai, runs in a tortuous course east and west. The volume of water in the Sutlej has sensibly diminished since the opening of the Sirhind Canal, and during the cold season it is easily fordable everywhere above its confluence with the Beās; below the confluence the stream is about 1,000 yards wide in the cold season, swelling to 2 or 3 miles in time of flood. The country is well wooded in its northern half, but very bare in the south; it is absolutely without hill or eminence of any description, even rock and stone being unknown.

Geology and botany.

There is nothing of geological interest in the District, which is situated entirely on the alluvium. In the north the spontaneous vegetation is that of the Central Punjab, in the south that of the desert, while in the Fāzilka subdivision several species of the Western Punjab, more particularly saltworts yielding *sajji* (barilla), are abundant. Trees are rare, except where planted; but the *tāli* or *shīsham* (*Dalbergia Sissoo*) is common on islands in the Sutlej. Along the banks of that river there are large brakes (locally called *belas*) of tall grasses (*Saccharum*, *Andropogon*, &c.) mixed with tamarisk, which are used for thatching, brush-making, and basket-weaving, also *mūnj* (used for cordage) and *khas-khas* (scented roots employed for screens, &c.).

Fauna.

Wolves are the only beasts of prey now found, and they are by no means common; but until the middle of the nineteenth century tigers were found on the banks of the Sutlej.

Hog abound, and 'ravine deer' (Indian gazelle) and antelope are fairly plentiful.

The climate does not differ from that of the Punjab plains generally, except that Ferozepore is proverbial for its dust-storms. Owing to the dryness of its climate, the city and cantonment of Ferozepore and the upland plains are exceptionally healthy; but the riverain tract is malarious in the extreme. Climate and temperature.

The annual rainfall varies from 11 inches at Muktsar to 20 at Zīra; of the rain at the latter place 17 inches fall in the summer months and 2 in the winter. The rainfall is very uncertain: the greatest amount received in any year between 1881 and 1903 was 25 inches at Ferozepore in 1882, and in four of the last twenty years one place or another has received absolutely no rain. An unusually heavy flood came down the Sutlej in August, 1900, and the level then rose 3 feet above the highest on record, a part of the town of Ferozepore being washed away. Rainfall.

The earliest known rulers appear to have been the Ponwār Rājputs, one of whose capitals may have been Janer, a place apparently mentioned by Al Baihaki as Hajnīr on the route from Meerut to Lahore. About the time of the first Muhammadan invasions a colony of Bhatti Rājputs from Jaisalmer settled in the neighbourhood of Muktsar, and the Manj, a branch of them, ousted the Ponwārs and became converts to Islām about 1288. The great Jat tribes—Dhāliwāls, Gils, and others—which now people the District, began to appear 200 years after the Bhattis. About 1370 the fort of Ferozepore was built by Fīroz Shāh III, and included in his new government of Sirhind. Up to a comparatively recent date it seems probable, as tradition avers, that the District was richly cultivated, and deserted sites and ruined wells in the tract bordering on the older course of the Sutlej bear witness to the former presence of a numerous population. Though no date can be absolutely determined for this epoch of prosperity, there are some grounds for the belief that the Sutlej flowed east of Ferozepore fort in the time of Akbar; for the *Ain-i-Akbarī* describes it as the capital of a large tract attached to the province of Multān, and not to Sirhind, as would probably have been the case had the river then run in its modern course. The shifting of the river from which the tract derived its fertility, and the ravages of war, were doubtless the chief causes of its decline. This probably commenced before the end of the sixteenth century, and in another hundred years History and archaeology.

the country presented the appearance of a desert. About the end of the sixteenth century the Sidhu Jats, from whom the Phūlkiān Rājās are descended, made their appearance; and in the middle of the seventeenth century most of the Jat tribes were converted to Sikhism by Har Rai, the seventh Gurū. In 1705 the tenth Gurū, Govind Singh, in his flight from Chamkaur, was defeated with great loss at Muktsar; in 1715 Nawāb Isa Khān, a Manj chief, who fifteen years before had built the fort of Kot Isa Khān, rebelled against the imperial authorities and was defeated and killed; and about the same time the Dogars, a wild, predatory clan which claims descent from the Chauhān Rājputs, settled near Pākpattan, and gradually spread up the Sutlej valley, finding none to oppose them, as the scattered Bhatti population which occupied it retired before the new colonists. At length, in 1740, according to tradition, they reached Ferozepore, which was then included in a district called the Lakha Jungle in charge of an imperial officer stationed at Kasūr. Three of these officials in succession were murdered by the Dogars, who seem to have had matters much their own way until the Sikh power arose.

In 1763 the Bhangī confederacy, one of the great Sikh sections, attacked and conquered Ferozepore under their famous leader, Gūjar Singh, who made over the newly acquired territory to his nephew, Gurbakhsh Singh. The young Sikh chieftain rebuilt the fort and consolidated his power on the Sutlej, but spent most of his time in other portions of the province. In 1792, when he seems to have divided his estates with his family, Ferozepore fell to Dhanna Singh, his second son. Attacked by the Dogars, by the Pathāns of Kasūr, and by the neighbouring principality of Raikot, the new ruler lost his territories piece by piece, but was still in possession of Ferozepore itself when Ranjīt Singh crossed the Sutlej in 1808, and threatened to absorb all the minor principalities which lay between his domain and the British frontier. But the British Government, established at Delhi since 1803, intervened with an offer of protection to all the Cis-Sutlej States; and Dhanna Singh gladly availed himself of the promised aid, being one of the first chieftains who accepted British protection and control. Ranjīt Singh, seeing the British ready to support their rights, at once ceased to interfere with the minor States, and Dhanna Singh retained unmolested the remnant of his dominions until his death in 1818. He left no son, but his widow succeeded to the principality during her lifetime; and on her death in 1835, the territory escheated to the British Government, under the conditions of the arrangement effected in 1809. The political importance of Ferozepore had been already recognized, and an officer was at once deputed to take possession of the new post. After the boundary had been carefully determined, the District was made over for a while to a native official; but it soon became desirable to make Ferozepore the permanent seat of a European Political officer. In 1839 Sir Henry (then Captain) Lawrence took charge of the station, which formed at that time the advanced outpost of British India in the direction of the Sikh power. Early accounts represent the country as a dreary and desert plain, where rain seldom fell and dust-storms never ceased. The energy of Captain Lawrence, however, combined with the unwonted security under British rule, soon attracted new settlers to this hitherto desolate region. Cultivation rapidly increased, trees began to fringe the waterside, trade collected round the local centres; and Ferozepore, which in 1835 was a deserted village, had in 1841 a population of nearly 5,000 persons. Four years later, the first Sikh War broke out. The enemy crossed the Sutlej opposite Ferozepore on December 16, 1845; and the battles of Mudki, Ferozeshāh, Alīwāl, and Sobraon, the first two within the limits of the present District, followed one another in rapid succession. Broken by their defeats, the Sikhs once more retired across the boundary river, pursued by the British army, which dictated the terms of peace beneath the walls of Lahore. The whole cis-Sutlej possessions of the Punjab kingdom passed into the hands of the East India Company, and the little principality of Ferozepore became at once the nucleus of an important British District. The existing area was increased by subsequent additions, the last of which took place in 1884. Since the successful close of the first Sikh campaign, the peace of the District has never been broken, except during the Mutiny of 1857. In May of that year, one of the two native infantry regiments stationed at Ferozepore broke out into revolt, and, in spite of a British regiment and some European artillery, plundered and destroyed the buildings of the cantonment. The arsenal and magazine, however, which gave the station its principal importance, were saved without loss of life to the European garrison. The mutineers were subsequently dispersed. The detachment of native infantry at Fāzilka was at the same time disarmed; and the levies raised by General Van Cortlandt, and in Fāzilka by Mr. Oliver, succeeded in preserving the peace of the

District, which on any show of weakness would have been in revolt from one end to the other. In 1884, when Sirsa District was broken up, the *tahsīl* of Fāzilka was added to Ferozepore.

The people.

The population of the District at the last three enumerations was: (1881) 747,329, (1891) 886,676, and (1901) 958,072, dwelling in 8 towns and 1,503 villages. It increased by 8 per cent. during the last decade, the increase being greatest in the Fāzilka *tahsīl* and least in Zīra. It is divided into the five *tahsīls* of FEROZEPORE, ZĪRA, MOGA, MUKTSAR, and FĀZILKA, the head-quarters of each being at the place from which it is named. The chief towns are the municipalities of FEROZEPORE, the head-quarters of the District, FĀZILKA, MUKTSAR, DHARMKOT, ZĪRA, and MAKHU.

The following table shows the chief statistics of population in 1901:—

Tahsīl.	Area in square miles.	Number of Towns.	Number of Villages.	Population.	Population per square mile.	Percentage of variation in population between 1891 and 1901.	Number of persons able to read and write.
Ferozepore	480	2	320	165,851	345·5	− 7·7	10,159
Zīra	498	3	342	176,462	354·3	+ 1·3	4,218
Moga	807	1	202	245,857	304·6	+ 4·3	11,378
Muktsar	937	1	320	172,445	184·0	+ 6·8	5,538
Fāzilka	1,355	1	319	197,457	145·7	+ 45·6	5,279
District total	4,352	8	1,503	958,072	222·7	+ 8·0	36,572

NOTE.—The figures for the areas of *tahsīls* are taken from revenue returns. The total District area is that given in the *Census Report*.

Muhammadans number 447,615, or 47 per cent. of the total; Hindus, 279,099, or more than 29 per cent.; and Sikhs, 228,355, or nearly 24 per cent. The language generally spoken is Punjābi of the Mālwai type, but on the borders of Bīkaner Bāgrī is spoken.

Castes and occupations.

By far the largest tribe are the Jats or Jāts (248,000). They are of the Mālwā type, described under LUDHIĀNA DISTRICT. The Arains (65,000) appear to be recent immigrants from Jullundur and Lahore. Small to begin with, their holdings in this District have become so subdivided, and their recent extravagance has plunged them so heavily into debt, that they present a complete contrast to their brethren in Ludhiāna. Rājputs number 82,000. The Dogars (16,000) are still mainly a pastoral tribe; they are noted cattle-thieves, and have been described as feeble-minded, vain, careless, thriftless, very self-indulgent, and incapable of serious effort. Gūjars number

14,000. The chief commercial tribes are the Aroras (24,000), Baniās (18,000), and Khattrīs (11,000). Of the artisan and menial tribes, the most important are the Chhīmbas (washermen, 15,000), Chamārs (leather-workers, 32,000), Chūhrās (scavengers, 95,000), Julāhās (weavers, 23,000), Kumhārs (potters, 35,000), Māchhis (fishermen, 20,000), Mochīs (cobblers, 23,000), Sonārs (goldsmiths, 8,000), Tarkhāns (carpenters, 31,000), Telis (oil-pressers, 16,000), and Lohārs (ironsmiths, 10,000). There are 14,000 barbers and 11,000 village minstrels. Ascetics include the Muhammadan Bodlas (1,200), whose powers of healing by incantation are as highly esteemed by the people, both Muhammadan and Hindu, as their curse is dreaded. Brāhmans number 18,000. The Bāwaris (11,000), Hārnis, and Sānsis (500) have been proclaimed as criminal tribes. Mahtams number 14,000. About 61 per cent. of the population are supported by agriculture.

Christian missions. The Ludhiāna American Presbyterian Mission has a station, occupied in 1871, at Ferozepore. The mission of the Presbyterian Church of the United States of America started work in 1881. The District in 1901 contained 240 native Christians.

General agricultural conditions. The conditions of the District vary with the distance from the hills, the annual rainfall decreasing by about 4 inches every 20 miles, while in every part the light soils of the uplands can resist drought much better than the clays of the riverain tract. In the north-east the rainfall is sufficient for ordinary tillage. In the centre the hard clay soils of the riverain require water to grow even ordinary crops in dry years, but the light upland soils do very well with the quantity of rain they usually receive. In the south there is no unirrigated cultivation in the riverain, and in the uplands the cultivation is extremely precarious.

Chief agricultural statistics and principal crops. The District is held mostly on the *bhaiyāchārā* and *pattīdāri* tenures, *zamīndāri* lands covering only 474 square miles.

The area for which details are available from the revenue records of 1903-4 is 4,078 square miles, as shown below :—

Tahsīl.	Total.	Cultivated.	Irrigated.	Cultivable waste.
Ferozepore . . .	486	371	144	65
Zīra	495	413	155	48
Moga . . .	807	756	268	16
Muktsar . . .	935	807	449	73
Fāzilka . . .	1,355	1,097	595	193
Total	4,078	3,444	1,611	395

Wheat and gram are the most important crops of the spring harvest, occupying 784 and 841 square miles respectively in 1903-4; barley covered 213 square miles. In the autumn harvest, the great and spiked millets occupied 193 and 128 square miles respectively. Some rice (21 square miles) is grown on the inundation canals, and maize (117 square miles) in the riverain. The pulse *moth* is the autumn crop of the sandy tracts beneath the great bank. Little sugar-cane or cotton is grown.

Improvements in agricultural practice. The cultivated area increased by 6 per cent. during the twelve years ending 1903-4, the increase being chiefly due to the extension of canal-irrigation. Little has been done towards improving the quality of the crops grown, and experiments tend to show that foreign seeds deteriorate after a year or two. The chief improvement in agricultural practice is the substitution of the spring cultivation for the less valuable autumn crops; forty years ago the autumn harvest occupied twice the area of the spring, and even now spring cultivation in the south of the District is insignificant. Loans under the Agriculturists' Loans Act are popular, and as a rule faithfully applied. During the five years ending 1904 Rs. 86,000 was advanced under this Act, and Rs. 1,600 under the Land Improvement Loans Act.

Cattle, horses, and sheep. The cattle of the riverain are greatly inferior to the upland breed, which is an extremely fine one. Before the introduction of British rule, the jungles round Muktsar were inhabited by an essentially pastoral population. Camels are much used in the sandy parts and the local breed is good. Ferozepore is an important horse-breeding District. There are two breeds of horses—a small wiry animal bred chiefly by the Dogars of the riverain, and a larger one bred inland. An important horse and cattle fair is held at Jalālābād in the Mamdot estate in February. Nine horse and eighteen donkey stallions are kept by the Army Remount department, and two pony stallions by the District board. Sheep are fairly numerous, and the wool of the country between Fāzilka and Bīkaner is much esteemed.

Irrigation. Of the total area cultivated in 1903-4, 1,611 square miles, or 47 per cent., were classed as irrigated. Of this area, 170 square miles were irrigated from wells, 79 from wells and canals, 1,361 from canals, and 519 acres from streams and tanks. In addition, 68 square miles, or 2 per cent., were subject to inundation from the Sutlej. The high lands of the south-east are irrigated by the Abohar branch of the Sirhind

Canal, while the riverain is watered by the Grey Inundation Canals. In the riverain wells are worked by Persian wheels, in the high lands by the rope and bucket. In both cases bullocks are used. There were 8,604 wells in use in 1904, besides 808 temporary wells, lever wells, and water-lifts.

Forests and minerals. Forests covering an area of 6 square miles are managed by the Deputy-Commissioner. Small groves of trees are generally found round wells; but there are no large plantations, and the scarcity of wood is felt to a considerable extent. *Kankar* is the only mineral product of value.

Arts and manufactures. The manufactures are confined almost entirely to the supply of local wants. Coarse cloths and blankets are woven from home-grown cotton and wool, and the carts made locally are of exceptional excellence. Mats are woven of Indian hemp and false hemp. Excellent lacquer-work on wood is produced. The arsenal at Ferozepore employed 1,199 hands in 1904.

Commerce and trade. The District exports wheat and other articles of agricultural produce, which are to a great extent carried by the producers direct to markets in Ludhiāna, Amritsar, Bahāwalpur, Lahore, Jullundur, and Hoshiārpur. The chief imports are sugar, cotton, sesamum, metals, piece-goods, indigo, tobacco, salt, rice, and spices. Ferozepore town is the chief trade centre.

Railways and roads. Ferozepore town lies on the North-Western Railway from Lahore to Bhatinda, and the Fāzilka *tahsīl* is traversed by the Southern Punjab Railway. Fāzilka town is also connected with Bhatinda by a branch of the Rājputāna-Mālwā (narrow gauge) Railway, which runs parallel to the North-Western Railway from Bhatinda to Kot Kapūra. A railway running from Ludhiāna through Ferozepore and Fāzilka to join the Southern Punjab Railway at M'Leodganj has recently been opened. Ferozepore town lies on the important metalled road from Lahore to Ludhiāna. The total length of metalled roads in the District is 81 miles and of unmetalled roads 828 miles. Of the former, 57 miles are under the Public Works department, and the rest under the District board. The Abohar branch of the Sirhind Canal and the Sutlej Navigation Canal form a waterway connecting Ferozepore town with Rūpar. Below its junction with the Beās, the Sutlej is navigable all the year round. Little use, however, is made of these means of water communication. There are twenty ferries on the Sutlej.

Famine. The District was visited by famine in 1759–60, and again in 1783–4, the year of the terrible *chālīsa* famine, when rain failed for three successive seasons and wheat sold at a seer and a quarter per rupee. Famine again occurred in 1803-4, 1817-8, 1833-4, 1842-3, 1848-9, 1856-7, and 1860-1. In 1868-9 there was famine, and Rs. 16,739 was spent in relief. The next famine was in 1896-7, by which time the extension of canal-irrigation and the improvement of communications had to a great extent prevented distress becoming really acute. Food for human beings was not scarce, as the stocks of grain were ample, but a good deal of suffering was caused by high prices. The total amount spent on relief was Rs. 33,952, and the greatest number relieved in any week was 4,149. In 1899-1900 scarcity was again felt. The greatest number on test works was 2,296, and the expenditure was Rs. 75,470, of which Rs. 61,435 was for works of permanent utility on canals.

District subdivisions and staff. The District is in charge of a Deputy-Commissioner, aided by six Assistant or Extra Assistant Commissioners, of whom one is in charge of the Fāzilka subdivision and one in charge of the District treasury. It is divided into the five *tahsīls* of Ferozepore, Zīra, Moga, Muktsar, and Fāzilka, each under a *tahsīldār* and a *naib-tahsīldār*, the Fāzilka *tahsīl* forming a subdivision.

Civil justice and crime. The Deputy-Commissioner as District Magistrate is responsible for criminal justice. Civil judicial work is under a District Judge, and both officers are subordinate to the Divisional Judge of the Ferozepore Civil Division, who is also Sessions Judge. There are four Munsifs, one at head-quarters and one at each outlying *tahsīl*, except Fāzilka. Dacoity and murder are especially common in the District. The most frequent forms of crime are cattle-theft and burglary.

Land revenue administration. Practically nothing is known of the revenue systems which obtained in Ferozepore previous to annexation. The *Ain-i-Akbarī* mentions Ferozepore as the capital of a large *pargana* in the Multān *Sūbah*. The Lahore and Kapūrthala governments seem to have taken their revenue in cash. They fixed the amount for short periods only, and sometimes collected in kind. From annexation onwards the revenue history has to be considered in three parts. The District proper is divided into two portions by the State of Farīdkot, while the revenue history of the Fāzilka *tahsīl*, which was added to the District in 1884, is distinct from either of those portions and possesses different natural features. Several summary assessments were made from annexation to 1852, when the regular settlement was commenced. This assessment, which increased the demand of the summary settlement by only 1 per cent., was sanctioned for a term of thirty years. The Muktsar *tahsīl* was annexed in 1855 and settled summarily. This settlement ran on till 1868, when (together with the Mamdot territory annexed in 1864) the *tahsīl* was regularly settled. The northern part of the District, including the Moga, Zīra, and Ferozepore *tahsīls*, was resettled between 1884 and 1888. Besides raising the demand from Rs. 4,80,000 to Rs. 7,30,000, a water rate was imposed of 6 and 12 annas per *ghumao* (five-sixths of an acre) on crops irrigated by the Grey Inundation Canals. This rate brings in about Rs. 30,000 a year. The Muktsar *tahsīl* was reassessed immediately afterwards, and the revenue raised from Rs. 1,76,000 to Rs. 2,65,000, excluding the canal rate, which was calculated to bring in a further Rs. 20,000.

The Fāzilka *tahsīl* was summarily settled after annexation, and the regular settlement was made in 1852–64. The revised settlement made in 1881 increased the revenue from Rs. 55,000 to Rs. 94,000. At the same time 51 villages on the Sutlej were placed under a fluctuating assessment, based on crop rates varying from Rs. 1–8–0 to 8 annas per acre. The *tahsīl* came again under assessment in February, 1900, when the revenue was increased by Rs. 71,000, excluding a large enhancement of occupiers' rates on canal-irrigated lands.

The rates of the present settlement range from R. 0–14–3 to Rs. 1–6–3 on 'wet' land, and from 7 annas to R. 0–13–10 on 'dry' land.

The collections of land revenue alone and of total revenue are shown below, in thousands of rupees :—

	1880–1.	1890–1.	1900–1.	1903–4.
Land revenue . .	5,19*	8,71	9,01	11,04
Total revenue . .	7,34*	12,97	15,13	17,78

* For the District as then constituted, excluding the Fāzilka *tahsīl*.

The District possesses six municipalities: FEROZEPORE, FĀZILKA, MUKTSAR, DHARMKOT, ZĪRA, and MAKHU. Outside these, local affairs are managed by the District board, which had in 1903–4 an income of Rs. 1,73,000. The expenditure was Rs. 1,61,000, public works being the largest item. **Local and municipal.**

The regular police force consists of 679 of all ranks, including 59 cantonment and 91 municipal police, under a Superintendent who usually has four inspectors to assist him. The village and town watchmen number 1,528. There are 18 police stations, 4 outposts, and 13 road-posts. The District jail at headquarters has accommodation for 424 prisoners. **Police and jails.**

Education. Ferozepore stands fourteenth among the twenty-eight Districts of the Province in respect of the literacy of its population. In 1901 the proportion of literate persons was 3·8 per cent. (6·7 males and 0·3 females). The number of pupils under instruction was 2,942 in 1880–1, 5,446 in 1890–1, 6,113 in 1900–1, and 6,387 in 1903–4. In the last year there were 10 secondary and 93 primary (public) schools, and 7 advanced and 90 elementary (private) schools, with 473 girls in the public and 289 in the private schools. The District possesses an Anglo-vernacular high school maintained by the Ferozepore municipality, the management of which was taken over by the Educational department in 1904, and two unaided high schools—the Har Bhagwān Dās Memorial high school at Ferozepore and the Dev Dharm high school at Moga. It also has 7 middle and 93 primary schools under the department, and 2 middle and 95 primary schools supported mainly by private enterprise. Indigenous education, however, is on the decline. The girls' schools, though few, show more signs of life than they did ten years ago, and there is healthy competition between the small mission school for girls and that of the Dev Samāj. The amount spent on education in 1903–4 was Rs. 72,000, of which the District board contributed Rs. 25,300; the Government grant was Rs. 5,000.

Hospitals and dispensaries. Besides the civil hospital and a mission hospital at Ferozepore, the District contains seven outlying dispensaries. These institutions in 1904 treated a total of 97,612 out-patients and 3,067 in-patients, and 7,781 operations were performed. The expenditure was nearly Rs. 23,000, of which Rs. 10,000 was derived from municipal and Rs. 12,000 from Local funds.

Vaccination. The number of successful vaccinations in 1903–4 was 24,321, representing 26 per 1,000 of the population.

[E. B. Francis, *District Gazetteer* (1888–9), *Settlement Report of the Northern Part of the District* (1893), *Settlement Report of Muktsar and Ilāka Mamdot* (1892), and *Customary Law of the Tahsīls of Moga, Zīra, and Ferozepore* (1890); J. Wilson, *General Code of Tribal Custom in the Sirsa District* (1883); C. M. King, *Settlement Report of Sirsa and Fāzilka Tahsīls* (1905).]

Ferozepore Tahsīl.—*Tahsīl* of Ferozepore District, Punjab, lying between 30° 44′ and 31° 7′ N. and 74° 25′ and 74° 57′ E., with an area of 486 square miles. It is bounded on the north-west by the Sutlej, which divides it from Lahore District. The lowlands along the river are irrigated by the Grey Canals, but the greater part of the *tahsīl* lies in an upland plateau of sandy loam. The population in 1901 was 165,851, compared with 179,606 in 1891. FEROZEPORE (population, 49,341) is the *tahsīl* head-quarters. It also contains the town of MUDKĪ (2,977) and 320 villages. The land revenue and cesses amounted in 1903–4 to 2·1 lakhs. The battle-fields of FEROZESHĀH and MUDKĪ are in this *tahsīl*.

Zīra Tahsīl.—*Tahsīl* of Ferozepore District, Punjab, lying between 30° 52′ and 31° 9′ N. and 74° 47′ and 75° 26′ E., with an area of 495 square miles. It is bounded on the north by the Sutlej, which divides it from Lahore and Amritsar Districts. The natural divisions of the country are the Bet, or alluvial lands along the river, irrigated by the Grey Canals; the Rohi or upland plateau, with a good loam soil; and a long narrow alluvial tract of more recent formation than the Rohi proper, between the Bet and the Rohi. The population in 1901 was 176,462, compared with 174,138 in 1891. The head-quarters are at the town of ZĪRA (population, 4,001). The *tahsīl* also contains the towns of MAKHU (1,355) and DHARMKOT (6,731), and 342 villages. The land revenue and cesses amounted in 1903–4 to 2·7 lakhs.

Moga Tahsīl.—*Tahsīl* of Ferozepore District, Punjab, lying between 30° 8′ and 30° 54′ N. and 74° 54′ and 75° 26′ E., with an area of 807 square miles. It is bounded on the south by Patiāla, and on the west by the Farīdkot State. It lies almost wholly in the upland plateau known as the Rohi, which has a good loam soil and is irrigated by the Sirhind Canal. The population in 1901 was 245,857, compared with 235,806 in 1891. MOGA (population, 6,725) is the head-quarters. The *tahsīl* also contains 202 villages. The land revenue and cesses amounted in 1903–4 to 4·7 lakhs. The village of MAHRĀJ is of some religious importance.

Muktsar Tahsīl (*Muktesar*).—*Tahsīl* of Ferozepore District, Punjab, lying between 30° 9′ and 30° 54′ N. and 74° 4′ and 74° 52′ E., with an area of 935 square miles. It is bounded on the north-west by the Sutlej, which divides it from Montgomery and Lahore Districts, on the east by Farīdkot, and on the south-east by Patiāla. On the west is a belt of alluvial land along the left bank of the Sutlej, irrigated by the Grey Canals. The middle portion of the *tahsīl* is a level plain with a firm soil, while north and south the country is sandy. The central and southern portions are irrigated by the Sirhind Canal. The population in 1901 was 172,445, compared with 161,492 in 1891. The head-quarters are at the town of MUKTSAR (population, 6,389). The *tahsīl* also contains 320 villages. The land revenue and cesses amounted in 1903–4 to 2·7 lakhs.

Fāzilka Tahsīl.—*Tahsīl* and subdivision of Ferozepore District, Punjab, lying between 29° 55′ and 30° 34′ N. and 73° 52′ and 74° 43′ E., with an area of 1,355 square miles. It is bounded north-west by the Sutlej, which divides it from the Dipālpur *tahsīl* of Montgomery District, and east by the Patiāla State. It is divided into three well-marked natural divisions: a narrow low-lying belt along the Sutlej, a somewhat broader strip of older alluvium, and a plain broken by sand-hills, which extends to the borders of Bīkaner and is irrigated by the Sirhind Canal. The population in 1901 was 197,457, compared with 135,634 in 1891. It contains the town of FĀZILKA (population, 8,505), the head-quarters, and 319 villages. The land revenue and cesses amounted in 1903–4 to 2·2 lakhs.

Mamdot Estate (*Muhammadot*).—Estate in the Ferozepore, Muktsar, and Fāzilka *tahsīls* of Ferozepore District, Punjab. Area, 83 square miles of proprietary land, with 309 held in *jāgīr*. It is held by the minor Nawāb of Mamdot, Ghulām Kutb-ud-dīn Khān, a Pathān, whose ancestor Kutb-ud-dīn Khān held the principality of KASŪR, but was expelled from it by Ranjīt Singh in 1807 and retired to Mamdot, which he had conquered from the Raikot chief in 1800. His son Jamāl-ud-dīn Khān held Mamdot as a fief of the Lahore kingdom till 1848, when he received the title of Nawāb, with the powers of a ruling chief, from the British Government; but the powers thus conferred were abused by Jamāl-ud-dīn Khān, and were therefore withdrawn, the State being annexed to British territory in 1855. It was, however, subsequently conferred as an estate on the Nawāb's younger brother Jalāl-ud-dīn Khān, who had rendered good service in 1848 and 1857. Jalāl-ud-dīn died in 1875, leaving a minor son, by name Nizām-ud-dīn Khān, and the estate was managed by the Court of Wards until 1884, when the ward came of age and took charge of it. He died in 1891, leaving an infant son and the estate heavily involved in debt. It is now again under control of the Court of Wards, and the young Nawāb is being educated at the Aitchison College, Lahore. The gross income of the estate, which is the finest in the Punjab, is now Rs. 3,80,000. It owes its prosperity mainly to the Grey Canals.

Abohar.—Ancient town in the Fāzilka *tahsīl* of Ferozepore District, Punjab, situated in 30° 9′ N. and 74° 16′ E. Population (1901), 5,439. Tradition ascribes its foundation to

Jaura, a grandson of the legendary Bhatti king, Rājā Rasālu, and it was the capital of Bhattiāna. It was named Uboh-har, or the 'pool of Uboh,' after Jaura's wife. It lay on the ancient high road from Multān to Delhi, and was visited by Ibn Batūta (A.D. 1332). In it was resident the family of Shams-i-Sirāj Afīf, the author of the *Tārikh-i-Fīroz Shāhi*, whose grandfather was collector of the district, then a dependency of Dipālpur. The place is now of no importance. It has a Government dispensary.

Dharmkot.—Town in the Zīra *tahsīl* of Ferozepore District, Punjab, situated in 30° 57′ N. and 75° 14′ E., 41 miles east of Ferozepore. Population (1901), 6,731. The town was originally known as Kotālpur, but was renamed after its occupation in 1760 by the Sikh chieftain, Tāra Singh, of the Dallewāla confederacy, who built a fort, now destroyed. The municipality was created in 1867. The income and expenditure during the ten years ending 1902–3 averaged Rs. 3,600. In 1903–4 the income was Rs. 3,900, chiefly from octroi; and the expenditure was Rs. 3,500. Dharmkot being situated near the grand trunk road, with a good bazar, and being the only town in the immediate neighbourhood, a considerable trade is carried on in piece-goods, brought to the market via Ludhiāna, and in grain. The town possesses a vernacular middle school maintained by the municipality, and a Government dispensary.

Fāzilka Town.—Head-quarters of the subdivision and *tahsīl* of the same name, Ferozepore District, Punjab, situated in 30° 33′ N. and 74° 3′ E., and the terminus of the Fāzilka extension of the Rājputāna-Mālwā Railway. It has been connected with Ludhiāna, Ferozepore, and the Southern Punjab Railway by a line recently constructed. Population (1901), 8,505. It was founded about 1846 on the ruins of a deserted village, named after a Wattu chief, Fāzil. It is a considerable grain mart and contains a wool press. The municipality was created in 1867. The income during the ten years ending 1902–3 averaged Rs. 21,300, and the expenditure Rs. 22,400. In 1903–4 the income was Rs. 16,000, chiefly derived from octroi; and the expenditure was Rs. 18,500. The town has an Anglo-vernacular middle school maintained by the municipality, and a Government dispensary.

Ferozepore Town.—Head-quarters of the District and *tahsīl* of Ferozepore, Punjab, situated on the old high bank of the Sutlej, in 30° 58′ N. and 74° 37′ E., on the North-Western Railway; distant by rail from Calcutta 1,198 miles, from Bombay 1,080, and from Karāchi 788. Population (1901), with cantonment, 49,341, including 24,314 Muhammadans, 21,304 Hindus, 1,665 Sikhs, and 1,753 Christians. The town was founded, according to tradition, in the time of Fīroz Shāh III, but was in a declining state at the period of British annexation, the population in 1838 being only 2,732. It was occupied by the British in 1835, on the death of Sardārni Lachhman Kunwar. It is now the seat of a thriving commerce, due principally to the exertions of Sir H. Lawrence, who induced many native traders to settle in the city, and more lately to the enterprise of an English merchant, who has erected a powerful cotton press in the vicinity. The main streets are wide and well paved, while a circular road which girdles the wall is lined by the gardens of wealthy residents. The memorial church, in honour of those who fell in the Sutlej campaign of 1845-6, was destroyed during the Mutiny, but since restored. A Sikh temple in honour of the men of the 36th Sikhs who fell holding Fort Sāragarhi and in the sortie from Fort Gulistān in 1897, erected by private subscriptions collected by the *Pioneer* newspaper, and opened in 1903 by the Lieutenant-Governor of the Punjab, testifies to the loyalty and valour of our former foes.

Ferozepore has a large and prosperous grain market, but is chiefly important for its cantonment, the population of which in 1901 was 25,866. One of the two arsenals in the Province is situated at Ferozepore, which in 1904 employed 1,199 hands. The garrison includes a battery of field artillery and a company of garrison artillery, a British infantry regiment, one regiment of native cavalry, and two battalions of native infantry. The income and expenditure from the cantonment funds during the ten years ending 1902-3 averaged Rs. 47,000.

The municipality was created in 1867. The municipal receipts during the ten years ending 1902-3 averaged Rs. 50,900, and the expenditure Rs. 49,000. In 1903-4 the income was Rs. 52,700, chiefly derived from octroi; and the expenditure was Rs. 45,100, including conservancy (Rs. 7,700), education (Rs. 11,700), medical (Rs. 8,400), public safety (Rs. 7,200), and administration (Rs. 5,500). The chief educational institutions are two Anglo-vernacular high schools, one of which, maintained by the municipality, was taken over by the Educational department in 1904, and an aided Anglo-vernacular middle school in cantonments. There is a civil hospital. The Ludhiāna American Presbyterian Mission maintains a hospital for males and a small school for girls.

Ferozeshāh (*Pharūshahr*).—Battle-field in the District and *tahsīl* of Ferozepore, Punjab, situated in 30° 53′ N. and

74° 50′ E., about 12 miles from the left bank of the Sutlej. It is famous for the attack made upon the formidably entrenched Sikh camp, on December 21, 1845, by the British forces under Sir Hugh Gough and Sir Henry Hardinge. After two days' severe fighting, the entrenchments were carried and the enemy completely routed, but not without heavy losses on the part of the conquerors. No traces of the earthworks now remain, but a monument erected upon the spot perpetuates the memory of the officers and men who fell in the engagement. The real name of the place, as called by the people, is Pharūshahr, corrupted into the historical name Ferozeshāh.

Mahrāj.—A collection of four large villages in the Moga *tahsīl* of Ferozepore District, Punjab, situated in 30° 19′ N. and 75° 14′ E. It is the head-quarters of a *pargana*, held almost entirely by the Mahrājki section (*al*) of the Sidhu Jats, the clan of which the Phūlkiān families of Patiāla, Nābha, and Jīnd are another section. A great excavation, from which was taken earth to build the town, is regarded as a sacred spot, offerings being made monthly to the guardian priest. The Mahrājkiāns, who own the surrounding country as *jāgīrdārs*, form a distinct community: physically robust, but litigious, insubordinate, and addicted to excessive opium-eating. Population (1901), 5,780. The place possesses a vernacular middle school and a Government dispensary.

Makhu.—Town in the Zīra *tahsīl* of Ferozepore District, Punjab, situated in 31° 6′ N. and 75° 4′ E., 30 miles north-east of Ferozepore town. Population (1901), 1,355. The municipality was created in 1867. The income during the ten years ending 1902–3 averaged Rs. 1,100, and the expenditure Rs. 1,000. In 1903–4 the income was Rs. 1,500, chiefly from octroi; and the expenditure was Rs. 1,000.

Mamdot Village.—Village in Ferozepore District, Punjab, and former capital of a State, situated in 30° 53′ N. and 74° 26′ E., on the open plain, about 2 miles south of the Sutlej. Population (1901), 2,631. The walls rise to a height of 50 feet, and have a rectangular form, with a round tower at each corner and in the middle of each face. More than two-thirds of the fort was carried away in 1877-8 by the Sutlej, and a branch of that river now flows under the walls of the remainder. Anciently known as Muhammadot, it formed the centre of an *ilāka*, which became depopulated during the Mughal period and was occupied by the Dogars about 1750. Shortly afterwards, the Dogars made themselves independent, but were soon reduced to subjection by Sardār Subha Singh, a Sikh chieftain.

With the assistance of the Rai of Raikot, they expelled the Sikhs; but the Rai made himself supreme at Mamdot, and the Dogars then revolted with the aid of Nizām-ud-dīn and Kutb-ud-dīn of Kasūr. Nizāmud-dīn was murdered by his three brothers-in-law, whom he had ousted from their *jāgīrs*. Kutb-ud-dīn eventually submitted to Ranjīt Singh, relinquishing Kasūr, but retaining Mamdot in *jagīr* subject to the service of 100 horse. Nizām-ud-dīn's son received a corresponding *jāgīr* in Gogaira, but laid claim to Mamdot. With the Dogars' aid he expelled Kutb-ud-dīn, but was finally recalled by the Mahārājā, who confirmed Jamāl-ud-dīn, son of Kutb-ud-dīn, in the succession. Jamāl-ud-dīn sided openly with the Sikhs in 1845, but rendered certain services towards the close of the campaign to the British Government, which requited him by maintaining him in possession of Mamdot as a protected chief with the title of Nawāb. Jamāl-ud-dīn, however, was guilty of serious misgovernment, and the Dogars especially, having incurred his resentment, suffered grave oppression. The British Government therefore, after an inquiry, deposed him in 1855, and annexed his territory. His estates were in 1864 conferred on his brother Jalāl-ud-dīn to the exclusion of his sons. The present Nawāb, Ghulām Kutb-ud-dīn, who succeeded in 1891, is the grandson of Jalāl-ud-dīn.

Moga Town.—Head-quarters of the *tahsīl* of the same name in Ferozepore District, Punjab, situated in 30° 49′ N. and 75° 10′ E., 35 miles south-east of Ferozepore town on the Ferozepore road. Population (1901), 6,725. The Tayyan fair is held here in the month of Chet (March–April). The chief educational institutions are the Dev Samāj Anglo-vernacular high school (unaided), and an Anglo-vernacular middle school maintained by the municipality. There is also a Government dispensary.

Mudkī.—Town in the District and *tahsīl* of Ferozepore, Punjab, situated in 30° 47′ N. and 74° 55′ E., on the road between Ferozepore and Ludhiāna. Population (1901), 2,977. It is memorable for the battle which inaugurated the first Sikh War, fought on December 18, 1845, on the plain 26 miles south of the Sutlej. Two days before this battle, the Sikhs had crossed the boundary river at Ferozepore. They were met by a much smaller British force at Mudkī, and driven from their position, with the loss of 17 guns, after a hard contest, in which the British lost a large proportion of officers. Monuments have been erected on the battle-field in honour of those who fell.

Muktsar Town (*Muktesar*).—Head-quarters of the *tahsīl* of the same name in Ferozepore District, Punjab, situated in 30° 28′ N. and 74° 31′ E., on the Fāzilka extension of the Rājputāna-Mālwā Railway. Population (1901), 6,389. Muktsar is the largest town and principal trade mart in the west of Ferozepore District. Apart from its commercial importance, the town is chiefly noticeable for a great Sikh festival, which takes place in January. It lasts for three days, and commemorates a battle fought in 1705–6 by Gurū Govind Singh against the pursuing imperial forces. There is a large tank in which pilgrims bathe, begun by the Mahārājā Ranjīt Singh, and continued and completed by the chiefs of Patiāla, Jīnd, Nābha, and Farīdkot. The municipality was created in 1867. The income during the ten years ending 1902–3 averaged Rs. 6,100, and the expenditure Rs. 4,900. In 1903–4 the income was Rs. 6,800, chiefly from octroi; and the expenditure was Rs. 6,200. There is a Government dispensary.

Zīra Town.—Head-quarters of the *tahsīl* of the same name in Ferozepore District, Punjab, situated in 30° 59′ N. and 74° 59′ E., 24 miles east of Ferozepore town. Population (1901), 4,001. The municipality was created in 1867. The income during the ten years ending 1902–3 averaged Rs. 4,200, and the expenditure Rs. 3,900. In 1903–4 the income was Rs. 4,800, chiefly from octroi; and the expenditure was Rs. 3,400. The town is of no commercial importance. It has a vernacular middle school maintained by the municipality, and a Government dispensary.

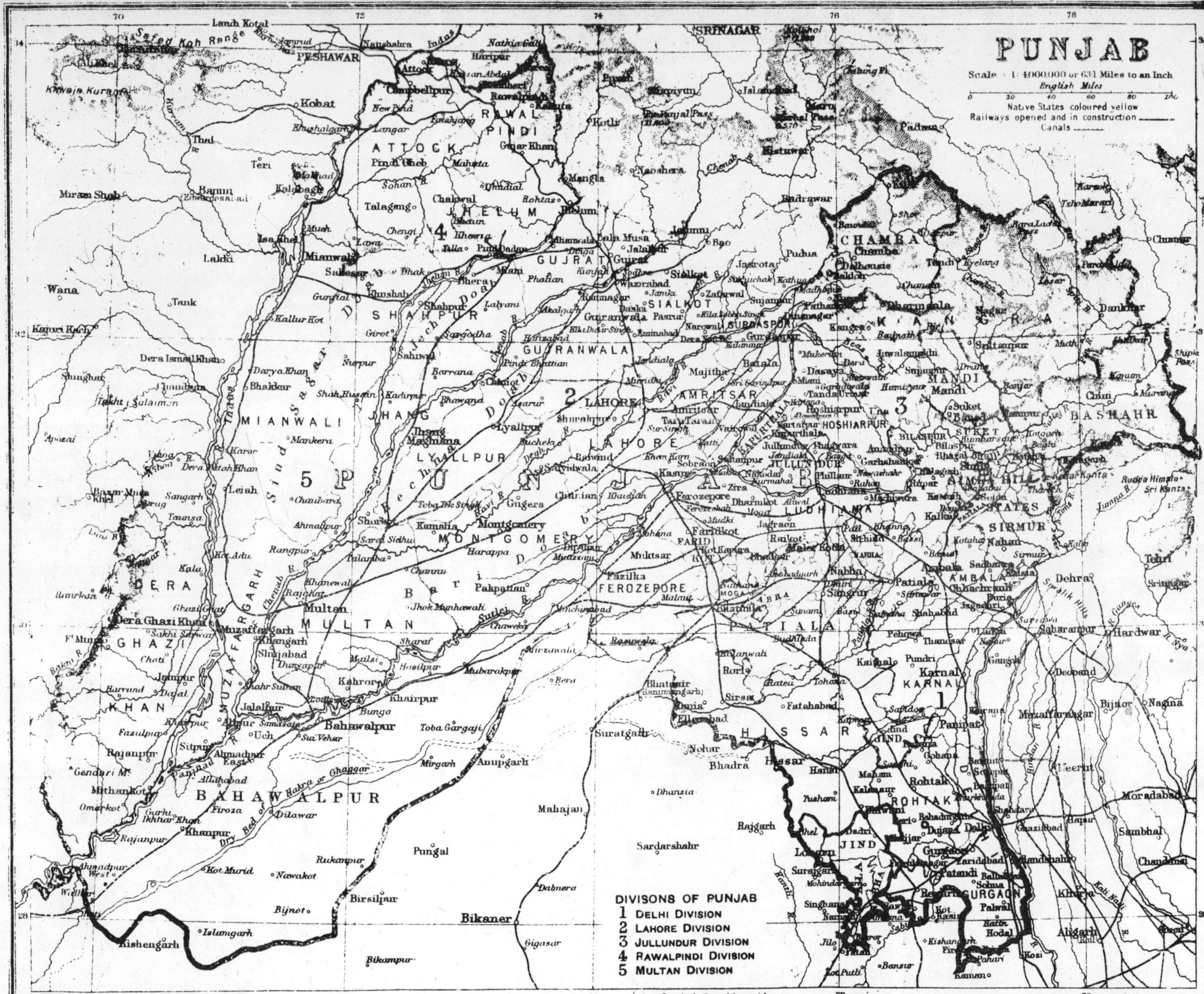

The Edinburgh Geographical Institute

J.G. Bartholomew.